Oxford starter Spanish dictionary

W9-ACY-875

Also available from Oxford University Press

Quick Take off in Spanish
Language learning pack with almost 3 hours of audio
that enables you to learn the essentials fast
Book and 2 cassettes 0–19–860660–5
Book and 2 CDs 0–19–860661–3

Quick Take off in Latin American Spanish
Book and 2 cassettes 0–19–860656–7
Book and 2 CDs 0–19–860657–5

Oxford Take off in Spanish
Language learning pack with almost 5 hours of audio
that takes you from complete beginner to intermediate level
Book and 4 cassettes 0–19–860276–6
Book and 4 CDs 0–19–860296–0

Oxford Take off in Latin American Spanish
Book and 4 cassettes 0–19–860302–9
Book and 4 CDs 0–19–860303–7

Oxford Colour Spanish Dictionary Plus
Colour headwords throughout
0–19–864562–7
0–19–864566–X (US edition)

Oxford Spanish Verbpack
0–19–860340–1

Oxford Spanish Wordpack
0–19–860337–1

Oxford Spanish Grammar
0–19–860343–6

Oxford Starter
Spanish Dictionary

Revised edition

Edited by

Ana Cristina Llompart
Jane Horwood
Carol Styles Carvajal

OXFORD
UNIVERSITY PRESS

XFORD
NIVERSITY PRESS

Great Clarendon Street, Oxford OX2 6DP

Oxford University Press is a department of the University of Oxford.
It furthers the University's objective of excellence in research, scholarship,
and education by publishing worldwide in

Oxford New York

Auckland Bangkok Buenos Aires Cape Town Chennai
Dar es Salaam Delhi Hong Kong Istanbul Karachi Kolkata
Kuala Lumpur Madrid Melbourne Mexico City Mumbai Nairobi
São Paulo Shanghai Taipei Tokyo Toronto

Oxford is a registered trade mark of Oxford University Press
in the UK and in certain other countries

Published in the United States
by Oxford University Press Inc., New York

© Oxford University Press 1997, 2000, 2003

British Library Cataloguing in Publication Data

Data available

Library of Congress Cataloging in Publication Data

The Oxford starter Spanish dictionary / edited by Ana Cristina Llompart,
Jane Horwood, Carol Styles Carvajal.—Rev. ed.
p. cm.
1. Spanish language—Dictionaries—English.   2. English language—
Dictionaries—Spanish.   I. Llompart, Cristina.   II. Horwood, Jane.
III. Carvajal, Carol Styles.
PC4640.O95 2000   463'.21—dc21   00-055087

ISBN 0-19-860716-4

10 9 8 7 6 5 4 3 2 1

Typeset in Swift and Arial by Latimer Trend & Company Ltd.
Printed in Italy by
«La Tipografica Varese S.p.A.» Varese

Contents

Contributors

Senior Editors
Ana Cristina Llompart
Jane Horwood
Carol Styles Carvajal

Editors
Haydn Kirnon
Bernadette Mohan

Dictionary know-how
Michael Britton

Prelims for revised edition
Jane Horwood
Carol Styles Carvajal
Graham Bishop

Proprietary terms
This dictionary contains some words which are, or are asserted to be, proprietary names or trade marks. Their inclusion does not imply that they have acquired for legal purposes a non-proprietary or general significance, nor is any other judgement implied concerning their legal status. In cases where the editors have some evidence that a word is used as a proprietary name or trade mark, this is indicated by the symbol ®, but no judgement concerning the legal status of such words is made or implied thereby.

Introduction

A fresh approach

Created to meet the specific needs of English speakers who are starting to learn Spanish, the *Oxford Starter Spanish Dictionary* takes a completely fresh approach to helping you make sense of the new language. We have changed the design of the entries to make them different from entries in traditional dictionaries. What exactly is it that makes the entries so different?

- they have a new, clearer layout
- they are designed to provide the information you need in a helpful, readable way with the minimum of clutter
- since you will be using the English–Spanish and the Spanish–English sides of the dictionary for different tasks, each side works differently and it shows in the way the information is presented.

Because of these major changes, you will find that the *Oxford Starter Spanish Dictionary* is a far more efficient language-learning tool for you as a beginner. Finding the right information quickly and easily will make Spanish more satisfying to learn.

A clearer layout

Each page of the dictionary presents the information you will need in entries which are well-spaced, easy to read, and which have a consistent layout both in English and Spanish. The main features of the new design are:

- bullet points and numbers to indicate the various uses of each word
- different typefaces as well as the symbol = to indicate the switch from one language to the other
- use of the symbol ! to indicate important grammar points
- use of the symbol ✶ to indicate informal or COLLOQUIAL words
- use of the symbol ◆ to indicate words which should be used with care.

More helpful and easy to use

The entries have been designed so that you can find the information you need quickly. Many of the conventions in traditional dictionaries which you may find confusing or offputting have been avoided, so:

- PARTS OF SPEECH and grammatical terms are written out in full for you. A separate section explains all the the terms used if you should need to find out more about them
- explanations of specific grammar points and notes on how a word is actually used are provided in short paragraphs at appropriate places in the dictionary text
- groups of words which behave in a similar way, or which present similar difficulties, are treated in a consistent manner which you will quickly come to recognize. In many entries, you are guided to other parts of the dictionary, to verb tables, for instance, where you will find all the forms

Words in capital letters are found in the glossary

of the main Spanish VERBS. You will also find handy language notes which deal with such concepts as colours, countries, and dates.

- The language used in the examples and in the signposts to the right translation has been carefully chosen to ensure that it is clear and up to date.

This dictionary, with its precise and lively examples, contains all the words you will need as a beginner and includes plenty of examples of British as well as American English in both the English–Spanish and Spanish–English texts.

Using the two sides of the dictionary to do different things

Each side of the dictionary has been separately designed to take account of the different ways in which you will use it.

The English–Spanish side is longer. Since you are moving from your own language into Spanish, you will need more detailed guidance. We have provided regular reminders about essential grammar rules. The signposts which pinpoint the precise CONTEXT in which a word is used are there to help you choose the right translation. These 'sense indicators' are also supported with a wide selection of useful examples.

The Spanish–English side makes the most of what you already know about your own language. The presentation of translations from Spanish is therefore more streamlined. There is detailed treatment of the more irregular and unpredictable features of Spanish which you may come across in newspapers and magazines, for example. A particularly useful feature is that the variations in spelling of IRREGULAR VERBS, ADJECTIVES and PLURAL NOUNS are all listed as separate entries in the word list. These words then send you to the main dictionary form where you will find the translation you are looking for.

Special features

To help you make the most of your Starter Dictionary, we have provided in this introductory section the following features:

A Guide to Pronunciation
Definitions of Grammatical Terms
A Key to the Design of the Entries
A Guide to Using the Entries
A Word Games section

Words in capital letters are found in the glossary

How to use the dictionary

Where to look for a word

Bilingual dictionaries are divided into two sections.

- The first section gives you a list of Spanish words followed by their English equivalents as well as information about the CONTEXTS in which they are used.

- The second section gives you a list of English words followed by the Spanish words which match their exact meaning according to the contexts in which they are used.

Decide first which section you need to look at.

Your Starter Dictionary is particularly good at listing as HEADWORDS the various forms that VERBS, NOUNS and ADJECTIVES may take in Spanish when they are being used to indicate TENSE, GENDER or NUMBER. From these more unpredictable forms, you will be referred to the main entry of the DICTIONARY FORM for the meaning and any further information.

What information does the dictionary provide you with?

Your dictionary gives you information which falls into three broad categories:

1. information about meaning

2. information about the grammatical characteristics of the words

3. information about the circumstances in which a word may be safely used — either from the point of view of CONTEXT (e.g. medical, sport, school contexts) or REGISTER (e.g. formal, polite, informal registers).

How to recognize the information given in the dictionary

Study carefully the diagrams given on pages x–xi **The Structure of Spanish–English and English–Spanish entries**. There you will see how the three categories of information mentioned above are displayed to help you.
If you need help finding out what PART OF SPEECH you are dealing with, have a look at the **Glossary of Grammatical Terms** on page xiii.

Finding meanings and translating

When you are looking up words for meaning in order to translate them either from your own language or from Spanish, dictionaries can only give you lists of choices. You must look carefully at the information provided to help you choose the right translation in English or in Spanish for the CONTEXT you are in.

If you look up the Spanish word for 'right', you need to be clear whether you mean 'right' as opposed to 'left' or whether you mean 'right' as opposed to 'wrong'.

Scan the whole ENTRY to find the word in Spanish which matches the meaning you need. The CONTEXT indicators or 'signposts' will help you to pinpoint this meaning. This will be easier to select when you are looking up Spanish words to translate into English since you will know what each of the choices given in English means and how it is used.

If the entry is a long one, first identify the PART OF SPEECH of the word you want to translate. When you have found the right section of the ENTRY, check the range of meanings covered in that section to find the appropriate one. For example:

- **'ring'** could be a verb, in which case the correct Spanish translation may be **'sonar'** which is also a verb

- **'ring'** could be a noun, in which case the correct Spanish equivalent might be **'un anillo'** (*a piece of jewelry*) or **'un círculo'** (*a circle*)

Your Starter Dictionary will give you the CONTEXT clearly so that you can decide on the appropriate word.

Words in capital letters are found in the glossary

Using the entries to find information about a word other than the meaning

- Sometimes you will want to use your dictionary simply to check the spelling of the FEMININE or PLURAL form of a NOUN or ADJECTIVE

- You may wish to check to see if the word has ACCENTS

- You may wish to check the GENDER of a noun

- You may wish to find out how a verb is spelled in a particular TENSE

- The entry will often tell you which pattern of VERB in the tables at the back is the one to use as a model

How to use the verb tables

Where you see a Spanish verb followed by a number in a box, look at the back of the dictionary where you will find tables of verbs. The number given against the verb indicates the spelling pattern that the verb follows.

For example: **'flotar'** and **'mojar'** are both followed by the number 1. In the verb tables this spelling pattern is represented by the verb **'hablar'**.

Verbs can be split into two parts: the STEM and the ENDING.
   e.g. **flot** + **ar** ; **moj** + **ar**

The endings of **'habl** + **ar'** should be used with the stems of **flot** + **ar** and **moj** + **ar** to form the tenses you need.

Where the verb is REGULAR the stem does not change, only the endings.

Where the verb is IRREGULAR the stem may alter as well. Just follow the pattern indicated.

e.g.	3	**pagar**	[**pag** + **ar**]	note how the **'g'** changes to 'gu' when the ending begins with **'e'**
	6	**contar**	[**cont** + **ar**]	note the change from **'o'** to **'ue'**
	45	**corregir**	[**correg** + **ir**]	note the change from **'e'** to **'i'**, and that the **'g'** of the stem changes to **'j'** when the ending begins with **'o'** or **'a'**

Getting to know your dictionary

In the central section of this dictionary pages 141–150 you will find a short section of games and exercises which will help you get to know your dictionary better and to use it more effectively. Your dictionary is a very important study aid which can greatly help you to find out how the Spanish language works and how to expand your vocabulary.

Words in capital letters are found in the glossary

The structure of Spanish–English entries

HEADWORD ········· **azul**

1 *adjective*

numbers indicating ········· = blue

grammatical ········· **2** *noun, masculine*

categories **el azul** = blue ······· translation clearly indicated by =

campesino/campesina *noun,*

masculine/feminine ······· FEMININE form of headword

un campesino/una campesina = a countryman/woman

= a peasant

lápiz *noun, feminine* ······· PART OF SPEECH plus GENDER

un lápiz = a pencil

a lápiz = in pencil

lápices de colores = crayons

compounds ········· **un lápiz de ojos** = an eyeliner

presented in block **un lápiz de labios** = a lipstick

at end of entry

molestar *verb* [1] ······· number of verb conjugation pattern

• = to bother

deja de molestar a tu hermano = stop bothering your brother

me molesta que no me ayuden = it annoys me that they don't help

bullet points

indicating a

separate meaning **!** *Note use of the subjunctive after*

of headword **molestar que** ·······

• = to disturb information on

'**no molestar**' = 'do not disturb' correct grammatical usage

• = (*when asking permission*)

¿te molesta si abro la ventana? do you mind if I open the window?

molestarse

• = to get upset

• **molestarse en hacer algo** = to bother to do something

oiga, oigo etc ▶ oír ······· cross-reference to headword

symbol drawing ·······

attention to

REGISTER **papá✶** *noun, masculine*

papá = dad, daddy

mis papás = my mom and dad, my mum and dad

Words in capital letters are found in the glossary

The structure of English–Spanish entries

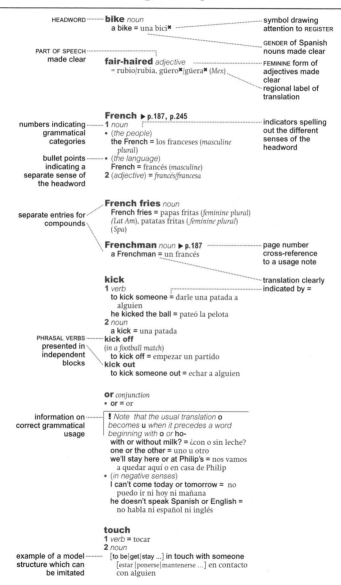

HEADWORD → **bike** *noun*
a bike = una bici✖ → symbol drawing attention to REGISTER

PART OF SPEECH made clear → GENDER of Spanish nouns made clear

fair-haired *adjective*
= rubio/rubia, güero✖/güera✖ (*Mex*) → FEMININE form of adjectives made clear
→ regional label of translation

French ▶ p.187, p.245
numbers indicating grammatical categories → **1** *noun* → indicators spelling out the different senses of the headword
• (*the people*)
the French = los franceses (*masculine plural*)
bullet points indicating a separate sense of the headword → • (*the language*)
French = francés (*masculine*)
2 (*adjective*) = francés/francesa

French fries *noun*
separate entries for compounds → French fries = papas fritas (*feminine plural*) (*Lat Am*), patatas fritas (*feminine plural*) (*Spa*)

Frenchman *noun* ▶ p.187 → page number cross-reference to a usage note
a Frenchman = un francés

kick → translation clearly indicated by =
1 *verb*
to kick someone = darle una patada a alguien
he kicked the ball = pateó la pelota
2 *noun*
a kick = una patada
PHRASAL VERBS presented in independent blocks → **kick off**
(*in a football match*)
to kick off = empezar un partido
kick out
to kick someone out = echar a alguien

or *conjunction*
• or = or
information on correct grammatical usage → **!** *Note that the usual translation* **o** *becomes* **u** *when it precedes a word beginning with* **o** *or* **ho-**
with or without milk? = ¿con o sin leche?
one or the other = uno u otro
we'll stay here or at Philip's = nos vamos a quedar aquí o en casa de Philip
• (*in negative senses*)
I can't come today or tomorrow = no puedo ir hoy ni mañana
he doesn't speak Spanish or English = no habla ni español ni inglés

touch
1 *verb* = tocar
2 *noun*
example of a model structure which can be imitated → [to be|get|stay ...] in touch with someone
[estar |ponerse|mantenerse ...] en contacto con alguien

Words in capital letters are found in the glossary

Glossary of grammatical terms

The list of words and definitions below contains most of the words which you will come across when learning a language and its grammar. Some are used in this dictionary; others you will see in grammars and textbooks.

Abbreviation
a shortened form of a word or phrase, e.g. (English) exam ▶ examination; (Spanish) Mr ▶ Sr.

Accent
1. (in writing) a mark associated with a letter, usually showing how the letter is pronounced, e.g. acute accent (é); tilde (ñ)
2. (in speech) a person's way of speaking

Adjective
a word describing a noun, e.g. a *green* shirt = una camisa *verde*; *my* house = *mi* casa

Adverb
a word that describes or modifies the meaning of a verb, an adjective or another adverb, e.g. he speaks *quickly* = habla *rápidamente; fairly* big = *bastante* grande; she sings *very badly* = canta *muy mal*

Agree, Agreement
when a word agrees with another, its spelling changes to match the number of that other word, e.g. one child = un niño; two child*ren* = dos niño*s*; it must also match it for gender, e.g. *the white* dog = *el* perro blanc*o*; *the white* house = *la* casa blanc*a*

Article
the definite article *the* = *el/la/los/las*, the indefinite article *a* or *an* = *un/una*, and the partitive articles *some* and *any* are all used before a noun. See DETERMINER

Auxiliary, Auxiliary verb
the verbs *estar* and *haber*, which are used in Spanish to form the perfect, pluperfect, or continous tenses, e.g. *he* comido = I have eaten; *habían* visto a Bob = they had seen Bob; *estaba* durmiendo = he was sleeping; also, less commonly in Spanish than in English, the verb *ser* when used to form the passive, e.g. la casa *fue* demolida = the house was demolished

Base form
see DICTIONARY FORM

Clause
a self-contained section of a sentence which contains a subject and a verb

Cognates
words which resemble each other in more than one language and which historically have the same origin, e.g. republic, república. They do not always retain the same meaning. See FALSOS AMIGOS

Colloquial
refers to a word or an expression used in relaxed, everyday situations. Colloquial language is usually spoken, or used in personal letters or informal writing

Comparative
the form of the adjective or adverb which allows a comparison to be made, e.g. big*ger* = *más* grande; *more* intelligent = *más* inteligente; *better* = *mejor*

Conditional
the form of the verb that expresses what might happen IF something else occurred first, e.g. *if* the weather was good, we *would go out* = *si* hiciera buen tiempo *saldríamos*

Conjunction
a word used to join clauses together, e.g. *and* = *y*, *but* = *pero*, *because* = *porque*

Consonant	a letter representing a sound such as *b*, *c*, *d*, *p*, *s*, *t*, *z*, etc. Consonants cannot form a complete sound unit or syllable without a vowel. See VOWEL
Construction	the way the words in a phrase or sentence work together grammatically
Context	the environment or surroundings within which a word occurs and which affect its meaning. Compare *the **tank** fired first* with *he filled the petrol **tank***. Information about the context of a word helps to pinpoint its exact sense. Knowing the sense and then using the dictionary signposts will guide you to the right translation
Definite article	see ARTICLE
Determiner	a word used before a noun to make clear what is being referred to. It describes the function of definite and indefinite articles as well as words like *this*, *my*, and *certain*, e.g. *this* money = *este dinero*; *my* cats = *mis* gatos; *certain* people = *ciertas* personas. In Spanish, the determiner will match the gender and the number of the noun it is referring to
Dictionary form	the form of a word given in the dictionary WORD LIST. For verbs, it is the spelling of the infinitive in English and Spanish; for Spanish nouns, the spelling of the masculine singular form (or the feminine singular form if there is no masculine form); for Spanish adjectives, the spelling of the masculine singular form
Direct object	the noun or pronoun directly affected by the verb, e.g. *she bought the book* = *compró el libro*; *he ate it* = *lo comió*; *help me* = *ayúdame*
Ending	that part of a noun or an adjective which can be changed to show gender or number, and of a verb to show number or tense. The ending doesn't change the basic meaning of the word
Entry	the information given in a dictionary about the word you have looked up; also the word itself. See HEADWORD
Exclamation	a sound, word or remark expressing a strong feeling such as anger, fear, or joy, e.g. ouch! = ¡ay!
Falsos amigos	a pair of words from two different languages which look alike but do not have the same meaning, e.g. *sensible* (English) = *having good sense* and *sensible* (Spanish) = *sensitive*
Feminine	one of the genders used in Spanish. See GENDER
Future	the tense of a verb that refers to something that will happen in the future: *I will leave* = *me iré*
Gender	marks nouns in Spanish as being either masculine or feminine (whether they refer to persons or things) whereas English does not make the distinction. Gender is most clearly indicated by the article used with the noun, e.g. *the* dog = *el* perro (masculine); *a* house = *una* casa (feminine). Pronouns and adjectives also carry gender information e.g. *he* eats = *él* come; *this* is my sister = *está* es mi hermana; a black hat = *un* sombrero *negro* (because the noun *sombrero* is masculine); the white cows = *las* vacas blanc*as*. Spanish also has the neuter pronouns *esto*, *eso*, and *aquello* and a neuter article, *lo*. See NEUTER

Gerund	the part of a verb used in Spanish to form continuous tenses in combination with an auxiliary verb. See PRESENT PARTICIPLE
Headword	the word used in the dictionary word list to begin each separate entry.
Imperative	a verb form for expressing commands, e.g. *close* the door = *cierra* la puerta; *be quiet!* = *icállense!*; *let's go* = *vamos*
Imperfect tense	the tense of the verb which refers to a continuous action or state in the past, e.g. the children *were singing* = los niños *cantaban*; or to something that used to happen regularly, e.g. I *used to read* a lot = *leía* mucho; we *went* there every Monday = *íbamos* allí todos los lunes
Impersonal verb	a verb whose action is not performed by a person or a thing, e.g. *it* is raining = está lloviendo; *it's* going to snow = va a nevar
Indefinite article	see ARTICLE
Indefinite pronoun	a pronoun that does not identify a specific person or object, e.g. *one* never knows = *uno* nunca sabe; they never tell *you* the truth = nunca *te* dicen la verdad; *something* = *algo*
Indicative	a verb form used when indicating or stating a fact, e.g. I don't understand = no entiendo; he wrote a letter = escribío una carta. See SUBJUNCTIVE
Indirect object	the noun or pronoun indirectly affected by the verb and often following a preposition, e.g. I wrote *to him* = *le* escribí. The direct object is aimed at the indirect object, e.g. she gave the book *to the boy* = dio el libro *al niño*; tell *us* a story = cuénta*nos* un cuento
Infinitive	the basic part or 'name' of a verb before it is altered to indicate tense or number, e.g. to sing = cantar; to decide = decidir. See DICTIONARY FORM
Interrogative	a form of wording used to ask questions
Intonation	the quality in a human voice which indicates an emotion (surprise, shock) or which shows that a speaker is asking a question, stating a fact, or giving an order
Inverted commas	punctuation marks used to indicate direct speech, e.g. 'come here,' she said
Irregular verb	a verb whose spelling is not predictable or does not follow a regular pattern when it changes to express tense, e.g. English *to be*, Spanish *ser*
Masculine	one of the genders used in Spanish. See GENDER
Neuter	one of the genders used in Spanish, which has the neuter pronouns *esto* = this, *eso* = that, and *aquello* = that, plus the neuter article, *lo*, which is used with adjectives, e.g. *eso* es *lo bueno* de *esto* = that's the good thing about this
Noun	a word which names a person, an animal, an object, a feeling, or an event, e.g. a student = un estudiante; a dog = un perro; a house = una casa; envy = la envidia; the storm = la tormenta

Number	a form of the word indicating whether it is singular, e.g. a boy = un niño, or plural, e.g. two boys = dos niños
Object	the person, thing, or idea affected by or referred to by a verb, e.g. he walked *the dog* = sacó *al perro* a pasear; we crossed *the road* = cruzamos *la calle*. See also DIRECT OBJECT, INDIRECT OBJECT
Partitive article	SEE ARTICLE
Part of speech	the grammatical term which describes the function of a word and categorizes it as *noun*, *verb*, *adjective*, *adverb*, etc. All the entries in this dictionary carry information about the part of speech of the word you look up
Past participle	the part of the verb used to form past tenses in combination with an auxiliary verb, e.g. I have *sung* = he *cantado*; we had *stayed* = habíamos *quedado*; she's *gone* to bed = se ha *acostado*
Past simple	the tense of the verb which refers to something that happened or was completed in the past: he *woke up* = *se despertó*; we *went* to the theatre = *fuimos* al teatro
Perfect tense	the tense of the verb which refers to an event taking place in a period of time that includes the present, e.g. I *have eaten* = he *comido*, the train *has arrived* = el tren *ha llegado*
Person	the 'person' of a verb shows you **who** or **what** is carrying out the action referred to by the verb. There are six persons in the singular: *I, you, he, she, it, one* and three in the plural: *we, you, they*
Phrasal verb	a form of the English verb which combines with a preposition or an adverb to produce a particular meaning, e.g. to *run away* = *huir*; to *carry on* working = *seguir* trabajando
Phrase	**1.** a self-contained section of a sentence which does not contain a full verb **2.** an expression with a particular meaning which can make it more difficult to translate word for word, e.g. to lay the table = poner la mesa; to be in love = estar enamorado
Pluperfect tense	the tense of the verb referring to (1) past events which precede (2) other events taking place in a more recent past, e.g. John (1) *had* already *left* when (2) I *arrived* = John ya (1) *había salido* cuando (2) *llegué*
Plural	the form of nouns and pronouns which refers to more than one of something, e.g. *boys, we, they.* Spanish ADJECTIVES also have plural forms, e.g. red shoe*s* = zapatos rojo*s*, to agree with the noun they are describing
Preposition	a word which stands in front of a noun or pronoun, connecting it to the rest of a sentence, e.g. *between* the chairs = *entre* las sillas; *with* us = *con* nosotros; *to* Madrid = *a* Madrid; *from* Bob = *de* Bob
Present Participle	the part of a verb used in English to form continuous tenses in combination with an auxiliary verb: they were *talking* = estaban *hablando*; it is *raining* = está *lloviendo*
Present tense	the tense of a verb referring to something that is happening now, e.g. I *am watching* television = *estoy viendo* televisión; she *understands* = ella *entiende*

Pronominal verb	a Spanish verb formed using the pronouns *me*, *te*, *se*, *nos*, and *os*, in which the pronoun refers to the subject of the verb, e.g. *bañarse*, *irse*. See also REFLEXIVE VERB
Pronoun	a word which takes the place of a noun, e.g. is it *your dog*? ▶ is it *yours*?; I sold *the car* ▶ I sold *it*; *my father* saw *my friend and me* ▶ *he* saw *us*
Reflexive verb	a type of pronominal verb whose object is the same as its subject; in Spanish used with a reflexive pronoun, e.g. lavar*se* = to wash *oneself*
Register	the style of language used in speech and writing which is suited (and which you can adapt) to the circumstances. These may range from very formal situations to very relaxed or informal contexts
Regular verb	a verb which follows a set pattern in its different forms and tenses and can be classified in a fixed group of verbs
Sentence	a set of words usually containing a subject and a verb, which can stand alone and make sense to make a statement, ask a question, or give a command
Singular	the form of nouns and pronouns which refers to just one of something, e.g. *boy*, *I*, *it*. See PLURAL.
Stem	the root or main part of a verb, adjective or other word, to which endings are added, e.g. the stem of *hablar* is *habl-*, the stem of *contento* is *content-*
Subject	the noun or pronoun which causes the action of a verb and can usually be identified by asking **who..?** or **what..?**, e.g. *he* wants to do it = *él* lo quiere hacer (although note that in Spanish the subject pronoun is often indicated by the verb ending, and is only given for emphasis or to avoid confusion); *the light* was too bright = *la luz* estaba demasiado fuerte
Subjunctive	a verb form that is used to express a desire, doubt, unlikelihood, and conditionality, e.g. it's unlikely *that he'll come* = no es probable *que venga*, I want *you to stay* =quiero *que te quedes*, if it *was/were* possible = si *fuera* posible. It often expresses how the speaker feels rather than the fact itself
Superlative	the form of the adjective which makes it 'the most', e.g. *the* big*gest* = *el más* grande; *the most* intelligent = *el más* inteligente; *the best* = *el mejor*
Syllable	part of a word which can form a spoken unit built around the **vowel** it contains, e.g. the English word **in-tel-li-ge**nt has four syllables, the Spanish word **in-te-li-g**en-**te** has five
Synonym	a word with the same (or almost the same) meaning as another, e.g. *enormous* and *gigantic*, *sure* and *certain*
Tense	the form of the verb which indicates a particular time frame – past: I *went* = yo *fui*; present: I *go* = yo *voy*; future: I *will go* = yo *iré*
Verb	a word which indicates what is being done or describes a situation, e.g. the children *are playing* = los niños *están jugando*; she *read* the book = ella *leyó* el libro; I *am* tired = *estoy* cansado

Vocabulary	words in their basic dictionary form, i.e. which are not affected by grammatical factors such as tense or number, e.g. (to) do = hacer; happy = contento; boy = niño
Vowel	a sound which forms the basis of the syllable and which can be spoken by itself, e.g. *a, i, e, o, u*. See CONSONANT, SYLLABLE
Word list	the list of headwords or vocabulary items found in a dictionary

The pronunciation of Spanish

Vowels

a is between the pronunciation of *a* in English *cat* and *arm*

e is like *e* in English *bed*

i is like *ee* in English *see* but a little shorter

o is like *o* in English *hot* but a little longer

u is like *oo* in English *too*

Consonants

b (1) in initial position or after **m** or **n** is like English *b*
      (2) in other positions is between English *b* and English *v*

c (1) before **e** or **i**: in European Spanish is like *th* in English *thin*; in Latin American Spanish is like *s* in English *stop*
      (2) in other positions is like *c* in English *cat*

ch is like *ch* in English *chip*

d (1) in initial position, after **m** or **n**, and after **l** is like English *d*
      (2) in other positions is like *th* in English *this*

f is like *f* in English *fat*

g (1) before **e** or **i** is like *ch* in Scottish *loch*
      (2) in initial position is like *g* in English *get*
      (3) in other positions is like (2) but a little softer

h is silent in Spanish, but see also **ch**

j is like *ch* in Scottish *loch*

k is like English *k*

l is like English *l*, but see also **ll**

ll is like *lli* in English *million*, except in the River Plate area, where it is like *s* in English *measure*

m is like English *m*

n is like English *n*

ñ is like English *ni* in English *opinion*

p is like English *p*

q is like English *k*

r is rolled; is more strongly rolled when double *r*, or in initial position

s is like *s* in English *sit*

t is like English *t*

v (1) in initial position or after **m** or **n** is like English *b*
      (2) in other positions is between English *b* and English *v*

w is like *g* in English *get* followed by English *w*

x is like English *x*

y is like English *y*

z in European Spanish is like *th* in English *thin*; in Latin American Spanish is like *s* in English *stop*

Spanish–English

a *preposition*
- *(indicating destination)* = to
  fuimos a la playa = we went to the beach
  se lo di a tu hermano = I gave it to your brother
- *(indicating time)* = at
  se fueron a la una = they left at one o'clock
  a la hora de comer = at lunchtime
- *(indicating date)*
  hoy estamos a jueves = today is Thursday
- *(indicating position)*
  está a la derecha = it's on the right
  estábamos sentados a la mesa = we were sitting at the table
- *(indicating manner)*
  ir a pie = to go on foot
- *(indicating distance)*
  el pueblo está a 40 km de Leeds = the village is 40 km from Leeds
- *(indicating price)*
  las manzanas están a 90 pesos el kilo = the apples cost 90 pesos a kilo
- *(used before people or people's names)*
  vi a Juan = I saw Juan
  ¿conoces a su madre? = do you know her mother?
- *(after certain verbs)*
  voy a ir = I'm going to go
  empezar a comer = to start eating

abajo *adverb*
- = below
  está en el cajón de abajo = it's in the drawer below
  = it's in the bottom drawer
- = downstairs
  viven abajo = they live downstairs
- *(Lat Am)* **abajo de** = under
  abajo de la cama = under the bed

abanico *noun, masculine*
  un abanico = a fan

abarrotería *noun, feminine (Mex)*
  una abarrotería = a grocery store, a grocer's

abarrotero/abarrotera *noun, masculine/feminine (Mex)*
  un abarrotero/una abarrotera = a storekeeper, a grocer

abarrotes *noun, masculine plural (C Am, Mex)*
  abarrotes = groceries

abecedario *noun, masculine*
  el abecedario = the alphabet

abeja *noun, feminine*
  una abeja = a bee

abierto/abierta *adjective*
- = open
  la puerta estaba abierta = the door was open
- *(if it's a faucet)* = running
  dejaste la llave abierta = you left the faucet running

abogado/abogada *noun, masculine/feminine*
  un abogado/una abogada = a lawyer

abordar *verb* 1 *(Mex)*
  = to board

abrazar *verb* 4
  = to hug

abrazo *noun, masculine*
  un abrazo = a hug
  me dio un abrazo = she gave me a hug
  un abrazo, Juan *(in a letter)* = best wishes, Juan

abrebotellas *noun, masculine (! does not change in the plural)*
  un abrebotellas = a bottle opener

abrelatas *noun, masculine (! does not change in the plural)*
  un abrelatas = a can opener

abreviatura *noun, feminine*
  una abreviatura = an abbreviation

abridor *noun, masculine*
  un abridor = a can opener
  = a bottle opener

abrigo *noun, masculine*
  un abrigo = a coat

abril *noun, masculine*
  abril = April

abrir *verb* 59
- = to open
- = to turn on
  abrir el gas = to turn the gas on

abrocharse *verb* 1
- *(if it's clothes, buttons)* = to do up
  se abrochó la chaqueta = she did up her jacket
- *(if it's a seatbelt)* = to fasten

absoluto/absoluta *adjective*
  = absolute

absorber verb 17
= to absorb

absurdo/absurda adjective
= absurd

abuelo/abuela noun,
masculine/feminine
un abuelo/una abuela = a
grandfather/grandmother
mis abuelos = my grandparents

aburrido/aburrida adjective
• = bored
• = boring

aburrir verb 41
= to bore
aburrirse
= to get bored

acá adverb
= here
¡ven acá! = come here!

acabar verb 1
• = to finish
acaba a las siete = it finishes at seven
acabé de pintarlo ayer = I finished
painting it yesterday
• = to end
cuando acabó la película = when the film
ended
• acabo de verlo = I've just seen him
acabarse
• = to be over
se acabó el colegio = school is over
• = to run out
• se les acabó el dinero a mis padres = my
parents ran out of money
se nos acabó el pan = we ran out of bread

academia noun, feminine
una academia = a school
una academia de idiomas = a language
school

acampar verb 1
= to camp

acaso adverb
por si acaso = just in case

accidente noun, masculine
un accidente = an accident

aceite noun, masculine
aceite = oil
aceite de oliva = olive oil

aceituna noun, feminine
una aceituna = an olive

acelerador noun, masculine
el acelerador = the accelerator

acento noun, masculine
un acento = an accent

aceptable adjective
= acceptable

aceptar verb 1
= to accept

acera noun, feminine
la acera = the sidewalk, the pavement

acercar verb 2
• = to bring closer/nearer
• = to pass
me acercó un cuchillo = he passed me a
knife
acercarse
• = to get nearer
• = to go/come nearer
acércate un poco = come a bit nearer

acero noun, masculine
acero = steel

ácido/ácida
1 adjective
• = sharp
• = acid
2 ácido noun, masculine
un ácido = an acid

acierto noun, masculine
un acierto = a success

acné noun, masculine
acné = acne

aconsejar verb 1
= to advise
me aconsejó que no fuera = he advised me
not to go

! Note the use of the subjunctive after
aconsejar que

acordarse verb 6
= to remember
acordarse de algo/alguien = to remember
something/someone

acostarse verb 6
= to go to bed
= to lie down

acostumbrado/acostumbrada
adjective
estar acostumbrado/acostumbrada a algo
= to be used to something

acostumbrarse verb 1
acostumbrarse a algo = to get used to
something

actitud noun, feminine
una actitud = an attitude

actividad noun, feminine
una actividad = an activity

activo/activa adjective
= active

A

acto *noun, masculine*
un acto = an act

actor/actriz *noun, masculine/feminine*
un actor/una actriz = an actor/actress

actuar *verb* [11]
= to act

Acuario *noun, masculine*
Acuario = Aquarius

acuario *noun, masculine/feminine*
un/una acuario = an Aquarius, an Aquarian

acuerda, acuerdo, etc ▶ acordar

acuerdo *noun, masculine*
un acuerdo = an agreement
llegaron a un acuerdo = they reached an
  agreement
de acuerdo = all right
estar de acuerdo = to agree

acuesta, acuesto, etc ▶ acostar

acusar *verb* [1]
= to accuse

adaptar *verb* [1]
= to adapt
adaptarse
= to adapt

adecuado/adecuada *adjective*
• = suitable
• = right

adelantar *verb* [1]
• (*if it's a car*) = to overtake
  (*if it's an appointment, meeting*) = to bring
   forward
• (*if it's a clock*) = to put forward

adelante
1 *adverb*
• = forward
  se cayó hacia adelante = he fell forward
• (*Lat Am*) adelante de = in front of
  adelante de mí = in front of me
2 *exclamation*
  ¡adelante! = come in!

adelgazar *verb* [4]
= to lose weight

además *adverb*
• = besides
  no quiero ir, además no tengo dinero = I
   don't want to go; besides, I don't have any
   money
• = what's more
  llega tarde y, además, no trabaja = he's
   always late, and what's more, he doesn't
   work
• además de = as well as

adentro *adverb*
• = inside
  vamos adentro = let's go inside

• (*Lat Am*) adentro de = inside
  adentro de la casa = inside the house

adhesivo/adhesiva *adjective*
• = sticky
• = adhesive

adiós *exclamation*
• (*on leaving a person or place*)
  ¡adiós! = goodbye!
• (*when passing someone in the street*)
  ¡adiós! = hello!

adivinar *verb* [1]
= to guess

adjetivo *noun, masculine*
un adjetivo = an adjective

administración *noun, feminine*
la administración = the administration

admiración *noun, feminine*
• admiración = admiration
• un signo de admiración = an exclamation
  point, an exclamation mark

admirar *verb* [1]
= to admire

adonde *adverb*
= where
el lugar adonde iban = the place where
  they were going

adónde *adverb*
= where
¿adónde vas? = where are you going?

adornar *verb* [1]
= to decorate

adorno *noun, masculine*
un adorno = an ornament
adornos de Navidad = Christmas
  decorations

adquiera, adquiero, etc ▶ adquirir

adquirir *verb* [47]
= to acquire

adrede *adverb*
= on purpose

aduana *noun, feminine*
la aduana = customs

adulto/adulta
1 *adjective*
= adult
2 *noun, masculine/feminine*
un adulto/una adulta = an adult

adverbio *noun, masculine*
un adverbio = an adverb

aéreo/aérea *adjective*
= air
el tráfico aéreo = air traffic
el puente aéreo = the shuttle

aeromozo/aeromoza noun, masculine/feminine (Lat Am)
un aeromozo/una aeromoza = a flight attendant

aeropuerto noun, masculine
un aeropuerto = an airport

afectar verb ①
= to affect

afeitarse verb ①
= to shave
= to shave off
se afeitó la barba = he shaved off his beard

aficionado/aficionada
1 adjective
• = keen
ser aficionado/aficionada a algo = to be keen on something
• (if it's an athlete, a sports player) = amateur
2 noun, masculine/feminine
un aficionado/una aficionada al fútbol = a football fan
un aficionado/una aficionada a la música = a music lover

afortunado/afortunada adjective
= lucky

africano/africana
1 adjective
= African
2 noun, masculine/feminine
un africano/una africana = an African

afuera adverb
• = outside
¡ven afuera! = come outside!
• (Lat Am) afuera de = outside
afuera del edificio = outside the building

afueras noun, feminine plural
las afueras = the outskirts

agarrar verb ①
• = to grab
• (Lat Am) = to take
• (Lat Am) = to catch
agarrar un resfriado = to catch a cold

agencia noun, feminine
una agencia = an agency

ágil adjective
= agile

agradezca, agradezco, etc
▶ agradecer

agosto noun, masculine
agosto = August

agotado/agotada adjective
• (if it's a person) = exhausted
• (if it's a book, record, etc) = sold out

agotar verb ①
= to use up

agradable adjective
= pleasant

agradecer verb ⑲
= to thank
agradecerle algo a alguien = to thank someone for something

agradecido/agradecida adjective
= grateful
le estoy muy agradecida = I am very grateful to you

agresivo/agresiva adjective
= aggressive

agrícola adjective
= agricultural

agricultor/agricultora noun, masculine/feminine
un agricultor/una agricultora = a farmer

agrio/agria adjective
= sour

agua noun, feminine
el agua = water

> **!** Note that although agua is feminine it is preceded by a masculine article in the singular

agua mineral con gas/sin gas = sparkling/still mineral water

aguacate noun, masculine
un aguacate = an avocado

aguantar verb ①
• = to bear
= to stand
• = to put up with
• = to hold
aguantar la respiración = to hold one's breath

águila noun, feminine
un águila = an eagle

> **!** Note that although águila is feminine it is preceded by a masculine article in the singular

• águila o sol (Mex) = heads or tails

aguja noun, feminine
• una aguja = a needle
• (of watch, clock) = a hand

agujero noun, masculine
un agujero = a hole

ahí adverb
= there
ponlo ahí = put it there

ahogarse verb ③
• = to suffocate
• = to drown

---

ahora *adverb*
= now
ahora mismo = right now
por ahora = for the time being

ahorrar *verb* [1]
= to save

ahorro *noun, masculine*
un ahorro = a saving
mis ahorros = my savings

aire *noun, masculine*
aire = air
aire acondicionado = air-conditioning
al aire libre = outdoors
estar al aire libre = to be outdoors
un concierto al aire libre = an open-air
concert

ajedrez *noun, masculine*
el ajedrez = chess

ajo *noun, masculine*
ajo = garlic

al

> ! Note that al *is a contraction of the
> preposition* a *and the definite article* el

• ir al cine = to go to the cinema
vimos al marido de Elena = we saw Elena's
husband
• *(used before an infinitive)*
al verme se puso a llorar = when he saw
me he started to cry
tengo que llamarlos al llegar a casa = I
have to phone them when I get home

ala *noun, feminine*
un ala = a wing

> ! Note that although ala *is feminine it is
> preceded by a masculine article in the
> singular*

alambre *noun, masculine*
alambre = wire

alargar *verb* [3]
• = to extend
decidieron alargar las vacaciones = they
decided to extend their vacation
• = to lengthen
alargar una falda = to lengthen a skirt
• = to stretch out
alargó la mano para tomar el libro = she
stretched out her hand to take the book
alargarse
• = to get longer
los días se iban alargando = the days were
getting longer
• = to go on
la reunión se alargó hasta la noche = the
meeting went on until night-time

alarma *noun, feminine*
una alarma = an alarm
una alarma contra incendios = a fire alarm

albañil *noun, masculine*
un albañil = a builder
= a bricklayer

albaricoque *noun, masculine* (Spa)
un albaricoque = an apricot

alberca *noun, feminine* (Mex)
una alberca = a swimming pool

albergue *noun, masculine*
un albergue = a hostel
un albergue juvenil = a youth hostel

albóndiga *noun, feminine*
una albóndiga = a meatball

álbum *noun, masculine*
un álbum = an album

alcachofa *noun, feminine*
una alcachofa = an artichoke

alcalde *noun, masculine*
el alcalde = the mayor

alcaldesa *noun, feminine*
la alcaldesa = the mayoress
= the mayor's wife

alcanzar *verb* [4]
• = to reach
no alcanzo al estante de arriba = I can't
reach the top shelf
• = to catch up with
corrió para alcanzarlos = she ran to catch
up with them
• = to pass
¿me alcanzas la mantequilla? = can you
pass me the butter?

alcohol *noun, masculine*
alcohol = alcohol

alcohólico/alcohólica
1 *adjective*
= alcoholic
2 *noun, masculine/feminine*
un alcohólico/una alcohólica = an
alcoholic

alegrarse *verb* [1]
= to cheer up
¡alégrate! = cheer up!
• alegrarse de algo:
se alegran de tu éxito = they are happy
about your success
me alegro de verte = it's nice to see you
se alegraron de venir = they were glad they
had come

alegre *adjective*
• *(if it's a person)* = cheerful
• *(if it's a color)* = bright

alegría *noun, feminine*
alegría = joy
= happiness

alemán/alemana
1 *adjective*
= German
2 *noun, masculine|feminine*
un alemán/una alemana = a German
3 alemán *noun, masculine*
el alemán (*the language*) = German

Alemania *noun, feminine*
Alemania = Germany

alfabeto *noun, masculine*
el alfabeto = the alphabet

alfiler *noun, masculine*
un alfiler = a pin

alfombra *noun, feminine*
• una alfombra = a rug
(*large*) = a carpet
• (*Lat Am: wall to wall*) la alfombra = the
carpet

algo *pronoun*
• = something
quiero preguntarte algo = I want to ask you
something
• = anything
¿vas a comprar algo? = are you going to
buy anything?

algodón *noun, masculine*
algodón = cotton

alguien *pronoun*
• = someone, somebody
alguien me dijo que estaba cerrado =
someone told me that it was shut
• = anyone, anybody
¿llamó alguien? = did anyone phone?

algún *adjective*
▶ alguno/alguna

alguno/alguna

> **!** *Note that* alguno *becomes* algún *before*
> *masculine singular nouns*

1 *adjective*
• (*in affirmative sentences*) = some
algunos alumnos = some pupils
lo haré algún día = I'll do it some day
• (*in questions*) = any
¿quieres ver alguna película en especial?
= do you want to see any movie in
particular?
• alguna cosa = something
= anything
¿trajeron alguna cosa para comer? = did
they bring anything to eat?
• alguna vez = ever
¿has montado alguna vez en globo? =
have you ever been up in a balloon?
• en algún lugar, en algún sitio, en alguna
parte (*in affirmative sentences*) =
somewhere
(*in questions*) =anywhere

2 *pronoun*
siempre hay alguno que falta = there is
always one missing
seguro que a alguno se le olvida = one of
them is bound to forget
¿te queda alguno? = have you any left?
algunos fueron a pie = some went on foot
algunos de ellos = some of them

alimentar *verb* 1
= to feed

alimento *noun, masculine*
alimento = food

allá *adverb*
= there

allí *adverb*
= there

almacén *noun, masculine*
• un almacén = a warehouse
(*a room*) = a storeroom
• (*SC*) un almacén = a grocery store, a
grocer's shop

almendra *noun, feminine*
una almendra = an almond

almíbar *noun, masculine*
el almíbar = syrup

almohada *noun, feminine*
una almohada = a pillow

almorzar *verb* 10
= to have lunch

almuerza, almuerzo, etc ▶ almorzar

almuerzo *noun, masculine*
el almuerzo = lunch

aló *exclamation* (*AmS*)
(*when answering the phone*) = hello?

alojarse *verb* 1
= to stay

alojamiento *noun, masculine*
alojamiento = accommodations,
accommodation

alquilar *verb* 1
• (*from a person or company*)
= to rent
= to hire
• (*to a person or company*)
= to rent out
= to let
= to hire out

alquiler *noun, masculine*
• (*money paid*) = hire charge
= rent
• de alquiler:
un coche de alquiler = a hire car
un apartamento de alquiler = a rented
apartment

A

alrededor *adverb*
- a mi alrededor = around me
  se sentaron alrededor suyo = they sat around her
- alrededor de = around
  formaron un círculo alrededor del árbol = they formed a circle around the tree
  llegaron alrededor de las once = they'll arrive at about eleven
- de alrededor:
  los pueblos de alrededor son muy bonitos = the surrounding villages are very pretty

alrededores *noun, masculine plural*
  los alrededores = the surrounding area
  (*of a town*) = the outskirts
  = the surroundings

altavoz *noun, masculine*
  un altavoz = a loudspeaker

alternativa *noun, feminine*
  una alternativa = an alternative

altitud *noun, feminine*
  la altitud = the altitude

alto/alta
1 *adjective*
- (*if it's a person, building*) = tall
- (*if it's a mountain, volume*) = high
- (*if it's the radio*) = loud
2 alto *adverb*
  = loud
  hablar alto = to speak loudly
3 alto *noun, masculine*
- el alto = the height
  tiene 4m de alto = it's 4m high
- pasarse un alto (*Méx*) = to go through a red light
  = to go through a stop sign

altura *noun, feminine*
- la altura = the height
  tiene 50m de altura = it's 50m high
- la altura = the altitude

aluminio *noun, masculine*
  aluminio = aluminum, aluminium

alumno/alumna *noun, masculine/feminine*
- un alumno/una alumna = a pupil
- un alumno/una alumna = a student

amable *adjective*
  = kind

ama de casa *noun, feminine*
  un ama de casa = a housewife

> **!** *Note that although* ama de casa *is feminine it is preceded by a masculine article in the singular*

amanecer 19
1 *verb*
  = to get light
  estaba amaneciendo = it was getting light

2 *noun, masculine*
  el amanecer = dawn, daybreak
  al amanecer = at dawn, at daybreak

amanezca ▶ amanecer

amante *noun, masculine/feminine*
  un/una amante = a lover

amar *verb*
  = to love

amargo/amarga *adjective*
  = bitter

amarillo/amarilla
1 *adjective*
  = yellow
2 amarillo *noun, masculine*
  el amarillo = yellow

ambición *noun, feminine*
  la ambición = ambition

ambiente *noun, masculine*
- el ambiente = the environment
- (*at work, at a party*)
  el ambiente = the atmosphere

ambiguo/ambigua *adjective*
  = ambiguous

ambos/ambas *adjective, pronoun*
  = both
  ambos libros = both books
  me gustan ambas = I like them both

ambulancia *noun, feminine*
  una ambulancia = an ambulance

amenaza *noun, feminine*
  una amenaza = a threat

amenazar *verb* 4
  = to threaten

americano/americana
1 *adjective*
  = American
2 *noun, masculine/feminine*
  un americano/una americana = an American

amigo/amiga *noun, masculine/feminine*
  un amigo/una amiga = a friend

amistad *noun, feminine*
  la amistad = friendship

amor *noun, masculine*
  el amor = love

amplio/amplia *adjective*
  = wide

ancho/ancha
1 *adjective*
- = wide
- (*referring to clothing*)
  siempre lleva jerseys anchos = she always wears baggy sweaters
  esta chaqueta me queda ancha = this jacket is too big for me

R Pl River Plate area   SC Southern Cone   Spa Spain

2 ancho *noun, masculine*
= width
¿cuánto mide de ancho? = how wide is it?
tiene 30cm de ancho = it is 30cm wide

anciano/anciana
1 *adjective*
= elderly
2 *noun, masculine/feminine*
un anciano/una anciana = an elderly man/woman
los ancianos = the elderly

ancla *noun, feminine*
un ancla = an anchor

> **!** *Note that although* ancla *is feminine it is preceded by a masculine article in the singular*

andar *verb* 14
• = to walk
tuvimos que ir andando = we had to walk
• = to work
el reloj no anda = the watch doesn't work
• (*Lat Am*) = to ride
andar [en bicicleta | a caballo | en moto …] = to ride [a bicycle | a horse | a motorcycle …]

andén *noun, masculine*
un andén = a platform
(*C Am*) = a sidewalk, a pavement

anduve, anduviste, etc ▶ andar

ángel *noun, masculine*
un ángel = an angel

ángulo *noun, masculine*
un ángulo = an angle

anillo *noun, masculine*
un anillo = a ring

aniversario *noun, masculine*
un aniversario = an anniversary

anoche *adverb*
= last night
antes de anoche = the night before last

anochecer 19
1 *verb*
= to get dark
estaba anocheciendo = it was getting dark
2 *noun, masculine*
el anochecer = dusk
al anochecer = at dusk

anochezca ▶ anochecer

anotar *verb* 1
= to make a note of

antártico/antártica *adjective*
= Antarctic

Antártida *noun, feminine*
la Antártida = Antarctica

ante *preposition*
= before
se puso ante el micrófono = she stood before the microphone
ante todo = above all

antena *noun, feminine*
una antena (*on a radio, television*) = an antenna, an aerial
(*of an insect*) = an antenna

antepasado/antepasada *noun, masculine/feminine*
un antepasado/una antepasada = an ancestor

anterior *adjective*
= previous
el día anterior = the previous day, the day before

antes *adverb*
• = before
la noche antes = the night before
antes de Navidad = before Christmas
antes de anoche/ayer = the night/day before yesterday
• = earlier
ayer llegó antes = yesterday she arrived earlier
• (*indicating order, priority*)
éste va antes = this one goes first
antes de hacer algo = before doing something
lo antes posible = as soon as possible

anticonceptivo *noun, masculine*
un anticonceptivo = a contraceptive

anticuado/anticuada *adjective*
= old-fashioned

antiguo/antigua *adjective*
• = old
estos muebles son muy antiguos = this furniture is very old
• = former
el antiguo campeón = the former champion
• = ancient
el antiguo Egipto = ancient Egypt

anual *adjective*
= annual

anunciar *verb* 1
• (*if it's a decision, news*) = to announce
• (*if it's a product*) = to advertise

anuncio *noun, masculine*
un anuncio = an advertisement, an ad
(*on TV*) = a commercial
(*on a billboard*) = a poster

año *noun, masculine*
un año = a year
el año que viene = next year
los años 60 = the 60s
un año bisiesto = a leap year
¡Feliz Año Nuevo! = Happy New Year!
¿cuántos años tienes? = how old are you?
tengo trece años = I'm thirteen

apagar *verb* [3]
• (*if it's a light, TV*) = to turn off
• (*if it's a fire, cigarette*) = to put out

apagón *noun*, *masculine*
un apagón = a power cut, a blackout

aparato *noun*, *masculine*
los aparatos eléctricos = electrical
    appliances
el dentista y todos sus aparatos = the
    dentist and all his equipment

aparcamiento *noun*, *masculine* (*Spa*)
un aparcamiento = a parking lot, a car park

aparcar *verb* [2] (*Spa*)
= to park

aparecer *verb* [19]
= to appear

aparezca, aparezco, etc ▶ aparecer

apariencia *noun*, *feminine*
apariencia = appearance

apartamento *noun*, *masculine*
un apartamento = an apartment, a flat

apartar *verb* [1]
• = to move away
apartó el coche de la acera = she moved
    the car away from the sidewalk
• = to move out of the way
aparté las cajas para poder pasar = I
    moved the boxes out of the way so I could
    get past
• = to set aside
aparta los que te gusten = set aside the
    ones that you like
• apartar los ojos de algo = to take one's eyes
    off something
apartarse
• = to move over
¡apártese!, ¡apártate! = move over!
• = to move away
apartarse de la ventana = to move away
    from the window

aparte *adverb*
• = aside, to one side
puso sus libros aparte = he put his books
    aside
lo llamó aparte = she called him to one side
• aparte de = apart from

apellido *noun*, *masculine*
el apellido = the surname

apenas *adverb*
• = hardly
apenas podía oírlo = I could hardly hear it
• = hardly ever
apenas viene a vernos = she hardly ever
    comes to see us
• = scarcely
hace apenas tres meses que murió = it's
    scarcely three months since she died

• apenas el jueves podré ir (*Mex*) = I won't
    be able to go till Thursday
• (*meaning shortly afterwards*)
apenas había llegado cuando sonó el
    teléfono = no sooner had he arrived than
    the phone rang

apéndice *noun*, *masculine*
el apéndice = the appendix

apetecer *verb* [19] (*Spa*)
me apetece ir al cine = I feel like going to
    the cinema
haz lo que te apetezca = do whatever you
    like

apetezca, apetezco, etc ▶ apetecer

apetito *noun*, *masculine*
el apetito = appetite

aplastar *verb* [1]
= to crush, = to squash

aplaudir *verb* [41]
= to applaud
= to clap

aplauso *noun*, *masculine*
un aplauso = a round of applause
aplausos = applause

apodo *noun*, *masculine*
un apodo = a nickname

apostar *verb* [6]
= to bet

apoyar *verb* [1]
• = to lean
apoya la escalera en la pared = lean the
    ladder against the wall
• = to rest
apoyó la cabeza en la almohada = she
    rested her head on the pillow
• = to support
todos apoyaron mi decisión = everyone
    supported my decision
apoyarse
apoyarse en algo = to lean on something

apoyo *noun*, *masculine*
apoyo = support

apreciar *verb* [1]
• = to be fond of
la aprecio mucho = I am very fond of her
• = to appreciate
aprecio tu interés = I appreciate your
    interest

aprender *verb* [17]
= to learn

apretar *verb* [7]
• (*if it's a lid, bolt*) = to tighten
• (*if it's a button*) = to press

- (referring to shoes, clothing)
  estos zapatos me aprietan = these shoes are too tight for me
- = to squeeze
  me apretó la mano = she squeezed my hand
- **apretar el puño** = to clench one's fist
- **apretar el acelerador** = to put one's foot on the accelerator

aprieta, aprieto, etc ▶ apretar

aprobar verb [6]
- (if it's an idea, behavior) = to approve of
- (if it's a test, subject) = to pass

apropiado/apropiada adjective
= appropiate, suitable

aprovechar verb [1]
- = to make good use of
  hay que aprovechar bien el tiempo = we have to make good use of our time
- (other uses)
  aproveché su visita para devolverle los libros = her visit gave me the chance to return her books to her
  quisiera aprovechar la oportunidad para darle las gracias = I would like to take the opportunity to thank you
  ¡qué aproveche! = enjoy your meal!

aproximado/aproximada adjective
= rough
un cálculo aproximado = a rough estimate

aprueba, apruebo, etc ▶ aprobar

apto/apta adjective
= suitable

apuesta, apuesto, etc ▶ apostar

apuntar verb [1]
- (if it's a name, address) = to note down
- (with your finger etc) = to point at
  me apuntó con el dedo = she pointed her finger at me
apuntarse
= to put one's name down
  me apunté para ir a la excursión = I put my name down for the trip

aquel/aquella
adjective
aquel/aquella = that
aquellos/aquellas = those
aquel día = that day
dame aquellos zapatos = give me those shoes

aquél/aquélla pronoun
aquél/aquélla = that one
aquéllos/aquéllas = those
aquélla es la que más me gusta = I like that one the most
aquéllos son de Juan = those are Juan's

aquello pronoun
¿qué es aquello de allí? = what's that over there?

aquí adverb
= here
ven aquí = come here
lo puse aquí abajo = I put it down here
- **por aquí:**
  por aquí, por favor = this way, please
  creo que está por aquí = I think it's around here
  está por aquí cerca = it's near here

árabe
1 adjective
= Arab
2 noun, masculine|feminine
un/una árabe = an Arab
3 árabe noun, masculine
el árabe (the language) = Arabic

araña noun, feminine
una araña = a spider

árbitro/árbitra noun, masculine|feminine
un árbitro/una árbitra (in football, boxing) = a referee
(in tennis, baseball) = an umpire

árbol noun, masculine
un árbol = a tree

arbusto noun, masculine
un arbusto = a bush

archivo noun, masculine
un archivo = an archive
(in computing) = a file

arco noun, masculine
- **un arco** = an arch
- (for shooting arrows, playing the violin) **un arco** = a bow
- (Lat Am: in football) **el arco** = the goal

arder verb [17]
= to burn

área noun, feminine
un área = an area

> **!** Note that although **área** is feminine it is preceded by a masculine article in the singular

arena noun, feminine
arena = sand

arete noun, masculine (Mex)
un arete = an earring

argentino/argentina
1 adjective
= Argentinian
2 noun, masculine|feminine
un argentino/una argentina = an Argentinian

---

argot noun, masculine
  argot = slang

Aries noun, masculine
  Aries = Aries

aries noun, masculine|feminine
  un/una aries = an Aries

aristocracia noun, feminine
  la aristocracia = the aristocracy

aritmética noun, feminine
  aritmética = arithmetic

arma noun, feminine
  un arma = a weapon

> ! Note that although **arma** is feminine it is
> preceded by a masculine article in the
> singular
> las armas = weapons, arms

armario noun, masculine
  un armario = a cupboard
  (for keeping clothes) = a closet, a wardrobe

armonía noun, feminine
  armonía = harmony

armónica noun, feminine
  una armónica = a harmonica

aro noun, masculine (SC)
  un aro = an earring

aroma noun, masculine
  un aroma = an aroma

arpa noun, feminine
  un arpa = a harp

> ! Note that although **arpa** is feminine it is
> preceded by a masculine article in the
> singular

arquitecto/arquitecta noun,
masculine|feminine
  un arquitecto/una arquitecta = an architect

arquitectura noun, feminine
  arquitectura = architecture

arrancar verb ②
* = to pull up
  arrancar una planta = to pull up a plant
* = to pull out
  no puedo arrancar este clavo = I can't pull
  this nail out
* = to tear off
  me arrancó un botón de la chaqueta = he
  tore a button off my jacket
* = to tear out
  arrancar una hoja de un libro = to tear a
  page out of a book
* = to start
  arrancó el coche = she started the car
* = to snatch
  me arrancó las llaves de la mano = she
  snatched the keys from my hand

arrastrar verb ①
  = to drag
arrastrarse
  = to crawl

arreglar verb ①
* = to mend
* (if it's a television, washing-machine) = to
  repair
* (if it's a room, the house) = to straighten
  (up), to tidy (up)
* = to sort out
  no sé cómo arreglar este asunto = I don't
  know how to sort this matter out
arreglarse
* = to get ready
  necesito dos minutos para arreglarme = I
  need two minutes to get ready
* = to get better
  a ver si se arreglan las cosas = let's see if
  things get better

arriba adverb
* = up
  está ahí arriba = it's up there
  ponlo más arriba = put it higher up
* de arriba:
  la parte de arriba = the top part
  el piso de arriba = the apartment above
  = the top apartment
  los vecinos de arriba = the upstairs
  neighbors
* arriba de (Lat Am):
  está arriba del armario = it's on top of the
  cupboard
  está arriba de mi dormitorio = it's above my
  bedroom

arriesgarse verb ③
* = to take a risk
* = to risk
  se arriesgan a que los despidan = they
  risk being fired

arrogante adjective
  = arrogant

arroz noun, masculine
  arroz = rice

arte noun, masculine
  el arte = art

> ! Note that **arte** is generally masculine in
> the singular and feminine in the plural:
> las artes = the arts

artesanía noun, feminine
  artesanía = crafts

artesano/artesana noun,
masculine|feminine
  un artesano/una artesana = a craftsman/a
  craftswoman

ártico/ártica adjective
  = Arctic

Ártico *noun, masculine*
el Ártico = the Arctic
= the Arctic Ocean

artículo *noun, masculine*
el artículo = the article
el artículo definido = the definite article

artificial *adjective*
= artificial

artista *noun, masculine/feminine*
un/una artista = artist

asa *noun, feminine*
un asa = a handle

> ! Note that although **asa** *is feminine it is preceded by a masculine article in the singular*

asado *noun, masculine*
un asado = a roast
(*Lat Am*) = a barbecue

asar *verb* 1
(*if it's meat*) = to roast
(*if it's a potato*) = to bake

ascensor *noun, masculine*
el ascensor = the elevator, the lift

asegurar *verb* 1
• = to assure
me aseguró que vendría = she assured me that she would come
• = to insure
aseguraron el cuadro en un millón = they insured the painting for a million
asegurarse
= to make sure
asegúrate de cerrar la puerta = make sure you shut the door

asesino/asesina *noun,*
masculine/feminine
un asesino/una asesina = a murderer

asfalto *noun, masculine*
el asfalto = asphalt

asfixiar *verb*
= to suffocate
• = to smother
asfixiarse
• = to suffocate

así
1 *adverb*
• = like this
así es mejor = it's better like this
• = like that
no te pongas así = don't be like that
2 *adjective* (! *never changes*)
= like that
él es así = he's like that

asiático/asiática
1 *adjective*
= Asian

2 *noun, masculine/feminine*
un asiático/una asiática = an Asian

asiento *noun, masculine*
un asiento = a seat
(*on a bicycle*) = a saddle

asignatura *noun, feminine*
una asignatura = a subject

asistir *verb* 41
= to attend
= to go to

asno *noun, masculine*
un asno = a donkey

asociación *noun, feminine*
una asociación = an association

asociar *verb* 1
= to associate
asociarse
asociarse a algo = to become a member of something
asociarse con alguien = to go into partnership with someone

aspecto *noun, masculine*
• (*referring to appearance*)
un niño de aspecto delicado = a delicate-looking boy
tienen un aspecto agradable = they look nice
¿qué aspecto tienen? = what do they look like?
• (*referring to health*)
no tienes buen aspecto = you don't look well
• un aspecto = an aspect

áspero/áspera *adjective*
= rough

aspiradora *noun, feminine,* **aspirador**
noun, masculine
una aspiradora, un aspirador = a vacuum cleaner, a Hoover
pasar la aspiradora, pasar el aspirador = to vacuum, to hoover

aspirina *noun, feminine*
una aspirina = an aspirin

asterisco *noun, masculine*
un asterisco = an asterisk

astrología *noun, feminine*
la astrología = astrology

astronauta *noun, masculine/feminine*
un/una astronauta = an astronaut

asunto *noun, masculine*
un asunto = a matter
es un asunto personal = it's a personal matter
no es asunto tuyo = it's none of your business

C Am Central America   **Lat Am** Latin America   **Mex** Mexico

asustar *verb* [1]
= to scare, to frighten
asustarse
= to get scared, to get frightened

atacar *verb*
= to attack

ataque *noun, masculine*
un ataque = an attack
un ataque cardíaco = a heart attack

atar *verb* [1]
= to tie
= to tie up
me ataron las manos = they tied my hands
up
atarse
= to do up
se ató los zapatos = he did up his shoes

atardecer
1 *verb*
= to get dark
atardecía = it was getting dark
2 *noun, masculine*
el atardecer = dusk
al atardecer = at dusk

atención *noun, feminine*
atención = attention
prestar atención = to pay attention

Atlántico *noun, masculine*
el Atlántico = the Atlantic

atlas *noun, masculine*
un atlas = an atlas

atleta *noun, masculine/feminine*
un/una atleta = an athlete

atlético/atlética *adjective*
= athletic

atletismo *noun, masculine*
el atletismo = athletics

atmósfera *noun, feminine*
la atmósfera = the atmosphere

atómico/atómica *adjective*
= atomic

atracar *verb* [2]
• (*if it's a bank*) = to hold up
• (*if it's a person*) = to mug

atraco *noun, masculine*
un atraco (*in a bank*) = a holdup
(*in the street*) = a mugging

atractivo/atractiva *adjective*
= attractive

atrapar *verb* [1]
= to catch

atrás *adverb*
• = back
ponlo más atrás = put it further back

• = at the back
con botones atrás = with buttons at the
back
quedarse atrás = to be left behind
• (*Lat Am*) **atrás de** = behind
atrás de mí = behind me

atrasado/atrasada *adjective*
• = slow
tengo el reloj atrasado = my watch is slow
• = behind
estamos *or* vamos atrasados en los
preparativos = we're behind in our
preparations

atrasar *verb* [1]
• = to postpone
atrasaron el comienzo del curso = they
postponed the start of the course
• = to delay
atrasaron la salida del avión = the flight
was delayed
• = to put back
atrasar los relojes una hora = to put the
clocks back an hour
• = to be slow, to lose time
este reloj atrasa = this clock is slow
atrasarse
• = to be slow, to lose time
este reloj se atrasa = this clock is slow
• = to be late (*Lat Am*)
el vuelo se atrasó = the flight was late

atreverse *verb* [17]
= to dare
no me atreví a llamar = I didn't dare call

atrevido/atrevida *adjective*
• = daring
• = sassy, cheeky

atropellar *verb* [1]
= to knock down
= to run over

atún *noun, masculine*
el atún = tuna

aula *noun, feminine*
un aula = a classroom
(*in a university*) = a lecture theater

! *Note that although* aula *is feminine it is
preceded by a masculine article in the
singular*

aumentar *verb* [1]
= to increase

aumento *noun, masculine*
un aumento = an increase

aun *adverb*
= even
ni aun con una caja más grande = not even
with a bigger box
aun así = even so

aún *adverb*
• = still
  es aún joven = he is still young
• = yet
  ¿aún no has terminado? = haven't you finished yet?
• = even
  éste es aún más barato = this one is even cheaper

aunque *conjunction*
• = although
• = even though
• = even if
  inténtalo, aunque sólo sea una vez = try it, even if only once

auricular
1 *noun, masculine*
  (*of a telephone*)
  el auricular = the receiver
2 auriculares *noun, masculine plural*
  los auriculares = the headphones

ausencia *noun, feminine*
  una ausencia = an absence

ausente *adjective*
  = absent

australiano/australiana
1 *adjective*
  = Australian
2 *noun, masculine/feminine*
  un australiano/una australiana = an Australian

austriaco/austriaca,
austríaco/austríaca
1 *adjective*
  = Austrian
2 *noun, masculine/feminine*
  un austriaco/una austriaca = an Austrian

auténtico/auténtica *adjective*
  = genuine, authentic

auto *noun, masculine* (*SC*)
  un auto = a car

autobiografía *noun, feminine*
  una autobiografía = an autobiography

autobús *noun, masculine*
  un autobús = a bus
  (*Lat Am*) = a coach

autocar *noun, masculine* (*Spa*)
  un autocar = a bus, a coach

autógrafo *noun, masculine*
  un autógrafo = an autograph

automático/automática *adjective*
  = automatic

automóvil *noun, masculine*
  un automóvil = a car

autopista *noun, feminine*
  una autopista = an expressway, a motorway

autor/autora *noun, masculine/feminine*
  un autor/una autora = an author

autoridad *noun, feminine*
  autoridad = authority

autoservicio *noun, masculine*
  un autoservicio = a self-service restaurant

autostop *noun, masculine*
  autostop = hitchhiking
  hacer autostop = to hitchhike

avalancha *noun, feminine*
  una avalancha = an avalanche

avanzar *verb* 4
  = to advance

ave *noun, feminine*
  un ave = a bird

> **!** *Note that although* **ave** *is feminine it is preceded by a masculine article in the singular*

avellana *noun, feminine*
  una avellana = a hazelnut

avenida *noun, feminine*
  una avenida = an avenue

aventar *verb* 7 (*Mex*)
  = to throw

aventón *noun, masculine* (*Mex*)
  un aventón = a ride, a lift

aventura *noun, feminine*
  una aventura = an adventure

avería *noun, feminine*
  una avería = a breakdown

aviación *noun, feminine*
  la aviación = aviation

avión *noun, masculine*
  un avión = a plane, an airplane, an aeroplane

avisar *verb* 1
• = to let know
  avísame cuando termines = let me know when you've finished
• = to warn
• (*Mex, Spa*) = to call
  avisar al médico = to call the doctor

aviso *noun, masculine*
• **un aviso** = a notice
• **un aviso** = a warning
  sin previo aviso, sin avisar = without prior warning
• (*Lat Am*) **un aviso** = an advertisement, an advert

avispa *noun, feminine*
  una avispa = a wasp

¡ay! *exclamation*
(*expressing pain*) = ouch!, ow!
(*expressing alarm*) = oh dear!

ayer *adverb*
= yesterday
ayer en *or* (*Spa*) **por** *or* (*R Pl*) **a la noche** =
last night

ayuda *noun, feminine*
ayuda = help

ayudante *noun, masculine/feminine*
un/una ayudante = an assistant

ayudar *verb* 1
= to help

ayuntamiento *noun, masculine*
el ayuntamiento = the town hall

azafata *noun, feminine*
una azafata = a flight attendant, an air
hostess

azúcar *noun, masculine/feminine*
azúcar = sugar

> **!** *Note that* azúcar *is always preceded by
> the masculine article even though it can
> have a feminine adjective:* el azúcar
> morena = *brown sugar*

azucarero *noun, masculine*
un azucarero = a sugar bowl

azul
1 *adjective*
= blue
2 *noun, masculine*
el azul = blue

azulejo *noun, masculine*
un azulejo = a tile

bachillerato *noun, masculine*
el bachillerato = high school education and
diploma

bahía *noun, feminine*
una bahía = a bay

bailar *verb* 1
= to dance

bailarín/bailarina *noun,*
masculine/feminine
un bailarín/una bailarina = a dancer

baile *noun, masculine*
• baile = dance
un baile nuevo = a new dance

• (*the activity*)
el baile = dancing

bajar *verb* 1
• = to go/come down
ya bajo = I'm coming down
el camino baja hasta la playa = the road
goes down to the beach
• = to get down
baja ese libro del estante = get that book
down from the shelf
• = to take down
voy a bajar estas cajas = I'm going to take
down these boxes
• = to bring down
¿me bajas un jersey? = can you bring
down a sweater for me?
• = to lower
bajar la vista/los ojos = to lower one's
eyes
• = to turn down
bajar la televisión = to turn down the
television
• (*if it's temperature, prices*) = to fall
• bajar la cabeza = to bow one's head
bajarse
bajarse de un coche = to get out of a car
bajarse del tren = to get off the train

bajo/baja
1 *adjective*
• = short
• (*if it's volume, level, a building*) = low
hablar en voz baja = to speak quietly
2 bajo *preposition*
= under
3 bajo *adverb*
• =low
volar bajo = to fly low
• = quietly, softly
hablar bajo = to speak quietly
4 bajo *noun, masculine*
• el bajo = the first floor, the ground floor
• el bajo (*of a dress, skirt*) = the hem
(*of trousers*) = the cuff, the turn-up

bala *noun, feminine*
una bala = a bullet

balcón *noun*
un balcón = a balcony

ballena *noun, feminine*
una ballena = a whale

balón *noun, masculine*
un balón = a ball

balonvolea *noun, masculine*
el balonvolea = volleyball

banco *noun, masculine*
• un banco = a bank
• un banco (*in a park*) = a bench
(*in a church*) = a pew

bandeja *noun, feminine*
una bandeja = a tray

bandera noun, feminine
una bandera = a flag

banqueta noun, feminine
• una banqueta = a stool
• (Mex) una banqueta = a sidewalk

bañador noun, masculine (Spa)
un bañador = a swimsuit

bañar verb ⊡
= to bath
bañarse
= to have a bath

bañera noun, feminine
una bañera = a bath, a bathtub

baño noun, masculine
• un baño = a bath
darse un baño = to have a bath
= to have a swim
• el baño = the bathroom
ir al baño = to go to the bathroom, to go to
the toilet

bar noun, masculine
un bar = a bar

baraja noun, feminine
una baraja = a deck of cards

barata noun, feminine (Mex)
una barata = a sale

barato/barata adjective
= cheap

barba noun, feminine
una barba = a beard
dejarse (la) barba = to grow a beard

barbacoa noun, feminine
una barbacoa = a barbecue
hacer una barbacoa = to have a barbecue

barbilla noun, feminine
la barbilla = the chin

barco noun, masculine
un barco = a boat

barra noun, feminine
• una barra (of chocolate, soap) = a bar
(of deodorant) = a stick
• (for curtains) una barra = a rod
• una barra de pan (Mex, Spa) = a stick, a
French loaf

barrer verb ⊡⊓
= to sweep

barrera noun, feminine
una barrera = a barrier

barriga noun, feminine
una barriga = a belly, a tummy
echar barriga = to develop a paunch

barrio noun, masculine
un barrio = a neighborhood, a
neighbourhood
el barrio Gótico = the Gothic quarter

barro noun, masculine
barro = mud
(for pottery) = clay

base noun, feminine
• una base = a base
• la base = the basis

bastante
1 adjective
• = enough
¿tenemos bastantes sillas? = do we have
enough chairs?
• = quite a lot of
vino bastante gente = quite a lot of people
came
2 pronoun
= enough
3 adverb
• = enough
no es bastante fuerte = he's not strong
enough
• = quite
es bastante guapa = she's quite pretty
me gusta bastante = I like it quite a lot

bastar verb ⊡
= to be enough

basura noun, feminine
la basura = the garbage, the rubbish
(container) = the garbage can, the dustbin
tirar algo a la basura = to throw something
away

basurero/basurera
1 noun, masculine/feminine
un basurero/una basurera = garbage
collector, dustman
2 basurero noun masculine
el basurero = the garbage can, the dustbin

batalla noun, feminine
una batalla = a battle

bate noun, masculine
un bate = a bat

batería noun, feminine
• una batería = a battery
• la batería = the drums

batido noun, masculine
un batido = a (milk)shake

batir verb ⊠⊓
• (if it's eggs) = to beat
• (if it's cream) = to whip
• (if it's a record) = to beat

baúl noun, masculine
un baúl = a trunk
(R Pl: in a car) = a trunk, a boot

bebe/beba noun, masculine/feminine
(R Pl)
un bebe/una beba = a baby

bebé noun, masculine
un bebé = a baby

bebedero *noun, masculine (Méx, SC)*
un bebedero = a drinking fountain

beber *verb* [17]
= to drink

bebida *noun, feminine*
una bebida = a drink

beca *noun, feminine*
una beca = a grant
= a scholarship

béisbol *or (Mex)* **beisbol** *noun, masculine*
el béisbol, el beisbol = baseball

belga
1 *adjective*
= Belgian
2 *noun, masculine/feminine*
un/una belga = a Belgian

Bélgica *noun, feminine*
Bélgica = Belgium

belleza *noun, feminine*
la belleza = beauty

bello/bella *adjective*
= beautiful

berenjena *noun, feminine*
una berenjena = an eggplant, aubergine

besar *verb* [1]
= to kiss

beso *noun, masculine*
un beso = a kiss

betabel *noun, feminine (Mex)*
una betabel = a beet, a beetroot

Biblia *noun, feminine*
la Biblia = the Bible

biblioteca *noun, feminine*
una biblioteca = a library

bibliotecario/bibliotecaria *noun, masculine/feminine*
un bibliotecario/una bibliotecaria = a librarian

bicho* *noun, masculine*
• un bicho = a bug
• un bicho = a critter, a creature

bici* *noun, feminine*
una bici = a bike

! *Note that* bici *is short for* bicicleta

bicicleta *noun, feminine*
una bicicleta = a bicycle

bien
1 *adverb*

• = well
lo has hecho muy bien = you've done it very well
¿qué tal estás? — muy bien, gracias = how are you? — very well, thank you
• = all right, OK
¿estás bien? = are you all right?
• = correctly
contestó bien = he answered correctly
• = good
• = nice
huele bien = it smells nice
• = properly
siéntate bien = sit properly
• ¡muy bien! = very good!, well done!
• hablar bien inglés/francés = to speak good English/French
• hacer bien:
hiciste bien llamándome = you did the right thing phoning me
• ¡está bien! *(agreeing to something)* = OK!
2 *noun, masculine*
• el bien = good
• *(Spa: in school)* = grade between 6 and 7 on a scale of 10

bienvenida *noun, feminine*
una bienvenida = a welcome
darle la bienvenida a alguien = to welcome someone

bienvenido/bienvenida *adjective*
= welcome

bigote *noun, masculine*
un bigote = a mustache, a moustache

bilingüe *adjective*
= bilingual

billar *noun, masculine*
el billar = billiards

billetera *noun, feminine,* **billetero** *noun, masculine*
una billetera, un billetero = a wallet, a billfold

biografía *noun, feminine*
una biografía = a biography

biología *noun, feminine*
la biología = biology

biólogo/bióloga *noun, masculine/feminine*
un biólogo/una bióloga = a biologist

biquini *noun, masculine*
un biquini = a bikini

birome *noun feminine (R Pl)*
una birome = a ballpoint pen

bisabuelo/bisabuela *noun, masculine/feminine*
un bisabuelo/una bisabuela = a great-grandfather/a great-grandmother
mis bisabuelos = my great-grandparents

bisnieto/bisnieta *noun,*
masculine/feminine
  un bisnieto/una bisnieta = a great-
    grandson/a great-granddaughter
  mis bisnietos = my great-grandchildren

blanco/blanca
1 *adjective*
  = white
  en blanco y negro = in black and white
2 *noun, masculine/feminine*
  un blanco/una blanca = a white
    man/woman
  los blancos = white people
3 blanco *noun, masculine*
• el blanco = the target
  dar en el blanco = to hit the target
• (*the color*) el blanco = white

blando/blanda *adjective*
  = soft
  (*if it's meat*) = tender

bloc *noun, masculine*
  un bloc = a writing pad

bloque *noun, masculine*
  un bloque = a block

bloquear *verb* 1
  = to block

blusa *noun, feminine*
  una blusa = a blouse

boca *noun, feminine*
• la boca = the mouth
• (*of tunnel*) la boca = the entrance
  la boca del metro *or* (*R Pl*) subte = the
    subway entrance, underground entrance
• boca abajo/arriba = face up/down
  (*referring to person*) = on one's stomach/on
    one's back

bocadillo *noun, masculine* (*Spa*)
  un bocadillo = a (filled) roll

bocina *noun, feminine*
• una bocina = a horn
• (*Lat Am: of a telephone*) la bocina = the
  receiver

boda *noun, feminine*
  una boda = a wedding

bodega *noun, feminine*
  una bodega = a wine cellar
  (*selling wine*) = a wine merchant's
  (*C Am*) = a grocery store, a grocer's

bofetada *noun, feminine*
  una bofetada = a slap

boina *noun, feminine*
  una boina = a beret

bola *noun, feminine*
  una bola = a ball
  una bola de nieve = a snowball

boletería *noun, feminine* (*Lat Am*)
  la boletería = the ticket office

boleto *noun, masculine*
  un boleto (*for lottery*) = a ticket
  (*Lat Am: for train, bus, etc*) = a ticket
  (*Mex: for the theater etc*) = a ticket

boli× *noun, masculine*
  un boli = a ballpoint pen

> ❗ *Note that* boli *is short for* bolígrafo

bolígrafo *noun, masculine*
  un bolígrafo = a ballpoint pen

bollo *noun, masculine*
  un bollo = a bun

bolsa *noun, feminine*
• una bolsa = a bag
• (*Mex*) una bolsa = a purse, a handbag

bolsillo *noun, masculine*
  un bolsillo = a pocket
  de bolsillo = pocket-size

bolso *noun, masculine*
  (*Spa*) un bolso = a handbag, a purse
  un bolso de viaje = an overnight bag

boludo/boluda❞ *noun,*
masculine/feminine (*R Pl*)
  un boludo/una boluda = an asshole

bomba *noun, feminine*
  una bomba = a bomb

bombero *noun, masculine/feminine,*
bombero/bombera *noun,*
masculine/feminine
  un/una bombero, un bombero/una
    bombera = a firefighter

bombilla *noun, feminine* (*Spa*)
  una bombilla = a light bulb

bombita *noun, feminine* (*R Pl*)
  una bombita = a light bulb

bombón *noun, masculine*
  un bombón = a chocolate
  (*Mex*) = a marshmallow

bonito/bonita *adjective*
  = pretty
  = nice
  = lovely

borde *noun, masculine*
• un borde = an edge
  (*of glass etc*) = a rim
• al borde de algo
  = on the brink *or* verge of something

bordo *noun, masculine*
  a bordo = on board

borracho/borracha
1 *adjective*
= drunk
2 *noun, masculine/feminine*
un borracho/una borracha = a drunk

borrador *noun, masculine*
• un borrador = a (rough) draft
(*for the blackboard*) = an eraser, a board
rubber
(*Mex, Spa: for pencil*) = an eraser, a rubber

borrar *verb* $\boxed{1}$
• = to erase, to rub out
• = to white out, to Tipp-Ex   out
• (*if it's the blackboard*) = to clean
• (*from a tape*) = to erase
• (*from a computer*) = to delete

bosque *noun, masculine*
un bosque = a forest
= a wood

bostezar *verb* $\boxed{4}$
= to yawn

bota *noun, feminine*
• una bota = a boot
• (*for wine*) una bota = a small wineskin

botar *verb* $\boxed{1}$ (*Lat Am*)
botar algo = to throw something out *or*
away
botar a alguien✱ (*from a job*) = to fire
someone
(*from a bar, etc*) = to throw someone out

bote *noun, masculine*
• un bote = a boat
• un bote (*of marmalade, jelly*) = a jar
(*of paint*) = a can, a tin
• (*Mex: for garbage*) un bote = a trash can, a
rubbish bin

botella *noun, feminine*
una botella = a bottle

botón *noun, masculine*
un botón = a button
(*of TV, etc*) = a button, a switch
(*Lat Am*) = a badge

boxeador/boxeadora *noun,*
masculine/feminine
un boxeador/una boxeadora = a boxer

boxear *verb* $\boxed{1}$
= to box

bragas *noun, feminine plural* (*Spa*)
unas bragas = a pair of panties

bragueta *noun, feminine*
la bragueta (*in trousers*) = fly, flies

brasier *noun, masculine* (*Mex*)
un brasier = a bra

brasileño/brasileña *or* (*Lat Am*)
brasilero/brasilera

1 *adjective*
= Brazilian
2 *noun, masculine/feminine*
un brasileño/una brasileña = a Brazilian

brazo *noun, masculine*
un brazo = an arm

brillante
1 *adjective*
= bright
= shiny
2 *noun, masculine*
un brillante = a diamond

brillar *verb* $\boxed{1}$
= to shine
= to sparkle

brisa *noun, feminine*
una brisa = a breeze

británico/británica
1 *adjective*
= British
2 *noun, masculine/feminine*
un británico/una británica = a British
man/woman

broma *noun, feminine*
una broma = a joke
hacerle *or* gastarle una broma a alguien =
to play a joke on someone

bromear *verb* $\boxed{1}$
= to joke

bronce *noun, masculine*
el bronce = bronze

bronceado/bronceada *adjective*
= tanned

bruja *noun, feminine*
una bruja = a witch

brújula *noun, feminine*
una brújula = a compass

buceador/buceadora *noun,*
masculine/feminine
un buceador/una buceadora = a diver

bucear *verb* $\boxed{1}$
= to dive

buen *adjective* ▶ bueno/buena

bueno/buena
1 *adjective*

> ! Note that bueno *becomes* buen *before*
> masculine singular nouns

• = good
son muy buenos conmigo = they are very
good to me
ser bueno para [los deportes | los idiomas | la
física ...] = to be good at [sport | languages |
physics ...]

R Pl River Plate area   SC Southern Cone   Spa Spain

* (*in greetings*)
¡buenos días! *or* (*R Pl*) **¡buen día!** = good morning
¡buen provecho! = enjoy your meal!
* **estar bueno/buena** (*referring to taste*) = to be nice
(*referring to condition of food*)
esta leche no está buena = this milk is off
* **¡qué bueno!** (*referring to food*) = it's really nice!
* **¡qué bueno!** (*Lat Am*) = great!
2 bueno *adverb*
= OK, all right
¿quieres un café? — bueno = do you want a coffee? — OK
* (*other uses*)
bueno, ya he terminado = well, I have finished now
¡bueno, basta ya! = right, that's enough!
¡bueno! (*Mex: answering the phone*) = hello!

buey *noun, masculine*
un buey = an ox

bufanda *noun, feminine*
una bufanda = a scarf

búho *noun, masculine*
un búho = an owl

burbuja *noun, feminine*
una burbuja = a bubble

burlarse *verb* [1]
burlarse de algo/alguien = to make fun of something/somebody

burro *noun, masculine*
un burro = a donkey

busca *noun, feminine*
a la *or* **en busca de algo** = in search of something

buscar *verb* [2]
* = to look for
* = to look
buscar en un cajón = to look in a drawer
(*in a book, list*) = to look up
* **ir a buscar a alguien** = to go to pick someone up

búsqueda *noun, feminine*
búsqueda = search

buzo *noun, masculine*
un buzo = a diver

buzón *noun, masculine*
un buzón = a mailbox, a letterbox

Cc

caballero *noun, masculine*
un caballero = a gentleman
caballeros (*in a store*) = menswear
caballeros (*toilets*) = Gentlemen

caballo *noun, masculine*
un caballo = a horse
(*in chess*) = a knight

cabello *noun, masculine*
el cabello = the hair

caber *verb* [27]
* = to fit
la mesa no cabe aquí = the table doesn't fit here
cabe otro más = there's room for one more
* = to hold
en el estadio caben 100.000 personas = the theater holds 100,000 people
* **caber por algo** = to go through something
no cabe por la puerta = it doesn't go through the door

cabeza *noun, feminine*
* **la cabeza** = the head
se tiró a la piscina de cabeza = he dived into the pool
caí de cabeza = I fell on my head
lavarse la cabeza = to wash one's hair
* **a la cabeza de**
= at the top of
= at the head of
* **cabeza abajo** = upside down
* **una cabeza de ajo(s)** = a head of garlic

cabina *noun, feminine*
una cabina telefónica *or* **de teléfonos** = a telephone box

cabra *noun, feminine*
una cabra = a goat

cabré, cabría, etc ▶ caber

cabrón/cabrona◄
1 *noun, masculine/feminine* (*Spa*)
un cabrón/una cabrona = a bastard/a bitch
2 cabrón◄ *noun, masculine*
un cabrón = a cuckold

cacahuete, cacahuate *noun, masculine*
un cacahuete, un cacahuate = a peanut

cacao *noun, masculine*
* **cacao** = cocoa
* (*Spa*) **cacao** = lipsalve

cacerola *noun, feminine*
una cacerola = a saucepan

cada *adjective*
= each
= every
cada uno = each
cada noche = every night, each night
cada dos días = every two days
cada cierto tiempo = every so often
cada vez más/menos = more and more/less and less
cada vez mejor/peor = better and better/worse and worse

cadena
1 *noun, feminine*
• **una cadena** = a chain
• **una cadena** (*Spa: of radio*) = a station
  (*Spa: of television*) = a channel
• **tirar de la cadena** = to flush the toilet
• **cadena perpetua** = life imprisonment
2 cadenas *noun, feminine plural*
cadenas = snow chains

cadera *noun, feminine*
la cadera = the hip

caer *verb* 28
= to fall
dejar caer algo = to drop something
caerse
= to fall (down)
se me cayó el vaso = I dropped the glass
se le cayó todo el pelo = all his hair fell out

café *noun, masculine*
• **café** = coffee
  un café negro *or* (*Spa*) **solo** = a black coffee
  un café con leche = a regular coffee, a white coffee
  un café cortado = a coffee with a dash of milk
• **un café** = a café
• (*Mex: the color*) **el café** = brown

cafetera *noun, feminine*
una cafetera = a coffeepot
una cafetera eléctrica = a coffee maker

caído/caída *past participle*
= fallen

caiga, caigo, etc ▶ caer

caimán *noun, masculine*
un caimán = an alligator

caja *noun, feminine*
• **una caja** = a box
  (*of beer*) = a crate
  (*of wine*) = a case
• **una caja** (*in a shop*) = a till
  (*in a supermarket*) = a checkout
• **una caja fuerte** = a safe

cajero/cajera *noun, masculine/feminine*
• **un cajero/una cajera** = a cashier
  (*in a supermarket*) = a checkout operator
• **un cajero automático** = a cash dispenser

cajón *noun, masculine*
un cajón = a drawer

cajuela *noun, feminine* (*Mex*)
la cajuela = the trunk, the boot

calabacín *noun masculine or* (*Mex*)
calabacita *noun, feminine*
una calabacín = a zucchini, a courgette

calamar *noun, masculine*
un calamar = a squid
calamares a la romana = fried squid in batter

calcetín *noun, masculine*
un calcetín = a sock
unos calcetines = a pair of socks

calculadora *noun, feminine*
una calculadora = a calculator

caldo *noun, masculine*
caldo = stock
= broth

calefacción *noun, feminine*
la calefacción = the heating

calendario *noun, masculine*
un calendario = a calendar

calentador *noun, masculine*
un calentador = a heater

calentar *verb* 7
• = to heat (up)
• (*if it's a stove etc*) = to give off heat
• (*if it's a car*) = to warm up
• **calentar los músculos** = to warm up
calentarse
• = to get hot
• = to get warm

calesita *noun, feminine* (*R Pl*)
una calesita = a merry-go-round

calidad *noun, feminine*
calidad = quality

calienta, caliento, etc ▶ calentar

caliente *adjective*
• = hot
• = warm

callado/callada *adjective*
= quiet
quedarse callado = to go quiet
= to keep quiet

callar *verb* 1
• = to go quiet
• = to be quiet
  ¡calla! = be quiet!/shut up!
callarse
• = to go quiet
• = to be quiet
• **¡cállate ya!** = be quiet!/shut up!

calle *noun, feminine*
una calle = a street
calle Lérida n° 9 = 9 Lerida Street

R Pl River Plate area   SC Southern Cone   Spa Spain

calma *noun, feminine*
calma = calm
en calma = calm
me lo tomé con calma = I took it easy
¡tengamos calma! = let's calm down
= let's keep calm

calor *noun, masculine*
el calor = the heat
tengo mucho calor = I'm very hot
hace calor = it's hot
¡qué calor! = it's so hot

calvo/calva *adjective*
= bald

calzoncillos *noun, masculine plural*
unos calzoncillos = a pair of underpants

cama *noun, feminine*
una cama = a bed
hacer *or* (*Lat Am*) **tender la cama** = to make
the bed
una cama individual *or* (*Lat Am*) **de una
plaza** = a single bed
una cama de matrimonio *or* (*Lat Am*) **de
dos plazas** = a double bed

cámara *noun, feminine*
una cámara fotográfica *or* **de fotos** = a
camera
una cámara de video *or* (*Spa*) **vídeo** = a
video camera

cambiar *verb* ☐1
• = to change
cambiar de [coche | canal | trabajo ...] = to
change [cars | channels | jobs ...]
cambiar de idea/opinión = to change one's
mind
• = to exchange
quisiera cambiar esta camisa por una
blusa = I'd like to exchange this shirt for
a blouse
• te cambio estos sellos por tu póster = I'll
swap you these stamps for your poster
• cambiar algo de lugar = to move
something
cambiarse
= to change
cambiarse de ropa = to change clothes
cambiarse de casa = to move house

cambio *noun, masculine*
• un cambio = a change
un cambio de horario = a change in the
timetable
un cambio para mejor/peor = a change for
the better/worse
• cambio = change
me dieron mal el cambio = they gave me
the wrong change
• el cambio = the exchange rate
¿a cuánto está el cambio? = what's the
exchange rate?
Cambio (*sign in a bank, street*) = Bureau de
Change
• a cambio (de) = in return (for)

caminar *verb* ☐1
= to walk
= to go for a walk

camino *noun, masculine*
• un camino = a road
= a path, a track
• el camino = the way
de camino a ... = on the way to ...
me queda de camino = it's on my way
ponerse en camino = to set off

camión *noun, masculine*
un camión = a truck, a lorry
(*Mex, C Am*) = a bus

camisa *noun, feminine*
una camisa = a shirt

camiseta *noun, feminine*
una camiseta = an undershirt, a vest
= a T-shirt

camisón *noun, masculine*
un camisón = a nightdress

camote *noun masculine* (*Mex*)
un camote = a sweet potato

campamento *noun, masculine*
un campamento = a camp
irse de campamento = to go camping

campana *noun, feminine*
una campana = a bell

campeón/campeona *noun,*
masculine/feminine
un campeón/una campeona = a champion

campesino/campesina *noun,*
masculine/feminine
un campesino/una campesina = a country
man/woman
= a peasant

campo *noun, masculine*
• el campo = the country
• el campo = the countryside
• el campo = the land
• un campo = a field
un campo de fútbol = a football field, a
football pitch
un campo de golf = a golf course

cana *noun, feminine*
una cana = a grey hair

canadiense
1 *adjective*
= Canadian
2 *noun, masculine/feminine*
un/una canadiense = a Canadian

canal *noun, masculine*
• un canal = a channel
= a canal
el canal de la Mancha = the English
Channel
• (*of television etc*) un canal = a channel

canario noun, masculine
un canario = a canary

cancelar verb 1
= to cancel

Cáncer noun, masculine
Cáncer = Cancer

cáncer
1 noun, masculine
cáncer = cancer
cáncer de mama = breast cancer
2 noun, masculine/feminine
un/una cáncer = a Cancer, a Cancerian

cancha noun, feminine
una cancha = a court
(Lat Am: for football) = a field, a pitch
(Lat Am: for polo) = a field

canción noun, feminine
una canción = a song
una canción de cuna = a lullaby

cangrejo noun, masculine
un cangrejo = a crab
= a crayfish

canguro
1 noun, masculine
un canguro = a kangaroo
2 noun, masculine/feminine (Spa)
un/una canguro = a babysitter

canica noun, feminine
una canica = a marble

cansado/cansada adjective
• = tired
estoy cansado de pedírtelo = I'm tired of
asking you
• = tiring

cansador adjective (SC)
= tiring

cansar verb 1
• = to tire (out)
• = to be tiring
• = to bore, to tire
le cansa mucho caminar = he gets very
tired walking
• = to be boring
esta música cansa = this music is boring
cansarse
= to get tired
cansarse de algo/de hacer algo = to get
tired of something/of doing something

cantante noun, masculine/feminine
un/una cantante = a singer

cantar verb 1
= to sing

cantidad noun, feminine
una cantidad = an amount
= a quantity
= a number
¡qué or cuánta cantidad de coches! = what
a lot of cars!
hay cantidad or cantidades de [gente |
peces ...] = there are lots of [people | fish ...]
¿qué or cuánta cantidad de leche pongo?
= how much milk do I add?
¿qué cantidad de niños hay? = how many
children are there?

cantina noun, feminine
• una cantina = a buffet, a cafeteria
• (Lat Am) una cantina = a bar

cañería noun, feminine
una cañería = a pipe

capa noun, feminine
• una capa = a layer
(of paint, varnish) = a coat
• una capa (garment) = a cape

capaz adjective
= capable, able
ser capaz de hacer algo
= to be capable of doing something, to be
able to do something
no fui capaz de terminarlo = I wasn't able to
finish it

capital noun, feminine
una capital = a capital

capitán/capitana
1 noun, masculine/feminine
(in sports)
un capitán/una capitana = a captain
2 capitán noun, masculine/feminine
(in the army)
un/una capitán = a captain

capítulo noun, masculine
un capítulo = a chapter
= an episode

capó noun, masculine
un capó = a hood, a bonnet

Capricornio noun, masculine
Capricornio = Capricorn

capricornio noun, masculine/feminine
un/una capricornio = a Capricorn

cara noun, feminine
la cara = the face
(of record, etc) = the side
tener cara de [enfermo | cansado ...] = to look
[ill | tired ...]
poner cara de [sorpresa | susto | alegría ...] =
to look [surprised | scared | happy ...]
cara o cruz = heads or tails

caracol noun, masculine
un caracol = a snail
(from the sea) = a winkle
(Lat Am) = a conch

C

carácter *noun, masculine*
carácter = character
= nature
es de carácter bondadoso = he has a kind
nature
tener buen/mal carácter = to be good-
natured/bad-tempered
tener mucho/poco carácter = to have a lot
of/not much personality

¡caramba! *exclamation*
• = goodness me!
• = dammit!

caramelo *noun, masculine*
• un caramelo = a candy, a sweet
un caramelo de menta = a mint
• caramelo = caramel

caravana *noun, feminine*
• una caravana (*of traffic*) = a backup, a
tailback
• (*Spa*) una caravana = a trailer, a caravan

carbón *noun, masculine*
el carbón = coal

cárcel *noun, feminine*
la cárcel = jail

cardíaco/cardíaca *adjective* ▶ ataque

carga *noun, feminine*
• una carga = a load
(*of plane, boat*) = a cargo
• (*of pen*) una carga = a refill
• (*of weapon*) una carga = a charge
• (*responsibility*) una carga = a burden

cargado/cargada *adjective*
• = loaded
el arma estaba cargada = the weapon was
loaded
venía cargada de bolsas = she was loaded
down with bags
• (*if it's coffee*) = strong

cargo *noun, masculine*
• un cargo = a post, a position
• el niño está a mi cargo = the child is in my
care
estoy a cargo de la empresa = I'm in
charge of the company
• me da cargo de conciencia = I feel guilty
about it
tener cargo de conciencia = to feel guilty

cariño *noun, masculine*
cariño = affection
tenerle cariño a alguien/algo = to be fond
of someone/something
tomarle or (*Spa*) cogerle cariño a
alguien/algo = to grow fond of
someone/something
cariños (*Lat Am*), con cariño (*Spa*) (*in
letters*) = love

cariñoso/cariñosa *adjective*
• = affectionate
• = warm

carnaval *noun, masculine*
un carnaval = a carnival

carne *noun, feminine*
carne = flesh
= meat
carne molida (*Lat Am*) or (*Spa, R Pl*)
picada = ground beef, mince

carné *noun, masculine*
un carné = a card
un carné de identidad = an identity card
un carné de conducir = a driver's licence, a
driving licence

carnicería *noun, feminine*
una carnicería = a butcher's

caro/cara *adjective*
= expensive
costar caro = to be expensive
pagar algo caro (*for a mistake, a misdeed*)
= to pay dearly for something

carpeta *noun, feminine*
una carpeta = a folder

carpintero/carpintera *noun,
masculine/feminine*
un carpintero/una carpintera = a carpenter

carrera *noun, feminine*
• una carrera = a race
echar una carrera = to have a race
echarle una carrera a alguien = to race
someone
las carreras de caballos = the races
una carrera de relevos = a relay race
• echar una carrera = to run
fui hasta la tienda de una carrera = I ran to
the shop
• una carrera = a degree course
hace la carrera de derecho = she is
studying law
• una carrera = a career
su carrera profesional = her professional
career

carretera *noun, feminine*
una carretera = a road

carrito *noun, masculine*
un carrito (*for baggage*) = a trolley
(*in supermarket*) = a shopping cart, a
trolley

carro *noun, masculine*
• un carro = a cart
• (*Lat Am*) un carro = a car
fui en carro = I went by car
• (*Mex: of a train*) un carro = a coach, a
carriage
un carro dormitorio = a sleeping
coach/carriage

carrusel *noun, masculine* (*Lat Am*)
un carrusel = a merry-go-round

carta *noun, feminine*
- **una carta** = a letter
  echar una carta (al correo) = to mail a letter, to post a letter
  una carta certificada/urgente = a registered/express letter
- **la carta** = the menu
- **una carta** = a card
  jugar a las cartas = to play cards

cartel *noun, masculine*
  un cartel = a poster
  = a sign

cartelera *noun, feminine*
  la cartelera = the theater/movie listings
  la cartelera de espectáculos = the entertainment guide
  la obra sigue en cartelera = the play is still on *or* running

cartera *noun, feminine*
  una cartera = a wallet
  (for documents) = a briefcase
  (for school) = a school bag
  (SC) = a purse, a handbag

cartero/cartera *noun, masculine/feminine*
  un cartero/una cartera = a mailman/mailwoman, a postman/postwoman

cartón *noun, masculine*
  cartón = cardboard

casa *noun, feminine*
- **una casa** = a house
- **una casa** = an apartment, a flat
- **mi casa** = my home
  vive en casa de sus padres = he lives at his parent's
  están en casa = they are at home

casado/casada *adjective*
  = married
  estar casado con alguien = to be married to someone

casarse *verb* [1]
  = to get married
  casarse con alguien = to get married to someone

cáscara *noun, feminine*
  cáscara = peel
  (of an egg, a nut) = shell
  (of a banana) = skin

casco
1 *noun, masculine*
- **un casco** = a helmet
- *(of a horse)* **un casco** = a hoof
- *(Mex, Spa)* **un casco** = an empty bottle
2 cascos *noun, masculine plural (Spa)*
  los cascos = the headphones

caseta *noun, feminine*
- **una caseta** = a kennel
- *(in exhibitions)* **una caseta** = a stand

casete
1 *noun, masculine/feminine*
  un/una casete = a cassette
2 casete *noun, masculine (Spa)*
  un casete = a cassette recorder/player

casi *adverb*
- = almost
  casi he terminado = I have almost finished
- = hardly
  no viene casi nunca = she hardly ever comes
  casi, casi = almost

casilla electrónica *noun, feminine*
  una casilla electrónica = an email address

caso *noun, masculine*
- **un caso** = a case
  en todo *or* **cualquier caso** = in any case
  el caso es que... = the thing is that...
  en caso de = in case of
  yo en tu caso... = if I were you...
- **hacer caso de algo** = to take notice of something
  hacerle caso a alguien = to take notice of someone

castaña *noun, feminine*
  una castaña = a chestnut

castaño/castaña *adjective*
  = brown

castañuelas *noun, feminine plural*
  las castañuelas = castanets

castellano/castellana
1 *adjective*
  = Castilian
2 *noun, masculine/feminine*
  un castellano/una castellana = a Castilian
3 castellano *noun, masculine*
  el castellano *(the language)* = Castilian
  = Spanish

> **!** Note that Castilian is the official language in Spain and the language that, with regional variants, is used in Latin America. Spanish speakers often use the word **castellano** *rather than* **español** *to refer to the Spanish language.*

castigar *verb* [3]
  = to punish
  castigar a alguien sin salir = to ground someone

castigo *noun, masculine*
  un castigo = a punishment

castillo *noun, masculine*
  un castillo = a castle
  un castillo de arena = a sandcastle

casualidad *noun, feminine*
 una casualidad = a coincidence
 de *or* **por casualidad** = by chance
 da la casualidad de que... = it so happens
  that...

catalán/catalana
 1 *adjective*
 = Catalan
 2 *noun, masculine/feminine*
 un catalán/una catalana = a Catalan
 3 catalán *noun, masculine*
 el catalán (*the language*) = Catalan

catarata *noun, feminine*
 una catarata = a waterfall

catarro *noun, masculine*
 un catarro = a cold
 agarrarse *or* (*Spa*) **coger un catarro** = to
  catch a cold

catedral *noun, feminine*
 una catedral = a cathedral

categoría *noun, feminine*
 una categoría = a category
 de categoría = first-rate
 de mucha categoría = first-rate
 de poca categoría = second-rate

católico/católica
 1 *adjective*
 = Catholic
 2 *noun, masculine/feminine*
 un católico/una católica = a Catholic

catorce *number*
 • = fourteen
 • (*in dates*) = fourteenth
   See **quince** *for examples*

causa *noun, feminine*
 una causa = a cause
 a causa de algo = due to something

causar *verb* 1
 = to cause

cavar *verb* 1
 = to dig

cayendo ▶ caer

caza *noun, feminine*
 la caza = hunting
 ir de caza = to go hunting

cazadora *noun, feminine* (*Spa*)
 una cazadora = a jacket

cazar *verb* 4
 • = to hunt
 • = to shoot

cebolla *noun, feminine*
 una cebolla = an onion

ceja *noun, feminine*
 una ceja = an eyebrow

celebración *noun, feminine*
 una celebración = a celebration

celebrar *verb* 1
 • = to celebrate
 • (*if it's a meeting, an election*) = to hold

celo *noun, masculine* (*Spa*)
 celo = Scotch   tape, Sellotape

celos *noun, masculine plural*
 celos = jealousy
 sentir *or* **tener celos de alguien** = to be
  jealous of someone
 darle celos a alguien = to make someone
  jealous

celoso/celosa *adjective*
 = jealous

celular *noun, masculine*
 un celular = a mobile phone

cementerio *noun, masculine*
 un cementerio = a cemetery

cemento *noun, masculine*
 cemento = cement

cena *noun, feminine*
 la cena = dinner, supper
 ¿qué quieres de cena? = what do you
  want for dinner?

cenar *verb* 1
 = to have dinner, to have supper
 les di de cenar = I gave them their dinner
 salir a cenar = to go out for a meal

cenicero *noun, masculine*
 un cenicero = an ashtray

centavo *noun, masculine*
 un centavo = a cent (*of dollar*)

centenar *noun, masculine*
 un centenar = a hundred
 centenares de personas = hundreds of
  people

centenario *noun, masculine*
 un centenario = a centenary

centígrado *adjective*
 = centigrade

centímetro *noun, masculine*
 un centímetro = a centimeter, a centimetre

céntimo *noun, masculine*
 un céntimo = a cent (*of euro*)

central
 1 *adjective*
 = central
 2 *noun, feminine*
 la central = (the) head office
 una central nuclear = a nuclear power
  station

---

centro noun, masculine
el centro = the center, the centre
un centro comercial = a shopping mall, a
shopping centre

ceño noun, masculine
fruncir el ceño = to frown

cepillar verb 1
= to brush
cepillarse
= to brush
se cepilló los dientes = he brushed his
teeth

cepillo noun, masculine
un cepillo = a brush
un cepillo de dientes = a toothbrush
un cepillo del pelo = a hairbrush

cera noun, feminine
la cera = wax

cerámica noun, feminine
cerámica = pottery
una cerámica = a piece of pottery

cerca adverb
• = nearby
hay un bar cerca = there is a bar nearby
• = close
el verano ya está cerca = summer is
getting close
• cerca de = near
está cerca del hospital = it's near the
hospital
son cerca de las tres = it's almost three
o'clock

cerdo/cerda
1 noun, masculine|feminine
un cerdo/una cerda = a pig
2 **cerdo** noun, masculine
cerdo = pork

cereal
1 noun, masculine (Lat Am)
cereal = cereal
2 **cereales** noun, masculine plural (Spa)
cereales = cereal

ceremonia noun, feminine
una ceremonia = a ceremony

cereza noun, feminine
• una cereza = a cherry
• (C Am) una cereza = a coffee bean

cerilla noun, feminine (Spa), **cerillo**
noun, masculine (C Am, Mex)
una cerilla/un cerillo = a match

cero noun, masculine
cero = zero, nought

cerrado/cerrada adjective
• = closed, shut
cerrado con llave/con cerrojo =
locked/bolted

• (if it's a faucet) = turned off
• (if it's an envelope) = sealed
• (if it's curtains) = drawn
• (if it's a space) = enclosed
• (if it's an accent) = broad

cerrar verb 7
• = to close, to shut
cerrar con llave/cerrojo = to lock/to bolt
• (if it's a faucet) = to turn off
• (if it's an envelope) = to seal
cerrarse
= to close
se me cerraban los ojos = my eyes were
closing
cerrarse de un portazo = to slam shut

certificado/certificada
1 adjective
• = registered
• = certified
2 **certificado** noun, masculine
un certificado = a certificate

cerveza noun, feminine
una cerveza = a beer
una cerveza rubia = a lager

césped noun, masculine
el césped = the grass
= the lawn

cesta noun, feminine
una cesta = a basket

chabacano noun, masculine (Mex)
un chabacano = an apricot

chaleco noun, masculine
un chaleco = a vest, a waistcoat
(knitted) = a sleeveless sweater
(SC) = a cardigan

champán, noun, masculine, **champaña**
noun, feminine
el champán, la champaña = champagne

champiñón noun, masculine
un champiñón = a mushroom

champú noun, masculine
champú = shampoo

chancho/chancha noun,
masculine|feminine (Lat Am)
un chancho/una chancha = a pig

chándal noun, masculine (Spa)
un chándal = a tracksuit

chapa noun, feminine
• una chapa = a metal sheet
• (Spa: of bottle) una chapa = a top
• una chapa = a badge
(of policeman) = a shield, a badge
• (Lat Am: on door, etc) una chapa = a lock
• (R Pl: of car) una chapa = a license plate, a
number plate

---

chaqueta noun, feminine
  una chaqueta = a jacket

charco noun, masculine
  un charco = a puddle

chavo/chava✘ noun, masculine|feminine (Mex)
  un chavo/una chava = a guy/a girl

checar verb 2 (Mex)
  = to check

cheque noun, masculine
  un cheque = a check, a cheque
  un cheque de viaje = a traveler's check, a traveller's cheque
  un cheque sin fondos = a bad check

chequear verb 1
• = to check
• (Lat Am) = to check in

chequeo noun, masculine
  un chequeo = a checkup

chícharo noun, masculine (Mex)
  un chícharo = a pea

chicle noun, masculine
  un chicle = a piece of chewing gum

chico/chica noun, masculine|feminine
  un chico/una chica = a boy/a girl
    = young man/woman
  unos chicos (boys and girls) = some children/some youngsters

chimenea noun, feminine
  una chimenea = a fireplace
    = a chimney

chinche noun, feminine (C Am, Mex, R Pl)
  una chinche = a thumbtack, a drawing pin

chincheta noun, feminine (Spa)
  una chincheta = a thumbtack, a drawing pin

chino/china
1 adjective
• = Chinese
• (Mex) = curly
2 noun, masculine|feminine
• un chino/una china = a Chinese man/woman
• (Mex) un chino/una china = a curly-haired man/woman
3 chino noun, masculine
• (the language)
  el chino = Chinese
• (Mex) chino = curly hair

chispa noun, feminine
• una chispa = a spark
• una chispa de [café | agua]✘ = a drop of [coffee | water]

chiste
1 noun, masculine
  un chiste = a joke
  contar un chiste = to tell a joke
  hacerle un chiste a alguien (Mex, SC) = to play a joke on someone
2 chistes noun, masculine plural (R Pl)
  chistes = comic strips

chocar verb 2
  = to crash, to collide
  chocar con or contra algo = to run or crash into something
  chocar contra alguien = to run into someone

chocolate noun, masculine
  chocolate = chocolate
  chocolate negro = dark chocolate
  chocolate con leche = milk chocolate
  (Lat Am) un chocolate = a chocolate

chocolatina noun, masculine (Spa)
  una chocolatina = a chocolate bar

chofer (Lat Am), **chófer** (Spa), noun, masculine
  un chofer, un chófer = a chauffeur
    = a driver

chompipe noun, masculine (C Am, Mex)
  un chompipe = a turkey

choque noun, masculine
  un choque = a crash, a collision

chuleta noun, feminine
  una chuleta = a chop

chupar verb 1
• = to suck
• = to absorb
chuparse
  chuparse el dedo = to suck one's thumb

churro noun, masculine
  un churro = a strip of fried dough

cicatriz noun, feminine
  una cicatriz = a scar

ciclista noun, masculine|feminine
  un/una ciclista = a cyclist

ciego/ciega
1 adjective
  = blind
  quedarse ciego = to go blind
2 noun, masculine|feminine
  un ciego/una ciega = a blind man/woman
  los ciegos = the blind

cielo noun, masculine
• el cielo = the sky
• el cielo = heaven

---

cien *number*
  = a/one hundred
  cien días = a hundred days
  cien por ciento *or (Spa)* **cien** = a hundred
    per cent
  cien mil = a hundred thousand
  ciento uno = one hundred and one

ciencia
1 *noun, feminine*
  la ciencia = science
2 ciencias *noun, feminine plural*
  ciencias *(subject)* = science

científico/científica
1 *adjective*
  = scientific
2 *noun, masculine/feminine*
  un científico/una científica = a scientist

ciento *number*
  = a/one hundred
  ciento veinte = a/one hundred and twenty
  cientos de personas = hundreds of people
• **por ciento** = per cent
  el tres por ciento = three per cent
    See also **tanto**

cierra, **cierro**, **etc** ▶ cerrar

cierto/cierta *adjective*
• = true
  es cierto = it's true
• = certain
  ciertas personas = certain people
  en cierta ocasión = once, on one occasion
• **por cierto** = by the way
    See also **punto**

cigarrillo *noun, masculine*
  un cigarrillo = a cigarette

cima *noun, feminine*
  la cima = the top

cinco *number*
• = five
  cinco niños = five children
  el cinco = (number) five
  tengo cinco = I have five (of them)
• *(in dates)* = fifth
  hoy es cinco *or (Spa)* **hoy es día cinco** =
    today is the fifth
  hoy estamos a cinco = today's the fifth
  el cinco de mayo = the fifth of May
• *(talking about the time)*
  son las cinco = it's five o'clock
  las siete y cinco = five after *or* past seven
  cinco para la una *or (R Pl, Spa)* **la una**
    menos cinco = five minutes to one
• *(talking about age)*
  tengo cinco años = I'm five (years old)
  hoy cumplo cinco años = I'm five today
  a los cinco años empecé a ir al colegio = I
    started school when I was five

cincuenta *number*
• = fifty
  cincuenta y uno, cincuenta y dos, *etc*
    = fifty-one, fifty-two, *etc.*
  el cincuenta = (number) fifty
  hay cincuenta = there are fifty (of them)
• *(talking about age)*
  tengo cincuenta años = I'm fifty (years
    old)
  hoy cumplo cincuenta años = I'm fifty
    today
  a los cincuenta años dejé de trabajar = I
    stopped working when I was fifty

cine *noun, masculine*
• **un cine** = a movie theater, a cinema
  ir al cine = to go to the movies, to go to the
    cinema
• **el cine** = cinema
  el mundo del cine = the world of cinema
• **el cine** = movies, films
  el cine mudo = silent movies, silent films
  hacer cine = to make movies, to make
    films

cinta *noun, feminine*
• **una cinta** = a ribbon
• *(of video, cassette)* **una cinta** = a tape
  una cinta virgen = a blank tape
• **una cinta transportadora** = a conveyor belt

cintura *noun, feminine*
  la cintura = the waist

cinturón *noun, masculine*
  un cinturón = a belt
  un cinturón de seguridad = a safety belt

circo *noun, masculine*
  un circo = a circus

circunstancia
1 *noun, feminine*
• **una circunstancia** = a reason
  por esta circunstancia = for this reason
• **una circunstancia** = a factor
2 circunstancias *noun, feminine plural*
  circunstancias = circumstances

ciruela *noun, feminine*
  una ciruela = a plum
  una ciruela pasa *or (SC)* **seca** = a prune

cirujano/cirujana *noun,*
masculine/feminine
  un cirujano/una cirujana = a surgeon

cisne *noun, masculine*
  un cisne = a swan

cita *noun, feminine*
• **una cita** = a quotation
• *(with doctor, dentist)* = an appointment
• *(with boyfriend, girlfriend)* = a date
  tener una cita con alguien = to have a date
    with someone
  (with a friend) = to have arranged to meet
    someone

C

ciudad *noun, feminine*
  una ciudad = a city
  = a town

ciudadano/ciudadana *noun,*
masculine/feminine
  un ciudadano/una ciudadana = a citizen

claro
1 *adjective*
• = clear
  dejar claro algo = to make something clear
• (*if it's a color*) = light
  azul claro = light blue
  ojos claros = green/blue/gray eyes
• (*if it's the sky*) = bright
2 *adverb*
  = clearly
  habla claro = speak clearly
  ¡claro! = of course!
  ¡claro que sí/no! = of course/of course not!
  ¡claro que quieres! = of course you want to!

clase *noun, feminine*
• = kind, sort, type
• = quality
  productos de primera clase = top-quality
    products
• (*in education*) una clase = a class, a lesson
  una clase particular = a private lesson
  dar clase de [inglés | latín | música ...] (*if it's a
    a teacher*) = to teach [English | Latin |
    music ...]
  (*Spa: if it's a pupil*) = to have [English | Latin |
    music ...] lessons
• (*room*) una clase = a classroom
• (*group of pupils*) la clase = the class
• (*social status*) clase = class
  clase alta/baja = upper/lower class
• (*when traveling*) clase = class
  primera clase = first class
  clase turista/preferente =
    economy/business class

clasificar *verb* 2
  = to classify

clave
1 *noun, feminine*
• una clave = a code
  un mensaje en clave = a coded message
• (*in music*) una clave = a clef
• la clave del éxito = the key to success
2 *adjective* (**!** *never changes*)
  = key

clavo *noun, masculine*
• un clavo = a nail
• (*spice*) un clavo = a clove

claxon *noun, masculine*
  un claxon = a horn

cliente/clienta *noun,*
masculine/feminine
  un cliente/una clienta = a customer
  (*of company, lawyer, etc*) = a client
  (*at hotel*) = a guest

clima *noun, masculine*
  el clima = the climate

clínica *noun, feminine*
  una clínica = a private hospital

clip *noun, masculine*
  un clip = a paperclip
• (*for hair*) un clip = a bobby pin, a hairgrip
• aretes *or* (*Spa*) pendientes de clip = clip-on
    earrings

cobarde
1 *noun, masculine/feminine*
  un/una cobarde = a coward
2 *adjective*
  = cowardly

cobija *noun, feminine* (*Lat Am*)
  una cobija = a blanket

cobrador/cobradora *noun,*
masculine/feminine
  un cobrador/una cobradora (*on bus, train*)
    = a conductor
  (*of debts*) = a collector

cobrar *verb* 1
• = to charge
  me cobraron de más/de menos = they
    overcharged me/undercharged me
  ¿me cobra las cervezas, por favor? = can I
    pay for the beers, please?
• = to earn
  ¿cuánto cobras al mes? = how much do
    you earn a month?
• = to get paid
  mañana cobro = I'm getting paid
    tomorrow
• (*if it's a debt*) = to recover
• (*if it's a check*) = to cash
• (*if it's one's pension, benefits*) = to draw

cobre *noun, masculine*
  el cobre = copper

cocer *verb* 23
  (*if it's vegetables, water*) = to boil
  (*if it's bread*) = to bake
  cocer a fuego lento = to simmer

coche *noun, masculine*
• un coche = a car
  fui en coche = I went by car
• (*of train*) un coche = a car, a carriage
  un coche cama/restaurante = a
    sleeping/dining car
• un coche bomberos = a fire truck, a fire
    engine

cocina *noun, feminine*
• una cocina = a stove, a cooker
• (*room*) una cocina = a kitchen
• la cocina española = Spanish cooking

- **un libro de cocina** = a cookbook, a cookery book

cocinar verb 1
= to cook
cocinar a fuego lento = to cook over a low heat

coco noun, masculine
un coco = a coconut

cocodrilo noun, masculine
un cocodrilo = a crocodile

código noun, masculine
un código = a code

codo noun, masculine
el codo = the elbow

coger verb 20 (Spa)

> **!** Note that **coger** is an offensive word in Mexico, River Plate and Venezuela. In those regions the words **agarrar** or **tomar** are used instead

- = to take
me cogió de la mano = he took me by the hand
coger el tren = to take the train
- = to catch
coger una pelota = to catch a ball
coger a un ladrón = to catch a thief
- = to get
coger un resfriado = to catch a cold
coger una entrada = to get a ticket
- = to pick
coger flores = to pick flowers
- **coger algo del suelo** = to pick something up off the floor
- **coger el teléfono** = to answer the phone
cogerse
= to grab hold of
se cogió a la cuerda = she grabbed hold of the rope

cogido/cogida past participle (Spa)
= taken
ir cogidos de la mano = to be hand in hand
See also **coger**

coincidencia noun, feminine
una coincidencia = a coincidence
se dio la coincidencia de que... = it so happened that...

coincidir verb 41
- (if it's dates, results) = to coincide
- (when discussing something) = to agree

coja, cojo, etc ▶ coger

cojín noun, masculine
un cojín = a cushion

cojo/coja
1 adjective
= lame
ser cojo = to be lame
estar cojo = to have a limp
ir/andar a la pata coja = to hop

2 noun, masculine/feminine
un cojo/una coja = a lame man/woman

col noun, feminine (Mex, Spa)
una col = a cabbage
coles de Bruselas = Brussels sprouts

cola noun, feminine
- **una cola** = a tail
- (at bus stop, bank)
una cola = a line, a queue
hacer cola = to line up, to queue up
ponerse a la cola = to join the line, to join the queue
saltarse la cola (Mex, Spa) = to jump the line, to jump the queue
- (of dress) **la cola** = the train
- (for sticking things together) **cola** = glue

colcha noun, feminine
una colcha = a bedspread

colchón noun, masculine
un colchón = a mattress

colección noun, feminine
una colección = a collection

coleccionar verb 1
= to collect

colega noun, masculine/feminine
un/una colega = a colleague

colegio noun, masculine
un colegio = a school
colegio público = public school (in USA), state school (in Britain)

colgado/colgada past participle
- (if it's a lamp etc) **colgado de algo** = hanging from something
- **el teléfono está mal colgado** = the telephone is off the hook

colgar verb 9
- = to hang
(if it's coat) = to hang up
(if it's a picture) = to put up
- (when phoning)
colgar el teléfono = to put the phone down
¡me colgó! = he hung up on me!
no cuelgue, por favor = please hold the line
colgarse
colgarse de algo = to hang from something

coliflor noun, feminine or (R Pl) noun, masculine
una coliflor, un coliflor = a cauliflower

colina noun, feminine
una colina = a hill

collar noun, masculine
un collar = a necklace
(for animal) = a collar

colmo noun, masculine
¡esto es el colmo! = this is the limit!
y para colmo = and to make matters worse

colocar verb 2
• = to place
colócalo en su lugar = put it in its place
• colocar a alguien = to find/give someone a
job
colocarse
• = to get a job
• colocarse al lado de la ventana = to
stand/sit next to the window

colombiano/colombiana
1 adjective
= Colombian
2 noun, masculine/feminine
un colombiano/una colombiana = a
Colombian

colonia noun, feminine
• una colonia = a colony
• (Mex) una colonia = a district
• colonia = (eau de) cologne

coloquial adjective
= colloquial

color noun, masculine
color = color, colour
¿de qué color es? = what color is it?
de colores = colored, coloured
una televisión en colores or (Spa) en color
or (Mex) a color = a color television
a todo color = full color, full colour

colorado/colorada adjective
= red
ponerse colorado = to turn red

colorear verb 1
= to color (in), to colour (in)

columna noun, feminine
• una columna = a column
• la columna vertebral = the spine

columpio noun, masculine
un columpio = a swing

coma
1 noun, feminine
una coma = a comma

> **!** Note that in Spanish a comma and not a
> point is used to mark decimal numbers:
> 2,7 instead of 2.7 (dos coma siete = two
> point seven)

2 coma noun, masculine
coma = coma
en estado de coma = in a coma

comba noun, feminine (Spa)
una comba = a jump rope, a skipping rope
saltar or jugar a la comba = to jump rope,
to skip

comedia noun, feminine
una comedia = a comedy

comedor noun, masculine
un comedor = a dining room
(in school, university) = a dining hall
(in factory) = a canteen

comentario noun, masculine
un comentario = a comment

comenzar verb 5
= to start, to begin

comer verb 17
• = to eat
(Mex, Spa) = to have lunch
(Lat Am) = to have dinner
¿qué hay de comer? = what's for
lunch/dinner?
• dar de comer a alguien = to feed someone
• (in chess, checkers) = to take

comercio noun, masculine
• el comercio = trade
• el comercio = the stores, the shops

cometa noun, feminine
una cometa = a kite

cometer verb 17
(if it's a crime) = to commit
(if it's a mistake) = to make

cómic noun, masculine (Spa)
• un cómic = a comic strip
• un cómic = a comic

cómico/cómica
1 adjective
= comic
2 noun, masculine/feminine
un cómico/una cómica = a comedy
actor/actress
un cómico/una cómica = a comedian

comida noun, feminine
comida = food
una comida = a meal
(Mex, Spa) la comida = lunch
(Lat Am) la comida = dinner
hacer la comida (Mex, Spa) = to cook
lunch
(Lat Am) = to cook dinner

comienza, comienzo, etc
▶ comenzar

comillas noun, feminine plural
comillas = quotation marks, inverted
commas
entre comillas = in quotation marks, in
inverted commas

como
1 adverb
• = as
duro como una piedra = as hard as rock

C Am Central America   Lat Am Latin America   Mex Mexico

- = like
  no eres como los demás = you're not like
  the rest
- = such as, like
  países como Grecia, Italia... = countries
  such as or like Greece, Italy...
- = about
  llegaron como a las siete = they arrived
  about seven
- **como mucho/poco** = at most/least
2 *conjunction*
- = if
  como no estudies no vas a aprobar = if
  you don't study, you won't pass

> ! *Note the use of the subjunctive after*
> como

- = as, since
  como tenía dinero, lo compré = since I had
  the money, I bought it
- = as
  como yo creía = as I thought
- = the way
  no me gustó como lo dijo = I didn't like the
  way he said it

cómo *adverb*
- = how
  ¿cómo estás? = how are you
  sé cómo lo hizo = I know how he did it
- (*in exclamations*)
  ¡cómo has cambiado! = you've really
  changed!
  ¡cómo! ¿no lo sabías? = what! you didn't
  know?
  ¡cómo no! = of course!
  ¿cómo? (*when you don't understand*) =
  sorry?, pardon?
- **¿cómo es?** = what's he/she/it like?
  ¿cómo te llamas? = what's your name?

cómodo/cómoda *adjective*
  = comfortable
  ponerse cómodo = to make oneself
  comfortable

compañero/compañera *noun*,
masculine|feminine
  un compañero/una compañera = a
  colleague
  un compañero de cuarto = a roommate
  un compañero de clase = a schoolmate

compañía *noun, feminine*
- **compañía** = company
  hacerle compañía a alguien = to keep
  someone company
  una compañía = a company, a firm

comparar *verb* 1
  = to compare

compartir *verb* 41
  = to share

competencia *noun, feminine*
- **la competencia** = the competition
- (*Lat Am*) **una competencia** = a competition

competición *noun, feminine* (*Spa*)
  una competición = a competition

competir *verb* 48
  = to compete

compita, compito, etc ▶ competir

completo/completa *adjective*
  = complete
  = full
  por completo = completely

complicado/complicada *adjective*
  = complicated

comportamiento *noun, masculine*
  comportamiento = behavior, behaviour

comportarse *verb* 1
  = to behave

compra *noun, feminine*
  una compra = a purchase
  las compras or (*Spa*) **la compra** = the
  shopping
  ir de compras = to go shopping
  hacer las compras or (*Spa*) **la compra** = to
  do the shopping

comprar *verb* 1
  = to buy
  comprarle algo a alguien = to buy
  something for someone
  = to buy something from someone
  le compré un libro para su cumpleaños = I
  bought him a book for his birthday
  le compré su coche viejo = I bought his
  old car from him

comprender *verb* 17
  = to understand

computación *noun, feminine* (*Lat Am*)
  computación = computing

computador *noun, masculine*,
computadora *noun, feminine* (*Lat Am*)
  un computador, una computadora = a
  computer

común *adjective*
- = common
- **en común:**
  hicieron el trabajo en común = they did the
  work together
  tener algo en común = to have something
  in common

comunicación *noun, feminine*
- **la comunicación** = communication
- (*when phoning*)
  se cortó la comunicación = I was/we were
  etc cut off

comunicar *verb* 2
- = to communicate
- (*Spa: if it's the phone*) = to be busy, to be
  engaged
  está comunicando = it's busy

C

- (*Lat Am: if it's someone phoning*) = to put through
  lo comunico = I'm putting you through

comunidad *noun, feminine*
  una comunidad = a community
  una comunidad de vecinos = a residents' association
  una comunidad autónoma (*in Spa*) = an autonomous region

comunión *noun, feminine*
  la comunión = communion
  hacer la primera comunión = to take one's first communion

con *preposition*
  = with
  córtalo con el cuchillo = cut it with the knife
  pan con mantequilla = bread and butter
  estar casado con alguien = to be married to someone

concha *noun, feminine*
  una concha = a shell

concierto *noun, masculine*
- **un concierto** = a concert
- **un concierto** = a concerto

concurso *noun, masculine*
  un concurso = a competition
  = a contest
  = a quiz

conde/condesa *noun,*
masculine/feminine
  un conde/una condesa = a count/a countess

condición *noun, feminine*
  una condición = a condition
  estar en malas condiciones = to be in bad condition
  con la condición de que... = on condition that...

conducir *verb* 43
- = to lead
- = to drive

conductor/conductora *noun,*
masculine/feminine
  un conductor/una conductora = a driver

conduje, condujo ▶ conducir

conduzca, conduzco, etc
▶ conducir

conejillo de Indias *noun, masculine*
  un conejillo de Indias = a guinea pig

conejo/coneja *noun,*
masculine/feminine
  un conejo/una coneja = a rabbit

conexión *noun, feminine*
  una conexión = a connection

conferencia *noun, feminine*
  una conferencia = a lecture, a talk
- **una conferencia de prensa** = a press conference
- (*Spa*) **una conferencia** = a long-distance call

confianza *noun, feminine*
  confianza = confidence
  de confianza = trustworthy
  tratar a alguien con confianza = to treat someone as a friend
  tener confianza con alguien
  = to trust someone
  = to be friends with someone

confiar *verb* 13
  confiar en alguien/en algo = to trust someone/something
  = to rely on someone/something

confirmar *verb* 1
  = to confirm

confitería *noun, feminine*
- **una confitería** = a cake shop (*also selling candy*)
- (*R Pl*) **una confitería** = a tearoom

confundir *verb* 41
  = to confuse
  confundir algo por algo = to mistake something for something
confundirse
- = to make a mistake/mistakes
  perdona, me he confundido = sorry, I've made a mistake
- = to get confused
  confundirse de [persona | casa | número ...] = to get the wrong [person | house | number ...]

confusión *noun, feminine*
- **una confusión** = a mistake
  = a mix-up
- **confusión** = confusion
  había una gran confusión = there was great confusion

confuso/confusa *adjective*
- = confused
- = confusing

congelador *noun, masculine*
  un congelador = a freezer

congelar *verb* 1
  = to freeze
congelarse
  = to freeze
  = to be freezing
  me estoy congelando = I'm freezing

conjugar *verb* 3
  = to conjugate

conmigo *pronoun*
- = with me
- = to me
  conmigo mismo = with myself
  = to myself

conocer verb 19
* = to know
  no las conozco = I don't know them
  conocer a alguien de vista/de oídas = to have seen someone/have heard of someone
  conocer a alguien de nombre = to know someone by name
* = to meet
  ¿dónde se conocieron? = where did you meet?

conocido/conocida
1 *adjective*
  = well-known
2 *noun, masculine/feminine*
  un conocido/una conocida = an acquaintance

conocimiento *noun, masculine*
* **conocimiento** = knowledge
* **sin conocimiento** = unconscious
  perder/recobrar el conocimiento = to lose/regain consciousness

conozca, conozco, etc ▶ conocer

conseguir verb 57
* = to achieve
* = to get
  conseguí que fuera I got him to go

> **!** *Note the use of the subjunctive after* conseguir que

consejo *noun, masculine*
  un consejo = a piece of advice
  mis consejos = my advice

conserje *noun, masculine/feminine*
  un/una conserje (*in a school*) = a custodian, a caretaker
  (*in a hotel*) = a receptionist
  (*of public building*) = a superintendent, a caretaker

considerar verb 1
  = to consider

consiga, consigo, consiguiendo, etc ▶ conseguir

consigna *noun, feminine*
  una consigna = a baggage room, a left-luggage office

consigo *pronoun*
* = with him/her
  Ana no lo llevaba consigo = Ana didn't have it with her
  consigo mismo/misma = with himself/herself
  = to himself/herself
* = with them
  todo lo que tenían consigo = everything they had with them
  consigo mismos = with themselves
  = to themselves

* (*referring to you — polite form*) = with you
  ¿lleva el pasaporte consigo? = do you have your passport with you?
  consigo mismo/misma = with yourself
  = to yourself

consistir verb 41
  consistir en algo = to consist of something

consonante *noun, feminine*
  una consonante = a consonant

constipado/constipada
1 *past participle*
* **estar constipado** = to have a cold
* (*Lat Am*) **estar constipado** = to be constipated
2 constipado *noun, masculine*
  un constipado = a cold

construir verb 51
  = to build

construya, construyendo, construyo, etc ▶ construir

consultar verb 1
* = to consult
* = to look up

contacto *noun, masculine*
  un contacto = a contact
  ponerse en contacto con alguien = to get in touch with someone

contaminación *noun feminine*
  la contaminación = the pollution

contar verb 6
* = to count
  contar hasta diez = to count up to twenty
* = to tell
  cuéntame lo que pasó = tell me what happened
* **contar con alguien/algo** = to count on *or* rely on someone/something

contenedor *noun, masculine*
* **un contenedor** = a container
  (*for garbage*) = a bin
  (*for rubble*) = a dumpster, a skip
* **un contenedor de vidrio** = a bottle bank

contenido *noun, masculine*
  el contenido = the contents

contento/contenta *adjective*
  = happy
  estamos contentos de verte = we are happy to see you

contestador *noun, masculine*
  un contestador (**automático**) = an answering machine

contestar verb 1
  = to answer
  = to reply

C

contigo *pronoun*
- = with you
- = to you
  - contigo mismo = with yourself
  - = to yourself

continente *noun, masculine*
- un continente = a continent

continuar *verb* ⟦11⟧
- = to continue, to carry on

contra *preposition*
- = against
  - en contra = against
- = into
  - chocó contra un árbol = he crashed into a tree
- llevarle la contra a alguien✱ = to contradict someone

contrario/contraria *adjective*
- = opposite
  - ser contrario a algo = to be opposed to something
  - al contrario = on the contrary
  - todo lo contrario = quite the opposite
  - llevarle la contraria a alguien✱ = to contradict someone

contrato *noun, masculine*
- un contrato = a contract

control *noun, masculine*
- control = control
- (*in education*) un control = a test

controlar *verb* ⟦1⟧
- = to control

convencer *verb* ⟦18⟧
- = to convince
- = to persuade

conveniente *adjective*
- = convenient
- = advisable

convenza, convezco, etc
▶ convencer

conversación *noun, feminine*
- una conversación = a conversation

convertir *verb* ⟦46⟧
- convertir agua en vino = to turn water into wine
- convertir pesos a *or* (*Spa*) en dólares = to convert pesos into dollars

convertirse
- convertirse en un monstro = to become a monster
- (*by magic*) = to turn into a monster
- convertirse al budismo = to convert to Buddhism

convierta, convierto, etc
▶ convertir

copa *noun, feminine*
- una copa = a glass (*with a stem*)
- una copa = a drink
  - tomar una copa = to have a drink
- (*of tree*) la copa = the top
- (*trophy*) una copa = a cup

copia *noun, feminine*
- una copia = a copy

copiar *verb* ⟦1⟧
- = to copy
- = to make a copy of
- = to copy down

corazón *noun, masculine*
- el corazón = the heart

corbata *noun, feminine*
- una corbata = a tie

corcho *noun, masculine*
- un corcho = a cork

cordero *noun, masculine*
- un cordero = a lamb

cordón *noun, masculine*
- un cordón = a cord
- un cordón = a (shoe)lace
- (*R Pl*) el cordón de la vereda = the curb, the kerb

coro *noun, masculine*
- un coro = a choir

corona *noun, feminine*
- una corona = a crown
- una corona = a wreath

correcto/correcta *adjective*
- = correct

corredor/corredora *noun, masculine/feminine*
- un corredor/una corredora = a runner
- (*on a bike*) = a cyclist

corregir *verb* ⟦45⟧
- = to correct
- (*if it's an exam etc*) = to grade, to mark

correo *noun, masculine*
- el correo = the mail, the post
  - echar una carta al correo = to mail a letter, to post a letter
- un correo (*Lat Am*) = a post office
- una oficina de correos (*Spa*) = a post office
- un correo electrónico = an email

correr *verb* ⟦17⟧
- = to run
  - subir las escaleras corriendo = to run up the stairs
  - salir corriendo de la habitación = to run out of a room
  - echar a correr = to start running
- (*in competition*) = to race

✱ in informal situations   C Am Central America   Lat Am Latin America   Mex Mexico

- = to hurry
  ¡corre, vístete! = hurry up, get dressed!
  hacer las cosas corriendo = to do things in a hurry
  me tengo que ir corriendo = I have to rush
- **correr** (**mucho**) (*if it's a car*) = to go very fast
  (*if it's a driver*) = to drive very fast
- (*if it's curtains*) = to draw
- (*if it's an object*) = to move (along/across etc)

corrida *noun, feminine*
  una corrida (**de toros**) = a bullfight

corriente
1 *adjective*
  = common
  = normal
2 *noun, feminine*
- **la corriente** = the current
- **una corriente** (**de aire**) = a draft, a draught
  hay *or* (*Spa*) **hace corriente** = there's a draft

corrija, **corrijo**, **etc** ▶ corregir
corrompido/corrompida,
corrupto/corrupta *adjective* = corrupt

cortar *verb* ⟦1⟧
- = to cut
  cortar una rama = to cut off a branch
  cortar un árbol = to chop down a tree
  cortar el césped *or* (*Lat Am*) **el pasto** = to mow the lawn
- (*when on the phone*)
  me cortó = he hung up on me
cortarse
- = to cut oneself
  se cortó el dedo = she cut her finger
  me corté el pelo = I've had my hair cut
  = I cut my hair
- (*when on the phone*)
  se cortó = I was, we were, *etc* cut off

cortaúñas *noun, masculine* (**!** *does not change in the plural*)
  un cortaúñas = a pair of nail clippers

corte *noun, masculine*
- **un corte** = a cut
  un corte de pelo = a haircut
- **un corte de digestión** = a stomach cramp

cortina *noun, feminine*
  una cortina = a curtain

corto/corta *adjective*
  = short

cosa *noun, feminine*
  una cosa = a thing
  ¿cómo van las cosas? = how are things?
  alguna cosa = something
  = anything
  ¿trajeron alguna cosa para comer? = did they bring anything to eat?
  cualquier cosa = anything
  alguna otra cosa = something else
  = anything else
  ¿quiere alguna otra cosa? = would you like anything else?

cosecha *noun, feminine*
  la cosecha = the harvest
  = the crop

coser *verb* ⟦17⟧
  = to sew

cosquillas *noun, feminine plural*
  tener cosquillas = to be ticklish
  hacerle cosquillas a alguien = to tickle someone

costa *noun, feminine*
  la costa = the coast

costar *verb* ⟦6⟧
- = to cost
  ¿cuánto cuesta? = how much is it?
  costar mucho *or* **caro** = to be expensive
  costar poco = to be cheap
- = to be hard
  me cuesta entenderlo = I find it hard to understand

costo *or* (*Spa*) **coste** *noun, masculine*
  el costo = the cost

costumbre *noun, feminine*
- **una costumbre** = a habit
  por costumbre = out of habit
  tengo la costumbre de madrugar = I'm in the habit of getting up early
  = I usually get up early
  antes tenía la costumbre de pasear después del trabajo = I used to go for a walk after work
- **una costumbre** = a custom

cotilla* (*Spa*)
1 *noun, masculine|feminine*
  un/una cotilla = a gossip
2 *adjective*
  eres muy cotilla = you're such a gossip

cotillear* *verb* ⟦1⟧ (*Spa*)
  = to gossip

crear *verb* ⟦1⟧
  = to create

crecer *verb* ⟦19⟧
  = to grow
  = to grow up

creer *verb* ⟦26⟧
  = to believe
  = to think
  ¿tú crees? = do you think so?
  no creo = I don't think so

crema *noun, feminine*
- **una crema** = a cream
- **crema** = *type of custard*
- (*from milk*) **crema** = cream

cremallera *noun, feminine*
  una cremallera = a zipper, a zip
  bajarse la cremallera = to undo one's zipper

creyendo, **creyó**, **etc** ▶ creer

crezca, **crezco**, **etc** ▶ crecer

crimen *noun*, *masculine*
un crimen = a serious crime
= a murder

cristal *noun*, *masculine*
el cristal = crystal
(*Spa: material*) el cristal = glass
(*Spa: section of window*) un cristal = a
window pane

cristiano/cristiana
1 *noun*, *masculine|feminine*
un cristiano/una cristiana = a Christian
2 *adjective*
= Christian

crítica *noun*, *feminine*
• una crítica = a criticism
• (*of film, play*) una crítica = a review
• la crítica = the critics

cruce *noun*, *masculine*
• un cruce = a crossing
(*where roads cross*) = a crossroads
• (*between animals, plants*) un cruce = a
cross

crucigrama *noun*, *masculine*
un crucigrama = a crossword

crudo/cruda *adjective*
• = raw
• = underdone

cruel *adjective*
= cruel

cruz *noun*, *feminine*
una cruz = a cross

cruzar *verb* 4
= to cross
cruzar las piernas = to cross one's legs
cruzarse
cruzarse de brazos = to fold one's arms

cuaderno *noun*, *masculine*
un cuaderno = a notebook
(*in school*) = an exercise book

cuadra *noun*, *feminine*
una cuadra = a block

cuadrado/cuadrada
1 *adjective*
= square
2 cuadrado *noun*, *masculine*
un cuadrado = a square

cuadro *noun*, *masculine*
• un cuadro = a picture
• una tela a cuadros = a checked material

cual *pronoun*
el/la cual/los/las cuales = who
= whom
= which
la mayoría de los cuales = most of whom
= most of which
lo cual = which
• por *or* con lo cual = therefore

cuál
1 *pronoun*
• = which (one)
¿cuál te llevas? = which one are you
taking?
• = what
¿cuál es el problema? = what's the
problem?
2 *adjective* (*Lat Am*)
= which
= what
¿en cuál casa vive? = which house does
she live in?

cualidad *noun*, *feminine*
una cualidad = a quality

cualquiera
1 *adjective*

> **!** *Note that before a noun or noun phrase*
> cualquiera *becomes* cualquier

= any
en cualquier momento = at any moment
un día cualquiera = any day
2 *pronoun*
• = anybody
• = anyone
• (*referring to two people or things*) = either
(*referring to more than two*) = whichever
¿cuál de los dos llevo? — cualquiera =
which one shall I take? — either (of them)
= which one shall I take? — whichever one
you want

cuando *conjunction*
• = when
cuando sea viejo = when I am old

> **!** *Note the use of the subjunctive after*
> cuando *to express something that will*
> *happen in the future*

• cuando quieras, quiera *etc* = whenever you
want, he/she wants, *etc*
cuando puedas, pueda *etc* = whenever you
can, he/she can *etc*

cuándo *adverb*
= when
¿desde cuándo vives aquí? = how long
have you been living here?

cuanto/cuanta
1 *adjective, pronoun*
cuanto/cuanta = as much as
cuantos/cuantas = as many as
unos cuantos [niños | días | casos ...] = a few
[children | days | cases ...]

le di todo cuanto tenía = I gave him everything I had
fueron sólo unos cuantos = only a few went
2 cuanto adverb
= as much as
toma cuanto quieras = take as much as you want

> **!** Note the use of the subjunctive after cuanto
> **cuanto antes** = as soon as possible
> **cuanto más/menos** = the more/the less
> **cuanto más tarde mejor** = the later the better
> **en cuanto** [llegue | pueda | termine ...] = as soon as [I arrive | I can | I finish ...]

> **!** Note the use of the subjunctive after en cuanto

cuánto/cuánta
1 adjective, pronoun
cuánto/cuánta = how much
cuántos/cuántas = how many
¿cuánta leche quieres? = how much milk do you want?
¿cuántos libros hay? = how many books are there?
• (in exclamations)
¡cuántos niños! = what a lot of children!
¡cuánto dinero tienes! = you've got so much money!
• (referring to time) = how long
¿cuánto (tiempo) tardaste? = how long did you take?
2 cuánto adverb, pronoun
• = how much
¿cuánto cuesta? = how much is it?
• (referring to measurements, size, etc)
¿cuánto mide de largo? = how long is it?
• (in exclamations)
¡cuánto llueve! = it's raining so much!

cuarenta number
= forty
See cincuenta for examples

cuarto/cuarta number
1 = fourth
See primero for examples
2 cuarto noun, masculine
• **un cuarto** = a room
el cuarto de estar = the living room
el cuarto de baño = the bathroom
• **un cuarto** = a bedroom
el cuarto de los niños = the children's room
• **un cuarto** = a quarter
(referring to time) = a quarter
son un cuarto para las dos or (R Pl, Spa)
son las dos menos cuarto = it's a quarter to two
las tres y cuarto = a quarter after three, a quarter past three

cuatro number
• = four

• (in dates) = fourth
See cinco for more examples

cuatrocientos/cuatrocientas number
= four hundred
See quinientos for examples

cubierto/cubierta
1 adjective
= covered
(it it's the sky) = overcast
2 cubierto noun, masculine
un cubierto = a piece of cutlery
los cubiertos = the cutlery

cubo noun, masculine
• **un cubo** = a cube
• (Spa) **un cubo** = a bucket
el cubo de la basura (Spa) = the garbage can, the dustbin
(in the kitchen) = the garbage can, the rubbish bin

cubrir verb 59
= to cover

cucaracha noun, feminine
una cucaracha = a cockroach

cuchara noun, feminine
una cuchara = a spoon
una cuchara de postre = a dessertspoon
una cuchara de servir = a tablespoon

cucharada noun, feminine
una cucharada = a spoonful

cucharilla, cucharita noun, feminine
una cucharilla de café/té = a coffee spoon/teaspoon

cuchilla noun, feminine
una cuchilla = a blade
una cuchilla de afeitar = a razor blade

cuello noun, masculine
• **el cuello** = the neck
(of shirt, dress) = the collar
• **un cuello alto** = a turtleneck, a polo neck
• **un cuello de pico** = a V neck

cuelga, cuelgo, etc ▶ colgar

cuenta, cuento, etc ▶ contar

cuenta noun, feminine
• **una cuenta** = a check, a bill
¿me trae la cuenta, por favor? = could I have the check, please? could I have the bill, please?
• (at the bank) **una cuenta** = an account
• **una cuenta** = a sum
hacer cuentas = to do some calculations
• (in phrases)
llevar la cuenta de algo = to keep count of something
tener algo en cuenta = to take something into account
más de la cuenta = too much
darse cuenta de algo = to realize something

cuento noun, masculine
- un cuento = a story
- un cuento = a tale
  un cuento de hadas = a fairy tale

cuerda noun, feminine
- una cuerda = a rope
  darle cuerda a un juguete/al reloj = to wind a toy/the clock up
- una cuerda = a jump rope, a skipping rope
  saltar a la cuerda = to jump rope, to skip

cuerno noun, masculine
  un cuerno = a horn

cuero noun, masculine
  el cuero = leather

cuerpo noun, masculine
  el cuerpo = the body

cuesta, cueste, etc ▶ costar

cuesta noun, feminine
  una cuesta = a slope
  ir cuesta abajo/cuesta arriba = to go uphill/downhill
  llevar algo/a alguien a cuestas = to carry something/someone on one's back

cueva noun, feminine
  una cueva = a cave

cueza, cuezo, etc ▶ cocer

cuidado
1 noun, masculine
  hacer algo con cuidado = to do something carefully
  tener cuidado con algo/alguien = to be careful with something/someone
  ten cuidado de no quemarte = be careful you don't burn yourself
  cuidado con el perro = beware of the dog
  cuidado con el escalón = mind the step
2 exclamation
  ¡cuidado! = watch out!/careful!

cuidar verb 1
- = to look after
- = to take care of
  cuidar de algo/alguien = to look after something/someone

culo noun, masculine

> ! Note that culo is an offensive word in most regions of Latin America

- el culo = the butt, the bum
- (of bottle, glass) el culo = the bottom

culpa noun, feminine
  culpa = fault
  mi, tu, su, etc culpa = my, your, his/her, etc fault
  no es culpa tuya = it's not your fault
  echarle la culpa a alguien = to blame someone
  tener la culpa de algo = to be to blame for something
  por culpa de algo/alguien = because of something/someone

culpable
1 adjective
  = guilty
2 noun, masculine/feminine
  el/la culpable = the culprit

cultivar verb 1
  = to cultivate
  = to grow

cultura noun, feminine
  la cultura = culture

cumpleaños noun, masculine
  un cumpleaños = a birthday
  ¡feliz cumpleaños! = Happy Birthday!

cumplir verb 41
- (referring to age, time) = to be
  hoy cumple quince años = she's fifteen today
  ¡que cumplas muchos más! = many happy returns!
  hoy cumplimos quince años de casados (Lat Am) = it's our fifteenth wedding anniversary today
- (if it's a jail sentence) = to serve
- (if it's a promise) = to keep
- (if it's an order, a task) = to carry out
- cumplió con su deber = he did his duty

cuna noun, feminine
  una cuna = a crib, a cot

cuñado/cuñada noun, masculine/feminine
  un cuñado/una cuñada = a brother-/sister-in-law

cupe,cupiera, cupo, etc ▶ caber

cura¹ noun, feminine
  una cura = a cure

cura² noun, masculine
  un cura = a priest

curioso/curiosa
1 adjective
  = curious
2 noun, masculine/feminine
  un curioso/una curiosa✱ = a busybody

curita noun, feminine (Lat Am)
  una curita = a Band-Aid®, a sticking plaster

curso noun, masculine
- un curso = a year
- un curso = a course

curva noun, feminine
  una curva = a curve
  (in road) = a bend

cuyo/cuya adjective
  = whose

#

dado noun, masculine
  un dado = a dice
danés/danesa
  1 adjective
  = Danish
  2 noun, masculine/feminine
  un danés/una danesa = a Dane
  3 danés noun, masculine
  el danés (the language) = Danish

daño noun, masculine
  hacerse daño = to hurt oneself
  ¿te hiciste daño? = did you hurt yourself?
  hacerle daño a alguien = to hurt someone
  ¿te hace daño el cinturón? = does your
    belt hurt you?

dar verb ⌐15¬
  = to give
  le di mi chaqueta a tu madre = I gave my
    jacket to your mother
  ¿me da un paquete de azúcar? = can I
    have a packet of sugar?
  = to turn on
  dar la luz = to turn on the light
  = to say
  dar las gracias = to say thank you
  = to give
  dales recuerdos de mi parte = give them
    my regards
  darle una noticia a alguien = to break a
    piece of news to someone
  (to cause)
  esto da [sed | hambre | calor …] = this makes
    you feel [thirsty | hungry | hot …]
  me dio un susto = he gave me a fright
  (referring to time)
  dieron las cinco = the clock struck five
  dar a:
  la ventana da al mar = the window
    overlooks the sea
  la puerta da a la plaza = the door leads to
    the square
    See also **clase** for more examples
darse
  darse un baño = to have a bath
  darse un golpe = to hit oneself
de preposition
  = of
  la puerta de la casa = the door of the house
  (indicating possession, ownership)
  el abrigo de María = María's coat
  están en casa de sus padres = they are at
    their parents'
  son de él = they're his
  la iglesia del pueblo = the village church
  la ciudad de Sevilla = Seville
  ciudad de México = Mexico city

(indicating origin) = from
  soy de Lima = I'm from Lima
  ¿cuánto se tarda de aquí a allá? = how
    long does it take from here to there?
  (describing people)
  una niña de diez años = a ten-year-old girl
  el señor del sombrero = the man with the
    hat
  la chica de la chaqueta verde = the girl in
    the green jacket
  (indicating material, content)
  una caja de madera = a wooden box
  una botella de vino = a bottle of wine
  (indicating subject)
  un libro de aventuras = an adventure book
  una película de misterio = a thriller
  la clase de inglés = the English lesson
  (indicating authorship) = by
  una canción de los Beatles = a song by the
    Beatles
  (with numbers, quantities)
  un billete de cincuenta dólares = a fifty-
    dollar bill
  la mitad de treinta = half of thirty
  (in comparisons)
  el más grande de todos = the biggest of all
  menos de diez = less than ten
  (in expressions of time)
  viajan de noche = they travel at night
  a las siete de la tarde = at seven in the
    evening

dé ▶ dar

debajo adverb
  = underneath
  ponte una camiseta debajo = wear a T-shirt
    underneath
  el de debajo = the one underneath
  debajo de = under
  debajo de la mesa = under the table
  el de debajo de todo = the one at the
    bottom
  por debajo de cero grados = below zero
    degrees
  pasó por debajo de la mesa = he went
    underneath the table

deber
  1 noun
  un deber = a duty
  2 deberes noun plural
  (in school)
  los deberes = homework
  3 verb ⌐17¬
  = to owe
  te debo disculpas = I owe you an apology
  deber hacer algo:
  (when used in the past or conditional)
  debiste or deberías or debías or debieras
    haber ido = you should have gone
  deberías estudiar más = you should study
    more
  (when used in the present)

debes portarte bien = you must behave
(*when used in the future*)
los estudiantes deberán esforzarse = the
students must *or* will have to make an
effort

debido/debida *adjective*
debido a algo = due to something

débil *adjective*
= weak

decena *noun, feminine*
una decena = ten
una decena de personas = about ten
people

decente *adjective*
= decent

decepcionar *verb* 1
= to disappoint
Madrid me decepcionó = I was
disappointed with Madrid

decidir *verb* 41
= to decide
decidirse
= to make up one's mind

décimo/décima
1 *number*
= tenth
See primero *for examples*
2 décimo *noun, masculine*
un décimo = a tenth

decir *verb* 53
= to say
= to tell
me lo dijo él = he told me
(*Spa: when answering the phone*)
diga *or* (*more polite*) dígame = hello?
(*inviting someone to talk*)
oye, Ana — dime = hey Ana! — yes?
querer decir = to mean
¿qué quiere decir esta palabra? = what
does this word mean?

decisión *noun, feminine*
una decisión = a decision

decorar *verb* 1
= to decorate

dedo *noun, masculine*
un dedo = a finger
= a toe
el dedo pulgar *or* gordo (*on the hand*) =
the thumb
(*on the foot*) = the big toe
el dedo meñique/índice = the small/index
finger
hacer dedo = to hitchhike

defecto *noun, masculine*
un defecto = a defect
= a fault
= a flaw
un defecto físico = a physical handicap

defender *verb* 21
= to defend
defenderse
= to defend oneself

definición *noun, feminine*
una definición = a definition

dejar *verb* 1
= to leave
dejé el vaso en la mesa = I left the glass on
the table
dejó el trabajo = he left his job
¡déjame en paz! = leave me alone!
(*to allow*) = to let
no la dejan ver la tele = they don't let her
watch TV
(*Spa*) = to lend
¿me dejas tu coche? = will you lend me
your car?, can I borrow your car?
dejar de hacer algo
= to stop doing something
= to give up doing something
¡deja de preguntar! = stop asking!
dejar de fumar = to give up smoking
dejarse
(*Spa*) = to leave
me dejé las llaves en casa = I left the keys
at home
dejarse barba = to grow a beard
dejarse el pelo largo = to grow one's hair
long
¡déjate de molestar! (*Lat Am*) stop being a
nuisance

del

> ! *Note that* del *is a contraction of the
> preposition* de *and the article* el, *as in* la
> caseta del perro (= la caseta de + el
> perro). *For usage see* de

delantal *noun, feminine*
un delantal = an apron
= a pinafore

delante *adverb*
= in front
estaban delante de mí = they were in front
of me
la fila de delante = the front row
por delante:
se abrocha por delante = it does up at the
front
tienes toda la vida por delante = you have
your whole life ahead of you

delegación *noun, feminine*
una delegación = a delegation
(*Mex*) una delegación = a police station

deletrear *verb*
= to spell

delfín *noun, masculine*
un delfín = a dolphin

delgado/delgada *adjective*
= thin

delicado/delicada *adjective*
= delicate

delicioso/deliciosa *adjective*
= delicious

delito *noun, masculine*
un delito = a crime

demás
1 *adjective*
los demás niños = the rest of the children, (the) other children
2 *pronoun*
¿dónde están los demás? = where are the others?
ayudar a los demás = to help others
lo demás = the rest

demasiado/demasiada
1 *adjective, pronoun*
demasiado/demasiada = too much
demasiados/demasiadas = too many
hay demasiada luz = there's too much light
había demasiada gente = there were too many people
demasiadas veces = too often, too many times
somos demasiados = there are too many of us
2 demasiado *adverb*
= too much
comimos demasiado = we ate too much
= too
es demasiado grande = it's too big
vas demasiado lento = you're going too slowly

demonio *noun, masculine*
el demonio = the devil

demos, dan, etc ▶ dar

den ▶ dar

dentífrico *noun, masculine*
dentífrico = toothpaste

dentista *noun, masculine/feminine*
un/una dentista = a dentist

dentro *adverb*
= inside
= indoors
vamos dentro = let's go inside, let's go in
está ahí dentro = it's in there
no se puede fumar dentro = you can't smoke indoors
de dentro, desde dentro = from the inside
se cierra desde dentro = it locks from the inside
está pintado por dentro = it's painted on the inside
dentro de:

dentro de la caja = in the box, inside the box
dentro de dos semanas = in two weeks time
dentro de lo posible = if possible

departamento *noun, masculine*
(*of a company, university*) un departamento = a department
(*Lat Am*) un departamento = an apartment, a flat

D

depender *verb* 17
= to depend
¿vas a ir? — depende = are you going? — it depends
depender de algo = to depend on something

dependiente/dependienta *noun masculine/feminine*
un dependiente/una dependienta = a sales clerk , a shop assistant

deporte *noun, masculine*
el deporte = sport
un deporte = a sport
hacer deporte = to play sports

deprisa *adverb*
= fast
escribía muy deprisa = he was writing very fast
¡deprisa, que llegamos tarde! = quick, we're late!

derecha *noun, feminine*
la derecha = the right
fue hacia la derecha = he went right
a la derecha = on the right
manejar *or* (*Spa*) conducir por la derecha = to drive on the right
la derecha = the right hand
(*in politics*) la derecha = the right
ser de derecha *or* (*Spa*) de derechas = to be right-wing

derecho/derecha
1 *adjective*
= straight
el árbol no crece derecho = the tree isn't growing straight
siéntate derecho = sit up straight
= right
la mano derecha = the right hand
2 derecho *adverb*
sigue todo derecho = go straight on
3 derecho *noun, masculine*
(*in law*) un derecho = a right
los derechos humanos = human rights
tener derecho a algo/a hacer algo = to have the right to something/to do something
¡no hay derecho! = it's not fair!

(*of a garment, fabric, piece of paper*)
el derecho = the right side
póntelo al derecho = put it on right side out

des ▶ dar

desabrochar *verb* 1
= to undo
le desabroché el abrigo = I undid his coat
desabrocharse
= to undo
se desabrochó la blusa = she undid her blouse
= to come undone
se le desabrochó la camisa = his shirt came undone

desagradable *adjective*
= unpleasant

desaparecer *verb* 19
= to disappear

desastre *noun, masculine*
un desastre = disaster

desatornillador *noun, masculine* (*C Am Mex*)
un desatornillador = a screwdriver

desayunar *verb* 1
= to have breakfast
¿desayunaste ya? = have you already had breakfast?
después de desayunar = after breakfast
normalmente desayuno café = I normally have coffee for breakfast
desayunarse (*Lat Am*)
= to have breakfast
se desayunó con tostadas = she had toast for breakfast

desayuno *noun, masculine*
el desayuno = breakfast

descansar *verb* 1
= to rest
necesita descansar = he needs to rest
(*from work*) = to have a break
vamos a descansar un rato = let's have a break

descanso *noun, masculine*
un descanso = a rest
necesitas un descanso = you need a rest
(*from work*) **un descanso** = a break
hacer un descanso = to take a break
(*in sport*) **el descanso** = half time
(*at the theater*) **un descanso** = an interval

desconocido/desconocida
1 *adjective*
= unknown
= unrecognizable
está desconocida (*Spa*) = she's changed so much
2 *noun, masculine/feminine*
un desconocido/una desconocida = a stranger

describir *verb* 60
= to describe

descripción *noun, feminine*
una descripción = a description

descrito ▶ describir

desde *preposition*
= from
nos llamó desde Roma = he called us from Rome
va desde la pared hasta la puerta = it goes from the wall to the window
= since
desde las tres en punto = since three o'clock
desde que llegó aquí = since she arrived here
= from
desde tres mil pesos = from three thousand pesos
desde un principio = right from the start
desde luego = of course

desembarcar *verb* 2
= to unload
desembarcaron la carga = they unloaded the cargo
(*if it's people*) = to disembark
los pasajeros desembarcaron = the passengers disembarked

desempleado/desempleada
1 *noun, masculine/feminine*
un desempleado/una desempleada = an unemployed person
2 *adjective*
= unemployed

desenchufar *verb* 1
= to unplug

deseo *noun, masculine*
un deseo = a wish
pide un deseo = make a wish
deseo = desire

desgracia *noun feminine*
una desgracia = a misfortune
tuvo la desgracia de perder la vista = he had the misfortune to lose his sight
por desgracia = unfortunately

desierto/desierta
1 *adjective*
= deserted
2 desierto *noun, masculine*
el desierto = the desert

desnudo/desnuda *adjective*
(*if it's a person*) = naked
(*if it's a part of the body*) = bare

desobedecer *verb* 19
= to disobey

desobedezca, desobedezco, etc
▶ desobedecer

---

desobediente
1 *adjective*
= disobedient
2 *noun, masculine/feminine*
eres un/una desobediente = you are very
disobedient

desorden *noun, masculine*
= mess
estaba todo en desorden = everything was
a mess

desorganizado/desorganizada
1 *adjective*
= disorganized
2 *noun, masculine/feminine*
**eres un desorganizado/una
desorganizada** = you are so disorganized

despacho *noun, masculine*
un despacho (*at work*) = an office
(*at home*) = a study

despacio *adverb*
= slowly
¡ve más despacio! = slow down!

despedida *noun, feminine*
una despedida = a goodbye
una fiesta de despedida = a farewell party

despedir *verb* 48
(*to say goodbye*)
iremos a despedirlos al aeropuerto = we'll
go to see them off at the airport
(*at work*) = to dismiss, to fire
despedirse
= to say goodbye

despegar *verb* 3
= to take off

despegue *noun, masculine*
= takeoff

despertador *noun, masculine*
un despertador = an alarm clock

despertar *verb* 7
= to wake up
despertarse
= to wake up

despida, despido, etc ▶ despedirse

despierta, despierto, etc
▶ despertar

despierto/despierta *adjective*
= awake

despistado/despistada
1 *adjective*
= absentminded
2 *noun, masculine/feminine*
es una despistada = she's very
absentminded

desplegar *verb* 8
= to unfold

despliega, despliego, etc
▶ desplegar

después *adverb*
= later
= afterwards
quedaron para después = they arranged to
meet later
se lo dijo mucho después = he told her
much later
poco después = shortly afterwards
¿qué dijo después? = what did she say
next?
después de = after
después de la película = after the movie
depués de ir al gimnasio = after going to
the gym
después de todo = after all
después de que hayas hecho los deberes
= when *or* after you've finished your
homework

! *Note the use of the subjunctive after*
después de que

destino *noun, masculine*
el destino = fate
(*of a train, plane, traveler*) **destino** =
destination
con destino a = bound for

destornillador *noun, masculine*
un destornillador = a screwdriver

detalle *noun, masculine*
un detalle = a detail

detective *noun, masculine/feminine*
un/una detective = a detective

detergente *noun, masculine*
un detergente = a laundry detergent, a
washing powder
(*SC*) = a dishwashing liquid, a washing-up
liquid

detestar *verb* 1
= to detest

detrás *adverb*
= behind
vienen detrás = they are coming behind
detrás de = behind
se escondió detrás de un árbol = he hid
behind a tree
= after
un cigarrillo detrás de otro = one cigarette
after another
por detrás:
se abrocha por detrás = it does up at the
back
nos atacaron por detrás = they attacked us
from behind

D

deuda noun, feminine
una deuda = a debt
tener una deuda = to be in debt

devolver verb 24
(if it's an object, a book) = to return
(if it's money) = to refund

devuelto, **devuelvo**, **etc** ▶ devolver

di ▶ dar

día noun, masculine
un día = a day
¿qué día es hoy? = what day is it today?
al or el día siguiente = the following day
el día anterior = the previous day
el otro día = the other day
[una vez | dos veces | doce horas …] al día =
  [once | twice | twelve hours …] a day
de día = during the day, in the daytime
hacerse de día = to get light
todos los días = every day
cada día = every day
un día festivo or (Lat Am) feriado = a public
  holiday
un día libre = a day off
el día trece de junio = the thirteenth of
  June
el día de los inocentes = April Fool's day
el día de los Reyes = the 6th of January
  (when Christmas presents are exchanged in
  Spain)
  (talking about the weather)
hoy hace un buen día = it is nice today

diablo noun, masculine
el diablo = the devil

diadema noun, feminine
una diadema = a tiara
una diadema = a hairband

diagrama noun, masculine
un diagrama = a diagram

diálogo noun, masculine
un diálogo = a conversation

diamante noun, masculine
un diamante = a diamond

diario/diaria
1 adjective
= daily
clases diarias = daily lessons
= everyday
gastos diarios = everyday expenses
a diario = every day
de diario = everyday
ropa de diario = everyday clothes
2 diario noun, masculine
un diario = a newspaper
un diario = a diary

dibujar verb 1
= to draw

dibujo noun, masculine
un dibujo = a drawing
hizo un dibujo = he drew a picture
estudiar dibujo = to study drawing
dibujos animados = cartoons

diccionario noun, masculine
un diccionario = a dictionary

dice, **dicho**, **etc** ▶ decir

diciembre noun, masculine
= December

dictado noun, masculine
un dictado = a dictation

diecinueve number
= nineteen
(in dates) = nineteenth
  See quince for examples

dieciocho number
= eighteen
(in dates) = eighteenth
  See quince for examples

dieciséis number
= sixteen
(in dates) = sixteenth
  See quince for examples

diecisiete number
= seventeen
(in dates) = seventeenth
  See quince for examples

diente noun, masculine
un diente = a tooth
un diente de ajo = a clove of garlic

diera, **dieras**, **etc** ▶ dar

diez number
= ten
(in dates) = tenth
  See cinco for examples

diferencia noun, feminine
una diferencia = a difference
diferencia de tamaño = difference in size

diferente adjective
= different

difícil adjective
= difficult

dificultad noun, feminine
una dificultad = a difficulty

diga, **digo**, **dije**, **etc** ▶ decir

dimos ▶ dar

Dinamarca noun, feminine
Dinamarca = Denmark

dinero noun, masculine
el dinero = money
dinero suelto (Mex, Spa) = small change
dinero en efectivo = cash

dinosaurio noun, masculine
un dinosaurio = a dinosaur

dio ▶ dar

dios noun, masculine
un dios = a god
¡Dios mío! = Good God!
¡por Dios! = for God's sake!

dirá, **diré**, **etc** ▶ decir

dirección noun, feminine
= address
¿me das tu dirección? = will you give me
your address?
= direction
en dirección contraria = in the opposite
direction
van en dirección a Lima = they are heading
toward Lima

directo/directa adjective
= direct
(if it's a train) = through
en directo = live

director/directora noun,
masculine/feminine
un director/una directora (of a company) =
a manager
(of a school) = a principal, a
headmaster/headmistress
(of a play, a film) = a director
(of a newspaper) = an editor
(of an orchestra, a choir) = a conductor

disco noun, masculine
un disco = a record

discoteca noun, feminine
una discoteca = a disco

disculpa noun, feminine
una disculpa = an apology
pedir disculpas = to apologize

disculparse verb [1]
= to apologize

diseño noun, masculine
un diseño = a design
estudiar diseño = to study design

disfraz noun, masculine
un disfraz = a costume, a fancy dress outfit
un disfraz = a disguise

disfrutar verb [1]
= to enjoy

disparo noun, masculine
un disparo = a shot

distancia noun, feminine
= distance
¿a qué distancia está el pueblo? = how far
is the village?
está a poca distancia de la frontera = it's
near the border

diste ▶ dar

distinto adjective
= different

D

distrito noun, masculine
un distrito = a district
el Distrito Federal = the Federal District

divertido/divertida adjective
= funny
= entertaining

dividir verb [41]
= to divide
= to share out

división noun, feminine
una división = a division

divorciado/divorciada
1 adjective
= divorced
2 noun, masculine/feminine
un divorciado/una divorciada = a divorcé, a
divorcée/a divorcée, a divorcee

doblar verb [1]
= to fold
= to bend
= to double
(if it's a movie) = to dub
doblar la esquina = to turn the corner

doble
1 adjective
= double
(if it's a whisky, gin, etc) = large
2 noun, masculine
el doble = twice as many/much
es el doble de ancho = it's twice as wide

doce number
= twelve
(in dates) = twelfth
See **cinco** for examples
(talking about the time)
son las doce del mediodía = it's twelve
noon
son las doce de la noche = it's twelve
midnight

doceavo/doceava number
= twelfth
See **primero** for examples

docena noun, feminine
una docena = a dozen
una docena de huevos = a dozen eggs

doctor/doctora noun,
masculine/feminine
un doctor/una doctora = a doctor

documento *noun, masculine*
un documento = a document

dólar *noun, masculine*
un dólar = a dolar

doler *verb* 22
= to hurt
¿te duele? = does it hurt?
me duele la mano = my hand hurts
me duele la cabeza = I have a headache

dolor *noun, masculine*
un dolor = a pain
un dolor en la espalda = a pain in my back
tengo dolor de muelas/de cabeza = I have
  a toothache/a headache

domingo *noun, masculine*
domingo = Sunday
Domingo de Ramos/de Resurrección =
  Palm/Easter Sunday
  See miércoles *for examples*

dominó *noun, masculine*
el dominó = dominoes

don *noun, masculine*
≈ Mr
don Miguel Ferrer ≈ Mr Miguel Ferrer

! *Note that* don *can also be used before
first names as a mark of respect*

dona *noun, feminine* (Mex)
una dona = a donut, a doughnut

donde *adverb*
= where
el lugar donde vivo = the place where I live
el lugar a donde viajaban = the place they
  were traveling to
la carretera por donde pasamos = the road
  we went along
ponlo donde quieras = put it wherever you
  want

! *Note the use of the subjunctive after*
donde

dónde *adverb*
= where
¿dónde vives? = where do you live?
¿dónde queda? = where is it?
¿por dónde se va a la estación? = how do
  you get to the station?
no sé por dónde se fueron = I don't know
  which way they went

donut *noun, masculine*
un donut = a donut, a doughnut

doña *noun, feminine*
≈ Mrs, Ms
doña Juana Lucas = Mrs Juana Lucas

! *Note that* doña *can also be used before
first names as a mark of respect*

dorado/dorada *adjective*
= golden
= gold

dormir *verb* 49
= to sleep
= to be asleep
= to get to sleep
no conseguí dormir al niño = I couldn't get
  the baby to sleep
dormirse
= to fall asleep
= to get to sleep
= to oversleep
se me ha dormido el brazo = my arm has
  gone to sleep

dormitorio *noun, masculine*
un dormitorio (*in a house*) = a bedroom
  (*in a school, barracks*) = a dormitory

dorso *noun, masculine*
el dorso = the back
el dorso [de la mano | del papel | de la carta ...]
  = the back [of the hand | paper | letter ...]
nadar de dorso (*Méx*) to swim (the)
  backstroke

dos *number*
= two
(*in dates*)
= second
  See cinco *for examples*

doscientos/doscientas *number*
= two hundred
  See quinientos *for examples*

doy ▶ dar

droga *noun, feminine*
una droga = a drug

drogadicto/drogadicta *noun,*
masculine/feminine
un drogadicto/ una drogadicta = a drug
  addict

droguería *noun, feminine* (Spa)
una droguería = *a shop that sells cleaning
  materials and products, paint, and other
  household items*

ducha *noun, feminine*
una ducha = a shower
darse una ducha = to take a shower

ducharse *verb* 1
= to take a shower

duda *noun, feminine*
una duda = a doubt
no tengo la menor duda = I have no doubts
  whatsoever
tener dudas *or* (*Spa*) estar en duda sobre
  algo = to have doubts about something

(*in a class, lecture*)
consultar dudas con el profesor = to sort
out queries with the teacher
¿tiene alguien alguna duda? = does
anybody have any queries?

dudar *verb* 1
= to doubt
dudo de su honestidad = I doubt his
honesty
dudo que venga = I doubt he'll come

! *Note the use of the subjunctive after*
dudar que
dudaba entre ir o quedarse = he didn't
know whether to go or to stay

duela, **duelo**, **etc** ▶ doler

dueño/dueña *noun, masculine/feminine*
un dueño/una dueña = an owner

duerma, **duermo**, **etc** ▶ dormir

dulce
1 *adjective*
= sweet
2 *noun, masculine* (*Lat Am*)
un dulce = a candy, a sweet

duodécimo/duodécima *adjective*
= twelfth

duque/duquesa *noun*
masculine/feminine
un duque/una duquesa = a duke/a duchess

durante *preposition*
= during
lo leí durante el viaje = I read it during the
journey
= for
trabajaron durante tres semanas = they
worked for three weeks

durar *verb* 1
= to last
duró mucho = it lasted a long time

duro/dura
1 *adjective*
= hard
= harsh
un castigo duro = a harsh punishment
= tough
un régimen duro = a tough regime
(*referring to food*)
un huevo duro = a boiled egg
la carne está dura = the meat is very
tough
ser duro/dura de oído = to be hard of
hearing
2 duro *adverb* (*Lat Am*)
= hard
estudiar duro = to study hard
3 duro *noun, masculine* (*Spa*)
un duro = a five-peseta coin

Ee

e *conjunction*
= and

! *Note that e is used instead of* y *when
the word that follows starts with* i *or* hi, *as
in* España e Inglaterra, *and in* padres e
hijos. *See* y *for uses*

echar *verb* 1
• = to throw
échale la pelota = throw him the ball
• = to put in
echar [gasolina | azúcar | leche ...] = to put
[some gasoline | sugar | milk ...] in
• = to give, to serve
¿te echo más vino? = can I give you some
more wine?
• **echar a alguien** (*from a job*) = to fire
someone
(*from a bar, theater*) = to throw someone
out
(*from school*) = to expel someone
• **echar de menos a alguien** = to miss
someone

eco *noun, masculine*
un eco = an echo

economía *noun, feminine*
la economía = the economy

económico/económica *adjective*
• = economic
• = economical

ecuador *noun, masculine*
el ecuador = the equator

edad *noun, feminine*
edad = age
¿qué edad tiene? = how old is she?
tengo un hijo de tu edad = I have a boy
your age

edificio *noun, masculine*
un edificio = a building

edredón *noun, masculine*
un edredón = a quilt
un edredón nórdico = a continental quilt, a
duvet

educación *noun, feminine*
• = education
educación física = physical education
• = upbringing
tuvo una educación muy estricta = he had
a very strict upbringing
• = manners
eso es de mala educación = that's bad
manners

educado/educada *adjective*
= polite
una persona bien/mal educada = a polite/rude person

efectivo/efectiva
1 *adjective*
= effective
2 efectivo *noun, masculine*
efectivo = cash
dinero en efectivo = cash
pagar en efectivo = to pay cash

efecto *noun, masculine*
hacer efecto = to take effect

egoísta
1 *noun, masculine/feminine*
eres un/una egoísta = you are so selfish
2 *adjective*
= selfish

ejemplo *noun, masculine*
un ejemplo = an example
por ejemplo = for example

ejercicio *noun, masculine*
un ejercicio = an exercise
hacer ejercicio = to exercise

ejército *noun, masculine*
un ejército = an army

ejote *noun, masculine (Mex)*
un ejote = a green bean

el *masculine article*

> **!** *The plural of* el *is* los, *and the feminine forms are* la *(singular) and* las *(plural). Note that the masculine article* el *is also used before feminine nouns which begin with a stressed* a- *or* ha- *sound, such as* el agua, el hada

• = the
  prefiero el abrigo rojo = I prefer the red coat
• **los perros son muy fieles** = dogs are very loyal
  me duele la cabeza = my head hurts
  se quitó los zapatos = he took his shoes off
• *(with proper names, titles, and names that indicate family ties)*
  el señor Rodríguez = Mr Rodríguez
  el hermano de Julia = Julia's brother
• *(with expressions of time)*
  llegan el quince de julio = they arrive on the fifteenth of July
  la semana que viene = next week
  voy a visitarla los lunes = I go to visit her on Mondays
  son las siete = it's seven o'clock
• **el/la/los/las de:**
  el de Jaime = Jaime's
  las del colegio = the ones from the school
  la de los ojos verdes = the one with green eyes
• **el/la /los/las que:**

el que te dije = the one I told you about
los/las que yo llevé = the ones I took
elige el/la que tú quieras = choose whichever you want
dame el/la que sea = give me any one
invitaré a los/las que yo quiera = I will invite whoever I want

> **!** *Note the use of the subjunctive after* el/la que, los/las que

él *pronoun*
• = he
• = him
  se lo di a él = I gave it to him
  él mismo = himself
  es de él = it's his

elástico/elástica *adjective*
= elastic

elección *noun, feminine*
• **una elección** = a choice
  no tengo elección = I have no choice
• **una elección** = an election
  las elecciones municipales = the local elections

electricidad *noun, feminine*
la electricidad = electricity

electricista *noun, masculine/feminine*
un /una electricista = an electrician

eléctrico/eléctrica *adjective*
= electric
= electrical

electrónico/electrónica *adjective*
= electronic

elefante *noun, masculine*
un elefante = an elephant

elegir *verb* 45
= to choose

elepé *noun, masculine*
un elepé = an LP

elija, elijo, elijiendo, etc ▶ elegir

ella *pronoun*
• = she
• = her
  se lo di a ella = I gave it to her
  ella misma = herself
  es de ella = it's hers

ellas *pronoun*
• = they
• = them
  See ellos *for examples*

ello *pronoun*
= it
ocúpate de ello = take care of it

ellos/ellas *pronoun*
- = they
- = them
  se lo dí a ellos/ellas = I gave it to them
  ellos mismos/ellas mismas = themselves
  es de ellos/ellas = it's theirs

elote *noun, masculine (C Am, Mex)*
un elote = a corncob, an ear of corn

embarazada
1 *adjective*
= pregnant
quedar *or* (*Spa*) quedarse embarazada =
  to get pregnant
está embarazada de seis meses = she's six
  months pregnant
2 *noun, feminine*
una embarazada = a pregnant woman

embarcar *verb* [2]
(*onto a plane*) = to board
(*onto a boat*) = to embark

embotellamiento *noun, masculine*
un embotellamiento = a traffic jam

emergencia *noun, feminine*
una emergencia = an emergency

empanada *noun, feminine*
una empanada (*Lat Am*) = a pastry
(*Spa*) = a pie

empate *noun, masculine*
un empate (*in sports*) = a tie, a draw
(*in an election*) = a tie

empecé ▶ empezar

empeorar *verb* [1]
- = to get worse
- = to make worse

empezar *verb* [5]
= to begin, to start

empiece, empieza, empiezo, etc
▶ empezar

empleado/empleada *noun*
masculine/feminine
un empleado/una empleada = an employee
(*in an office*) = an office worker, a clerk
(*in a shop*) = a clerk, a shop assistant

empleo *noun, masculine*
un empleo = a job
estar sin empleo = to be unemployed

empujar *verb* [1]
= to push

en *preposition*
- = in
  = into
  en primavera = in spring
  meterse en la cama = to get into bed
- = on
  en la mesa = on the table

- = at
  viven en el número quince = they live at
    number fifteen
  ahora está en casa = she's at home now
  en la noche (*Lat Am*) = at night
- = by
  en [coche | barco | avión …] = by [car | boat |
    plane …]
  iba en bicicleta = she was riding a bike

encendedor *noun, masculine*
un encendedor = a lighter

encender *verb* [21]
- = to switch on
  = to turn on
  encender [la televisión | la calefacción | la
    luz …] = to turn on [the television | the
    heating | the light …]
- = to light
  encender [el fuego | una vela | una cigarrillo …]
    = to light [the fire | a candle | a cigarette …]

encendido/encendida *adjective*
- (*if it's a television, radio*) = on
- (*if it's a fire, match, etc.*) = lit, lighted

enchufar *verb* [1]
- = to plug in
  enchufar la plancha = to plug the iron in
- = to switch on
  = to turn on

enchufe *noun, masculine*
un enchufe = a plug

enciclopedia *noun, feminine*
una enciclopedia = an encyclopedia

encienda, enciendo, etc ▶ encender

encima *adverb*
- = on
  le puse una piedra encima = I put a stone
    on it
  lo dejé ahí encima = I left it up there
- encima de:
  encima de la mesa = on the table
  está encima del refrigerador = it's on top of
    the fridge
  su sala está encima de mi cuarto = her
    living-room is over my bedroom
- el de encima = the top one
- por encima de:
  = above
  = over
  por encima de las rodillas = above the
    knees
  por encima de la valla = over the fence
  temperaturas por encima de veinte grados
    = temperatures over twenty degrees

E

encontrar verb 6
= to find
no lo encuentro = I can't find it
encontrarse
• = to find
  me encontré una cartera = I found a wallet
• = to meet
  se encontraron en la calle = they met on
  the street

encuentra, **encuentro**, **etc**
▶ encontrar

enemigo/enemiga noun,
masculine/feminine
un enemigo/una enemiga = an enemy

energía noun, feminine
energía = energy
la energía eléctrica = electricity

enero noun, masculine
= January

enfadado/enfadada adjective (Spa)
= angry
= annoyed

enfadar verb 1 (Spa)
= to make angry
= to annoy
me hizo enfadar = he made me angry
enfadarse
= to get angry
= to get annoyed

enfermarse verb 1 (Lat Am)
= to fall ill

enfermedad noun, feminine
una enfermedad = an illness
= a disease

enfermero/enfermera noun,
masculine/feminine
un enfermero/una enfermera = a nurse

enfermo/enferma
1 adjective
= ill
= sick
caer enfermo/enferma = to fall ill
2 noun, masculine/feminine
un enfermo/una enferma = a sick person

enfrente adverb
= opposite
está enfrente del cine = it's opposite the
movie house

engordar verb 1
• = to put on weight
  he engordado mucho = I have put on a lot
  of weight
• = to be fattening

enhorabuena noun, feminine
¡enhorabuena! = congratulations!
darle la enhorabuena a alguien = to
congratulate someone

enojado/enojada adjective (Lat Am)
= angry
= annoyed

enojar verb 1 (Lat Am)
= to make angry
= to annoy
me hizo enojar = he made me angry
enojarse
= to get angry
= to get annoyed

enorme adjective
= enormous

ensalada noun, feminine
una ensalada = a salad

ensaladera noun, feminine
una ensaladera = a salad bowl

ensayo noun, masculine
un ensayo = a test
(for a play) = a rehearsal
(a short piece of writing) = an essay

enseguida adverb
= at once, straight away

enseñanza noun, feminine
= teaching
= education

enseñar verb 1
• = to teach
• = to show
  ¿me enseñas las fotos? = will you show
  me the photographs?

ensuciar verb 1
= to get dirty
ensuciarse
te has ensuciado la cara = you've got your
face dirty
me ensucié la camisa de café = I got coffee
on my shirt

entender verb 21
= to understand
te entendí mal = I misunderstood you
dar a entender = to imply
entiende mucho de [fotografía | motos |
jardinería ...] = he knows a lot about
[photography | bikes | gardening ...]

entero/entera adjective
• = whole
  la semana entera = the whole week
• (not broken) = intact
• (if it's milk) = full-cream

entienda, **entiendo**, **etc** ▶ entender

entonces adverb
= then

entrada noun, feminine
• = entry
  'prohibida la entrada' = 'no entry'

- = entrance
sólo hay una entrada = there's only one entrance
- = ticket
= admission
'entrada libre' = 'free admission', 'open to the public'
- (*Spa: when buying a house, a car*)
una entrada = a deposit

entrar *verb* 1
= to come in
= to go in
déjame entrar = let me in
- **entrar en:**
= to go into
entramos en *or* (*Lat Am*) **a la cocina** = we went into the kitchen
= to fit into
no entra en el cajón = it doesn't fit in the drawer
= to join
entrar en *or* **a una organización** = to join an organization
- = to start
entro a trabajar a las nueve = I start work at nine

entre *preposition*
- = between
se puso entre ellos dos = he stood between them
- = among
entre amigos = among friends
entre otras cosas = among other things
- = in
entre paréntesis = in parentheses *or* brackets
- = by
dividir veinte entre cinco = to divide twenty by five

entregar *verb* 3
- = to give
= to hand over
- **entregar un paquete** = to deliver a parcel
- **entregarle un premio a alguien** = to present someone with a prize
entregarse
= to surrender

entrenador/entrenadora *noun, masculine/feminine*
un entrenador/una entrenadora = a coach

entrenar *verb* 1
= to train

entrevista *noun, feminine*
una entrevista = an interview

enviar *verb* 13
= to send

envolver *verb* 24
= to wrap

envuelto ▶ envolver

episodio *noun, masculine*
un episodio = an episode

época *noun, feminine*
época = time
= times
= age

equilibrio *noun, masculine*
equilibrio = balance
mantener/perder el equilibrio = to keep/lose one's balance

equipaje *noun, masculine*
equipaje = baggage, luggage
equipaje de mano = hand baggage, hand luggage

equipo *noun, masculine*
un equipo = a team

equivocado/equivocada *adjective*
= wrong

equivocarse *verb* 2
= to make a mistake
= to be wrong
me equivoqué = I made a mistake
me equivoqué de casa/teléfono = I got the wrong house/number
en eso se equivoca = he's wrong about that

era, erais, eras, eres, etc ▶ ser

error *noun, masculine*
un error = a mistake

eructar *verb* 1
= to burp

eructo *noun, masculine*
un eructo = a burp

es ▶ ser

esa *adjective*
= that

ésa *pronoun*
= that one

esas *adjective*
= those

ésas *pronoun*
= those ones

escala *noun, feminine*
- (*when traveling*) **una escala** = a stopover
hacer escala en Roma = to stop over in Rome
- (*in music*) **una escala** = a scale

escalera *noun, feminine*
- **una escalera** = a staircase
una escalera de incendios = a fire escape
una escalera mecánica = an escalator
- **una escalera (de mano)** = a ladder

R Pl River Plate area   SC Southern Cone   Spa Spain

escalón *noun, masculine*
un escalón = a step

escalofrío *noun, masculine*
un escalofrío = a shiver
tener escalofríos = to shiver

escándalo *noun, masculine*
• un escándalo = a scandal
• un escándalo = a racket
armar un escándalo = to make a racket

escaparate *noun, masculine (Spa)*
un escaparate = a shop window

escaparse *verb* ⒈
= to escape

escarabajo *noun, masculine*
un escarabajo = a beetle

escena *noun, feminine*
una escena = a scene

escenario *noun, masculine*
un escenario = a stage

esclavo/esclava *noun,*
masculine/feminine
un esclavo/una esclava = a slave

escoba *noun, feminine*
una escoba = a broom

escocés/escocesa
1 *adjective*
= Scottish
• (*if it's whisky*) = Scotch
• (*if it's a pattern*) = tartan
2 *noun, masculine/feminine*
un escocés/una escocesa = a Scot

Escocia *noun, feminine*
= Scotland

escoger *verb* 20
= to choose

escoja, escojo, etc ▶ escoger

escolar
1 *adjective*
= school
las vacaciones escolares = the school
vacation *or* holidays
2 *noun masculine/feminine*
un/una escolar = a schoolboy/-girl

esconder *verb* 17
= to hide
esconderse
= to hide

escondido/escondida *adjective*
= hidden

Escorpión, Escorpio *noun, masculine*
Escorpion = Scorpio

escorpión, escorpio *noun,*
masculine/feminine
un/una escorpión, un/una escorpio
= a Scorpio

escribir *verb* 60
• = to write
• = to spell

escrito ▶ escribir

escritor/escritora *noun,*
masculine/feminine
un escritor/una escritora = a writer

escuchar *verb* ⒈
= to listen
= to listen to

escuela *noun, feminine*
una escuela = a school

escupir *verb* 41
= to spit
me escupió = he spat at me

ese/esa *adjective*
= that

ése/ésa *pronoun*
= that one

esfuerzo *noun, masculine*
un esfuerzo = an effort
hacer un esfuerzo = to make an effort

eso *pronoun*
= that
por eso = that's why
¡eso es! = that's it!

esos/esas *adjective*
= those

ésos/ésas *pronoun*
= those (ones)

espacio *noun, masculine*
= space
= room

espaguetis *noun, masculine plural*
los espaguetis = spaghetti

espalda *noun, feminine*
le espalda = the back
de espaldas:
estaba de espaldas a la ventana = she had
her back to the window
me puse de espaldas a la clase = I stood
with my back to the class
nadar de espaldas = to swim (the)
backstroke

espantapájaros *noun, masculine*
un espantapájaros = a scarecrow

España *noun, feminine*
España = Spain

español/española
1 *adjective*
= Spanish
2 *noun, masculine/feminine*
un español/una española = a Spaniard

3 español *noun, masculine*
el español (*the language*) = Spanish

espárrago *noun, masculine*
espárrago = asparagus

especia *noun, feminine*
una especia = a spice

especial *adjective*
= special
en especial = especially
= in particular

espectáculo *noun, masculine*
• un espectáculo (*on television, at a theater etc*) = a show
• un espectáculo = a sight

espejo *noun, masculine*
un espejo = a mirror
el espejo retrovisor = the rear-view mirror

espera *noun, feminine*
una espera = a wait
una lista de espera = a waiting list
una sala de espera = a waiting room

esperar *verb* 1
• = to wait
= to wait for
la estuve esperando tres horas = I was waiting for her for three hours
• = to expect
los espero a eso de las diez = I'm expecting them at around ten o'clock
• = to hope
eso espero, espero que sí = I hope so
espero que te guste = I hope you like it

> ! *Note the use of the subjunctive after* esperar que

espeso/espesa *adjective*
= thick

espinaca *noun, feminine*
las espinacas = spinach

esponja *noun, feminine*
una esponja = a sponge

esposo/esposa *noun, masculine/feminine*
un esposo/una esposa = a husband/a wife

espuma *noun, feminine*
espuma = foam
(*of beer*) = froth
(*of soap*) = lather
(*for styling hair*) = mousse

esqueleto *noun, masculine*
un esqueleto = a skeleton

esquí *noun, masculine*
• un esquí = a ski
• (*sport*) el esquí = skiing
hacer esquí = to ski
esquí acuático = water-skiing

esquiar *verb* 13
= to ski

esquimal
1 *adjective*
= Eskimo
2 *noun, masculine/feminine*
un/una esquimal = an Eskimo

esquina *noun, feminine*
una esquina = a corner

esta *adjective*
= this

ésta *pronoun*
= this (one)

está ▶ estar

estación *noun, feminine*
• una estación = a station
una estación de buses/de tren = a bus/train station
una estación de servicio = a gas station, a petrol station
• una estación de esquí = a ski resort
• una estación = a season

estacionar *verb* 1 (*Lat Am*)
= to park

estadio *noun, masculine*
un estadio = a stadium

estado *noun, masculine*
• un estado = a state
• estado = condition
el cuadro está en buen estado = the picture is in good condition
en mal estado (*if it's food*) = to be off
(*if it's a house, road*) = to be in a bad state
• estado civil = marital status

Estados Unidos *noun, masculine plural*
(los) Estados Unidos (de América) = the United States (of America)

estáis ▶ estar

estanco *noun, masculine*
un estanco = a tobacconist's

estanque *noun, masculine*
un estanque = a pond

estante *noun, masculine*
un estante = a shelf

estar *verb* 16
• = to be
últimamente está muy amable = he's being very nice lately
¿cómo estás? = how are you?
estoy [alegre | enfermo | cansado …] = I'm [happy | ill | tired …]
está de viaje = he's away on a trip
están sin trabajo = they're unemployed
¿dónde está Juan? = where is Juan?
estaré allí tres días = I'll be there for three days
estar [casado | soltero | divorciado …] (*Spa*) = to be [married | single | divorced …]

E

está casada con un inglés = she's married to an Englishman

hoy estamos a tres de enero = it's the third of January today

¿a cuánto están los tomates? = how much are the tomatoes

- (*Spa: referring to how clothes suit or fit you*) = to be
  me está largo = it's too long for me
  no te está bien = it doesn't fit you
- (*as auxiliary verb*) = to be
  está mintiendo = he's lying
  estába dormido = he was sleeping
  está roto = it's broken

estarse
- = to keep
  ¡estáte quieto! = keep still!
- se está bien al sol = it's nice in the sun

estatua *noun, feminine*
una estatua = a statue

este *noun, masculine*
- el este = the east
  al este de Quito = to the east of Quito
- = easterly
  vientos del este = easterly winds

este/esta *adjective*
= this

éste/ésta *pronoun*
= this (one)

esté, estén ▶ estar

estéreo *noun, masculine*
un estéreo = a stereo

estés ▶ estar

estilo *noun, masculine*
un estilo = a style
o algo por el estilo = or something like that
eran todos por el estilo = they were all similar

estirar *verb* 1
= to stretch

esto *pronoun*
= this
¿de quién es esto? = whose is this?

estómago *noun*
el estómago = the stomach

estornudar *verb* 1
= to sneeze

estoy ▶ estar

estrecho/estrecha *adjective*
= narrow
= tight
un pasillo estrecho = a narrow corridor
estos pantalones me quedan estrechos = these trousers are too tight for me

estrella *noun, feminine*
una estrella = a star

estrellarse *verb* 1
= to crash

estricto/estricta *adjective*
= strict

estropear *verb* 1
- (*if it's a plan, holiday*) = to spoil
- (*if it's a television, car, toy*) = to break
- (*if it's a dress, carpet*) = to ruin

estructura *noun feminine*
una estructura = a structure

estudiante *noun, masculine/feminine*
un/una estudiante = a student

estudiar *verb* 1
= to study
= to learn
estudiar inglés = to study English
estudiar la lección = to learn the lesson

estudio
1 *noun, masculine*
- un estudio = a study
  el estudio de la naturaleza = the study of nature
  estudios de derecho = law studies
- estudio de mercado = market research
- un estudio = a studio apartment
  un estudio (*for artist, photographer, etc; room in a house*) = a study
2 estudios *noun, masculine plural*
= education

estufa *noun, feminine*
- una estufa = a heater
  una estufa eléctrica/de gas = an electric heater/a gas heater
- (*Mex*) una estufa = a stove, a cooker

estúpido/estúpida
1 *adjective*
= stupid
2 *noun, masculine/feminine*
es un estúpido/una estúpida = he's/she's really stupid

estuve, estuvo, etc ▶ estar

etapa *noun, feminine*
una etapa = a stage
por *or* en etapas = in stages

etcétera *noun, masculine*
= etcetera, and so on

etiqueta *noun, masculine*
una etiqueta = a label
= a price tag

euro *noun, masculine*
un euro = a euro

Europa *noun, feminine*
Europa = Europe

C Am Central America   **Lat Am** Latin America   **Mex** Mexico

europeo/europea
1 *adjective*
= European
2 *noun, masculine or feminine*
un europeo/una europea = a European

evitar *verb* ⬚1
= to avoid
= to prevent
no se puede evitar = it can't be avoided
si puedo/puede evitarlo = if I can help it/if you, he, she can help it

exacto/exacta *adjective*
• = exact
= accurate
son 1.000 pesos exactos = that's 1,000 pesos exactly

exagerar *verb* ⬚1
= to exaggerate

examen *noun, masculine*
un examen = an exam, a test
hacer un examen = to take an exam
aprobar *or* pasar un examen = to pass an exam
un examen de recuperación (*Spa*) = a retake exam, a resit
un examen tipo test = a multiple-choice test
los exámenes finales = the finals

excelente *adjective*
= excellent

excepto *preposition*
= except

excusa *noun, feminine*
una excusa = an excuse

existir *verb* ⬚41
= to exist
no existen pruebas = there's no evidence

éxito *noun, masculine*
un éxito = a success
(*song*) = a hit
tener éxito = to succeed
(*if it's a song*) = to be a hit

experiencia *noun, feminine*
una experiencia = an experience
tengo mucha experiencia = I have a lot of experience

experto/experta *noun, masculine/feminine*
un experto/una experta = an expert

explicar *verb* ⬚2
= to explain

explotar *verb* ⬚1
= to explode

exportar *verb* ⬚1
= to export

exposición *noun, feminine*
una exposición = an exhibition
(*of a subject*) = a presentation

expresión *noun, feminine*
una expresión = an expresion

exterior
1 *adjective*
• = outer
la capa exterior = the outer layer
la parte exterior del objeto = the outside of the object
• = foreign
la política exterior = foreign policy
2 *noun, masculine*
el exterior = the outside, the exterior

externo/externa *adjective*
= external

extinguidor *noun, masculine* (*Lat Am*)
un extinguidor = a fire extinguisher

extintor *noun, masculine* (*Spa*)
un extintor = a fire extinguisher

extranjero/extranjera
1 *adjective*
= foreign
2 *noun, masculine/feminine*
un extranjero/una extranjera = a foreigner
3 extranjero *noun, masculine*
estar en el extranjero = to be abroad

extrañar *verb* ⬚1
• me extraña que no te lo haya dicho = I'm suprised that *or* I find it surprising that he hasn't told you

> **!** *Note the use of the subjunctive after* extrañar que

• (*Lat Am*) = to miss
extrañar a un amigo = to miss a friend

extraño/extraña
1 *adjective*
= strange
2 *noun, masculine/feminine*
un extraño/una extraña = a stranger

extremo/extrema
1 *adjective*
= extreme
2 extremo *noun, masculine*
• un extremo = an extreme
• (*of rope, corridor, etc*) un extremo = an end

E

f

fábrica *noun, feminine*
una fábrica = a factory

fácil *adjective*
= easy

factura *noun, feminine*
una factura = a bill

facultad *noun, feminine*
una facultad = a faculty
la Facultad de Medicina = the Faculty of
  Medicine
la facultad = university
ir a la facultad = to go to university

falda *noun, feminine*
una falda = a skirt

falla *noun, feminine*
una falla = a flaw
(*Lat Am: of a machine etc*) = a fault

fallar *verb* 1
= to miss
me falló la puntería, fallé el tiro = I missed
= to fail
fallaron los frenos = the brakes failed
= to go wrong
el plan falló = the plan went wrong
fallarle a alguien = to let someone down

fallo *noun, masculine (Spa)* ▶ falla

falso/falsa *adjective*
= false
= fake

falta *noun, feminine*
una falta de ortografía = a spelling mistake
(*in school*) una falta = an absence
ponerle falta a alguien = to mark someone
  as absent
(*in football*) una falta = a foul
falta de algo = lack of something
falta de [cariño | dinero | tiempo ...] = lack of
  [love | money | time ...]
falta de educación = lack of manners
eso es una falta de educación = that's bad
  manners
hacer falta:
hace falta revisarlo = it needs to be
  revised
no hace falta que te quedes = you don't
  need to stay

┌─────────────────────────────────────┐
│ **!** *Note the use of the subjunctive after*
│ hacer falta que
└─────────────────────────────────────┘

nos hace falta más dinero = we need more
  money
ya no me hace falta = I don't need it any
  more
le hace mucha falta = he really needs it

faltar *verb* 1
= to be missing
faltan dos niños = there are two children
  missing
(*talking about time*)
faltan dos horas para llegar = it's another
  two hours before we arrive
¿les falta mucho para terminar? = do you
  have long to go before you finish?
aún falta mucho tiempo para las
  vacaciones = the vacation is still a long
  way away
les falta [disciplina | dinero | apoyo ...] = they
  lack [discipline | money | support ...]
me falta cuerda = I need more rope

fama *noun, feminine*
la fama = fame
fama = reputation
tener fama de [gracioso | despistado | cruel ...]
  = to have a reputation for being [funny |
  absent-minded | cruel ...]
tener buena/mala fama = to have a
  good/bad reputation

familia *noun, feminine*
la familia = the family

familiar
1 *adjective*
= familiar
= family
2 *noun, masculine/feminine*
un/una familiar = a relative

famoso/famosa *adjective*
= famous, well-known

fantasía *noun, feminine*
fantasía = fantasy
= imagination

fantasma *noun, masculine*
un fantasma = a ghost

fantástico/fantástica *adjective*
= fantastic

farmacia *noun, feminine*
una farmacia = a pharmacy, a chemist's
(*as a subject*) farmacia = pharmacy
estudiar farmacia = to study pharmacy

farola *noun, feminine*
una farola = a street light

favor *noun, masculine*
un favor = a favor, a favour
estar a favor de algo = to be in favor of
  something

favorito/favorita *adjective*
= favorite, favourite

febrero *noun, masculine*
febrero = February

fecha *noun, feminine*
una fecha = a date
¿qué fecha es hoy?, ¿a qué fecha estamos? = what's the date today?
el año pasado por estas fechas = this time last year
fecha de caducidad (*for medicines*) = expiration date, expiry date
(*for food*) = use-by date

feliz *adjective*
= happy

femenino/femenina
1 *adjective*
= feminine
= women's
= female
2 femenino *noun, masculine*
el femenino = the feminine

feo/fea *adjective*
= ugly

feria *noun, feminine*
una feria = a fair
(*Mex*) **feria** = small change

feriado/feriada *adjective* (*Lat Am*) ▶ día

ferretería *noun, feminine*
una ferretería = a hardware store, an ironmonger's

ferrocarril *noun, masculine*
un ferrocarril = a railroad, a railway

festivo/festiva *adjective* ▶ día

fiarse *verb* [13]
= to trust
= to believe
fiarse de alguien = to trust someone
no te fíes de lo que dice = don't believe what he says

fideo
1 *noun, masculine*
un fideo = a noodle
2 fideos *noun, masculine plural* (*R Pl*)
fideos = pasta

fiebre *noun, feminine*
fiebre = temperature
tener fiebre = to have a fever, to have a temperature
(*an illness*) **una fiebre** = a fever

fiesta *noun, feminine*
una fiesta = a party
una fiesta = a holiday
hoy es fiesta = today's a holiday

figura *noun, feminine*
una figura = a figure

fijo/fija *adjective*
= fixed
(*if it's a job, an employee*) = permanent

fila *noun, feminine*
una fila = a row
= a line

fin *noun, masculine*
el fin = the end
un fin de semana = a weekend
a fin de mes/año = at the end of the month/year
a fines de abril/siglo = at the end of April/the century
al fin, por fin = at last
en fin, ya veremos = well, we'll see

final
1 *adjective*
= final
2 *noun, masculine*
el final = the end
(*of a movie*) = the ending
al final
= at the end
= in the end
a finales de [mes | año | semana…] = at the end of [the month | year | week…]
2 *noun, feminine*
una final = a final

finlandés/finlandesa
1 *adjective*
= Finnish
2 *noun, masculine/feminine*
un finlandés/una finlandesa = a Finn
3 finlandés *noun, masculine*
el finlandés (*the language*) = Finnish

firmar *verb* [1]
= to sign

física *noun, feminine*
la física = physics

flama *noun, feminine* (*Mex*)
una flama = a flame

flan *noun, masculine*
un flan = a crème caramel

flauta *noun, feminine*
una flauta = a flute
una flauta dulce = a recorder

flecha *noun, feminine*
una flecha = an arrow

fleco *noun, masculine* (*Mex*) ▶ flequillo

flequillo *noun, masculine*
un flequillo = bangs, a fringe

flojo/floja
1 *adjective*
= loose, slack
(*if it's coffee, tea*) = weak
(*if it's wind*) = light
(*Lat Am: if it's a person*) **flojo/floja** ✶ = lazy

F

estar flojo en [inglés | química |
  matemáticas …] = to be weak at [English |
  chemistry | maths …]
2 *noun, masculine/feminine (Lat Am)*
  un flojo/una floja✖ = a lazybones

flor *noun, feminine*
  una flor = a flower

florero *noun, masculine*
  un florero = a vase

floristería *noun, feminine*
  una floristería = a flower shop

flotar *verb* [1]
  = to float

foco *noun, masculine*
  un foco = a spotlight
  (*Mex*) = a light bulb

folleto *noun, masculine*
  un folleto = a leaflet, a flier
  = a brochure
  = a booklet

fondo *noun, masculine*
  el fondo = the bottom
  un pozo sin fondo = a bottomless well
  (*of a corridor, road*) el fondo = the end
  al fondo del pasillo = at the end of the
    corridor
  (*of a room*) el fondo = the back
  a fondo = in depth
  = thoroughly
  en el fondo = deep down

fontanero/fontanera *noun,*
masculine/feminine (Spa)
  un fontanero/una fontanera = a plumber

forma *noun, feminine*
  una forma = a shape
  tiene forma redonda = it's round
  forma = way
  esa no es forma de contestar = that's no
    way to answer
  es mi forma de ser = that's the way I am
  (*Mex: a paper*) una forma = a form
  estar/ponerse en forma = to be/get fit

formal *adjective*
  = formal
  = reliable
  = well-behaved

formar *verb* [1]
  = to form
  = to make up

fortuna *noun, feminine*
  una fortuna = a fortune
  por fortuna = fortunately

fósforo *noun, masculine*
  un fósforo = a match

foto *noun, feminine*
  una foto = a photo
  sacar *or* tomar *or* (*Spa*) hacer una foto = to
    take a photo

fotocopia *noun, feminine*
  una fotocopia = a photocopy

fotografía *noun, feminine*
  una fotografía = photograph
  (*the art*) la fotografía = photography

fotógrafo/fotógrafa *noun,*
masculine/feminine
  un fotógrafo/una fotógrafa = a
    photographer

fracasar *verb* [1]
  = to fail

fracaso *noun, masculine*
  un fracaso = a failure

frágil *adjective*
  = fragile

frambuesa *noun, feminine*
  una frambuesa = a raspberry

francés/francesa
1 *adjective*
  = French
2 *noun, masculine/feminine*
  un francés/una francesa = a
    Frenchman/Frenchwoman
3 francés *noun, masculine*
  el francés (*the language*) = French

Francia *noun, feminine*
  France = France

frase *noun, feminine*
  una frase = a sentence
  = a phrase

frazada *noun, feminine (Lat Am)*
  una frazada = a blanket

frecuente *adjective*
  = frequent
  = common
  no es muy frecuente = it doesn't happen
    very often

fregadero *noun, masculine*
  un fregadero = a sink

fregar *verb* [8]
  = to wash

fregona *noun, feminine (Spa)*
  una fregona = a mop

freír *verb* [61]
  = to fry

freno *noun, masculine*
  un freno = a brake
  el freno de mano = the handbrake
  poner/quitar el freno = to put on/release
    the brake

✖ in informal situations   **C Am** Central America   **Lat Am** Latin America   **Mex** Mexico

frente
1 *noun, feminine*
  la frente = the forehead
2 *noun, masculine*
  el frente = the front
  al frente:
  dar un paso al frente = to move one step
    forward
  pasar al frente (*Lat Am*) = to go/come up to
    the front
  al frente de la empresa = in charge of the
    company

fresa *noun, feminine*
  una fresa = a strawberry

fresco/fresca
1 *adjective*
  (*if it's vegetables*) = fresh
  (*if it's weather, water*) = cool
2 fresco *noun, masculine*
  hace fresco = it's a bit chilly

fría, frío, etc ▶ freír

friega, friego, friegue, etc ▶ fregar

frigorífico *noun, masculine* (*Spa*)
  un frigorífico = a fridge

frío/fría
1 *adjective*
  = cold
2 frío *noun, masculine*
  hace frío = it's cold
  tener frío, pasar frío = to be cold
  ¡tengo tanto frío! = I'm so cold!
  tomar *or* (*Spa*) **coger frío** = to catch cold

frito/frita *adjective*
  = fried

frontera *noun, feminine*
  la frontera = the border

fruta *noun, feminine*
  fruta = fruit

frutero *noun, masculine*
  un frutero = a fruit bowl

frutilla *noun, feminine* (*SC*)
  una frutilla = a strawberry

fruto *noun, masculine*
  un fruto = a fruit
  frutos secos = nuts and dried fruits

fue ▶ ser, ir

fuego *noun, masculine*
  fuego = fire
  hacer fuego = to light a fire
  prenderle fuego a algo = to set fire to
    something
  fuego = a light
  ¿me da fuego? = could you give me a
    light?
  fuegos artificiales = fireworks
    See also cocer, cocinar

fuente *noun, feminine*
  una fuente = a spring
  = a fountain

fuera, fuéramos, etc ▶ ser, ir

fuera *adverb*
  = out
  = outside
  por fuera:
  es verde por fuera = it's green on the
    outside
  pintamos la casa por fuera = we painted
    the outside of the house
  fuera de la casa = outside the house
  fuimos a comer fuera = we went out for a
    meal
  fuera de juego = offside
  = away
  = abroad

fueron ▶ ser, ir

fuerte
1 *adjective*
  = strong
  (*if it's rain, a meal*) = heavy
  (*if it's an increase*) = big
  (*if it's a pain, cold*) = bad
  (*if it's a noise*) = loud
2 *adverb*
  = hard
  = tight, tightly
  apretar una tuerca = to screw a bolt in
    tightly
  = loud, loudly
  poner la música fuerte = to turn the music
    up loud

fuerza *noun, feminine*
  fuerza = force
  = strength
  tengo mucha fuerza = I'm very strong
  a la fuerza = by force

fui, fuimos, fuiste, etc ▶ ser, ir

fumador/fumadora *noun,*
masculine/feminine
  un fumador/una fumadora = a smoker

fumar *verb* [1]
  = to smoke

función *noun, feminine*
  una función = a function
  (*at a theater*) **una función** = a performance

funcionar *verb* [1]
  = to work

furgoneta *noun, feminine*
  una furgoneta = a van

furioso/furiosa *adjective*
  = furious

fusil *noun, masculine*
  un fusil = a rifle

futbito *noun, masculine* (*Spa*)
  futbito = five-a-side football

F

fútbol or (*C Am, Mex*) **futbol** *noun, masculine*
  fútbol = soccer, football

futbolín
1 *noun, masculine*
  futbolín = table football
2 futbolines *noun, masculine plural* (*Spa*)
  los futbolines = the local amusement
  arcade

futbolista *noun, masculine/feminine*
  un/una futbolista = a footballer

futuro *noun, masculine*
  el futuro = the future

gafas *noun, feminine plural*
  gafas = glasses
  llevar or usar gafas = to wear glasses

galería *noun, feminine*
  una galería = a gallery

Gales *noun, masculine*
  Gales, el país de Gales = Wales

galés/galesa
1 *adjective*
  = Welsh
2 *noun, masculine/feminine*
  un galés/una galesa = a Welshman/a
  Welshwoman
3 galés *noun, masculine*
  el galés (*the language*) = Welsh

gallego/gallega
1 *adjective*
  = Galician
2 *noun, masculine/feminine*
  un gallego/una gallega = a Galician
3 gallego *noun, masculine*
  el gallego (*the language*) = Galician

galleta *noun, feminine*
  una galleta = a cookie, a biscuit
  = a cracker

gallina *noun, feminine*
  una gallina = a hen

gallo *noun, masculine*
  un gallo = a cock

gamba *noun, feminine* (*Spa*)
  una gamba = a shrimp, a prawn

gana *noun, feminine*
  no me da la gana = I don't want to
  haz lo que te dé la gana = do as you please
  hacer algo de buena/mala gana = to do
  something willingly/unwillingly
  hacer algo sin ganas = to do something
  half-heartedly
  tener ganas de hacer algo
  = to feel like doing something
  = to look forward to doing something

ganador/ganadora
1 *adjective*
  = winning
2 *noun, masculine/feminine*
  un ganador/una ganadora = a winner

ganar *verb* [1]
  = to earn
  = to win

gancho *noun, masculine*
  un gancho = a hook

ganso/gansa *noun, masculine/feminine*
  un ganso/una gansa = a goose

garage (*Lat Am*), **garaje** (*Spa*) *noun, masculine*
  un garage = a garage

garantía *noun, feminine*
  una garantía = a guarantee

garbanzo *noun, masculine*
  un garbanzo = a chickpea

garganta *noun, feminine*
  la garganta = the throat
  me duele la garganta = I have a sore throat

gas *noun, masculine*
  gas = gas

gaseosa *noun, feminine*
  una gaseosa = a soda, a lemonade

gasolina *noun, feminine*
  gasolina = gas, petrol

gasolinera *noun, feminine*
  una gasolinera = a gas station, a petrol
  station

gastar *verb* [1]
  = to spend
  = to use
  gastaron toda el agua = they used (up) all
  the water

gasto *noun, masculine*
  un gasto = an expense

gato/gata *noun, masculine/feminine*
  un gato/una gata = a cat

gemelo/gemela
1 *adjective*
= twin
hermanos gemelos = twin brothers
2 *noun, masculine/feminine*
un gemelo/una gemela = a twin
3 gemelos *noun, masculine plural*
unos gemelos = a pair of binoculars
4 gemelo *noun, masculine*
un gemelo = a cuff link

Géminis *noun, masculine*
Géminis = Gemini

géminis *noun, masculine/feminine*
un/una géminis = a Gemini, a Geminian

generación *noun, feminine*
una generación = a generation

general
1 *adjective*
= general
en general = in general, on the whole
por lo general = generally, usually
2 *noun, masculine/feminine*
un/una general = a general

generoso/generosa *adjective*
= generous

genio *noun, masculine*
genio = temper
tener mal genio = to be bad-tempered
estar de mal genio = to be in a bad mood
un genio = a genius

gente *noun, feminine*
gente = people
había mucha gente = there were a lot of people

geografía *noun, feminine*
la geografía = geography

gerente *noun, masculine/feminine*
un/una gerente = a manager

gesto *noun, masculine*
un gesto = a gesture

gigante/giganta *noun,*
masculine/feminine
un gigante/una giganta = a giant

gilipollas◆ *noun, masculine/feminine*
(Spa) **(! *does not change in the plural*)**
un/una gilipollas = a jerk

gimnasia *noun, feminine*
la gimnasia = gymnastics
hice dos horas de gimnasia = I worked out for two hours

gimnasio *noun, masculine*
un gimnasio = gymnasium, gym

girar *verb* 1
= to turn

gitano/gitana *noun, masculine/feminine*
un gitano/una gitana = a gypsy

globo *noun, masculine*
un globo = a balloon
un globo terráqueo = a globe

gobierno *noun, masculine*
un gobierno = a government

gol *noun, masculine*
un gol = a goal

golfo *noun, masculine*
un golfo = a gulf
el Golfo de México = the Gulf of Mexico

golpe *noun, masculine*
un golpe = a blow
me di un golpe en la cabeza = I banged my head
le dio un golpe en la espalda = she hit him on the back
un golpe = a knock
la ventana se cerró de un golpe = the window slammed shut

golpear *verb* 1
= to bang
= to beat
= to hit

goma *noun, feminine*
goma = rubber
una goma (elástica) = a rubber band, an elastic band
una goma (de borrar) = an eraser, a rubber
goma de pegar = glue

gorra *noun, feminine*
una gorra = a cap

gorro *noun, masculine*
un gorro = a cap

gota *noun, feminine*
una gota = a drop

gozar *verb* 4
= to enjoy
gozar de algo/haciendo algo = to enjoy something/doing something

grabadora *noun, feminine*
una grabadora = a tape recorder

grabar *verb*
= to tape

gracia *noun, feminine*
una gracia = a joke
tener gracia = to be funny
hacerle gracia a alguien = to make someone laugh
= to amuse someone
no me hace gracia = I don't find it funny

G

¡muchas gracias! = thank you very much!
darle las gracias a alguien = to thank
somebody
gracias a alguien/algo = thanks to
somebody/something

grado *noun, masculine*
un grado = a degree
tres grados bajo cero = three degrees
below zero

gramática *noun, feminine*
la gramática = grammar

gramo *noun, masculine*
un gramo = a gram

gran ▶ grande

Gran Bretaña *noun, feminine*
Gran Bretaña = Great Britain

grande *adjective*

> **!** *Note that* **grande** *becomes* **gran** *before
> singular nouns*

= big, large
una gran cantidad = a large quantity
= great
es un gran escritor = he's a great writer
(*referring to age*)
cuando sea grande = when I grow up
mi hijo ya es grande = my son is grown up
See also **parte**

granizado *noun, masculine*
un granizado = *a drink served on crushed ice*
un granizado de limón = *an iced lemon
drink*

granja *noun, feminine*
una granja = a farm

grapa *noun, feminine*
una grapa = a staple

grapadora *noun, feminine*
una grapadora = a stapler

grapar *verb* 1
= to staple

grasa *noun, feminine*
grasa = grease
= fat

grasiento/grasienta *adjective*
= greasy

gratis *adjective, adverb*
= free

grave *adjective*
= serious
está grave = he's seriously ill

Grecia *noun, feminine*
Grecia = Greece

griego/griega
1 *adjective*
= Greek

2 *noun, masculine/feminine*
un griego/una griega = a Greek
3 griego *noun, masculine*
el griego (*the language*) = Greek

grifo *noun, masculine* (*Spa*)
un grifo = a faucet, a tap

gripe *or* (*Mex*) **gripa** *noun, feminine*
gripe = flu
tener gripe = to have the flu

gris
1 *adjective*
= gray, grey
2 *noun, masculine*
el gris = gray, grey

gritar *verb* 1
= to shout

grito *noun, masculine*
un grito = a shout
= a cry

grueso/gruesa *adjective*
= thick

grupo *noun, masculine*
un grupo = a group

guante *noun, masculine*
un guante = a glove

guapo/guapa *adjective*
= good-looking

guardabarros *noun, masculine* (**!** *does
not change in the plural*)
un guardabarros (*on a car*) = a fender, a
mudguard
(*on a bicycle*) = a mudguard

guardar *verb* 1
= to keep
= to put away

guardia *noun, masculine/feminine*
un/una guardia = a police officer, a
policeman/a policewoman

guarro/guarra✗ *adjective* (*Spa*)
= filthy

guau *exclamation*
¡guau! = woof!, bow-wow!

güero/güera✗ *adjective* (*Mex*)
= blond, blonde

guerra *noun, feminine*
una guerra = a war
la Primera/Segunda Guerra Mundial = the
First/Second World War

guía
1 *noun, feminine*
una guía = a guide, a guidebook
una guía turística = a tourist guide
una guía telefónica = a telephone
directory

2 *noun, masculine/feminine*
un/una **guía** = a guide

guiar *verb* 13
= to guide

guiñar *verb* 1
= to wink

guiño *noun, masculine*
un **guiño** = a wink

guisante *noun, masculine (Spa)*
un **guisante** = a pea

guitarra *noun, feminine*
una **guitarra** = a guitar

gusano *noun, masculine*
un **gusano** = a worm

gustar *verb* 1
me gusta **nadar** = I like swimming
la película no me **gustó** = I didn't like the movie
le gustan los **perros** = he/she likes dogs

gusto *noun, masculine*
gusto = taste
tiene buen **gusto** = he has good taste
= pleasure
mucho *or* tanto **gusto** = pleased to meet you

ha ▶ haber

haba *noun, feminine*
un **haba** = a broad bean

> **!** *Note that although* haba *is feminine it is preceded by a masculine article in the singular*

habéis ▶ haber

haber *verb* 29
• *(used to form past tenses)* = to have
han **terminado** = they have finished
no lo había **visto** = I hadn't seen it
• **hay** = there is
= there are
no hay **suficiente** = there isn't enough
hay tres **entradas** = there are three entries
• **hay que:**
hay que **revisarlo** = it needs revising
hay que comprar **pan** = we have to buy bread
hay que **hacerlo** = it must be done
• gracias — no hay de **qué** = thank you — don't mention it

habitación *noun, feminine*
una **habitación** = a bedroom
(in a hotel) = a room
una habitación **individual** = a single room

habitante *noun, masculine/feminine*
un/una **habitante** = an inhabitant

hablar *verb*
• = to speak
hablar **italiano** = to speak Italian
• = to talk
hablar de algo/**alguien** = to talk about something/someone

habrán, habré, etc ▶ haber

hacer *verb* 30
• = to make
hacer [la cama | la cena | un vestido ...] = to make [the bed | dinner | a dress ...]
hacer un **esfuerzo** = to make an effort
• = to do
¿qué haces **aquí**? = what are you doing here?
hacer los **deberes** = to do one's homework
• *(when talking about the weather)*
hace [frío | calor | sol ...] = it's [cold | hot | sunny ...]
hizo mal tiempo *or (Spa)* hizo **malo** = the weather was bad
• *(when talking about time)*
hace dos años que no nos **vemos** = we haven't seen each other for two years
me jubilé hace cinco **años** = I retired five years ago
¿hace mucho que **esperas**? = have you been waiting long?
desde hace/desde **hacía** = for
no la había visto desde hacía dos **años** = I hadn't seen her for two years

hacerse
• = to make
se hace ella misma la **ropa** = she makes her own clothes
se va a hacer un traje para la **boda** = he is going to have a suit made for the wedding
• = to become
= to get
se hizo **famosa** = she became famous
hacerse **viejo** = to get old
• hacerse **daño** = to hurt oneself

hacia *preposition*
• = toward(s)
íbamos hacia la **playa** = we were going toward(s) the beach
• = at about
llegará hacia las **dos** = he'll arrive at about 2 o'clock

haga, hago, etc ▶ hacer

hamaca noun, feminine
- una **hamaca** = a hammock
- (R Pl) una **hamaca** = a swing
  = a rocking chair

hambre noun, feminine
  el **hambre** = hunger

> ! Note that although **hambre** is feminine it
> is preceded by a masculine article in the
> singular

  tener **hambre** = to be hungry
  tengo **hambre** = I'm hungry

hamburguesa noun, feminine
  una **hamburguesa** = a hamburger

han ▶ haber

harán, **haré**, **etc** ▶ hacer

harina noun, feminine
  la **harina** = flour

harto/harta
1 adjective
  = fed up
  estar **harto** de algo = to be fed up with
    something
2 harto adverb (Lat Am)
- = very
  es **harto** difícil = it's very difficult
- = a lot
  comimos **harto** = we ate a lot

has ▶ haber

hasta
1 preposition
- = until, till
  esperé **hasta** las tres = I waited until three
  no será or (Mex) **será** publicado **hasta**
    mayo = it won't be published till May
- = as far as
  nadaron **hasta** la roca = they swam as far
    as the rock
- = up to
  el ascensor sólo sube **hasta** el tercer piso
    = the elevator only goes up to the third
    floor
- = down to
  el pelo le llega **hasta** la cintura = her hair
    goes down to her waist
- **hasta** [mañana | luego | esta tarde ...] = see you
    [tomorrow | later | this afternoon ...]
2 adverb
  = even
  hasta yo lo sé hacer = even I can do it

hay ▶ haber

haz ▶ hacer

he ▶ haber

hebilla noun, feminine
  una **hebilla** = a buckle

hecho/hecha
1 past participle of hacer
- = made
  está **hecho** de madera = it's made of wood
  hecho a mano = handmade
- = done
  la cena aún no está **hecha** = dinner is not
    ready yet
2 adjective
  un filete de carne bien **hecho**/poco **hecho**
    (Spa) = a well-done/rare steak
3 hecho noun, masculine
  un **hecho** = a fact

helado/helada
1 adjective
- = frozen
  el lago está **helado** = the lake is frozen
- = freezing
  estoy **helada** = I'm freezing
2 helado noun, masculine
  un **helado** = an ice cream

helicóptero noun, masculine
  un **helicóptero** = a helicopter

hemos ▶ haber

herida noun, feminine
  una **herida** = an injury
  = a wound

herido/herida adjective
  = injured
  = wounded

hermanastro/hermanastra noun,
masculine/feminine
  un **hermanastro** = a stepbrother
  = a half brother
  una **hermanastra** = a stepsister
  = a half sister

hermano/hermana noun,
masculine/feminine
  un **hermano**/una **hermana** = a brother/a
    sister
  ¿tienes **hermanos**? = do you have any
    brothers or sisters?

hermoso/hermosa adjective
  = beautiful

héroe noun, masculine
  un **héroe** = a hero

heroína noun, feminine
  una **heroína** = a heroine

herramienta noun, feminine
  una **herramienta** = a tool

hervir verb 46
  = to boil

hice ▶ hacer

hielo noun, masculine
  hielo = ice
  un cubito de **hielo** = an ice cube

hierba noun, feminine
- la hierba = the grass
- una hierba = a herb

hierro noun, masculine
hierro = iron

hierve, hiervo, etc ▶ hervir

hígado noun, masculine
el hígado = the liver

hijo/hija noun, masculine/feminine
un hijo/una hija = a son/a daughter
¿tienes hijos? = do you have any children?

hilo noun, masculine
hilo = thread

himno noun, masculine
un himno = a hymn
el himno nacional = the national anthem

hipo noun, masculine
hipo = hiccups
tener hipo = to have hiccups

hipopótamo noun, masculine
un hipopótamo = a hippopotamus

hispanohablante
1 adjective
= Spanish-speaking
2 noun, masculine/feminine
un/una hispanohablante = a Spanish
speaker

historia noun, feminine
- la historia = history
- una historia = a story

histórico/histórica adjective
- = historical
- = historic

hizo ▶ hacer

hoja noun, feminine
- una hoja = a leaf
- (of paper) una hoja = a sheet

hola exclamation
¡hola! = hello!

holá exclamation (R Pl)
(when answering the phone) hello?

Holanda noun, feminine
Holanda = Holland

holandés/holandesa
1 adjective
= Dutch
2 noun, masculine/feminine
un holandés/una holandesa = a
Dutchman/a Dutchwoman
3 holandés noun, masculine
el holandés (the language) = Dutch

hombre noun, masculine
un hombre = a man

hombro noun, masculine
el hombro = the shoulder

honesto/honesta adjective
= honest

honor noun, masculine
honor = honor, honour

hora noun, feminine
- una hora = an hour
horas de consulta/visita (at the doctor's or
dentist's) = surgery/visiting hours
- la hora = the time
siempre empieza a la misma hora = it
always begins at the same time
¿tiene hora, por favor? = have you got the
time, please?
¿me da la hora? = can you tell me the
time?
¿qué hora es? = what time is it?
- pedir hora con el médico = to make an
appointment at the doctor's

horario noun, masculine
un horario (for trains, airplanes) = a
schedule, a timetable
(at school) = a timetable
horario de atención al público (in a shop or
bank) = opening hours

horizonte noun, masculine
el horizonte = the horizon

hormiga noun, feminine
una hormiga = an ant

hormigón noun, masculine
hormigón = concrete

horno noun, masculine
un horno = an oven
un horno microondas = a microwave oven

horóscopo noun, masculine
el horóscopo = the horoscope

horrible adjective
= horrible, awful

hospital noun, masculine
un hospital = a hospital

hostal noun, masculine
un hostal = a cheap hotel

hotel noun, masculine
un hotel = a hotel

hoy adverb
= today
hoy en día = nowadays, these days
el diario de hoy = today's newspaper
los jóvenes de hoy = the youth of today

hube, hubo, etc ▶ haber

hueco/hueca
1 adjective
= hollow

H

2 hueco *noun, masculine*
 un hueco = a space
 = a hollow

huela, huelo, etc ▶ oler

huelga *noun, feminine*
 una huelga = a strike
 estar en huelga *or* (*Spa*) **de huelga** = to be
  on strike
 ir a la huelga *or* **hacer huelga** *or* (*Spa*)
  ponerse en huelga = to go on strike

hueso *noun, masculine*
 un hueso = a bone

huésped *noun, masculine/feminine*
 un/una huésped = a guest

huevo *noun, masculine*
 un huevo = an egg
 un huevo duro/frito = a hard-boiled/fried
  egg
 huevos revueltos = scrambled eggs

huir *verb* [51]
 = to flee, to escape

hule *noun, masculine* (*Mex*)
 hule = rubber

humano/humana
1 *adjective*
 = human
 un ser humano = a human being
2 *noun, masculine/feminine*
 los humanos = human beings, humans

húmedo/húmeda *adjective*
 = damp
 = wet
 = moist

humo *noun, masculine*
 = smoke
 = fumes

humor *noun, masculine*
 • = mood
 estar de buen/mal humor = to be in a
  good/bad mood
 • = humor, humour

hundir *verb* [41]
 = to sink
hundirse
 = to sink

huracán *noun, masculine*
 un huracán = a hurricane

hurra *exclamation*
 ¡hurra! = hurrah!, hooray!

huyas, huyo, etc ▶ huir

I i

iba, iban, etc ▶ ir

ida *noun, feminine*
 la ida = the outward journey
 a la ida = on the way there
 un boleto (*Lat Am*) *or* (*Spa*) **billete de ida y
  vuelta** = a round trip ticket, a return
  ticket

idea *noun, feminine*
 una idea = an idea

idéntico/idéntica *adjective*
 = identical

identidad *noun, feminine*
 identidad = identity
 un documento de identidad = an identity
  card

idioma *noun, masculine*
 un idioma = a language

idiota
1 *adjective*
 = stupid
2 *noun, masculine/feminine*
 un/una idiota = an idiot

ido/ida ▶ ir

iglesia *noun, feminine*
 una iglesia = a church

igual
1 *adjective*
 son los dos iguales = they are both the
  same
 es igual al mío = it's the same as mine
 mi abrigo es igual a *or* que éste = my coat
  is the same as this one
2 *adverb*
 • = equally
 cantan igual de bien = they both sing
  equally well
 • = the same
 se escriben igual = they are written the
  same
 • = maybe
 igual se ha perdido = maybe he's got lost
 • es igual de alto/inteligente/gordo que yo
  = he's as tall/intelligent/fat as I am
 • igual que = just like, the same as
 se llama Juan, igual que yo = his name is
  Juan, just like mine

ilegal *adjective*
 = illegal

ilusión *noun, masculine*
 • una ilusión = an illusion

- **mi mayor ilusión es volar en globo** = my greatest dream is to fly in a balloon
  hacerse ilusiones = to build up one's hopes
- **me hace mucha ilusión ir** (*Spa*) = I am looking forward to going
  ¡qué ilusión! (*Spa*) = how wonderful!

ilustración *noun, feminine*
  una ilustración = an illustration

imagen *noun, feminine*
  una imagen = an image

imaginación *noun, feminine*
  la imaginación = the imagination

imbécil
1 *adjective*
  = stupid
2 *noun, masculine|feminine*
  un/una imbécil = an idiot

impaciente *adjective*
  = impatient

impermeable *noun, masculine*
  un impermeable = a raincoat

impersonal *adjective*
  = impersonal

importación *noun, feminine*
  importación = importation
  artículos de importación = imported goods
  las importaciones = imports

importancia *noun, feminine*
  importancia = importance
  sin importancia = unimportant
  no tiene importancia = it doesn't matter

importante *adjective*
  = important

importar *verb* 1
- = to matter
  no importa = it doesn't matter
  no me importa ir sola = I don't mind going on my own
  no me importa lo que ellos digan = I don't care what they say
- = to import

imposible *adjective*
  = impossible

incluido/incluida *adjective*
  somos diez, los niños incluidos = there are ten of us including the children
  todo incluido = all in, all inclusive

incluir *verb* 51
  = to include

incluso *adverb*
  = even

incluya, incluyo, etc ▶ incluir

incómodo/incómoda *adjective*
  = uncomfortable

inconveniente *noun, masculine*
  un inconveniente = a problem
  = a drawback

incorrecto/incorrecta *adjective*
  = incorrect

increíble *adjective*
  = incredible

independencia *noun, feminine*
  independencia = independence

independiente *adjective*
  = independent

indicar *verb* 2
  = to show
  = to indicate
  = to point out

índice *noun, masculine*
- **un índice** = an index
- **el índice** = the index finger, the forefinger

indio/india
1 *adjective*
  = Indian
2 *noun*
  un indio/una india = an Indian

individual *adjective*
- = individual
- (*if it's a bed, a room*) = single

individuo/individua *noun, masculine|feminine*
  un individuo/una individua = an individual
  = a person

industria *noun, feminine*
  una industria = an industry

infarto *noun, masculine*
  un infarto = a heart attack

inferior *adjective*
- = lower
- = inferior

infierno *noun, masculine*
  el infierno = hell

influencia *noun, feminine*
  influencia = influence

informal *adjective*
- = informal, casual
- = unreliable

informar *verb* 1
  = to inform

informática *noun, feminine*
  la informática = computing

ingeniero/ingeniera *noun, masculine|feminine*
  un ingeniero/una ingeniera = an engineer

Inglaterra *noun, feminine*
  Inglaterra = England

inglés/inglesa
1 *adjective*
= English
2 *noun, masculine/feminine*
un inglés/una inglesa = an Englishman/Englishwoman
3 inglés *noun, masculine*
el inglés (*the language*) = English

ingrediente *noun, masculine*
un ingrediente = an ingredient

inicial *adjective*
= initial

injusto/injusta *adjective*
= unfair

inmigración *noun, masculine*
inmigración = immigration

inmigrante *noun, masculine/feminine*
un/una inmigrante = an immigrant

inocente *adjective*
• = innocent
• = naive

inolvidable *adjective*
= unforgettable

insecto *noun, masculine*
un insecto = an insect

insistir *verb* 41
= to insist

inspector/inspectora *noun,*
masculine/feminine
un inspector/una inspectora = an inspector

instalar *verb* 1
= to install
= to put in
= to put up
= to put

instante *noun, masculine*
un instante = a moment

instituto *noun, masculine*
• un instituto = an institute
• (*Spa*) un instituto = a high school, a secondary school

instrucción
1 *noun, feminine*
una instrucción = an instruction
2 instrucciones *noun, feminine plural*
instrucciones = directions

instructor/instructora *noun,*
masculine/feminine
un instructor/una instructora = an instructor

instrumento *noun, masculine*
un instrumento = an instrument

insuficiente
1 *adjective*

• = insufficient
• = inadequate
• = poor
2 *noun, masculine* (*Spa*)
un insuficiente = a fail

insulto *noun, masculine*
un insulto = an insult

inteligencia *noun, feminine*
la inteligencia = intelligence

inteligente *adjective*
= intelligent

intención *noun, feminine*
una intención = an intention
no fue mi intención = I didn't mean to
tener buenas intenciones = to mean well

intentar *verb* 1
= to try

intercambio *noun, masculine*
un intercambio = an exchange

interés *noun, masculine*
interés = interest
tener interés en algo = to be interested in something

interesante *adjective*
= interesting

interesar *verb* 1
no me interesa la política = I am not interested in politics
le interesa oír tu opinión = he's interested in hearing your opinion
interesarse
= to show an interest

interior
1 *adjective*
• = inner
= inside
• = domestic
2 *noun, masculine*
el interior = the inside
= the interior

intermedio
1 *adjective*
• = intermediate
• = medium
2 *noun, masculine*
un intermedio = a break
= an interval

internacional *adjective*
= international

internado *noun, masculine*
un internado = a boarding school

Internet noun, *masculine*
el Internet = the Internet

interno/interna
1 *adjective*
• = internal
= inner
• = domestic
2 noun, *masculine/feminine*
un interno/una interna = a boarder

intérprete noun, *masculine/feminine*
un/una intérprete = an interpreter

interrumpir verb 41
= to interrupt

interruptor noun, *masculine*
un interruptor = a switch

íntimo/íntima *adjective*
= intimate
= private
un amigo íntimo = a close friend

inundación noun, *feminine*
una inundación = a flood

inútil *adjective*
= useless

invasión noun, *feminine*
una invasión = an invasion

inventar verb 1
= to invent
inventarse
= to make up

invento noun, *masculine*
un invento = an invention

invernadero noun, *masculine*
un invernadero = a greenhouse
el efecto invernadero = the greenhouse
effect

investigación noun, *feminine*
una investigación = an investigation
(*scientific*) = a piece of research

invierno noun, *masculine*
el invierno = winter

invisible *adjective*
= invisible

invitación noun, *feminine*
una invitación = an invitation

invitado/invitada noun,
masculine/feminine
un invitado/una invitada = a guest

invitar verb 1
= to invite
te invito a una copa = I'll buy you a drink
me invitó a comer a un restaurante = he
took me out for a meal
esta vez te invito yo = this time it's is on me

ir verb 54
• = to go
fuimos a México = we went to Mexico
vamos a casa = let's go home
ir [a pie | en coche | en tren ...] = to go [on foot |
by car | by train ...]
fui a ayudarla = I went to help her
¿qué tal van las cosas? = how are things
going?
• = to come
¡ya voy! = I'm coming!
• = to be
iba con su novio = she was with her
boyfriend
• = to have
iba con un peinado muy raro = she had a
really strange hairstyle
• ir a hacer algo:
voy a estudiar medicina = I'm going to
study medicine
vete a comprar pan = go and buy some
bread
• ir haciendo algo:
voy acostumbrándome = I'm getting used
to it
vete vistiéndote = start getting dressed
• ¡vamos! = come on!
• ¡vaya!:
¡vaya, si es Fernando! = what a surprise,
it's Fernando!
¡vaya, se rompió! = oh, dear! it has broken
irse
• = to leave
nos fuimos a las siete = we left at seven
irse de casa = to leave home
• = to go
me voy al trabajo = I'm going to work

Irlanda noun, *feminine*
Irlanda = Ireland

irlandés/irlandesa
1 *adjective*
= Irish
2 noun, *masculine/feminine*
un irlandés/una irlandesa = an
Irishman/Irishwoman

irregular *adjective*
= irregular

isla noun, *feminine*
una isla = an island

italiano/italiana
1 *adjective*
= Italian
2 noun, *masculine/feminine*
un italiano/una italiana = an Italian
3 italiano noun, *masculine*
el italiano (*the language*) = Italian

I

izquierda noun, feminine
  la izquierda = the left
  ir hacia la izquierda = to go left
  a la izquierda = on the left
  manejar or (Spa) **conducir por la izquierda**
    = to drive on the left
  la izquierda = the left hand
  (in politics) **la izquierda** = the left
  ser de izquierda or (Spa) **izquierdas** = to be
    left-wing

izquierdo/izquierda adjective
  = left

Jj

jabón noun, masculine
  el jabón = the soap

jabonera noun, feminine
  una jabonera = a soapdish

jaguar noun, masculine
  un jaguar = a jaguar

jalar verb [1]
  (Lat Am) = to pull
  (Mex) = to take

jamás adverb
  = never
  nunca jamás = never ever
  = never again

jamón noun, masculine
  el jamón = ham
  jamón cocido, jamón (de) York = cooked
    ham
  jamón serrano = type of cured ham similar to
    Parma ham

Japón noun, masculine
  (el) **Japón** = Japan

jardín noun, masculine
  un jardín = a garden
  un jardín de niños or (Spa) **de infancia** = a
    nursery school

jardinero/jardinera noun,
masculine/feminine
  un jardinero/una jardinera = a gardener

jarra noun, feminine
  una jarra = a pitcher, a jug

jarro noun, masculine
  un jarro = a pitcher, a jug

jaula noun, feminine
  una jaula = a cage

jefe/jefa noun, masculine/feminine
  un jefe/una jefa = a boss
  (of a department) = a head
  (of a group) = a leader
  jefe de estado/gobierno = head of
    state/government

jerez noun, masculine
  el jerez = sherry

jersey noun, masculine
  un jersey = a sweater, a jumper

Jesucristo noun, masculine
  Jesucristo = Jesus Christ

jícama noun, feminine (Mex)
  una jícama = a yam bean

jirafa noun, feminine
  una jirafa = a giraffe

jitomate noun, masculine (Mex)
  un jitomate = a tomato

joven
1 adjective
  = young
2 noun, masculine/feminine
  un/una joven = a young man/young
    woman
  los jóvenes de hoy = the young people of
    today

joya noun, feminine
  una joya = a piece of jewelry, a piece of
    jewellery
  mis joyas = my jewelry

joyería noun, feminine
  una joyería = a jeweler's, a jeweller's

jubilado/jubilada
1 adjective
  = retired
2 noun, masculine/feminine
  un jubilado/una jubilada = a pensioner

judía noun, feminine (Spa)
  una judía = a bean
  una judía verde = a green bean

judío/judía
1 adjective
  = Jewish
2 noun, masculine/feminine
  un judío/una judía = a Jew

juega, juego, etc ▶ jugar

juego noun, masculine
  un juego = a game
  hacer juego con algo = to match
    something
  (of knives, plates) **un juego** = a set

juegue ▶ jugar

jueves noun, masculine (**!** does not
change in the plural)
  el jueves = Thursday
    See **miércoles** for more examples.

C Am Central America   **Lat Am** Latin America   **Mex** Mexico

juez *noun, masculine/feminine*
  un/una juez = a judge

jugador/jugadora *noun,*
masculine/feminine
  un jugador/una jugadora = a player

jugar *verb* 12
  = to play
  jugar tenis *or (R Pl, Spa)* **al tenis** = to play
    tennis
  jugar a las cartas = to play cards

jugo *noun, masculine*
  jugo = juice
  jugo de naranja = orange juice

juguete *noun, masculine*
  un juguete = a toy

juguetería *noun, feminine*
  una juguetería = a toy store, a toyshop

julio *noun, masculine*
  julio = July

jungla *noun, feminine*
  la jungla = the jungle

junio *noun, masculine*
  junio = June

juntar *verb* 1
  = to put together
  juntaron todos los pupitres = they put all
    the desks together
  = to join
  hay qué juntar los dos extremos = you
    have to join the two ends
  (Lat Am) = to collect
  juntar sellos = to collect stamps
juntarse
  = to move closer together
  = to get together

junto/junta *adjective, adverb*
  = together
  ponlos juntos = put them together
  lo queremos hacer juntos = we want to do
    it together
  viven juntas = they live together
  junto a = by, next to
  junto con = with

justicia *noun, feminine*
  la justicia = justice

justo/justa
1 *adjective*
  = fair
  = tight
  me queda un poco justo = it's a bit tight for
    me
  = right
  la cantidad justa = the right amount
  = just enough
  tengo el dinero justo = I have just enough
    money

2 justo *adverb*
  = just
  justo donde yo pensaba = just where I
    thought
  llegó justo a las 8 = he arrived at 8 o'clock
    exactly

juventud *noun, feminine*
  la juventud = young people
  (period) = youth

juzgar *verb* 3
  = to judge

K k

kilo *noun, masculine*
  un kilo = a kilo

kilogramo *noun, masculine*
  un kilogramo = a kilogram

kilómetro *noun, masculine*
  un kilómetro = a kilometer, a kilometre

kiosco *noun, masculine*
  un kiosco = a newsstand
  (selling sweets, cigarettes) = a kiosk

L l

la
1 *feminine article*
  = the
  la niña = the girl
    See **el** *for more examples*
2 *pronoun*
• = her
  la vi ayer = I saw her yesterday
• = it
  la vas a romper = you're going to break it

labio *noun, masculine*
  un labio = a lip

lado *noun, masculine*
  un lado = a side
  en el lado derecho = on the right-hand side
  de un lado a otro = from one place to
    another
  la casa de al lado = the house next door
  al lado de = next to
  a mi lado = next to me
  de lado = sideways
  duerme de lado = he sleeps on his side
  en otro lado = somewhere else

en todos lados = everywhere
en algún lado = somewhere
en cualquier lado = anywhere
en ningún lado = nowhere
= anywhere
por un lado..., pero por otro (lado)... = on
  the one hand..., but on the other hand...

ladrar verb [1]
= to bark

ladrillo noun, masculine
un ladrillo = a brick

ladrón/ladrona noun,
masculine/feminine
un ladrón/una ladrona = a thief
= a burglar
= a bank robber

lagarto noun, masculine
un lagarto = a lizard

lago noun, masculine
un lago = a lake

lágrima noun, feminine
una lágrima = a tear

lamer verb [17]
= to lick

lámpara noun, feminine
una lámpara = a lamp

lana noun, feminine
la lana = wool

langosta noun, feminine
una langosta = a lobster

lanzar verb [4]
• = to throw
• = to launch

lapicera noun, feminine (SC)
una lapicera = a pen

lápiz noun, masculine
un lápiz = a pencil
a lápiz = in pencil
lápices de colores = crayons
un lápiz de ojos = an eyeliner
un lápiz de labios = a lipstick

largo/larga
1 adjective
= long
2 largo noun, masculine
el largo = the length
¿cuánto mide de largo? = how long is it?
a lo largo de = along
(referring to time) = throughout

las plural feminine article, pronoun
See **los/las** for examples

lástima noun, feminine
una lástima = a pity, a shame
¡qué lástima! = what a shame!

lata noun, feminine
• una lata = a can, a tin
• una lata✖ = a pain
¡qué lata! = what a pain!

látigo noun, masculine
un látigo = a whip

latín noun, masculine
el latín = Latin

latino/latina adjective
= Latin

lavabo noun, masculine
un lavabo = a washbowl, a washbasin

lavadora noun, feminine
una lavadora = a washing machine

lavandería noun, feminine
una lavandería = a Laundromat   , a
  launderette

lavaplatos noun, masculine (**!** does not
change in the plural)
un lavaplatos = a dishwasher

lavar verb [1]
= to wash
lavarse
= to wash (oneself), to have a wash
lavarse el pelo = to wash one's hair

lavatorio noun, masculine (SC)
un lavatorio = a washbowl, a washbasin

lavavajillas noun, masculine (**!** does not
change in the plural)
un lavavajillas (detergent) = a dish liquid,
  a washing-up liquid
(machine) = a dishwasher

lazo noun, masculine
• un lazo = a bow
• un lazo = a ribbon

le pronoun
• = him/her
= to him/her
• (referring to you — polite form) = you
= to you
• = it
hay que ponerle más fertilizante = you
  have to give it more fertilizer

> **!** Note that sometimes the only thing that
> will indicate whether le is translated by
> him, her, you or it is the context

tengo que decirle algo = I have to tell
  him/her/you something

> **!** Note that le becomes se when it's
> followed by another pronoun: se lo dije
> and not le lo dije

lección noun, feminine
una lección = a lesson

---

leche *noun, feminine*
 la leche = milk
 leche descremada *or* (*Spa*) desnatada = skim milk, skimmed milk

lechuga *noun, feminine*
 una lechuga = a lettuce

lectura *noun, feminine*
 la lectura = reading

leer *verb* 26
 = to read

lejos *adverb*
 = far
 lejos de = far from
 de *or* desde lejos = from a distance

lengua *noun, feminine*
• la lengua = the tongue
• lengua = language

lenguaje *noun, masculine*
 un lenguaje = a language

lente
1 *noun, masculine or feminine*
 un/una lente = a lens
 lentes de contacto = contact lenses
2 lentes *noun, masculine plural* (*Lat Am*)
 lentes = glasses
 llevar *or* usar lentes = to wear glasses

lenteja *noun, feminine*
 una lenteja = a lentil

lentilla *noun, feminine* (*Spa*)
 una lentilla = a contact lens

lento/lenta *adjective*
 = slow

Leo *noun, masculine*
 Leo = Leo

leo *noun, masculine/feminine*
 un/una leo = a Leo

león/leona *noun, masculine/feminine*
 un león/una leona = a lion/a lioness

leopardo *noun, masculine*
 un leopardo = a leopard

les *pronoun*
• = them
 = to them
• = you
 = to you

> **!** *Note that sometimes the only thing that will indicate whether* les *is translated by* them *or* you *is the context*

 tengo que pedirles un favor = I have to ask them a favor
 (*referring to you*) = I have to ask you a favour

> **!** *Note that* les *becomes* se *when it's followed by another pronoun:* se lo dije *and not* les lo dije

letra *noun, feminine*
• una letra = a letter
• letra = handwriting
 tener buena letra = to have good handwriting
• (*of a song*) la letra = the words

letrero *noun, masculine*
 un letrero = a sign, a notice

levantar *verb* 1
 = to lift
 = to raise
 = to pick up
levantarse
 = to stand up
 = to get up

ley *noun, feminine*
 una ley = a law

leyó ▶ leer

liberar *verb* 1
 = to free
 = to liberate

libertad *noun, feminine*
 la libertad = freedom

Libra *noun, masculine*
 Libra = Libra

libra
1 *noun, feminine*
 una libra = a pound
2 *noun, masculine/feminine*
 un/una libra = a Libra, a Libran

libre *adjective*
 = free

librería *noun, feminine*
• una librería = a bookstore, a bookshop
• (*Spa*) una librería = a bookcase

libro *noun, masculine*
 un libro = a book

líder *noun, masculine/feminine, or* (*Mex*)
líder, lideresa *noun, masculine/feminine*
 un/una líder = a leader

ligero/ligera *adjective*
• = light
• = slight

límite *noun, masculine*
 un límite = a limit

limpiaparabrisas *noun, masculine*
 (**!** *does not change in the plural*)
 el limpiaparabrisas = the windshield wipers, the windscreen wipers

limpiar *verb* 1
 = to clean

limpieza *noun, feminine*
 limpieza = cleanliness
 = cleaning
 hacer la limpieza = to do the cleaning
 limpieza en seco = drycleaning

L

limpio/limpia *adjective*
= clean

lindo/linda *adjective*
* = cute
* = lovely
* (*Lat Am*) = nice

línea *noun, feminine*
una línea = a line

linterna *noun, feminine*
una linterna = a flashlight, a torch

líquido *noun, masculine*
un líquido = a liquid

liso/lisa *adjective*
* = flat
* = smooth
* (*if it's hair*) = straight

lista *noun, feminine*
* una lista = a list
una lista de espera = a waiting list
* (*at school*) la lista = the roll call, the register
pasar lista = to take the roll call , to take the register

listo/lista *adjective*
* = clever
* estar listo/lista = to be ready

literatura *noun, feminine*
la literatura = literature

litro *noun, masculine*
un litro = a liter, a litre

llama *noun, feminine*
* una llama = a flame
* (*animal*) una llama = a llama

llamada *noun, feminine*
una llamada = a call
una llamada a cobro revertido *or* (*Mex*) **por cobrar** = a collect call, a reverse-charge call

llamar *verb* 1
* = to call
* = to phone, to call, to ring
llamar a alguien por teléfono = to phone someone
llamarse
= to be called
¿cómo te llamas? = what's your name?

llano/llana *adjective*
= flat

llanta *noun, feminine* (*Lat Am*)
una llanta = a tire, a tyre

llave *noun, feminine*
* una llave = a key
* (*a tool*) una llave = a wrench, a spanner
* (*Lat Am*) una llave = a faucet, a tap
* la llave del gas = the gas jet, the gas tap
* (*in music*) una llave = a clef

llavero *noun, masculine*
un llavero = a key ring

llegada *noun, feminine*
la llegada = the arrival

llegar *verb* 3
* = to arrive
llegaron a Francia = they arrived in France
llegar a casa = to get home
llegar tarde/temprano = to be late/early
llegar a tiempo = to be on time
no me llegó la carta = I didn't get the letter
¿falta mucho para llegar? = is there much further to go?
* = to reach
¿llegas a la estantería de arriba? = can you reach the top shelves?
* llegar hasta = to come up/down to
= to go up/down to
el agua llegó hasta la ventana = the water came up to the window
el camino llega hasta el pueblo = the road goes up to the village
* llegar a ser = to become

llenar *verb* 1
* = to fill
= to fill up
llena la botella de agua = fill the bottle with water
llenó el suelo de basura = he covered the floor with garbage
* = to fill out, to fill in

lleno/llena *adjective*
= full
lleno de = full of
= covered with

llevar *verb* 1
* = to take
* = to carry
* = to wear
llevaré un vestido rojo = I'll wear a red dress
* no llevo dinero = I don't have any money on me
* = to lead
el camino que lleva a la playa = the road that leads to the beach
* (*referring to time*)
llevo una semana estudiando = I've been studying for a week
¿cuánto tiempo llevas en Inglaterra? = how long have you been in England?
me llevó mucho (tiempo) = it took me a long time
* (*referring to age*)
le llevo cuatro años a mi marido = I'm four years older than my husband
llevarse
* = to take
se llevó mis llaves = he took my keys
* llevarse bien/mal con alguien = to get on/not to get on with someone

llorar *verb* 1
= to cry

llover *verb* 22
= to rain

llueva, **llueve** ▶ llover

lluvia *noun, feminine*
la lluvia = the rain

lo
1 *article*
lo interesante es... = the interesting thing
   is...
prefiero lo dulce = I prefer sweet things
• lo de:
  lo de Ana me preocupa = I'm worried
    about Ana
  lo de su hijo fue terrible = what happened
    to his son was terrible
  todo esto es lo de Juan = all this is Juan's
  iremos a lo de María (*R Pl*) = we'll go to
    María's
• lo mío, lo tuyo, *etc*:
  todo esto es lo mío = all this is mine
• lo que = what
  eso no es lo que yo dije = that's not what I
    said
  lo que sea = whatever
2 *pronoun*
• = him
  lo vi ayer = I saw him yesterday
• = it
  lo vas a romper = you are going to break it
  ya lo sé = I know

lobo *noun, masculine*
un lobo = a wolf

local *noun, masculine*
el local = the premises

loco/loca
1 *adjective*
= crazy, mad
2 *noun, masculine/feminine*
un loco/una loca = a madman/madwoman

lograr *verb* 1
• = to achieve
• = to manage
  lograr que alguien haga algo = to get
    someone to do something

  ! *Note the use of the subjunctive after*
  lograr que

lomo *noun, masculine*
• el lomo = the back
• (*of a book*) el lomo = the spine
• (*of meat*) lomo = loin of pork
  (*of beef*) = sirloin steak

loncha *noun, feminine*
una loncha = a slice

loro/lora *noun, masculine/feminine*
un loro/una lora = a parrot

los/las
1 *article*
= the
  See el *for examples*
2 *pronoun*
= them

lotería *noun, feminine*
la lotería = the lottery
jugar a la lotería = to play the lottery

lucha *noun, feminine*
una lucha = a fight
= a struggle
lucha libre = wrestling

luchar *verb* 1
• = to fight
• = to struggle
• = to wrestle

luego *adverb*
• = later
• = then, afterwards
• (*Mex*) = soon
= quickly

lugar *noun, masculine*
• un lugar = a place
  en algún lugar = somewhere
  en cualquier lugar = anywhere
  en ningún lugar = nowhere
  = anywhere
  en otro lugar = somewhere else
• lugar = position
  en primer/último lugar (*in a race etc*) = in
    first/last position
  (*when listing reasons etc*) = first/last of all
• en lugar de = instead of
• yo en tu lugar = if I were you

lujo *noun, masculine*
un lujo = a luxury
de lujo = luxury

luna *noun, feminine*
la luna = the moon

lunes *noun, masculine* (**!** *does not change
in the plural*)
el lunes = monday
  See miércoles *for more examples*

luz *noun, feminine*
• la luz = the light
  las luces = the lights
• la luz = electricity

L

Mm

macarrones *noun, masculine plural*
macarrones = macarroni

macedonia *noun, feminine*
una macedonia (**de frutas**) = a fruit salad

maceta *noun, feminine*
una maceta = a flowerpot

machista
1 *adjective*
= sexist
2 *noun, masculine*
un machista = a sexist

madera *noun, feminine*
madera = wood
= lumber, timber
una madera = a piece of wood
una mesa de madera = a wooden table

madre *noun, feminine*
una madre = a mother

madrina *noun, feminine*
una madrina (*of a baby*) = a godmother
(*at a wedding*) = *woman who accompanies the groom, usually his mother*

madrugada *noun, feminine*
la madrugada = dawn, daybreak
a las tres de la madrugada = at three o'clock in the morning

madrugar *verb* ³
= to get up early

maduro/madura *adjective*
• (*if it's a fruit*) = ripe
• (*if it's a person*) = mature

maestro/maestra *noun,*
masculine/feminine
un maestro/una maestra = a teacher
(*of a discipline, an art*) = a master

magdalena *noun, feminine* (*Spa*)
una magdalena = a cup cake, a fairy cake

magia *noun, feminine*
la magia = magic

mágico/mágica *adjective*
= magic

magnético/magnética *adjective*
= magnetic

magnetofón, magnetófono *noun,*
masculine
un magnetofón = a tape recorder

magnífico/magnífica *adjective*
= wonderful

mago/maga *noun, masculine/feminine*
un mago/una maga = a magician

Majestad *noun, feminine*
Su Majestad = His/Her Majesty

mal
1 *adjective* (**!** *never changes*)

! *Note that* mal *is the shortened form of* malo, *used before a masculine noun*

• = bad
un mal día = a bad day
• = ill
• = wrong
2 *adverb*
• = badly
• = wrongly
entender mal = to misunderstand
el café me hace mal (*Lat Am*) = coffee doesn't agree with me
• te oigo muy mal = I can hardly hear you
• el pescado huele/sabe mal = the fish smells/tastes bad
olía muy mal allí dentro = there was a horrible smell in there
• portarse mal = to misbehave
• ¡menos mal! = thank goodness!
3 *noun, masculine*
el mal = evil

maleducado/maleducada
1 *adjective*
= rude
2 *noun, masculine/feminine*
ser un maleducado/una maleducada = to be rude

maleta *noun, feminine*
una maleta = a suitcase
hacer la(s) maleta(s) = to pack

maletero *noun, masculine*
el maletero = the trunk, the boot

maletín *noun, masculine*
un maletín = a briefcase
(*of a doctor*) = a bag

malla *noun, feminine*
• una malla = a leotard
• (*R Pl*) una malla (**de baño**) = a swimsuit

malo/mala
1 *adjective*
• = bad
• = poor
mala calidad = poor quality
ser malo para los deportes/los idiomas = to be bad at sports/languages
• = naughty
eres muy malo = you are very naughty
• el guiso esta malo (*referring to condition of food*) = the stew has gone bad *or* is off
(*referring to taste*) = the stew doesn't taste nice
• estar malo (*Mex, Spa*) = to be sick, ill

mamá* *noun, feminine*
mamá = mom, mommy; mum, mummy

mancha *noun, feminine*
una mancha = a stain

manchar *verb* [1]
= to mark, to stain
mancharse
= to get dirty
me manché los pantalones = I got my
  trousers dirty

mandar *verb* [1]
• = to send
  mandar una postal = to send a postcard
• le gusta mandar = he likes telling people
  what to do
• (*Lat Am*) mandé a arreglar el coche = I'm
  having my car fixed
  me mandaron venir = they sent for me
• ¿mande? (*Mex*) = sorry?, pardon?

mandarina *noun, feminine*
una mandarina = a mandarin, a tangerine

mandíbula *noun, feminine*
la mandíbula = the jaw

manejar *verb* [1]
• (*if it's a machine, a tool*) = to handle
• (*Lat Am*) = to drive

manera *noun, feminine*
manera = way
a mi manera, a tu manera, *etc* = my way,
  your way, *etc*
de ninguna manera = no way
de todas maneras = anyway
de cualquier manera = anyway
= any which way, any old how
es su manera de ser = that's the way he is
no hay manera de [abrirlo | entenderlo |
  saberlo …] = it is impossible to [open |
  understand | know …]

manga *noun, feminine*
una manga = a sleeve

mango *noun, masculine*
• (*of a knife etc*) un mango = a handle
• (*fruit*) un mango = a mango

manguera *noun, feminine*
una manguera = a hose

manillar *noun, masculine* (*Spa*)
el manillar = the handlebars

mano *noun, feminine*
• una mano = a hand
  decir adiós con la mano = to wave goodbye
  dame la mano = give me your hand

(*when congratulating someone*) = shake
  my hand
ir de la mano = to be hand in hand
tener algo a mano = to have something at
  hand
está a mano derecha/izquierda = it's on the
  right-/left-hand side
hacer algo a mano = to do something by
  hand
echarle una mano a alguien = to give
  someone a hand
de segunda mano = second hand
• (*of paint*) una mano = a coat

manta *noun, feminine*
una manta = a blanket

manteca *noun, feminine*
• = fat
• = lard
• (*R Pl*) = butter

mantel *noun, masculine*
un mantel = a tablecloth

mantendrá, mantendría, etc
▶ mantener

mantener *verb* [37]
= to keep

mantengo, mantenga, etc
▶ mantener

mantequilla *noun, feminine*
mantequilla = butter

M

mantuve, mantuvo, etc ▶ mantener

manzana *noun, feminine*
una manzana = an apple

mañana
1 *noun, feminine*
la mañana = the morning
en la *or* (*Spa*) por la *or* (*R Pl*) a la mañana =
  in the morning
a la mañana siguiente = the following
  morning
a las ocho de la mañana = at eight o'clock
  in the morning
2 *adverb*
= tomorrow
pasado mañana = the day after tomorrow
mañana por la mañana = tomorrow
  morning

mapa *noun, masculine*
un mapa = a map

maquillaje *noun, masculine*
maquillaje = makeup

maquillarse *verb* [1]
= to put one's makeup on

máquina *noun, feminine*
una máquina = a machine
una máquina fotográfica *or* de fotos = a
  camera
una máquina de escribir = a typewriter
escribir algo a máquina = to type
  something

maquinilla *noun, feminine (Spa)*
una maquinilla (**de afeitar**) = an electric razor

mar *noun, masculine*
el mar = the sea
por mar = by sea

maratón *noun, masculine/feminine*
un/una maratón = a marathon

maravilla *noun, feminine*
una maravilla = a wonder
es una maravilla = it's wonderful

maravilloso/maravillosa *adjective*
= wonderful
= marvelous, marvellous

marca *noun, feminine*
una marca = a mark
(*for products*) = a brand, a make
(*in sports*) = a record
un producto de marca = a brand-name product
ropa de marca = designer clothes

marcar *verb* 2
* = to mark
* (*when phoning*) = to dial
* (*in sports*) = to score
* = to say
  el reloj marcaba las seis = the clock said six o'clock

marco *noun, masculine*
* (*currency*) un marco = a mark
* (*for pictures*) un marco = a frame

marea *noun, feminine*
la marea = the tide

mareado/mareada *adjective*
* = sick, queasy
* = dizzy, giddy

marear *verb* 1
* = to make ... feel sick *or* queasy
  = to make ... feel dizzy *or* giddy
* (*with questions, explanations*) = to confuse
marearse
= to feel sick
= to get dizzy

margarina *noun, feminine*
margarina = margarine

margarita *noun, feminine*
una margarita = a daisy

margen *noun, masculine*
el margen = the margin

marido *noun, masculine*
un marido = a husband

marina *noun, feminine*
la marina = the navy

marinero *noun, masculine*
un marinero = a sailor

mariposa *noun, feminine*
una mariposa = a butterfly

marisco *noun, masculine*
los mariscos *or* (Spa) el marisco = seafood

mármol *noun, masculine*
el mármol = marble

marrón
1 *adjective*
= brown
2 *noun, masculine*
el marrón = brown

martes *noun, masculine* (**!** *does not change in the plural*)
el martes = Tuesday
See **miércoles** *for more examples*

martillo *noun, masculine*
un martillo = a hammer

marzo *noun, masculine*
marzo = March

más
1 *adjective/adverb*
* = more
  necesito más tiempo = I need more time
  es más valiente/organizado que yo = he's braver/more organized than me
  más de tres días = more than three days
  no me lo digas más = don't tell me any more
  más alto que yo = taller than me
  más negro que el carbón = as black as coal
  no voy a esperar más = I am not going to wait any longer
* el jugador de más altura/habilidad = the tallest/most skillful player
  el que más me gusta = the one I like the best
* nadie más que tú = only you
  no tiene más que veinte mil pesos = he only has twenty thousand pesos
* = else
  ¿algo más? = anything else?
  nada más = nothing else
  ¿qué más quieres? = what else do you want?
* (*in exclamations*) = so
  ¡este camino es más largo! = this road is so long!
  ¡qué agua más limpia! = this water is so clean!
* de más:
  hay cinco copias de más = there are five copies too many
  ¿alguien tiene una entrada de más? = does anyone have a spare ticket?
* más o menos = more or less
2 *preposition*
más = plus
dos más cuatro son seis = two plus four is six

---

masculino
1 *adjective*
= male
= men's
= masculine
2 *noun, masculine*
el masculino = the masculine

matar *verb* 1
= to kill
matarse
• = to kill oneself
• = to get killed

matemáticas *noun, feminine*
las matemáticas = mathematics, math,
maths

material
1 *adjective*
= material
2 *noun, masculine*
material = material
= equipment

matrícula *noun, feminine*
• (*for a course*) la matrícula = registration
• (*for a car*) una matrícula = a license
number, a registration number
= a license plate, a number plate

matrimonio *noun, masculine*
• el matrimonio = marriage
• un matrimonio = a married couple

mayo *noun, masculine*
mayo = May

máximo/máxima *adjective*
= maximum

mayonesa *noun, feminine*
la mayonesa = mayonnaise

mayor
1 *adjective*
• = greater/greatest
mi mayor deseo = my greatest wish
la mayor parte del tiempo = most of the
time
• (*Spa*) = bigger/biggest
un tamaño mayor = a bigger size
• = older/oldest
es el hermano mayor = he's the oldest
brother
ella es bastante mayor que yo = she's quite
a bit older than me
• = grown-up
cuando los niños sean mayores = when
the children are grown-up
las personas mayores = grown-ups
hacerse mayor = to grow up
ser mayor de edad = to be of age
• (*Spa*) = higher
una mayor temperatura = a higher
temperature
• al por mayor = wholesale

2 *noun, masculine/feminine*
el mayor/la mayor = the oldest
3 mayores *noun, masculine plural*
los mayores (*adults*) = the grown-ups
(*old*) = the elderly

mayoría *noun, feminine*
la mayoría = the majority
la mayoría de = most (of)

mayúscula *noun, feminine*
una mayúscula = a capital letter
con *or* en mayúsculas = in capital letters

me *pronoun*
• = me
= to me
me lo dijo = she told me
me lo dio = she gave it to me
me lavé la cara = I washed my face
me puse el abrigo = I put my coat on
• (*when someone else does the action*)
me tengo que cortar el pelo = I have to
have my hair cut
• = myself
tengo que cuidarme = I have to look after
myself
no me he movido de aquí = I haven't
moved from here

mecánica *noun, feminine*
mecánica = mechanics

mecánico/mecánica
1 *adjective*
= mechanical
2 *noun, masculine/feminine*
un mecánico/una mecánica = a mechanic

mecedora *noun, feminine*
una mecedora = a rocking chair

mechero *noun, masculine* (*Spa*)
un mechero = a lighter

medalla *noun, feminine*
una medalla = a medal

media
1 *noun, feminine*
• la media = the average
• (*garment*) una media = a stocking
(*Lat Am*) = a sock
2 medias *noun, feminine plural*
• medias = pantyhose, tights
• a medias:
hicimos el trabajo a medias = we did the
work between the two of us
pagamos a medias = we paid half each
See also medio

mediados *noun, masculine plural*
a mediados de = in the middle of

medianoche *noun, feminine*
la medianoche = midnight
a medianoche = at midnight

M

medicamento noun, masculine
un medicamento = a medicine

medicina noun, feminine
medicina = medicine

médico/médica noun,
masculine/feminine
un/una médico, un médico/una médica = a
doctor

medida noun, feminine
una medida = a measure
(size) = a measurement

medio/media
1 adjective
• = half
• medio paquete = half a packet
media pensión = half board
a medio camino = halfway
• = average
la temperatura media = the average
temperature
• (referring to time)
las cinco y media = half past five
media hora = half an hour
tres días y medios = three and a half days
2 adverb
= half
estaba medio dormido = he was half asleep
3 medio noun, masculine
• un medio = a way
ése es el medio de ganar = that's the way
to win
por cualquier medio = by any means
por todos los medios = by all possible
means
por medio de = through
• el medio = the middle
me gusta el del medio = I like the one in
the middle
ponerse en medio = to get in the way
quitarse de en medio or del medio = to get
out of the way
• los medios de comunicación = the media
• medios (económicos) = means, resources

medio ambiente noun, masculine
el medio ambiente = the environment

mediodía noun, masculine
mediodía = midday, noon, lunchtime
a mediodía = at midday, at lunchtime

medir verb 48
• = to measure
• (referring to height) ¿cuánto mides? = how
tall are you?
mido 1,80 m = I'm 1.80 m

Mediterráneo noun, masculine
el Mediterráneo = the Mediterranean

mejicano/mejicana
▶ mexicano/mexicana

mejilla noun, feminine
la mejilla = the cheek

mejillón noun, masculine
un mejillón = a mussel

mejor
1 adjective
= better/best
cuanto más grande mejor = the bigger the
better
es mejor que no vengan = it's better if they
don't come
mi mejor amiga = my best friend
2 adverb
• = better/best
ahora canta mejor = he sings better now
el que mejor trabaja = the best worker
el que mejor funciona = the one that works
the best
lo mejor que puedo = as best as I can
• (when giving suggestions)
mejor no vamos = it's better if we don't go
mejor siéntate ahí = you'd be better sitting
over there
• a lo mejor = maybe
a lo mejor se han perdido = maybe they
have got lost
3 noun, masculine/feminine
el/la mejor = the best (one)

mejorar verb 1
= to improve

mellizo/melliza
1 adjective
= twin
2 noun, masculine/feminine
un mellizo/una melliza = a twin, a twin
brother/sister

melocotón noun, masculine (Spa)
un melocotón = a peach

melón noun, masculine
un melón = a melon

membrillo noun, masculine
un membrillo = a quince

memoria noun, feminine
la memoria = memory
aprenderse algo de memoria = to learn
something by heart

mencionar verb 1
= to mention

mendigo/mendiga noun,
masculine/feminine
un mendigo/una mendiga = a beggar

menor
1 adjective
• = less
de menor importancia = of less importance
• = smaller/smallest
el menor detalle = the smallest detail

- = younger/youngest
  mi hermano menor = my younger brother
  soy la menor del grupo = I'm the youngest
  of the group
  es bastante menor que yo = he's quite a bit
  younger than me
  el menor [esfuerzo | ruido | gasto …] **posible** =
  as little [effort | noise | expense …] as
  possible
2 *noun, masculine/feminine*
  el/la menor = the younger/youngest
  un/una menor = a minor

menos
1 *adjective/adverb*
  = less
  = fewer
  gastar menos dinero = to spend less money
  tengo menos que tú = I have less than you
  cada vez menos = less and less
  el menos dañado de todos = the least
  damaged of all
  el que menos se queja = the one who
  complains the least
  tiene menos errores = it has fewer
  mistakes
  el que tiene menos empleados = the one
  with the fewest employees
  menos de tres dólares = less than three
  dollars
  hay cinco copias de menos = we're five
  copies short
  al menos = at least
  por lo menos = at least
  a menos que = unless
  ¡menos mal! = thank goodness!
2 *preposition*
- = except
  todos menos éste = all of them except this
  one
- (*R Pl Spa: when telling the time*)
  las doce menos cinco = five of or to twelve
- (*in temperatures, math*) = minus
  tres grados bajo cero = minus three
  degrees
  trece menos cinco son ocho = thirteen
  minus five is eight

mensaje *noun, masculine*
  un mensaje = a message

menta *noun, feminine*
  menta = mint
  un caramelo de menta = a mint

mente *noun, feminine*
  la mente = the mind

mentir *verb* 46
  = to lie

mentira *noun, feminine*
  una mentira = a lie

mentiroso/mentirosa *noun,*
masculine/feminine
  un mentiroso/una mentirosa = a liar

menú *noun, masculine*
  un menú = a menu
  el menú del día = the set menu

menudo/menuda *adjective*
- = small
- (*Spa: in exclamations*)
  ¡menudo coche! = what a fantastic car!
- **a menudo** = often

mercado *noun, masculine*
  un mercado = a market

merecer *verb* 19
  = to deserve
merecerse
  = to deserve

merendar *verb* 7
  = to have a snack in the afternoon
  merendamos leche con galletas = we had
  milk and biscuits in the afternoon

merezca, merezco, etc ▶ merecer

merienda, meriendo, etc
  ▶ merendar

mermelada *noun, feminine*
  mermelada = jam
  = marmalade
  mermelada de naranja = marmalade

mero/mera*
1 *adjective* (*C Am, Mex*)
  uno mero = just one
  en la mera esquina = right on the corner
  el mero día de su cumpleaños = the very
  day of his birthday
2 mero *adverb* (*Mex*)
  = nearly, almost
  ya mero llegamos = we are almost there

mes *noun, masculine*
  un mes = a month
  el mes pasado/que viene = last/next
  month
  dos veces al or por mes = twice a month

mesa *noun, feminine*
  una mesa = a table
  sentarse a la mesa = to sit at the table
  poner/quitar la mesa = to lay/clear the
  table

mestizo/mestiza
1 *adjective*
  = (of) mixed race
2 *noun, masculine/feminine*
  un mestizo/una mestiza = a man/woman of
  mixed race

metal *noun, masculine*
  el metal = metal

metálico/metálica *adjective*
- = metal, metallic
- **en metálico** = in cash

M

meter verb 17
* = to put
  mete estos papeles en el cajón = put these papers in the drawer
* = to fit
  podemos meter dos más en el coche = we can fit two more in the car
* **meter un gol** = to score a goal
meterse
* = to get in/into
  se metió en el coche = she got into the car
  se me metió jabón en los ojos = I got soap in my eyes
* = to get involved
  no te metas en lo que no te importa = mind your own business

método noun, masculine
  un método = a method

métrico adjective
  = metric

metro noun, masculine
* **un metro** = a meter, a metre
* **el metro** = the subway, the underground

mexicano/mexicana
1 adjective
  = Mexican
2 noun, masculine/feminine
  un mexicano/una mexicana = a Mexican

mezcla noun, feminine
  una mezcla = a mixture, a mix
  (of coffee, tea) = a blend

mezclar verb 1
* = to mix
* = to get mixed up
mezclarse
  mezclarse con alguien = to mix with someone
  mezclarse en algo = to get mixed up in something

mi adjective
  = my

mí pronoun
  = me
  es mejor para mí = it's better for me
  me lo dijo a mí = he told me
* **mí mismo/mí misma** = myself
  sólo pensaba en mí mismo = I was only thinking of myself

micrófono noun, masculine
  un micrófono = a microphone

microondas noun, masculine (! does not change in the plural)
  un microondas = a microwave

microscopio noun, masculine
  un microscopio = a microscope

mida, midiendo midió, mido, etc
▶ medir

miedo noun, masculine
  miedo = fear
  tener miedo = to be scared, to be afraid
  tener miedo de hacer algo = to be afraid of doing something
  me da miedo la oscuridad = I'm afraid of the dark
  le da miedo volar = he's afraid of flying
  no me da miedo = I'm not afraid

miel noun, feminine
  la miel = honey

miembro
1 noun, masculine
  un miembro = a limb
2 noun, masculine/feminine
  un/una miembro = a member

mienta, miento, etc ▶ mentir

mientras
1 adverb
* = in the meantime
  mientras tanto = in the meantime
* **mientras más tiene, más quiere** (Lat Am) = the more he has, the more he wants
2 conjunction
* = while
  disfrútalo mientras dure = enjoy it while it lasts
* = as long as
  mientras no se oponga = as long as he/she doesn't object

! Note the use of the subjunctive after the conjunction mientras

miércoles noun, masculine (! does not change in the plural)
  miércoles = Wednesday
  llegaron el miércoles = they arrived on Wednesday
  el miércoles pasado = last Wednesday
  el miércoles próximo or **que viene** = next Wednesday
  todos los miércoles = every Wednesday
  un miércoles sí y otro no = every other Wednesday
  Miércoles de Ceniza = Ash Wednesday

miga noun, feminine
  una miga = a crumb
  migas de pan = breadcrumbs

mil number
  = a/one thousand
  veinte mil dólares = twenty thousand dollars
  miles de personas = thousands of people
  mil cincuenta = one thousand and fifty

milagro noun, masculine
  un milagro = a miracle

mili✗ noun, feminine (Spa)
  la mili = military service

milímetro *noun, masculine*
un milímetro = a millimeter, a millimetre

militar
1 *adjective*
= military
2 *noun, masculine|feminine*
un/una militar = a soldier

milla *noun, feminine*
una milla = a mile

millón *number*
un millón = a million

millonario/millonaria *noun,*
masculine|feminine
un millonario/una millonaria = a
  millionaire

minoría *noun, feminine*
una minoría = a minority

mintamos, **mintió**, **etc** ▶ mentir

minúscula *noun, feminine*
una minúscula = a small *or* lower-case
  letter
con *or* en minúsculas = in small letters

minúsculo/minúscula *adjective*
• = minute, tiny
• letra minúscula = small *or* lower-case letter

minusválido/minusválida
1 *adjective*
= disabled
2 *noun, masculine|feminine*
un minusválido/una minusválida = a
  disabled man/woman

minuto *noun, masculine*
un minuto = a minute

mío/mía
1 *adjective*
= mine
mío/mía/míos/mías = mine
2 *pronoun*
el mío/la mía/los míos/las mías = mine
  See **tuyo** *for more examples*

mirada *noun, feminine*
una mirada = a look
= a glance
echarle una mirada a algo = to look at
  something
= to glance at something
bajar la mirada = to look down

mirar *verb* $\boxed{1}$
• = to look
miré abajo = I looked down
mirar por la ventana = to look through the
  window
¡mira qué cuadro! = look at that picture!
• = to watch
mirar una película = to watch a movie
• mirar fijamente = to stare

mirarse
mirarse en el espejo = to look at oneself in
  the mirror

mismo/misma
1 *adjective*
• = same
en el mismo lugar = in the same place
lo mismo = the same (thing)
yo mismo/tú mismo, *etc* = myself/yourself,
  etc
• very
en este mismo momento = at this very
  moment
2 *pronoun*
el mismo/la misma = the same one
los mismos/las mismas = the same ones
da lo mismo = it doesn't matter
me da lo mismo uno que otro = I don't
  mind *or* care which one
3 mismo *adverb*
= just
= right
ahí mismo = just there
ahora mismo = right now
enfrente mismo del cine = right opposite
  the movie house
ayer mismo lo vi = I saw him just yesterday
lo haré hoy mismo = I'll do it today

misterio *noun, masculine*
un misterio = a mystery

misterioso/misteriosa *adjective*
= mysterious

mitad *noun, feminine*
una mitad = a half
la mitad del dinero = half (of) the money
partir algo por la mitad = to split
  something in half
llénalo hasta la mitad = fill it halfway
a mitad de precio = half-price
a mitad de camino = halfway
en la mitad de la película = halfway
  through the movie
a *or* en la mitad de la reunión = in the
  middle of the meeting

mito *noun, masculine*
un mito = a myth

mochila *noun, feminine*
una mochila = a backpack

mocos *noun, masculine plural*
tener mocos = to have a runny nose
límpiate los mocos = wipe your nose

moda *noun, feminine*
la moda = fashion
ir a la moda = to be trendy
estar de moda = to be in fashion
pasarse de moda = to go out of fashion

modales *noun, masculine plural*
modales = manners

M

modelo
1 *noun, masculine*
  un modelo = a model
2 *noun, masculine|feminine*
  un/una modelo = a model

moderno/moderna *adjective*
  = modern

modesto/modesta *adjective*
  = modest

modo *noun, masculine*
  modo = way
  no hay otro modo = there's no other way
  a mi modo, a tu modo, *etc* = my way, your way, *etc*
  de todos modos = anyway
  'modo de empleo' = 'instructions for use'
  ni modo✘ (*Lat Am*) = no way

mojar *verb* 1
• = to get...wet
• = to dip
mojarse
• = to get wet
• = to wet
  mojarse el pelo = to wet one's hair

molestar *verb* 1
• = to bother
  deja de molestar a tu hermano = stop bothering your brother
  me molesta que no me ayuden = it annoys me that they don't help me

  ! *Note use of the subjunctive after* molestar que

• = to disturb
  'no molestar' = 'do not disturb'
• (*when asking permision*)
  ¿te molesta si abro la ventana? = do you mind if I open the window?
molestarse
• = to get upset
• molestarse en hacer algo = to bother to do something

molestia *noun, feminine*
• una molestia = a feeling of discomfort
• ¿podría apartarse un poco si no es molestia? = would you mind moving away a little?
• no es ninguna molestia = it's no trouble at all
  tomarse la molestia de hacer algo = to take the trouble to do something

molesto/molesta *adjective*
• = annoying
  = unpleasant
• estar molesto/molesta con alguien = to be upset with someone

molino *noun, masculine*
  un molino = a mill
  un molino de agua/viento = a watermill/windmill

momento *noun, masculine*
  un momento = a moment
  = a minute
  a partir de ese momento = from that moment on
  cuando llegue el momento = when the time comes
  de momento = at the moment
  de un momento a otro = any minute now
  en cualquier momento = at any time
  en este momento = right now
  por el momento = for the time being

moneda *noun, feminine*
• una moneda = a coin
• la moneda mexicana = the Mexican currency

monedero *noun, masculine*
  un monedero = a change purse, a purse

monja *noun, feminine*
  una monja = a nun

monje *noun, masculine*
  un monje = a monk

mono/mona
1 *adjective*
  = pretty
  = lovely
  = cute
2 *noun, masculine|feminine*
  un mono/una mona = a monkey

monopatín *noun, masculine*
  un monopatín = a skateboard
  = a scooter

monstruo *noun, masculine*
  un monstruo = a monster

montaña *noun, feminine*
• una montaña = a mountain
• una montaña rusa = a roller coaster

montar *verb* 1
• = to ride
  montar a caballo = to ride a horse
  montar en bicicleta = to ride a bicycle
• = to get on/in
  montar en un coche = to get in a car
• = to assemble
• montar un negocio = to set up a business
• montar una tienda = to put up a tent
montarse
  = to get on/in
  montarse en el coche/en el tren = to get in the car/on the train

montón *noun, masculine*
• un montón = a pile
  un montón de hojas = a pile of leaves
• un montón de✘ = loads of
  un montón de llamadas = loads of calls

monumento *noun, masculine*
  un monumento = a monument

morder *verb* 22
= to bite

mordisco *noun, masculine*
un mordisco = a bite
dar un mordisco = to bite

moreno/morena *adjective*
= brown
= dark
piel morena = brown/dark skin
ser moreno/morena *(referring to skin)* = to be dark
(referring to hair) = to be dark-haired
estar moreno/morena = to be brown, to be tanned

morir *verb* 62
= to die
morirse
= to die
me muero de frío = I'm freezing
se murió de frío = he died of cold

mora *noun, feminine*
una mora = a blackberry

moro/mora
1 *adjective*
= Moorish
2 *noun, masculine/feminine*
un moro/una mora = a Moor
(Spa) = a North African

mosca *noun, feminine*
una mosca = a fly

mostaza *noun, feminine*
mostaza = mustard

mostrador *noun, masculine*
un mostrador *(in a shop)* = a counter
(in a pub) = a bar
(at the airport) = a check-in desk

mostrar *verb* 6
= to show

motivo *noun, masculine*
un motivo = a reason
= a cause

moto✶ *noun, feminine*
una moto = a bike

> ! *Note that* moto *is short for* motocicleta

motocicleta *noun, feminine*
una motocicleta = a motorcycle

motor *noun, masculine*
un motor = an engine

mover *verb* 22
= to move
moverse
= to move

movimiento *noun, masculine*
un movimiento = a movement
estar en movimiento = to be in motion

muchacho/muchacha *noun,*
masculine/feminine
un muchacho/una muchacha = a boy/a girl

muchedumbre *noun, feminine*
una muchedumbre = a crowd

mucho/mucha
1 *adjective*
• mucho/mucha = much, a lot of
muchos/muchas = many, a lot of
• tengo [mucha sed | mucho sueño | mucho frío ...] = I'm very [thirsty | tired | cold ...]
hace mucho calor = it's very hot
• *(referring to time)*
hace mucho tiempo = a long time ago
por mucho tiempo = for a long time
2 *pronoun*
• mucho/mucha = much, a lot
muchos/muchas = many, a lot
muchos de ellos se quejaron = many *or* a lot of them complained
• mucho *(referring to time)*
hace mucho que se fueron = it's a long time since they went away
aún falta mucho para las vacaciones = the vacation is still a long way off
queda mucho para llegar = it's still a long way/time before we get there
no se quedó mucho = he didn't stay long
3 mucho *adverb*
= much, a lot
hemos gastado mucho = we've spent a lot
eso es mucho para nosotros = that's too much for us
no me gusta mucho = I don't like it much
mucho antes/después = long before/after
como mucho = at most
ni mucho menos = far from it
trabajan mucho = they work very hard
lo siento mucho = I'm very sorry

mudanza *noun, feminine*
una mudanza = a move, a removal
estar de mudanza = to be in the process of moving

mudarse *verb* 1
= to move

mudo/muda
1 *adjective*
= dumb
2 *noun, masculine/feminine*
un mudo/una muda = a mute

mueble *noun, masculine*
un mueble = a piece of furniture
los muebles = the furniture

muela *noun, feminine*
una muela = a (back) tooth

muera, muero, etc ▶ morir

muerda, muerdo, etc ▶ morder

muerte *noun, feminine*
la muerte = death

M

muerto/muerta
1 *adjective*
= dead
muerto/muerta de✱:
muerto/muerta de cansancio/de sueño = dead tired
muerto/muerta de frío = freezing cold
muerto/muerta de hambre = starving
muerto/muerta de sed = dying of thirst
2 *noun, masculine/feminine*
un muerto/una muerta = a dead man/woman
hubo tres muertos en el incendio = three people died in the fire

muestra, **muestro**, **etc** ▶ mostrar

mueva, **muevo**, **etc** ▶ mover

mujer *noun, feminine*
- **una mujer** = a woman
- **mi mujer** = my wife

muleta *noun, feminine*
una muleta = a crutch
andar con muletas = to be on crutches

multa *noun, feminine*
una multa = a fine
ponerle una multa a alguien = to fine someone

multiplicar *verb* [2]
= to multiply

mundial
1 *adjective*
= world
de fama mundial = world-famous
2 *noun, masculine*
el mundial = the world championship

mundo *noun, masculine*
el mundo = the world
todo el mundo = the whole world
= everybody

municipal *adjective*
- = municipal
- = local

muñeca *noun, feminine*
- **una muñeca** = a doll
- **la muñeca** = the wrist

muñeco *noun, masculine*
- **un muñeco** = a doll
  = a toy animal
- **un muñeco de nieve** = a snowman

muralla *noun, feminine*
una muralla = a wall

murciélago *noun, masculine*
un murciélago = a bat

muriendo, **murió** ▶ morir

murmullo *noun, masculine*
un murmullo = a murmur

murmurar *verb* [1]
- = to mutter
- = to whisper
- = to gossip

muro *noun, masculine*
un muro = a wall

músculo *noun, masculine*
un músculo = a muscle

museo *noun, masculine*
un museo = a museum

música *noun, feminine*
la música = music

musical *adjective*
= musical

músico/música *noun, masculine/feminine*
un músico/una música = a musician

muslo *noun, masculine*
un muslo = a thigh
(*of chicken*) = a leg

musulmán/musulmana
1 *adjective*
= Muslim
2 *noun, masculine/feminine*
un musulmán/una musulmana = a Muslim

muy *adverb*
- = very
  es muy tarde = it's very late
  son muy trabajadores = they work very hard
  muy bien = very well
  Muy Sr mío, Muy Sra mía (*in formal letters*) = Dear Sir/Madam
- = too
  es muy grande para mí = it's too big for me

Nn

nacer *verb* [19]
= to be born

nacimiento *noun, masculine*
un nacimiento = a birth
es sordo de nacimiento = he was born deaf

nación *noun, feminine*
una nación = a nation

nacional *adjective*
- = national
- = domestic

nacionalidad *noun, feminine*
nacionalidad = nationality

nada
1 *pronoun*
- nada = nothing
  = anything
  no pasó nada = nothing happened
  no necesito nada = I don't need
    anything
  ¿no quieres nada de París? = don't you
    want anything from Paris?
- (*Spa: in tennis*) nada = love
  quince nada = fifteen love
- de nada (*to someone who has said 'thank
  you'*) = you're welcome
- nada más = just
  uno nada más = just one
- nada más = nothing else
  = anything else
  no compramos nada más = we didn't buy
    anything else
  nada más gracias = that's all, thank you
2 *adverb*
  = at all
  no estudia nada = he doesn't study at all

nadar *verb* [1]
  = to swim
    See espalda, dorso, pecho

nadie *pronoun*
  = nobody
  = anybody
  nadie vino *or* no vino nadie = nobody came
  no vi a nadie = I didn't see anybody

nafta *noun, feminine* (*R Pl*)
  nafta = gas, petrol

naipe *noun, masculine*
  un naipe = a card

naranja
1 *noun, feminine*
  una naranja = an orange
2 *adjective* (**!** *never changes*)
  = orange
3 *noun, masculine*
  el naranja (*the color*) = orange

nariz *noun, feminine*
  la nariz = the nose

nata *noun, feminine* (*Spa*)
  nata = cream

natación *noun, feminine*
  la natación = swimming

naturaleza *noun, feminine*
  la naturaleza = nature

navaja *noun, feminine*
- una navaja = a penknife
  = a knife
- (*for shaving*) una navaja = a razor

navegar *verb* [3]
  = to sail

Navidad *noun, feminine*
  la Navidad = Christmas
  feliz Navidad = Merry Christmas, Happy
    Christmas

nazca, nazco, etc ▸ nacer

necesario/necesaria *adjective*
  = necessary
  no es necesario que preguntemos = we
    don't need to ask

> **!** *Note the use of the subjunctive after* ser
> necesario que

necesidad *noun, feminine*
- una necesidad = a need
  no hay necesidad = there's no need
- la necesidad = necessity

necesitar *verb* [1]
  = to need

negativo/negativa *adjective*
  = negative

negocio *noun, masculine*
- un negocio = a business
  un viaje de negocios = a business trip
- (*SC*) un negocio = a store, a shop

negro/negra
1 *adjective*
  = black
2 *noun, masculine/feminine*
  un negro/una negra = a black man/woman
3 negro *noun, masculine*
  el negro = black

nervioso/nerviosa *adjective*
- = nervous
  poner nervioso/nerviosa a alguien = to
    make somebody nervous
  (*to irritate*) = to get on someone's nerves
- = worked up
  ponerse nervioso/nerviosa = to get worked
    up

neumático *noun, masculine*
  un neumático = a tire, a tyre

nevar *verb* [7]
  = to snow

nevera *noun, feminine*
  una nevera = a fridge

ni *conjunction*
  no me escribió ni me telefoneó = he didn't
    ring me nor did he phone me
  allí no está ni aquí tampoco = it's not there
    and not here either
  ni yo mismo lo sé = not even I know
  ni ... ni ... = neither ... nor ...
  ni siquiera la conozco = I don't even know
    her

nido *noun, masculine*
  un nido = a nest

N

niebla *noun, feminine*
la niebla = fog
hay niebla = it's foggy

nieto/nieta *noun, masculine/feminine*
un nieto/una nieta = a
grandson/granddaughter
mis nietos = my grandchildren

nieva, nieve, etc ▶ nevar

nieve *noun, feminine*
la nieve = the snow

ningún *adjective*
▶ ninguno/ninguna

ninguno/ninguna
1 *adjective*

> **!** *Note that* ninguno *becomes* ningún
> *before masculine singular nouns*

no veo ningún animal = I don't see any
animals
no hay ninguna razón = there is no reason
2 *pronoun*
• = neither
ninguno de los dos vino = neither of them
came
• = none
¿cuál quieres? — ninguno = which one do
you want? — none of them

niño/niña *noun, masculine/feminine*
un niño/una niña = a boy/girl

nivel *noun, masculine*
un nivel = a level

no *adverb*
= no
= not
no te muevas = don't move
tu eres Pedro ¿no? = you're Pedro, aren't
you?
no me gusta nada = I don't like it at all
no salen nunca = they never go out
no gastaron nada = they didn't spend
anything

noche *noun, feminine*
la noche = the night
= the evening
esta noche = tonight
= this evening
a las nueve de la noche = at nine o'clock in
the evening
en la *or* (*Spa*) por la *or* (*RPl*) a la noche = in
the evening/at night
el martes en la noche = Tuesday
evening/night
[trabajar | conducir | estudiar …] de noche = [to
work | drive | study …] at night
hacerse de noche = to get dark
¡buenas noches! (*as a greeting*) = good
evening!
(*when leaving, going to bed*) = good night!

Nochebuena *noun, feminine*
la Nochebuena = Christmas Eve

Nochevieja *noun, feminine*
la Nochevieja = New Year's Eve

nocturno/nocturna *adjective*
• = night
• = evening

nomás✱ *adverb* (*Lat Am*)
así nomás = just like that
es aquí nomás = it's just here
pase nomás = come on in

nombre *noun, masculine*
• un nombre = a name
• (*printed on a form*) **nombre** = first name
• (*in grammar*) un nombre = a noun

nordeste, noreste *noun, masculine*
el nordeste = the north-east

norma *noun, feminine*
una norma = a rule

normal *adjective*
• = normal
• = ordinary

noroeste *noun, masculine*
el noroeste = the north-west

norte *noun, masculine*
el norte = the north
See **este** *for more examples*

noruego/noruega
1 *adjective*
= Norwegian
2 *noun, masculine/feminine*
un noruego/una noruega = a Norwegian
3 noruego *noun, masculine*
el noruego (*the language*) = Norwegian

nos *pronoun*
• = us
= to us
nos lo dijo = he told us
nos lo dio = he gave it to us
vamos a lavarnos las manos = let's wash
our hands
nos pusimos los abrigos = we put our
coats on
• (*when someone else does the action*)
nos tenemos que hacer ropa = we have to
have some clothes made
• = ourselves
nos tenemos que cuidar más = we have to
look after ourselves more
nos divertimos mucho = we had a good
time
• = each other
nos queremos = we love each other

nosotros/nosotras *pronoun*
• = we

• = us
nos lo dijo a nosotras = he told us
nosotros mismos = ourselves

nota *noun, feminine*
• **una nota** = a note
• (*in school*) **una nota** = a grade, a mark
sacar buenas notas = to get good grades/marks
tomar nota de algo = to write something down

notar *verb* [1]
= to notice
se nota que ... = you can tell that ...

noticia *noun, feminine*
una noticia = a piece of news
tengo una noticia = I have some news
escuchar las noticias = to listen to the news
tener noticias de alguien = to hear from someone

novecientos/novecientas *number*
= nine hundred
See **quinientos** *for examples*

novela *noun, feminine*
una novela = a novel

noveno/novena *number*
= ninth
See **primero** *for examples*

noventa *number*
= ninety
See **cincuenta** *for examples*

noviembre *noun, masculine*
noviembre = November

novio/novia *noun, masculine/feminine*
• **un novio/una novia** = a boyfriend/girlfriend
• **un novio/una novia** = a fiancé/a fiancée
• **el novio/la novia** = the groom/bride
los novios = the bride and groom

nube *noun, feminine*
una nube = a cloud

nublado/nublada *adjective*
= cloudy
está nublado = it's cloudy

nuca *noun, feminine*
la nuca = the back of the neck

nudillo *noun, masculine*
un nudillo = a knuckle

nudo *noun, masculine*
un nudo = a knot
hacer un nudo = to tie a knot

nuera *noun, feminine*
una nuera = a daughter-in-law

nuestro/nuestra
1 *adjective*
nuestro/nuestra/nuestros/nuestras = our
2 *pronoun*
el nuestro/la nuestra/los nuestros/las nuestras = ours
See **tuyo** *for more examples*

nueve *number*
• = nine
• (*in dates*) = ninth
See **cinco** *for examples*

nuevo *adjective*
= new

nuez *noun, feminine*
• **una nuez** = a walnut
• **la nuez** = the Adam's apple

número *noun, masculine*
un número = a number
(*of shoes*) = a size

nunca *adverb*
= never
= ever
casi nunca = hardly ever
nunca más = never again
nunca jamás = never ever
= never again

ñapa *noun, feminine* (*Lat Am*)
= small amount of extra goods given free

ñono /ñona *adjective*
= drippy, wet

o *conjunction*
= or
diez o doce = ten or twelve

obedecer *verb* [19]
= to obey
= to do as one is told

obedezca, obedezco, etc
▶ **obedecer**

obediente *adjective*
= obedient

objeto *noun, masculine*
un objeto = an object

obligar *verb* 3
obligar a alguien a hacer algo = to make someone do something, to force someone to do something

obra *noun, feminine*
una obra = a deed
(*in a theater*) **una obra** = a play
(*literary, artistic*) = a work
una obra = a building site
estamos de obras = we are having some building work done
la calle está en obras = there are roadworks in the street

obrero/obrera *noun, masculine/feminine*
un obrero/una obrera = a worker

observación *noun, feminine*
una observación = an observation

obstáculo *noun, masculine*
un obstáculo = an obstacle

obstante: no obstante *conjunction*
= nevertheless

obtendré, obtendría, etc ▶ obtener

obtener *verb* 37
= to obtain
= to get

**obtenga, obtengo, obtuve, etc
▶** obtener

obvio/obvia *adjective*
= obvious

ocasión *noun, feminine*
una ocasión = an occasion
= an opportunity

océano *noun, masculine*
un océano = an ocean

ochenta *number*
= eighty
See **cincuenta** for examples

ocho *number*
= eight
(*in dates*) = eighth
See **cinco** for examples

ochocientos/ochocientas *number*
= eight hundred
See **quinientos** for examples

octavo/octava *number*
= eighth
See **primero** for examples

ocupado/ocupada *adjective*
(*if it's a person*) = busy

(*if it's a telephone*) = busy, engaged
(*if it's a seat*) = taken

ocurrir *verb* 41
= to happen
¿qué les ha ocurrido? = what's happened to them?

ocurrirse
se me ha ocurrido que... = it's just occurred to me that...
si se te ocurre algo... = if you think of anything...

odiar *verb* 1
= to hate

oeste *noun, masculine*
el oeste = the west
See **este** for more examples

ofender *verb* 17
= to offend

ofenderse
= to take offense

oferta *noun, feminine*
una oferta = an offer
estar de oferta = to be on offer

oficial *adjective*
= official

oficina *noun, feminine*
una oficina = an office
la oficina de información y turismo = the tourist information office

ofrecer *verb* 19
= to offer

ofrezca, ofrezco, etc ▶ ofrecer

oído *noun, masculine*
el oído = the ear
se lo dije al oído = I whispered it in her ear
el oído = hearing

oiga, oigo, etc ▶ oír

oír *verb* 55
= to hear
= to listen to
me gusta oír música = I like to listen to music

ojalá *exclamation*
¡ojalá vengan! = I hope they come!
¡ojalá fuera mía! = I wish it was mine!

! Note the use of the subjunctive after ojalá

ojo
1 *noun, masculine*
un ojo = an eye
el ojo de la cerradura = the keyhole
2 *exclamation*
¡ojo! = careful!

ola *noun, feminine*
una ola = a wave

oler verb [25]
= to smell
oler a algo = to smell of something

olimpiada, **olimpíada** noun, feminine
la olimpiada, las olimpiadas = the
  Olympics

olla noun, feminine
una olla = a pot
una olla a presión = a pressure cooker

olor noun, masculine
un olor = a smell

olvidar verb [1]
= to forget
olvidarse
olvidarse de algo/de hacer algo = to forget
  something/to do something

ombligo noun, masculine
el ombligo = the navel, the belly button

omitir verb [41]
= to omit, to leave out

once number
= eleven
(in dates) = eleventh
  See **cinco** for examples

onceavo/onceava number
= eleventh

operación noun, feminine
una operación = an operation

operar verb [1]
= to operate (on)
operarse
= to have an operation
se operó del corazón = he had a heart
  operation

opinar verb [1]
= to think
= to express an opinion

opinión noun, feminine
una opinión = an opinion

oportunidad noun, feminine
una oportunidad = an opportunity
(Lat Am) **una oportunidad** = an occasion

oposición noun, feminine
oposición = opposition
(Spa) **una oposición** = a public competitive
  exam

optimista
1 adjective
= optimistic
2 noun, masculine/feminine
un/una optimista = an optimist

orden
1 noun, masculine
orden = order
por orden alfabético = in alphabetical
  order

2 noun, feminine
una orden = an order

ordenador noun, masculine (Spa)
un ordenador = a computer

ordenar verb [1]
= to put in order
= to straighten up, to tidy up
(Lat Am) = to order

oreja noun, feminine
una oreja = an ear

organización noun, feminine
una organización = an organization

organizar verb [4]
= to organize

orgullo noun, masculine
orgullo = pride

orgulloso/orgullosa adjective
= proud

oriente noun, masculine
el oriente = the east

oro noun, masculine
el oro = gold

orquesta noun, feminine
una orquesta = an orchestra
= a band

ortografía noun, feminine
ortografía = spelling

os pronoun (Spa)
= you
= to you
os lo dijo = he told you
os lo di = I gave it to you
lavaos las manos = wash your hands
¿os habéis puesto los abrigos? = have you
  put your coats on?
(when someone else does the action)
os tenéis que cortar el pelo = you have to
  have your hair cut
= yourselves
os tenéis que cuidar más = you have to
  look after yourselves more
¿os lo pasasteis bien? = did you have a
  good time?
= each other
¿os veis mucho? = do you see each other
  often?

oscuro adjective
= dark

oso noun, masculine
un oso = a bear

otoño noun, masculine
el otoño = the fall, the autumn

otro/otra
1 *adjective*
  otro/otra = another
  = other
  otros/otras = other
  = another
  el otro día = the other day
  dame otro vaso = give me another glass
  me trajeron otros libros/otros dos libros =
    they brought me some other/another two
    books
  otra cosa = something else
  (*in the negative*) = nothing else
  = anything else
  otra vez = again
2 *pronoun*
  otro/otra = another (one)
  otros/otras = others
  el otro, la otra = the other (one)

oveja *noun, feminine*
  una oveja = a sheep

oxidado/oxidada *adjective*
  = rusty

oxígeno *noun, masculine*
  el oxígeno = oxygen

oyendo, **oyó** ▶ oír

ozono *noun, masculine*
  el ozono = ozone

Pp

---

paciencia *noun, feminine*
  paciencia = patience

paciente
1 *adjective*
  = patient
2 *noun, masculine/feminine*
  un/una paciente = a patient

padre *noun, masculine*
  un padre = a father
  mis padres = my parents

padrino *noun, masculine*
  el padrino (*of a baby*) = the godfather
  (*at a wedding*) = man who gives away and
    accompanies the bride, usually her father

pagar *verb* ③
• = to pay
• = to pay for

página *noun, feminine*
  una página = a page

pago *noun, masculine*
  un pago = a payment

país *noun, masculine*
  un país = a country

Países Bajos *noun, masculine plural*
  los Países Bajos = the Netherlands

paisaje *noun, masculine*
  el paisaje = the landscape, the scenery

paisano/paisana *noun,*
masculine/feminine
  un paisano/una paisana = a fellow
    countryman/countrywoman

paja *noun, feminine*
• **paja** = straw
• (*for drinking through*) **una paja** = a straw

pájaro *noun, masculine*
  un pájaro = a bird

pala *noun, feminine*
  una pala = a shovel
  = a spade

palabra *noun, feminine*
  una palabra = a word

palacio *noun, masculine*
  un palacio = a palace

paleta *noun feminine*
• **una paleta** = a paletta
• (*Lat Am*) **paleta** = beach tennis
• (*Mex*) **una paleta** (**helada**) = a Popsicle , an
  ice lolly

pálido/pálida *adjective*
  = pale
  ponerse pálido = to go pale

palito helado *noun, masculine* (*R Pl*)
  un palito helado = a Popsicle , an ice lolly

palmera *noun, feminine*
  una palmera = a palm tree

palo *noun, masculine*
• **un palo** = a stick
• (*in golf*) **un palo** = a club

paloma *noun, feminine*
  una paloma = a dove
  = a pigeon

palomitas de maíz *noun, feminine*
plural
  palomitas de maíz = popcorn

pan *noun, masculine*
  el pan = bread
  pan integral = wholemeal bread
  un pan = a loaf of bread
  un pan de molde = a tin loaf

panadería *noun, feminine*
  una panadería = a bakery

---

pánico *noun, masculine*
pánico = panic

panorama *noun, masculine*
un panorama = a view

pantaletas *noun, feminine plural* (*C Am, Mex*)
unas pantaletas = a pair of panties, a pair of knickers

pantalla *noun, feminine*
* una pantalla (*in a cinema, of a computer*) = a screen
* (*of a lamp*) una pantalla = a lampshade

pantalón *noun, masculine,* **pantalones** *noun, masculine plural*
un pantalón, unos pantalones = a pair of pants, a pair of trousers

pañal *noun, masculine*
un pañal = a diaper, a nappy

pañuelo *noun, masculine*
* un pañuelo = a handkerchief
* un pañuelo = a scarf

papa *noun, feminine* (*Lat Am*)
una papa = a potato
papas fritas = French fries, chips = potato chips, potato crisps

papá* *noun, masculine*
papá = dad, daddy
mis papás = my mom and dad, my mum and dad

papel *noun, masculine*
* papel = paper
un papel = a piece of paper
papel de aluminio = tinfoil
papel de envolver *or* de regalo = wrapping paper
papel higiénico = toilet paper
* (*in a movie, a play*) un papel = a role

papelera *noun, feminine or* (*SC*)
papelero *noun, masculine*
una papelera, un papelero = a waste-paper basket
= a litter basket, a litter bin

papelería *noun, feminine*
una papelería = a stationery store, a stationer's

paquete *noun, masculine*
un paquete = a parcel, a packet

par
1 *adjective*
= even
2 *noun, masculine*
un par = a pair
un par de preguntas = a couple of questions

para *preposition*
* = for
¿para qué es? = what's it for?
* = by
debe estar listo para mañana = it must be ready by tomorrow
* = to
es muy grande para llevarlo = it's too big to carry
* (*indicating direction*)
van para [casa | el aeropuerto | Sevilla ...] = they are going [home | to the airport | to Seville ...]
* (*Lat Am: when telling the time*)
son cinco para las siete = it is five to seven
* para que = so that

parabrisas *noun, masculine* (**!** *does not change in the plural*)
un parabrisas = a windshield, a windscreen

paracaídas *noun, masculine* (**!** *does not change in the plural*)
un paracaídas = a parachute

parachoques *noun, masculine* (**!** *does not change in the plural*)
un parachoques = a bumper, a fender

parado/parada
1 *adjective*
* (*Spa*) = unemployed
* estar parado/parada (*Lat Am*) = to be standing
2 *noun, masculine/feminine* (*Spa*)
un parado/una parada = an unemployed person
3 parada *noun, feminine*
una parada = a stop
una parada de autobús = a bus stop
una parada de taxis = a taxi stand, a taxi rank

paradero *noun, masculine* (*Lat Am*)
un paradero = a bus stop

paraguas *noun, masculine* (**!** *does not change in the plural*)
un paraguas = an umbrella

paraíso *noun, masculine*
el paraíso = paradise

parar *verb* [1]
* = to stop
parar de hacer algo = to stop doing something
* (*in sports*) = to save
* (*Lat Am*) = to stand (up)
* (*Lat Am*) = to go on strike
pararse
* = to stop
* (*Lat Am*) = to stand up

parchís *noun, masculine* (*Spa*)
parchís = ludo

P

parecer verb 19
- = to seem
  = to look
  parece de metal = it looks like metal
  al parecer, según parece = apparently
  parece ser que = it seems that
  parece que va a llover = it looks like it's going to rain
  parece mentira = it is difficult to believe
- **me parece mal** = I don't think it's right
  nos parece necesario = we think it's necessary
  ¿qué te parece el plan? = what do you think of the plan?

parecerse
  parecerse a algo = to be like something
  parecerse a alguien = to look like someone
  = to be like someone

parecido/parecida adjective
- = similar
- = alike
  ser parecido/parecida a alguien = to look like someone
  = to be like someone

pared noun, feminine
  una pared = a wall

pareja noun, feminine
- **una pareja** = a pair
  = a couple
- **mi pareja** = my partner

parezca, parezco, etc ▶ parecer

pariente noun, masculine/feminine
  un/una pariente = a relative

parlamento noun, masculine
  el parlamento = parliament

paro noun, masculine
- (at work) **un paro** = a strike
  estar de or **en paro** = to be on strike
- (Spa) **el paro** = unemployment
  estar en paro = to be unemployed

párpado noun, masculine
  un párpado = an eyelid

parque noun, masculine
  un parque = a park
  un parque de atracciones or (R Pl) **de diversiones** = an amusement park

párrafo noun, masculine
  un párrafo = a paragraph

parrilla noun, feminine
  una parrilla = a grill
  a la parrilla = grilled

parte noun, feminine
- **parte** = part
  esta parte del país = this part of the country
  la gran or **mayor parte del tiempo** = most of the time
  en alguna parte = somewhere, anywhere
  en cualquier parte = anywhere
  en otra parte = somewhere else
  en todas partes = everywhere

- **una parte** = a share
  mi parte del premio = my share of the prize
- **¿de parte de quién?** = who's calling? (on the phone)
  dale recuerdos de mi parte = give him my regards

participar verb 1
  = to participate, to take part

partida noun, feminine
  una partida = a game

partido noun, masculine
- **un partido** = a match
- **un partido** = a party
- (Lat Am) **un partido de ajedrez** = a game of chess

pasa noun, feminine
  una pasa = a raisin

pasado/pasada
1 adjective
- = last
  el sábado pasado = last Saturday
  pasados dos meses = after two months
- (when telling the time)
  son las tres pasadas = it's past three o'clock
2 pasado noun, masculine
  el pasado = the past

pasajero/pasajera noun, masculine/feminine
  un pasajero/una pasajera = a passenger

pasaporte noun, masculine
  un pasaporte = a pasport

pasar verb 1
- = to go/come past
  pasaron tres autobuses seguidos = three buses went past one after the other
  pasar por un lugar = to go past a place
  pasaré por su oficina mañana = I'll stop by at her office tomorrow
  dejar pasar a alguien = to let someone through
  pasar por la aduana = to go through customs
- = to come/go in
  ¡pase! = come in!
- = to cross
  pasar la frontera = to cross the border
- (when talking about time) = to pass
  pasaron tres días = three days passed
  ha pasado mucho tiempo = it's been a long time
- = to spend
  ¿dónde vas a pasar las Navidades? = where are you going to spend Christmas?
  pasarlo bien/mal = to have a good/bad time
- = to happen
  ¿qué pasó? = what happened?
  ¿qué pasa? = what's the matter?
  les ha debido pasar algo = something must have happened to them

• = pass
¿**me pasas la sal?** = can you pass me the salt?
pasarse
• = to go too far
pasarse de estación/de casa = to go past the station/house
• (*if it's fruit*) = to go bad
(*if it's milk, fish*) = to go off

pasatiempo *noun, masculine*
un pasatiempo = a hobby

Pascua *noun, feminine*
la Pascua = Easter

pasear *verb* [1]
• = to walk
• = to go for a walk
llevar al perro a pasear = to take the dog for a walk
pasear en bicicleta = to go for a ride
pasear en coche = to go for a drive

paseo *noun, masculine*
un paseo = a walk
= a ride
= a drive
ir a dar un paseo = to go for a walk
ir a dar un paseo en bicicleta = to go for a ride
ir a dar un paseo en coche = to go for a drive

pasillo *noun, masculine*
un pasillo = a corridor

paso *noun, masculine*
• **un paso** = a step
dar un paso = to take a step
paso a paso = step by step
oí pasos = I heard footsteps
• **de paso** = on the way
= in passing
me pilla de paso = it's on my way
mencionar algo de paso = to mention something in passing
• '**ceda el paso**' = 'yield', 'give way'
'**prohibido el paso**' = 'no entry'
• **un paso de cebra** = a zebra crossing
un paso de peatones = a crosswalk, a pedestrian crossing
un paso subterráneo = an underpass

pasta *noun, feminine*
• **una pasta** = a paste
• (*food*) **la pasta** = pasta
• (*Spa*) **una pasta** = a cookie, a biscuit

pastel *noun, masculine*
un pastel = a cake

pastelería *noun, feminine*
una pastelería = a cake shop

pastilla *noun, feminine*
• **una pastilla** = a tablet, a pill
• (*of soap*) **una pastilla** = a bar

pata *noun, feminine*
una pata = a leg
(*of a cat, dog*) = a paw

patada *noun, feminine*
una patada = a kick

patata *noun, feminine* (*Spa*)
una patata = a potato
See **papa** *for examples*

patín *noun, masculine*
un patín = a roller skate
= an ice skate

patinar *verb* [1]
• = to skate
• = to ice-skate
• = to skid
• = to slip

patio *noun, masculine*
un patio = a courtyard
= a playground

pato/pata *noun, masculine/feminine*
una pato/una pata = a duck

pausa *noun, feminine*
una pausa = a pause, a break
hacer una pausa = to have a break

pavo/pava *noun, masculine/feminine*
un pavo/una pava = a turkey
un pavo real = a peacock

payaso/payasa *noun, masculine/feminine*
un payaso/una payasa = a clown

paz *noun, feminine*
la paz = peace
dejar a alguien en paz = to leave someone alone
hacer las paces = to make (it) up

peatón *noun, masculine*
un peatón = a pedestrian

peca *noun, feminine*
una peca = a freckle

pecado *noun, masculine*
un pecado = a sin

pecho *noun, masculine*
el pecho = the chest
= the breast
nadar de pecho = to do (the) breaststroke

pechuga *noun, feminine*
la pechuga = the breast

pedal *noun, masculine*
un pedal = a pedal

pedazo *noun, masculine*
un pedazo = a piece, a bit
hacerse pedazos = to smash to pieces

P

pedir verb [48]
• = to ask
  me pidió información = she asked me for
    information
  les pedí que me ayudasen = I asked them
    to help me
• (*in a restaurant*) = to order

pegamento noun, masculine
  pegamento = glue

pegar verb [3]
• = to hit
  pegarle a alguien = to hit someone
• (*if it's a stamp*) = to stick
• (*if it's a broken object*) = to glue (together)
pegarse
  = to stick
  no se pega = it doesn't stick

pegatina noun, feminine (Spa)
  una pegatina = a sticker

peinado noun, masculine
  un peinado = a hairstyle

peinar verb [1]
  = to comb
  = to brush
peinarse
  = to comb one's hair
  = to brush one's hair

peine noun, masculine
  un peine = a comb

pelar verb [1]
  = to peel
  = to shell

peldaño noun, masculine
  un peldaño = a step

pelea noun, feminine
• una pelea = a fight
• una pelea = an argument

pelear verb [1]
• = to fight
• = to quarrel
pelearse
• = to fight
• = to quarrel

película noun, feminine
  una película = a movie, a film
  una película cómica or **de risa** = a comedy
  una película de terror = a horror movie
  una película de suspense (Spa) or (Lat
    Am) de suspenso = a thriller

peligro noun, masculine
  un peligro = a danger
  estar en peligro/fuera de peligro = to be in
    danger/out of danger

peligroso/peligrosa adjective
  = dangerous

pelirrojo/pelirroja adjective
  = red-haired, ginger

pellizcar verb
  = to pinch

pelo noun, masculine
• el pelo = hair
  tiene el pelo rubio = he has blond hair
• (*of an animal*) = fur

pelota noun, feminine
  una pelota = a ball

peluca noun, feminine
  una peluca = a wig

peluquería noun, feminine
  una peluquería = a hairdresser's

peluquero/peluquera noun,
masculine/feminine
  un peluquero/una peluquera = a
    hairdresser

pena noun, feminine
• = sadness
• = pity, shame
  sentir or **tener pena** = to feel sad
  me da pena que no estén aquí = I'm sad
    that they are not here
  ¡qué pena que se haya roto! = what a
    shame it has broken!

  > ! Note the use of the subjunctive after
  > pena que

• (*Lat Am*)
  ¡qué pena! = how embarrassing!
  le da pena pedírselo = he is embarrassed to
    ask her
• **merecer** or **valer la pena** = to be worth it
• **la pena de muerte** = the death penalty

pendejo/pendeja✱ noun,
masculine/feminine (Lat Am)
  un pendejo/una pendeja = a nerd

penique noun, masculine
  un penique = a penny

pensamiento noun, masculine
  un pensamiento = a thought

pensar verb [7]
  = to think
  pensar en algo = to think about something

pensión noun, feminine
• una pensión = a pension
• una pensión = a guesthouse
  pensión completa = full board

peor
1 adjective
  = worse/worst
2 adverb
  = worse
3 noun, masculine/feminine
  el/la peor = the worst (one)

pepino noun, masculine
un pepino = a cucumber

pequeño/pequeña
1 adjective
• = small, little
un paquete pequeño = a small parcel
un niño pequeño = a little boy
• = young
es muy pequeño para ir solo = he's too
  young to go on his own
mi hermano pequeño = my younger
  brother
2 noun, masculine/feminine
un pequeño/una pequeña = a small
  boy/girl
el pequeño/la pequeña = the younger
= the youngest

pera noun, feminine
una pera = a pear

perder verb 21
• = to lose
• = to miss
perder [un tren | una oportunidad | un vuelo ...]
  = to miss [a train | an opportunity | a flight ...]
• perder (el) tiempo = to waste time
perderse
= to get lost

pérdida noun, feminine
una pérdida = a loss
una pérdida de tiempo = a waste of time

perdón
1 noun, masculine
perdón = forgiveness
pedirle perdón a alguien = to apologize to
  someone
2 ¡perdón! exclamation
= sorry!
= excuse me!

perdonar verb 1
= to forgive
perdonarle algo a alguien = to forgive
  someone for something
perdona or (more polite) perdone = sorry
= excuse me

perejil noun, masculine
el perejil = parsley

perezoso/perezosa adjective
= lazy

perfeccionar verb 1
• = to improve
• = to perfect

perfecto/perfecta adjective
= perfect

perfume noun, masculine
un perfume = a perfume

periódico noun, masculine
un periódico = a newspaper

periodista noun, masculine/feminine
un periodista/una periodista = a journalist

periodo, **período** noun, masculine
un periodo = a period

perla noun, feminine
una perla = a pearl

permanecer verb 19
= to remain

permanente
1 adjective
= permanent
2 noun, feminine or (Mex) noun, masculine
una/un permanente = a perm

permanezca, permanezco, etc
▶ permanecer

permiso noun, masculine
• permiso = permission
• un permiso = a permit
• un permiso = a leave
estar de permiso = to be on leave
• con permiso (when entering) = may I come
  in?
(when wishing to get past) = excuse me

permitir verb 41
= to allow, to let
¿me permite? = may I?

pero conjunction
= but

perro/perra noun, masculine/feminine
• un perro/una perra = a dog
• un perro caliente = a hot dog

persiana noun, feminine
una persiana = a blind

persona noun, feminine
una persona = a person
muchas personas = a lot of people

personaje noun, masculine
un personaje = a character

persuadir verb 41
= to persuade

pertenecer verb 19
= to belong

pertenezca, pertenezco, etc
▶ pertenecer

pesa noun, feminine
una pesa = a weight
hacer pesas = to do weightlifting

pesadilla noun, feminine
una pesadilla = a nightmare

P

pesado/pesada
1 *adjective*
- = heavy
- **un libro muy pesado** = a very tedious book
  Juan es muy pesado✖ = Juan is a pain in the neck *or* such a bore

2 *noun, masculine/feminine*
  ser un pesado/una pesada✖ = to be a pain in the neck *or* a bore

pesar *verb* [1]
- = to weigh
- = to be heavy
  ¿te pesa mucho? = is it too heavy for you?

pesca *noun, feminine*
  la pesca = fishing
  ir de pesca = to go fishing

pescadería *noun, feminine*
  una pescadería = a fish shop, a fishmonger's

pescado *noun, masculine*
- **el pescado** = fish
- **un pescado** = a fish

pescador/pescadora *noun, masculine/feminine*
  un pescador/una pescadora = a fisherman/fisherwoman

pescar *verb* [2]
- = to fish
  ir a pescar = to go fishing
- = to catch
  pescar un salmón = to catch a salmon

pesero *noun, masculine (Mex)*
  un pesero = a minibus

peseta *noun, feminine*
  una peseta (*former Spanish currency*) = a peseta

pesimista
1 *adjective*
  = pessimistic
2 *noun, masculine/feminine*
  un/una pesimista = a pessimist

peso *noun, masculine*
- **un peso** = a weight
- **un peso** = a (pair of) scales
- (*currency in many Latin American countries*) **un peso** = a peso

pestaña *noun, feminine*
  una pestaña = an eyelash

petaca *noun, feminine (Mex)*
  una petaca = a suitcase

pétalo *noun, masculine*
  un pétalo = a petal

petróleo *noun, masculine*
  el petróleo = oil

pez *noun, masculine*
  un pez = a fish
  un pez de colores = a goldfish

piano *noun, masculine*
  un piano = a piano

picadura *noun, feminine*
  una picadura = a bite
  = a sting

picante *adjective*
  = hot, spicy

picar *verb* [2]
- = to bite
  = to sting
- (*if it's carrots, onions etc*) = to chop
- (*R Pl, Spa*) = to grind, to mince

pico *noun, masculine*
- (*of a bird*) **un pico** = a beak
- (*of a mountain*) **un pico** = a peak
- **y pico** = and a bit

pida, pido, pidió, etc ▶ pedir

pie *noun, masculine*
  un pie = a foot
  ir a pie = to go on foot
  estar de pie = to be standing
  ponerse de pie = to stand up

piedra *noun, feminine*
  una piedra = a stone

piel *noun, feminine*
  piel (*of a person, fruit*) =skin
  (*of a potato, lemon*) = peel
  (*of a fox, rabbit*) = fur

piensa, pienso etc ▶ pensar

pierna *noun, feminine*
  una pierna = a leg

pieza *noun, feminine*
- **una pieza** = a piece
  (*of an engine*) = a part
- (*Lat Am*) **una pieza** = a bedroom
  (*in a hotel*) = a room

pijama *noun, masculine*
  un pijama = a pair of pajamas, a pair of pyjamas

pila *noun, feminine*
- (*for a torch, radio, etc*) **una pila** = a battery
- (*in the kitchen*) **una pila** = a sink

píldora *noun, feminine*
  una píldora = a pill

pileta *noun, feminine (R Pl)*
- **una pileta** = a sink
  = a washbowl, a washbasin
- **una pileta** = a swimming pool

piloto *noun, masculine/feminine*
  un/una piloto = a pilot

pimentón *noun, masculine*
  el pimentón = paprika

pimienta *noun, feminine*
la pimienta = pepper

pimiento *noun, masculine*
un pimiento = a pepper

pimpón *noun, masculine*
el pimpón = ping-pong

pinchar *verb* 1
• = to prick
= to be prickly
• = to burst
= to puncture
= to get a puncture

pinchazo *noun, masculine*
un pinchazo = a puncture

pino *noun, masculine*
un pino = a pine tree

pinta *noun, feminine*
• una pinta = a pint
• ¡qué pinta más buena!✱ = it looks really
delicious!
tiene pinta de estudiante✱ = he looks like a
student

pintar *verb* 1
= to paint

pintor/pintora *noun, masculine/feminine*
un pintor/una pintora = a painter

pintura
1 *noun, feminine*
pintura = painting
= paint
2 pinturas *noun, feminine plural* (*Mex, Spa*)
pinturas = color crayons

pinza
1 *noun, feminine*
• (*of a crab*) una pinza = a pincer
• (*for hair*) una pinza = a bobby pin, a
hairgrip
• (*for laundry*) una pinza = a clothespin, a
clothes peg
2 pinzas *noun, feminine plural*
unas pinzas = a pair of tweezers

piña *noun, feminine*
• una piña = a pineapple
• un piña = a pine cone

pipa *noun, feminine*
una pipa = a pipe

pirámide *noun, feminine*
una pirámide = a pyramid

pisar *verb* 1
pisar a alguien = to step on someone's foot
pisar algo = to step on/in something

piscina *noun, feminine*
una piscina = a swimming pool

Piscis *noun, masculine*
Piscis = Pisces

piscis *noun, masculine/feminine*
un/una piscis = a Pisces

piso *noun, masculine*
• piso = floor
el primer piso = the second floor (*US
English*), the first floor (*British English*)
un edificio de cinco pisos = a five-story
building
• (*Spa*) un piso = an apartment, a flat

pista *noun, feminine*
• (*in a mystery, riddle*) una pista = a clue
• (*for racing*) una pista = a track
• (*for dancing*) = a dance floor
• una pista de esquí = a ski slope
una pista de hielo = an ice rink
una pista de tenis (*Spa*) = a tennis court

pistola *noun, feminine*
una pistola = a gun

pitar *or* (*Lat Am*) **pitear** *verb* 1
• = to whistle
• (*in a car*) = to hoot

pito *noun, masculine*
un pito = a whistle

piyama *noun, masculine/feminine* (*Lat Am*)
un/una pyjama = a pair of pajamas, a pair
of pyjamas

pizarra *noun, feminine*
una pizarra = a blackboard

placer *noun, masculine*
placer = pleasure

plan *noun, masculine*
un plan = a plan

plancha *noun, feminine*
• una plancha = an iron
• a la plancha = grilled

planchar *verb* 1
= to iron
= to do the ironing

planear *verb* 1
= to plan

planeta *noun, masculine*
un planeta = a planet

plano
1 *adjective*
= flat
2 *noun, masculine*
un plano = a map, a plan

planta *noun, feminine*
• una planta = a plant
• (*of a building*) una planta = a floor
• la planta del pie = the sole of the foot

plantar *verb* 1
= to plant

P

plasticina *(SC)* ▶ plastilina

plástico *noun, masculine*
el plástico = plastic

plastilina *noun, feminine*
la plastilina = Plasticine

plata *noun, feminine*
* la plata = silver
* *(S Am)* plata = money
tener mucha plata = to have a lot of money

plataforma *noun, feminine*
una plataforma = a platform

plátano *noun, masculine*
* un plátano = a banana
* un plátano = a plantain

platicar *verb* [2]
* *(C Am, Mex)* = to talk
* *(Mex)* = to tell

plato *noun, masculine*
un plato = a plate
(for a cup) = a saucer
(for food) = a dish
el primer/segundo plato = the first/second course

playa *noun, feminine*
la playa = the beach
= the seaside

playera *noun, feminine*
* *(Spa)* una playera = a canvas shoe
* *(Mex)* una playera = a T-shirt

plaza *noun, feminine*
* *(in a town)* una plaza = a square
* *(Spa)* una plaza = a market
* *(on a bus, plane)* una plaza = a seat
* *(on a course)* una plaza = a place
* *(at work)* una plaza = a position
* una plaza de toros = a bullring

plegar *verb* [8]
= to fold

pleno/plena *adjective*
en pleno centro = right in the middle
= right in the center
en pleno invierno = in the middle of winter
a plena luz del día = in broad daylight

pliega, pliego, pliegue, etc ▶ plegar

plomo *noun, masculine*
el plomo = lead

pluma *noun, feminine*
* una pluma = a feather
* una pluma = a pen
una pluma atómica *(Mex)* = a ballpoint pen

plural
1 *noun, masculine*
el plural = the plural
2 *adjective*
= plural

población *noun, feminine*
* la población = the population
* una población = a city
= a town
= a village

pobre
1 *adjective*
= poor
2 *noun, masculine/feminine*
un/una pobre = a poor man/woman

pobreza *noun, feminine*
la pobreza = poverty

poco/poca
1 *adjective*
poco/poca = little, not much
pocos/pocas = few, not many
con poco entusiasmo = with little enthusiasm
unos pocos días = a few days
2 *pronoun*
* poco/poca = little, not much
pocos/pocas = a few/not many
he comprado poco = I haven't bought much
pocos lo saben = only a few know about it
un poco = a little (bit)
poco a poco = little by little, gradually
* por poco = nearly
por poco se cae = he nearly fell
* hace poco que vive aquí = she hasn't lived here for very long
ya falta poco = it won't be long now
se quedó poco = he didn't stay long
3 poco *adverb*
me gusta poco = I don't like it much
son muy poco responsables = they're very irresponsible
es poco interesante = it is not very interesting

poder
1 *noun*
el poder = power
2 *verb* [31]
* = to be able to
no puedo levantarlo = I can't lift it
¿puedo entrar? = may I come in?, can I come in?
* podrías haberte hecho daño = you could have hurt yourself
puede que no lo sepa = he might not know
¿cómo has podido hacerme esto? = how could you do this to me?
podríamos ir al cine = we could go to the movies
* puede ser = it might be
puede que vengan... = maybe they'll come...

> **!** *Note the use of the subjunctive after* puede que

podrá, podré, podría, etc ▶ poder

podrido/podrida *adjective*
= rotten

poema *noun, masculine*
un poema = a poem

poesía *noun, feminine*
* la poesía = poetry
* una poesía = a poem

poeta, poeta/poetisa *noun,
masculine/feminine*
un poeta/una poeta, un poeta/una poetisa
= a poet

polaco/polaca
1 *adjective*
= Polish
2 *noun, masculine/feminine*
un polaco/una polaca = a Pole
3 polaco *noun, masculine*
el polaco (*the language*) = Polish

policía
1 *noun, masculine/feminine*
un/una policía = a policeman/policewoman
2 *noun, feminine*
la policía = the police

política *noun, feminine*
* la política = politics
* una política = a policy

político/política
1 *noun, masculine/feminine*
un político/una política = a politician
2 *adjective*
* = political
* mi familia política = my in-laws

pollito *noun, masculine*
un pollito = a chick

polo *noun, masculine*
* el polo norte/sur = the North/South Pole
* (*sport*) el polo = polo
* (*Spa*) un polo = a Popsicle , an ice lolly

Polonia *noun, feminine*
Polonia = Poland

polución *noun, feminine*
la polución = pollution

polvo
1 *noun, masculine*
* = dust
* = powder
2 polvos *noun, masculine plural*
polvos = face powder

pomelo *noun, masculine*
un pomelo = a grapefruit

ponchar *verb* 1 (*Mex*)
se nos ponchó una llanta = we had a
puncture

pondría, pondrías, etc ▶ poner

poner *verb* 32
* = to put
  ponlo en el cajón = put it in the drawer
* = to put on
  ponle el abrigo al niño = put the baby's coat
  on
* = to give
  ¿te pongo un poco más? = shall I give you
  a bit more?
* poner la tele = to put the TV on
* = to set
  pon el despertador a las siete = set the
  alarm for seven
* poner una tienda = to open a shop
* poner una película (*Spa*) = to show a movie
* poner a alguien [nervioso | contento | triste ...]
  = to make someone [nervous | happy | sad ...]
ponerse
* = to become
  ponerse enfermo = to get sick, to fall ill
  ponerse contento = to cheer up
* = to put on
  se puso los zapatos = he put his shoes on
* ponerse de pie = to stand up
* ponerse a hacer algo = to start doing
  something
  se puso a cantar = he started singing
* ponerse al teléfono (*Spa*) = to come to the
  phone

ponga, pongo, etc ▶ poner

poni *noun, masculine*
un poni = a pony

popular *adjective*
= popular

por *preposition*
* = by
  por avión = by plane
  uno por uno = one by one
* = for
  lo hice por ti = I did it for you
* = because of
  no salimos por la lluvia = we didn't go out
  because of the rain
* (*indicating position*)
  por la derecha = on the right
  viajar por el mundo = to travel around the
  world
  pasamos por el museo = we went past the
  museum
  pasar por la puerta = to go through the
  door
* por la mañana = in the morning
  por la noche = at night
  vino por el día = he came for the day
* por teléfono = on the telephone
  lo dijeron por el radio = it was on the radio
* = per
  cinco libras por hora = five pounds per
  hour *or* an hour

P

- **por qué** = why
  ¿por qué no lo dijiste? = why didn't you say so before?
- **por eso** = that's why
  por eso no vino = that's why he didn't come
- **por supuesto** = of course
- **por si (acaso)** = (just) in case

porcentaje noun, masculine
  un porcentaje = a percentage

poro noun, masculine (Mex)
  un poro = a leek

porque conjunction
  = because

portero/portera noun, masculine/feminine
  un portero/una portera = a porter
  = a superintendent, a caretaker

portugués/portuguesa
1 adjective
  = Portuguese
2 noun, masculine/feminine
  un portugués/una portuguesa = a Portuguese
3 portugués noun, masculine
  el portugués (the language) = Portuguese

posibilidad noun, feminine
  una posibilidad = a possibility
  tener muchas posibilidades de hacer algo = to have a good chance of doing something

posible
1 adjective
  = possible
  hacer todo lo posible = to do one's best
2 adverb
  lo antes posible = as soon as possible
  lo hice lo mejor posible = I did my best

posición noun, feminine
  una posición = a position

positivo/positiva adjective
  = positive

posterior adjective
- = rear, back
  la parte posterior = the back, the rear
- = later

postizo/postiza adjective
  = false

postre noun, masculine
  un postre = a dessert

pozo noun, masculine
  un pozo = a well

practicar verb 2
  = to practice, to practise

precio noun, masculine
  un precio = a price

precioso/preciosa adjective
- = beautiful
- = precious

preciso/precisa adjective
- = precise
  el lugar preciso = the precise spot
  en el momento preciso = at the right moment
- **es preciso que vayas** = you must go, you have to go
  no es preciso que lo cambies = there's no need for you to change it

  ! Note the use of the subjunctive after ser preciso que
  si es preciso = if necessary

preferir verb 46
  = to prefer
  preferiría no verla = I would rather not see her

prefiera, prefiero, etc ▶ preferir

pregunta noun, feminine
  una pregunta = a question
  hacer una pregunta = to ask a question

preguntar verb 1
  = to ask
  el jefe ha estado preguntado por ti = the boss has been asking for you
  le pregunté por su madre = I asked after his mother
preguntarse
  = to wonder

premio noun, masculine
  un premio = a prize

prender verb 17
- = to light
  prender un cigarrillo = to light a cigarette
  prenderle fuego a algo = to set fire to something
- (Lat Am) = to switch on, to turn on

prensa noun, feminine
  la prensa = the press, the newspapers

preocupar verb 1
  = to worry
preocuparse
  = to worry, to get worried

preparación noun, feminine
- **preparación** = preparation
- (for a job)
  ¿que preparación tiene? = what experience does he have?
  = what has he studied?
- (in sports) **preparación** = training

preparar verb 1
  = to prepare
prepararse
  = to get ready

preposición *noun, feminine*
una preposición = a preposition

presencia *noun, feminine*
presencia = presence

presentar *verb* [1]
• = to introduce
les presentó a su mujer = he introduced them to his wife
• = to present
presentar un programa = to present a program
presentarse
• = to introduce oneself
• = to take
presentarse a un examen = to take an exam
• presentarse a un concurso = to enter a competition

presente *noun, masculine*
el presente = the present

presidencia *noun, feminine*
la presidencia = the presidency
= the chairmanship

presidente/presidenta *noun, masculine/feminine*
un presidente/una presidenta = a president
= a chairman/chairwoman

preso/presa
1 *adjective*
estar preso/presa = to be in prison
2 *noun, masculine/feminine*
un preso/una presa = a prisoner

préstamo *noun, masculine*
un préstamo = a loan

prestar *verb* [1]
= to lend
prestarle algo a alguien = to lend something to someone
¿me prestas tu coche? = can I borrow your car?

presumido/presumida
1 *adjective*
= conceited
= arrogant
= vain
2 *noun, masculine/feminine*
ser un presumido/una presumida = to be vain

presumir *verb* [41]
= to show off

primavera *noun, feminine*
la primavera = spring

primer *adjective* ▶ primero/primera

primero/primera *number*
! Note that primero *becomes* primer *before masculine singular nouns*
= first
el primero/la primera = the first
de primera calidad = top quality
• (*in dates*) = first

primo/prima *noun, masculine/feminine*
un primo/una prima = a cousin

princesa *noun, feminine*
una princesa = a princess

principal *adjective*
= main
lo principal = the main thing

príncipe *noun, masculine*
un príncipe = a prince
los príncipes = the prince and princess

principiante/principianta *noun, masculine/feminine*
un principiante/una principianta = a beginner

principio *noun, masculine*
el principio = the beginning
al principio = at the beginning

prisa *noun, feminine*
prisa = hurry, rush
tener prisa = to be in a hurry
darse prisa = to hurry
meter prisa a alguien = to rush someone
de prisa ▶ deprisa

prisión *noun, feminine*
una prisión = a prison

prisionero/prisionera *noun, masculine/feminine*
un prisionero/una prisionera = a prisoner

privado/privada *adjective*
= private

privilegio *noun, masculine*
un privilegio = a privilege

probable *adjective*
= probable, likely
poco probable = unlikely

probar *verb* [6]
• = to try
nunca he probado el vodka = I have never tried vodka
• = to taste
¿has probado la salsa? = have you tasted the sauce?
• = to test
probar una máquina = to test a machine
• = to prove
probó su inocencia = he proved his innocence
probarse
= to try on

problema noun, masculine
un problema = a problem

proceso noun, masculine
un proceso = a process

producir verb 43
= produce

producto noun, masculine
un producto = a product

produje, **produzca**, **etc** ▶ producir

profesión noun, feminine
una profesión = a profession

profesional adjective
= professional

profesor/profesora noun,
masculine|feminine
un profesor/una profesora = a teacher
(at a university) = a professor, a lecturer
un profesor/una profesora particular = a
private tutor

profundo/profunda adjective
= deep

programa noun, masculine
un programa = a program, a programme
(in school, college etc) = a syllabus, a
curriculum

progresar verb 1
= to progress

progreso noun, masculine
el progreso = progress

prohibido/prohibida adjective
= forbidden
'prohibido pisar el césped' = 'keep off the
grass'
'prohibido el paso', 'prohibida la entrada'
= 'no entry'
'prohibido fumar' = 'no smoking'

prohibir verb 52
• = to forbid
= to ban
te lo prohíbo = I forbid you
'se prohíbe fumar' = 'no smoking'

promesa noun, feminine
una promesa = a promise

prometer verb 17
= to promise

pronombre noun, masculine
un pronombre = a pronoun

pronto adverb
• = soon
= quickly
lo más pronto posible = as soon as possible
termínalo pronto = finish it quickly
de pronto = suddenly

• (Spa) = early
se levantan pronto = they get up early

pronunciar verb 1
= to pronounce

propina noun, feminine
una propina = a tip

propio/propia adjective
• = own
mi propio hijo = my own son
• = himself/herself
la propia dueña los atendió = the owner
herself served them

propósito noun, masculine
un propósito = an intention, a purpose
a propósito = on purpose
= by the way

protección noun, feminine
protección = protection

proteger verb 20
= to protect

protestante
1 adjective
= Protestant
2 noun, masculine|feminine
un/una protestante = a Protestant

provecho noun, masculine
provecho = benefit
sacar provecho de algo = to benefit from
something
¡buen provecho! = enjoy your meal!

proverbio noun, masculine
un proverbio = a proverb

próximo/próxima adjective
= next

proyecto noun, masculine
un proyecto = a plan
= a project

proyector noun, masculine
un proyector = a projector

prueba noun, feminine
• una prueba = a proof
• una prueba = a test

prueba, **pruebo**, **etc** ▶ probar

psicólogo/psicóloga noun,
masculine|feminine
un psicólogo/una psicóloga = a
psychologist

psiquiatra noun, masculine|feminine
un/una psiquiatra = a psychiatrist

pub noun, masculine
un pub = a bar that is open till late at night and
has music

publicar verb 2
= to publish

---

publicidad noun, feminine
* la publicidad = publicity
* la publicidad = the advertisements
  = advertising
  después de la publicidad = after the break
  = after this message

público/pública
1 adjective
  = public
2 público noun, masculine
  el público = the public
  = the audience

pude, pudo, etc ▶ poder

pudrirse verb 63
  = to rot

pueblo noun, masculine
* un pueblo = a village
* el pueblo = the people

pueda, puedo, etc ▶ poder

puente noun, masculine
  un puente = a bridge

puerco/puerca
1 adjective
  puerco/puerco✱ = dirty
2 noun, masculine/feminine
  un puerco/una puerca = a pig
3 puerco noun, masculine (Mex)
  puerco = pork

puerta noun, feminine
* una puerta = a door
* una puerta = a gate
  la puerta de embarque (at an airport) = the
  gate

puerto noun, masculine
  un puerto = a port, a harbor, a harbour

pues conjunction
  pues, no sabía = oh, I didn't know
  pues mira, se hace así = you see, it's done
  like this
  pues no = well, no
  pues si no te gusta, no lo compres = if you
  don't like it, don't buy it
  ¡pues claro que iré! = of course I'll go!

puesto¹ noun, masculine
* un puesto = a position, a place
  en primer puesto = in first position
* (at work) un puesto = a job
* un puesto de periódicos = a newspaper
  stand

puesto²/puesta adjective
* (if it's the table) = laid
* llevaba el sombrero puesto = he had his
  hat on
  no lo envuelva, me lo llevo puesto = don't
  wrap it, I'll wear it now

pulgada noun, feminine
  una pulgada = an inch

pulgar noun, masculine
* el pulgar = the thumb
* el pulgar = the big toe

pulir verb 41
  = to polish

pulmón noun, masculine
  el pulmón = the lung

pulpo noun, masculine
  un pulpo = an octopus

pulsera noun, feminine
  una pulsera = a bracelet

pulso noun, masculine
* pulso = pulse
  tomarle el pulso a alguien = to take
  someone's pulse
* tener buen pulso = to have a steady hand
  me tiembla el pulso = my hand is shaking

punta noun, feminine
  una punta = a point
  = a tip
  = an end
  sacar punta a un lápiz = to sharpen a
  pencil

puntada noun, feminine
  una puntada = a stitch

puntilla noun, feminine
  de or (Lat Am) en puntillas = on tiptoe

punto noun, masculine
* un punto = a point
  hasta cierto punto = up to a point
  un punto de vista = a point of view
* un punto = a dot
  un punto (final) = a period, a full stop
  un punto y coma = a semicolon
  dos puntos = a colon
  puntos suspensivos = suspension points,
  dot, dot, dot
* un punto = a stitch
* estar a punto de hacer algo
  = to be about to do something
  = to be on the verge of doing something
* (Spa) hacer punto = to knit
  de punto (Spa) = knitted
* llegar en punto = to arrive on the dot

puntuación noun, feminine
* puntuación = punctuation
* (in exams) puntuación = grades, marks

puntual adjective
  = punctual
  llegar puntual = to arrive on time

puñetazo noun, masculine
  un puñetazo = a punch

puño noun, masculine
* un puño = a fist
* (of a shirt) un puño = a cuff
* (of an umbrella) un puño = a handle

P

pupitre noun, masculine
  un pupitre = a desk

puré noun, masculine
  puré = purée
  = mash

puro[1] noun, masculine
  un puro = a cigar

puro[2]/**pura** adjective
  = pure

puse, puso, etc ▶ poner

puta⚫ noun, feminine
  una puta = a whore

puzzle noun, masculine
  un puzzle = a jigsaw (puzzle)

Qq

---

que
1 pronoun
  = who, that
  la chica que trabaja conmigo = the girl
    who works with me
  = which, that
  la casa que compraron = the house they
    bought
    See **el** for translations of **el que/la que/los**
    que/las que
2 conjunction
  = that
  dijo que no vendría = he said (that) he
    wouldn't come
  = than
  es más alto que yo = he's taller than me
  (when expressing a wish)
  ¡que te diviertas! = have a good time!
  ¡que no llame! = I hope she doesn't phone!

  ! Note the use of the subjunctive after
  que

qué
1 pronoun
  = what
  ¿qué es esto? = what's this?
  no sé qué decir = I don't know what to say
  ¿qué tal van las cosas?, ¿qué tal? = how
    are things?
  ¡qué de libros! = what a lot of books!
  ¡qué va! = no way!
2 adjective
  = what
  ¿qué hora es? = what time is it?
  (in exclamations) = what a
  ¡qué playa más limpia! = what a clean
    beach!

3 adverb
  = how
  ¡qué bonito! = how beautiful!
  ¡qué bien! = great!

quebrar verb [7]
  = to break
quebrarse
  = to break
  se quebró un brazo (Lat Am) = he broke his
    arm

quedar verb [1]
  = to be left
  no queda pan = there is no bread left
  me quedan treinta libras = I have thirty
    pounds left
  quedan tres minutos para el final = there
    are three minutes left to the end
  aún queda mucho tiempo = there's still
    plenty of time
  nos quedan tres kilómetros = we still have
    three kilometers to go
  te queda media hora = you have half an
    hour left
  (when talking about clothes, color, etc)
  me queda grande = it's too big for me
  te queda muy bien = it suits you
  (Spa)
  quedamos en el bar = we arranged to meet
    at the bar
  ¿quedamos esta tarde? = shall we meet
    this afternoon?
quedarse
  = to stay
  quedarse con algo = to keep something
  quedarse + adjective:
  quedarse ciego = to go blind
  quedarse callado/quieto = to keep
    still/quiet
  quedarse sentado = to remain or stay
    seated
  quedarse dormido = to fall asleep
  quedarse solo = to be left alone
  me quedé mirando = I sat/stood there
    watching

queja noun, feminine
  una queja = a complaint

quejarse verb [1]
  = to complain
  quejarse de algo = to complain about
    something

quemadura noun, feminine
  una quemadura = a burn

quemar verb [1]
  = to burn
  = to scald
  = to burn down
  = to be hot
quemarse
  = to burn oneself

⚫ considered offensive   **C Am** Central America   **Lat Am** Latin America   **Mex** Mexico

me quemé la lengua = I burnt my tongue
= to scald oneself
= to get (sun)burnt
= to burn
= to burn down

querer *verb* 34
= to love
te quiero = I love you
= to want
¿quieres verlos? = do you want to see them?
quiere que la ayudemos = she wants us to help her

! *Note the use of the subjunctive after* querer que

quiero *or* **quisiera una habitación doble** = I would like a double room
quisiera preguntarle... = I would like to ask you...
querer decir = to mean
lo hice sin querer = I didn't mean to do it
hacer algo queriendo = to do something on purpose
quererse
= to love each other

querido/querida *adjective*
= dear

querrá, querré, querría, etc
▶ querer

quesadilla *noun, feminine* (Mex)
una quesadilla = *a tortilla filled with a savory mixture and topped with melted cheese*

queso *noun, masculine*
queso = cheese

quien *pronoun*
= who
= whom
= that
fue ella quien me lo pidió = she's the one who asked me
la persona con quien hablé = the person I spoke to

quién *pronoun*
= who
= which
¿quién de ellos es el dueño? = which of them is the owner?
¿de quién es este libro? = whose book is this?

quiera, quiere, etc ▶ querer

quieto/quieta *adjective*
= still

química *noun, feminine*
la química = chemistry

quince *number*
= fifteen
quince niños = fifteen children
el quince = (number) fifteen
tengo quince = I have fifteen (of them)
(*in dates*) = fifteenth
hoy es quince *or* (Spa) **hoy es día quince** = today is the fifteenth
hoy estamos a quince = today's the fifteenth
el quince de mayo = the fifteenth of May
(*talking about age*) = fifteen
tengo quince años = I'm fifteen (years old)
hoy cumplo quince años = I'm fifteen today
a los quince años cambié de colegio I changed schools at fifteen

quinceañero/quinceañera *noun, masculine/feminine*
un quinceañero/una quinceañera = a teenager

quincena *noun, feminine*
una quincena = two weeks, a fortnight

quiniela
1 *noun, feminine* (Spa)
una quiniela = a sports lottery ticket (*in USA*), a pools coupon (*in Britain*)
2 quinielas *noun, feminine* (Spa)
las quinielas = the sports lottery (*in USA*), the pools (*in Britain*)

quinientos/quinientas *number*
= five hundred
quinientos uno, quinientos dos, etc = five hundred and one, five hundred and two, etc

quinto/quinta
1 *adjective*
= fifth
See **primero** for examples
2 quinto *noun, masculine*
un quinto = a fifth

quiosco *noun, masculine*
un quiosco = a newsstand
= an ice-cream stand
= a drinks stand
= a kiosk

quise, quiso, etc ▶ querer

quitar *verb* 1
= to take off
= to remove
= to take away
quitarle algo a alguien = to take something from someone
quitarse
= to take off
quitarse los zapatos = to take one's shoes off
(*if it's a pain*) = to go away

quizá, quizás *adverb*
= perhaps

Q

Rr

rábano *noun, masculine*
un rábano = a radish

rabia *noun, feminine*
• rabia = anger
me pegó con rabia = he hit me in anger
me da rabia su actitud = his attitude drives
me mad, his attitude really annoys me
le da rabia no haberte visto = he's really
upset not to have seen you
me da rabia tener que irme ahora = what a
shame I have to go now
¡qué rabia! = how annoying!
(*expressing disappointment*) = what a
shame!
• (*disease*) la rabia = rabies

rabo *noun, masculine*
un rabo (*of animal*) = a tail
(*of fruit, leaf*) = a stalk

racimo *noun, masculine*
un racimo = a bunch

ración *noun, feminine*
una ración = a portion

radiador *noun, masculine*
un radiador = a radiator

radio *noun, masculine* (*Lat Am*) or (*Spa,
SC*) *noun, feminine*
un/una radio = radio
escuchar el/la radio = to listen to the radio

raíz *noun, feminine*
una raíz = a root
echar raíces = to take root

rallar *verb* 1
= to grate

rama *noun, feminine*
una rama = a branch

rana *noun, feminine*
una rana = a frog

rápido/rápida *adjective*
= quick, swift

raqueta *noun, feminine*
una raqueta = a racket

raro/rara *adjective*
• = strange, odd
• = rare

rasguño *noun, masculine*
un rasguño = a scratch

rata *noun, feminine*
una rata = a rat

rato *noun, masculine*
un rato = a while
hace (un) rato que te llamó = he rang you a
while ago
hace (un) rato que está ahí = she's been
there for a while
al rato = after a while
al poco rato = soon afterwards
. a ratos = on and off
en mis ratos libres = in my spare time
pasar un buen/mal rato = to have a
great/bad time

ratón *noun, masculine*
un ratón = a mouse

raya *noun, feminine*
• una raya = a line
• (*in designs*) una raya = a stripe
una camiseta a rayas = a striped T-shirt
• (*in hair*) la raya = the part, the parting
llevar la raya a un lado or (*Lat Am*) a un
costado = to have a side part or parting

rayar *verb* 1
= to scratch

rayo *noun, masculine*
un rayo (*of sun, light*) = a ray
(*in storms*) = a bolt/flash of lightning
un rayo láser = a laser beam
rayos X = X-rays

raza *noun, feminine*
una raza = a race
un perro de raza = a pedigree dog

razón *noun, feminine*
una razón = a reason
tener razón = to be right
no tener razón = to be wrong

reacción *noun, feminine*
una reacción = a reaction

real *adjective*
• = real
• = true
• = royal

realidad *noun, feminine*
la realidad = reality
hacerse realidad = to become true
en realidad = actually

rebaja
1 *noun, feminine*
una rebaja = a reduction
2 rebajas *noun, feminine plural*
las rebajas = the sales
estar de rebajas = to have a sale on

rebajar *verb* 1
• = to reduce
se lo rebajo a cincuenta dólares = I'll
reduce it to fifty dollars for you
me rebajó dos mil pesos = he gave me a
two thousand pesos discount
• = to bring down
rebajar el precio = to bring down the price

rebanada noun, feminine
una rebanada = a slice

rebelde
1 adjective
• = rebel
• = rebellious
2 noun, masculine|feminine
un/una rebelde = a rebel

rebobinar verb
= to rewind

rebotar verb [1]
(if it's a ball) = to bounce
(if it's a bullet) = to ricochet
rebotó en la pared = it bounced/ricocheted
off the wall

recado noun, masculine
un recado = a message

recámara noun, feminine (Mex)
una recámara = a bedroom

recepción noun, feminine
la recepción = reception

recepcionista noun,
masculine|feminine
un/una recepcionista = a receptionist

receta noun, feminine
• (for cooking) una receta = a recipe
• (from the doctor) una receta = a
prescription

recibir verb [41]
• = to receive
recibir ayuda = to receive help
• = to meet
fuimos a recibirlos a la estación = we went
to meet them at the station
• = to welcome

recibo noun, masculine
un recibo = a receipt

recién adverb
• el recién nacido/la recién nacida = the
newborn baby
los recién llegados = the newcomers
los recién casados = the newlyweds
'recién pintado' = 'wet paint'
• (Lat Am) = just
recién llego = I've just arrived

reciente adjective
= recent

recoger verb [20]
• (if it's fruit, information) = to collect
• (from the floor) = to pick up
• (if it's a person, a parcel) = to pick up, to
fetch
• (if it's garbage) = to take away
• (if it's a room, a house) = to straighten (up),
to tidy (up)
• (if it's the table) = to clear

recogerse
recogerse el pelo = to tie one's hair back

recomendar verb [7]
= to recommend

recompensa noun
una recompensa = a reward

reconocer verb [19]
• (if it's a person, place) = to recognize
• (if it's a mistake) = to admit

reconozca etc ▶ reconocer

récord noun, masculine
un récord = a record
batir un récord = to break a record

recordar verb [6]
• = to remember
• recordarle algo a alguien
= to remind someone about something
= to remind someone of something
me recuerda a su madre = she reminds me
of her mother
recuérdame que la llame mañana =
remind me to phone her tomorrow

> **!** Note the use of the subjunctive after
> recordar que

recreo noun, masculine
el recreo = the recess, the break

rectángulo noun, masculine
un rectángulo = a rectangle

recto/recta
1 adjective
= straight
2 recto adverb
siga todo recto = carry straight on

recuerda, recuerdo, etc ▶ recordar

recuerdo
1 noun, masculine
• un recuerdo = a memory
• un recuerdo = a souvenir
2 recuerdos noun, masculine plural
recuerdos = regards

red noun, feminine
una red = a net
la Red = the Net

redacción noun, feminine
una redacción = an essay

redondo/redonda adjective
• = round
• (Mex: if it's a ticket) = round-trip, return

reducir verb [43]
= to reduce

reduje, reduzca, reduzco, etc
▶ reducir

R

reemplazar verb 4
= to replace

referirse verb 46
= to refer

refiera, refiero, refiramos, refirió,
etc ▶ referirse

reflejo
1 adjective
= reflex
2 noun, masculine
* un reflejo = a reflex
tener reflejos rápidos = to have fast
reflexes
* (in the mirror) un reflejo = a reflection
3 **reflejos** noun, masculine plural
reflejos = highlights

refrán noun, masculine
un refrán = a saying

refresco noun, masculine
un refresco = a soft drink

regadera noun, feminine
* una regadera = a watering can
* (Mex) una regadera = a shower
= a shower head

regalar verb 1
* = to give (as a gift)
* = to give away

regalo noun, masculine
un regalo = a gift, a present

regañar verb 1
= to tell off, to scold

regar verb 8
= to water

régimen noun, masculine
un régimen = a diet
ponerse a régimen = to go on a diet

región noun, feminine
una región = a region

registro noun, masculine
* (book) un registro = register
* (office) un registro = a registry
un registro civil = a registry, a registry
office
* (by the police) un registro = a search

regla noun, feminine
* una regla = a rule
* (for measuring) una regla = a rule, a ruler
* (in a woman) la regla = the period
tener la regla, estar con la regla = to have
one's period
* en regla = in order

regresar verb 1
* = to return, to come/go back
* (Lat Am) = to return, to give back
= to send back

regreso noun, masculine
regreso = return

regular
1 adjective
* = regular
* = poor
2 adverb
¿qué tal va el trabajo? — regular = how's
work going? — so-so
lee regular = her reading is not very good

reina noun, feminine
la reina = the queen

reino noun, masculine
un reino = a kingdom
el Reino Unido = the United Kingdom

reír verb 50
= to laugh
echarse a reír = to burst out laughing
reírse
= to laugh
reírse de algo/alguien = to laugh at
something/someone
reírse a carcajadas = to roar with laughter

reja noun, feminine
una reja = a grille
= a railing

relación noun, feminine
una relación (between facts, events) = a
connection
(between people) = a relationship
relaciones diplomáticas/comerciales =
diplomatic/trade relations
relaciones públicas = public relations

relacionar verb 1
= to relate
relacionarse
relacionarse con alguien = to mix with
someone

relajar verb 1
= to relax
relajarse
= to relax

relámpago noun, masculine
un relámpago = a flash of lightning
un viaje/una visita relámpago = a lightning
trip/visit

religión noun, feminine
la religión = religion

religioso/religiosa adjective
= religious

relleno/rellena
1 adjective
(if it's a cake) = filled
(if it's a chicken, pepper, etc) = stuffed
2 **relleno** noun, masculine
relleno (for cakes) = filling
(for chicken, peppers, etc) = stuffing

reloj *noun, masculine*
un reloj = a clock
= a watch
un reloj de sol = a sundial
un reloj despertador = an alarm clock
un reloj de pulsera = a wristwatch

relojería *noun, feminine*
una relojería = a watchmaker's

remedio *noun, masculine*
* un remedio = a remedy
  (*for a problem*) = a solution
  si no hay más remedio = if there's no other
  option
  no tener más remedio que ... = to have no
  other option but ...
* (*Lat Am*) un remedio = a medicine

remitente
1 *noun, masculine/feminine*
el/la remitente = the sender
2 *noun, masculine*
el remitente = the return address

remolacha *noun, feminine*
una remolacha = a beet, a beetroot

remover *verb* 22
* (*if it's soil*) = to turn over
* (*Spa: if it's a salad*) = to toss
* (*Spa: if it's a liquid*) = to stir

remueva, remuevo, etc ▶ remover

renglón *noun, masculine*
un renglón = a line

rentar *verb* 1 (*Mex*)
= to rent

reparar *verb* 1
* = to repair
* = to mend

repartir *verb* 41
* (*if it's post, goods*) = to deliver
* (*if it's money*) = to share out
* (*if it's leaflets*) = to hand out
* (*in card games*) = to deal

repasar *verb* 1
* = to check
* (*for an exam*) = to review, to revise

repaso *noun, masculine*
un repaso = a review, a revision
darle un repaso a los apuntes = to review
one's notes, to revise one's notes

repente: de repente *adverb*
= suddenly, all of a sudden

repentino/repentina *adjective*
= sudden

repetir *verb* 48
* = to repeat
* = to do/say again
* (*when eating*) = to have a second helping
* (*in school*) = to repeat a year

repita, repitió, repito, etc ▶ repetir

repollo *noun, masculine*
un repollo = a cabbage

reportaje *noun, masculine*
un reportaje (*in the newspaper*) = an article
(*on television*) = a report
(*Lat Am*) = an interview

reportero/reportera *noun,*
masculine/feminine
un reportero/una reportera = a reporter

representante *noun,*
masculine/feminine
un/una representante = a representative
(*of actor, actress*) = an agent

representar *verb* 1
* = to represent
* (*if it's a play*) = to perform
* (*if it's a role*) = to play

república *noun, feminine*
una república = a republic

resbalar *verb* 1
* = to slip
* (*if it's the floor*) = to be slippery
resbalarse
= to slip
resbalarse con algo = to slip on something

reserva *noun, feminine*
una reserva = a reservation

reservar *verb* 1
= to reserve, to book

resfriado *noun, masculine*
un resfriado = a cold
agarrar *or* (*Spa*) coger un resfriado = to
catch a cold

residencia *noun, feminine*
* residencia = residence
* (*for students*) una residencia = a
  dormitory, a hall of residence
  una residencia de ancianos = an old
  people's home

respaldo *noun, masculine*
el respaldo = the back

respecto *noun, masculine*
respecto a, con respecto a = with regard
to, regarding

respetable *adjective*
= respectable

respetar *verb* 1
= to respect

respeto *noun, masculine*
respeto = respect

respirar *verb* 1
= to breath
respirar hondo = to take a deep breath

R

responder verb ⟨17⟩
- = to answer, to reply
- = to respond

responsabilidad noun, feminine
responsabilidad = responsibility

responsable
1 adjective
= responsible
2 noun, masculine/feminine
el/la responsable (in a shop, office) = the person in charge
(of a mistake, crime) = the person responsible

respuesta noun, feminine
una respuesta = an answer, a reply

restar verb ⟨1⟩
= to subtract, to take away

restaurante noun, masculine
un restaurante = a restaurant

resto
1 noun, masculine
el resto = the rest
2 restos noun, masculine plural
los restos = the remains
(of food) = the leftovers

resultado noun, masculine
el resultado = the result
dar resultado = to work

resultar verb ⟨1⟩
- (if it's a plan, idea) = to work
- resultar [fácil | aburrido | caro …] = to be [easy | boring | expensive …]

resumen noun, masculine
un resumen = a summary

retraso noun, masculine
un retraso = a delay
el vuelo de Caracas lleva retraso = the flight from Caracas is delayed
llegaron con veinte minutos de retraso = they arrived twenty minutes late

retrato noun, masculine
un retrato = a portrait

reunión noun, feminine
una reunión = a meeting
(of friends) = a gathering

reunirse verb ⟨64⟩
= to meet

revancha noun, feminine
- la revancha = revenge
tomarse la revancha = to take (one's) revenge
- (when playing games) la revancha = the return game

revelar verb ⟨1⟩
- (if it's a secret) = to reveal
- (if it's a photograph) = to develop

reverso noun, masculine
el reverso (of paper, cloth) = the back
(of coin, medal) = the reverse

revés noun, masculine
- el revés (of paper, material) = the back
(of garment) = the inside
- al revés = upside down
= inside out
= back to front
= the other way around
= the wrong way around
- del revés = inside out

revisar verb ⟨1⟩
- (if it's a machine, document) = to check
- (Lat Am) = to search, to go through

revisión noun, feminine
una revisión = a check
(of an installation) = an inspection
(medical) = a checkup
(Spa: for a car) = a service

revisor/revisora noun, masculine/feminine (Spa)
un revisor/una revisora = a ticket inspector

revista noun, feminine
una revista = a magazine

revolución noun, feminine
una revolución = a revolution

revolver verb ⟨24⟩
= to stir

rey noun, masculine
un rey = a king
los reyes (the couple) = the King and Queen
los Reyes Magos = the Three Wise Men

rezar verb ⟨4⟩
= to pray
rezar una oración = to say a prayer

ría, rían, etc ▶ reír

rico/rica
1 adjective
= rich
- (if it's food) = nice
- (if it's a baby, a puppy) = sweet, cute
2 noun, masculine/feminine
los ricos = the rich

ridículo noun, masculine
hacer el ridículo = to make a fool of oneself
dejar or poner a alguien en ridículo = to make someone look stupid

ridículo/ridícula adjective
= ridiculous

ríe, ríen, etc ▶ reír

riega, riego, riegue, etc ▶ regar

riesgo noun, masculine
un riesgo = a risk
correr un riesgo = to run a risk, to take a risk

rifa *noun, feminine*
　una rifa = a raffle

rincón *noun, masculine*
　un rincón = a corner
　un bonito rincón de España = a beautiful
　　spot in *or* corner of Spain
　estará en cualquier rincón = it could be
　　anywhere
　mirar por todos los rincones = to look in
　　every nook and cranny

riña *noun, feminine*
　• una riña = a quarrel, a row
　• una riña = a fight

riñón
1 *noun, masculine*
　un riñón = a kidney
2 riñones *noun, masculine plural*
　los riñones = the lower part of the back
　me duelen los riñones = my back hurts

río *noun, masculine*
　un río = a river

rió ▶ reír

riqueza *noun, feminine*
　la riqueza = wealth

risa
1 *noun, feminine*
　la risa = laughter
　¡qué risa! = what a laugh!
　darle risa a alguien = to make someone
　　laugh
　me da risa pensarlo = thinking about it
　　makes me laugh
　me dio la risa = I started laughing
　morirse de la risa = to die laughing
　　See also **película**
2 risas *noun, feminine plural*
　risas = laughter

ritmo *noun, masculine*
　• el ritmo = the rhythm
　llevar el ritmo = to keep time
　• el ritmo = the pace, the speed
　a este ritmo = at this pace

rizo *noun, masculine*
　un rizo = a curl

robar *verb* ⑴
　= to steal
　= to rob
　= to break into
　= to rip off

robo *noun, masculine*
　un robo = a robbery
　= a theft
　= a burglary
　= a break-in
　= a rip-off

roca *noun, feminine*
　una roca = a rock

rodaja *noun, feminine*
　una rodaja = a slice
　en rodajas = sliced

rodear *verb* ⑴
　= to surround

rodilla *noun, feminine*
　una rodilla = a knee
　ponerse de rodillas = to kneel down

rojo/roja
1 *adjective*
　= red
　ponerse rojo = to blush
　al rojo vivo = red hot
2 rojo *noun, masculine*
　el rojo = red

rollo *noun, masculine*
　• un rollo = a roll
　• (*Spa*) un rollo✱ = a bore, a pain
　sus padres son un rollo = his parents are a
　　bore *or* a real pain
　un rollo de libro = a really boring book

romántico/romántica *adjective*
　= romantic

rompecabezas *noun, masculine* (**!** *does
not change in the plural*)
　un rompecabezas = a jigsaw (puzzle)
　= a puzzle, a riddle

romper *verb* ⑷⓪
　• = to break
　• (*if it's paper, material*) = to tear
　• (*if it's shoes*) = to wear out
　• romper con alguien = to split up with
　　someone
romperse
　= to break
　se rompió un brazo = he broke his arm

ron *noun, masculine*
　el ron = rum

roncar *verb* ⑵
　= to snore

ronronear *verb* ⑴
　= to purr

ropa *noun, feminine*
　la ropa = clothes
　ropa interior = underwear

ropero *noun, masculine*
　un ropero = a wardrobe

rosa
1 *noun, feminine*
　una rosa = a rose
2 *adjective* (**!** *never changes*)
　= pink
3 *noun, masculine*
　el rosa (*the colour*) = pink

R

rosado/rosado
1 *adjective*
= pink
2 rosado *noun, masculine*
• (*wine*) **un rosado** = a rosé
• (*the colour*) **el rosado** = pink

rosario *noun, masculine*
un rosario = a rosary

roto/rota *adjective*
= broken
(*if it's paper, material*) = torn
(*if it's shoes*) = worn-out

rotulador *noun, masculine* (*Spa*)
un rotulador = a felt-tip pen

rubio/rubia *adjective*
= blond

rueda *noun, feminine*
una rueda = a wheel
= a tire, a tyre
se me pinchó una rueda = I got a puncture

ruedo *noun, masculine*
el ruedo = the bullring

rugir *verb* 44
= to roar

ruido *noun, masculine*
un ruido = a noise

ruidoso/ruidosa *adjective*
= noisy

ruina *noun, feminine*
ruina = ruin
estar en la ruina = to be ruined
en ruinas = in ruins

rulo *noun, masculine*
un rulo = a curler, a roller
(*SC*) = a curl

rumbo *noun, masculine*
rumbo = direction
(*of boat, plane*) = course
poner rumbo a = to set course for
un avión con rumbo a Santiago = a plane
bound for Santiago

rumor *noun, masculine*
un rumor = a rumor, a rumour
corre el rumor de que se va = there's a
rumor going around that he's leaving

ruso/rusa
1 *adjective*
= Russian
2 *noun, masculine/feminine*
un ruso/una rusa = a Russian
3 ruso *noun, masculine*
el ruso (*the language*) = Russian

ruta *noun, feminine*
una ruta = a route

rutina *noun, feminine*
la rutina = the routine
las preguntas de rutina = the routine
questions

Ss

sábado *noun, masculine*
el sábado = Saturday
See **miércoles** *for more examples*

sábana *noun, feminine*
una sábana = a sheet

saber *verb* 35
• = to know
no se sabe = nobody knows
¡y yo qué sé!, ¡qué sé yo! = how should I
know?
• = to find out
¿cómo lo supo? = how did she find out?
• **saber hacer algo** = to know how to do
something
no sé nadar = I can't swim
• **saber de alguien** = to hear from someone
¿qué sabes de Ana? = have you heard
from Ana?
• **saber a algo** = to taste of something
sabe bien/dulce = it tastes nice/sweet
saber mal = to have a nasty taste
sabe a limón = it tastes of lemon
saberse
saberse algo de memoria = to know
something by heart

sabor *noun, masculine*
un sabor = a taste, a flavor, a flavour

sabrá, sabré, sabría, etc ▶ saber

sabroso/sabrosa *adjective*
• (*if it's food*) = delicious
• (*Lat Am*) **sabroso/sabrosa✖** = nice

sacacorchos *noun, masculine* (**!** *does
not change in the plural*)
un sacacorchos = a corkscrew

sacapuntas *noun, masculine* (**!** *does not
change in the plural*)
un sacapuntas = a pencil sharpener

sacar *verb* 2
• = to take (out), to get (out)
sacar al perro a pasear = to take the dog
out for a walk
• = to put out
sacó la cabeza por la ventana = he put his
head out of the window

* = to take off
  no puedo sacar la tapa = I can't take the lid off
* (*if it's a ticket, passport*) = to get
* (*if it's a book, record*) = to bring out
* (*if it's a conclusion*) = to draw
* (*if it's a photograph*) = to take
* (*if it's a stain*) = to remove

sacarse
* = to take out
  sacarse las manos de los bolsillos = to take one's hands out of one's pockets
  se sacó una muela = he had his tooth out
* = to get
  se sacó el carnet de identidad = he's got his identity card
  me saqué una buena nota en el examen (*Lat Am*) = I got a good grade *or* mark in the exam
* = to take off
  se sacó los zapatos = he took his shoes off

sacerdote *noun, masculine*
  un sacerdote = a priest

saco *noun, masculine*
* **un saco** = a sack
  un saco de dormir = a sleeping bag
* (*Lat Am*) **un saco** = a jacket

sacudir *verb* 41
* = to shake
  = to shake off
* (*Mex, SC*) = to dust

sacudirse
  = to brush
  = to brush off

Sagitario *noun, masculine*
  Sagitario = Sagittarius

sagitario *noun, masculine|feminine*
  un/una sagitario = a Sagittarius

sagrado/sagrada *adjective*
  = holy
  = sacred

sal *noun, feminine*
  la sal = salt

sala *noun, feminine*
  una sala = a room
  (*in a hospital*) = a ward
  una sala de estar = a living room
  una sala de espera = a waiting room
  una sala de exposiciones = a gallery

salado/salada *adjective*
  = salty

salario *noun, masculine*
  un salario = a salary

salchicha *noun feminine*
  una salchicha = a sausage

saldrá, **saldré**, **saldría**, **salga**, **salgo**, etc ▶ salir

salida *noun, feminine*
* **la salida** = the exit
* (*of plane, train*) **la salida** = the departure
* **a la salida** = on the way out

salir *verb* 56
* = to go out
  salen todas las noches = they go out every night
* = to come out
  sal de ahí = come out of there
* = to leave
  salen mañana = they're leaving tomorrow
* = to turn out
  todo salió bien = everything turned out OK
* = to work out
  sale a 3.000 pesos cada uno = it works out at 3.000 pesos each
* (*referring to the way one does something*)
  no me sale = I can't do it
  le sale muy bien la paella = he makes a really good paella
* **me salió un grano** = I have a spot
  te está saliendo sangre = you're bleeding

salirse
* = to come off
  se salió el asa = the handle came off
* = to leave
  salirse del colegio = to leave school
* = to leak
  se sale el gas = the gas is leaking
* = to overflow
  el agua se salió de la bañera = the bathtub overflowed

salmón
1 *noun, masculine*
* **un salmón** = a salmon
* **el salmón** (*the color*) = salmon pink
2 *adjective* (**!** *never changes*)
  = salmon pink

salón *noun, masculine*
* (*in a hotel*) **un salón** = a reception room
* (*Spa*) **un salón** = a living room
* (*Mex*) **un salón** = a classroom
* **un salón de belleza** = a beauty salon

salpicadera *noun, feminine* (*Mex*)
▶ guardabarros

salpicar *verb* 2
  = to splash

salsa *noun, feminine*
* **una salsa** = a sauce
* **salsa** = gravy

saltamontes *noun, masculine* (**!** *does not change in the plural*)
  un saltamontes = a grasshopper

saltar *verb* 1
* = to jump
  saltó al suelo = he jumped onto the floor

saltarse

S

• (*if it's a line, page, etc*) = to skip, to miss
saltarse un stop/un semáforo = to go
through a stop sign/a red light

salto *noun, masculine*
un salto = a jump, a leap
(*of a bird, a kangaroo, etc*) = a hop
(*from a diving board*) = a dive
dar saltos = to jump, to leap
(*if it's a bird, kangaroo, etc*) = to hop
dar saltos de alegría = to jump for joy
se levantó de un salto de la silla/la cama =
he jumped up from his chair/out of bed

salud *noun, feminine*
la salud = health
estar bien de salud = to be in good health
¡salud! (*when drinking*) = cheers!
(*Lat Am: when someone sneezes*) = bless
you!

saludar *verb* [1]
= to greet
= to say hello to
lo/la saluda atentamente (*in letters*) = yours
faithfully

saludo
1 *noun, masculine*
un saludo = a greeting
2 saludos *noun, masculine plural*
saludos = regards

salvaje *adjective*
= wild

salvar *verb* [1]
= to save
salvarse
= to survive

salvavidas *noun, masculine* (**!** *does not
change in the plural*)
un salvavidas = a life jacket

salvo: a salvo *adverb*
estar a salvo = to be safe

San *adjective*
= Saint

sandalia *noun, feminine*
una sandalia = a sandal

sandía *noun, feminine*
una sandía = a watermelon

sangrar *verb* [1]
= to bleed

sangre *noun, feminine*
la sangre = blood
me salió *or* (*Spa*) **me hice sangre** = I bled

sano/sana *adjective*
= healthy
sano y salvo = safe and sound

santo/santa
1 *adjective*
= holy
Santo Tomás = Saint Thomas
2 *noun, masculine/feminine*
un santo/una santa = a saint
3 santo *noun, masculine*
mi santo = my saint's day

sapo *noun, masculine*
un sapo = a toad

sarampión *noun, masculine*
el sarampión = measles

sardina *noun, feminine*
una sardina = a sardine

sargento *noun, masculine/feminine*
un/una sargento = a sergeant

sartén *noun, feminine or* (*Lat Am*) *noun,
masculine/feminine*
una/un sartén = a frying pan

sastre *noun, masculine/feminine*
un/una sastre = a tailor

satisfacción *noun, feminine*
satisfacción = satisfaction

satisfecho/satisfecha *adjective*
• = satisfied
• = pleased

saxofón *noun, masculine*
un saxofón = a saxophone

se *pronoun*
• = himself/herself/itself
se quemó = he burnt himself
se lavó la cara = he/she washed his/her
face
• = themselves
se quemaron = they burnt themselves
se vistieron = they got dressed
• (*referring to you — polite form*)
= yourself/yourselves
no se culpe = don't blame yourself
¿se hicieron daño? = have you hurt
yourselves?
• (*when someone else does the action*)
se cortaron el pelo = they had their hair
cut
se va a operar = he's/she's going to have an
operation
• = each other
se ayudan mucho = they help each other a
lot
• (*impersonal use*)
se ve bien desde aquí = you can see well
from here
se está bien allí = it's nice there
• (*passive use*)
se dice que... = it is said that...
se vendió rápidamente = it was sold very
quickly

C Am Central America   **Lat Am** Latin America   **Mex** Mexico

• (*in instructions*)
se calienta la leche = heat the milk

> **!** *Note that* **se** *is used also in many pronominal verbs, such as* **irse, caerse, subirse, volverse,** *etc. Many of these verbs are reflexive in Spanish but not in English:* **se cayó** = he fell down. *See these verbs for meaning and use.*

• = him/her
= to him/her
se lo dije = I told her
• = them
= to them
se lo di a los dos = I gave it to both of them
> *See* **le, les** *for more information*

sé ▶ saber

secador *noun, masculine*
un secador (**de pelo**) = a hairdryer

secadora *noun, feminine*
• **una secadora** = a tumble dryer
• (*Mex*) **una secadora** = a hairdryer

secar *verb* [2]
= to dry
secarse
• = to dry up
• = to dry
se secó las lágrimas = he dried his tears

sección *noun, feminine*
• **una sección** = a section
• (*in a shop, company*) **una sección** = a department

seco/seca *adjective*
= dry
= dried

secretario/secretaria *noun, masculine/feminine*
• **un secretario/una secretaria** = a secretary
• (*Mex*) **un secretario/una secretaria** = a secretary of state, a minister

secreto *noun, masculine*
un secreto = a secret

secuestrar *verb* [1]
• = to kidnap
• = to hijack

sed *noun, feminine*
sed = thirst
tener sed = to be thirsty

seda *noun, feminine*
seda = silk

seguida: en seguida *adverb*
• = at once, straightaway

seguir *verb* [57]
• = to follow
seguir a alguien = to follow someone

• = to carry on, to continue
seguir adelante = to carry on
sigue trabajando en un colegio = he is still working at a school

según
1 *preposition*
• = according to
• = depending on
según cómo me sienta = depending on how I feel

> **!** *Note the use of the subjunctive after* **según como**

2 *adverb*
= it depends
¿vas a ir? — según = will you go? – it depends
3 *conjunction*
= as
según vayan terminando = as they finish

> **!** *Note the use of the subjunctive after* **según**

segundo/segunda
1 *number*
= second
> *See* **primero** *for examples*
2 segundo *noun, masculine*
• **un segundo** = a second
• **el segundo** = the main course

seguridad *noun, feminine*
• = safety
• = security
• = certainty
no lo sé con seguridad = I don't know for certain
• **seguridad en uno mismo** = self-confidence

seguro/segura
1 *adjective*
• = safe
• = secure
• = sure
¿es seguro que vienen? = are they coming for sure?
2 seguro *adverb*
las tiene él seguro = he's definitely got them
3 seguro *noun, masculine*
un seguro = an insurance

seis *number*
• = six
• (*in dates*) = sixth
> *See* **cinco** *for examples*

seiscientos/seiscientas *number*
= six hundred
> *See* **quinientos** *for examples*

selección *noun, feminine*
una selección = a selection
la selección (**nacional**) = the national team

sello *noun, masculine*
un sello = a stamp

S

selva noun, feminine
la selva = the jungle

semáforo noun, masculine
un semáforo = a set of traffic lights
pasarse or (Spa) saltarse un semáforo en rojo = to go through a red light

semana noun, feminine
una semana = a week
la semana pasada/que viene = last/next week
entre semana = during the week
la Semana Santa = Easter

semanal adjective
= weekly

sembrar verb [7]
• = to sow
• = to plant

semilla noun, feminine
una semilla = a seed

sencillo/sencilla
1 adjective
= simple
= straightforward
2 **sencillo** noun, masculine
• (Mex) sencillo = change
• (Mex, Spa) un sencillo = a one-way ticket, a single (ticket)
• (a record) un sencillo = a single

sensación noun, feminine
una sensación = a feeling

sensato/sensata adjective
= sensible

sensible adjective
= sensitive

sentado/sentada adjective
= seated
= sitting

sentar verb [7]
• = to sit
• = to suit
la chaqueta te sienta bien = the jacket suits you
• el café me sienta mal = coffee doesn't agree with me
sentarse
= to sit (down)

sentido noun, masculine
• un sentido = a sense
(of a word) = a meaning
• (of a road, someone moving) un sentido = a direction
una calle de sentido único = a one-way street
• estar sin sentido = to be unconscious
quedarse sin sentido = to lose consciousness

sentimiento noun, masculine
un sentimiento = a feeling

sentir verb [46]
• = to feel
sentir frío = to feel cold
siento alegría = I feel happy
• = to hear
sentí un ruido = I heard a noise
• siento lo que ha pasado = I am sorry about what has happened
lo siento mucho = I'm very sorry
sentirse
= to feel

seña
1 noun, feminine
una seña = a sign
les hice señas para que se callaran = I gestured to them to be quiet
2 **señas** noun, feminine plural
unas señas = an address

señal noun, feminine
una señal = a sign
= a mark
= a signal

señor/señora
1 noun, masculine|feminine
un señor/una señora = a gentleman/a lady
el Señor García = Mr García
la Señora de García = Mrs García
¡oiga, señora! = excuse me, (madam)!
2 **señora** noun, feminine
mi señora = my wife

señorita noun, feminine
una señorita = a young lady
la Señorita García = Miss or Ms García

sepa, sepan, etc ▶ saber

separado/separada adjective
• = separate
• = separated

separar verb [1]
• = to separate
• = to move away
separa la silla de la pared = move the chair away from the wall
separarse
= to get separated

septiembre noun, masculine
= September

séptimo/séptima number
= seventh
See **primero** for examples

sequía noun, feminine
una sequía = a drought

ser *verb* 36
* = to be
  es [flaco | muy amable | soltero …] = he's [thin | very kind | single …]
  ¿cómo son? = what are they like?
  = what do they look like?
  soy ingeniero = I'm an engineer
  era verano = it was summer
  ¿cuánto es? = how is that (altogether)?
  es de madera = it's wooden
  eso es = that's right
* (*passive use*)
  fue despedido = he was fired
* a no ser que = unless
* como/donde/cuando sea = however/wherever/whenever
  lo que sea = whatever
* o sea = so
  = that is
  o sea que no fuiste = so you didn't go
  toda mi familia, o sea, mis padres mi hermana y yo = all my family, that is my parents, my sister, and I

será, seré, sería, etc ▶ ser

serie *noun, feminine*
  una serie = a series

serio/seria *adjective*
  = serious
  en serio = seriously
  lo digo en serio = I'm serious, I mean it

serpiente *noun, feminine*
  una serpiente = a snake
  una serpiente (de) cascabel = a rattlesnake

servicio *noun, masculine*
* un servicio = a service
* los servicios = the restroom, the toilet(s)
* el servicio militar = military service

servilleta *noun, feminine*
  una servilleta = a napkin

servir *verb* 48
* = to serve
  servir la comida = to serve the food
* = to be used for
  sirve para sujetar los libros = it can be used to hold the books
  ¿para qué sirve? = what's it for?
  esto no sirve = this is no good
  no sirves para nada = you're useless
servirse
  (*if it's food*) = to help oneself (to)

sesenta *number*
  = sixty
  See cincuenta *for examples*

sesión *noun, feminine*
  una sesión = a session
  (*of a movie*) = a showing
  (*of a play*) = a performance

setecientos/setecientas *number*
  = seven hundred
  See quinientos *for examples*

setenta *number*
  = seventy
  See cincuenta *for examples*

sexo *noun, masculine*
  el sexo = the sex

sexto/sexta
1 *number*
  = sixth
  See primero *for examples*
2 sexto *noun, masculine*
  un sexto = a sixth

si *conjunction*
* = if
  si tu quieres = if you want
  si lo hubiese sabido… = if only I had known…

  ! Note the use of the subjunctive after si

* = whether
  no sé si comprarlo o no = I don't know whether to buy it or not

sí¹ *adverb*
  = yes
  ¿lo conoces? — sí = do you know him? — yes, I do
  él no ha estado pero yo sí = he's never been there but I have

sí² *personal pronoun*
* = himself/herself/itself
  sí (mismo)/sí (misma) = himself/herself
  sólo piensa en sí (mismo) = he only thinks of himself
* (*referring to you — polite form*)
  = yourself/yourselves
  léalo para sí/léanlo para sí = read it to youself/read it to yourselves
* entre sí = between themselves
  = among themselves

sida, SIDA *noun, masculine*
  el sida = AIDS

sidra *noun, feminine*
  la sidra = cider

siempre *adverb*
  = always
  como siempre = as usual
  lo de siempre = the usual thing
  desde siempre = always
  siempre que… = whenever…

sienta, siento, etc ▶ sentarse, sentir

sierra *noun, feminine*
* una sierra = a saw
* la sierra = the (range of) mountains
  la sierra de Guadarrama = the Guadarrama mountain range

S

siesta noun, feminine
  una siesta = a siesta, a nap
  echarse✶ or dormir la siesta = to have a
  nap

siete number
• = seven
• (in dates) = seventh
    See **cinco** for examples

siga, **sigan**, **etc** ▶ seguir

siglo noun, masculine
  un siglo = a century

significado noun, masculine
  el significado = the meaning

significar verb [2]
  = to mean

signo noun, masculine
  un signo = a sign
  un signo de admiración = an exclamation
    point, an exclamation mark
  un signo de interrogación = a question
    mark

sigo, **sigue** ▶ seguir

siguiente
1 adjective
  = following
  = next
2 noun, masculine|feminine
  el/la siguiente = the next one

siguió ▶ seguir

silbar verb [1]
• = to whistle
• = to boo

silbato noun, masculine
  un silbato = a whistle

silbido noun, masculine
  un silbido = a whistle

silencio noun, masculine
  el silencio = the silence
  ¡silencio! = quiet!

silla noun, feminine
  una silla = a chair
  una silla de ruedas = a wheelchair
  una silla de montar = a saddle

sillón noun, masculine
  un sillón = an armchair

símbolo noun, masculine
  un símbolo = a symbol

simpático/simpática adjective
• = nice
• = friendly

simple adjective
  = simple

sin preposition
  = without
  aún está sin terminar = it's not finished yet

sincero/sincera adjective
  = sincere

singular noun, masculine
  el singular = the singular

sino conjunction
  = but

sinónimo
1 adjective
  = synonymous
2 noun, masculine
  un sinónimo = a synonym

sintieron, **sintió** ▶ sentir

sinvergüenza noun, masculine|feminine
  un/una sinvergüenza = a scoundrel

sirena noun, feminine
• una sirena = a siren
• (in children's stories) una sirena = a
    mermaid

sistema noun, masculine
  un sistema = a system

sitio noun, masculine
• un sitio = a place
  en algún sitio = somewhere
  en ningún sitio = nowhere
  en cualquier sitio = anywhere
  en otro sitio = somewhere else
• (to sit) un sitio = a seat
• (space) sitio = room
  no hay sitio = there's no room
• (Mex) un sitio = a taxi stand, a taxi rank
• un sitio web = a website

situación noun, feminine
  una situación = a situation
  = a position

situado/situada adjective
  = situated

sobra
1 de sobra adjective|adverb
• = plenty of
  con dinero de sobra = with plenty of
    money
• = spare
  tengo una entrada de sobra = I have a
    spare ticket
• = very well
  lo sabes de sobra = you know very well
• estar de sobra:
  aquí estamos de sobra = we are not
    wanted/needed here
2 sobras noun, feminine plural
  sobras = leftovers

sobrar *verb* 1
- = to be left over
  sobró vino de la fiesta = there was wine left over from the party
  me sobran cinco mil pesos de ayer = I have five thousand pesos left from yesterday
- = to be too much/too many
  sobra dinero = there's too much money
  sobran dos entradas = there are two tickets too many
  me sobran dos cartas = I have two cards too many
  nos sobra tiempo = we have plenty of time
- **tú aquí sobras** = you're not wanted/needed here
- **y aún nos sobran diez dólares** = and we still have ten dollars to spare

sobre
1 *noun, masculine*
- **un sobre** = an envelope
- **un sobre de sopa** = a packet of soup
2 *preposition*
- = on
  está sobre la mesa = it's on the table
- = over
  el avión pasó sobre la ciudad = the plane flew over the city
- = about
  un libro sobre la guerra = a book about the war
- = above
  sobre el nivel del mar = above sea level
  sobre todo = above all

sobresaliente *noun, masculine* (*Spa*)
un sobresaliente = *an 8.5/a 9 out of 10*

sobrevivir *verb* 41
= to survive

sociedad *noun, feminine*
la sociedad = society
una sociedad anónima = a limited company

socio/socia *noun, masculine/feminine*
un socio/una socia = a member
(*in a company*) = a partner

socorro *noun, masculine*
socorro = help

sofá *noun, masculine*
un sofá = a sofa

sois ▶ ser

sol *noun, masculine*
- **el sol** = the sun
  al salir/al ponerse el sol = at da...
  hace sol = it's sunny
  tomar el sol = to sunbathe
- (*Peruvian currency*) **un sol** = a sol

solamente ▶ sólo

soldado *noun, masculine/feminine*
un/una soldado = a soldier

soleado/soleada *adjective*
= sunny

soler *verb* 22
- (*in the present*)
  suele llover = it usually rains
  suelen venir los lunes = they usually come on Mondays
- (*in the past*)
  solían salir juntos = they used to go out together

sólido/sólida *adjective*
- = solid
- = sound

solo/sola *adjective*
- = alone
  quedarse solo = to be left alone
  estar a solas = to be alone
- = lonely
- = by oneself
  lo hice sola = I did it by myself

sólo *adverb*
= only

soltar *verb* 6
- = to let go
  me soltó la mano = she let go of my hand
- = to let out
  suelta un poco de cuerda = let out a bit of rope
  soltó un grito = he let out a cry
- **soltar a un prisionero** = to release a prisoner
- **soltar una carcajada** = to burst out laughing
soltarse
- = to let go

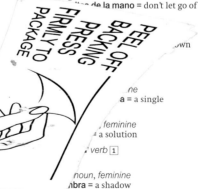

...te de la mano = don't let go of

...own

...ne
...a = a single

...feminine
... a solution

...*verb* 1

...noun, feminine
...bra = a shadow
- **la sombra** = the shade
- **sombra de ojos** = eyeshadow

sombrero *noun, masculine*
un **sombrero** = a hat
un **sombrero de copa** = a top hat

sombrilla *noun, feminine*
una **sombrilla** = a parasol
= a sunshade

somos, **son** ▶ ser

sonar *verb* [6]
• = to sound
suena bonito = it sounds nice
¿qué suena? = what's that noise
me suena ese nombre = that name sounds
    familiar to me
• (*if it's an alarm*) = to go off
(*if it's a telephone, bell*) = to ring
sonarse
sonarse la nariz = to blow one's nose

sonido *noun, masculine*
un **sonido** = a sound

sonreír *verb* [50]
= to smile

sonría, **sonríe**, **sonrió**, **etc** ▶ sonreír

sonrisa *noun, feminine*
una **sonrisa** = a smile

sopa *noun, feminine*
una **sopa** = a soup

soplar *verb* [1]
• = to blow
• = to blow out

sorbo *noun, masculine*
un **sorbo** = a sip

sordo/sorda
1 *adjective*
= deaf
2 *noun, masculine/feminine*
un **sordo**/una **sorda** = a deaf man/woman

sordomudo/sordomuda
1 *adjective*
= deaf and dumb
2 *noun, masculine/feminine*
un **sordomudo**/una **sordomuda** = a deaf-
    mute

sorprender *verb* [17]
• = to surprise
la sorprendí robando el dinero = I caught
    her stealing the money
• = to catch (unawares)
sorprenderse
= to be surprised

sorprendido/sorprendida *adjective*
= surprised

sorpresa *noun, feminine*
una **sorpresa** = a surprise

sospecha *noun, feminine*
una **sospecha** = a suspicion

sospechar *verb* [1]
= to suspect

sospechoso/sospechosa *adjective*
= suspicious

sostén *noun, masculine*
un **sostén** = a bra

sostener *verb* [37]
= to hold

soy ▶ ser

su *adjective*
• = his/her/its
• = their
• (*referring to you — polite form*)
= your

> **!** *Note that sometimes the only thing that*
> *will indicate whether* **su** *is translated by*
> *his, her, its, their or your is the context:*
> **¿es éste su coche?** = is this his/her car?
> = is this their car?
> = is this your car?

• (*impersonal use*)
cada uno tiene que traer su (propia) tienda
    = everyone has to bring their own tent

suave *adjective*
• = soft
• = smooth
• = gentle

subida *noun, feminine*
una **subida** = a rise

subir *verb* [41]
• = to go/come up
subir las escaleras = to go up the stairs
subir a un coche = to get into a car
• = to put up
el gobierno subió los precios = the
    government put up prices
• = to take/bring up
subí las cajas al piso de arriba = I took the
    boxes upstairs
sube el cuadro un poco más = put the
    picture a bit higher
• (*if it's the volume*) = to turn up
sube el radio = turn up the radio
• (*if it's a curtain, blind*) = to raise
• (*if it's the temperature*) = to rise
• (*if it's the tide*) = to come in
subirse
• = to climb
subirse a un árbol = to climb (up) a tree
• **subirse a un avión** = to get on a plane

subjuntivo *noun, masculine*
el **subjuntivo** = the subjunctive

submarino *noun, masculine*
un **submarino** = a submarine

subrayar *verb* [1]
= to underline

subte✱ *noun, masculine (R Pl)*
el subte = the subway, the underground

❗ *Note that* **subte** *is short for* **subterráneo**

subterráneo/subterránea
1 *adjective*
= underground
2 subterráneo *noun, masculine (R Pl)*
el subterráneo = the subway, the
underground

suburbio *noun, masculine*
• **un suburbio** = a suburb
• *(poor area)* = a slum

suceder *verb* ⒄
• *(if it's an event)* = to happen
• *(to the throne)* = to succeed

suceso *noun, masculine*
un suceso = an event
= an incident

suciedad *noun, feminine*
la suciedad = dirt

sucio/sucia *adjective*
= dirty

sucursal *noun, feminine*
una sucursal *(of a bank)* = a branch
(of a company) = an office

sudadera *noun, feminine*
una sudadera = a sweatshirt

sudar *verb* ⑴
= to sweat

sudeste *noun, masculine*
el sudeste = the south-east

sudoeste *noun, masculine*
el sudoeste = the south-west

sudor *noun, masculine*
sudor = sweat, perspiration

Suecia *noun, feminine*
Suecia = Sweden

sueco/sueca
1 *adjective*
= Swedish
2 *noun, masculine/feminine*
un sueco/una sueca = a Swede
3 sueco *noun, masculine*
el sueco *(the language)* = Swedish

suegro/suegra *noun,*
masculine/feminine
un suegro/una suegra = a father-in-law/
a mother-in-law
mis suegros = my parents-in-law

suela, suelas, etc ▶ soler

sueldo *noun, masculine*
un sueldo = a salary

suelo *noun, masculine*
el suelo = the floor

suelo ▶ soler

suelta, suelte, suelto, etc ▶ soltar

suelto/suelta
1 *adjective*
= loose
2 suelto *noun, masculine (Mex, Spa)*
suelto = small change

suena, suene, sueno, etc ▶ sonar

sueña, sueñe, sueño, etc ▶ soñar

sueño *noun, masculine*
un sueño = a dream
tener sueño = to be sleepy
darle sueño a alguien = to make someone
feel sleepy

suerte *noun, feminine*
= luck
dar buena/mala suerte = to bring good/bad
luck
una número de (la) suerte = a lucky
number
por suerte = fortunately
echar algo a suertes *(Spa)* = to toss for
something

suéter *noun, masculine*
un suéter = a sweater

suficiente
1 *adjective*
= enough
2 *noun, masculine (Spa)*
un suficiente = a pass

sufrir *verb* ⒀
• = to suffer
• **sufrir un accidente** = to have an accident
• **sufrir un cambio** = to undergo a change

sugerencia *noun, feminine*
una sugerencia = a suggestion

sugerir *verb* ⒁
= to suggest

sugiera, sugiero, sugirieron, etc
▶ sugerir

suicidarse *verb* ⑴
= to commit suicide

suicidio *noun, masculine*
un suicidio = a suicide

Suiza *noun, feminine*
Suiza = Switzerland

suizo/suiza
1 *adjective*
= Swiss
2 *noun, masculine/feminine*
un suizo/una suiza = a Swiss

S

sujeto/sujeta *adjective*
= secured
= fastened
tener sujeto a alguien = to have hold of
someone

suma *noun, feminine*
una suma = a sum

sumar *verb* ⟨1⟩
= to add (up)

supe, supiste, etc ▶ saber

superar *verb* ⟨1⟩
• to exceed
• (*if it's a difficulty*) = to overcome
(*if it's a trauma*) = to get over
• (*if it's a record*) = to beat

superior *adjective*
• = superior
• = top
• = upper

supermercado *noun, masculine*
un supermercado = a supermarket

superstición *noun, feminine*
una superstición = a superstition

supersticioso/supersticiosa
adjective
= superstitious

supervisar *verb* ⟨1⟩
= supervise

superviviente *noun, masculine/feminine*
un/una superviviente = a survivor

supondrá, supondré, supondría,
etc ▶ suponer

suponer *verb* ⟨32⟩
= to suppose
supongamos que... = let's suppose that...

suponga, supongo, etc ▶ suponer

suprimir *verb* ⟨41⟩
• = to supress
• = to delete

supuesto: por supuesto
= of course

supuse, supuso ▶ suponer

sur *noun, masculine*
el sur = the south
See **este** *for more examples*

sureste *noun, masculine*
▶ sudeste

suroeste *noun, masculine*
▶ sudoeste

suspender *verb* ⟨17⟩
• = to suspend
• (*Spa*) = to fail

suspense *noun, masculine* (*Spa*)
suspense = suspense
See also **película**

suspenso *noun, masculine*
• (*Lat Am*) **suspenso** = suspense
See also **película**
• (*Spa*) **un suspenso** = a fail

suspirar *verb* ⟨1⟩
= to sigh

suspiro *noun, masculine*
un suspiro = a sigh

sustancia *noun, feminine*
una sustancia = a substance

sustantivo *noun, masculine*
un sustantivo = a noun

sustituir *verb* ⟨51⟩
• = to replace
• = to stand in for
• = to substitute

sustituto/sustituta *noun,*
masculine/feminine
un sustituto/una sustituta = a replacement
(*temporary*) = a substitute
(*for a doctor*) = a covering doctor, a locum

susto *noun, masculine*
un susto = a fright

susurrar *verb* ⟨1⟩
= to whisper

sutil *adjective*
= subtle

suyo/suya *adjective, pronoun*
• **suyo/suya/suyos/suyas** = his/hers/its
el coche no es suyo = the car isn't his/hers
• **suyo/suya/suyos/suyas** = theirs
fueron con un amigo suyo = they went
with a friend of theirs
• (*referring to you — polite form*)
suyo/suya/suyos/suyas = yours
perdone, ¿es esto suyo? = excuse me, is
this yours?

! *Note that sometimes the only thing that
will indicate whether* **suyo/suya/suyos/**
suyas *is translated by* **his, hers, its, theirs**
or **yours** *is the context:*
usé las suyas = I used his/hers
= I used theirs
= I used yours

---

tabaco *noun, masculine*
 tabaco = tobacco
 (*Spa*) = cigarettes

tacaño/tacaña
 1 *adjective*
 = mean
 2 *noun, masculine/feminine*
 un tacaño/una tacaña = a skinflint

tachar *verb* 1
 = to cross out

taco *noun, masculine*
 • un taco = a taco
 • (*SC*) un taco = a heel
 • (*Spa*) un taco✗ = a swearword

tacón *noun, masculine*
 un tacón = a heel
 = a high heel
 zapatos de tacón = high-heeled shoes

tal
 1 *adjective*
 • = such (a)
  nunca dije tal cosa = I never said such a
  thing
  en tales circunstancias = in such
  circumstances
 • en tal caso = in that case
 • un tal García = someone called García
 2 *adverb*
 • ¿qué tal estás✗? = how are you?
  ¿que tal es la película✗? = what's the movie
  like?
 • tal vez = maybe
 • tales como... = such as...

talento *noun, masculine*
 talento = talent

talla *noun, feminine*
 una talla = a size

taller *noun, masculine*
 un taller = a workshop
 (*for cars*) = a garage, a repair shop

talón *noun, masculine*
 el talón = the heel

tamaño *noun, masculine*
 tamaño = size

también *adverb*
 = also, too, as well

tambor *noun, masculine*
 un tambor = a drum

tampoco *adverb*
 él tampoco lo sabe = he doesn't know it
 either
 él no va ni yo tampoco = he isn't going and
 neither am I

tan *adverb*
 • = so
  es tan inteligente = he's so clever
 • = such
  era un trabajo tan difícil = it was such a
  difficult job
  ¡qué paisaje tan bonito! = what a lovely
  landscape!
 • ¿qué tan ricos son? (*Lat Am*) = how rich
  are they?
 • tan [alto | rico | listo ...] como... = as [tall | rich |
  clever ...] as...

tanque *noun, masculine*
 un tanque = a tank

tanto/tanta
 1 *adjective*
  tanto/tanta = so much
  tantos/tantas = so many
  tanto vino = so much wine
  tantos coches = so many cars
  tanta cantidad = so much
  tanto tiempo = so long
  no hace tanto tiempo = it hasn't been so
  long
  tanto/tanta...como... = as much... as...
  tantos/tantas...como... = as many... as...
  tanto/tanta... que... = so much... that...
  tantos/tantas... que... = so many... that...
 2 *pronoun*
 • tanto/tanta = so much
  tantos/tantas = so many
  no necesitamos tanto/tantos = we don't
  need so much/so many
 • tanto = so long
  hace tanto que no los veo = I haven't seen
  them for so long
 • por lo tanto = therefore
 • entre tanto, mientras tanto = in the
  meantime
 3 *tanto adverb*
 • = so
  me alegro tanto = I'm so glad
 • = so much
  tanto como = as much as
 • = so long
  siempre tardas tanto = you always take so
  long
 • = so often
  no salen tanto = they don't go out so often
 • ¿qué tanto te gusta? (*Lat Am*) = how much
  do you like it?
 4 **tanto** *noun masculine*
 • un tanto (*in sports*) = a point
  (*in football*) = a goal
 • un tanto por ciento = a percentage

T

R Pl River Plate area   SC Southern Cone   Spa Spain

tapa
1 *noun, feminine*
una tapa (*of a jar, box*) = a lid
(*of a book*) = a cover
2 tapas *noun, feminine plural* (*Spa*)
tapas (*food*) = tapas

tapar *verb* 1
• = to cover
• = to put the lid/top on
• = to fill
tapar un agujero = to fill a hole
• = to block
estás tapando la luz = you are blocking the light
quítate, me estás tapando = move, you are in my way

tapete *noun, masculine* (*Mex*)
un tapete = a carpet

tapón *noun, masculine*
un tapón (*of a bottle*) = a cork
(*for the sink, bath, etc*) = a plug
(*Spa: of bottle*) = a top

taquilla *noun, feminine*
la taquilla = the ticket office
= the box office

tardar *verb* 1
• = to take
se tarda tres horas en llegar = it takes three hours to get there
¡cuánto tardan! = they are taking so long!
tardaron mucho tiempo = they took a long time
• = to be long
no tardo nada = I won't be long

tarde
1 *noun, feminine*
= afternoon
= evening
en la (*Spa*) **por la** or (*RPl*) **a la tarde** = in the afternoon
= in the evening
¡buenas tardes! = good afternoon/evening!
2 *adverb*
= late
llegar tarde = to be late
hacerse tarde = to get late
se me hace tarde, mejor me voy = it's getting late, I'd better go
tarde o temprano = sooner or later

tarea *noun, feminine*
• **una tarea** = a task
las tareas de la casa = the housework
• (*in school*) **la tarea** or (*Lat Am*) **las tareas** = homework

tarjeta *noun, feminine*
una tarjeta = a card

tarta *noun, feminine* (*Spa*)
una tarta = a cake

Tauro *noun, masculine*
Tauro = Taurus

tauro *noun, masculine/feminine*
un/una tauro = a Taurus, a Taurean

taxista *noun, masculine/feminine*
un/una taxista = a taxi driver

taza *noun, feminine*
una taza = a cup

te *pronoun*
• = you
= to you
te lo dije = I told you
te lo di ayer = I gave it to you yesterday
¿te lavaste la cara? = did you wash your face?
ponte el abrigo = put your coat on
• (*when someone else does the action*)
tienes que cortarte el pelo = you have to have your hair cut
• = yourself
cuídate = look after yourself
muévete = move

té *noun, masculine*
té = tea

teatro *noun, masculine*
el teatro = the theater, the theatre

tebeo *noun, masculine* (*Spa*)
un tebeo = a comic

techo *noun, masculine*
el techo = the ceiling
(*Lat Am: of a house*) = the roof

tecla *noun, feminine*
una tecla = a key

técnico/técnica
1 *adjective*
= technical
2 *noun, masculine/feminine*
un técnico/una técnica = a technician

tecnología *noun, feminine*
la tecnología = technology

tejado *noun, masculine*
el tejado = the roof

tejer *verb* 17
• = to weave
• = to knit

tela *noun, feminine*
tela = material, fabric, cloth
una tela = a piece of material

telaraña *noun, feminine*
una telaraña = a spider's web
= a cobweb

tele✖ *noun, feminine*
la tele = the TV, the telly

> **!** *Note that* **tele** *is short for* televisión
> *See* **televisión** *for more examples*

---

telediario *noun, masculine (Spa)*
el telediario = the news

telefonear *verb* 1
= to phone, to telephone, to call

teléfono *noun, masculine*
• un teléfono = a telephone
• un teléfono = a phone number
• un teléfono móvil = a mobile phone

telegrama *noun, masculine*
un telegrama = a telegram

telenovela *noun, feminine*
una telenovela = a soap opera

telescopio *noun, masculine*
un telescopio = a telescope

televisión *noun, feminine*
• la televisión = the television
ver (la) televisión = to watch television
• una televisión = a television (set)

televisor *noun, masculine*
un televisor = a television (set)

tema *noun, masculine*
un tema = a subject, a topic
(*in music*) = a theme

temblar *verb* 7
• = to tremble
• = to shake
• (*with cold*) = to shiver
• (*if it's the ground, a building*) = to shake
• ¡está temblando! (*Lat Am*) = it's an
earthquake!

temer *verb* 17
• = to fear
• = to be afraid of
no temas = don't be afraid
temerse
= to be afraid
me temo que no es posible = I'm afraid
that's not possible

temperatura *noun, feminine*
la temperatura = the temperature

temprano *adverb*
= early

tender *verb* 21
• = to hang out
tender la ropa = to hang the washing out
• tender la cama (*Lat Am*) = to make the bed
• tiende a enojarse = he tends to get
annoyed
tenderse
= to lie down

tenedor *noun, masculine*
un tenedor = a fork

tendrá, tendré, tendría, etc ▶ tener

tener *verb* 37
• = to have
tuvimos una pelea = we had a fight
tengo la gripe = I have the flu

tiene el pelo corto = she has long hair
• = to be
tengo cuarenta años = I'm forty years old
tiene dos metros de alto = it is two meters
tall
tener paciencia/cuidado = to be
patient/careful
tener [hambre | calor ...] = to be [hungry |
hot ...]
tener celos de alguien = to be jealous of
someone
• = to feel
tener sueño = to feel sleepy
• tener que hacer algo = to have to do
something
tienes que estudiar más = you must study
more
tendría que preguntárselo a mi madre = I
would have to ask my mother
• tener + *past participle*:
lo tengo terminado = I've already finished
it
nos tiene preocupados = we are worried
about him

tenga, tengo, etc ▶ tener

tenis *noun, masculine*
el tenis = tennis
tenis de mesa = table tennis

tenista *noun, masculine/feminine*
un/una tenista = a tennis player

tensión *noun, feminine*
• tensión = tension
• tensión = voltage
• (*Spa*) la tensión = blood pressure

teñir *verb* 65
= to dye
teñirse
= to dye one's hair

tercer *adjective*
▶ tercero/tercera

tercero/tercera *number*

> **!** *Note that* tercero *becomes* tercer
> *before masculine singular nouns*

= third
See primero *for examples*

terminar *verb* 1
• = to finish
terminar de hacer algo = to finish doing
something
• = to end up
vas a terminar en la cárcel = you're going
to end up in jail
terminó aceptándolo = he accepted it in
the end
terminó disculpándose = he ended up
apologizing
• termina en punta = it is pointed

terminarse
* = to be over
  se nos terminó el pan = we ran out of bread

termómetro *noun, masculine*
  un termómetro = a thermometer
  ponerle el termómetro a alguien = to take someone's temperature

ternero/ternera
1 *noun, masculine/feminine*
  un ternero/una ternera = a calf
2 ternera *noun, feminine*
  ternera = veal .

terraza *noun, feminine*
* una terraza = a balcony
* una terraza = a roof terrace
* una terraza = *an area with tables outside a bar or café where people can sit*

terremoto *noun, masculine*
  un terremoto = an earthquake

terrible *adjective*
  = terrible

terreno *noun, masculine*
  terreno = land
  un terreno = a piece of land

territorio *noun, masculine*
  territorio = territory

terror *noun, masculine*
  terror = terror

terrorismo *noun, masculine*
  el terrorismo = terrorism

tesoro *noun, masculine*
  un tesoro = a treasure

tetera *noun, feminine*
  una tetera = a teapot
  (*Lat Am*) = a kettle

texto *noun, masculine*
  un texto = a text
  = a text message

ti *personal pronoun*
* = you
  es para ti = it's for you
  no me apetece, ¿y a ti? = I don't feel like it, do you?
* ti (mismo)/ti (misma) = yourself
  sólo piensas en ti (mismo) = you only think of yourself

tiburón *noun, masculine*
  un tiburón = a shark

tiembla, tiemblo, etc ▶ temblar

tiempo
1 *noun, masculine*
* tiempo = time

¡cuánto tiempo sin verte! = I haven't seen you for ages!
  a tiempo = on time
  al mismo tiempo = at the same time
  al poco tiempo = shortly afterwards
  por un tiempo = for a while
  hace mucho tiempo que no los veo = I haven't seen them for a long time
  ¿cuánto tiempo hace que lo conoces? = how long have you known him for?
* (*in grammar*) el tiempo = the tense
* tiempo = weather
  hace buen tiempo = the weather is nice
* el primer tiempo (*in sports*) = the first half
2 tiempos *noun, masculine plural*
  en mis tiempos = in my time
  en aquellos tiempos = in those days

tienda, tiendo, etc ▶ tender

tienda *noun, feminine*
* una tienda = a store, a shop
* una tienda de campaña = a tent

tierra *noun, feminine*
  tierra = land
  = earth, soil
  = ground
  tomar tierra = to land
  la Tierra = the Earth

tigre/tigresa *noun, masculine/feminine*
  un tigre/una tigresa = a tiger/a tigress

tijera *noun, feminine*
  una(s) tijera(s) = a pair of scissors
  dame las tijeras = pass me the scissors

timbre *noun, masculine*
* un timbre = a bell
* (*Mex*) un timbre = a stamp

tímido/tímida *adjective*
  = shy

tinta *noun, feminine*
  tinta = ink

tinto
1 *adjective*
  = red
2 *noun, masculine*
  el tinto = red wine

tintorería *noun, feminine*
  una tintorería = a dry cleaner's

tiña, tiñeron, tiño, tiñó, etc ▶ teñir

tío/tía *noun, masculine/feminine*
  un tío/una tía = an uncle/an aunt
  mis tíos = my aunt and uncle

tiovivo *noun, masculine* (*Spa*)
  un tiovivo = a merry-go-round

típico/típica *adjective*
* = typical
* = traditional

---

tipo noun, masculine
* **tipo** = kind, sort
  = type
* **el tipo** = the body, the figure

tirar verb [1]
* = to throw
* = to throw away
* = to knock over
  tirar una puerta abajo = to knock a door down
* **tirar de la cuerda** = to pull the rope
* **verde tirando a azul** = bluish green
tirarse
  = to throw oneself
  tirarse al agua = to jump into the water
  tirarse de cabeza = to dive in head first

tirita noun, feminine (Spa)
  una tirita = a Band-Aid , a sticking plaster

tiro noun, masculine
  un tiro = a shot
  le dispararon or **le pegaron un tiro** = they shot him

títere
1 noun, masculine
  un títere = a puppet
2 títeres noun, masculine plural
  unos títeres = a puppet show

título noun, masculine
* **un título** = a title
* (of chapter) **un título** = a heading
* (in education) **un título** = a degree

tiza noun, feminine
  tiza = chalk
  una tiza = a (piece of) chalk

tlapalería noun, feminine (Mex)
  una tlapalería = a hardware store

toalla noun, feminine
  una toalla = a towel

tobillo noun, masculine
  un tobillo = an ankle

tobogán noun, masculine
  un tobogán = a slide

tocadiscos noun, masculine
  un tocadiscos = a record player

tocar verb [2]
* = to touch
  me tocó la mano = he touched my hand
* (at the door) = to knock
* **tocar un disco/un instrumento** = to play a record/an instrument
* **tocar el timbre** = to ring the bell
* = to blow
  tocar una bocina = to blow a horn
* **les tocó la lotería** = they won the lottery
* **te toca fregar los platos/jugar** = it's your turn to do the dishes/to play

tocarse
  = to touch
  tocarse la nariz = to touch one's nose

tocino noun, masculine
* **tocino** = pork fat
* (Lat Am) **tocino** = bacon

todavía adverb
* = yet
* = still
* = even
  todavía mejor = even better

todo/toda
1 adjective
* = all
  todo mi dinero = all my money
* = whole
  toda la semana = the whole week
2 pronoun
* = everything
  yo pago por todo = I'll pay for everything
* = all
  ¿han llegado ya todos? = are they all there?
* **ante todo** = above all
* **un poco de todo** = a bit of everything
* **sobre todo** = especially
  = above all
* **todo lo que quieras** = as much as you like
  = for as long as you like
3 todo adverb
  = all
  = completely

tomar verb [1]
* = to take
  me tomó del brazo = she took me by the arm
  tomar el tren = to take the train
* (when handing something to someone)
  toma, tus llaves = here are your keys
* (Spa) = to have
  ¿qué quieres tomar? = what are you going to have?
* (Lat Am) = to drink
tomarse
* = to take
  tomarse unas vacaciones = to take a vacation
* **tomarse una foto** (Lat Am) = to have one's picture taken

tomate noun, masculine
  un tomate = a tomato

tonelada noun, feminine
  una tonelada = a ton

tono noun, masculine
* **tono** = tone
* **un tono** = a shade

tontería noun, feminine
  eso es una tontería = that's silly

T

tonto/tonta
1 *adjective*
= silly
2 *noun, masculine/feminine*
un tonto/una tonta = a fool
hacer el tonto (*Spa*) = to play the fool

torcer *verb* 23
• = to twist
me torció el brazo = he twisted my arm
• = to turn
tuerce a la derecha = turn to the right
torcerse
= to twist
= to sprain

torcido/torcida *adjective*
• = crooked
• = twisted
• = bent
• = sprained
tengo el tobillo torcido = I've twisted my ankle

torero/torera *noun, masculine/feminine*
un torero/una torera = a bullfighter

tormenta *noun, feminine*
una tormenta = a storm

tornillo *noun, masculine*
un tornillo = a screw

toro
1 *noun, masculine*
un toro = a bull
2 toros *noun, masculine plural*
los toros = bullfighting

toronja *noun, feminine* (*Lat Am*)
una toronja = a grapefruit

torpe *adjective*
= clumsy

torre *noun, feminine*
• una torre = a tower
= an apartment block, a tower block
• (*in chess*) una torre = a rook, a castle

torta *noun, feminine*
• una torta (*Lat Am*) = a pie
(*Mex*) = a sandwich
(*SC*) = a cake

tortilla *noun, feminine*
una tortilla = a tortilla
= an omelet, an omelette
una tortilla de papas (*Lat Am*) *or* (*Spa*) de patatas = a Spanish omelet, a Spanish omelette

tortuga *noun, feminine*
una tortuga = a tortoise
= a turtle

torturar *verb* 1
= to torture

tos *noun, feminine*
tos = cough
me dio (la) tos = I started coughing

toser *verb* 17
= to cough

tostada *noun, feminine*
• una tostada = a piece of toast
tostadas = toast
• (*Mex*) una tostada = a fried corn tortilla

tostador *noun, masculine*, **tostadora** *noun, feminine*
un tostador, una tostadora = a toaster

tostar *verb* 6
• = to toast
• = to roast

total
1 *adjective*
= total
2 *noun, masculine*
el total = the total
en total = altogether

trabajador/trabajadora
1 *adjective*
= hard-working
2 *noun, masculine/feminine*
un trabajador/una trabajadora = a worker

trabajar *verb* 1
= to work

trabajo *noun, masculine*
• el trabajo = work
estar sin trabajo = to be out of work
el trabajo de la casa = the housework
• un trabajo = a job
• (*in school*) un trabajo = a project
= an essay

tractor *noun, masculine*
un tractor = a tractor

tradición *noun, feminine*
la tradición = tradition

tradicional *adjective*
= traditional

traducción *noun, feminine*
una traducción = a translation

traducir *verb* 43
= to translate

traductor/traductora *noun, masculine/feminine*
un traductor/una traductora = a translator

traduje, traduzca, traduzco, etc
▶ traducir

traer *verb* 33
= to bring
me trajo a casa = he brought me home

tráfico noun, masculine
el tráfico = the traffic

tragar verb [3]
= to swallow
tragarse
= to swallow

tragedia noun, feminine
una tragedia = a tragedy

trágico/trágica adjective
= tragic

traiga, traigo, traje, etc ▶ traer

traje noun, masculine
un traje = a suit
(in the theater) = a costume
un traje de baño = a pair of swimming
trunks
= a swimsuit

trampa noun, feminine
una trampa = a trap
hacer trampa(s) = to cheat

trampolín noun, masculine
un trampolín = a springboard
= a diving board

tranquilo/tranquila adjective
= quiet
= calm

transformar verb [1]
= to transform
transformarse
= to be transformed

transparente adjective
= transparent

transporte noun, masculine
el transporte = transportation, transport

tranvía noun, masculine
un tranvía = a streetcar, a tram

trapo noun, masculine
un trapo = a cloth
un trapo del polvo = a dust cloth, a duster

tras preposition
• = after
• = behind

trasero/trasera adjective
= back
= rear

trasnochar verb [1]
= to stay up late
= to stay up all night

tratar verb [1]
• = to treat
tratar algo con cuidado = to be careful
with something
• to try
tratar de hacer algo = to try to do
something

tratarse
tratarse de algo = to be about something

través: a través de preposition
• = through
• = across

travieso/traviesa adjective
= naughty

trece number
• = thirteen
• (in dates) = thirteenth
See **quince** for examples

treinta number
• = thirty
• (in dates) = thirtieth
See **cinco** and **cincuenta** for examples

tren noun, masculine
un tren = a train

trenza noun, feminine
una trenza = a braid, a plait

trepar verb [1]
= to climb (up)

tres number
• = three
• (in dates)
= third
See **cinco** for examples

trescientos/trescientas number
= three hundred
See **quinientos** for examples

triángulo noun, masculine
un triángulo = a triangle

trigo noun, masculine
el trigo = wheat

trillizos/trillizas noun,
masculine/feminine plural
trillizos/trillizas = triplets

trimestre noun, masculine
un trimestre = a quarter
(in education) = a term

triple
1 adjective
= triple
2 noun, masculine
es el triple de caro = it's three times more
expensive

tripulación noun, feminine
la tripulación = the crew

triste adjective
= sad
= gloomy

tristeza noun, feminine
tristeza = sadness

T

triunfo noun, masculine
  un triunfo = a triumph

trofeo noun, masculine
  un trofeo = a trophy

trombón noun, masculine
  un trombón = a trombone

trompeta noun, feminine
  una trompeta = a trumpet

tronco noun, masculine
  un tronco = a trunk
  = a log

trono noun, masculine
  el trono = the throne

tropezar verb 5
  = to trip
  tropezar con algo = to trip over something
tropezarse
  = to trip
  tropezarse con algo = to trip over
    something

trópico noun, masculine
  el trópico = the tropics

tropiece, tropiezo, etc ▶ tropezar

trozo noun, masculine
  un trozo = a piece

trucha noun, feminine
  una trucha = a trout

truco noun, masculine
  un truco = a trick

trueno noun, masculine
  un trueno = a clap of thunder
  truenos = thunder

tu adjective
  = your

tú pronoun
  = you
  tú (mismo)/tú (misma) = yourself

tubo noun, masculine
  un tubo = a tube

tuerza, tuerzo ▶ torcer

tuesta, tueste, tuesto, etc ▶ tostar

tumba noun, feminine
  una tumba = a grave
  = a tomb

tumbar verb 1
  = to knock down
tumbarse
  = to lie down

turismo noun, masculine
  el turismo = tourism
  hacer turismo = to travel
  = to go sightseeing
  = to tour

turista noun, masculine/feminine
  un/una turista = a tourist

turno noun, masculine
  un turno = a turn
  (at work) = a shift

turrón noun, masculine
  turrón = type of nougat eaten at Christmas

tutear verb 1
  = to address someone using the familiar **tú** form
tutearse
  = to address each other using the familiar **tú**
    form

tutor/tutora noun, masculine/feminine
  un tutor/una tutora = a course tutor, a class
    teacher
  (at university) = a tutor

tuvo, tuvieron, tuviste, etc ▶ tener

tuyo/tuya
1 adjective
  tuyo/tuya/tuyos/tuyas = yours
  eso es un problema tuyo = that's your
    problem
  un amigo tuyo = a friend of yours
2 pronoun
  el tuyo/la tuya/los tuyos/las tuyas = yours

Uu

u conjunction

  ! Note that u is used instead of o before
  o- or ho-
  = or
  diez u once = ten or eleven

último/última
1 adjective
  = last
  = latest
  (in a pile) = top
2 noun, masculine/feminine
  el último/la última = the last one
  (in a pile) = the top one
3 último adverb (SC)
  = last

últimamente adverb
  = recently, lately

un/una article
  un/una = a, an
  unos/unas = some, a few
  una mesa = a table
  compró unos vasos = he bought some
    glasses
  unos días = a few days

unos/unas (*to express approximate number*) = about
unas tres horas = about three hours
   See also **uno/una**

único/única
1 *adjective*
= only
es hijo único = he's an only child
= unique
2 *noun, masculine|feminine*
el único/la única = the only one

unidad *noun, feminine*
una unidad = a unit

unido/unida *adjective*
= close
= united

uniforme
1 *adjective*
= uniform
2 *noun, masculine*
un uniforme = a uniform

Unión Europea *noun, feminine*
la Unión Europea = the European Union

unir *verb* 41
= to join
unirse
= to join together

universidad *noun, feminine*
una universidad = a university

uno/una
1 *adjective, pronoun*

> **!** *Note that* **uno** *becomes* **un** *before masculine singular nouns*

= one
tienen un solo hijo = they only have one son
uno en uno = one by one
unos/unas
= some
unos lo sabían y otros no = some knew and some didn't
= about
unos dos kilos = about two kilos
2 uno *number*
el uno = (number) one
(*Spa: in dates*) = first
   See **cinco** for more examples

uña *noun, feminine*
una uña = a nail

urgencia
1 *noun, feminine*
una urgencia = an emergency
2 urgencias *noun, feminine plural*
urgencias = accident and emergency

urgente *adjective*
= urgent

usado/usada *adjective*
= worn
= secondhand

usar *verb* 1
= to use
= to wear

uso *noun, masculine*
uso = use

usted *pronoun*

> **!** *Note that this is the polite singular form of address, but in Colombia and Chile it is also used instead of the familiar form of address* **tú**

= you
usted (mismo)/usted (misma) = yourself

ustedes *plural pronoun*

> **!** *Note that this is both the polite and the familiar plural form of address, except in Spain where the familiar form of address is* **vosotros**

= you
ustedes (mismos)/ustedes (mismas) = yourselves

utensilio *noun, masculine*
un utensilio = a utensil
= a tool

útil *adjective*
= useful

uva *noun, feminine*
una uva = a grape

Vv

vaca *noun, feminine*
una vaca = a cow

vacaciones *noun, feminine plural*
unas vacaciones = a vacation, a holiday
las vacaciones de verano = the summer vacation, the summer holidays

vacío/vacía *adjective*
= empty

vagón *noun, masculine*
un vagón = a coach, a car, a carriage

vainilla *noun, feminine*
vainilla = vanilla

valdrá, valdré, valdría, etc ▶ valer

valer *verb* 38
= to be worth
= to cost

valga, **valgo**, **etc** ▶ valer

válido/**válida** *adjective*
= valid

valiente *adjective*
= brave

valle *noun, masculine*
un valle = a valley

valor *noun, masculine*
valor = courage
valor = value

vanidoso/**vanidosa** *adjective*
= vain

vano/**vana** *adjective*
= vain
en vano = in vain

vapor *noun, masculine*
vapor = steam

vaquero
1 *noun, masculine*
un vaquero = a cowboy
2 vaqueros *noun, masculine plural*
unos vaqueros = a pair of jeans

variedad *noun, feminine*
variedad = variety

varón
1 *noun, masculine*
un varón = a man, a male
tuvieron un varón = they had a boy
2 *adjective*
= male

vasco/**vasca**
1 *adjective*
= Basque
2 *noun, masculine/feminine*
un vasco/una vasca = a Basque
3 vasco *noun, masculine*
el vasco (*the language*) = Basque

vaso *noun, masculine*
un vaso = a glass

vecino/**vecina**
1 *adjective*
= neighboring, neighbouring
2 *noun, masculine/feminine*
un vecino/una vecina = a neighbor, a neighbour

vegetariano/**vegetariana**
1 *adjective*
= vegetarian
2 *noun, masculine/feminine*
un vegetariano/una vegetariana = a vegetarian

vehículo *noun, masculine*
un vehículo = a vehicle

veía, **veían**, **etc** ▶ ver

veinte *number*
= twenty

(*in dates*) = the twentieth
See **cinco** and **cincuenta** for examples

vela *noun, feminine*
una vela = a candle
(*on a ship*) una vela = a sail

velocidad *noun, feminine*
velocidad = speed

vena *noun, feminine*
una vena = a vein

vencer *verb* 18
= to beat
= to overcome

venda *noun, feminine*
una venda = a bandage

vendedor/**vendedora** *noun, feminine*
un vendedor/una vendedora = a stallholder
= a salesclerk, a shop assistant
= a salesman/saleswoman

vender *verb* 17
= to sell
'se vende' = 'for sale'

vendrá, **vendré**, **vendría**, **etc**
▶ venir

veneno *noun, masculine*
un veneno = a poison

venenoso/**venenosa** *adjective*
= poisonous

venga, **vengo**, **etc** ▶ venir

venir *verb* 58
= to come
venir por *or* (*Spa*) a por alguien = to come to pick someone up
venir por *or* (*Spa*) a por algo = to come to pick up something
= to come back
no vengas tarde = don't come back late
[la semana | el mes | el año ...] que viene = next [week | month | year ...]

venta *noun, feminine*
una venta = a sale
estar en venta = to be for sale

ventaja *noun, feminine*
una ventaja = an advantage

ventana *noun, feminine*
una ventana = a window

ventanilla *noun, feminine*
(*of a vehicle*) una ventanilla = a window
(*at a theater, cinema, etc*) la ventanilla = the box office

ventilador *noun, masculine*
un ventilador = a fan

C Am Central America   Lat Am Latin America   Mex Mexico

ver *verb* **39**
= to see
no lo veo = I can't see it
= to watch
ver (la) televisión = to watch television
a ver:
a ver, ¿cuál es el problema? = okay, what's
　the problem?
¿a ver? = let's see
verse
= to meet (up)
= to see each other

verano *noun, masculine*
el verano = the summer

verbo *noun, masculine*
un verbo = a verb

verdad *noun, feminine*
la verdad = the truth
ser verdad = to be true
éste es mejor ¿verdad? = this one is better,
　isn't it?
tú lo sabes ¿verdad? = you know it, don't
　you?
de verdad = really
= real
¿de verdad que la viste? = did you really
　see her?
de verdad que lo siento = I am really sorry
una pistola de verdad = a real gun

verdura *noun, feminine*
una verdura = a vegetable

verde
1 *adjective*
= green
2 *noun, masculine*
el verde = green

vereda *noun, feminine* (*SC*)
la vereda = the sidewalk, the pavement

vergüenza *noun, feminine*
vergüenza = embarrassment
me da vergüenza pedírselo = I'm
　embarrassed to ask her
vergüenza = shame
no tienes vergüenza = you have no shame

verso *noun, masculine*
un verso = a verse

vestíbulo *noun, masculine*
un vestíbulo = a hall
= a lobby
= a foyer

vestido/vestida
1 *adjective*
= dressed
siempre va bien vestido = he is always well
　dressed
iba vestida de verde = she was wearing
　green
2 vestido *noun, masculine*
un vestido = a dress

vestir *verb* **48**
= to dress
vestirse
= to dress, to get dressed

veterinario/veterinaria *noun,*
masculine/feminine
un veterinario/una veterinaria = a
　veterinarian, a veterinary surgeon

vez *noun, feminine*
una vez más = one more time
dos veces = twice
tres veces al mes = three times a month
lo vi una vez = I saw it once
a la vez = at the same time
a veces = sometimes
de vez en cuando = from time to time,
　now and again
érase una vez = once upon a time

vía *noun, feminine*
la vía = the track
la vía férrea = the railroad track, the
　railway track

viaje *noun, masculine*
un viaje = a journey, a trip
están de viaje = they are away

viajero/viajera *noun,*
masculine/feminine
un viajero/una viajera = a traveler, a
　traveller
= a passenger

víctima *noun, feminine*
una víctima = a victim

victoria *noun, feminine*
una victoria = a victory
(*in sports*) = a win

vida *noun, feminine*
la vida = life

video *or* (*Spa*) **vídeo**, *noun, masculine*
un video, un vídeo = a video
= a video cassette recorder
= a videotape, a videocassette

videocámara *noun, feminine*
una videocámara = a video camera

videoclub *noun, masculine*
un videoclub = a video library

videojuego *noun, masculine*
un videojuego = a video game

vidrio *noun, masculine*
vidrio = glass
(*Lat Am*) **un vidrio** = a window pane
limpiar los vidrios = to clean the windows

viejo/vieja
1 *adjective*
= old
2 *noun, masculine/feminine*
un viejo/una vieja = an old man/an old
　woman

V

R Pl River Plate area　**SC** Southern Cone　**Spa** Spain

viento *noun, masculine*
  el viento = the wind

viernes *noun, masculine* (**!** *does not change in the plural*)
  el viernes = Friday
  Viernes Santo =Good Friday
  See **miércoles** *for more examples*

villancico *noun, masculine*
  un villancico = a carol

vinagre *noun, masculine*
  el vinagre = vinegar

vine, viniste, vino, etc ▶ venir

vino *noun, masculine*
  el vino = wine

violencia *noun, feminine*
  la violencia = violence

violento/violenta *adjective*
  = violent

violín *noun, masculine*
  un violín = a violin

Virgo *noun, masculine*
  Virgo = Virgo

virgo *noun, masculine/feminine*
  un/una virgo = a Virgo, a Virgoan

visa *noun, feminine or* (*Spa*) **visado** *noun, masculine*
  una visa, un visado = a visa

visita *noun, feminine*
  una visita = a visit
  = a visitor

visitar *verb* 1
  = to visit

víspera *noun, feminine*
  la víspera = the day before
  la víspera del accidente = the day before
    the accident

vista *noun, feminine*
  la vista = sight, eyesight
  ¡hasta la vista! = see you!
  una vista = a view

vistieron, vistió, etc ▶ vestir

visto *past participle* ▶ ver

vitamina *noun, feminine*
  una vitamina = a vitamin

viudo/viuda *noun, masculine/feminine*
  un viudo/una viuda = a widower/a widow

vivir *verb* 41
  = to live
  = to be alive

vivo/viva *adjective*
  = alive
  un concierto en vivo = a live concert

vocabulario *noun, masculine*
  el vocabulario = the vocabulary

volante *noun, masculine*
  un volante = a steering wheel

volar *verb* 6
  = to fly

volcán *noun, masculine*
  un volcán = a volcano

vóleibol, voleibol *noun, masculine*
  el vóleibol = volleyball

voltear *verb* 1 (*Lat Am*)
  = to turn over
  = to turn inside out
voltearse
  = to turn around

voltereta *noun, feminine*
  una voltereta = a somersault

volumen *noun, masculine*
  el volumen = the volume

voluntad *noun, feminine*
  la voluntad = the will
  fuerza de voluntad = willpower

voluntario/voluntaria
  1 *adjective*
  = voluntary
  2 *noun, masculine/feminine*
  un voluntario/una voluntaria = a volunteer

volver *verb* 24
  = to go/come back
  volví a mi país = I went back to my country
  = to be back
  volveré a las cinco = I'll be back at five
  volver a hacer algo = to do something
    again
volverse
  = to turn around
  = to become
  se ha vuelto muy presumido = he's become
    very vain

vosotros/vosotras *personal pronoun* (*Spa*)
  = you
  vosotros mismos/vosotras mismas =
    yourselves

votar *verb* 1
  = to vote

voto *noun, masculine*
  un voto = a vote

voz *noun, feminine*
  una voz = a voice
  en voz alta/baja = in a loud/quiet voice

vuelo *noun, masculine*
  un vuelo = a flight

vuelta *noun, feminine*
  una vuelta = a turn
  dale otra vuelta = give it another turn
  dar una vuelta = to go for a walk/drive
  la vuelta = the return
  a la vuelta = on the way back

---

dar (la) vuelta a algo:
dar (la) vuelta a la esquina = to turn the corner
dar (la) vuelta a la página = to turn the page
dar (la) vuelta al colchón = to turn the mattress over
dar (la) vuelta a un vaso = to turn a glass upside down/the right way up
dar vuelta a la llave = to turn the key
dar vueltas alrededor de algo = to go around something
dar la vuelta al mundo = to go around the world

vuelva, **vuelvo**, **etc** ▶ volver

vuestro/**vuestra** (*Spa*)
1 *adjective*
vuestro/**vuestra**/**vuestros**/**vuestras** = your
2 *pronoun*
el vuestro/**la vuestra**/**los vuestros**/**las vuestras** = yours
See **tuyo** for more examples

wáter *noun, masculine*
el wáter = the toilet

Web *noun, masculine*
el Web = the Web

xilófono *noun, masculine*
un xilófono = a xylophone

Yy

y *conjunction*
= and
Pepe y Laura = Pepe and Laura
son las seis y veinte = it's twenty after six, it's twenty past six

a las diez y media = at ten thirty
cincuenta y cinco = fifty-five

ya
1 *adverb*
• = already
ya lo he hecho = I've done it already
• = now
ha estado enfermo pero ya está mejor = he's been ill but he's better now
• ¡**ya voy!** = I'm coming!
¡**ya casi está!** = it's almost ready
• (*referring to the future*)
ya veremos = we'll see
ya lo terminarás = you'll get it finished
• (*in negative sentences*)
= any more, any longer
ya no está enfadada = she's not angry any more
• (*in interrogative sentences*) = yet
¿**ya se decidió?** = has he decided yet?
• (*to emphasize*)
¡**ya lo sé!** = I know!
¡**ya lo creo!** = you bet!
• (*to show that you understand*)
esto va aquí — ya = this goes here – right *or* I see
• **ya que** = since
2 *exclamation*
¡**ya!** (*ironic*) = of course

yate *noun, masculine*
un yate = a yacht

yema *noun, feminine*
• **una yema** = a yolk
• **una yema** = a fingertip

yerno *noun, masculine*
un yerno = a son-in-law

yo *pronoun*
• = I
yo que tú = if I were you
• = me
soy yo = it's me
yo (mismo)/**yo (misma)** = myself

yogur *noun, masculine*
un yogur = a yogurt, yoghurt

yudo *noun, masculine*
yudo = judo

zanahoria *noun, feminine*
una zanahoria = a carrot

zapallo *noun, masculine* (*SC*)
un zapallo = a pumpkin

zapatería *noun, feminine*
  una **zapatería** = a shoe store, a shoe
  shop

zapatero/zapatera *noun,*
masculine/feminine
  un **zapatero/una zapatera** = a shoe-
  maker

zapatilla *noun, feminine*
  una **zapatilla** = a slipper
  (*for sports*) = a sneaker, a trainer
  (*Mex*) = a woman's shoe

zapato *noun, masculine*
  un **zapato** = a shoe

zíper *noun, masculine (C Am, Mex)*
  un **zíper** = a zipper, a zip

zodíaco, **zodiaco** *noun, masculine*
  el **zodíaco** = the Zodiac

zona *noun, feminine*
  una **zona** = an area
  = a zone

zoológico *noun, masculine*
  un **zoológico** = a zoo

zorro/zorra *noun, masculine/feminine*
  un **zorro/una zorra** = a fox/a vixen

zumbido *noun, masculine*
  un **zumbido** = buzzing

zumo *noun, masculine (Spa)*
  zumo = juice
  zumo de naranja = orange juice

zurdo/zurda
  1 *adjective*
    = left-handed
    = left-footed
  2 *noun, masculine/feminine*
    un **zurdo/una zurda** = a left-hander
    = a left-footed person

Dictionary know-how

This section contains a number of short exercises which will help you to use your dictionary more effectively. You will find answers to all of the exercises at the end of the section.

1 Noun or adjective?

Here is an extract from a Spanish advertisement for swimming pool installation. See if you can find thirteen different nouns and underline them, and nine different adjectives and circle them (or make two lists). If you are not sure of some words, look them up in the Spanish/English half of the dictionary and see if the term 'noun' or 'adjective' is used to describe them.

¿TE GUSTA NADAR? ¿TE GUSTA LA SENSACIÓN DE TIRARTE AL AGUA PURA, AZUL, LIMPIA Y PROFUNDA?

Ya puedes. En tu propia casa. Más de tres millones de españoles ya gozan de este lujo con nuestras modernas piscinas de diseño original y precio económico. Tenemos veinte años de experiencia en instalar piscinas cubiertas y por lo tanto ahora somos expertos en este campo.

Venga, permítete el lujo. Lánzate.

---

2 Which gender?

Here are some English nouns which appear in the English–Spanish half of the dictionary. Find out what their Spanish equivalents are and make two separate lists, masculine nouns and feminine nouns.

bag	hat	shop	door
pencil	animal	tiger	island
train	library	magic	nickname
milk	mussel	pear	rain
belt	saucer	thunderstorm	parents
waitress	worm		

3 **Spot the pronoun**

Each of the following phrases appears in the Spanish–English half of this dictionary in entries where a pronoun is the headword. In each one, underline the pronoun(s) and give the English equivalent(s).

¿de quién es esto?

lo vi ayer

la vas a romper

me lo dio

¿te lavaste la cara?

tengo que pedirles un favor

ocúpato de ello

es para ti

4 **Where's the verb?**

Rearrange the following to form correct sentences and underline the verb in each case. Some variations in the word order may be possible.

te para despacio entienda que habla

de cinco tren minutos el dentro llegará

el tienda recuerda la Roberto no de nombre

una lado del siempre verano mar alquilamos al en casa

su en columpio primo jardín mi tiene un rojo

5 **Spot the adverb**

Here is a list of seventeen Spanish words. Eleven of them are adverbs and six are not. Underline the ones which are not, or make a list, and say what they are. If you are not sure of some of them, look them up in the Spanish–English half of the dictionary.

abajo	**caso**	**entrevista**	**mente**
abeja	**delante**	**fuera**	**mientras**
acaso	**deprisa**	**incluso**	**prisa**
además	**enseguida**	**limpiaparabrisas**	**recién**
afuera			

6 **Subject or object?**

We have left out the subjects and objects from this account in Spanish. Choose suitable words from the list below in order to complete it. When you have finished, list the subjects and objects separately. Remember, word order is much more flexible in Spanish than in English.

> .... del pueblo salieron varias veces a cazar ....
>
> .... pero siempre logró escaparse. Todas las noches arrancaba .... que se cultivaban en los campos. Al final .... atraparon .... cerca del pueblo y .... metieron en una jaula. Sin embargo esa noche, mientras .... celebraba .... , un nino travieso soltó al pobre animal. .... del pueblo estaban tan preocupadas que no dejaron salir a .... , de manera que .... del niño travieso se vio obligado a ofrecer .... de 2.000 rupias a quien le trajera la cola del animal.

la gente	las plantas
sus niños	el padre
el elefante peligroso	lo
los habitantes	una recompensa
las madres	unos jóvenes
lo	una fiesta

7 **Word search**

Here is a grid in which are hidden the following twelve Spanish words: agarrar, amor, ancho, diente, eso, gusano, hija, morder, nieve, silla, sucio, vaso. They may appear horizontally, vertically or diagonally, and in either direction. When you have found them, ring them, then list them in their correct categories (masculine nouns, feminine nouns, etc)

H	E	T	N	E	I	D	A	J	U
R	A	P	R	E	D	R	O	M	A
E	A	W	I	G	H	O	S	I	L
I	V	R	E	U	E	S	O	M	L
P	O	E	R	S	N	H	A	B	I
S	H	N	I	A	Y	I	Z	O	S
G	C	O	R	N	G	J	E	U	T
E	N	U	T	O	P	A	C	H	U
V	A	S	O	X	L	I	F	A	N
S	I	L	N	A	O	J	R	D	E

8 Accents are important

Here is part of a letter typed by somebody who does not know how to find the accents on a word processor. Use your dictionary to help you put them in:

> Querida Teresa:
>
> Muchas gracias por las flores que recibi ayer. Son preciosas.
>
> Esta manana me encontre con Carmen en la calle Mayor ¿sabes que? hace poco conocio a un pintor ingles y esta a punto de irse con el a Londres. Ademas termino la carrera y se consiguio una beca para seguir estudiando alli. Es increible, ¿no? Claro que es una persona simpatica, pero es muy timida y encima bastante fea, la pobrecita. Bueno, pues ¿tu como estas? ¿Que piensas hacer en el verano? ¿Por que no vienes con nosotros a la playa?, siempre lo pasamos muy bien alli . . . .

9 Find the ending

Use your knowledge of Spanish and the dictionary, in particular the verb tables on pages 339–52, to give the correct form of the verb in parentheses.

¿Cuánto (**ganar**) ud.?
How much do you earn?

Normalmente (**almorzar**) a las doce
I usually have lunch at twelve o'clock

(**Pedir**) la cuenta
He asked for the bill

Tú lo (**ver**) más tarde
You'll see him later

(**Jugar**) con los niños en el jardín
She used to play with the children in the garden

(**Llegar**) el domingo
I arrived on Sunday

(**Pertenecer**) a ese club
I belong to that club

10 Find the preposition

Use your dictionary to find the English for the following Spanish sentences and underline the English and Spanish prepositions.

Dejé de fumar hace seis meses

El mantel estaba cubierto de manchas

Los obligó a abrir la caja fuerte

Es muy mala para la química

Iba acompañada de su madre

11 Find the verb

Some words in English can be both nouns and verbs e.g. race. In this exercise you have to find the following English words in the English–Spanish half of the dictionary and then give the Spanish for the verb only.

answer	**insult**	**finish**
block	**joke**	**rest**
camp	**kiss**	**sentence**
dance	**laugh**	**trick**
envy	**market**	**video**
fish	**notice**	**water**
glue	**paint**	**yell**

12 Choosing the right word

Very often you cannot use a word exactly as it is given in the dictionary. In the case of adjectives, you have to make sure that you select the form which is appropriate to the noun you are using. Use your dictionary and your own knowledge to find the correct form of the adjective to match the nouns in the following sentences.

Mi padre es .... pero mi madre es ....   (*Irish*) (*German*)

Tienen una casa .... con unas habitaciones ....   (*beautiful*) (*huge*)

Carmen es muy .... pero sus hermanos son ....   (*tall*) (*short*)

Raquel y su madre están muy .... allí   (*happy*)

Es muy .... idea   (*good*)

Las inmigrantes .... llevaban pañuelos ....
(*Russian*) (*old*) (*white*)

La rabia es una de las enfermedades más .... de controlar (*difficult*)

13 **Translating phrasal verbs**

Use your dictionary to find the correct translation for the following English sentences containing phrasal verbs.

a button came off my jacket

to take down a poster

to give up smoking

I took off my shoes

to get worked up

14 **Form the subjunctive**

It's important not to be afraid of the subjunctive, because it is so common in Spanish. Using the English–Spanish side of the dictionary and the verb tables on page 339–52, translate these sentences into Spanish.

stay here until I call you [referring to one person]

I'll walk unless it rains

you needn't send the letter today

put this helmet on so that you don't hurt yourself

it's likely that they'll lose

it's no wonder he hasn't got a girlfriend

15 **Falsos amigos**

Some Spanish words look the same as, or very similar to English words, but in fact have a different meaning. These are known as 'falsos amigos' or false friends. Use your dictionary to find the meanings of the following Spanish words:

asistir	**librería**
avisar	**quieto**
embarazada	**remover**
éxito	**sensible**
fábrica	**suceso**
largo	**wáter**

16 **False friends**

Now use your dictionary to find a Spanish meaning for each of these English 'lookalikes'.

to advise	**library**
assistance	**quiet**
embarrassed	**remove**
exit	**sensible**
fabric	**success**
large	**water**

17 **Male or female?**

Many Spanish nouns also have a feminine form. This is particularly true of words denoting an occupation—un abogado, una abogada. Some simply change from -o to -a for the feminine form, but not all do. Use your dictionary to find the feminine form of the following nouns:

un soldado	**un policía**
un director	**un presidente**
un actor	**un bailarín**
un poeta	**un astronauta**

18 **Find the sentence**

Use your dictionary to find the Spanish equivalents of the following English sentences

(a) I'd like to change jobs

(b) we arrived at the right time

(c) before the train leaves

(d) he's not up yet

(e) her work means a lot to her

(f) what's happening?

(g) how long is the movie?

(h) the meal came to 25 dollars

(i) stamps sold here

(j) painting is great fun

19 **Which meaning?**

Some words have more than one meaning and it's important to check that you have chosen the right one. In this dictionary the different meanings of a word are marked by a bullet point •

We have given you one meaning of the Spanish words below. Use your dictionary to find another one.

un departamento	• a department	**una llama**	• a flame
una escala	• a stopover	**manejar**	• to handle
formal	• formal	**raro**	• strange
importar	• to matter	**repasar**	• to check
justo	• fair	**sentar**	• to sit
una lata	• a can	**la tensión**	• voltage

20 **Crossword**

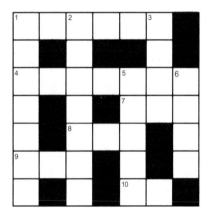

Across

1 to avoid
4 we go out, leave
   we went out, left
7 bear
8 without
9 celery with the end cut off
10 yes

Down

1 to teach
2 church
3 rivers
5 monkeys
6 alone

Answers

1

Nouns: sensación, agua, casa, millones, españoles, lujo, piscinas, diseño, precio, años, experiencia, expertos, campo

Adjectives: pura, azul, limpia, profunda, propia, modernas, original, económico, cubiertas

2

Masculine nouns: sombrero, tigre, animal, apodo, platillo, mejillón, cinturón, padres, gusano, tren, làpiz

Feminine nouns: bolsa, tienda, puerta, isla, leche, biblioteca, magia, pera, lluvia, tormenta eléctrica, camarera, (mesera, moza)

3

¿de quien es **esto**?
whose is this?

lo vi ayer
I saw him yesterday

la vas a romper
you're going to break it

me lo dio
she gave it to me

¿**te** lavaste la cara?
did you wash your face?

tengo que pedir**les** un favor
I have to ask them a favor

ocúpate de **ello**
take care of it

es para **ti**
it's for you

4

habla despacio para que te **entienda**

el tren **llegará** dentro de cinco minutos

Roberto no **recuerda** el nombre de la tienda

en verano siempre **alquilamos** una casa al lado del mar

mi primo **tiene** un columpio rojo en su jardín

5

abeja, entrevista, mente, prisa are feminine nouns

caso, limpiaparabrisas are masculine nouns

6

Los habitantes del pueblo salieron varias veces a cazar el elefante peligroso pero siempre logró escaparse. Todas las noches arrancaba las plantas que se cultivaban en los campos. Al final lo atraparon unos jóvenes cerca del pueblo y lo metieron en una jaula. Sin embargo, esa noche, mientras la gente celebraba una fiesta, un niño travieso soltó al pobre animal. Las madres del pueblo estaban tan preocupadas que no dejaron salir a sus niños, de manera que el padre del niño travieso se vio obligado a ofrecer una recompensa de 2.000 rupias a quien le trajera la cola del animal.

Subjects: los habitantes, unos jóvenes, la gente, las madres, el padre

Objects: el elefante peligroso, las plantas, lo, lo, una fiesta, sus niños

7

amor, diente, gusano, vaso are masculine nouns

hija, nieve, silla are feminine nouns

ancho, sucio are adjectives

agarrar, morder are verbs

eso is a pronoun

8

Querida Teresa:

Muchas gracias por las flores que recibí ayer. Son preciosas. Esta mañana me encontré con Carmen en la calle Mayor ¿sabes qué? Hace poco conoció a un pintor inglés y está a punto de irse con él a Londres. Además terminó la carrera y se consiguió una beca para seguir estudiando allí. Es increíble,¿no? Claro que es una persona simpática, pero es muy tímida y encima bastante fea, la pobrecita. Bueno, pues ¿tú cómo estás? ¿Qué piensas hacer en el verano? ¿Por qué no vienes con nosotros a la playa? siempre lo pasamos muy bien allí ...

9

gana
almuerzo
pidió
verás
jugaba
llegué
pertenezco

10

Dejé **de** fumar hace seis meses
I gave up smoking six months ago

El mantel estaba cubierto **de** manchas
The tablecloth was covered in stains

Los obligó **a** abrir la caja fuerte
He forced them to open the safe

Es muy mala **para** la química
She is very bad at chemistry

Iba acompañada **de** su madre
She was accompanied by her mother

11
contestar insultar terminar acabar
bloquear bromear descansar
acampar besar sentenciar
bailar reírse engañar
envidiar comercializar grabar
pescar notar regar
pegar pintar gritar

12
irlandés alemana
preciosa enormes
alta bajos
contentas
buena
rusas viejas blancos
difíciles

13
se le cayó un botón a la chaqueta
quitar un cartel
dejar de fumar
me quité los zapatos
exaltarse

14
quédate aquí hasta que te llame
quédese aquí hasta que lo/la llame [polite form]
iré a pie a no ser que llueva
no hace falta que mandes la carta hoy
ponte este casco para que no te hagas daño
póngase este casco para que no se haga daño [polite form]
es probable que pierdan
no es de extrañar que no tenga novia

15
asistir = *to attend*
avisar = *to let know*
embarazada = *pregnant*
éxito = *success*
fábrica = *factory*
largo = *long*
librería = *bookstore, bookshop*
quieto = *still*
remover = *to stir, to turn over, to toss*
sensible = *sensitive*
suceso = *event, incident*
wáter = *toilet*

16
assistance = ayuda
embarrassed = avergonzado
exit = salida
fabric = tela, tejido
large = grande
library = biblioteca
quiet = silencioso, tranquilo
remove = quitar
sensible = sensato, prudente, cómodo y práctico
success = éxito
water = agua

17
una soldado
una directora
una actriz
una poetisa, una poeta
una policía
una presidenta
una bailarina
una astronauta

18
(a) quisiera cambiar de trabajo
(b) llegamos en un buen momento
(c) antes de que salga el tren
(d) no se ha levantado todavía
(e) su trabajo es muy importante para ella
(f) ¿qué pasa?
(g) ¿cuánto dura la película?
(h) la comida costó 25 dolares
(i) los sellos se venden aquí
(j) la pintura es una gran diversión

19

un departamento	a department an apartment
una escala	a stopover a scale
formal	formal reliable well-behaved
importar	to matter to import
justo	fair tight right just enough
una lata	a can a pain (nuisance)
una llama	a flame a llama
manejar	to handle to drive
raro	strange rare
repasar	to check to review, revise
sentar	to sit to suit
la tensión	voltage tension blood pressure

20

Aa

a, an *indefinite article*
a = un/una
he's a dentist = es dentista
what a good idea! = ¡qué buena idea!

> **!** a *is not translated before a person's profession, or in the phrase* what a

ability *noun*
ability = capacidad (*feminine*)
he doesn't have the ability to do it = no tiene capacidad para hacerlo

able *adjective*
• (*having the ability*)
to be able to [stand up | travel | work ...] = poder [levantarse | viajar | trabajar ...]
• (*capable*) = capaz
an able pupil = un alumno capaz

aboard
1 *preposition* = a bordo de
2 *adverb*
to go aboard = subir a bordo

about

> **!** About *is often used in combinations with verbs, for example,* mess about, run about. *To find the correct translations for this type of verb, look up the separate dictionary entries at* mess, run *etc*

1 *preposition*
• (*on the subject of*) = sobre
it's a book about the First World War = es un libro sobre la Primera Guerra Mundial
he wants to see you about something = quiere verte acerca de algo
I know nothing about this matter = no sé nada (con) respecto a este asunto
2 *adverb*
• (*approximately*) = como
I have about 5 dollars left = me quedan como 5 dólares
we left at about seven o'clock = nos fuimos como a las siete
• (*on the point of*)
to be about to = estar a punto de
to be about to go = estar a punto de ir

above
1 *preposition* = encima de
his room is above the kitchen = su cuarto está encima de la cocina
above all = sobre todo
2 *adverb*
I have the room above = ocupo el cuarto de arriba
children aged twelve and above = niños a partir de 12 anos

abroad *adverb*
to travel abroad = viajar al extranjero
to live abroad = vivir en el extranjero

absent *adjective*
= ausente
to be absent from school = faltar al colegio

accent *noun*
an accent = un acento
with a Mexican accent = con acento mexicano

accept *verb*
= aceptar

accident
1 *noun*
an accident = un accidente
by accident (*by chance*) = por casualidad
(*unintentionally*) = sin querer

**accommodation,
accommodations** (*US English*) *noun*
accommodation = alojamiento (*masculine*)
hotel accommodation = alojamiento en hotel

accompany *verb*
= acompañar

account *noun*
• (*in a bank*)
an account = una cuenta
• to take something into account = tomar algo en cuenta

accountant *noun*
an accountant = un contador/una contadora (*Lat Am*), un/una contable (*Spa*)

accurate *adjective*
an accurate watch = un reloj preciso
are these measurements accurate? = ¿estas medidas son exactas?
an accurate description = una descripción exacta

accuse *verb*
= acusar
to accuse someone of lying = acusar a alguien de mentir

across *preposition*

> **!** *The combination of a verb of movement* + across *is translated by the verb* cruzar

to go across the street = cruzar la calle
to run across the street = cruzar la calle corriendo

- (*through*)
  a journey across the desert = un viaje a través del desierto
- (*on the other side of*)
  she lives across the street = vive al otro lado de la calle

act *verb*
- (*to take action*) = actuar
- (*to perform as an actor*) = actuar

activity *noun*
  an activity = una actividad

actor *noun*
  an actor = un actor

actress *noun*
  an actress = una actriz

actually *adverb*
- (*in fact*)
  I haven't actually read the book yet = la verdad es que no he leído el libro todavía
- (*really*) = de verdad
  did he actually say that? = ¿de verdad dijo eso?
- (*exactly*) = exactamente
  what actually happened? = ¿qué pasó exactamente?

adapt *verb*
- (*if it's a play, an engine etc*) = adaptar
- (*to get used to*) = adaptarse
  she quickly adapted to the new school = pronto se adaptó al nuevo colegio

add *verb*
- = añadir
  you have to add lemon juice = hay que añadir jugo de limón
- (*in arithmetic*) = sumar

address *noun*
  an address = una dirección
  (*on a form*) = un domicilio

adhesive *noun*
  an adhesive = un adhesivo

adjust *verb*
- (*if it's an instrument*) = ajustar
- (*to get used to*) = adaptarse
  it takes time to adjust to a new job = se necesita tiempo para adaptarse a un trabajo nuevo

administration *noun*
  administration = administración (*feminine*)

admire *verb*
  = admirar

admission *noun*
  (*price of entry*)
  admission = entrada (*feminine*)

admit *verb*
- (*to recognize, to confess*) = admitir, reconocer

- **to be admitted to hospital** = ingresar en el hospital

adolescent *noun*
  an adolescent = un/una adolescente

adopt *verb*
  = adoptar

adore *verb*
  = adorar
  she adores her grandparents = adora a sus abuelos
  they adore traveling abroad = les encanta viajar al extranjero

adult *noun*
  an adult = un adulto/una adulta

advance *noun*
  in advance = con antelación
  to pay in advance = pagar por adelantado

advantage *verb*
- (*a positive point*)
  an advantage = una ventaja
  to have an advantage over someone = tener ventaja sobre alguien
- **to take advantage of an opportunity** = aprovechar una oportunidad
  they are taking advantage of you = se están aprovechando de ti

adventure *noun*
  an adventure = una aventura

advert, advertisement *noun*
  an advert, an advertisement = un anuncio, un aviso (*Lat Am*)

advertising *noun*
  advertising = publicidad (*feminine*)

advice *noun*
  advice = consejos (*masculine plural*)
  a piece of advice = un consejo

advise *verb*
  = aconsejar
  to advise someone to stay = aconsejarle a alguien que se quede

  ! *Note the use of the subjunctive after* aconsejarle a alguien que

aerial *noun* (*British English*)
  an aerial = una antena

aeroplane *noun* (*British English*)
  an aeroplane = un avión

affect *verb*
  (*to have an effect*) = afectar a
  this doesn't affect me = esto no me afecta

afford *verb*
  I'd like to go, but I can't afford it = me gustaría ir, pero no puedo permitirme el lujo
  he can't afford a car = no le alcanza el dinero para comprar un coche

afraid *adjective*
* (*scared*)
  to be afraid = tener miedo
  I'm afraid of mice = les tengo miedo a los ratones
* (*expressing a regret*)
  I'm afraid I can't go with you = me temo que no te puedo acompañar

Africa *noun* ▶ p. 187
  Africa = África (*feminine*)

African ▶ p. 187
1 *noun*
  an African = un africano/una africana
2 *adjective* = africano/africana

after ▶ p. 319
1 *preposition*
* = después de
  they left after breakfast = se fueron después del desayuno
  the day after tomorrow = pasado mañana
  after all = después de todo
* (*US English—when talking about time*)
  it's twenty after four = son las cuatro y veinte
2 *adverb* = después
  soon after = poco después
3 *conjunction*
  after we finished, we went to bed = después de que terminamos, nos acostamos
  after seeing the movie, I went home = después de ver la película, me fui a casa

afternoon *noun* ▶ p. 319
  an afternoon = una tarde
  Friday afternoon = el viernes en la tarde, el viernes por la tarde (*Spa*)
  in the afternoon = en la tarde, por la tarde (*Spa*)
  at six o'clock in the afternoon = a las seis de la tarde
  good afternoon = buenas tardes

aftershave *noun*
  an aftershave = una loción para después de afeitarse, un aftershave

afterward (*US English*), **afterwards** (*British English*) *adverb*
  = después
  they left not long afterwards = se fueron poco después

again *adverb*
  = otra vez, de nuevo
  are you going to do it again? = ¿lo vas a hacer otra vez?, ¿lo vas a hacer de nuevo?

> **!** Very often there will be a specific Spanish verb to translate the idea of doing something 'again'—e.g. start again = recomenzar, to do the work again = rehacer el trabajo *etc*

  she read the letter again = releyó la carta
  to begin again = volver a empezar

against *preposition*
* (*close to*) = contra
  she left her bike against the wall = dejó la bicicleta contra la pared
* (*not in favor of*) = en contra de
  to be against hunting = estar en contra de la caza

age *noun* ▶ p. 154
  age = edad (*feminine*)

ago *adverb*
  a month/two years ago = hace un mes/dos años

agree *verb*
* (*to have the same opinion*) = estar de acuerdo
  I don't agree with you = no estoy de acuerdo contigo
* (*to give one's consent*)
  we agreed to meet next week = quedamos en encontrarnos la semana que viene
* (*to reach a decision*)
  to agree on a price = ponerse de acuerdo en un precio

agreement *noun*
  an agreement = un acuerdo

agriculture *noun*
  agriculture = agricultura (*feminine*)

ahead *adverb*
* (*in advance*)
  they went on ahead = se adelantaron
* (*in front*)
  he was ahead of us = estaba delante de nosotros
  to be ahead of the other pupils = estar más avanzado/avanzada que los demás alumnos

AIDS *noun*
  AIDS = el sida, el SIDA

aim
1 *noun*
* (*a purpose*)
  an aim = un objetivo
* (*when using a weapon*)
  to take aim at someone = apuntarle a alguien
2 *verb*
* **to aim to win** (*to try*) = intentar ganar
  (*to intend*) = tener la intención de ganar
* **to aim a gun at someone** = apuntarle a alguien con una pistola

air
1 *noun*
  air = aire (*masculine*)
2 *verb*
  (*if it's clothes, linen*) = airear, orear
  to air a room = ventilar una habitación

air-conditioning *noun*
  the air-conditioning = el aire acondicionado

Age

Where English says **to be X years old**, Spanish says **tener X años** (*to have X years*).

How old?

how old are you?	= ¿cuántos años tienes?
what age is she?	= ¿qué edad tiene?
he is twenty years old	= tiene veinte años
he is twenty	
he is twenty years of age	

Aged

he was aged twenty	= tenía veinte años
a baby aged eleven months	= un bebé de once meses

Younger/older/the same age

he is younger than you	= es más joven que tú
she is older than John	= es mayor que John
he's two years older than me	= es dos años mayor que yo
she's the same age as me	= tiene la misma edad que yo

X-year-old

a fifty-year-old	= una persona de cincuenta años
a five-year-old	= un niño/una niña de cinco años

Approximate ages

he is about thirty	= tiene alrededor de treinta años, tiene unos treinta años
she's in her forties	= tiene cuarenta y tantos
she's in her early forties	= tiene poco más de cuarenta años
she's in her late forties	= tiene cerca de cincuenta años

---

aircraft *noun*
an aircraft = un avión

air force *noun*
the air force = la fuerza aérea

air hostess *noun*
an air hostess = una azafata, una
aeromoza (*Lat Am*)

airline *noun*
an airline = una línea aérea

airmail *noun*
airmail = correo aéreo (*masculine*)
by airmail = por vía aérea

airplane *noun* (*US English*)
an airplane = un avión

airport *noun*
an airport = un aeropuerto

alarm *noun*
an alarm = una alarma

alarm clock *noun*
an alarm clock = un despertador

album *noun*
an album = un álbum

alcohol *noun*
alcohol = alcohol (*masculine*)

alike *adjective*
= parecido/parecida

alive *adjective*
= vivo/viva

all
1 *adjective*
= todo/toda (+ *singular*), todos/todas
(+ *plural*)
all the boys/girls = todos los chicos/todas
las chicas
2 *pronoun*
= todo
that's all = eso es todo
3 *adverb*
to be all alone = estar completamente
solo/sola

---

allergic *adjective*
  to be allergic to something = ser alérgico/alérgica a algo

allergy *noun*
  an allergy = una alergia

allow *verb*
  = permitir
  'smoking is not allowed' = 'no se permite fumar'

allowance *noun*
  (*from parents*) **a monthly allowance** = una mensualidad, una mesada (*Lat Am*)

all right *adjective*
* (*when giving an opinion*)
  the play was all right = la obra no estaba mal
* (*when talking about health*) = bien
  are you all right? = ¿estás bien?
* (*when asking for an opinion*)
  is it all right if I go? = ¿está bien si me voy?
* (*when agreeing*) = de acuerdo

almond *noun*
  an almond = una almendra

almost *adverb*
  = casi
  I've almost finished = casi he terminado
  they almost missed the plane = por poco pierden el avión, casi pierden el avión

alone
  1 *adjective* = solo/sola
  2 *adverb*
  to live alone = vivir solo/sola

along *preposition*
  = por
  she walked along the sidewalk = caminó por la acera
  there are benches along the street = hay bancos a lo largo de la calle

aloud *adverb*
  = en voz alta

already *adverb*
  = ya
  it's already eight o'clock = ya son las ocho

also *adverb*
  = también

alternative *noun*
  an alternative = una alternativa

although *conjunction*
  = aunque

altogether *adverb*
  (*in total*) = en total

always *adverb*
  = siempre

amateur *noun*
  an amateur = un/una amateur

amazed *adjective*
  = asombrado/asombrada

amazing *adjective*
  = increíble

ambassador *noun*
  an ambassador = un embajador/una embajadora

ambition *noun*
  ambition = ambición (*feminine*)

ambitious *adjective*
  = ambicioso/ambiciosa

ambulance *noun*
  an ambulance = una ambulancia

America *noun* ▶ p. 187
* (*the USA*)
  America = Estados Unidos (*masculine plural*), Norteamérica (*feminine*)
* (*the continent*)
  America = América (*feminine*)

American ▶ p. 187
  1 *noun*
  an American = un/una estadounidense, un norteamericano/una norteamericana
  2 *adjective*
  an American city = una ciuded norteamericana
  the American embassy = la embajada de los Estados Unidos

among, amongst *preposition*
* (*in the midst of*) = entre
  I found it among the newspapers = lo encontré entre los periódicos
* (*one of*)
  Japan is among the richest countries in the world = el Japón es uno de los países más ricos del mundo

amount *noun*
  an amount = una cantidad

amusement park *noun*
  an amusement park = un parque de diversiones, un parque de atracciones (*Spa*)

amusing *adjective*
  = divertido/divertida

an *indefinite article* ▶ a

ancestor *noun*
  an ancestor = un antepasado/una antepasada

anchor *noun*
  an anchor = un ancla (*feminine*)

and *conjunction*

> **!** *Note that the usual translation* y *becomes* e *when it precedes a word beginning with* i- *or* hi-

* = y

she visited France and Spain = visitó Francia y España
Pedro and Isabel = Pedro e Isabel
bread and butter = pan con mantequilla
I'll go and see = iré a ver
* (*in numbers*)
  a hundred and ten = ciento diez
  nine hundred and seventy-two = novecientos setenta y dos

angel *noun*
an angel = un ángel

anger *noun*
anger = ira (*feminine*), enojo (*masculine*), enfado (*masculine*) (*Spa*)

angry *adjective*
= enojado/enojada, enfadado/enfadada (*Spa*)
to be angry with someone = estar enojado con alguien, estar enfadado con alguien (*Spa*)
to get angry = enojarse, enfadarse (*Spa*)

animal *noun*
an animal = un animal

ankle *noun* ▶ p. 235
the ankle = el tobillo

anniversary *noun*
an anniversary = un aniversario
a wedding anniversary = un aniversaria de boda de casados

announcement *noun*
an announcement = un anuncio

annoy *verb*
= molestar

annoyed *adjective*
= enojado/enojada, enfadado/enfadada (*Spa*)
are you annoyed with me? = ¿estás enojado conmigo?, ¿estás enfadado conmigo? (*Spa*)

annoying *adjective*
* (*if it's a person*) = pesado/pesada
* (*if it's a noise*) = molesto/molesta

annual
1 *noun*
(*a book*)
an annual = un anuario
2 *adjective* = **anual**

anonymous *adjective*
= anónimo/anónima

another
1 *adjective* = otro/otra
another 25 copies = otras 25 copias
I'll come back another day = vuelvo otro día
2 *pronoun* = otro/otra

answer
1 *noun*

* (*a reply*)
  an answer = una respuesta
  there's no answer (*at the door, on the phone*) = no contestan
* (*a solution*)
  an answer = una solución
2 *verb* = contestar
  to answer a question = contestar una pregunta
  she answered the phone = contestó el teléfono
  would you answer the door? = ¿puedes abrir la puerta?
answer back
= contestar

answering machine *noun*
an answering machine = un contestador automático

ant *noun*
an ant = una hormiga

antenna *noun*
(*of a television or radio*)
an antenna = una antena

antique *noun*
an antique = una antigüedad

anxious *adjective*
* (*worried*) = preocupado/preocupada
  he is anxious about the exam results = está preocupado por los resultados de los exámenes
* (*keen*)
  to be anxious to do something = estar deseoso/desosa de hacer algo

any
1 *adjective*
* (*in questions*)
  is there any sugar? = ¿hay azúcar?
  do you have any money? = ¿tienes dinero?
* (*with a negative*)
  we don't have any beer = no tenemos cerveza
  she doesn't have any brothers = no tiene hermanos
* (*whatever*) = cualquier
  come any day you want = ven cualquier día que quieras
2 *pronoun*
  I need some ink—do you have any? = necesito tinta—¿tienes?
  I don't have any = no tengo

anybody, **anyone** *pronoun*
* (*in questions*)
  is there anybody at home? = ¿hay alguien en casa?
* (*with the negative*) = nadie
  there isn't anybody there = no hay nadie allí
  they don't want anybody to know = no quieren que nadie lo sepa

---

C Am Central America   Lat Am Latin America   Mex Mexico

* (*everybody*)
  anybody can come = puede venir
  cualquiera

anything *pronoun*
* (*in questions*) = algo
  do you have anything to eat? = tienes algo
  para comer?
* (*with the negative*) = nada
  he doesn't want to do anything = no quiere
  hacer nada
* (*everything*)
  he would do anything for her = haría
  cualquier cosa por ella

anyway *adverb*
= de todos modos

anywhere *adverb*
* (*in questions*)
  have you seen my shoes anywhere? = has
  visto mis zapatos por algún lado?
  are you going anywhere tonight? = ¿vas a
  algún lado esta noche?
* (*with the negative*)
  I can't find them anywhere = no los
  encuentro por ningún lado
  you're not going anywhere = no vas a ir a
  ningún lado
* (*any place*)
  we can go anywhere = podemos ir a
  cualquier lado

apart *adjective*
  they don't like to be apart = no les gusta
  estar separados
  apart from = aparte de

apartment *noun*
  an apartment = un apartamento, un
  departamento (*Lat Am*), un piso (*Spa*)

**apartment building, apartment
house** (*US English*) *noun*
  an apartment building = un edificio de
  apartamentos, un edificio de
  departamentos (*Lat Am*), una casa de
  pisos (*Spa*)

ape *noun*
  an ape = un simio

apologize *verb*
  = pedir perdón
  we apologize for the delay = rogamos
  disculpen el retraso

apology *noun*
  an apology = una disculpa

appear *verb*
* (*to seem*) = parecer
  she appears to be happy = parece estar
  contenta
* (*to come into view*) = aparecer

appendix *noun*
  the appendix = el apéndice

appetite *noun*
  appetite = apetito (*masculine*)

applaud *verb*
  = aplaudir

applause *noun*
  applause = aplausos (*masculine plural*)
  a round of applause = un aplauso

apple *noun*
  an apple = una manzana

appliance *noun*
  an appliance = un aparato
  electrical appliances = electrodomésticos
  (*masculine plural*)

application *noun*
  (*for a job*)
  an application = una solicitud

application form *noun*
  an application form = una solicitud

apply *verb*
  (*to send a job application*)
  to apply for a job = solicitar un trabajo

appointment *noun*
  an appointment (*arrangement to meet*) =
  una cita
  (*with doctor, hairdresser*) = una hora, una
  cita (*Lat Am*)
  to make an appointment = concertar una
  cita
  **I have an appointment at the doctor's at
  one o'clock** = tengo hora con el médico a
  la una, tengo cita con el médico a la una

appreciate *verb*
* (*to be grateful for*) = agradecer
  I appreciate your concern = agradezco tu
  interés
* (*if it's good food or wine*) = apreciar

approach *verb*
  = acercarse
  to approach someone/something =
  acercarse a alguien/algo

approve *verb*
  my mother doesn't approve of him = a mi
  madre no le gusta
  they approved of the idea = la idea les
  parecía muy buena

approximately *adverb*
  it is approximately 10 kilometers from here
  = está a unos diez kilómetros de aquí
  at approximately 5 o'clock = a eso de las
  cinco

apricot *noun*
  an apricot = un chabacano (*Mex*), un
  damasco (*SC*), un albaricoque (*Spa*)

April *noun* ▶ **p. 192**
  April = abril (*masculine*)

apron noun
an apron = un delantal

aquarium noun
an aquarium = un acuario

Aquarius noun
• (the sign)
Aquarius = Acuario
I'm Aquarius = soy Acuario, soy de Acuario
• (a person)
an Aquarius = un/una acuario

arch noun
an arch = un arco

architect noun
an architect = un arquitecto/una arquitecta

architecture noun
architecture = arquitectura (feminine)

area noun
an area (of country) = una zona
(of city) = un barrio

argue verb
= discutir
to argue about money = discutir por el
dinero
to argue about politics = discutir de
política

argument noun
• (a quarrel)
an argument = una discusión
to have an argument with someone =
discutir con alguien
• (reasons for or against)
an argument = un argumento

Aries noun
• (the sign)
Aries = Aries
I'm Aries = soy Aries, soy de Aries
• (a person)
an Aries = un/una aries

arithmetic noun
arithmetic = aritmética (feminine)

arm noun ▶ p. 235
the arm = el brazo

armchair noun
an armchair = un sillón

arms noun
arms = armas (feminine plural)

army noun
the army = el ejército
to be in the army = ser militar

around
1 preposition = alrededor de
they were sitting around the table =
estaban sentados alrededor de la mesa
to go around the world = dar la vuelta
alrededor del mundo

2 adverb

> **!** Around often occurs in combinations
> with verbs, eg run around, turn around
> etc. To find the correct translations for
> this type of verb, look up the separate
> dictionary entries at run, turn etc

• (approximately) = como
I have around 5 dollars left = me quedan
unos 5 dólares
I'll be there at around four o'clock = estaré
allí como a las cuatro
• (available, nearby)
will you be around tomorrow? = vas a estar
aquí mañana?
they live around here = viven por aquí

arrange verb
to arrange a vacation in Italy = organizar
unas vacaciones en Italia
to arrange an appointment = concertar una
cita
they arranged to meet later = quedaron en
encontrarse más tarde

arrangement noun
to make an arrangement or arrangements
to leave early = quedar en irse temprano

arrest verb
= detener

arrival noun
the arrival = la llegada

arrive verb
= llegar

arrow noun
an arrow = una flecha

art noun
art = arte (masculine)
(as school subject) = expresion artística
(feminine)

art gallery noun
an art gallery = un museo de Bellas Artes

artificial adjective
= artificial

artist noun
an artist = un artista/una artista

artistic adjective
= artístico

arts noun
the arts = las artes

as
1 conjunction
• (like) = como
she arrived late as usual = llegó tarde
como siempre
let's leave the room as it is = dejemos el
cuarto así como está
• (because, since) = como
as you were out, I left a message = como
habías salido, dejé un mensaje

C Am Central America   Lat Am Latin America   Mex Mexico

A

- (*while*) = mientras
  I watched him as he counted the money =
  lo vigilé mientras contaba el dinero
  I used to live there as a child = vivía allí
  cuando era niño/niña
- (*when used with* the same)
  my coat is the same as yours = mi abrigo
  es igual que el tuyo
  they have the same car as us = tienen el
  mismo coche que nosotros
2 *preposition*
  she works as a receptionist = trabaja de
  recepcionista
  he was dressed as a pirate = estaba
  vestido de pirata
3 *adverb*
  I'm as tired as you = estoy tan cansada
  como tú
  I ran as fast as possible = corrí lo más
  rápido que pude
  as for = en cuanto a
  as for us = en cuanto a nosotros
  as from tomorrow = a partir de mañana

ash *noun*
  ash = ceniza (*feminine*)

ashamed *adjective*
  to be ashamed = estar
  avergonzado/avergonzada
  he is ashamed of what he has done = está
  avergonzado de lo que ha hecho

ashtray *noun*
  an ashtray = un cenicero

Asia *noun* ▶ p. 187
  Asia = Asia (*feminine*)

Asian ▶ p. 187
1 *noun*
  an Asian = un asiático/una asiática
2 *adjective* = asiático/asiática

ask *verb*
  to ask = preguntar
  he asked me my name = me preguntó mi
  nombre
  to ask permission to go outside = pedir
  permiso para salir
  to ask someone to call = pedirle a alguien
  que llame

  ! Note the use of the subjunctive after
  | pedirle a alguien que

  to ask a question = hacer una pregunta
- (*to invite*)
  to ask a friend to dinner = invitar a un
  amigo a cenar
- (*to inquire*)
  did you ask about the plane tickets? =
  ¿preguntaste por los boletos de avión?
ask for
  to ask for money = pedir dinero
  to ask for someone (*on the phone*) =
  preguntar por alguien

asleep *adjective*
  to be asleep = estar dormido/dormida
  to fall asleep = dormirse
aspirin *noun*
  an aspirin = una aspirina
assassinate *verb*
  = asesinar
assemble *verb*
- (*gather*) = reunirse
- (*construct*) = armar
assignment *noun*
  (*for school*)
  an assignment = un trabajo
assistance *noun*
  assistance = ayuda (*feminine*)
assistant *noun*
- (*a helper*)
  an assistant = un ayudante/una ayudante
- (*British English—in a shop*) ▶ **shop**
  assistant
association *noun*
  an association = una asociación
assume *verb*
  = suponer
assure *verb*
  = asegurar
astronaut *noun*
  an astronaut = un astronauta/una
  astronauta
at *preposition*
- (*when talking about position or place*) = en
  at home = en casa

  ! You will find translations for phrases
  like at the top, at the front of, at the
  back of *etc in the entries for* top, front,
  | back *etc*

- (*at the house, shop, practice of*)
  we'll be at Laura's = estaremos en casa de
  Laura, estaremos donde Laura (*Lat Am*)
  I have an appointment at the dentist's =
  tengo cita con el dentista
- (*when talking about time*) = a
  it starts at 7 o'clock = empieza a las siete
- (*when talking about age*) = a
  at four years of age = a los cuatro años

  ! There are many verbs which involve the
  use of at, such as look at, laugh at *etc*.
  For translations look up the separate
  | dictionary entries for look, laugh *etc*

athlete *noun*
  an athlete = un atleta/una atleta
athletics *noun*
  athletics (*in the US*) = los deportes
  (*in Britain*) = el atletismo
Atlantic *noun*
  the Atlantic = el Atlántico
atlas *noun*
  an atlas = un atlas

atmosphere *noun*
(*air*)
the atmosphere = la atmósfera

attach *verb*
to be attached to the wall = estar
sujeto/sujeta a la pared
to attach a letter to an application =
adjuntar una carta a una solicitud

attack
1 *verb*   = atacar
2 *noun*
an attack = un ataque

attempt
1 *verb* = intentar
to attempt to break the world record =
intentar batir el récord mundial
2 *noun*
an attempt = un intento
to make an attempt to escape = intentar
escapar

attend *verb*
to attend a wedding = asistir a una boda
to attend the village school = ir a la escuela
del pueblo

attention *noun*
attention = atención (*feminine*)
to get someone's attention = atraer la
atención de alguien
to pay attention to someone/something =
prestar atención a alguien/algo

attic *noun*
an attic (*used for storage*) = un desván, un
altillo
(*used as accommodation*) = un ático

attitude *noun*
an attitude = una actitud

attract *verb*
= atraer
to attract someone's attention = atraer la
atención de alguien

attractive *adjective*
= atractivo/atractiva

audience *noun*
• (*at a cinema, theater, or concert*)
the audience = el público
• (*for a radio or TV program*)
the audience = la audiencia

August *noun* ▶ p. 192
August = agosto (*masculine*)

aunt *noun*
an aunt = una tía

au pair *noun*
an au pair = una au pair

Australia *noun* ▶ p. 187
Australia = Australia (*feminine*)

Australian ▶ p. 187
1 *noun*
an Australian = un australiano/una
australiana
2 *adjective* = australiano/australiana

Austria *noun* ▶ p. 187
Austria = Austria (*feminine*)

Austrian ▶ p. 187
1 *noun*
an Austrian = un austríaco/una austríaca,
un austriaco/una austriaca
2 *adjective* = austríaco/austríaca,
austriaco/austriaca

author *noun*
an author (*of an article*) = un autor/una
autora
(*of a book*) = un escritor/una escritora

authority *noun*
• (*power*)
authority = autoridad (*feminine*)
• the authorities = las autoridades

autograph *noun*
an autograph = un autógrafo

automatic *adjective*
= automático/automática

autumn *noun*
autumn = otoño (*masculine*)
in autumn = en el otoño

available *adjective*
(*on sale*)
there are places available on the 6
o'clock flight = hay asientos disponibles
en el vuelo de las seis
tickets for the concert are still available =
todavía quedan entradas para el
concierto

average
1 *noun*
an average = un promedio, una media
2 *adjective* = medio/media

avoid *verb*
• (*to prevent*) = evitar
to avoid making noise = evitar hacer
ruido
• (*to keep away from*)
to avoid someone = evitar a alguien

awake *adjective*
= despierto/despierta
I'm wide awake now = estoy totalmente
despierta ahora
they kept me awake all night = no me
dejaron dormir en toda la noche

award
1 *noun*
(*a prize*)
an award = un premio

2 *verb*
he was awarded first prize = le otorgaron
  el primer premio

aware *adjective*
• (*conscious*)
  to be aware of a problem = ser consciente
  de un problema, estar consciente de un
  problema (*Mex*)
• (*up to date*)
  to be aware of what's happening = estar al
  tanto de lo que está pasando

away *adverb*
• (*absent*)
  John is away today = John no está hoy
• (*when talking about distances*)
  to be far away = estar muy lejos
  Boston is 80 km away = Boston está a
  80 km de aquí

> **!** *Away is often used in combinations with
> verbs, for example,* go away, run away.
> *To find the correct translations for this
> type of verb, look up the separate
> dictionary entries at* go, run *etc*

awful *adjective*
• **the movie was awful** = la película fue
  terrible
  the weather was awful = hacía muy mal
  tiempo
• (*unwell*)
  I feel awful = me siento muy mal, me siento
  fatal

awkward *adjective*
  it's a very awkward situation = es una
  situación muy incómoda
  I felt very awkward = me sentí muy
  incómodo

ax (*US English*), **axe** (*British English*) *noun*
  an axe = un hacha (*feminine*)

---

baby *noun*
  a baby = un bebé, un niño/una niña, un
  bebe/una beba (*R Pl*)

baby buggy, **baby carriage** *noun*
(*US English*)
  a baby buggy = un cochecito

babysitter *noun*
  a babysitter = un/una babysitter, un/una
  canguro (*Spa*)

back
1 *noun*

• (*a part of the body*) ▶ **p. 235**
  the back = la espalda
• (*the rear of something*)
  at the back of the shop = en el fondo de la
  tienda
  the back of a chair = el respaldo de una
  silla
  the back of a car = la parte trasera de un
  coche
• (*the reverse side of something*)
  write your name on the back of the check
  = escriba su nombre al dorso del cheque

2 *adverb*

> **!** *Back is often used in combinations with
> verbs, for example,* come back, get back,
> give back *etc. To find the correct
> translations for this type of verb, look up
> the separate dictionary entries at* come,
> get, give *etc*

  to be back = estar de vuelta
  I'll be back in five minutes = vuelvo dentro
  de cinco minutos
• (*before in time*)
  back in February = en febrero
  back in 1972 = (ya) en 1972

3 *verb*
(*support*)
  = respaldar, apoyar
back down = volverse atrás

back door *noun*
  the back door = la puerta trasera

background *noun*
• (*of a picture or photograph*)
  the background = el fondo
• (*of a person*)
  she is from a poor background = su
  familia es pobre

back seat *noun*
  the back seat = el asiento trasero

back to front *adverb*
  your sweater is on back to front = te has
  puesto el suéter al revés

backward (*US English*), **backwards**
(*British English*) *adverb* = hacia atrás

bacon *noun*
  bacon = tocino (*masculine*), bacon
  (*masculine*) (*Spa*), panceta (*feminine*)
  (*R Pl*)

bad *adjective*
• (*not good*)
  = malo/mala

> **!** *Note that* malo *becomes* mal *when it
> appears before a masculine singular
> noun*

  a bad movie = una película mala
  that's not a bad idea = no es mala idea
  how was the play?—not bad = ¿qué tal la
  obra?—no estaba mal

R Pl River Plate area   **SC** Southern Cone   **Spa** Spain

- (*serious*) = grave
  a bad accident = un accidente grave
- (*wicked*) = malo/mala

badge *noun*
- **a badge** = una chapa, un botón (*Lat Am*)
  (*worn by a policeman*) = una placa de
  policía

badly *adverb*
- (*not well*) = mal
  he did badly in his exams = le fue mal en
  los exámenes
- (*seriously*)
  he was badly injured = resultó gravemente
  herido

badminton *noun* ▶ p. 306
  badminton = bádminton (*masculine*)

bad-tempered *adjective*
  to be bad-tempered = tener mal genio

bag *noun*
- **a bag** = una bolsa
- (*baggage*)
  she packed her bags = hizo las maletas

baggage *noun*
  baggage = equipaje (*masculine*)

bake *verb*
- **to bake bread** = hacer pan
  to bake a dish in the oven = hacer una
  comida al horno
- (*to make cakes or bread*)
  he likes baking (*making cakes*) = le gusta
  hacer pasteles
  (*making bread*) = le gusta hacer pan

baker *noun*
  a baker = un panadero/una panadera

bakery *noun*
  a bakery = una panadería

balance
1 *noun*
- (*physical*)
  balance = equilibrio (*masculine*)
- (*in a bank account*)
  a balance = un saldo
2 *verb*
- (*to place*) = mantener en equilibrio
- (*remain steady*) = mantener el equilibrio

balcony *noun*
  a balcony = un balcón

bald *adjective*
  = calvo, pelón (*Mex*), pelado (*SC*)
  to go bald = quedarse calvo (*or* pelón *etc*)

ball *noun*
- (*for playing football, rugby, tennis, cricket
  or basketball*)
  a ball = una pelota, un balón
- (*for playing baseball or golf*)
  a ball = una pelota, una bola

- (*a dance*)
  a ball = un baile

ballet *noun*
  ballet = ballet (*masculine*)

balloon *noun*
  a balloon = un globo

ballpoint pen *noun*
  a ballpoint pen = un bolígrafo, una pluma
  atómica (*Mex*), una birome (*R Pl*)

ban *verb*
  = prohibir

banana *noun*
  a banana = un plátano, una banana (*R Pl*),
  un banano (*C Am*)

band *noun*
  (*a musical group*)
  a band = un grupo

bandage
1 *noun*
  a bandage = un vendaje
2 *verb* = vendar

Band-Aid *noun* (*US English*)
  a Band-Aid = una curita , una tirita   (*Spa*)

bang
1 *noun*
- (*a loud noise*)
  a bang = un estrépito
- (*an explosion*)
  a bang = una explosión
2 *verb*
- (*to hit*)
  he banged his head on the ceiling = se dio
  un golpe en la cabeza con el techo
  he banged his fist on the table = golpeó la
  mesa con el puño
- (*to shut loudly*)
  she banged the door = dio un portazo

bangs *noun* (*US English*)
  bangs = flequillo (*masculine*), cerquillo
  (*masculine*) (*Lat Am*), fleco (*masculine*)
  (*Mex*)

bank *noun*
- (*a financial institution*)
  a bank = un banco
- (*of a river or lake*)
  the bank = la orilla

bank account *noun*
  a bank account = una cuenta bancaria

bank holiday *noun* (*British English*)
  a bank holiday = un día festivo, un día
  feriado (*Lat Am*)

bank note *noun*
  (*British English*)
  a bank note = un billete de banco

C Am Central America   Lat Am Latin America   Mex Mexico

bankrupt *adjective*
= en bancarrota
to go bankrupt = quebrar

bank statement *noun*
a bank statement = un estado de cuenta

baptize *verb*
= bautizar

bar *noun*
- (*a place*)
  a bar = un bar
- (*a counter*)
  a bar = una barra
- (*on a cage or window*)
  a bar = un barrote
- **a bar of soap** = una pastilla de jabón, una barra de jabón (*R Pl*)
  a bar of chocolate = una barra de chocolate

barbecue *noun*
- (*a cooking utensil*)
  a barbecue = una barbacoa, un asador (*Lat Am*)
- (*a social occasion*)
  a barbecue = una barbacoa, un asado (*Lat Am*)

barbed wire, barbwire (*US English*) *noun*
  barbed wire = alambre de púas (*masculine*), alambre de espino (*masculine*) (*Spa*)

bare *adjective*
- (*uncovered*)
  to have bare feet = estar descalzo/decalza
  the walls were bare = las paredes estaban desnudas
- (*empty*) = vacío/vacía

barely *adverb*
= apenas

bargain
1 *noun*
- (*a cheap thing*)
  a bargain = una ganga
- (*a business agreement*)
  a bargain = un trato
2 *verb*
- (*to haggle*) = regatear
- (*to negotiate*) = negociar

bark
1 *noun*
- (*of a dog*)
  a bark = un ladrido
- (*of a tree*)
  the bark = la corteza
2 *verb* = ladrar

barmaid *noun*
  a barmaid = una mesera, una camarera (*Spa*)

barman *noun* (*British English*)
  a barman = un barman, un camarero (*Spa*)

barn *noun*
  a barn = un granero

barrel *noun*
  a barrel = un barril

barricade *noun*
  a barricade = una barricada

barrier *noun*
  a barrier = una barrera

barrister *noun*
  a barrister = un abogado/una abogada

bartender *noun* (*US English*)
  a bartender = un barman, un camarero (*Spa*)

base
1 *noun*
- (*the bottom part of something*)
  the base of a wall = la base de una pared
  the base of a tree/a lamp = el pie de un árbol/una lámpara
- (*a place*)
  a base = una base
2 *verb*
  she is based in London = tiene su base en Londres
  the film is based on a true story = la película está basada en una historia real

baseball *noun* ▶ p. 306
  baseball = béisbol (*masculine*)

basement *noun*
  a basement = un sótano

basic *adjective*
= básico/básica

basically *adverb*
= básicamente

basin *noun*
- (*for washing up*)
  a basin = una palangana
- (*a washbasin*)
  a basin = un lavabo

basis *noun*
  (*for action or negotiation*)
  basis = base (*feminine*)

basket *noun*
  a basket = una canasta, una cesta

basketball *noun* ▶ p. 306
  basketball = baloncesto (*masculine*), básquetbol (*masculine*) (*Lat Am*)

bat *noun*
- (*animal*)
  a bat = un murciélago
- (*for playing baseball or cricket*)
  a bat = un bate

bath *noun*
- (*a wash*)
  to have a bath, to take a bath (*US English*) = bañarse

R Pl River Plate area   **SC** Southern Cone   **Spa** Spain

- (a tub)
  a bath = una bañera, una tina (Lat Am)
  he's in the bath = se está bañando

bathroom noun
  a bathroom = un cuarto de baño

battery noun
  a battery (for a radio, a clock or a torch) =
  una pila
  (for a car) = una batería

battle noun
  a battle = una batalla

bay noun
  a bay = una bahía

be verb
- (describing permanent qualities) = ser
  she is [young | tall | rich ...] = es [joven | alta |
  rica ...]
  it is Monday = es lunes
  it is late = es tarde
- (describing transitional state or mood) =
  estar
  I'm [worried | sad | okay ...] = estoy
  [preocupado | triste | bien ...]
  the water was hot = el agua estaba caliente
  the car is broken = el coche está estropeado

  ! Note that ser and estar can imply fine
  differences in meaning: es delgado = he
  is thin, implying that he has always been
  thin; está delgado = he is thin, implying
  that he has lost weight recently; las
  manzanas son buenas = apples are good,
  talking about apples in general; las
  manzanas están buenas = the apples are
  good, referring to the particular apples
  that the speaker has

- (exist)
  there is/are = hay
  **there is a tree/there are three trees in the
  garden** = hay un árbol/tres árboles en el
  jardín
- (describing a job) = ser
  I am a journalist = soy periodista
- (talking about health) = estar
  how are you = ¿como estás?
  I'm very well = estoy muy bien
- (talking about cost)
  how much is it? = ¿cuánto cuesta?,
  ¿cuánto es?
- (to be situated) = estar
  where is the library? = ¿dónde está la
  biblioteca?
- (talking about going to a place or traveling)
  I've never been to Greece = nunca he
  estado en Grecia
- (in the following expressions to be is
  translated by tener)
  I'm hot/cold = tengo calor/frío
  to be hungry/thirsty = tener hambre/sed
  to be afraid = tener miedo
  how old are you? = ¿cuántos años tienes?
  I'm 30 = tengo 30 años

- (talking about the weather)
  the weather is fine = hace buen tiempo
  it's hot/cold today = hace calor/frío hoy
- (in continuous sentences)
  he is reading = está leyendo
  it was snowing = nevaba, estaba nevando
  we are going to Paris tomorrow = mañana
  vamos a París
- (in passive sentences)
  it was built in 1903 = fue construido en
  1903, se construyó en 1903, lo
  construyeron en 1903
  the house has been sold = la casa se ha
  vendido
  it is known that ... = se sabe que ...

  ! The passive is less common in Spanish
  than it is in English; passive sentences in
  English are more usually translated using
  the pronoun se, or the third person plural,
  as shown in the examples above

- (in questions at the end of sentences)
  it's a lovely house, isn't it? = es una casa
  muy linda, ¿verdad?

  ! See estar and ser for a fuller treatment
  of the uses of these verbs

beach noun
  a beach = una playa

bead noun
  a bead = una cuenta

beak noun
  a beak = un pico

beam noun
- (made of wood)
  a beam = una viga
- (of light)
  a beam = un rayo

bean noun
  a bean = un frijol, un poroto (SC), una
  alubia (Spa)

bear
  1 noun
  a bear = un oso
  2 verb
- (to tolerate a person) = aguantar
- (to tolerate a sight, a noise, a taste or a
  smell) = soportar
- (to carry) = llevar

beard noun
  a beard = una barba

bearded adjective
  = barbudo/barbuda

beat verb
- (to hit) = pegar
- (to be victorious over) = ganarle a
  she beat me at tennis = me ganó al tenis
  beat up = pegarle a
  to beat someone up = pegarle a alguien

C Am Central America   **Lat Am** Latin America   **Mex** Mexico

beautiful *adjective*
- (*if it's scenery*) = precioso/preciosa, hermoso/hermosa
- (*if it's a woman or child*) = precioso/preciosa

beauty *noun*
beauty = belleza (*feminine*)

because
1 *conjunction* = porque
2 because of = debido a

become *verb*
to become President = asumir la presidencia
to become rich = hacerse rico
they became friends = se hicieron amigos

bed *noun*
a bed = una cama
to go to bed = acostarse

bedroom *noun*
a bedroom = un dormitorio, un cuarto, una pieza (*Lat Am*), una recámara (*Mex*)

bee *noun*
a bee = una abeja

beef *noun*
beef = carne de vaca (*feminine*), carne de res (*feminine*) (*Mex*), ternera (*feminine*) (*Spa*)

beer *noun*
- (*the product*)
  beer = cerveza (*feminine*)
- (*a glass of beer*)
  a beer = una cerveza

beet (*US English*), **beetroot** (*British English*) *noun*
a beet = una remolacha, un betabel (*Mex*)

before
1 *preposition*
- (*in time*) = antes de
  before Christmas = antes de Navidad
  the day before yesterday = anteayer
- (*in front of*)
  = ante
  the match took place before a crowd of five thousand spectators = el partido se desarrolló ante cinco mil espectadores
2 *adverb*
  = antes
  two weeks before = dos semanas antes
3 *conjunction*
  I would like to see him before I go = quisiera verlo antes de irme
  before the train leaves = antes de que salga el tren

  ! *Note the use of the subjunctive after* antes de que

beg *verb*
- (*to beg for food or money*) = mendigar

- (*to ask*) = pedir
  I beg your pardon = le pido perdón

beggar *noun*
a beggar = un mendigo/una mendiga

begin *verb*
= empezar, comenzar
to begin work, to begin working = empezar a trabajar, comenzar a trabajar
to begin with (*at first*) = al principio
(*first of all*) = para empezar

beginner *noun*
a beginner = un/una principiante

beginning *noun*
the beginning = el comienzo, el principio
in the beginning = al principio
at the beginning of May = al principio de Mayo

behalf *noun*
in behalf of (*US English*), on behalf of (*British English*)
I am phoning in behalf of my sister = llamo de parte de mi hermana
he was acting in her behalf = actuaba en representación de ella

behave *verb*
= comportarse
to behave oneself = comportarse bien

behavior (*US English*), **behaviour** (*British English*) *noun*
behavior = comportamiento (*masculine*)

behind
1 *preposition* = detrás de, atrás de (*Lat Am*)
2 *adverb*
- to stay behind = quedarse
  he looked behind = miró hacia atrás
- (*late*)
  he is behind with his work = está atrasado con el trabajo

beige *adjective* ▶ p. 183
= beige (**!** *never changes*), beis (**!** *never changes*) (*Spa*)

Belgian ▶ p. 187
1 *noun*
a Belgian = un/una belga
2 *adjective* = belga

Belgium *noun* ▶ p. 187
Belgium = Bélgica (*feminine*)

belief *noun*
a belief = una creencia

believe *verb*
= creer
to believe in God = creer en Dios

bell *noun*
- (*in a church*)
  a bell = una campana

B

• (*on a door or bicycle*)
  a bell = un timbre

belong *verb*
• (*to be the property of*)
  to belong to = pertenecer a
• (*to be a member of*)
  to belong to a club = ser socio de un club
  to belong to a union = estar
  afiliado/afiliada a un sindicato
• (*to be kept or stored*) = ir
  those plates belong in the kitchen = esos
  platos van en la cocina

belongings *noun*
  belongings = pertenencias (*feminine
  plural*)

below
1 *preposition* = debajo de, abajo de (*Lat Am*)
2 *adverb*
  the room below = el cuarto de abajo

belt *noun*
  a belt = un cinturón

bench *noun*
  a bench = un banco

bend
1 *noun*
  (*turning in a road*)
  a bend = una curva
2 *verb*
• (*to bow*)
  to bend one's leg = doblar la pierna
• (*to make something crooked*)
  to bend = torcer
• (*to lean forward or stoop*)
  to bend = inclinarse
  she bent forward = se inclinó hacia
  adelante
  bend down = agacharse

beneath
1 *preposition* = bajo
2 *adverb*
  the room beneath = el cuarto de abajo

benefit
1 *noun*
  (*advantage*)
  a benefit = una ventaja
2 *verb*
  to benefit someone = beneficiar a alguien

bent *adjective*
  = torcido/torcida

berry *noun*
  a berry = una baya

beside *preposition*
  = al lado de, junto a
  he is sitting beside me = está sentado a mi
  lado, está sentado junto a mí
  I live beside the sea = vivo a la orilla del
  mar

best
1 *noun*
  the best = el mejor/la mejor
  she did her best to convince me = hizo
  todo lo que pudo para convencerme
2 *adjective* = mejor
  the best restaurant in town = el mejor
  restaurante de la ciudad
3 *adverb*
  blue suits you best = el azul es el color que
  mejor te queda
  I did it as best I could = lo hice lo mejor
  que pude

bet
1 *noun*
  a bet = una apuesta
2 *verb* = apostar
  to bet on a horse = apostar a un caballo

betray *verb*
  = traicionar

better
1 *adjective* = mejor
  her new film is better than the rest = su
  nueva película es mejor que las demás
  to get better = mejorar
2 *adverb* = mejor
  he speaks French better than I do = habla
  francés mejor que yo

between
1 *preposition* = entre
  between now and next year = de aquí al
  año que viene
2 *adverb*
  in between = en medio

beware *verb*
  beware! = ¡atención!
  beware of the dog! = ¡cuidado con el perro!

beyond *preposition*
  = más allá de

bicycle *noun*
  a bicycle = una bicicleta

big *adjective*
• (*large*) = grande

  ! Note that **grande** *becomes* **gran** *when it
  is used before a singular noun*
  ---

  a big garden = un jardín grande, un gran
  jardín
• (*important or considerable*)
  a big mistake = un gran error
• (*older*) = mayor

bike *noun*
  a bike = una bici✶

bikini *noun*
  a bikini = un bikini

bilingual *adjective*
  = bilingüe

bill *noun*
- (*in a restaurant*)
  a bill = una cuenta, una adición (*R Pl*)
- (*for gas, electricity, telephone, repairs*)
  a bill = una factura
- (*in a hotel or guesthouse*)
  a bill = una cuenta
- (*US English—paper money*)
  a bill = un billete

billion *noun*
- (*US English—a thousand million*)
  a billion = mil millones (*masculine plural*)
- (*British English—a million million*)
  a billion = un billón

bin *noun*
  a bin (*in a kitchen*) = un cubo de basura, un tacho de basura (*SC*), un bote de basura (*Mex*)
  (*for wastepaper*) = una papelera

binoculars *noun*
  binoculars = gemelos (*masculine plural*)

biology *noun*
  biology = biología (*feminine*)

bird *noun*
  a bird (*small*) = un pájaro, (*large*) = un ave (*feminine*)

birth *noun*
  a birth = un nacimiento
  she gave birth to a boy = dio a luz a un niño

birthday *noun*
  a birthday = un cumpleaños
  happy birthday! = ¡feliz cumpleaños!

biscuit *noun* (*British English*)
  a biscuit = una galleta, una galletita (*R Pl*)

bishop *noun*
  a bishop = un obispo

bit *noun*
- (*a piece*)
  a bit = un pedazo, un trozo
- (*a little*)
  a bit = un poco
  a bit expensive = un poco caro

bite
1 *noun*
- (*from a dog or snake*)
  a bite = una mordedura
- (*from an insect*)
  a bite = una picadura
2 *verb*
- (*of a person or dog*) = morder
  she bites her nails = se come las uñas
- (*of an insect*) = picar

bitter *adjective*
  = amargo/amarga

black *adjective* ▶ **p. 183**
  = negro/negra

blackberry *noun*
  a blackberry = una mora

blackboard *noun*
  a blackboard = una pizarra

B

blackcurrant *noun*
  a blackcurrant = una grosella negra

blackmail
1 *noun*
  blackmail = chantaje (*masculine*)
2 *verb* = chantajear

bladder *noun*
  the bladder = la vejiga

blade *noun*
  (*of a knife or sword*)
  a blade = una hoja
  a blade of grass = una brizna de hierba

blame
1 *noun*
  to put the blame on someone = echarle la culpa a alguien
2 *verb*
  to blame someone for something = echarle a alguien la culpa de algo

blank *adjective*
  a blank sheet of paper = una hoja de papel en blanco
  a blank cassette = una cinta virgen

blanket *noun*
  a blanket = una manta, una cobija (*Lat Am*), una frazada (*Lat Am*)

blast *noun*
  a blast = una explosión

blaze
1 *noun*
  (*in a building or street*)
  a blaze = un incendio
2 *verb* = arder

bleach *noun*
  bleach = lejía (*feminine*), cloro (*masculine*) (*Lat Am*), blanqueador (*masculine*) (*Mex*)

bleed *verb*
  = sangrar
  his nose is bleeding = le sangra la nariz

bless *verb*
  = bendecir

blind
1 *adjective* = ciego/ciega
  to go blind = quedarse ciego/ciega
2 *verb*
- (*to make someone lose their sight*) = dejar ciego/ciega
- (*to dazzle*) = deslumbrar
3 *noun*
  (*on a window*)
  a blind = una persiana

blink *verb*
= parpadear

blister *noun*
a blister = una ampolla

blizzard *noun*
a blizzard = una ventisca

block
1 *noun*
• (*a large piece*)
a block = un bloque
• (*a building*)
a block of flats (*British English*) = un edificio de apartamentos, un edificio de departamentos (*Lat Am*), una casa de pisos (*Spa*)
an office block = un edificio de oficinas
2 *verb*
(*to obstruct*) = bloquear
block out
to block out the light = tapar la luz
block up
to block up a hole = tapar un agujero

blond, **blonde**
1 *noun*
a blond = un rubio/una rubia, un güero✱/una güera✱ (*Mex*)
2 *adjective* = rubio/rubia, güero✱/güera✱ (*Mex*)

blood *noun*
blood = sangre (*feminine*)

bloom *verb*
= florecer

blouse *noun*
a blouse = una blusa

blow
1 *verb* = soplar
the wind was blowing = soplaba el viento
the referee blew his whistle = el árbitro hizo sonar el silbato
2 *noun*
a blow = un golpe
his death was a terrible blow for her = su muerte fue un golpe terrible para ella
blow out
to blow out a candle = apagar una vela
blow up
• (*in an explosion*)
they blew up the building = hicieron saltar el edificio por los aires
• (*to inflate*)
to blow up a balloon = inflar un globo, hinchar un globo (*Spa*)

blue *adjective* ▶ p. 183
= azul

blunt *adjective*
(*not sharp*)
= desafilado/desafilada

blush *verb*
= sonrojarse

board
1 *noun*
• (*a piece of wood*)
a board = una tabla
• (*a committee*)
a board = una junta
• (*for chess or checkers*)
a board = un tablero
• (*a blackboard*)
a board = una pizarra
• (*accommodation*)
board and lodging = comida y alojamiento
• on board = a bordo
2 *verb*
to board a [plane | ship | train ...] = embarcarse

boarding card, boarding pass
noun
a boarding card = una tarjeta de embarque, un pase de abordar (*Mex*)

boarding school *noun*
a boarding school = un internado

boast *verb*
= alardear

boat *noun*
a boat = un barco

body *noun* ▶ p. 235
the body = el cuerpo
a dead body = un cadáver

boil *verb*
• to boil water = hervir agua
to boil an egg = cocer un huevo
• (*to come to the boil*) = hervir

boiled egg *noun*
a boiled egg (*soft*) = un huevo pasado por agua, un huevo tibio (*Mex*), (*hard*) un huevo duro

boiler *noun*
a boiler = una caldera

boiling *adjective*
boiling water = agua hirviendo

bolt
1 *noun*
• (*a lock*)
a bolt = un pestillo
• (*a screw*)
a bolt = un perno
2 *verb*
to bolt a door = cerrar una puerta con pestillo

bomb
1 *noun*
a bomb = una bomba
2 *verb* = bombardear

bond *noun*
a bond = un lazo

---

bone *noun*
- **a bone** = un hueso
- (*of a fish*)
  a bone = una espina

bonnet *noun*
- (*a baby's hat*)
  a bonnet = un gorrito
- (*a lady's hat*)
  a bonnet = un sombrero (de ala pequeña)
- (*British English—of a car*)
  the bonnet = el capó, el capote (*Mex*)

bonus *noun*
- (*a payment*)
  a bonus = una bonificación
- (*an advantage*)
  a bonus = una ventaja

book
1 *noun*
  a book = un libro
2 *verb*
  to book [a room | a seat | a table …] = reservar
  [un cuarto | un asiento | una mesa …]
  the flight is fully booked = el vuelo está
  completo

bookcase *noun*
  a bookcase = una biblioteca, una librería
  (*Spa*), un librero (*Mex*)

booking *noun*
  a booking = una reserva, una reservación
  (*Lat Am*)
  to make a booking = hacer una reserva,
  hacer una reservación

bookshop, **bookstore** (*US English*)
noun
  a bookshop = una librería

boom *noun*
  (*in the economy*)
  a boom = un boom

boot *noun*
- (*footwear*)
  a boot = una bota
- (*British English—of a car*)
  the boot = el maletero, la cajuela (*Mex*), el
  baúl (*R Pl*)

border
1 *noun*
- (*a frontier*)
  a border = una frontera
- (*an edge*)
  a border = un borde
2 *verb*
  (*if it's a country*) = limitar con
  Chile borders Argentina = Chile limita con
  Argentina

bore *verb*
  = aburrir

bored *adjective*
  = aburrido/aburrida
  to be bored = estar aburrido/aburrida
  to get bored = aburrirse

boredom *noun*
  boredom = aburrimiento (*masculine*)

boring *adjective*
  = aburrido/aburrida
  to be boring = ser aburrido/aburrida

born *adjective*
  to be born = nacer

borrow *verb*
  I borrowed some money from him = le pedí
  prestado dinero
  can I borrow your keys? = ¿me prestas las
  llaves?, ¿me dejas las llaves? (*Spa*)

boss *noun*
  the boss = el jefe/la jefa

bossy *adjective*
  = mandón/mandona

both
1 *adjective*
  both books are red = ambos libros son
  rojos, los dos libros son rojos
  both my sons = mis dos hijos
2 *pronoun* = ambos/ambas, los dos/las dos
3 *conjunction*
  both Anne and Brian came = tanto Anne
  como Brian vinieron
  both in Europe and America = tanto en
  Europa como en los Estados Unidos

bother *verb*
- (*to worry*) = preocupar
- (*to inconvenience*) = molestar
  I'm sorry to bother you = siento molestarla
- (*to take the trouble*)
  you needn't bother to wait = no hace falta
  que esperes
  please don't bother = no te molestes

bottle *noun*
  a bottle = una botella

bottle opener *noun*
  a bottle opener = un abrebotellas, un
  destapador (*Lat Am*)

bottom
1 *noun*
- (*the lowest part*)
  the bottom of the hill/stairs = el pie de la
  colina/las escaleras
  at the bottom of the page = al final de la
  página
  at the bottom of the garden = al fondo del
  jardín
- (*the underside*)
  the bottom (*of a box*) = la parte de abajo
  (*of a bottle*) = el fondo
- **to be bottom of the class** = ser el último/la
  última de la clase

R Pl River Plate area   SC Southern Cone   Spa Spain

• (*part of the body*)
  the bottom = el trasero
2 *adjective*
  the bottom shelf = el estante de abajo
bounce *verb*
  (*of a ball*) = rebotar, picar (*Lat Am*), botar
  (*Mex, Spa*)
bound *adjective*
• **it was bound to happen** = tenía que
  suceder
  it's bound to create problems = seguro que
  va a crear problemas
• (*heading in the direction of*)
  a train bound for London = un tren con
  rumbo a Londres
boundary *noun*
  a boundary = un límite
bow¹ *noun*
• (*a knot*)
  a bow = un lazo, un moño (*Lat Am*)
• (*a weapon*)
  a bow = un arco
bow²
1 *noun*
  a bow = una reverencia, una venia (*SC*)
2 *verb*
  (*as a mark of respect*) = hacer una
  reverencia, hacer una venia (*SC*)
bowl
1 *noun*
• (*for food*)
  a bowl = un cuenco
  a fruit bowl = un frutero, una frutera (*SC*)
  a salad bowl = una ensaladera
• (*for washing*)
  a bowl = una palangana
2 *verb*
  (*in sports*) = lanzar
bowling *noun*
  bowling = bolos (*masculine plural*),
  bowling (*masculine*)
box *noun*
  a box = una caja
boxer *noun*
  a boxer = un boxeador
boxing *noun*
  boxing = boxeo (*masculine*)
boy *noun*
  a boy = un chico, un niño
boyfriend *noun*
  a boyfriend = un novio
bra *noun*
  a bra = un sostén, un brasier (*Mex*), un
  sujetador (*Spa*)
bracelet *noun*
  a bracelet = una pulsera

bracket *noun*
  a bracket = un paréntesis
braid *noun*
  (*US English—in hair*)
  a braid = una trenza
brain *noun*
  the brain = el cerebro
brake
1 *noun*
  a brake = un freno
  (*in a car*) = un freno de mano
2 *verb* = frenar
branch *noun*
• (*of a tree*)
  a branch = una rama
• (*of a shop or business*)
  a branch = una sucursal
brand *noun*
  (*a make*)
  a brand = una marca
brand-new *adjective*
  = flamante
brandy *noun*
  brandy = coñac (*masculine*)
brass *noun*
  brass = latón (*masculine*)
brave *adjective*
  = valiente
Brazil *noun* ▶ **p. 187**
  Brazil = (el) Brasil
bread *noun*
  bread = pan (*masculine*)
break
1 *noun*
• (*a pause*)
  a break = un descanso
  to take a break = tomarse un descanso
• (*a holiday*)
  the summer break = las vacaciones de
  verano
2 *verb*
• (*to crack, smash or damage*) = romper
• (*to become damaged*) = romperse
• (*to injure*)
  he broke his arm = se rompió el brazo, se
  quebró el brazo (*Lat Am*)
• (*not to keep*)
  to break a promise = no cumplir una
  promesa
  to break the rules = infringir las reglas
• (*to tell*)
  I had to break the news to her = me tocó a
  mí darle la noticia
break down
  (*to stop working*) = estropearse,
  descomponerse (*Lat Am*)

---

break in
the thieves broke in through a window = los ladrones se metieron por una ventana
break into
to break into a car = entrar en un coche (para robar)
our house was broken into = nos entraron a robar
break out
• (to start suddenly)
the fire broke out in the basement = el incendio se declaró en el sótano
• (to escape) = escaparse
break up
• (to disperse)
the crowd broke up = la muchedumbre se dispersó
• (if it's a couple) = romper

breakfast noun
breakfast = desayuno (masculine)
to have breakfast = desayunar

breast noun
a breast = un pecho

breath noun
breath = aliento (masculine)
to be out of breath = estar sin aliento
to hold one's breath = aguantar la respiración
to have bad breath = tener mal aliento

breathe verb
= respirar

breed
1 noun
a breed = una raza
2 verb
(to rear) = criar

breeze noun
a breeze = una brisa

brew verb
• (if it's beer) = fabricar
• (if it's tea) = preparar

bribe verb
to bribe someone = sobornar a alguien

brick noun
a brick = un ladrillo
a brick wall = una pared de ladrillo

bride noun
a bride = una novia

bridge noun
a bridge = un puente

brief adjective
= breve

bright adjective
bright blue = azul vivo (! never changes)
the light was too bright = la luz estaba demasiada fuerte
this room is not very bright = no hay mucha luz en este cuarto

brilliant adjective
(very clever) = brillante

bring verb
• (take along) = traer
he brought me flowers = me trajo flores
• (to transport)
to bring someone home = traer a alguien a casa
• (to lead) = llevar
the path brings you to the village = el camino lleva al pueblo
bring back
• (to return) = devolver
• (to take home) = traer
bring down
to bring down prices = bajar los precios
bring up
(to raise and educate) = criar

Britain noun ▶ p. 187
(Great) Britain = Gran Bretaña (feminine)

British ▶ p. 187
1 plural noun
the British = los británicos
2 adjective = británico/británica

broad adjective
• (wide) = ancho/ancha
• (wide-ranging)
a broad range of programs = una amplia gama de programas
• in broad daylight = a plena luz del día

broadcast
1 noun
a broadcast = una transmisión, un programa
2 verb = transmitir

brochure noun
a brochure = un folleto

broil verb (US English)
= asar a la parrilla, asar al grill

broiler noun (US English)
a broiler = una parrilla, un grill

broke adjective
to be broke = estar pelado✗/pelada✗

broken adjective
= roto/rota
• (if it's a bone) roto/rota, quebrado/quebrada (Lat Am)

bronze
1 noun
bronze = bronce (masculine)
2 adjective = de bronce

brooch noun
a brooch = un prendedor

broom noun
a broom = una escoba

brother *noun*
a brother = un hermano

brother-in-law *noun*
a brother-in-law = un cuñado

brown *adjective* ▶ p. 183
- (*if it's eyes, clothes, shoes*) = marrón
  (**!** *never changes*), café (**!** *never changes*) (*Mex*)
- (*it it's someone's hair*) = castaño/castaña
- (*if it's natural skin color*) = moreno/morena
- (*tanned*) = bronceado/bronceada
- brown rice/bread = arroz/pan integral
  brown sugar = azúcar morena

bruise
1 *noun*
a bruise = un moretón
2 *verb*
I bruised my knee = me magullé la rodilla

brush
1 *noun*
- (*for hair, teeth, clothes, shoes*)
  a brush = un cepillo
- (*a broom*)
  a brush = una escoba
- (*for painting*)
  a (paint)brush (*small*) = un pincel, (*large*) = una brocha
2 *verb* = cepillar
she brushed her hair = se cepilló el pelo
I brushed my teeth = me cepillé los dientes

bubble *noun*
- (*of air or gas*)
  a bubble = una burbuja
- (*of soap*)
  a bubble = una pompa
  to blow bubbles = hacer pompas

bucket *noun*
a bucket = un balde, un cubo (*Spa*), una cubeta (*Mex*)

build *verb*
= construir

builder *noun*
a builder (*a contractor*) = un/una contratista
(*a laborer*) = un/una albañil

building *noun*
a building = un edificio

built-in *adjective*
= empotrado/empotrada

built-up *adjective*
= urbanizado/urbanizada

bulb *noun*
- (*a light bulb*)
  a bulb = una bombilla, una bombita (*R Pl*), una bujía (*C Am*), un foco (*Mex*)
- (*of a plant*)
  a bulb = un bulbo

Bulgaria *noun* ▶ p. 187
Bulgaria = Bulgaria (*feminine*)

bull *noun*
a bull = un toro

bullet *noun*
a bullet = una bala

bulletin *noun*
a bulletin = un boletín

bully
1 *noun*
a bully = un matón/una matona
2 *verb*
to bully someone = intimidar a alguien

bump
1 *noun*
- (*on a part of the body or on a surface*)
  a bump = un golpe
- (*a jolt*)
  a bump = una sacudida
2 *verb*
he bumped his head = se dio un golpe en la cabeza
he bumped into the door = se dio contra la puerta

bumpy *adjective*
a bumpy road = una calle llena de baches

bun *noun*
- (*sweet*)
  a bun = un bollo
- (*bread roll*)
  a bun = un panecillo, un bolillo (*Mex*)

bunch *noun*
a bunch of flowers = un ramo de flores
a bunch of grapes = un racimo de uvas
a bunch of keys = un manojo de llaves

bundle *noun*
a bundle of clothes (*tied up*) = un lío de ropa, (*loose*) = una pila de ropa
a bundle of letters = un paquete de cartas

bunk *noun*
a bunk = una litera

burden *noun*
a burden = una carga

bureaucrat *noun*
a bureaucrat = un/una burócrata

burger *noun*
a burger = una hamburguesa

burglar *noun*
a burglar = un ladrón/una ladrona

burglar alarm *noun*
a burglar alarm = una alarma antirrobo

burglary *noun*
a burglary = un robo

burn
1 noun
a burn = una quemadura
2 verb
• **to burn** = quemar
to burn garbage = quemar basura
to burn one's fingers = quemarse los dedos
• (when cooking)
I've burnt the toast = se me quemaron las tostadas
• **a burning building** = un edificio en llamas
burn down = incendiar
the house burned down = la casa se incendió

burst verb
= reventar
to burst a balloon = reventar un globo
the pipe burst = la cañería se reventó
• **to burst into tears** = echarse a llorar
• **to burst into a room** = irrumpir en un cuarto
burst out
to burst out laughing = echarse a reír

bury verb
= enterrar

bus noun
a bus = un autobús, un bus, un camión (C Am, Mex)

bush noun
a bush = un arbusto

business noun
• (commercial activities)
business = negocios (masculine)
she has gone to London on business = fue a Londres por negocios
• (a company)
a business = un negocio
• (a trade or profession)
the insurance business = el negocio de los seguros
the hotel business = la industria hotelera
• (matters that concern a person)
that's my business = eso es asunto mío
it's none of your business = no te metas en lo que no te importa

businessman noun
a businessman = un hombre de negocios

businesswoman noun
a businesswoman = una mujer de negocios

bus stop noun
a bus stop = una parada, un paradero (Lat Am)

busy adjective
• (occupied) = ocupado/ocupada
• (full of activity)
he leads a very busy life = tiene una vida muy ajetreada

• (full of people or traffic)
the town is very busy on Saturdays = los sábados hay mucho movimiento en la ciudad
a busy market = un mercado muy concurrido
• (if it's a phone) (US English)
to be busy = estar ocupado, estar comunicando (Spa)

but
1 conjunction = pero
not one but two = no uno sino dos
2 preposition
we have nothing to drink but water = no tenemos nada que beber salvo agua
they invited everyone but Tom = invitaron a todos menos a Tom

butcher noun
a butcher = un carnicero/una carnicera

butter noun
butter = mantequilla (feminine), manteca (feminine) (R Pl)

butterfly noun
a butterfly = una mariposa

button noun
a button = un botón

buy verb
= comprar
he bought me a book = me compró un libro

buzz verb
(if it's a bee, fly etc) = zumbar

by preposition
• **we entered by the back door** = entramos por la puerta trasera
he was bitten by a dog = lo mordió un perro
to pay by check = pagar con cheque
• **by oneself** = solo/sola
she did it by herself = lo hizo sola
• (by means of)
to travel by bus = viajar en autobús
we went there by bicycle = fuimos allí en bicicleta
• (beside)
it's by the door = está al lado de la puerta
by the sea = junto al mar
• (used to indicate the painter or author) = de
a book by Charles Dickens = un libro de Charles Dickens
• (when talking about time)
will it be ready by five o'clock? = ¿estará listo para las cinco?
he should be here by now = ya debería estar aquí

- (*indicating an amount, a rate*)
  to increase by 20% = subir en un veinte
  por ciento
  to pay by the hour = pagar por hora
- (*in measurements*) = por
  20 meters by 20 meters = 20 metros por 20
  metros

cab *noun*
  a cab = un taxi

cabbage *noun*
  a cabbage = un repollo, una col (*Mex, Spa*)

cabin *noun*
- (*in a boat*)
  a cabin = un camarote
- (*in a plane*)
  a cabin = una cabina
- (*a house made of wood*)
  a cabin = una cabaña

cable *noun*
  a cable = un cable

cable TV *noun*
  cable TV = televisión por cable (*feminine*),
  cablevisión (*feminine*) (*Lat Am*)

café *noun*
  a café = un café

cage *noun*
  a cage = una jaula

cake *noun*
  a cake = un pastel, una tarta (*Spa*), una
  torta (*SC*)

calculator *noun*
  a calculator = una calculadora

calendar *noun*
  a calendar = un calendario

calf *noun*
- (*a young cow*)
  a calf = un ternero/una ternera
- (*part of the leg*)
  the calf = la pantorrilla

call
1 *verb*
- (*to name*) = llamar
  he's called Philip = se llama Philip
- (*to describe as*)
  he called me a liar = me llamó mentiroso
- (*to call out to*) = llamar
- (*to telephone*)
  to call someone = llamar a alguien

- (*to summon*) = llamar
  to call a taxi = llamar un taxi
- (*to arrange*)
  to call a meeting = convocar una reunión
- (*to pay a visit*) = pasar
- (*to stop en route*)
  the train calls at Reading = el tren para en
  Reading
2 *noun*
  a call = una llamada
  to give someone a call = llamar a alguien
call back
- (*to return*) = volver a pasar
- (*to phone back*) = volver a llamar
call off = suspender
call on
  (*to visit*)
  to call on someone = pasar a visitar a
  alguien
call up = llamar (por teléfono)

call box *noun* (*British English*)
  a call box = una cabina telefónica

calm
1 *adjective*
  she's a very calm person = es una persona
  muy tranquila
  keep calm! = ¡calma!
2 *noun*
  calm = calma (*feminine*)
3 *verb*
- **to calm someone** = calmar a alguien
- (*to become less violent*) = calmarse
calm down = calmarse

camel *noun*
  a camel = un camello

camera *noun*
- (*for taking photographs*)
  a camera = una cámara, una máquina
  fotográfica
- (*in TV studio*)
  a (television) camera = una cámara

camp
1 *noun*
- (*group of tents, huts*)
  a camp = un campamento
  a holiday camp = una colonia de
  vacaciones
2 *verb* = acampar
  to go camping = ir de camping

campsite *noun*
  a campsite = un camping

can¹ *verb*
- (*to have the ability*) = poder
  can you come? = ¿puedes venir?
- (*with verbs of perception*)
  I can hear you better now = ahora te oigo
  mejor
  can they see us? = ¿nos ven?

! When talking about seeing, hearing, and understanding, you do not translate can

- (to be allowed) = poder
  can I smoke? = ¿puedo fumar?
- (to know how to) = saber
  she can swim = sabe nadar
  can you speak German? = ¿sabes (hablar) alemán?
- (when asking, offering or suggesting) = poder
  can I help you? = ¿te puedo ayudar?

can² noun
a can = una lata, un bote (Spa)

Canada noun ▶ p. 187
Canada = (el) Canadá

Canadian ▶ p. 187
1 noun
a Canadian = un/una canadiense
2 adjective = canadiense

canal noun
a canal = un canal

cancel verb
= cancelar

cancer noun
- (the disease)
  cancer = cáncer (masculine)
- (the sign)
  Cancer = Cáncer
  I'm Cancer = soy Cáncer, soy de Cáncer
- (a person)
  a Cancer = un/una cáncer

candle noun
- (in a room, restaurant, on a cake)
  a candle = una vela
- (in a church)
  a candle = un cirio, una veladera (Mex)

candy noun (US English)
- (confectionery)
  candy = golosinas (feminine plural)
- (a sweet)
  a candy = un caramelo, un dulce (Mex)

canoe noun
a canoe = una canoa

can opener noun
a can opener = un abrelatas

cap noun
- (with a peak)
  a cap = una gorra
- (for a pen, marker, bottle)
  a cap = una tapa

capable adjective
= capaz
to be capable of = ser capaz de
to be capable of doing something = ser capaz de hacer algo

capital
1 noun
- (money, wealth)
  capital = capital (masculine)
- (a city)
  the capital = la capital
- (a letter)
  a capital = una mayúscula
2 adjective
a capital letter = una letra mayúscula

Capricorn noun
- (the sign)
  Capricorn = Capricornio
  I'm Capricorn = soy Capricornio, soy de Capricornio
- (a person)
  a Capricorn = un/una capricornio

capsize verb
= volcarse

captain noun
- (of a ship, sports team)
  the captain = el capitán/la capitana
- (of an airplane)
  the captain = el/la comandante

capture verb
= capturar

car noun
- a car = un coche, un carro (Lat Am), un auto (SC)
- (American English—of a train)
  a car = un vagón

caravan noun (British English)
a caravan = una caravana, un rulot (Spa), una casa rodante (SC)

card noun
- (for greetings, correspondence)
  a card = una tarjeta
- (for playing games)
  a card = una carta

care
1 noun
care = cuidado (masculine)
to take care crossing the street = tener cuidado al cruzar la calle
to take care of the children = cuidar a los niños
2 verb
I don't care = me da igual
to care about someone/something = preocuparse por alguien/algo

career noun
a career = una carrera

careful adjective
(cautious) = cuidadoso/cuidadosa, prudente
to be careful = tener cuidado

careless adjective
to be careless = ser descuidado/descuidada

carousel *noun*
- (*a merry-go-round*)
  a carousel = unos caballitos, un carrusel
  (*Lat Am*), una calesita (*R Pl*), un tiovivo
  (*Spa*)
- (*for baggage*)
  a carousel = una cinta transportadora, un
  carrusel (*Spa*)

car park *noun* (*British English*)
  a car park = un aparcamiento, un
  estacionamiento (*Spa*)

carpenter *noun*
  a carpenter = un carpintero/una carpintera

carpet *noun*
- (*covering the entire floor*)
  a carpet = una alfombra (de pared a pared),
  una moqueta (*Spa*), una moquette (*R Pl*)
- (*a mat*)
  a carpet = una alfombra, un tapete (*Mex*)

carriage *noun*
- (*horse-drawn*)
  a carriage = un carruaje, un coche
- (*British English—of a train*)
  a carriage = un vagón

carrot *noun*
  a carrot = una zanahoria

carry *verb*
- (*to hold*) = llevar
- (*to move*)
  to carry the baggage upstairs = subir el
  equipaje
  to carry the boxes downstairs = bajar las
  cajas
carry on
- (*to continue*) = seguir
  carry on working, carry on with your work
  = sigue trabajando

cartoon *noun*
  (*a movie*)
  a cartoon = unos dibujos animados

case[1] *noun*
  it's raining? in that case I'm taking a taxi =
  ¿llueve? en ese caso voy a tomar un taxi
  in case = por si
  keep the rest in case you need it later =
  guarda el resto por si la necesitas más
  tarde

case[2] *noun*
- (*a suitcase*)
  a case = una maleta, una petaca (*Mex*),
  una valija (*R P*)
- (*for glasses*)
  a case = un estuche
- (*a crate*)
  a case = una caja

cash
1 *noun*
  cash = dinero en efectivo (*masculine*)
2 *verb* = cobrar

cash desk *noun* (*British English*)
  a cash desk = una caja

cassette *noun*
  a cassette = una cinta, un/una cassette

cassette player *noun*
  a cassette player = un pasacintas, un
  cassette (*Spa*)

castle *noun*
  a castle = un castillo

cat *noun*
  a cat = un gato/una gata

catch *verb*
- (*to capture*)
  to catch a fish = pescar un pez
  to catch a rabbit = atrapar un conejo
  to catch a thief = pillar a un ladrón, agarrar
  a un ladrón, coger a un ladrón (*Spa*)
- (*to take hold of*) = agarrar, coger (*Spa*)
  to catch the ball = agarrar la pelota, coger
  la pelota (*spa*)
- (*to trap, snag*)
  he caught his finger in the door = se pilló
  el dedo en la puerta, se agarró el dedo en
  la puerta (*Lat Am*)
  to catch the plane to Madrid = tomar *or*
  (*Spa*) coger el avión a Madrid
- (*to take by surprise*)
  to catch someone stealing = pillar a
  alguien robando, coger a alguien
  robando (*Spa*)
- (*to hear*) = oír
- **to catch flu** = contagiarse de gripe
  to catch a cold = resfriarse
catch up
  you'll have to work very hard to catch up =
  tendrás que trabajar mucho para ponerte
  al día

caterpillar *noun*
  a caterpillar = una oruga, un azotador
  (*Mex*)

cathedral *noun*
  a cathedral = una catedral

cattle *noun*
  cattle = ganado (*masculine*)

cauliflower *noun*
  a cauliflower = una coliflor

cause
1 *noun*
  (*of an accident, a death*)
  the cause = la causa
2 *verb*
  = causar

cautious *adjective*
  = cauteloso/cautelosa

cave *noun*
  a cave = una cueva

CD *noun*
  a CD = un disco compacto, un compact-disc

CD player *noun*
  a CD player = un (reproductor de) compact-disc

ceiling *noun*
  a ceiling = un techo

celebrate *verb*
  = celebrar, festejar

celery *noun*
  celery = apio (*masculine*)

cell *noun*
  (*in a prison*)
  a cell = una celda

cellar *noun*
  a cellar = un sótano

cement *noun*
  cement = cemento (*masculine*)

cemetery *noun*
  a cemetery = un cementerio

cent *noun*
  a cent (*of dollar*) = un centavo
  (*of euro*) = un céntimo

center (*US English*), **centre** (*British English*) *noun*
• (*a place for meetings, activities*)
  a center = un centro
• (*the middle*)
  the center = el centro

centimeter (*American English*), **centimetre** (*British English*) *noun*
  a centimeter = un centímetro

central heating *noun*
  central heating = calefacción central (*feminine*)

centre *noun* (*British English*) ▶ center

century *noun* ▶ **p. 192**
  a century = un siglo

certain *adjective*
• (*sure*) = seguro/segura
  no-one knows for certain = nadie lo sabe con seguridad
• (*particular*) = cierto/cierta
  they only open on certain days = sólo abren ciertos días

certainly *adverb*
  will you be able to help us?—certainly = ¿podrás ayudarnos?—desde luego

certificate *noun*
  a certificate = un certificado

chain *noun*
• a chain = una cadena

• (*a series of shops*)
  a chain = una cadena

chair *noun*
  a chair = una silla

chalk *noun*
  chalk = tiza (*feminine*)

champagne *noun*
  champagne = champán (*masculine*), champaña (*feminine*)

champion *noun*
  a champion = un campeón/una campeona

championship *noun*
  a championship = un campeonato

chance *noun*
• (*likelihood*)
  a chance = una posibilidad
  there is a chance that she'll agree = es posible que acepte

  ! Note the use of the subjunctive after es posible que

• (*an opportunity*)
  a chance = una oportunidad
  to have the chance to travel abroad = tener la oportunidad de viajar al extranjero
• by chance = por casualidad

change
1 *noun*
  a change = un cambio
• (*a different experience*)
  let's go to the cinema for a change = vamos al cine para variar
• (*cash*)
  change = cambio (*masculine*), sencillo (*masculine*) (*Lat Am*), feria (*feminine*) (*Mex*)
2 *verb*
• (*to become different, make different*) = cambiar
  to change color = cambiar de color
• (*to replace*) = cambiar
  to change a tire = cambiar un neumático
• (*to exchange in a shop*) = cambiar
  I'd like to change jobs = quisiera cambiar de trabajo
• (*when talking about one's clothes*) = cambiarse
  to get changed = cambiarse
• (*when using transport*) = cambiar
• (*when dealing with foreign currency*) = cambiar

changing room *noun* (*British English*)
• (*in a swimming pool, sports center*)
  a changing room = un vestuario, un vestidor (*Mex*)
• (*in a store*)
  a changing room = un probador

channel noun
(a TV station)
a channel = un canal

Channel noun
the (English) Channel = el Canal de la Mancha

Channel Tunnel noun
the Channel Tunnel = el Eurotúnel

chapter noun
a chapter = un capítulo

character noun
(in a book, play or film)
a character = un personaje

charge
1 verb
• (to ask a price or payment)
to charge someone for delivery = cobrarle a alguien por la entrega
they'll charge you for the gasoline = te cobrarán la gasolina
• (to run)
the bull charged at us = el toro arremetió contra nosotros
2 noun
• (a price or fee)
a charge = un cobro
• in charge
who is the person in charge? = ¿quién es el/la responsable?
she's in charge of the organization = está a cargo de la organización

charming adjective
= encantador/encantadora

charter flight noun
a charter flight = un vuelo chárter

chase verb
= perseguir

chat
1 verb = charlar, conversar (Lat Am), platicar (Mex)
2 noun
a chat = una charla, una conversación (Lat Am), una plática (Mex)

cheap adjective
= barato/barata

cheat
1 verb = hacer trampa(s)
2 noun
a cheat = un tramposo/una tramposa

check
1 verb
• (to verify) = comprobar
• (to inspect) = revisar
2 noun
• (an inspection for quality, security)
a check = una revisión

• (US English—a bill)
the check = la cuenta, la adición (R Pl)
• (US English—in banking)
a check = un cheque
check in
• (at the airport) = facturar el equipaje, chequear el equipaje (Lat Am)
• (at a hotel) = registrarse
check out
to check out of the hotel = irse del hotel

checkbook noun (US English)
a checkbook = una chequera, un talonario (de cheques) (Spa)

checkers noun (US English) ▶ p. 306
checkers = damas (feminine plural)

checkout noun
a checkout = una caja

checkup noun
a checkup = un chequeo
to have a checkup = hacerse un chequeo

cheek noun ▶ p. 235
(part of the body)
the cheek = la mejilla

cheeky adjective
= descarado/descarada

cheerful adjective
= alegre

cheese noun
cheese = queso (masculine)

chef noun
a chef = un jefe/una jefa de cocina

chemist noun
(British English—in a shop)
a chemist = un farmacéutico/una farmacéutica
a chemist's = una farmacia

chemistry noun
chemistry = química (feminine)

cheque noun (British English)
a cheque = un cheque

chequebook noun (British English)
a chequebook = una chequera, un talonario (de cheques) (Spa)

cherry noun
a cherry = una cereza

chess noun ▶ p. 306
chess = ajedrez (masculine)

chest noun ▶ p. 235
(part of the body)
the chest = el pecho

chestnut
1 noun
a chestnut = una castaña

2 *adjective* ▶ **p. 183**
= castaño/castaña

chest of drawers *noun*
a chest of drawers = una cómoda

chew *verb*
to chew food = masticar la comida
to chew gum = mascar chicle

chewing gum *noun*
chewing gum = chicle (*masculine*)

chicken *noun*
• (*the bird*)
a chicken = un pollo
• (*the meat*)
chicken = pollo (*masculine*)

child *noun*
• a child = un niño/una niña
a group of children = un grupo de niños
• (*a son or daughter*)
a child = un hijo/una hija
have you any children? = ¿tiene hijos?

chilly *adjective*
= frío/fría

chimney *noun*
a chimney = una chimenea

chin *noun* ▶ **p. 235**
the chin = la barbilla

china *noun*
china = loza (*feminine*)
(*fine china*) = porcelana (*feminine*)

China *noun* ▶ **p. 187**
China = (la) China

Chinese ▶ **p. 187, p. 245**
1 *adjective* = chino/china
a Chinese (**man/woman**) = un chino/una
china
2 *noun*
• (*the language*)
Chinese = chino (*masculine*)
• (*the people*)
the Chinese = los chinos

chips *noun*
• (*US English—in packet*)
chips = papas fritas (*feminine plural*) (*Lat
Am*), patatas fritas (*feminine plural*) (*Spa*)
• (*British English—French fries*)
chips = papas fritas (*feminine plural*) (*Lat
Am*), patatas fritas (*feminine plural*) (*Spa*)

chocolate *noun*
chocolate = chocolate (*masculine*)
a chocolate = un bombón, un chocolate
(*Lat Am*)

choice *noun*
• (*an option*)
a choice = una elección
we had no choice = no tuvimos más
remedio

• (*a selection*)
a choice = un surtido, una selección

choir *noun*
a choir = un coro

choke
1 *verb*
to choke = asfixiarse
to choke someone = estrangular a alguien
2 *noun*
(*of a car*)
the choke = el choke, el estárter, el
ahogador (*Mex*), el cebador (*R Pl*)

choose *verb*
= elegir, escoger

chore *noun*
a chore = una tarea

christen *verb*
= bautizar

Christian name *noun*
a Christian name = un nombre de pila

Christmas *noun*
Christmas = Navidad (*feminine*)
Christmas (**Day**) = el día de Navidad
Merry Christmas! = ¡Feliz Navidad!

Christmas carol *noun*
a Christmas carol = un villancico

Christmas Eve *noun*
Christmas Eve = Nochebuena (*feminine*)

church *noun*
a church = una iglesia

cigarette *noun*
a cigarette = un cigarrillo

cigarette lighter *noun*
a cigarette lighter = un encendedor, un
mechero (*Spa*)

cinema *noun*
a cinema = un cine

circle *noun*
a circle = un círculo

circumstances *noun*
circumstances = circunstancias (*feminine
plural*)
under the circumstances = dadas las
circunstancias

circus *noun*
a circus = un circo

citizen *noun*
• (*of a country*)
a citizen = un ciudadano/una ciudadana
• (*of a city or town*)
a citizen = un/una habitante

city *noun*
a city = una ciudad

civilized adjective
= civilizado/civilizada

civil servant noun
a civil servant = un empleado público/una empleada pública, un funcionario/una funcionaria (del Estado)

clap
1 verb = aplaudir
2 noun
• (applause)
to give someone a clap = aplaudir a alguien
• a clap of thunder = un trueno

clarinet noun
a clarinet = un clarinete

class noun
• (a group of students)
a class = una clase
• (a lesson)
a class = una clase
• (a group of people in society)
a social class = una clase social

classical adjective
= clásico/clásica

classroom noun
a classroom = un aula (feminine), una clase

claw noun
a claw (of a cat, tiger) = una garra
(of a crab, lobster) = una pinza

clay noun
clay = arcilla (feminine)

clean
1 adjective = limpio/limpia
2 verb = limpiar
to have a jacket cleaned = hacer limpiar una chaqueta
clean up = limpiar
to clean up after someone = limpiar lo que ensucia alguien

clear
1 adjective
• (easy to understand, making sense)
= claro/clara
• (obvious)
it is clear that no one is happy = está claro que nadie está contento
• (easy to see or hear)
the photo is not very clear = la foto no está muy nítida
she has a clear voice = tiene una voz clara
• (transparent) = transparente
• (with no rain or cloud) = despejado/despejada
• (free, not blocked—if it's a road or space) = despejado/despejada

• (free from spots)
she has very clear skin = tiene muy buen cutis
2 verb
• (to remove obstacles, to empty)
to clear the table = levantar la mesa, quitar la mesa (Spa)
to clear the building = desalojar el edificio
to clear the snow off the road = quitar la nieve del camino
can you clear your books out of the way? = ¿puedes quitar los libros de en medio?
to clear one's throat = carraspear
clear away
to clear away the books and toys = recoger los libros y los juguetes
clear up
• if the weather clears up, we'll go out = si despeja, saldremos
• to clear up the kitchen = arreglar la cocina

clever adjective
• (intelligent) = inteligente
to be clever at mathematics = ser bueno/buena para las matemáticas
• (smart) = ingenioso/ingeniosa
a clever idea = una idea ingeniosa
• (skillful) = hábil

client noun
a client = un/una cliente

climate noun
a climate = un clima

climb verb
to climb (up) a tree = trepar a un árbol
we climbed to the top = subimos hasta la parte de arriba
to climb a mountain = escalar una montaña
to climb over a wall = pasar por encima de una pared

clinic noun
• (in state hospital)
a clinic = un consultorio
• (private hospital)
a clinic = una clínica

cloakroom noun
(for coats)
a cloakroom = un guardarropa

clock noun
a clock = un reloj

close[1]
1 adjective
• (near) = próximo/próxima, cercano/cercana
• (as a friend or relation)
a close relation = un pariente cercano
he's a close friend = es un amigo íntimo
• it's very close today = está muy pesado hoy
2 adverb
the station is very close = la estación está muy cerca
to live close (by) = vivir muy cerca
come closer, I can't see you = acércate, que no te veo

- **close to** (*when talking about location*) = cerca de
- **close to** (*when talking about a situation*)
  to be close to tears = estar a punto de llorar

close² *verb*
= cerrar
close down = cerrar

closed *adjective*
= cerrado/cerrada

closet *noun* (*US English*)
(*a cupboard*)
a closet = un armario, un placard (*R Pl*)
(*for clothes*)
a closet = un armario, un closet (*Lat Am*), un placard (*R Pl*)

cloth *noun*
- (*material*)
  cloth = tela (*feminine*)
- (*for household use*)
  a cloth = un trapo

clothes *noun*
clothes = ropa (*feminine*)

cloud *noun*
a cloud = una nube

cloudy *adjective*
= nublado

clown *noun*
a clown = un payaso/una payasa

club *noun*
- (*an association*)
  a club = un club
- (*a nightclub*)
  a club = un club nocturno
- (*for playing golf*)
  a club = un palo de golf

clue *noun*
- (*in an investigation*)
  a clue = una pista
- (*in a crossword*)
  a clue = una clave

clumsy *adjective*
= torpe

coach
1 *noun*
- (*British English—a bus*)
  a coach = un autobús, un autocar (*Spa*), un ómnibus (*R Pl*)
- (*a person in charge of training*)
  a coach = un entrenador/una entrenadora
- (*British English—of a train*)
  a coach = un vagón
2 *verb* = entrenar

coal *noun*
coal = carbón (*masculine*)

coat *noun*
- (*a garment*)
  a coat (*for men*) = un abrigo, un sobretodo (*R Pl*), (*for women*) = un abrigo, un tapado (*R Pl*)
- (*of an animal*)
  the coat = el pelaje
- **a coat of paint/dust** = una capa de pintura/polvo

coat hanger *noun*
a coat hanger = una percha

cobweb *noun*
a cobweb = una telaraña

cocktail *noun*
a cocktail = un cóctel

cocoa *noun*
(*the drink*)
cocoa = chocolate (*masculine*), cocoa (*feminine*) (*Lat Am*)

coconut *noun*
a coconut = un coco

coffee *noun*
- (*the product*)
  coffee = café (*masculine*)
- (*a cup of coffee*)
  a coffee = un café

coffin *noun*
a coffin = un ataúd, un cajón (*Lat Am*)

coin *noun*
a coin = una moneda

coincidence *noun*
a coincidence = una casualidad, una coincidencia

Coke *noun*
- (*the product*)
  Coke = Coca-Cola (*feminine*)
- (*a glass or can of Coke*)
  a coke = una Coca-Cola

cold
1 *adjective* = frío/fría
  to be cold, to feel cold = tener frío
  I am very cold = tengo mucho frío
  it's cold in the classroom = hace frío en el aula
  you'll get cold if you don't come in = te vas a enfriar si no entras
2 *noun*
- (*lack of heat*)
  the cold = el frío
- (*illness*)
  a cold = un resfriado, un constipado (*Spa*), un resfrío (*SC*)
  to have a cold = estar resfriado

collapse *verb*
= derrumbarse
  the building collapsed = el edificio de derrumbó
  she collapsed onto the floor = cayó desplomada al suelo

R Pl River Plate area   SC Southern Cone   Spa Spain

collar *noun*
- (*on a shirt or jacket*)
  a collar = un cuello
- (*for a pet*)
  a collar = un collar

colleague *noun*
  a colleague = un/una colega

collect *verb*
- (*to gather*)
  to collect information = reunir información
- (*to make a collection of*) = coleccionar,
  juntar (*Lat Am*)
  he collects stamps = colecciona
  estampillas, junta estampillas
- (*to pick up*) = recoger
  will you come and collect us? = ¿vendrás a
  recogernos?
- (*to take away*) = recoger
  they collect the mail at midday = recogen el
  correo al mediodía

collection *noun*
- (*a set of collected objects*)
  a collection = una colección
- (*money collected for charity, in church*)
  a collection = una colecta

college *noun*
- (*university*)
  a college = una universidad
- (*for vocational training*)
  a college = una escuela, un instituto

collide *verb*
  to collide (with someone/something) =
  chocar (con alguien/algo)

collision *noun*
  a collision = un choque

color (*US English*), **colour** (*British
English*)
1 *noun* ▶ **p. 183**
  a color = un color
  what color is the car? = ¿de qué color es el
  coche?
2 *verb* = colorear

color film (*US English*), **colour film**
(*British English*) *noun*
  a color film = una película de color

colorful (*US English*), **colourful** (*British
English*) *adjective*
  = de colores muy vivos

color television (*US English*), **colour
television** (*British English*) *noun*
  a color television = una televisión en
  colores, una televisión en color (*Spa*)

comb
1 *noun*
  a comb = un peine

2 *verb*
  to comb one's hair = peinarse

come *verb*
- **to come** = venir
  I'm coming! = ¡ya voy!
  be careful when you come down the stairs
  = ten cuidado al bajar la escalera
  he won't come into the house = no entrará
  en la casa, no entrará a la casa (*Lat Am*)
  he's coming for me at 10 o'clock = me
  viene a buscar a las 10
- (*to reach*)
  turn left when you come to the traffic lights
  = doble a la izquierda cuando llegue al
  semáforo
- (*to attend*)
  will you be able to come to the meeting? =
  ¿podrá venir a la reunión?
- (*to be a native or product of*)
  she comes from Italy = es italiana
  the strawberries all come from Spain =
  todas las fresas vienen de España
- (*referring to a position in a contest*)
  to come first = llegar el primero/la primera
come around
  (*to visit*) = venir
  **they're coming around for dinner this
  evening** = vienen a cenar esta tarde
come back = volver, regresar
come down
- (*descend*) = bajar
- (*to be reduced*) = bajar
come in
- (*to enter*) = entrar
- (*to arrive*) = llegar
  the train comes in at 5 o'clock = el tren
  llega a las 5
come off
  a button came off my jacket = se le cayó un
  botón a la chaqueta
come on
- (*to start to work*) = encenderse
- (*when encouraging someone*)
  come on, hurry up! = ¡vamos, date prisa!
come out
- (*to go out*) = salir
- (*to become available*) = salir
  the magazine comes out every month = la
  revista sale todos los meses
- (*to fall out*)
  one of my contact lenses came out = se
  me cayó uno de los lentes de contacto
- (*to wash out*) = salir
- (*be revealed*) = revelarse, salir a la luz
come round (*British English*) ▶ **come
around**
come to
  (*to amount to*)
  the meal came to 25 dollars = la comida
  costó 25 dólares
come up
- (*ascend*) = subir
  to come up to someone = acercársele a
  alguien

Colors

Adjectives

There are no significant differences between Spanish and English as regards the uses of adjectives of color.

what color is it/are they?	¿de qué color es/son?
it's blue	es azul
it's a blue dress	es un vestido azul

Nouns

In Spanish the names of colors are all masculine. They always preceded by the definite article:

I prefer blue	prefiero **el** azul
blue doesn't go with brown	**el** azul no combina con **el** marrón

When it follows a preposition:

*do you have it **in** blue?*	¿lo tienen **en** azul?
*she was dressed **in** blue*	estaba vestida **de** azul
*the man **in** blue*	el hombre **de** azul

When talking about shades of color:

deep/dark blue	azul intenso/oscuro
a light blue hat	un sombrero azul claro

- (*to occur*)
  something came up and I couldn't go =
  surgió algo y no pude ir

comfortable *adjective*
= cómodo/cómoda

comforter *noun* (*American English*)
a comforter = un edredón

commercial
1 *adjective* = comercial
2 *noun*
a commercial = un anuncio, una aviso (*Lat Am*)

commit *verb*
- (*to carry out*)
  to commit a crime = cometer un delito
  to commit suicide = suicidarse
- **to commit oneself** = comprometerse

common
1 *adjective*
- (*widespread*) = común
  it's a common problem = es un problema común
2 *noun*
  in common = en común
  we have nothing in common = no tenemos nada en común

communicate *verb*
= comunicarse

community *noun*
a community = una comunidad

company *noun*
- (*a business*)
  a company = una compañía, una empresa
- (*the presence of other people*)
  company = compañía (*feminine*)

compare *verb*
= comparar
to compare Spain with Italy = comparar España con Italia
compared with, compared to = comparado/comparada con, en comparación con

compartment *noun*
a compartment = un compartimento

compass *noun*
a compass = una brújula

competition *noun*
- (*rivalry*)
  competition = competencia (*feminine*)
- (*rival people or products*)
  the competition = la competencia
- (*a contest*)
  a competition (*sporting*) = una competencia, una competición (*Spa*), (*non-sporting*) = un concurso

complain *verb*
= quejarse
to complain about the noise = quejarse por el ruido

complete
1 *adjective*
(*total*)

R Pl River Plate area   SC Southern Cone   Spa Spain

it was a complete disaster = fue un desastre total
this is a complete waste of time = esto es una absoluta pérdida de tiempo
2 *verb*
• (*to finish*) = terminar, acabar
• (*to fill in*) = llenar
to complete a form = llenar un formulario

completely *adverb*
= completamente

complicate *verb*
= complicar

complicated *adjective*
= complicado/complicada

compliment
1 *noun*
a compliment = un cumplido
2 *verb*
to compliment someone = felicitar a alguien

comprehensive (**school**) *noun*
(*British English*)
a comprehensive (**school**) = un instituto de enseñanza secundaria

compulsory *adjective*
= obligatorio/obligatoria

computer *noun*
a computer = una computadora (*Lat Am*), un computador (*Lat Am*), un ordenador (*Spa*)

computing *noun*
computing = informática (*feminine*), computación (*feminine*)

concentrate *verb*
(*to pay attention*) = concentrarse

concerned *adjective*
• (*anxious*) = preocupado/preocupada
to be concerned about someone = estar preocupado/preocupada por alguien
• (*involved*)
to be concerned with something = ocuparse de algo

concert *noun*
a concert = un concierto

concrete *noun*
concrete = hormigón (*masculine*), concreto (*masculine*) (*Lat Am*)

condemn *verb*
• (*to sentence*)
to condemn someone to death = condenar a alguien a muerte
• (*to censure*)
= condenar

condition *noun*
• (*physical state*)
condition = estado (*masculine*), condiciones (*feminine plural*)
the car is in good condition = el coche está en buen estado, el coche está en buenas condiciones
• **on condition that** = con la condición de que
you can go on condition that her parents bring you home = pudes ir con la condición de que sus padres te traigan a casa

! *Note the use of the subjunctive after* con la condición de que

conductor *noun*
• (*of an orchestra*)
a conductor = un director/una directora de orquesta
• (*a bus conductor*)
a conductor = un cobrador/una cobradora

cone *noun*
• (*the shape*)
a cone = un cono
• (*for ice-cream*)
a cone = un cucurucho, un barquillo (*Mex*)

confectionery *noun*
confectionery = productos de confitería (*masculine*)

conference *noun*
• (*for business, for academics*)
a conference = una conferencia
• (*of a political party*)
a conference = un congreso

confidence *noun*
• (*trust*)
confidence = confianza (*feminine*)
to have confidence in someone = tener confianza en alguien
• (*self-confidence*)
confidence = confianza en sí mismo/misma (*feminine*)

confident *adjective*
(*self-confident*) = seguro/segura de sí mismo/misma

confidential *adjective*
= confidencial

conflict *noun*
a conflict = un conflicto

confused *adjective*
to get confused = confundirse
I'm confused = estoy confundido/confundida

confusing *adjective*
= confuso/confusa

congratulate *verb*
= felicitar

congratulations noun
congratulations! = ¡enhorabuena!,
¡felicitaciones! (Lat Am)

connection noun
• (a link between events, statements)
a connection = una conexión
• (in travel)
I missed my connection = perdí la
conexión, perdí la combinación

conquer verb
= conquistar

conscious adjective
• (awake) = consciente
• (aware) = consciente

consequence noun
a consequence = una consecuencia

considerate adjective
= atento/atenta

consideration noun
to take something into consideration =
tomar algo en cuenta

construct verb
= construir

consult verb
= consultar

contact
1 noun
contact = contacto (masculine)
to be in contact with someone = estar en
contacto con alguien
2 verb = ponerse en contacto con

contact lens noun
a contact lens = un lente de contacto (Lat
Am), una lentilla (Spa)

contain verb
= contener

container noun
a container = un recipiente

content adjective
to be content with something =
contentarse con algo

contents noun
• (of a bag, box, jar)
the contents = el contenido
• (of a book)
the contents = el índice de materias

contest noun
a contest (sporting) = una competencia,
una competición (Spa), (non-sporting) =
un concurso

continent noun
(large mass of land)
a continent = un continente

continental quilt noun (British English)
a continental quilt = un edredón

continue verb
= continuar, seguir
to continue to talk, to continue talking =
continuar hablando, seguir hablando

continuous adjective
= continuo/continua

contraceptive noun
a contraceptive = un anticonceptivo

contract
1 noun
a contract = un contrato
2 verb = contraerse

contradict verb
= contradecir

contradiction noun
a contradiction = una contradicción

contrast noun
a contrast = un contraste

contribute verb
• (to give money) = contribuir
• (to participate)
to contribute to a discussion = participar
en una discusión

control
1 noun
to be in control of an organization = dirigir
una organización
to lose control of a car = perder el control
de un coche
she lost control and started shouting =
perdió el control y empezó a gritar
2 verb
(to be in charge of)
to control a region = controlar una región
to control traffic = dirigir el tráfico

convenient adjective
• (useful, practical) = práctico/práctica
it's more convenient to take the bus = es
más práctico tomar el autobús
• (suitable) = conveniente
it's a convenient place to meet = es un
lugar conveniente para encontrarse

conversation noun
a conversation = una conversación

convince verb
= convencer

cook
1 verb
• (to prepare food)
I like to cook = me gusta cocinar
to cook a meal = preparar una comida
to cook the vegetables = preparar las
verduras
• (to be cooked in the oven) = hacerse
2 noun
a cook = un cocinero/una cocinera

cookbook *noun*
a cookbook = un libro de cocina

cooker *noun* (*British English*)
a cooker = una cocina, una estufa (*Mex*)

cookery book *noun* (*British English*)
a cookery book = un libro de cocina

cookie *noun* (*US English*)
a cookie = una galleta, una galletita (*R Pl*)

cooking *noun*
cooking = cocina (*feminine*)
to do the cooking = cocinar

cool
1 *adjective*
• (*fresh, not hot*) = fresco/fresca
it's much cooler today = hace mucho más fresco hoy, está mucho más fresco hoy
a cool drink = una bebida fresca
• (*calm*) = tranquilo/tranquila
stay cool! = ¡tranquilo!
2 *verb*
leave the soup to cool = dejar enfriar la sopa
cool down
• (*to get colder*) = enfriarse
• (*to calm down*) = calmarse

cooperate *verb*
= cooperar

cope *verb*
how do you cope without a washing machine? = ¿cómo te las arreglas sin lavadora?
I can't cope = no puedo más

copper *noun*
(*the metal*)
copper = cobre (*masculine*)

copy
1 *noun*
• (*an imitation*)
a copy = una copia
• (*a book, newspaper*)
a copy = un ejemplar
2 *verb* = copiar
copy down, copy out = copiar

cork *noun*
• (*in a bottle*)
a cork = un corcho
• (*the material*)
cork = corcho (*masculine*)

corkscrew *noun*
a corkscrew = un sacacorchos

corn *noun*
• (*US English—maize*)
corn = maíz (*masculine*)
• (*British English—wheat*)
corn = trigo (*masculine*)
• (*on the toe or foot*)
a corn = un callo

corner *noun*
• (*of a room, a cupboard*)
a corner = un rincón
• (*of a street, a page, a table*)
a corner = una esquina
• (*in football, hockey*)
a corner = un córner

corpse *noun*
a corpse = un cadáver

correct
1 *adjective* = correcto/correcta
the correct answer/pronunciation = la respuesta/la pronunciación correcta
2 *verb* = corregir

corridor *noun*
a corridor = un pasillo

cost *verb*
= costar
how much does it cost? = ¿cuánto cuesta?

costume *noun*
• (*a style of dress*)
a costume = un traje
• (*for party, disguise*)
a costume = un disfraz

cosy *adjective* (*British English*)
= acogedor/acogedora

cot *noun* (*British English*)
a cot = una cuna

cottage *noun*
a cottage = una casita

cottage cheese *noun*
cottage cheese = requesón (*masculine*)

cotton *noun*
• (*the material*)
cotton = algodón (*masculine*)
• (*the thread*)
cotton = hilo (*masculine*)
• (*US English—absorbent cotton*)
cotton = algodón (*masculine*)

cotton wool *noun* (*British English*)
cotton wool = algodón (*masculine*)

cough
1 *verb* = toser
2 *noun*
a cough = una tos
to have a cough = tener tos

could *verb*
• (*had the ability*)
I couldn't move = no me podía mover
• (*knew how to*)
she could read at the age of 3 = sabía leer a los 3 años
I couldn't speak German = no sabía hablar alemán

Countries, cities, and nationalities

In Spanish, countries ending in an unstressed -**a** are feminine (*España, Gran Bretaña, Francia* etc).
All other countries are masculine (*Egipto, Chile, Canadá*).

While the use of the definite article before the name of a country is not generally necessary,
there are some countries which are always preceded by the definite article:

La India	= India
El Reino Unido	= the United Kingdom
El Salvador	= El Salvador

Cities which end in an unstressed -**a** are feminine (*Mérida, Lima, Valencia* etc), and the rest are
masculine (*Londres, París, Madrid*)

The continents are all feminine: *África, Asia, Europa, América*.

Nationalities

Note the different use of capital letters in English and Spanish; adjectives and nouns never have
capital letters in Spanish:

a Spanish student	= un estudiante español
a Spaniard	= un español

English sometimes has a special word for a person of a specific nationality; in Spanish the same
word is almost always both an adjective and a noun:

Danish	= danés
a Dane	= un danés
the Danes	= los daneses

- (*with verbs of perception*)
  I couldn't see a thing = no veía nada
  he could hear them = los oía
  they couldn't understand me = no me
  entendían

  > **!** *When talking about seeing, hearing,*
  > *and understanding, you do not translate*
  > *could*

- (*when implying that something might have
  happened*)
  you could have died! = ¡podrías haberte
  matado!
- (*when indicating a possibility*)
  they could be wrong = puede que estén
  equivocados

  > **!** *Note the use of the subjunctive after*
  > puede que

  a bike could be useful = una bicicleta
  podría ser útil
- (*when asking, offering, or suggesting*)

  > **!** *The conditional is often used in Spanish*
  > *to make polite requests, suggestions etc*

  could I speak to Annie? = ¿podría hablar
  con Annie?
  we could ask Gary = podríamos
  preguntarle a Gary

count *verb*
= contar
**there will be five of us counting the
children** = seremos cinco, los niños
incluidos

count on
  to count on someone = contar con alguien

counter *noun*
- (*where customers are served*)
  a counter (*in a shop*) = un mostrador
  (*in a bank, post office*) = una ventanilla
  (*in a bar*) = una barra
- (*for a board game*)
  a counter = una ficha

country *noun*
- (*a state*)
  a country = un país
- (*the countryside*)
  the country = el campo

countryside *noun*
  the countryside = el campo

couple *noun*
- (*when counting*)
  a couple = un par
  a couple of days = un par de días
- (*two people*)
  a couple = una pareja
  (*if married*) = un matrimonio

courage *noun*
  courage = valor (*masculine*)

course *noun*
- (*a series of lessons or lectures*)
  a course = un curso

R Pl River Plate area   SC Southern Cone   Spa Spain

- (part of a meal)
  a course = un plato
  the main course = el plato fuerte, el plato principal
- **of course** = claro, por supuesto
  of course not = claro que no, por supuesto que no

court noun
- (a lawcourt)
  a court = un tribunal, (the building) = un juzgado
- (for playing sports)
  a court = una cancha (Lat Am), una pista (Spa)
  a tennis court = una cancha de tenis, una pista de tenis

courtyard noun
  a courtyard = un patio

cousin noun
  a cousin = un primo/una prima

cover
1 verb
- (to protect) = cubrir
- (to coat) = cubrir
  to be covered in spots = estar cubierto/cubierta de manchas
- (to insure) = asegurar
  to be covered against theft = estar asegurado/asegurada contra el robo
2 noun
- (a lid)
  a cover = una tapa, una cubierta
- (for a cushion, comforter)
  a cover = una funda
- (a blanket)
  a cover = una manta, una cobija (Lat Am), una frazada (Lat Am)
- (on a book, an exercise book)
  a cover = una tapa, una cubierta
- (of a magazine)
  a cover = una portada

cow noun
  a cow = una vaca

coward noun
  a coward = un/una cobarde

cowboy noun
  a cowboy = un vaquero

cozy adjective (US English)
  = acogedor/acogedora

crab noun
  a crab = un cangrejo, una jaiba (Lat Am)

crack
1 verb
- (to damage) = rajar
- (to get damaged) = rajarse
  the mirror cracked during the move = el espejo se rajó durante la mudanza

- (to get broken) = cascarse
  one of the eggs cracked = uno de los huevos se cascó
2 noun
  a crack = una rendija
  (in a wall, a pavement) = una grieta
  (in a cup, a mirror) = una rajadura

cradle noun
  a cradle = una cuna

crafty adjective
  = astuto/astuta

cramp noun
  a cramp = un calambre, una rampa (Spa)
  I've got (a) cramp in my leg = me ha dado un calambre en la pierna

crane noun
  (machine)
  a crane = una grúa

crash
1 noun
- (an accident)
  a crash = un accidente, un choque
  to have a car crash = tener un accidente de automóvil
- (a loud noise)
  a crash = un estrépito
2 verb
  to crash into a tree = estrellarse contra un árbol
  the plane crashed = el avión se estrelló

crate noun
  a crate = un cajón (de embalaje), una jaula

crawl verb
  (to move on one's hands and feet) = arrastrarse
  (of a baby) = gatear

crayon noun
  (a pencil)
  a crayon = un lápiz de color
  (made of wax)
  a crayon = una crayola   , un crayón (Mex, R Pl)

crazy adjective
  = loco/loca
  to go crazy = volverse loco/loca
  to be crazy about someone = estar loco/loca por alguien

cream
1 noun
- (to eat)
  cream = crema (de leche) (feminine), nata (feminine) (Spa)
- (lotion)
  cream = crema (feminine)
2 adjective ▶ **p. 183**
  = color crema (**!** never changes)

C Am Central America   **Lat Am** Latin America   **Mex** Mexico

create *verb*
= crear
to create a good impression = causar una buena impresión

creative *adjective*
= creativo/creativa

crèche *noun* (*British English*)
a crèche = una guardería

credit
1 *noun*
(*in business, banking*)
credit = crédito (*masculine*)
2 *verb*
to credit money to an account = depositar dinero en una cuenta, ingresar dinero en una cuenta (*Spa*)

credit card *noun*
a credit card = una tarjeta de crédito

crib *noun* (*American English*)
a crib = una cuna

crime *noun*
• (*a criminal act*)
a crime (*a wrongful act*) = un delito
(*a murder*) = un crimen
• (*in society in general*)
crime = delincuencia (*feminine*)

criminal *noun*
a criminal = un/una delincuente, (*serious*) = un/una criminal

crisis *noun*
a crisis = una crisis

crisps *noun* (*British English*)
crisps = papas fritas (*feminine plural*) (*Lat Am*), patatas fritas (*feminine plural*) (*Spa*)

criticize *verb*
= criticar

crooked *adjective*
a crooked line = una línea torcida, una línea chueca (*Lat Am*)
the picture is crooked = el cuadro está torcido, el cuadro está chueco (*Lat Am*)

cross
1 *verb*
• (*to go across*) = cruzar
to cross the road = cruzar la calle
• (*other uses*)
to cross one's legs = cruzar las piernas
our letters crossed = nuestras cartas se cruzaron
2 *noun*
a cross = una cruz
3 *adjective* (*British English*)
= enojado/enojada (*Lat Am*), enfadado/enfadada (*Spa*)
to get cross = enojarse (*Lat Am*), enfadarse (*Spa*)

cross off = tachar
cross out = tachar

crossroads *noun*
a crossroads = un cruce

crosswalk *noun* (*US English*)
a crosswalk = un paso de peatones

crossword *noun*
a crossword = un crucigrama, unas palabras cruzadas (*SC*)

crow *noun*
a crow = un cuervo

crowd
1 *noun*
• (*a large number of people*)
a crowd = una muchedumbre, un gentío
• (*the people watching a game or play*)
the crowd = el público
2 *verb*
they crowded into the hall = entraron en tropel a la sala

crowded *adjective*
a crowded train = un tren abarrotado de gente, un tren lleno de gente
the beach was too crowded = había demasiada gente en la playa

crown *noun*
a crown = una corona

cruel *adjective*
= cruel

cruelty *noun*
cruelty = crueldad (*feminine*)

cruise *noun*
a cruise = un crucero
to go on a cruise = hacer un crucero

crush *verb*
= aplastar

crust *noun*
the crust = la corteza, la costra
a crust of bread = un mendrugo

crutch *noun*
a crutch = una muleta
to be on crutches = andar con muletas

cry
1 *verb* = llorar
2 *noun*
a cry = un grito
cry out = gritar

cub *noun*
a cub = un cachorro

cucumber *noun*
a cucumber = un pepino

cuddle *noun*
a cuddle = un abrazo

cuff *noun*
  a cuff = un puño

cul-de-sac *noun*
  a cul-de-sac = una calle sin salida, una
    calle cortada (*R Pl*)

culprit *noun*
  the culprit = el/la culpable

culture *noun*
• culture = cultura (*feminine*)
• (*a civilization or society*)
  a culture = una cultura

cunning *adjective*
  = astuto/astuta

cup *noun*
• a cup = una taza
• (*a trophy*)
  a cup = una copa

cupboard *noun*
  a cupboard = un armario

curb *noun*
  (*on a sidewalk*)
  the curb = el bordillo (de la acera), el borde
    de la banqueta (*Mex*), el cordón de la
    vereda (*R Pl*)

cure
1 *verb* = curar
2 *noun*
  (*for an illness*)
  a cure = una cura

curious *adjective*
  = curioso/curiosa

curl *noun*
  a curl = un rizo, un rulo (*SC*), un chino
    (*Mex*)

curly *adjective*
  = rizado/rizada, crespo/crespa (*SC*),
    chino/china (*Mex*)

currency *noun*
  a currency = una moneda

current *noun*
  (*flow of electricity, water*)
  the current = la corriente

curry *noun*
• (*a dish*)
  a curry = un curry
• (*the powder*)
  curry = curry (*masculine*)

curtain *noun*
  a curtain = una cortina

cushion *noun*
  a cushion = un cojín, un almohadón

custard *noun* (*British English*)
  custard = natillas (*feminine plural*)

custom *noun*
  a custom = una costumbre

customer *noun*
  a customer = un/una cliente

customs *noun*
  customs = aduana (*feminine*)
  to go through customs = pasar por la
    aduana

cut
1 *verb* = cortar
  cut the bread into small pieces = corta el
    pan en trocitos
  to cut one's finger = cortarse el dedo
  to have one's hair cut = cortarse el pelo
2 *noun*
• (*a wound*)
  a cut = un tajo, un corte
• (*a reduction*)
  a cut = un recorte

cut down
  to cut down a tree = cortar un árbol, talar
    un árbol

cut out
  to cut a photo out of a magazine = recortar
    una foto de una revista

cut up = cortar en pedazos

cute *adjective*
• (*sweet*) = mono/mona, cuco/cuca, rico/rica
    (*SC*)
• (*US English—attractive*) = guapo/guapa
• (*US English—cunning*) = listo/lista,
    vivo/viva (*Lat Am*)

cutlery *noun*
  cutlery = cubiertos (*masculine plural*)

CV *noun* (*British English*)
  a CV = un currículum, un historial
    personal

cycle *verb*
  to cycle to school = ir a la escuela en
    bicicleta
  to go cycling = salir en bicicleta

cycling *noun*
  cycling = ciclismo (*masculine*)

cyclist *noun*
  a cyclist = un/una ciclista

cynical *adjective*
  = cínico/cínica

Czech Republic *noun* ▶ p. 187
  the Czech Republic = la República Checa

Dd

dad, **Dad** *noun*
Dad = papá (*masculine*)

daddy *noun*
my daddy = mi papi

daffodil *noun*
a daffodil = un narciso

daisy *noun*
a daisy = una margarita

damage
1 *noun*
damage = daño (*masculine*)
the storm did a lot of damage = la
tormenta causó grandes daños
2 *verb*
to damage a building = dañar un edificio
smoking seriously damages your health =
fumar perjudica seriamente la salud

damp
1 *noun*
damp = humedad (*feminine*)
2 *adjective* = húmedo/húmeda

dance
1 *noun*
a dance = un baile
2 *verb* = bailar

dancer *noun*
a dancer = un bailarín/una bailarina

dancing *noun*
dancing = baile (*masculine*)

Dane *noun* ▶ p. 187
a Dane = un danés/una danesa

danger *noun*
danger = peligro (*masculine*)
to be in danger = estar en peligro

dangerous *adjective*
= peligroso/peligrosa

Danish ▶ p. 187, p. 245
1 *noun*
(*the language*)
Danish = el danés
2 *adjective* = danés/danesa

dark
1 *noun*
the dark = la oscuridad
2 *adjective*
• (*lacking in light*) = oscuro/oscura
it's getting dark = está oscureciendo, se está
haciendo de noche
• (*if it's a color or piece of clothing*) =
oscuro/oscura
a dark blue dress = un vestido azul oscuro

• (*if it's a person's hair*) = oscuro/oscura
• (*if it's a person's coloring*) = moreno/morena

darkness *noun*
darkness = oscuridad (*feminine*)

darling *noun*
my darling = mi amor

dart *noun* ▶ p. 306
a dart = un dardo
to play darts = jugar a los dardos

date
1 *noun* ▶ p. 192
a date = una fecha
2 *verb* = fechar
the letter is dated February 1 = la carta está
fechada el 1 de febrero

daughter *noun*
a daughter = una hija

daughter-in-law *noun*
a daughter-in-law = una nuera

dawn *noun*
dawn = el amanecer

day *noun* ▶ p. 192
a day = un día

day care center *noun* (*US English*)
a day care center = una guardería

daylight *noun*
in broad daylight = a plena luz del día

dazzle *verb*
= deslumbrar

dead
1 *adjective* = muerto/muerta
the dead man/woman = el muerto/la
muerta
2 *noun*
the dead = los muertos

deaf *adjective*
= sordo/sorda

deal
1 *noun*
• (*a business agreement*)
a deal = un acuerdo
• (*when talking about an amount or quantity*)
a great deal of = muchísimo/muchísima
2 *verb*
to deal the cards = dar las cartas, repartir
las cartas
deal with
to deal with a problem = ocuparse de un
problema

dear
1 *adjective*
• (*expensive*) = caro/cara

Dates

The days of the week

The names of the days of the week begin with a lower case letter in Spanish:

Monday	= lunes	*Thursday*	= jueves	*Sunday*	= domingo
Tuesday	= martes	*Friday*	= viernes		
Wednesday	= miércoles	*Saturday*	= sábado		

They are preceded by an article in spoken Spanish. Note that **on** is not translated.

the course starts on Tuesday = el curso empieza el martes
we don't work on Saturdays = no trabajamos los sábados

The months of the year

The names of the months of the year begin with a lower case letter in Spanish:

January	= enero	*May*	= mayo	*September*	= septiembre *or* setiembre
February	= febrero	*June*	= junio	*October*	= octubre
March	= marzo	*July*	= julio	*November*	= noviembre
April	= abril	*August*	= agosto	*December*	= diciembre

The names of the months can be preceded by **el mes de**:

I spent May in Vienna = pasé el mes de mayo en Viena

Years and decades

The years after 1000 are referred to in thousands rather than hundreds:

1936 = mil novecientos treinta y seis   *1492* = mil cuatrocientos noventa y dos

When referring to decades, the plural article is used:

the sixties = los sesenta
the nineties = los noventa

Centuries

Ordinal numbers are used for the first to the ninth centuries:

the 4th century = el siglo cuarto   *the 8th century* = el siglo octavo

For the tenth century both the cardinal and the ordinal numbers are acceptable:

the 10th century = el siglo décimo, el siglo diez

From the 11th century onward, cardinal numbers are used.

the 12th century = el siglo doce   *the 20th century* = el siglo veinte

Dates

Unlike English, Spanish uses cardinal numbers for the date:

today is the 6th = hoy es seis

In most other contexts, the article **el** is required:

my birthday is on May 6 = mi cumpleaños es el 6 de mayo
she died on February 10th = murió el diez de febrero

Note that the ordinal number is preferred for the first day of the month in Latin America, whereas the use of the cardinal number is more common in Spain.

February 1st = el primero de febrero (*Lat Am*)   = el uno de febrero (*Spa*)

Asking the date

what's the date?	= ¿a cuánto estamos?
it's the 6th	= estamos a seis
what's the date today?	= ¿qué fecha es hoy?
today is November 20th	= hoy es 20 de noviembre
what day is it today?	= ¿qué día es hoy?
today is Monday	= hoy es lunes *or* estamos a lunes

- (in letter writing) = querido/querida
  Dear Anne = Querida Anne
  Dear Sir/Madam = Estimado
  Señor/Estimada Señora, Muy señor
  mío/señora mía
- (loved) = querido/querida
  Paul is a very dear friend = Paul es un
  amigo muy querido
2 exclamation
  oh dear! = ¡ay por Dios!

death noun
  death = muerte (feminine)

debit verb
  = debitar

debt noun
  a debt = una deuda
  to be in debt = tener deudas

decade noun ▶ p. 192
  a decade = una década

December noun ▶ p. 192
  December = diciembre (masculine)

decide verb
  = decidir

decision noun
  a decision = una decisión

deck noun
- (of a ship)
  the deck = la cubierta
- **a deck of cards** (US English) = una baraja,
  un mazo de cartas (SC)

declare verb
  = declarar

decorate verb
- (with ornaments) = adornar, decorar (Lat
  Am)
- **to decorate a house** (with paint) = pintar
  una casa, (with wallpaper) = empapelar
  una casa

decoration noun
- (the act)
  decoration = decoración (feminine)
- (an ornament)
  a decoration = un adorno

dedicated adjective
  to be dedicated to something = estar
  dedicado/dedicada a algo

deep adjective
  = profundo/profunda
  how deep is the lake? = ¿qué profundidad
  tiene el lago?
  the lake is 20 meters deep = el lago tiene
  20 metros de profundidad

deer noun
  a deer = un ciervo

defeat
1 noun
  a defeat = una derrota
2 verb
  to defeat the enemy = derrotar al enemigo,
  vencer al enemigo
  the team was defeated = el equipo sufrió
  una derrota

defense (US English), **defence** (British
English) noun
  a defense = una defensa

defend verb
  = defender

definite adjective
- (precise) = definitivo/definitiva
  a definite answer = una respuesta
  definitiva
- (obvious)
  a definite improvement = una clara mejora
- (certain) = seguro/segura

definitely adverb
  it's definitely true = es indudablemente
  cierto
  she definitely said she would come =
  seguro que dijo que vendría

definition noun
  a definition = una definición

defy verb
  = desafiar

degree noun
- (from university)
  a degree = un título
- (in measurements)
  a degree = un grado

deliberate adjective
  = deliberado/deliberada

deliberately adverb
  = adrede, a propósito

delicatessen noun
  a delicatessen = una charcutería, una
  fiambrería (SC), una salchichonería
  (Mex)

delicious adjective
  = delicioso/deliciosa

delighted adjective
  = encantado/encantada

deliver verb
  to deliver goods = entregar mercancías
  to deliver the mail = repartir el correo

demand
1 noun
- (a request)
  a demand = una petición, un pedido (Lat
  Am)

- (*a claim*)
  a demand = una exigencia
  2 *verb* = exigir

demolish *verb*
= demoler, derribar

demonstration *noun*
- (*by protesters*)
  a demonstration = una manifestación
- (*of a new machine or model etc*)
  a demonstration = una demostración

Denmark *noun* ▶ **p. 187**
Denmark = Dinamarca (*feminine*)

dentist *noun*
a dentist = un dentista/una dentista

deny *verb*
= negar

department *noun*
- (*a part of a firm or institution*)
  a department = un departamento
- (*a division of government*)
  a department = un ministerio, una
  secretaría (*Mex*)
- (*in a large store*)
  a department = una sección
- (*in a university*)
  a department = un departamento, una
  facultad
- (*in a school*)
  a department = un departamento

department store *noun*
a department store = unos grandes
almacenes, una tienda de departamentos
(*Mex*)

departure *noun*
departure = salida (*feminine*)

depend *verb*
to depend on someone/something =
depender de alguien/algo

deposit
1 *noun*
- (*an initial payment on a purchase*)
  a deposit = una entrega inicial, una
  entrada (*Spa*)
- (*paid when renting a house or apartment*)
  a deposit = un depósito
- (*in a bank account*)
  a deposit = un depósito, un ingreso (*Spa*)
  2 *verb* = depositar

depressed *adjective*
= deprimido/deprimida

depression *noun*
depression = depresión (*feminine*)

deprive *verb*
to deprive someone of something = privar
a alguien de algo

depth *noun*
depth = profundidad (*feminine*)
to examine something in depth = estudiar
algo a fondo

deputy
1 *noun*
a deputy (*second-in-command*) = un
segundo/una segunda
(*substitute*) = un/una suplente
2 *adjective*
the deputy director = el subdirector/la
subdirectora

describe *verb*
= describir

description *noun*
a description = una descripción

desert
1 *noun*
a desert = un desierto
2 *verb*
- (*to abandon*) = abandonar
- (*if it's a soldier*) = desertar

deserve *verb*
= merecer

design
1 *noun*
a design = un diseño
the design of a machine/room = el diseño
de una máquina/un cuarto
2 *verb*
= diseñar
the house was designed for a hot climate
= la casa fue diseñada para un clima
cálido
to design clothes = diseñar ropa

designer *noun*
a designer = un diseñador/una diseñadora
a fashion designer = un diseñador/una
diseñadora de modas

desire
1 *noun*
desire = deseo (*masculine*)
2 *verb* = desear

desk *noun*
- (*piece of furniture*)
  a desk = un escritorio
- (*of a pupil in a classroom*)
  a desk = un pupitre
- (*in a hotel*)
  the desk = la recepción

despair *noun*
despair = desesperación (*feminine*)
in despair = en la desesperación

desperate *adjective*
= desesperado/desesperada

dessert *noun*
a dessert = un postre

destroy *verb*
= destruir

destruction *noun*
destruction = destrucción (*feminine*)

detached *adjective*
a detached house (*British English*) = una casa no adosada

detail *noun*
a detail = un detalle
to go into details = entrar en detalles

detailed *adjective*
= detallado/detallada

detective *noun*
• a (police) detective = un/una agente oficial
• a private detective = un/una detective

determined *adjective*
= decidido/decidida
he was determined to go ahead = estaba decidido a seguir adelante

develop *verb*
• (*to elaborate*) = desarrollar
• (*to grow*) = desarrollarse

development *noun*
• (*the act of developing*)
development = desarrollo (*masculine*)
• (*a change*)
there has been a development in the situation = ha cambiado la situación

devil *noun*
the devil = el diablo, el demonio

dew *noun*
dew = rocío (*masculine*)

dial
1 *noun*
• (*of a clock or watch*)
a dial = una esfera
• (*of a telephone*)
a dial = un disco
2 *verb* = marcar, discar (*Lat Am*)

diamond *noun*
a diamond = un diamante

diaper *noun* (*US English*)
a diaper = un pañal

diary *noun*
• (*for writing personal thoughts*)
a diary = un diario
• (*for appointments*)
a diary = una agenda

dice *noun*
a dice = un dado

dictionary *noun*
a dictionary = un diccionario

die *verb*
= morir

diet *noun*
a diet = un régimen, una dieta
to be/go on a diet = estar/ponerse a régimen, estar/ponerse a dieta

difference *noun*
a difference = una diferencia

different *adjective*
= diferente, distinto/distinta

difficult *adjective*
= difícil

difficulty *noun*
a difficulty = una dificultad

dig *verb*
= cavar
dig up
to dig up a garden = levantar un jardín

dilute *verb*
= diluir

dining room *noun*
a dining room = un comedor

dinner *noun*
a dinner = una cena, una comida (*Lat Am*)
to have dinner = cenar, comer (*Lat Am*)

direct
1 *adjective* = directo/directa
2 *adverb* = directamente
3 *verb*
• (*when giving directions*)
could you direct me to the post office? = ¿me podría indicar el camino a la oficina de correos?
• (*if it's a movie or a play*) = dirigir

direction *noun*
• (*the way*)
direction = dirección (*feminine*)
• (*to show someone how to get somewhere*)
directions = indicaciones (*feminine plural*)

director *noun*
• (*of a movie or play*)
a director = un director/una directora
• (*of a company*)
a director = un directivo/una directiva

dirt *noun*
dirt = suciedad (*feminine*), mugre (*feminine*)

dirty *adjective*
= sucio/sucia
to get dirty = ensuciarse

disadvantage *noun*
a disadvantage = un inconveniente, una desventaja

disagree *verb*
= no estar de acuerdo
I disagree with you = no estoy de acuerdo contigo

disappear *verb*
= desaparecer

disappoint *verb*
= decepcionar

disappointing *adjective*
= decepcionante

disappointment *noun*
disappointment = decepción (*feminine*)

disapprove *verb*
to disapprove of an idea = desaprobar una idea
she disapproves of his friends = no tiene buen concepto de sus amigos

disaster *noun*
a disaster = un desastre

discipline *noun*
discipline = disciplina (*feminine*)

disco *noun*
a disco = una discoteca

discover *verb*
= descubrir

discovery *noun*
a discovery = un descubrimiento

discuss *verb*
to discuss politics = hablar de política

disease *noun*
a disease = una enfermedad

disguise
1 *noun*
a disguise = un disfraz
2 *verb* = disfrazar
she disguised herself as a witch = se disfrazó de bruja

disgust
1 *noun*
disgust = asco (*masculine*)
2 *verb* = darle asco a

disgusting *adjective*
= asqueroso/asquerosa

dish *noun*
a dish = un plato
to wash the dishes = fregar los platos, lavar los trastes (*C Am, Mex*)

dishonest *adjective*
= deshonesto/deshonesta

dishwasher *noun*
a dishwasher = un lavaplatos, un lavavajillas

disk *noun*
(*in computing*)
a disk = un disco

dislike *verb*
I dislike him = no me gusta
they disliked the idea = no les gusta la idea

dismiss *verb*
• (*from a job*) = despedir
• (*to reject*)
to dismiss an idea = descartar una idea

disobey *verb*
= desobedecer

display
1 *noun*
(*of objects for sale*)
a book display = una exposición de libros
2 *verb*
(*put on show*) = exponer

dispute *noun*
• (*a controversy, clash*)
a dispute = una polémica, una controversia
• (*a quarrel*)
a dispute = una disputa

disrupt *verb*
to disrupt someone's routine = desbaratar la rutina de alguien
to disrupt the traffic = afectar al tráfico

distance *noun*
distance = distancia (*feminine*)

distant *adjective*
= distante, lejano/lejana

distinguish *verb*
= distinguir

distract *verb*
= distraer

distressed *adjective*
= afligido/afligida

distribute *verb*
= repartir, distribuir

disturb *verb*
don't disturb him, he's busy = no lo molestes , que está ocupado
that noise is disturbing me = ese ruido me molesta

disturbing *adjective*
• (*worrying, upsetting*) = inquietante
• (*alarming*) = alarmante

dive
1 *noun*
(*from a diving board*)
a dive = un salto, un clavado (*Lat Am*)
2 *verb*
• (*from a height*) = tirarse, echarse un clavado (*Lat Am*)
he dived into the water = se tiró al agua
• (*under surface*) = sumergirse
to go diving = ir a hacer submarinismo

divide *verb*
= dividir
six divided by two is three $(6 \div 2 = 3)$ = seis dividido entre dos es igual a tres, seis dividido por dos es igual a tres $(6 \div 2 = 3)$

D

diving board *noun*
a diving board = un trampolín

division *noun*
division = división (*feminine*)

divorce
1 *noun*
a divorce = un divorcio
2 *verb*
to divorce someone = divorciarse de alguien
to get divorced = divorciarse

DIY *noun* (*British English*)
DIY = bricolaje (*masculine*)

dizzy *adjective*
to feel dizzy = estar mareado/mareada

do *verb*
• to do = hacer
what has he done with the newspaper? = ¿qué hizo con el periódico?
to do the cooking = preparar la comida
• (*when used as an auxiliary verb*)
do you speak English? = ¿hablas inglés?
I don't like cats = no me gustan los gatos
do you eat fish?—yes, I do = ¿comes pescado?—sí
I didn't do anything = no hice nada
don't shut the door! = ¡no cierres la puerta!
I love chocolate—so do I = me encanta el chocolate—a mí también
who wrote it?—I did = ¿quién lo escribió?—yo
he lives in London, doesn't he? = vive en Londres, ¿verdad?
• (*to be enough*)
ten pounds will do = con diez libras está bien
that box will do = esa caja está bien
• (*to perform*)
he did well/badly = le fue bien/mal
do up
• (*fasten*) = abrochar
• to do up a house = arreglar una casa
do with
it's got something to do with computers = tiene algo que ver con las computadoras
it has nothing to do with you = no tiene nada que ver contigo
do without
I can do without the television = puedo prescindir de la televisión

dock *noun*
a dock = una dársena

doctor *noun*
a doctor = un médico/una médica, un doctor/una doctora

document *noun*
a document = un documento

dog *noun*
a dog = un perro/una perra

doll *noun*
a doll = una muñeca

dollar *noun*
a dollar = un dólar

dolphin *noun*
a dolphin = un delfín

dominate *verb*
= dominar

donation *noun*
a donation = un donativo, una donación

donkey *noun*
a donkey = un burro, un asno

door *noun*
a door = una puerta

doorbell *noun*
a doorbell = un timbre

dormitory *noun*
a dormitory = un dormitorio

dose *noun*
a dose = una dosis

double
1 *adjective*
• (*if it's an amount or helping*) = doble
• (*when spelling or giving a number*)
Anne is spelt with a double 'n' = Anne se escribe con dos enes
three double five (*British English*) = tres cinco cinco
2 *adverb*
= el doble
he is double my age = tiene el doble de mi edad
3 *noun*
(*in tennis*)
doubles = dobles (*masculine plural*)
4 *verb*
= doblar

double bed *noun*
a double bed = una cama de matrimonio, una cama de dos plazas (*Lat Am*)

double-decker *noun*
a double-decker = un autobús de dos pisos

double room *noun*
a double room = una habitación doble

doubt
1 *noun*
doubt = duda (*feminine*)
there is no doubt that he is innocent = no cabe duda de que es inocente
2 *verb* = dudar
I doubt that he will come = dudo que venga

! Note the use of the subjunctive after dudar que

dough *noun*
dough = masa (*feminine*)

doughnut, donut (US English) noun
a doughnut = un dónut, una dona (Mex)

down

> **!** Down is often used in combinations
> with verbs, for example, cool down, fall
> down, sit down. To find the correct
> translations for this type of verb, look up
> the separate dictionary entries at cool,
> fall, sit etc.

1 adverb
down in Brixton = en Brixton
to go down = bajar
they've gone down to the country = se
fueron al campo
I'm down here! = ¡estoy aquí abajo!
where is he?—down there = ¿dónde
está?—está allí abajo
2 preposition
to go down a street = bajar por una calle
he ran down the slope = corrió cuesta
abajo
the library is just down the street = la
biblioteca está un poco más allá

downstairs adverb
= abajo
he's downstairs = está abajo
to go downstairs = bajar las escaleras

dozen noun
a dozen = una docena
a dozen eggs = una docena de huevos

draft noun (US English)
(cold air)
a draft = una corriente de aire

drag verb
= arrastrar

drain
1 noun
• (a pipe)
a drain = un sumidero, un resumidero (Lat
Am)
• (a plughole)
a drain = un desagüe
2 verb
to drain the vegetables = escurrir las
verduras

drama noun
• (theater)
drama = teatro (masculine)
• (a play)
a drama = un drama

dramatic adjective
= dramático/dramática

drapes noun (US English)
drapes = cortinas (feminine plural)

draught (British English) noun ▶ draft

draughts noun (British English) ▶ p. 306
draughts = damas (feminine plural)

draw
1 verb
• (with a pen or pencil)
to draw = dibujar
to draw a picture = hacer un dibujo
to draw a line = trazar una línea
she drew his portrait = le hizo un retrato
• (to pull)
to draw the curtains = correr las cortinas
• (to remove) = sacar
he drew a knife from his pocket = sacó una
navaja del bolsillo
• (to attract) = atraer
• (in a football match or game of tennis) =
empatar
• (if it's a date or event)
to draw near = acercarse
2 noun
• (in sport)
a draw = un empate
• (in a lottery)
a draw = un sorteo
draw up
to draw up a contract = redactar un
contrato

drawer noun
a drawer = un cajón, una gaveta (Mex)

drawing noun
a drawing = un dibujo

dream
1 noun
a dream = un sueño
2 verb = soñar

dress
1 noun
a dress = un vestido
2 verb
• (to put one's clothes on) = vestirse
• (to put clothes on someone) = vestir
dress up
• (to put on smart clothes) = ponerse elegante
• (to put on a costume) = disfrazarse

dressing gown noun
a dressing gown = una bata

dried adjective
dried fruits/flowers = frutas/flores secas
dried milk = leche en polvo

drill
1 noun
a drill = un taladro
(of a dentist) = un torno
2 verb
to drill a hole in the wall = hacer un agujero
con un taladro en la pared

drink
1 verb = beber, tomar (Lat Am)
2 noun
• a drink = una bebida
to have a drink of milk = tomar un poco de
leche

C Am Central America   Lat Am Latin America   Mex Mexico

- (*alcohol*)
  drink = bebida (*feminine*)
  to have a drink = tomar una copa

drive
1 *noun*
- (*in a car*)
  to go for a drive = ir a dar un paseo en coche
- (*a path*)
  a drive = un camino
2 *verb*
  (*in a vehicle*) = manejar, conducir (*Spa*)
  to drive a car = manejar un coche
  he drives to work = va a trabajar en coche
  she drove me home = me llevó a casa en coche

driver *noun*
  a driver = un/una chofer (*Lat Am*), un/una chófer (*Spa*)

driver's license (*US English*), driving licence (*British English*) *noun*
  a driver's license, a driving licence = una licencia de conducción, un permiso de conducir (*Spa*), una licencia (de manejar) (*C Am, Mex*)

drop
1 *noun*
- (*of liquid*)
  a drop = una gota
- (*a decrease*)
  a drop in temperature = un descenso de la temperatura
2 *verb*
- (*to fall*) = caerse
- (*to let fall*)
  she dropped her bag (*accidentally*) = se le cayó la bolsa, (*intentionally*) = dejó caer la bolsa
- **the temperature has dropped** = la temperatura ha bajado
drop in = pasar
  he dropped in to see me = pasó a verme
drop out
  to drop out of school = abandonar los estudios
  he dropped out of the race = abandonó la carrera

drought *noun*
  a drought = una sequía

drown *verb*
- (*to die*) = ahogarse, morir ahogado
- (*to kill*) = ahogar

drug
1 *noun*
- (*an addictive substance*)
  a drug = una droga
  to be on drugs = drogarse
- (*a medicine*)
  a drug = un medicamento

2 *verb*
  to drug someone = drogar a alguien

drug addict *noun*
  a drug addict = un drogadicto/una drogadicta

druggist *noun* (*American English*)
  a drugggist = un farmacéutico/una farmacéutica

drugstore *noun* (*US English*)
  a drugstore = *un establecimiento que vende medicamentos, cosméticos, periódicos y una gran variedad de artículos*

drum *noun*
  a drum = un tambor
  she plays the drums = toca la batería

drunk *adjective*
  to be drunk = estar borracho/borracha

dry
1 *adjective* = seco/seca
2 *verb*
  to dry wet clothes = secar la ropa mojada
  the clothes took a long time to dry = la ropa tardó en secarse
  to dry oneself = secarse
  he dried his hands = se secó las manos
  to dry the dishes = secar los platos

dryer *noun*
- (*for clothes*)
  a dryer = una secadora
- (*for hair*)
  a hair = un secador, una secadora (*Mex*)

duchess *noun*
  a duchess = una duquesa

duck
1 *noun*
- (*the bird*)
  a duck = un pato/una pata
- (*the meat*)
  duck = pato (*masculine*)
2 *verb*
  (*to lower one's head*)
  to duck = agachar la cabeza

due *adjective*
- (*owing or owed*)
  the balance due = el saldo pendiente
- (*expected*)
  the train is due at 2 o'clock = el tren tiene prevista su llegada a las dos

duke *noun*
  a duke = un duque

dull *adjective*
- (*if it's a color*) = apagado/apagada
- (*if it's a person or book*) = aburrido/aburrida
- (*if it's the weather*) = gris

dumb *adjective*
(*unable to speak*) = mudo/muda

dump *verb*
= tirar, botar (*Lat Am except R Pl*)

during *preposition*
= durante

dusk *noun*
dusk = anochecer (*masculine*)

dust
1 *noun*
dust = polvo (*masculine*)
2 *verb*
to dust the furniture = quitarles el polvo a
los muebles, sacudir los muebles (*Mex,
SC*)

dustbin *noun* (*British English*)
a dustbin = un cubo de la basura, un tacho
de la basura (*SC*), un bote de la basura
(*Mex*)

dustman *noun* (*British English*)
a dustman = un basurero

dustpan *noun*
a dustpan = una pala, un recogedor

Dutch ▶ p. 187, p. 245
1 *noun*
• (*the language*)
Dutch = holandés (*masculine*)
• (*the people*)
the Dutch = los holandeses
2 *adjective* = holandés/holandesa

duty *noun*
• (*moral obligation*)
duty = deber (*masculine*), obligación
(*feminine*)
• (*a task*)
to take up one's duties = asumir las
funciones
• to be on duty (*if it's a policeman, fireman*) =
estar de servicio, (*if it's a nurse, doctor*) =
estar de turno, estar de guardia
• (*a tax*)
a duty = un impuesto

duvet *noun* (*British English*)
a duvet = un edredón

dye
1 *noun*
dye = tintura (*feminine*)
2 *verb* = teñir
she dyed the dress red = tiñó el vestido de
rojo
to dye one's hair = teñirse el pelo

Ee

each
1 *adjective* = cada (**!** *never changes*)
each time I see him = cada vez que lo veo
2 *pronoun* = cada uno/cada una
they are ten dollars each = cuestan diez
dólares cada uno

each other *pronoun*
to love each other = quererse el uno al otro
to help each other = ayudarse el uno al
otro

eager *adjective*
I am eager to meet him = tengo muchas
ganas de conocerlo

eagle *noun*
an eagle = un águila (*feminine*)

ear *noun* ▶ p. 235
an ear = una oreja

early
1 *adverb* = temprano
to get up early = levantarse temprano
earlier in the year = más temprano en el
año
I'm a bit early = llegué un poco temprano
2 *adjective*
to have an early lunch = almorzar
temprano
to take the early train = tomar el primer
tren

earn *verb*
= ganar

earring *noun*
an earring = un pendiente, un arete (*Lat
Am*), un aro (*SC*)

earth *noun*
earth = tierra (*feminine*)
the earth = la tierra

earthquake *noun*
an earthquake = un terremoto

easily *adverb*
= fácilmente

east
1 *noun*
east = este (*masculine*)
the East (*of a country*) = el Este
(*the Orient*) = el Oriente
2 *adjective* = este (**!** *never changes*)
the east coast = la costa este
an east wind = un viento del este
3 *adverb*
it is east of Dallas = está al este de Dallas
we went east = fuimos hacia el este

C Am Central America　**Lat Am** Latin America　**Mex** Mexico

Easter noun
  Easter = Pascua (feminine)
  at Easter = en Semana Santa

Easter egg noun
  an Easter egg = un huevo de Pascua

easy adjective
  = fácil

eat verb
  = comer

echo noun
  an echo = un eco

economic adjective
  = económico/económica

economy noun
  the economy = la economía

economy class noun
  economy class = clase turista (feminine)

edge noun
• (of a road, table, object)
  the edge = el borde
• (of a lake, a river)
  the edge = la orilla
• (of a blade or knife)
  the edge = el filo

educate verb
  = educar

education noun
  education = educación (feminine)

effect noun
  an effect = un efecto

effective adjective
  = eficaz

effort noun
  an effort = un esfuerzo
  to make an effort = hacer un esfuerzo,
  esforzarse

egg noun
  an egg = un huevo

eggcup noun
  an eggcup = una huevera

Egypt noun ▶ p. 187
  Egypt = Egipto (masculine)

eight number ▶ p. 154, p. 319
  eight = ocho (masculine) (**!** never changes)
  see also five

eighteen number ▶ p. 154, p. 319
  eighteen = dieciocho (masculine) (**!** never
  changes) see also five

eighth
1 adjective = octavo/octava
2 noun ▶ p. 192
  (a part)
  an eighth = una octava parte

eighty number ▶ p. 154
  eighty = ochenta (masculine) (**!** never
  changes) see also five

either
1 pronoun
  take either (of them) = toma cualquiera de
  los dos
  which one do you want?—I don't want
  either of them = ¿cuál quieres?—no quiero
  ninguna de las dos
2 adjective
  take either road = toma cualquiera de las
  dos rutas
  I can't see either child = no veo a ninguno
  de los niños
3 adverb = tampoco
  I can't do it either = yo tampoco puedo
  hacerlo
4 conjunction
  they are coming on either Tuesday or
  Wednesday = vienen el martes o el
  viernes

elastic band noun (British English)
  an elastic band = una goma (elástica), una
  liga (Mex), una gomita (R Pl)

elbow noun ▶ p. 235
  the elbow = el codo

elder adjective
  = mayor

elderly adjective
  = anciano/anciana
  an elderly man/woman = un anciano/una
  anciana

eldest adjective
  = mayor
  the eldest son/daughter = el hijo/la hija
  mayor
  I'm the eldest = soy el/la mayor

elect verb
  = elegir

election noun
  an election = unas elecciones

electric adjective
  = eléctrico/eléctrica

electrician noun
  an electrician = un/una electricista

electricity noun
  electricity = electricidad (feminine)

elegant adjective
  = elegante

element noun
  (a part or a unit)
  an element = un elemento

elephant noun
  an elephant = un elefante

E

elevator noun (US English)
 an elevator = un ascensor

eleven number ▶ p. 154, p. 319
 eleven = once (*masculine*) (**!** *never changes*) *see also* **five**

else adverb
 someone else = otro/otra, otra persona
 nothing else = nada más
 everyone else = todos los demás/todas las demás
 everything else = todo lo demás
 what else did he say? = ¿qué más dijo?
 was anybody else at the meeting? = ¿había alguien más en la reunión?
 take your umbrella or else you'll get wet = lleva el paraguas o si no te vas a mojar

elsewhere adverb
 to go/search elsewhere = ir a/buscar en otro lugar
 elsewhere in Britain = en otras partes de Gran Bretaña

email noun
 an email = un correo electrónico
 an email address = una casilla electrónica

embark verb
 (*when sailing*) = embarcar(se)

embarrass verb
 = avergonzar
 to feel embarrassed = sentirse avergonzado/avergonzada

embarrassment noun
 embarrassment = vergüenza (*feminine*)

embassy noun
 an embassy = una embajada

emerge verb
• (*if it's a person or animal*) = salir
 he emerged from the building = salió del edificio
• (*to become apparent*) = surgir
 a new problem has emerged = ha surgido un problema nuevo

emergency noun
• an emergency = una emergencia
 in an emergency = en caso de emergencia
 it's an emergency! = ¡es una situación de emergencia!
• (*medical*)
 an emergency = una urgencia

emergency exit noun
 an emergency exit = una salida de emergencia

emigrate verb
 = emigrar

emotion noun
 emotion = emoción (*feminine*)

emotional adjective
• (*if it's a person*) = emotivo/emotiva
• (*if it's a scene or moment*) = conmovedor/conmovedora

emperor noun
 an emperor = un emperador

emphasize verb
 = enfatizar

employ verb
 = emplear

employee noun
 an employee = un empleado/una empleada

employer noun
 an employer = un empleador/una empleadora

employment noun
 employment = empleo (*masculine*)

empty
 1 adjective = vacío/vacía
 2 verb = vaciar

encourage verb
 = animar
 she/it ∿d me to carry on = me animó a seguir adelante

encyclop(a)edia noun
 an encyclop(a)edia = una enciclopedia

end
 1 noun
• (*the final part*)
 the end = el fin
 at the end of the year = a fin de año
 at the end of May = a fines de mayo
 in the end I telephoned him = al final lo llamé por teléfono
• (*the furthest part*)
 the end of a stick/rope = el extremo de un palo/una cuerda
 at the end of the street = al final de la calle
 at the end of the garden = al fondo del jardín
 2 verb
• (*to finish*) = terminar, acabar
• (*to come to an end*) = terminar, acabar

endure verb
• (*to survive*) = soportar
• (*to last*) = perdurar

enemy noun
 an enemy = un enemigo/una enemiga

energetic adjective
• (*full of energy*) = lleno/llena de energía
• (*requiring energy*) = enérgico/enérgica

energy noun
 energy = energía (*feminine*)

engaged adjective
 to get engaged = prometerse, comprometerse (*Lat Am*)
 they are engaged = están prometidos, están comprometidos

- (*if it's a phone*) (*British English*)
to be engaged = estar ocupado, estar comunicando (*Spa*)

engagement *noun*
- **an engagement** (*a pledge to marry*) = un compromiso
(*period as fiancés*) = un noviazgo
- (*an appointment*)
an engagement = un compromiso

engine *noun*
- (*of a car or airplane*)
an engine = un motor
- (*of a train*)
an engine = una locomotora

engineer *noun*
an engineer = un ingeniero/una ingeniera

England *noun* ▶ **p. 187**
England = Inglaterra (*feminine*)

English ▶ **p. 187, p. 245**
1 *noun*
- (*the people*)
the English = los ingleses
- (*the language*)
English = inglés (*masculine*)
2 *adjective* = inglés/inglesa

Englishman *noun* ▶ **p. 187**
an Englishman = un inglés

Englishwoman *noun* ▶ **p. 187**
an Englishwoman = una inglesa

enjoy *verb*
= disfrutar de
he enjoys life = disfruta de la vida
to enjoy oneself = divertirse
he enjoys traveling = le gusta viajar

enjoyable *adjective*
= agradable

enormous *adjective*
= enorme

enough
1 *pronoun*
we have had enough to eat = hemos comido bastante
that's enough = basta
I've had enough = estoy harto/harta
2 *adverb*
is it big enough? = ¿es lo suficientemente grande?
you don't go out enough = no sales lo suficiente
3 *adjective* (*singular*) = bastante, suficiente
(*plural*) = bastantes, suficientes
have you enough money? = ¿tienes bastante dinero?
there aren't enough chairs = no hay suficientes sillas

ensure *verb*
= asegurar

enter *verb*
- (*to go into*) = entrar en, entrar a (*Lat Am*)
he entered the room = entró en el cuarto, entró al cuarto (*Lat Am*)
- (*to come in*) = entrar
they were unable to enter = no pudieron entrar
- (*to participate in*)
to enter a competition = presentarse a un concurso
to enter a race = inscribirse en una carrera

E

entertain *verb*
- (*of a book, film, show*) = entretener
- (*of a host*)
to entertain guests = recibir a los invitados

enthusiasm *noun*
enthusiasm = entusiasmo (*masculine*)

enthusiastic *adjective*
= entusiasta
to be enthusiastic about something = estar entusiasmado/entusiasmada con algo

entrance *noun*
an entrance = una entrada

entry *noun*
entry = entrada (*feminine*)

envelope *noun*
an envelope = un sobre

environment *noun*
the environment = el medio ambiente

envy
1 *noun*
envy = envidia (*feminine*)
2 *verb* = envidiar

episode *noun*
(*of a story, TV series*)
an episode = un capítulo, un episodio

equal
1 *adjective* = igual
2 *verb* = ser igual a
six and four equals 10 = 6 más 4 es igual a 10

equality *noun*
equality = igualdad (*feminine*)

equator *noun*
the equator = el ecuador

equipment *noun*
equipment = equipo (*masculine*)
sports equipment = artículos de deportes (*masculine plural*)

eraser *noun*
an eraser = una goma (de borrar)

error *noun*
an error = un error

escalator *noun*
an escalator = una escalera mecánica

R Pl River Plate area   SC Southern Cone   Spa Spain

escape
1 *noun*
• *(from prison)*
 an escape = una fuga
• *(of gas, air)*
 an escape = un escape
2 *verb*
 (from a place) = escaparse

especially *adverb*
= especialmente

essay *noun*
 (written by a pupil or student)
 an essay = una redacción

essential *adjective*
= esencial

establish *verb*
= establecer

estimate
1 *noun*
• *(rough calculation)*
 an estimate = un cálculo estimado
• *(a quote for a client)*
 an estimate = un presupuesto
2 *verb* = calcular
 the estimated time of arrival = la hora
 prevista de llegada

euro *noun*
 a euro = un euro

eurocheque *noun*
 a eurocheque = un eurocheque

Europe *noun* ▶ p. 187
 Europe = Europa *(feminine)*

European ▶ p. 187
1 *noun*
 a European = un europeo/una europea
2 *adjective* = europeo/europea

European Union *noun*
 the European Union = la Unión Europea

even¹ *adverb*
• **he didn't even try** = ni siquiera lo intentó
 she even works when she's on vacation =
 trabaja incluso cuando está de vacaciones
• *(used to emphasize a comparison)*
 it's even colder today = hoy hace más frío
 todavía
 he's even richer than her = es todavía más
 rica que ella

even² *adjective*
• *(flat or smooth)* = plano/plana
 an even surface = una superficie plana
• *(when talking about numbers)* = par
 an even number = un número par

evening *noun* ▶ p. 319
 the evening *(before dark)* = la tarde, *(after
 dark)* = la noche
 Friday evening = el viernes en la
 tarde/noche, el viernes por la tarde/noche
 (Spa)
 in the evening = en la tarde/la noche, por la
 tarde/la noche *(Spa)*
 at 6 o'clock in the evening = a las seis de la
 tarde
 good evening = buenas tardes/buenas
 noches

event *noun*
 an event = un acontecimiento

eventually *adverb*
= finalmente, al final

ever *adverb*
• *(at any time)*
 nothing ever happens here = nunca pasa
 nada aquí
 nobody will ever know = nadie lo sabrá
 nunca
 have you ever been to Greece? = ¿has
 estado alguna vez en Grecia?
 I hardly ever go there = casi nunca voy allí
• *(always)*
 as ever = como siempre

every *adjective*
 every time I meet her = cada vez que la
 encuentro
 every day = cada día
 every second day, every other day = un
 día sí y otro no, un día por medio *(SC)*

everybody *pronoun*
 everybody = todos, todo el mundo

everyday *adjective*
= de todos los días

everyone *pronoun* ▶ everybody

everything *pronoun*
 everything = todo

everywhere *adverb*
 we looked for it everywhere = lo buscamos
 por todos lados
 they go everywhere by car = van a todos
 lados en coche

evidence *noun*
• *(proof)*
 evidence = pruebas *(feminine plural)*
• **to give evidence** = prestar declaración

evil
1 *noun*
 evil = mal *(masculine)*
2 *adjective* = malvado/malvada

exact *adjective*
= exacto/exacta

exactly *adverb*
= exactamente

C Am Central America   **Lat Am** Latin America   **Mex** Mexico

exaggerate *verb*
= exagerar

exaggeration *noun*
exaggeration = exageración (*feminine*)

exam *noun*
an exam = un examen

examination *noun*
(*at school*)
an examination = un examen

examine *verb*
= examinar

example *noun*
an example = un ejemplo
for example = por ejemplo

excellent *adjective*
= excelente

except *preposition*
= menos

exception *noun*
an exception = una excepción

exchange
1 *noun*
(*of information, students*)
an exchange = un intercambio
2 *verb*
to exchange something for something =
cambiar algo por algo

excite *verb*
= excitar

excited *adjective*
= entusiasmado/entusiasmada
to get excited = entusiasmarse

exciting *adjective*
= emocionante

exclude *verb*
= excluir

excuse
1 *noun*
• (*to justify something*)
an excuse = una excusa
to make excuses = poner excusas
• (*a pretext*)
an excuse = una excusa, un pretexto
2 *verb*
• (*to forgive*) = disculpar, perdonar
excuse me! = ¡discúlpame!, ¡perdóname!
• (*to justify*) = excusar, justificar

execute *verb*
= ejecutar

exercise
1 *noun*
• (*a piece of work*)
an exercise = un ejercicio
• (*to keep fit*)
exercises = ejercicios (*masculine plural*)

2 *verb*
(*to keep fit*) = hacer ejercicio

exercise book *noun*
an exercise book = un cuaderno

exhaust *noun*
(*of a car*)
the exhaust = el tubo de escape, el caño de
escape (*R Pl*), el mofle (*C Am*)

exhausted *adjective*
= agotado/agotada

exhibition *noun*
an exhibition = una exposición

existence *noun*
existence = existencia (*feminine*)

exit *noun*
an exit = una salida

exotic *adjective*
= exótico/exótica

expect *verb*
= esperar

expense *noun*
expense = gasto (*masculine*)
they had a good laugh at my expense = se
partieron de risa a costa mía

expenses *noun*
expenses = gastos (*masculine plural*)

expensive *adjective*
= caro/cara

experience
1 *noun*
an experience = una experiencia
2 *verb*
to experience happiness/pain =
experimentar alegría/dolor

expert *noun*
an expert = un experto/una experta

explain *verb*
= explicar

explanation *noun*
an explanation = una explicación

explode *verb*
• (*to go off*) = explotar, estallar
• (*to set off*) = explosionar

exploit *verb*
= explotar

explore *verb*
= explorar

explosion *noun*
an explosion = una explosión

export
1 *noun*
an export = un artículo de exportación
2 *verb* = exportar

E

expose *verb*
(*to reveal*) = poner al descubierto
(*to uncover or display*) = exponer

express
1 *adjective*
an **express train** = un tren expreso, un tren rápido
2 *verb* = expresar
to **express oneself** = expresarse

expression *noun*
an **expression** = una expresión

extent *noun*
(*of knowledge, wealth*)
extent = amplitud (*feminine*)
(*of damage*)
extent = alcance (*masculine*)
(*degree*)
to a **certain extent** = hasta cierto punto
to a **large extent** = en gran parte

external *adjective*
= externo/externa

extinct *adjective*
(*if it's an animal or species*) =
extinto/extinta
to **become extinct** = extinguirse

extra
1 *noun*
(*an additional thing*)
an **extra** = un extra
(*an actor in a film*) = un/una extra
2 *adjective*
I need an **extra bed** = necesito una cama más
I brought an **extra pair** = traje un par de más
3 *adverb*
to **pay extra** = pagar más

extraordinary *adjective*
= extraordinario/extraordinaria

extravagant *adjective*
(*if it's a person*) =
derrochador/derrochadora

extreme
1 *noun*
an **extreme** = un extremo
2 *adjective* = extremo/extrema

extremely *adverb*
= extremadamente

eye *noun* ▶ p. 235
an **eye** = un ojo

eyebrow *noun*
an **eyebrow** = una ceja

eyelash *noun*
an **eyelash** = una pestaña

eyelid *noun*
an **eyelid** = un párpado

eye shadow *noun*
eye shadow = sombra de ojos (*feminine*)

eyesight *noun*
eyesight = vista (*feminine*)

Ff

fabric *noun*
a **fabric** = una tela, un tejido

face
1 *noun*
(*of a person*) ▶ **p. 235**
the **face** = la cara
to **make a face** = hacer una mueca
(*of a clock or watch*)
the **face** = la esfera, la carátula (*Méx*)
2 *verb*
(*to be opposite*)
the **house facing ours** = la casa que está frente a la nuestra
(*to look toward*)
my **room faces the sea** = mi cuarto da al mar
(*if it's a building*)
to **face north** = estar orientado al norte
(*to confront*)
to **be faced with a problem** = enfrentarse a un problema
face up to = hacer frente a

fact *noun*
a **fact** = un hecho
in **fact** = de hecho

factory *noun*
a **factory** = una fábrica

fade *verb*
(*if it's a fabric*) = perder color, desteñirse
(*if it's a color*) = apagarse
(*if it's an image or sound*) = fundirse

fail *verb*
(*not to succeed*)
he tried to prevent the accident but he **failed** = intentó evitar el accidente pero falló
(*in an exam*) = ser reprobado/reprobada (*Lat Am*), suspender (*Spa*)
he **failed the exam** = fue reprobado en el examen, suspendió el examen
(*not to allow to pass*)
to **fail a candidate** = reprobar a un candidato (*Lat Am*), suspender a un candidato (*Spa*)
(*not to work*)
the **brakes failed** = fallaron los frenos

---

failure *noun*
  (*an unsuccessful person*)
  a failure = un fracaso
  (*a breakdown*)
  engine failure = falla mecánica (*feminine*),
    fallo mecánico (*masculine*) (*Spa*)
  a power failure = un apagón

faint
  1 *verb*
  = desmayarse
  2 *adjective*
  (*if it's a light or sound*) = débil
  (*if it's a hope*) = ligero/ligera

fair
  1 *noun*
  a fair = una feria
  2 *adjective*
  (*if it's hair*) = rubio/rubia, güero✱/güera✱
    (*Mex*)
  (*if it's skin*) = blanco/blanca
  (*just or reasonable*) = justo/justa
  tomorrow the weather will be fair =
    mañana hará buen tiempo

fair-haired *adjective*
  = rubio/rubia, güero✱/güera✱ (*Mex*)

fairly *adverb*
  (*rather*) = bastante

fairy *noun*
  a fairy = un hada (*feminine*)

fairy story, fairy tale *noun*
  a fairy story = un cuento de hadas

faith *noun*
  (*religious belief*)
  faith = fe (*feminine*)
  (*confidence*)
  faith = confianza (*feminine*)
  to have faith in someone = tener fe en
    alguien

faithful *adjective*
  = fiel

fall
  1 *noun*
  (*of a person or object*)
  a fall = una caída
  (*a decrease*)
  a fall in prices = una bajada de precios
  a fall in temperatures = un descenso de las
    temperaturas
  the fall of the government = la caída del
    gobierno
  (*US English—autumn*)
  the fall = el otoño
  in the fall = en el otoño
  2 *verb*
  (*physically*) = caerse
  to fall down the stairs = caerse por las
    escaleras
  (*to decrease*) = bajar

  (*become*)
  to fall asleep = dormirse
  to fall in love with someone = enamorarse
    de alguien
fall down
  (*of a person*) = caerse
  (*of a building*) = venirse abajo
fall off = caerse
fall out = caerse
  his hair is falling out = se le cae el pelo
fall over = caerse

false *adjective*
  (*not true*) = falso/falsa
  (*fake*) = postizo/postiza
  false teeth = dentadura postiza (*feminine*)

familiar *adjective*
  = familiar
  that name sounds familiar to me = ese
    nombre me suena

family *noun*
  a family = una familia

famous *adjective*
  = famoso/famosa

fan *noun*
  (*hand-held*)
  a fan = un abanico
  (*mechanical*)
  a fan = un ventilador
  (*an enthusiast*)
  a jazz fan = un aficionado/una aficionada
    al jazz
  an Oasis fan = un/una fan de Oasis
  a rugby fan = un/una hincha de rugby

fancy *adjective*
  a fancy hotel = un hotel de lujo
  fancy clothes = la ropa fina

fancy dress *noun* (*British English*)
  fancy dress = disfraz (*masculine*)

fantastic *adjective*
  (*wonderful*) = fantástico/fantástica

fantasy *noun*
  (*a dream*)
  a fantasy = un sueño
  (*unreality*)
  a fantasy = una fantasía

far
  1 *adverb*
  (*in distance*) = lejos
  it's very far = está muy lejos
  how far is Leicester from London? = ¿a
    qué distancia está Leicester de Londres?,
    ¿qué tan lejos está Leicester de Londres?
    (*Lat Am*)
  (*in time*)
  I can't remember that far back = no
    recuerdo cosas tan lejanas
  Christmas isn't far away = falta poco para
    Navidad

F

R Pl River Plate area   SC Southern Cone   Spa Spain

(*very much*)
far better = muchísimo mejor
far more = muchísimo más
by far
he's by far the tallest = es con mucho el
    más alto, es (de) lejos el más alto (*Lat Am*)
so far = hasta ahora
2 *adjective*
    (*extreme*) = extremo/extrema
    the far north/south = el extremo norte/sur
    (*other*)
    at the far end of the room = al otro extremo
        de la habitación

fare *noun*
    (*on a bus or on the subway*)
    the fare = el precio del boleto (*Lat Am*), el
        precio del billete (*Spa*)
    (*on a train or plane*)
    the fare = el precio del pasaje, el precio del
        billete (*Spa*)

farm *noun*
    a farm (*small*) = una granja, (*large*) = una
        hacienda

farmer *noun*
    a farmer = un agricultor/una agricultora

farther
1 *adverb*
    it was farther than I thought = estaba más
        lejos de lo que pensaba
    the train drew farther and farther away = el
        tren alejaba cada vez más
2 *adjective*
    at the farther end of the street = al otro
        extremo de la calle

fascinate *verb*
    = fascinar

fascinating *adjective*
    = fascinante

fashion *noun*
    fashion = moda (*feminine*)
    to be in/go out of fashion = estar/pasar de
        moda

fashionable *adjective*
    (*if it's clothes or designs*) = a la moda
    (*if it's places, people, or ideas*) = de moda

fast
1 *adjective*
    (*not slow*)
    = rápido/rápida
    (*if it's a clock or watch*)
    my watch is five minutes fast = mi reloj
        (se) adelanta cinco minutos
2 *adverb* = rápido, rápidamente
3 *verb* = ayunar

fasten *verb*
    to fasten a coat = abrochar un abrigo
    to fasten one's shoelaces = atarse los
        cordones, amarrarse los cordones (*Lat
        Am*), amarrarse las agujetas (*Mex*)
    fasten your seatbelts = abróchense los
        cinturones

fat
1 *adjective* = gordo/gorda
    to get fat = engordar
2 *noun*
    fat = grasa (*feminine*)

fatal *adjective*
    a fatal accident = un accidente fatal
    a fatal mistake = un error de consecuencias
        fatales

father *noun*
    a father = un padre

Father Christmas *noun*
    Father Christmas = Papá Noel (*masculine*)

father-in-law *noun*
    a father-in-law = un suegro

fattening *adjective*
    to be fattening = engordar

faucet *noun* (*US English*)
    a faucet = una llave, una canilla (*R Pl*), un
        grifo (*Spa*)

fault *noun*
    (*responsibility*)
    fault = culpa (*feminine*)
    it's my fault = yo tengo la culpa
    (*a defect*)
    a fault (*in goods*) = una falla
    (*in a machine*) = una falla, un fallo (*Spa*)
    (*in a person*) = un defecto

favor (*US English*), **favour** (*British
English*)
1 *noun*
    (*a kind act*)
    a favor = un favor
    he did me a favor = me hizo un favor
    (*advantage*)
    the circumstances are in his favor = las
        circunstancias están a su favor
    in favor of
    to be in favor of = estar a favor de
2 *verb*
    (*to benefit*) = favorecer
    (*to prefer*) = estar a favor de
    (*to treat specially*)
    to favor someone = favorecer a alguien

favorite (*US English*), **favourite** (*British
English*)
1 *adjective* = preferido/preferida
2 *noun*
    (*in a race or contest*)
    the favorite = el favorito/la favorita

(a person)
a favorite = un preferido/una preferida

fax
1 *noun*
  a fax = un fax
2 *verb* = faxear

fear
1 *noun*
  fear = miedo *(masculine)*
2 *verb* = temer

feast *noun*
  a feast = un banquete

feather *noun*
  a feather = una pluma

February *noun* ▶ p. 192
  February = febrero *(masculine)*

fed up *adjective*
  = harto/harta
  I'm fed up with this situation = estoy harta
  de esta situación

fee *noun*
  an admission fee = una entrada
  a membership fee = una cuota (de socio)
  school fees = cuota del colegio *(feminine)*,
  colegiatura *(feminine)* *(Mex)*
  a doctor's fees = los honorarios de un
  médico

feeble *adjective*
  = débil

feed *verb*
  (to give food to) = dar de comer a
  (to eat) = comer

feel *verb*
  (emotionally, physically)
  to feel sad = sentirse triste
  to feel hot/cold = tener calor/frío
  I don't feel very well = no me siento muy
  bien
  I didn't feel any pain = no sentí ningún
  dolor
  (to touch) = tocar
  (to want)
  I feel like a glass of water = tengo ganas de
  tomar un vaso de agua, me apetece un
  vaso de agua *(Spa)*
  I don't feel like it = no tengo ganas, no me
  apetece *(Spa)*

feeling *noun*
  (emotional)
  a feeling of sadness = una sensación de
  tristeza
  I have a feeling he's right = tengo la
  sensación de que tiene razón
  (physical)
  a feeling = una sensación

female
1 *adjective*

(when talking about animals) = hembra
(when talking about humans) =
  femenino/femenina
2 *noun*
  (a woman)
  a female = una mujer
  (an animal)
  a female = una hembra

feminine
1 *noun*
  (in grammar)
  the feminine = el femenino
2 *adjective* = femenino/femenina

feminist
1 *noun*
  a feminist = una feminista/un feminista
2 *adjective* = feminista

fence *noun*
  (around a garden, field etc)
  a fence = una cerca, un cerco *(Lat Am)*

ferry *noun*
  a ferry = un transbordador

fertile *adjective*
  = fértil

festival *noun*
  (a holiday or feast)
  a festival = una fiesta
  (an artistic or theatrical event)
  a festival = un festival

fetch *verb*
  (to go and get) = ir a buscar

fever *noun*
  fever = fiebre *(feminine)*

few
1 *adjective*
  (not many) = pocos/pocas
  the few people who came = las pocas
  personas que vinieron, los pocos que
  vinieron
  (several)
  over the next few days = durante los
  próximos días
  fewer people = menos gente
2 *pronoun* = pocos/pocas
  there are so few of them = son tan pocos
  fewer than ten people = menos de diez
  personas
3 a few
  a few houses = algunas casas
  a few of them = algunos de ellos
  I would like a few more = quisiera unos
  cuantos más

fiber *(US English)*, **fibre** *(British English)*
  (a material)
  a fiber = una fibra
  (in diet)
  fiber = fibra *(feminine)*

F

fiction *noun*
  fiction = ficción (*feminine*)

fiddle *verb*
  to fiddle with something = juguetear con algo

field *noun*
  a field = un campo

fierce *adjective*
  = feroz

fifteen *number* ▶ **p. 154, p. 319**
  fifteen = quince (*masculine*) (**!** *never changes*) *see also* **five**

fifth
  1 *adjective* = quinto/quinta
  2 *noun* ▶ **p. 192**
    (*a part*)
    a fifth = una quinta parte

fifty *number* ▶ **p. 154, p. 319**
  fifty = cincuenta (*masculine*) (**!** *never changes*) *see also* **five**

fight
  1 *noun*
    (*physical*)
    a fight = una pelea
    (*a quarrel*)
    a fight = una pelea
    (*a struggle*)
    a fight = una lucha
  2 *verb*
    (*physically*) = pelear
    (*to quarrel*) = pelear
    (*to struggle*) = luchar
    (*to combat*)
    to fight poverty = luchar contra la pobreza
    (*to engage in*)
    to fight a war = librar una guerra

fighting *noun*
  (*between armies*)
  fighting = enfrentamientos (*masculine plural*)
  (*brawling*)
  fighting = peleas (*feminine plural*)

figure *noun*
  (*a number*)
  a figure = una cifra
  (*a person*)
  a figure = una figura
  (*referring to a person's body*)
  to have a good figure = tener buena figura, tener buen tipo

file
  1 *noun*
    (*for papers or documents*)
    a file = una carpeta
    (*in computing*)
    a file = un archivo

(*for nails*)
  a (**nail**) file = una lima (de uñas)
  in single file = en fila india
  2 *verb*
    to file a document = archivar un documento
    to file one's nails = limarse las uñas

filing cabinet *noun*
  a filing cabinet = un archivero, un archivador (*Mex*)

fill *verb*
  (*to make full*) = llenar
  (*to become full*) = llenarse
  fill in = rellenar

film
  1 *noun*
    (*in cinema or television*)
    a film = una película
    (*for a camera*)
    a film = una película (fotográfica)
  2 *verb* = filmar

filthy *adjective*
  = mugriento/mugrienta

final
  1 *adjective*
    (*last*) = último/última
    (*definitive*)
    the final result = el resultado final
  2 *noun*
    (*in sport*)
    a final = una final

finally *adverb*
  = finalmente

finance
  1 *noun*
    (*funds*)
    finance = financión (*feminine*), financiamiento (*masculine*) (*Lat Am*)
  2 *verb* = financiar

financial *adjective*
  (*referring to a system*) = financiero/financiera
  financial difficulties = dificultades económicas

find *verb*
  = encontrar
  I found it hard to concentrate = me resultaba difícil concentrarme
  find out
    to find out the truth = descubrir la verdad
    if he ever finds out = si algún día se llega a enterar

fine
  1 *adjective*
    (*very good, excellent*)
    a fine novel = una novela excelente
    the weather is fine = hace buen tiempo
    a fine day = un día estupendo

(in good health or spirits)
I feel fine = estoy muy bien
2 *adverb* = muy bien
3 *noun*
  a fine = una multa
4 *verb*
  to fine someone = multar a alguien

finger *noun* ▶ p. 235
  a finger = un dedo

fingernail *noun*
  a fingernail = una uña

fingerprint *noun*
  a fingerprint = una huella digital

finish
1 *verb*
  (to end) = terminar, acabar
  I've finished writing my book = terminé de
    escribir mi libro
  (to come to an end) = terminar, acabar
2 *noun*
  (the end)
  the finish = el fin, el final
  (in a race)
  the finish = la llegada

Finland *proper noun* ▶ p. 187
  Finland = Finlandia *(feminine)*

fire
1 *noun*
  fire = fuego *(masculine)*
  to set fire to a house = prenderle fuego a
    una casa
  to be on fire = estar en llamas
  to catch fire = prender fuego
  (an accident)
  a fire = un incendio
2 *verb*
  (to shoot)
  to fire at someone = dispararle a alguien
  to fire a gun = disparar una pistola
  (to dismiss) = despedir

fire department *(US English)*, **fire
brigade** *(British English) noun*
  the fire department = el cuerpo de
    bomberos

fire engine *noun (British English)* ▶ fire
truck

fire extinguisher *noun*
  a fire extinguisher = un extinguidor *(Lat
    Am)*, un extintor *(Spa)*

firefighter *noun*
  a firefighter = un/una bombero

fireman *noun*
  a fireman = un bombero

fireplace *noun*
  a fireplace = una chimenea

fire truck *noun (US English)*
  a fire truck = un coche de bomberos, un
    carro de bomberos *(Mex)*, un autobomba
    (R Pl)

fireworks *noun*
  fireworks = fuegos artificiales *(masculine
    plural)*

firm
1 *noun*
  a firm = una empresa, una firma, una
    compañía
2 *adjective* = firme

F

first
1 *noun* ▶ p. 192
  (in a sequence or group)
  the first = el primero/la primera
  (the beginning)
  at first = al principio
2 *adjective* = primero/primera

> **!** Note that **primero** *becomes* **primer**
> *when it appears before a masculine*
> *singular noun*

  the first day = el primer día
  at first sight = a primera vista
3 *adverb*
  (before others)
  to arrive first = llegar primero
  he came first in the exam = sacó la mejor
    nota en el examen
  (to begin with) = primero, en primer lugar
  first of all = primero, en primer lugar
  (for the first time) = por primera vez

first aid *noun*
  first aid = primeros auxilios *(masculine
    plural)*

first class *adverb*
  to travel first class = viajar en primera
    clase

first-class *adjective*
  a first-class hotel = un hotel de primera
    clase
  a first-class stamp *(British English)* = una
    estampilla urgente *(Lat Am)*, un timbre
    urgente *(Mex)*, un sello urgente *(Spa)*

first floor *noun*
  the first floor *(US English)* = la planta baja
    (British English) = el primer piso

first name *noun*
  a first name = un nombre de pila

fish
1 *noun*
  (an animal)
  a fish = un pez
  (as food)
  fish = pescado *(masculine)*
2 *verb* = pescar

R Pl River Plate area   **SC** Southern Cone   **Spa** Spain

fisherman *noun*
  a fisherman = un pescador

fishing *noun*
  fishing = pesca (*feminine*)
  to go fishing = ir a pescar

fist *noun*
  a fist = un puño

fit
1 *adjective*
  (*suitable, appropriate*)
  he's not fit to be king = no es digno de ser
    rey
  the water is not fit to drink = el agua no es
    potable
2 *noun*
  a fit = un ataque
  he had a fit = le dio un ataque
  a fit of coughing = un acceso de tos
3 *verb*
  (*to be the right size*)
  it fits me perfectly = me queda perfecto
  these shoes don't fit = estos zapatos no me
    quedan bien
  (*to match*)
  it fits your description = cuadra con tu
    descripción

fit in
  (*into a room, car etc*)
  will you all fit in? = ¿van a caber todos?

fitness *noun*
  (*physical*) fitness = estado físico
    (*masculine*)

five *number* ▶ p. 154, p. 319
  five = cinco (*masculine*) (**!** *never changes*)
  five apples = cinco manzanas
  I have five of them = tengo cinco
  two fives are ten (2 × 5 = 10) = dos
    (multiplicado) por cinco (son) diez (2 ×
    5 = 10)

fix *verb*
  (*to repair*) = arreglar
  (*to establish*) = fijar
  to fix [a date | price | limit …] = fijar [una fecha |
    un precio | un límite …]

fizzy *adjective*
  = gaseoso/gaseosa

flag *noun*
  a flag = una bandera

flame *noun*
  a flame = una llama

flash
1 *noun*
  (*from a light*)
  a flash = un destello
  (*in photography*)
  a flash = un flash
2 *verb*
  (*to shine*) = destellar

to flash one's headlights = hacer una señal
  con los faros

flashlight *noun* (*US English*)
  a flashlight = una linterna

flask *noun*
  (*for tea or coffee*)
  a flask = un termo

flat
1 *adjective*
  (*if it's a surface*) = plano/plana
  to have a flat tire = tener una rueda
    desinflada
2 *noun* (*British English*)
  a flat = un apartamento, un departamento
    (*Lat Am*), un piso (*Spa*)

flatter *verb*
  (*to please*) = halagar
  (*to praise excessively*) = adular

flavor (*US English*), **flavour** (*British
English*)
1 *noun*
  a flavor = un sabor
2 *verb* = sazonar

flaw *noun*
  a flaw = un defecto

flea *noun*
  a flea = una pulga

flee *verb*
  = huir
  they fled the country = huyeron del país

flesh *noun*
  flesh = carne (*feminine*)

flexible *adjective*
  = flexible

flicker *verb*
  (*if it's a flame, light, or image*) = parpadear

flight *noun*
  (*in a plane*)
  a flight = un vuelo
  (*of a bird*)
  flight = vuelo (*masculine*)

flight attendant *noun*
  a flight attendant = un/una sobrecargo, un
    aeromozo/una aeromoza (*Lat Am*)

float *verb*
  (*in water*) = flotar
  (*in the air*) = flotar en el aire

flock *noun*
  (*of sheep, goats, geese*)
  a flock = un rebaño
  (*of birds*)
  a flock = una bandada

flood
1 *noun*
(*of a river*)
a flood = una inundación
2 *verb*
(*to overflow*) = desbordarse
(*to fill with water*) = inundar

floor *noun*
(*of a room, a vehicle*)
the floor = el suelo
(*a story*)
a floor = un piso

florist *noun*
a florist = un/una florista

flour *noun*
flour = harina (*feminine*)

flow
1 *verb*
blood flowed from the wound = sangre le
salía de la herida
the river flows into the sea = el río
desemboca en el mar
2 *noun*
the flow of traffic = la circulación

flower
1 *noun*
a flower = una flor
2 *verb* = florecer, florear (*Mex*)

flu *noun*
flu = gripe (*feminine*), gripa (*feminine*)
(*Mex*)

fluent *adjective*
he speaks fluent Spanish = habla español
con fluidez

fluff *noun*
fluff = pelusa (*feminine*)

fluid *noun*
(*in biology, chemistry*)
a fluid = un fluido
(*liquid nourishment*)
a fluid = un líquido

flush *verb*
to flush the toilet = tirar de la cadena,
jalarle a la cadena (*Lat Am except SC*)

flute *noun*
a flute = una flauta

fly
1 *verb*
(*if it's a bird, insect, airplane, kite etc*) =
volar
(*if it's an air passenger*) = ir en avión
(*if it's a pilot*)
to fly a plane = pilotar un avión, pilotear
un avión (*Lat Am*)
the ship was flying the British flag = el
barco llevaba la bandera británica

2 *noun*
a fly = una mosca
fly away = irse volando

foam *noun*
foam = espuma (*feminine*)

focus
1 *noun*
(*in photography*)
the picture is not in focus = la foto está
desenfocada
(*the center*)
he was the focus of attention = fue el
centro de atención
2 *verb*
to focus a camera = enfocar una cámara
(*to concentrate*)
to focus on employment = concentrarse en
la cuestión del paro

fog *noun*
fog = niebla (*feminine*)

foggy *adjective*
it was foggy = había niebla

fold
1 *verb* = plegar, doblar
he folded his arms = cruzó los brazos
2 *noun*
(*in fabric, paper, skin*)
a fold = un pliegue

follow *verb*
= seguir
she followed him into the room = entró en
el cuarto tras él
the winners were as follows ... = los
ganadores fueron los siguientes ...

following
1 *adjective* = siguiente
2 *preposition*
following the accident = tras el accidente

fond *adjective*
to be fond of someone = tenerle cariño a
alguien

food *noun*
food = comida (*feminine*)

fool
1 *noun*
a fool = un/una idiota
2 *verb*
to fool someone = engañar a alguien

foolish *adjective*
= tonto/tonta

foot *noun*
(*of a person*) ▶ p. 235
the foot = un pie
on foot = a pie, andando
(*of an animal*)
the foot = la pata

F

(*in measurements*)
a foot = un pie (= *30.48 cm*)

football *noun* ▶ **p. 306**
(*soccer*) = fútbol (*masculine*), futbol
  (*masculine*) (*Mex*)
(*American football*) = fútbol americano
  (*masculine*), futbol americano
  (*masculine*) (*Mex*)

footprint *noun*
a footprint = una huella

footstep *noun*
a footstep = un paso

for *preposition*
= para
the letter is for me = la carta es para mí
to work for a company = trabajar para una
  compañía
we went for a swim = fuimos a nadar
he was criticized for his behavior = fue
  criticado por su comportamiento
it's impossible for me to stay = me es
  imposible quedarme
(*when talking about time*)
I haven't seen him for three years = hace
  tres años que no lo veo
he will be in Chicago for a year = va a estar
  en Chicago por un año
she read for two hours = leyó durante dos
  horas
I've been waiting for three hours = hace
  tres horas que estoy esperando
(*indicating distance*)
we drove for 80 kilometers = hicimos 80
  kilómetros
(*indicating the cost or amount of
  something*)
he bought it for 50 pounds = lo compró por
  50 libras
(*representing*)
what is the Spanish for 'badger' = ¿cómo
  se dice 'badger' en español?

forbid *verb*
= prohibir
he forbade the children to go out = a los
  niños les prohibió salir

force
1 *noun*
force = fuerza (*feminine*)
by force = a la fuerza
(*in the police or military*)
the police force = la policía
the (armed) forces = las fuerzas armadas
2 *verb*
he forced them to accept = los obligó a
  aceptar
force open
= forzar

forecast
1 *noun*
forecast = previsión (*feminine*)
the weather forecast = el pronóstico del
  tiempo
2 *verb*
(*if it's a result*) = prever
(*if it's the weather*) = pronosticar

forehead *noun*
the forehead = la frente

foreign *adjective*
= extranjero/extranjera

foreigner *noun*
a foreigner = un extranjero/una extranjera

forest *noun*
a forest = un bosque

forever *adverb*
(*for all time*) = para siempre
(*always*) = siempre
he is forever complaining = siempre se está
  quejando

forge *verb*
= falsificar

forgery *noun*
a forgery = una falsificación

forget *verb*
= olvidar, olvidarse de

forgive *verb*
= perdonar
she forgave him for what he had done = le
  perdonó por lo que había hecho

fork *noun*
a fork = un tenedor

form
1 *noun*
(*a type or kind*)
form = forma (*feminine*)
(*a document*)
a form = un formulario
(*a shape*)
a form = una forma
(*referring to mood or fitness*)
form = forma (*feminine*)
to be in good form = estar en buena forma
(*British English—a class in a school*)
a form = un año
2 *verb*
(*to create*) = formar
(*to become created*) = formarse

formal *adjective*
(*official*) = formal
(*not casual*)
formal dress = traje de etiqueta
  (*masculine*)
(*if it's language*) = formal

former adjective
(previous) = antiguo/antigua

> ❗ antiguo/antigua come before the noun

the former Prime Minister = la antigua
primera ministra
his former wife = su ex-esposa

formula noun
a formula = una fórmula

fortnight noun (British English)
a fortnight = quince días (masculine plural)

fortunate adjective
= afortunado/afortunada

fortunately adverb
= afortunadamente

fortune
(wealth)
a fortune = una fortuna
(luck)
fortune = suerte (feminine)
to tell someone's fortune = decirle la
buenaventura a alguien

forty number ▶ p. 154, p. 319
forty = cuarenta (masculine) (❗ never
changes) see also five

forward
1 adjective
(at the front) = hacia adelante
(cheeky) = descarado/descarada
2 adverb (US English)
= hacia adelante
3 verb
to forward a letter = enviar una carta

forwards adverb (British English)
= hacia adelante

fossil noun
a fossil = un fósil

found verb
= fundar

foundation noun
(a basis)
a foundation = una base
(in building)
foundations = cimientos (masculine plural)
(a cosmetic)
foundation = base (feminine)

founder noun
the founder = el fundador/la fundadora

fountain noun
a fountain = una fuente

four number ▶ p. 154, p. 319
four = cuatro (masculine) (❗ never
changes) see also five

fourteen number ▶ p. 154, p. 319
fourteen = catorce (masculine) (❗ never
changes) see also five

fourth
1 adjective = cuarto/cuarta
2 noun ▶ p. 192
(a part)
a fourth = una cuarta parte

fox noun
a fox = un zorro

fraction noun
a fraction = una fracción

fracture
1 noun
a fracture = una fractura
2 verb
he fractured his leg = se fracturó la pierna

fragile adjective
= frágil

fragment noun
a fragment = un fragmento

frame
1 noun
(of a picture, door, window)
a frame = un marco
(of a tennis racket)
a frame = la montura
(for glasses)
frames = el/la armazón
2 verb = enmarcar

France noun ▶ p. 187
France = Francia (feminine)

frank adjective
= franco/franca

fraud noun
fraud = fraude (masculine)

freckle noun
a freckle = una peca

free
1 adjective
(in liberty) = libre
to set someone free = dejar a alguien en
libertad, poner a alguien en libertad
(not costing anything) = gratis
(not occupied, available) = libre
is this seat free? = ¿está libre este asiento?
2 adverb
(without payment) = gratis
3 verb
(if it's an animal) = soltar
(if it's a person) = dejar en libertad, poner
en libertad

freedom noun
freedom = libertad (feminine)

freeze verb
(in cold weather) = helarse, congelarse
(when preserving food) = congelar

F

R Pl River Plate area   SC Southern Cone   Spa Spain

(to feel cold)
I'm freezing = estoy helado/helada, estoy
   congelado/congelada
to freeze to death = morir
   congelado/congelada
(to fix at a certain level)
to freeze prices = congelar los precios

freezer *noun*
   a freezer = un congelador

French ▶ **p. 187, p. 245**
1 *noun*
   (the people)
   the French = los franceses *(masculine*
      plural)
   (the language)
   French = francés *(masculine)*
2 *adjective* = francés/francesa

French fries *noun*
   French fries = papas fritas *(feminine plural)*
      (Lat Am), patatas fritas *(feminine plural)*
      (Spa)

Frenchman *noun* ▶ **p. 187**
   a Frenchman = un francés

Frenchwoman *noun* ▶ **p. 187**
   a Frenchwoman = una francesa

frequent *adjective*
   = frecuente

frequently *adverb*
   = con frecuencia

fresh *adjective*
   = fresco/fresca

freshen up *verb*
   = arreglarse

Friday *noun* ▶ **p. 192**
   Friday = viernes *(masculine)*

fridge *noun*
   a fridge = un refrigerador *(Lat Am)*, un
      frigorífico *(Spa)*, una heladera *(R Pl)*

fried *adjective*
   = frito/frita

friend *noun*
   a friend = un amigo/una amiga
   to make friends = hacer amigos

friendly *adjective*
   (if it's a person) = simpático/simpática
   (if it's a smile, gesture, letter etc) = amable

friendship *noun*
   friendship = amistad *(feminine)*

fright *noun*
   to give someone a fright = darle un susto a
      alguien

frighten *verb*
   = asustar

frightened *adjective*
   = asustado/asustada
   to be frightened = tener miedo
   she is frightened of dogs = les tiene miedo
      a los perros

frightening *adjective*
   = espantoso/espantosa

fringe *noun* *(British English)*
   a fringe = un flequillo, un cerquillo *(Lat*
      Am), un fleco *(Mex)*

frog *noun*
   a frog = una rana

from *preposition*
   (referring to a point of origin) = de
   he is from London = es de Londres
   the journey from Manchester to
      Birmingham = el viaje de Manchester a
      Birmingham
   we live ten minutes from the city center =
      vivimos a diez minutos de la ciudad
   (referring to a point in time)
   the shop is open from 8am to 6pm = la
      tienda está abierta desde las 8 de la
      mañana hasta las 6 de la tarde
   from June to August = desde junio hasta
      agosto
   from then on = a partir de ahí
   50 years from now = dentro de cincuenta
      años
   (because of)
   from experience I would say that . . . =
      según mi experiencia diría que . . .
   I know him from work = lo conozco del
      trabajo

front
1 *noun*
   the front of a building = la fachada de un
      edificio, el frente de un edificio
   (of a garment)
   the front = la delantera
   (the forward section)
   the front = el frente, la parte delantera
   sit in front = siéntate delante
   in front of = delante de
2 *adjective*
   = delantero/delantera
   the front seat = el asiento delantero
   the front wheel = la rueda delantera

front door *noun*
   the front door = la puerta de la calle

frontier *noun*
   a frontier = una frontera

front page *noun*
   the front page = la primera plana

front seat *noun*
   the front seat = el asiento delantero

frost *noun*
   (sub-zero temperature)
   frost = helada *(feminine)*

(*frozen dew*)
frost = escarcha (*feminine*)
frost over = helarse, cubrirse de escarcha

frosty *adjective*
= helado/helada

frown *verb*
= fruncir el ceño

frozen *adjective*
= congelado/congelada

fruit *noun*
fruit = fruta (*feminine*)
a piece of fruit = una fruta

frustrate *verb*
= frustrar

frustrating *adjective*
= frustrante

fry *verb*
= freír

frying pan *noun*
a frying pan = una sartén, un sartén (*Lat Am*)

fuel *noun*
fuel = combustible (*masculine*)

fulfill (*US English*), **fulfil** (*British English*) *verb*
to fulfill a duty = cumplir con un deber
to fulfill an ambition = hacer realidad una ambición

full *adjective*
= lleno/llena
the streets were full of people = las calles estaban llenas de gente
(*completely booked*) = lleno/llena
the train was full = el tren estaba lleno
(*complete*)
you don't know the full story = no conoces toda la historia
to pay the full price = pagar el precio íntegro
his full name = su nombre completo
(*maximum*)
at full speed = a toda velocidad

full moon *noun*
a full moon = una luna llena

full stop *noun* (*British English*)
a full stop = un punto

full-time *adverb*
= a tiempo parcial

fumes *noun*
fumes = gases (*masculine plural*)

fun *noun*
fun = diversión (*feminine*)
to have fun = divertirse
painting is great fun = la pintura es una gran diversión

function
1 *noun*
(*a purpose or role*)
a function = una función
(*a reception*)
a function = una recepción
2 *verb* = funcionar

fund
1 *noun*
(*a reserve of money*)
a fund = un fondo
(*cash reserves*)
funds = fondos (*masculine plural*)
2 *verb* = financiar

funeral *noun*
a funeral = un entierro

funny *adjective*
(*amusing*) = divertido/divertida
(*bizarre*) = raro/rara
it's funny that he hasn't phoned = es raro que no haya llamado

> **!** Note the use of the subjunctive after **es raro que**

fur
1 *noun*
(*on an animal*)
fur = pelaje (*masculine*)
(*on a coat or jacket*)
fur = piel (*feminine*)
2 *adjective* = de piel, de pieles (*Spa*)

furious *adjective*
= furioso/furiosa

furnish *verb*
= amueblar, amoblar (*Lat Am*)

furniture *noun*
furniture = muebles (*masculine plural*)
a piece of furniture = un mueble

further
1 *adverb*
it was further than I thought = estaba más lejos de lo que pensaba
how much further is it? = ¿cuánto más allá queda?
(*to a greater extent*)
prices fell even further = los precios bajaron aún más
2 *adjective*
(*additional*)
without further delay = sin perder más tiempo

fuss
1 *noun*
a fuss = un escándalo
to make a fuss = hacer un escándalo
2 *verb* = preocuparse

F

future
1 *noun*
  the future = el futuro
  in future = de ahora en adelante
2 *adjective* = futuro/futura

gale *noun*
  (*a wind*)
  a gale = un vendaval

gallery *noun*
  (*a museum*)
  a gallery = un museo
  (*a commercial showcase*)
  a gallery = una galería (de arte)

game *noun*
  a game = un juego
  a game of football/tennis = un partido de fútbol/tenis
  a game of chess = una partida de ajedrez, un partido de ajedrez (*Lat Am*)

games *noun* ▶ **p. 306**
  (*British English—in school*)
  games = deportes (*masculine plural*)

game show *noun*
  a game show = un programa concurso

gang *noun*
  (*a group of friends, young people*)
  a gang = una pandilla
  (*a group of criminals*)
  a gang = una banda, una pandilla

gap *noun*
  a gap (*in a fence or hedge*) = un hueco
  (*between buildings, cars*) = un espacio
  (*a period of time*)
  a gap = un intervalo, una interrupción

garage *noun*
  (*for parking*)
  a garage = un garaje, un garage (*Lat Am*), una cochera (*Mex*)
  (*for repairing cars, selling point*)
  a garage = un taller, un garage (*Lat Am*)
  (*British English—for fuel*)
  a garage = una gasolinera, una estación de nafta (*R Pl*)

garbage *noun* (*US English*)
  garbage = basura (*feminine*)

garbage can *noun* (*US English*)
  a garbage can = un cubo de la basura, un tacho de la basura (*SC*), un bote de la basura (*Mex*)

garbage collector, **garbage man**
noun (*US English*)
  a garbage collector = un basurero

garden *noun*
  a garden = un jardín

gardener *noun*
  a gardener = un jardinero/una jardinera

gardening *noun*
  gardening = jardinería (*feminine*)

garlic *noun*
  garlic = ajo (*masculine*)

garment *noun*
  a garment = una prenda (de ropa)

gas *noun*
  gas = gas (*masculine*)
  (*US English—petrol*)
  gas = gasolina (*feminine*), nafta (*feminine*) (*R Pl*)

gasoline *noun* (*US English*)
  gasoline = gasolina (*feminine*), nafta (*feminine*) (*R Pl*)

gas station *noun* (*US English*)
  a gas station = una gasolinera, una estación de nafta (*R Pl*)

gate *noun*
  (*an entrance*)
  a gate (*to a garden*) = una verja, una cancela (*Spa*), un portón (*SC*)
  (*to a town, a prison*) = una puerta
  (*to a field*) = un portón, una tranquera (*Lat Am*)
  (*in an airport*)
  a gate = una puerta de embarque

gather
  (*to come together*) = reunirse
  (*to collect*) = juntar, recoger

gay *adjective*
  = homosexual, gay (**!** *never changes*)

gear *noun*
  (*in a vehicle, on a bike*)
  a gear = una marcha, un cambio
  to be in first gear = estar en primera
  (*equipment*)
  gear = equipo (*masculine*)
  (*clothing*)
  my football gear = mi ropa de fútbol

Gemini *noun*
  (*the sign*)
  Gemini = Géminis
  I'm Gemini = soy Géminis, soy de Géminis
  (*a person*)
  a Gemini = un/una géminis

general
1 *noun*
  a general = un/una general
  in general = en general
2 *adjective* = general

general knowledge *noun*
general knowledge = cultura general (*feminine*)

generation *noun*
a generation = una generación

generous *adjective*
= generoso/generosa

genius *noun*
a genius = un genio

gentle *adjective*
(*if it's a heat, a breeze, a murmur*) = suave
(*if it's a person*) = dulce

gentleman *noun*
(*a man*) = un señor
(*a polite man*) = un caballero

genuine *adjective*
(*real*) = auténtico/auténtica

geography *noun*
geography = geografía (*feminine*)

germ *noun*
a germ = un microbio, un germen

German ▶ p. 187, p. 245
1 *adjective* = alemán/alemana
2 *noun*
(*a person*)
a German = un alemán/una alemana
(*the language*)
German = alemán (*masculine*)

Germany *noun* ▶ p. 187
Germany = Alemania (*feminine*)

get *verb*

> **!** *The word* get *is extremely common in English and does not have a multi-purpose Spanish equivalent. This entry covers the most frequent uses of* get *but to find translations for other expressions using* get—to get angry, to get better, to get wet *etc, look up the entries at* angry, better, wet *etc*

(*to become*)
to get old = envejecer
to get worried = preocuparse
to get jealous = ponerse celoso/celosa
the situation is getting complicated = la situación se complica

> **!** *Note that there is very often a single verb translation for the English*
> get + adjective

(*to ask or persuade*)
I'll get him to lend me the money = le pediré que me preste el dinero
get her to call me = dile que me llame
(*to cause to be done or happen*)
to get the car cleaned = hacer limpiar el coche
you got your hair cut = te cortaste el pelo

(*to arrive*) = llegar
I called when we got there = llamé cuando llegamos allí
(*to be*)
you'll get killed = te vas a matar
a few chairs got broken = se rompieron unas cuantas sillas
(*to obtain*)
I got a job in publishing = conseguí un trabajo en el campo editorial
to get a present for someone, to get someone a present = comprarle un regalo a alguien
I'll get something to eat at the station = comeré algo en la estación
get some rest = descansa un poco
(*to receive*) = recibir
I got a letter from Mark = recibí una carta de Mark
to get good marks = sacar buenas notas
(*to fetch*) = buscar
he's gone to get help = fue a buscar ayuda
(*to prepare*)
to get breakfast = preparar el desayuno
(*to experience*)
to get a shock = llevarse un shock
(*to have the opportunity*)
I hope I get to use the computer = espero poder usar la computadora
(*to catch or fall ill with*) = agarrar, coger (*Spa*)
she got a cold = se resfrió
(*to use for transport*)
we can get the train = podemos tomar el tren, podemos coger el tren (*Spa*)
(*to make progress*)
to be getting somewhere = avanzar

> **!** *For the translation of* to have got (*meaning* to have), *see the entries* have *and* got. *For a translation of* I've got to [go | work | eat *etc ...*] *see the entry* got

get about ▶ get around
get across
(*to cross*) = cruzar
get along
(*to cope*) = arreglárselas
(*to have a good relationship*) = llevarse bien
I get along well with her = me llevo bien con ella
get around
I need a car to get around = necesito un coche para desplazarme
get away
(*to escape*) = escaparse
get back
(*to return*) = volver, regresar
(*to regain*)
did you get your money back? = ¿te devolvieron el dinero?
get in
(*to enter*) = entrar
get off
(*to leave a bus or train*) = bajarse
he fell as he was getting off the train = se cayó al bajar del tren
(*to remove*) = quitar

G

get on
(*to climb aboard a bus or train*) = subirse
to get on the train = subirse al tren
(*to have a good relationship*) = llevarse bien
I get on well with her = me llevo bien con
  ella
get out
(*to leave*) = salir
(*to bring out*) = sacar
to get the furniture out of the house = sacar
  los muebles de la casa
get over
(*to recover from*)
to get over a shock = reponerse de un
  shock
get through
(*to contact by phone*)
to get through to someone = comunicarse
  con alguien
get together = reunirse
get up = levantarse

ghost *noun*
a ghost = un fantasma

giant *noun*
a giant = un gigante/una giganta

gift *noun*
(*a present*)
a gift = un regalo
(*a talent*)
a gift = un don
he has a gift for languages = tiene talento
  para los idiomas

ginger
1 *noun*
ginger = jengibre (*masculine*)
2 *adjective* ▶ **p. 183**
she has ginger hair = es pelirroja
a ginger cat = un gato rojizo

girl *noun*
(*a baby or child*)
a girl = una niña
(*a young woman*)
a girl = una chica, una muchacha

girlfriend *noun*
(*in a couple*)
a girlfriend = una novia
(*a female friend*)
a girlfriend = una amiga

give *verb*
to give = dar
I gave him the photos = le di las fotos
I gave them to him = se los/las di
give me the newspapers = dame los
  periódicos
give them to me = dámelos/dámelas
(*to pass on*)
to give someone a message = darle un
  mensaje a alguien
(*to allow*) = dar
I was given two weeks to do the work = me
  dieron dos semanas para hacer el trabajo

give away
(*to give*) = regalar
(*to reveal*) = revelar
give back = devolver, regresar (*Lat Am*)
give in = ceder
give out = repartir
give up
to give up smoking = dejar de fumar
to give up a job = renunciar a un empleo
(*to surrender*)
to give oneself up to the police =
  entregarse a la policía
give way
(*to collapse*) = ceder, romperse
(*British English—when driving*) = ceder el
  paso

glad *adjective*
I am very glad to see you = me alegro
  mucho de verte
I'm glad that you're coming = me alegro de
  que vengas

! Note the use of the subjunctive after
alegrarse de que

glass *noun*
(*the material*)
glass = vidrio (*masculine*), cristal
  (*masculine*) (*Spa*)
(*for drinking*)
a glass = un vaso

glasses *noun*
glasses = gafas (*feminine plural*), lentes
  (*masculine plural*) (*Lat Am*), anteojos
  (*masculine plural*) (*Lat Am*)

glitter *verb*
= relumbrar

globe *noun*
(*the earth*)
the globe = el globo
(*a model of the earth*)
a globe = un globo terráqueo

gloomy *adjective*
(*dark*) = sombrío/sombría
(*sad*) = lúgubre

glove *noun*
a glove = un guante

glow
1 *noun*
a glow = un brillo
2 *verb*
(*to give off light*) = brillar
the lamp glowed = la lámpara brillaba, la
  lámpara resplandecía

glue
1 *noun*
glue = goma de pegar (*feminine*),
  pegamento (*masculine*)
2 *verb*
(*to stick*) = pegar

go
1 *verb*

> **!** *Generally*, to go *is translated by* ir(se). *There are a great many verbs such as* go away, go back, go round *etc, which are listed at the end of this entry. For translations of expressions like* I'm going to [leave | go to London | learn to drive …] *see the entry* going

(*to get from one place to another*) = ir
where are you going? = ¿dónde vas?, ¿adónde vas?
we went to the cinema = fuimos al cine
to go shopping = ir de compras
let's go and see them, let's go see them = vamos a verlos
to go into a room = entrar en un cuarto, entrar a un cuarto (*Lat Am*)
(*to leave*)
he's going at the end of the month = se va a fin de mes
the train goes at 6 o'clock = el tren sale a las seis
(*when talking about time*)
the time goes quickly = el tiempo pasa volando
there are only three days to go before Christmas = faltan sólo tres días para Navidad
(*to disappear*)
the money's gone (*spent*) = el dinero se acabó
I left my bike here and now it's gone = dejé mi bici aquí y ahora ha desaparecido
(*to become*)
to go red = enrojecerse
to go pale = palidecer
to go blind = quedarse ciego/ciega
to go mad, to go crazy = volverse loco/loca
(*in polite enquiries*)
how's it going? = ¿qué tal?
everything's going very well = todo va muy bien
how did the exam go? = ¿qué tal el examen?
(*match*)
the skirt and blouse go well together = la falda y la blusa combinan bien
the dress doesn't really go with your jacket = en realidad el vestido no queda bien con tu chaqueta
two burgers to go = (*US English*) = dos hamburguesas para llevar
2 *noun*
(*a turn*)
a go = un turno
it's your go = te toca a ti
(*a try*)
to have a go at doing something = intentar hacer algo
have another go = inténtalo de nuevo
go across = cruzar
go after = perseguir
go ahead = seguir adelante
go along = ir

go around
to go around a corner = doblar una esquina
(*to walk around, to visit*)
to go around the museums = visitar los museos
(*to become known*)
there's a rumor going around that you're leaving = corre el rumor de que te vas
(*to be enough*)
is there enough bread to go around? = ¿hay suficiente pan para todo el mundo?
go away = irse
go back = volver, regresar
to go back to sleep = volverse a dormir
go by = pasar
go down = bajar
go for
(*to attack*) = atacar
go in
(*to enter*) = entrar
(*to return inside*) entrar de nuevo
go off
(*to explode*) = estallar
(*to ring*) = sonar
my alarm clock didn't go off = no sonó el despertador
(*to leave*) = irse
(*to go bad, sour*) = echarse a perder
(*to be switched off*) = apagarse
go on
(*to continue*) = seguir
to go on talking = seguir hablando
(*to happen*) = pasar
what's going on? = ¿qué pasa?
(*to be switched on*) = encenderse, prenderse (*Lat Am*)
go out
(*to leave the house*) = salir
to go out for a walk = salir a dar un paseo
(*as a boyfriend, girlfriend*)
to go out with someone = salir con alguien
(*to be switched off, to stop burning*) = apagarse
go over
(*to check*) = revisar
(*to revise*) = repasar
go round (*British English*) ▶ go around
go through
(*to experience*)
to go through a difficult time = pasar por un período difícil
(*to search*) = registrar, revisar (*Lat Am*)
go up
(*by stairs, elevator*) = subir
he went up to bed = subió a dormir
(*to rise*) = subir, aumentar
go without = pasar sin

goal *noun*
(*the structure*)
the goal = la portería, el arco (*Lat Am*)

(*a point*)
a goal = un gol
(*an objective*)
a goal = una meta

goalkeeper *noun*
a goalkeeper = un portero/una portera, un arquero/una arquera (*Lat Am*)

goat *noun*
a goat = una cabra

god *noun*
a god = un dios
God = Dios

goddaughter *noun*
a goddaughter = una ahijada

goddess *noun*
a goddess = una diosa

godfather *noun*
a godfather = un padrino

godmother *noun*
a godmother = una madrina

godson *noun*
a godson = un ahijado

going
(*expressing the near future*)
to be going to = ir a
I'm going to leave = voy a irme
this peace is not going to last = esta paz no va a durar
we were going to phone you = te íbamos a llamar

gold
1 *noun*
(*the metal*)
gold = oro (*masculine*)
2 *adjective* = de oro

goldfish *noun*
a goldfish = un pez de colores

golf *noun* ▶ **p. 306**
golf = golf (*masculine*)

golf course *noun*
a golf course = un campo de golf, una cancha de golf (*Lat Am*)

good
1 *adjective*
good = bueno/buena

> **!** Note that **bueno** becomes **buen** when it appears before a masculine singular noun

a good book = un buen libro
we've got some good news = tenemos buenas noticias
he's good at chemistry = es bueno para la química
to have good eyesight = tener buena vista
spinach is good for you = las espinacas son buenas para la salud
I don't feel too good = no me siento muy bien

if the weather's good, we'll go out = si hace buen tiempo saldremos
(*talking about food*)
the coffee is very good = el café está muy bueno, el café está buenísimo
that tastes good = eso tiene buen sabor
the cake looks good = el pastel tiene buena pinta
(*well-behaved*)
the dog's very good = el perro es muy bueno
be good! = ¡pórtate bien!
2 *noun*
(*use*)
it's no good complaining = no sacarás nada con quejarte
the change will do you good = el cambio te hará bien
for good = para siempre
3 *exclamation*
(*when pleased, satisfied*)
good! = ¡qué bueno!
(*when praising, encouraging*)
good! = ¡muy bien!

goodbye *noun, exclamation*
goodbye = adiós

good-looking *adjective*
= guapo/guapa, buen mozo/buena moza (*Lat Am*)

goodnight *exclamation*
goodnight = buenas noches

goods *noun*
(*items for sale*)
goods = artículos (*masculine plural*), mercancías (*feminine plural*)

goose *noun*
a goose = un ganso

gooseberry *noun*
a gooseberry = una grosella espinosa

gorilla *noun*
a gorilla = un gorila

gossip
1 *noun*
(*harmful talk*)
gossip = chismes (*masculine plural*), cotilleo✱ (*masculine*) (*Spa*)
to have a gossip = chismorrear✱, cotillear✱ (*Spa*)
(*a person*)
a gossip = un chismoso/una chismosa
2 *verb* = chismorrear✱, cotillear✱ (*Spa*)

got: **to have got** *verb* (*British English*)
(*to have*) = tener
I've got a lot of work to do = tengo mucho trabajo que hacer
have you got a cold? = ¿estás resfriada?
(*to be obliged*)
to have got to = tener que
I have got to work = tengo que trabajar

---

government *noun*
a government = un gobierno

GP *noun*
a GP = un médico/una médica de medicina general

grab *verb*
to grab someone by the arm = agarrar a alguien del brazo
he tried to grab my purse = intentó arrebatarme el monedero

graceful *adjective*
= lleno/llena de gracia

grade *noun*
(*quality of an object, a material*)
the grade = la calidad
(*a mark*)
a grade = una nota
(*US English—a class*)
a grade = un año, un curso

grade school *noun* (*US English*)
grade school = escuela primaria (*feminine*)

gradually *adverb*
= poco a poco, de a poco (*Lat Am*)

gram, **gramme** *noun*
a gram = un gramo

grammar *noun*
grammar = gramática (*feminine*)

grandchild *noun*
a grandchild = un nieto/una nieta
the grandchildren = los nietos

granddaughter *noun*
a granddaughter = una nieta

grandfather *noun*
a grandfather = un abuelo

grandmother *noun*
a grandmother = una abuela

grandparents *noun*
grandparents = abuelos (*masculine plural*)

grandson *noun*
a grandson = un nieto

grape *noun*
a grape = una uva

grapefruit *noun*
a grapefruit = una toronja (*Lat Am*), un pomelo (*SC, Spa*)

grass *noun*
grass = hierba (*feminine*)
(*the lawn*)
the grass = el césped, la hierba, el pasto (*Lat Am*), la grama (*C Am*)

grasshopper *noun*
a grasshopper = un saltamontes

grateful *adjective*
= agradecido/agradecida

grave *noun*
a grave = una tumba, una sepultura

graveyard *noun*
a graveyard = un cementerio, un panteón (*Mex*)

gray (*US English*) *adjective* ▶ p. 183
= gris
(*used of hair*)
to have gray hair = ser canoso/canosa, tener el pelo canoso
she is going gray = le están saliendo canas

G

grease *noun*
grease = grasa (*feminine*)

greasy *adjective*
your hands are greasy = tienes las manos grasientas
a greasy overall = un overol cubierto de grasa
to have greasy hair = tener el pelo graso, tener el pelo grasoso (*Lat Am*)

great *adjective*
(*when stressing size, amount, importance*)
= grande
the great cities of Europe = las grandes ciudades de Europa
a great improvement = una gran mejora

! Note that grande becomes gran before a singular noun

(*when showing enthusiasm*)
it's a great idea = es una idea estupenda
(that's) great! = ¡qué bien!, ¡fenomenal!

Great Britain *noun* ▶ p. 187
Great Britain = Gran Bretaña (*feminine*)

great-grandfather *noun*
a great-grandfather = un bisabuelo

great-grandmother *noun*
a great-grandmother = una bisabuela

Greece *noun* ▶ p. 187
Greece = Grecia (*feminine*)

greedy *adjective*
= glotón/glotona

Greek ▶ p. 187, p. 245
1 *adjective* = griego/griega
2 *noun*
(*a person*)
a Greek = un griego/una griega
(*the language*)
Greek = griego (*masculine*)

green *adjective* ▶ p. 183
= verde

greenhouse *noun*
a greenhouse = un invernadero

grey *adjective* (*British English*) ▶ gray

greyhound *noun*
  a greyhound = un galgo

grief *noun*
  grief = dolor (*masculine*)

grill
1 *noun*
  (*British English—on a stove*)
  a grill = un grill, un gratinador
  (*on a barbecue*)
  a grill = una parrilla
2 *verb*
  (*British English—to cook on a stove*) =
    hacer al grill
  (*to cook over charcoal*) = hacer a la parrilla

grin
1 *noun*
  a grin = una sonrisa
2 *verb* = sonreír

grind *verb*
  (*if it's coffee or wheat*) = moler
  (*US English—if it's meat*) = moler, picar
    (*R Pl, Spa*)

groan *verb*
  to groan (*in pain*) = gemir
  (*when annoyed*) = gruñir

grocer *noun*
  a grocer = un tendero/una tendera, un
    abarrotero/ una abarrotera (*Mex*), un
    almacenero/una almacenera (*SC*)
  a grocer's shop (*British English*) = una
    tienda de comestibles, una tienda de
    abarrotes (*C Am, Mex*), un almacén (*SC*)

grocery *noun*
  a grocery = una tienda de comestibles, una
    tienda de abarrotes (*C Am, Mex*), un
    almacén (*SC*)

ground *noun*
  the ground = el suelo
  to get up off the ground = levantarse
  (*a piece of land*)
  a piece of ground = un terreno

ground beef *noun* (*US English*)
  ground beef = carne molida (*feminine*),
    carne picada (*feminine*) (*R Pl, Spa*)

ground floor *noun* (*British English*)
  the ground floor = la planta baja

grounds *noun*
  (*part of a property*)
  grounds = parque (*masculine*), jardines
    (*masculine plural*)
  (*reasons*)
  to have grounds for complaint = tener
    motivo de queja

group *noun*
  (*a number of people*)
  a group = un grupo

  (*a musical band*)
  a group = un grupo, un conjunto

grow *verb*
  (*to get big, strong*) = crecer
  (*to cultivate*) = cultivar
  (*to get long*) = crecer
  my nails are growing = mis uñas están
    creciendo
  (*to let grow*)
  to grow a beard = dejarse la barba
  (*to become*) = volverse
  to grow old = envejecerse
  (*to increase in size, importance*)
  the population will grow = la población va a
    aumentar
grow up = hacerse mayor

grumble *verb*
  = refunfuñar
  to grumble about the weather = quejarse
    del tiempo

guarantee
1 *verb* = garantizar
2 *noun*
  a guarantee = una garantía

guard
1 *verb*
  to guard the president = proteger al
    presidente
  to guard the palace = vigilar el palacio
2 *noun*
  (*in a prison*)
  a guard = un carcelero/una carcelera
  (*at a bank*)
  a guard = un/una guarda de seguridad
  (*in the army*)
  a guard = una guardia
  to be on guard = estar de guardia

guard dog *noun*
  a guard dog = un perro guardián

guess *verb*
  = adivinar
  guess who's here? = ¿adivina a quién está
    aquí?
  to guess right = acertar, atinar(le) (*Mex*)

guest *noun*
  (*a person invited to stay*)
  a guest = un invitado/una invitada
  (*a client at a hotel*)
  a guest = un/una huésped

guesthouse *noun* (*British English*)
  a guesthouse = una pensión

guide
1 *noun*
  (*a book*)
  a guide = una guía

(*a person*)
a guide = un/una guía
a tour guide = un/una guía de turismo,
un/una guía de turistas (*Mex*)
2 *verb* = guiar

guidebook *noun*
a guidebook = una guía

guided tour *noun*
a guided tour = una visita guiada

guilty *adjective*
= culpable

guitar *noun*
a guitar = una guitarra

gum *noun*
(*part of the body*) ▶ **p. 235**
the gum = la encía
(*chewing gum*)
gum = chicle (*masculine*)
a piece of gum = un chicle
(*British English — glue*)
gum = goma de pegar (*feminine*)

gun *noun*
(*a pistol*)
a gun = una pistola
(*a rifle*)
a gun = un fusil, una escopeta

gym *noun*
(*a gymnasium*)
a gym = un gimnasio

gymnasium *noun*
a gymnasium = un gimnasio

gymnastics *noun*
gymnastics = gimnasia (*feminine*)

gypsy *noun*
a gypsy = un gitano/una gitana

habit *noun*
a habit = una costumbre

hail
1 *noun*
hail = granizo (*masculine*)
2 *verb* = granizar

hair *noun*
(*on head*) ▶ **p. 235**
hair = pelo (*masculine*)
to have black hair = tener el pelo negro
(*a single strand*)
a hair = un pelo

(*on the body*)
hair = vello (*masculine*)
(*on an animal*)
the hair = el pelo

hairbrush *noun*
a hairbrush = un cepillo

haircut *noun*
a haircut = un corte de pelo
to have a haircut = cortarse el pelo

hairdresser *noun*
a hairdresser = un peluquero/una
peluquera
a hairdresser's (**shop**) = una peluquería

hairdrier *noun*
a hairdrier = un secador, una secadora
(*Mex*)

hairstyle *noun*
a hairstyle = un peinado

half
1 *noun*
half = mitad (*feminine*)
to cut something in half = cortar algo por la
mitad
(*in fractions*)
a half = un medio
(*a period in a game*)
a half = un tiempo
2 *adjective*
(*when talking about quantities*)
half a liter of milk = medio litro de leche
two and a half cups of flour = dos tazas y
media de harina
3 *pronoun*
(*when talking about quantities, numbers*)
he has already spent half of his salary = ya
gastó la mitad de su sueldo
half the pupils walk to school = la mitad de
los alumnos van al colegio a pie
(*when talking about time, age*) ▶ **p. 319**
an hour and a half = una hora y media
it's half (**past**) **three** = son las tres y media
he's three and a half = tiene tres años y
medio
4 *adverb*
the bottle is half empty = la botella está
medio vacía
the door was half closed = la puerta estaba
entreabierta

half an hour *noun*
half an hour = media hora (*feminine*)

half hour *noun*
a half hour = media hora (*feminine*)

half term *noun* (*British English*)
half term = vacaciones de mitad de
trimestre (*feminine plural*)

hall *noun*
(*in a house, an apartment*)
a hall = un vestíbulo, una entrada
(*for public events*)
a hall = una sala, un salón

ham *noun*
 ham = jamón (*masculine*)
hamburger *noun*
 (*a burger*)
 a hamburger = una hamburguesa
 (*US English—ground beef*)
 hamburger = carne molida (*feminine*),
  carne picada (*feminine*) (*R Pl, Spa*)
hammer
1 *noun*
 a hammer = un martillo
2 *verb* = martillear
hand
1 *noun*
 (*part of the body*) ▶ **p. 235**
 the hand = la mano
 they were holding hands = iban de la
  mano, iban tomados de la mano, iban
  cogidos de la mano (*Spa*)
 (*help*)
 to lend a hand = echar una mano
 (*on a clock or watch*)
 a hand = una manecilla
 on the one hand . . ., on the other . . . = por
  un lado . . ., por otro lado . . .
2 *verb*
 to hand a book to someone, to hand
  someone a book = pasarle un libro a
  alguien
hand around
 to hand around the biscuits = pasar las
  galletas
hand in = entregar
hand out = repartir, distribuir
hand over = entregar
hand round (*British English*) ▶ hand
around

handbag *noun*
 a handbag = una cartera, un bolso (*Spa*),
  una bolsa (*Mex*)

handbrake *noun*
 (*US English—on a bicycle*)
 a handbrake = un freno (de pastilla)
 (*British English—in a car*)
 a handbrake = un freno de mano

handicapped *adjective*
 = minusválido/minusválida
 mentally handicapped = minusválido
  psíquico/minusválida psíquica

handkerchief *noun*
 a handkerchief = un pañuelo

handle
1 *noun*
 a handle (*on a door*) = un picaporte
 (*on a drawer*) = un tirador
 (*on a bag*) = un asa (*feminine*)
 (*on a cup, a saucepan*) = un asa (*feminine*)
 (*on a spade, a knife*) = un mango
2 *verb*

(*to deal with, cope with*)
 to handle a situation = manejar una
  situación
 (*to control, manage*)
 to handle a car = manejar un coche
 to know how to handle children = saber
  tratar a los niños

handlebars *noun*
 the handlebars = el manillar, el manubrio
 (*Lat Am*)

handsome *adjective*
 = guapo/guapa, buen mozo/buena moza
 (*Lat Am*)

handwriting *noun*
 handwriting = letra (*feminine*)

handy *adjective*
 the guidebook was very handy = la guía
  resultó ser muy útil
 to come in handy = venir muy bien

hang *verb*
 (*to attach to a hook, coat hanger, line*)
 to hang a picture on the wall = colgar un
  cuadro en la pared
 to hang clothes in a wardrobe = colgar la
  ropa en un ropero
 (*to be attached*)
 there was a lightbulb hanging from the
  ceiling = la bombilla colgaba del techo
 (*to kill*) = ahorcar
 he was hanged = lo ahorcaron
hang on
 (*to wait*) = esperar
hang on to
 she was hanging on to the rope = se
  aferraba a la cuerda
hang out
 your shirt is hanging out = tienes la camisa
  afuera
 to hang out the washing = tender la ropa
hang up
 (*to attach to a hook, coat hanger*) = colgar
 (*to put the phone down*) = colgar, cortar
 (*SC*)

happen *verb*
 = pasar, suceder, ocurrir
 what's happening? = ¿qué pasa?
 what happened to you? = ¿qué te pasó?

happy *adjective*
 to make someone happy = hacer feliz a
  alguien
 to be happy (with something) = estar
  contento/contenta (con algo)

harbor (*US English*), **harbour** (*British
English*) *noun*
 a harbor = un puerto

hard
1 *adjective*

(*firm, stiff*) = duro/dura
to go hard = endurecerse
(*difficult*) = difícil
it's hard to understand = es difícil de
  entender
(*harsh, tough*)
a hard winter = un invierno crudo, un
  invierno severo
hard luck! = ¡mala suerte!
she's a hard woman = es una mujer muy
  dura
2 *adverb*
to work hard = trabajar duro
they hit him hard = le pegaron muy fuerte

hard-boiled *adjective*
a hard-boiled egg = un huevo duro

hardly *adverb*
(*barely*) = apenas

hardware *noun*
(*for computers*)
hardware = hardware (*masculine*)
(*for use in the home, garden*)
hardware = ferretería (*feminine*)

hardware store (*US English*),
hardware shop (*British English*) *noun*
a hardware store = una ferretería, una
  tlapalería (*Mex*)

hardworking *adjective*
= trabajador/trabajadora

hare *noun*
a hare = una liebre

harm
1 *verb*
to harm someone = hacerle daño a alguien
to harm the environment = dañar el medio
  ambiente
2 *noun*
to do harm to someone = hacerle daño a
  alguien
there's no harm in trying = nada se pierde
  con intentar

harmful *adjective*
a harmful gas = un gas nocivo
the harmful effects of alcohol = el efecto
  perjudicial del alcohol

harmless *adjective*
= inofensivo/inofensiva

harp *noun*
a harp = un arpa (*feminine*)

harsh *adjective*
a harsh climate = un clima riguroso
to live in harsh conditions = vivir en
  condiciones duras
a harsh light = una luz fuerte

harvest *noun*
the harvest (*of wheat, fruit*) = la cosecha
  (*of grapes*) = la vendimia

hat *noun*
a hat = un sombrero

hatch *verb*
(*if it's a chick*) = salir del cascarón

hate *verb*
= odiar

hatred *noun*
hatred = odio (*masculine*)

haunted *adjective*
= embrujado/embrujada

have
1 *verb*
to have, to have got (*British English*) =
  tener
she has a dog = tiene un perro
(*to eat, drink, smoke*)
to have a sandwich = comer un sándwich
to have a glass of wine = tomar una copa
  de vino
to have a cigarette = fumar un cigarrillo
to have dinner = cenar, comer (*Lat Am*)
(*to get*)
I had a letter from Bob yesterday = recibí
  una carta de Bob ayer
we have had no news from her = no hemos
  tenido noticias suyas
(*to hold or organize*)
to have a party = hacer una fiesta
to have a meeting = hacer una reunión
(*to spend*)
I'll have a good time in Paris = lo voy a
  pasar bien en París
(*to suffer*)
to have flu = tener gripe
to have a headache = tener dolor de
  cabeza
(*to get something done*)
to have the house painted = hacer pintar
  la casa
she had her hair cut = se cortó el pelo
(*to give birth to*) = tener
2 *auxiliary verb*
(*when used to form a past tense*)
I've lost my bag = he perdido la bolsa,
  perdí la bolsa (*Lat Am*)
have you seen Tom? = ¿has visto a Tom?,
  ¿viste a Tom? (*Lat Am*)
I had seen her = la había visto
they have arrived = han llegado, llegaron
  (*Lat Am*)
(*in questions and short answers*)
you've met her, haven't you? = ya la
  conoces ¿no?
you haven't lost the key, have you? = ¿no
  habrás perdido la llave
3 to have to = tener que
I have to study = tengo que estudiar
have on
to have a coat on = tener puesto un abrigo

H

hay *noun*
hay = heno (*masculine*)

hazelnut *noun*
a hazelnut = una avellana

he *pronoun*
he = él
he went to the theater = fue al teatro
he did it = él lo hizo
I work in London but he doesn't = yo
trabajo en Londres pero él no

> ! Although él *is given as the translation of*
> he, *it is in practice used only for*
> *emphasis, or to avoid ambiguity*

head
1 *noun*
(*part of the body*) ▶ **p. 235**
the head = la cabeza
(*the front or the top*)
at the head of the list = a la cabeza de la
lista, encabezando la lista
(*the top part of an object, tool*)
the head of a nail = la cabeza de un clavo
the head of a hammer = la cabeza de un
martillo
(*British English—a principal*)
a head = un director/una directora
(*a person in charge*)
the head (*of an organization*) = el
director/la directora
(*of a family, government*) = el jefe/la jefa
2 *verb*
(*to be in charge of*)
to head a team = capitanear un equipo
(*to be bound for*)
I was heading home = me dirigía a casa
where are you heading?, where are you
headed? = ¿para dónde vas?
(*in football*)
to head the ball = cabecear el balón
head for
I headed for the exit = me dirigí hacia la
salida

headache *noun*
a headache = un dolor de cabeza

headlamp, headlight *noun*
a headlamp = un faro, un foco (*Lat Am*)

headline *noun*
(*in a newspaper*)
a headline = un titular
(*on TV, radio*)
the news headlines = el resumen
informativo

headphones *noun*
a pair of headphones = unos auriculares,
unos cascos (*Spa*)

headquarters *noun*
the headquarters (*of a company*) = la
oficina central

(*of an army*) = el cuartel

headteacher *noun* (*British English*)
a headteacher = un director/una directora

heal *verb*
to heal someone = curar a alguien
the wound has healed = la herida ha
cicatrizado

health *noun*
health = salud (*feminine*)
to be in good health = estar bien de salud

healthy *adjective*
(*in good health*) = sano/sana
(*good for the health*) = sano/sana, saludable

heap *noun*
a heap = un montón, una pila

hear *verb*
to hear = oír
(*to learn, discover*)
to hear the news = enterarse de lo que ha
pasado
did you hear who won? = ¿sabes quién
ganó?
(*to listen to*) = escuchar
(*to have news from*)
we haven't heard from her = no sabemos
nada de ella
hear of
I've never heard of the place = nunca he
oído hablar del lugar

heart *noun*
(*part of the body*) ▶ **p. 235**
the heart = el corazón
(*the center*)
the office is right in the heart of London =
la oficina se encuentra en el corazón de
Londres
(*when talking about knowledge*)
by heart = de memoria

heart attack *noun*
a heart attack = un ataque al corazón, un
infarto

heat
1 *verb*
to heat some water = calentar agua
to heat a house = calefaccionar una casa
2 *noun*
(*warmth*)
the heat = el calor
(*on a cooker*)
to cook at a low heat = cocinar a fuego
lento
(*a round in a sporting contest*)
a heat = una (prueba) eliminatoria
heat up
to heat up some soup = calentar un poco
de sopa

heater *noun*
a heater = un calentador, un calefactor, una
estufa

heating noun
heating = calefacción (feminine)

heatwave noun
a heatwave = una ola de calor

heaven noun
heaven = cielo (masculine)

heavy adjective
(in weight)
to be heavy = pesar mucho, ser pesado/pesada
how heavy is it? = ¿cuánto pesa?
(in quantity, intensity)
the traffic is very heavy = la circulación está muy densa
to be a heavy smoker = fumar mucho
(with rich ingredients) = pesado/pesada
a heavy meal = una comida pesada

hedge noun
a hedge = un seto

hedgehog noun
a hedgehog = un erizo

heel noun
(part of the foot) ▶ p. 235
the heel = el talón
(part of a shoe)
a heel = un tacón, un taco (SC)

height noun
(of a person)
height = estatura (feminine)
(of a building or tree)
height = altura (feminine)

helicopter noun
a helicopter = un helicóptero

hell noun
hell = infierno (masculine)

hello exclamation
hello (when greeting someone) = hola
(on the phone) = sí, aló (S Am), diga (Spa), bueno (Mex), holá (R Pl)
Catherine says hello = Catherine te manda saludos

helmet noun
a helmet = un casco

help
1 verb
(to be of assistance) = ayudar
to help someone to escape = ayudar a alguien a escapar
can I help you? (in a shop) = ¿qué desea?
(to serve)
to help oneself = servirse
(to avoid)
she couldn't help laughing = no pudo contener la risa
I just can't help it = no lo puedo remediar
2 exclamation
help! = ¡socorro!

3 noun
help = ayuda (feminine)
the map wasn't much help = el mapa no sirvió mucho
help out
I helped him out = le di una mano

helpful adjective
(willing to help) = amable, servicial
(useful) = útil

helpless adjective
(defenseless) = indefenso/indefensa
(having no power)
to be helpless to do something = ser incapaz de hacer algo
(through disability)
the accident left her helpless = el accidente la dejó incapacitada

hem noun
a hem = un dobladillo

hen noun
(chicken)
a hen = una gallina

her
1 pronoun
(when used as a direct object) = la
I know/don't know her = la conozco/no la conozco

❗ Note that la comes before the verb in Spanish

(when used as an indirect object) = le
I never talk to her = nunca le hablo
I wrote her a letter = le escribí una carta

❗ Note that le comes before the verb in Spanish

(when used as an indirect object pronoun together with a direct object pronoun) = se
I gave it to her = se lo di
he's not going to say it to her = no se lo va a decir

❗ Note that se comes before the direct object pronoun

(when telling someone to do something)
catch her! = ¡atrápenla!
give the money to her = dale el dinero (a ella)
give them to her = dáselos

❗ Note that la, le, and se come after the verb in Spanish

(when telling someone not to do something)
don't look at her! = ¡no la mires!
don't give her my phone number! = ¡no le des mi número de teléfono!
don't show them to her! = ¡no se los muestres!

! Note that la, le and se come before the verb in Spanish

(when used after prepositions and with to be) = ella
we did it for her = lo hicimos por ella
I have nothing against her = no tengo nada en contra de ella, no tengo nada en contra suya
she had her dog with her = tenía el perro consigo
it's her = es ella
2 adjective
= su (+ singular), sus (+ plural)

! For her used with parts of the body,
▶ **p. 235**

herb noun
a herb = una hierba, un yuyo (R Pl)

herd noun
a herd (of cattle) = una manada, una tropa (R Pl)
(of goats) = un rebaño
(of pigs) = una manada

here adverb
(at a point close to the person speaking) = aquí, acá
I'm up here = estoy aquí arriba
(when drawing attention to something)
here's the bus stop = aquí está la parada de autobuses
here they are = aquí están
here comes the train = aquí viene el tren
(when giving something)
here, take my pencil = toma, te doy mi lápiz
here's my telephone number = aquí tienes mi número de teléfono
(present)
she's not here at the moment = no está en este momento

hers pronoun
hers (singular) = suyo/suya, de ella
(plural) = suyos/suyas, de ella
they're hers = son suyos/suyas, son de ella
hers is blue = el suyo/la suya es azul, el/la de ella es azul
a friend of hers = un amigo suyo, un amigo de ella

herself pronoun
(translated by a reflexive verb in Spanish)
she didn't hurt herself = no se hizo daño, no se lastimó (Lat Am)
she bought herself a hat = se compró un sombrero
(used for emphasis)
she said it herself = lo dijo ella misma
she did it by herself = lo hizo sola

hesitate verb
= dudar
don't hesitate to tell her = no dude en decírselo

hi exclamation
hi! = ¡hola!

hiccup, **hiccough** noun
to have hiccups = tener hipo

hide verb
(to conceal)
= esconder
to hide (oneself) = esconderse
(to keep secret) = ocultar
she couldn't hide her joy = no pudo ocultar su alegría

hide and seek noun
to play hide and seek = jugar al escondite, jugar a las escondidas (Lat Am)

hideous adjective
= espantoso/espantosa

hiding place noun
a hiding place = un escondite, un escondrijo

hi-fi noun
a hi-fi = un equipo de alta fidelidad, un hi-fi

high
1 adjective
(having great height) = alto/alta
the mountains are high = las montañas son altas
how high is the tower? = ¿qué altura tiene la torre?
it's 200 meters high = tiene 200 metros de altura, tiene 200 metros de alto
(in number, intensity, speed)
prices are high = los precios son altos
the train travels at a high speed = el tren viaja a alta velocidad
(in quality)
the standard is very high = el nivel es muy alto
(shrill)
to have a high voice = tener una voz aguda
a high note = una nota alta
2 adverb
(when talking about a place)
don't go any higher or you'll fall = no subas más o te vas a caer

high heels noun
high heels = zapatos de tacón alto (masculine plural), zapatos de taco alto (masculine plural) (SC)

Highlands noun
the Highlands = las Highlands, las tierras altas

highlights noun
(on TV, radio)
the match highlights = las jugadas más importantes del partido

(*in hair*)
highlights = reflejos (*masculine plural*),
luces (*feminine plural*) (*Mex*), claritos
(*masculine plural*) (*R Pl*)

high school noun (*US English*)
a high school = un colegio secundario
mixto, un liceo (*SC*), un instituto (*Spa*)

highway noun
a highway (*US English*) = una carretera
(*British English*) = una vía pública

hijack verb
= secuestrar

hike
1 noun
a hike = una caminata, una excursión
2 verb
to go hiking = ir de caminata, ir de
excursión

hill noun
a hill (*low*) = una colina, un cerro
(*high*) = una montaña
(*a slope*)
a hill = una cuesta

him pronoun
(*when used as a direct object*) = lo
I know/don't know him = lo conozco/no lo
conozco

> **!** Note that lo comes before the verb in
> Spanish

(*when used as an indirect object*) = le
she never talks to him = no le habla nunca
I wrote him a letter = le escribí una carta

> **!** Note that le comes before the verb in
> Spanish

(*when used as an indirect object pronoun
together with a direct object pronoun*) =
se
I have to give them to him = tengo que
dárselos
he's not going to say it to him = no se lo va
a decir

> **!** Note that se comes before the direct
> object pronoun

(*when telling someone to do something*)
catch him! = ¡atrápenlo!
give the money to him = dale el dinero
give it to him = dáselo

> **!** Note that lo, le, and se come after the
> verb in Spanish

(*when telling someone not to do
something*)
don't look at him! = ¡no lo mires!
don't give him my phone number! = ¡no le
des mi número de teléfono!
don't show them to him! = ¡no se los
muestres!

> **!** Note that lo, le, and se come before the
> verb in Spanish

(*when used after prepositions and with* to
be) = él
we did it for him = lo hicimos por él
I've got nothing against him = no tengo
nada en contra de él, no tengo nada en
contra suya
he had his dog with him = tenía el perro
consigo
it's him = es él

himself pronoun
(*translated by a reflexive verb in Spanish*)
he wants to enjoy himself = quiere
divertirse
he bought himself a hat = se compró un
sombrero
(*used for emphasis*)
he said it himself = lo dijo él mismo
he did it by himself = lo hizo solo

hip noun ▶ p. 235
the hip = la cadera

hire
1 verb
(*to rent*) = alquilar
(*to lend for payment*) = alquilar
(*to employ*) = contratar
2 noun
car hire (*British English*) = alquiler de
coches (*masculine*)
boats for hire = se alquilan barcos
hire out (*British English*)
= alquilar

his
1 adjective
= su (+ *singular*), sus (+ *plural*)

> **!** For his used with parts of the body,
> ▶ p. 235

2 pronoun (*singular*) = suyo/suya, de él
(*plural*) = suyos/suyas, de él
they're his = son suyos/suyas, son de él
his is blue = el suyo/la suya es azul, el/la de
él es azul
a friend of his = un amigo suyo, un amigo
de él

history noun
history = historia (*feminine*)

hit
1 verb
(*to strike*)
to hit a tennis ball = darle a una pelota de
tenis
to hit someone on the head = pegarle a
alguien en la cabeza
don't hit me! = ¡no me pegues!
to hit one's head on the door = pegarse en
la cabeza con la puerta
(*to have a collision with, to knock down*)
I hit the tree = choqué con el árbol
he was hit by a truck = lo atropelló un
camión

H

(*strike*)
to hit a target = dar en un objetivo
the port was hit = bombardearon el puerto
2 *noun*
a hit = un éxito
to be a big hit = tener mucho éxito

hitchhike *verb*
= hacer autostop, hacer dedo, ir de aventón
(*Mex*)

hitchhiker *noun*
a hitchhiker = un/una autoestopista

hoarse *adjective*
= ronco/ronca

hobby *noun*
a hobby = un pasatiempo, un hobby

hold
1 *verb*
to hold someone's hand = tomar a alguien
de la mano, agarrar a alguien de la mano,
coger a alguien de la mano (*Spa*)
they were holding hands = iban de la
mano
he was holding some coins in his hand =
tenía unas monedas en la mano
(*to arrange*)
to hold a meeting = celebrar una reunión
the party will be held in the school = la
fiesta tendrá lugar en la escuela
(*to have*)
to hold the world record = tener el récord
mundial
to hold a Spanish passport = tener
pasaporte español
(*other uses*)
to hold someone responsible = hacer
responsable a alguien de algo
hold the line please = no cuelgue, por
favor, no corte, por favor (*SC*)
2 *noun*
to get hold of the ball = agarrar la pelota,
coger el balón (*Spa*)
to get hold of someone = localizar a
alguien, ubicar a alguien (*Lat Am*)
hold back
to hold back the tears = contener las
lágrimas
hold on
(*to wait*) = esperar
hold on please (*on phone*) = no cuelgue,
por favor, no corte, por favor (*SC*)
(*so as not to fall*)
hold on tight! = ¡agárrate fuerte!
hold on to
to hold on to someone/something =
agarrarse a alguien/algo
hold up
(*to raise*) = levantar
(*to delay*)
to hold someone up = retrasar a alguien
(*to rob*) = atracar, asaltar

hole *noun*
(*in clothes, material*)
a hole = un agujero
(*in the ground*)
a hole = un hoyo
(*in a wall*)
a hole = un boquete
a rabbit hole = una madriguera
a mouse hole = una ratonera

holiday *noun*
(*British English—a vacation*)
a holiday = unas vacaciones
to go on holiday = ir de vacaciones
the school holidays = las vacaciones
(escolares)
(*a national or religious festival*)
a (public) holiday = un día festivo, un
feriado (*Lat Am*)

Holland *noun* ▶ **p. 187**
Holland = Holanda (*feminine*)

home
1 *noun*
a home (*a house, a place to live*) = una casa
(*a family environment*) = un hogar
to leave home = irse de casa
(*native country*)
home = patria (*feminine*)
(*for elderly people*)
a retirement home = una residencia de
ancianos
at home (*in one's house*) = en casa
at home (*comfortable*)
to feel at home = sentirse a gusto
make yourselves at home = pónganse
cómodos, están en su casa
2 *adverb*
to go home (*to one's house*) = volver a casa
(*to one's home country*) = volver a su país
I met her on my way home = me encontré
con ella cuando volvía a casa
to be home = estar en casa

homeless *adjective*
to be homeless = estar sin hogar, estar sin
techo

home-made *adjective*
= hecho/hecha en casa

homesick *adjective*
he is homesick (*for his family*) = echa de
menos a su familia, extraña a su familia
(*Lat Am*)
(*for his country*) = echa de menos a su país,
extraña a su país (*Lat Am*)

homework *noun*
homework = deberes (*masculine plural*),
tareas (*feminine plural*)

homosexual *noun*
a homosexual = un homosexual/una
homosexual

honest *adjective*
  (*trustworthy*)
  honest = honesto/honesta,
    honrado/honrada
  (*frank, sincere*) = sincero/sincera
  to be honest, I'd rather stay here = para
    serte sincero, prefiero quedarme aquí

honestly *adverb*
  to answer a question honestly = contestar
    sinceramente a una pregunta
  I honestly don't know = de verdad que no
    lo sé

honey *noun*
  honey = miel (*feminine*)

honeymoon *noun*
  a honeymoon = una luna de miel
  to go to Greece on honeymoon = irse a
    Grecia de luna de miel

honor (*US English*), **honour** (*British English*)
1 *noun*
  honor = honor (*masculine*)
  it's a great honor for us to meet them =
    conocerlos es un gran honor para
    nosotros
2 *verb*
  (*to show respect for*)
  **I would be honored to represent my
    country** = representar a mi país sería un
    honor para mí
  to honor a promise = cumplir con una
    promesa

hood *noun*
  (*to cover the head*)
  a hood = una capucha
  (*US English—of a car*)
  the hood = el capó, el capoté (*Mex*)

hoof *noun*
  a hoof (*of a horse*) = un casco, una pezuña
    (*Mex*), un vaso (*R Pl*)
  (*of a cow*) = una pezuña

hook *noun*
  (*for hanging clothes*)
  a hook = una percha, un gancho
  (*for hanging pictures*)
  a hook = un gancho
  (*for fastening a garment*)
  a hook = un ganchito
  (*on the telephone*)
  to leave the phone off the hook = dejar el
    teléfono descolgado

Hoover , **hoover** (*British English*)
1 *noun*
  a Hoover = una aspiradora, un aspirador
2 *verb* = pasar la aspiradora, aspirar (*Lat Am*)
  to hoover the house = pasar la aspiradora
    por la casa, aspirar la casa

hop *verb*
  (*to jump on one leg*) = saltar a la pata coja,
    saltar con un solo pie
  (*to move lightly*)
  the bird hopped up to me = el pájaro se me
    acercó dando saltitos

hope
1 *verb* = esperar
  I hope it's true = espero que sea verdad

> **!** *Note that* **esperar que** *is followed by the
> subjunctive*

  to hope to travel abroad = esperar viajar al
    extranjero
  I hope so/not = espero que sí/no
2 *noun*
  (*the belief that things will work out*)
  hope = esperanza (*feminine*)
  (*a chance*)
  a hope = una esperanza

hopeless *adjective*
  (*without hope of success*)
  a hopeless attempt = un intento
    desesperado
  it's hopeless! = ¡es inútil!

horizon *noun*
  the horizon = el horizonte

horn *noun*
  (*on a car, bus*)
  a horn = un claxon, una bocina
  to blow the horn = tocar el claxon, tocar la
    bocina
  (*of an animal*)
  a horn = un cuerno, un asta (*feminine*), un
    cacho (*S Am*)
  (*musical instrument*)
  a horn = un cuerno

horoscope *noun*
  a horoscope = un horóscopo

horrible *adjective*
  = horrible

horror *noun*
  horror = horror (*masculine*)

horse *noun*
  a horse = un caballo

hose *noun*
  a hose (*for watering the garden*) = una
    manguera
  (*for putting out fires*) = una manguera
    contra incendios

hospital *noun*
  a hospital = un hospital
  to be in hospital = estar en el hospital, estar
    hospitalizado/hospitalizada, estar
    internado/internada (*SC*)

hospitality *noun*
  hospitality = hospitalidad (*feminine*)

H

R Pl River Plate area   **SC** Southern Cone   **Spa** Spain

host *noun*
(*to guests, visitors*)
a host = un anfitrión/una anfitriona
(*on a radio or TV program*)
a host = un presentador/una presentadora

hostage *noun*
a hostage = un/una rehén
to take someone hostage = tomar a alguien como rehén

hostel *noun*
(*for refugees, workers, young people*)
a hostel = un hogar
(*a youth hostel*)
a hostel = un albergue juvenil

hostess *noun*
(*to guests, visitors*)
a hostess = una anfitriona
(*an air hostess*)
a hostess = una azafata, una aeromoza (*Lat Am*)
(*on a radio or TV program*)
a hostess = una presentadora

hostile *adjective*
= hostil

hot *adjective*
(*very warm*)
to be hot, to feel hot = tener calor
it's too hot in the office = hace demasiado calor en la oficina
it gets very hot in the summer = hace mucho calor en el verano
a hot climate = un clima cálido
a hot meal = una comida caliente
(*strong, with a lot of spice*) = picante

hot dog *noun*
a hot dog = un perro caliente, un pancho (*R Pl*)

hotel *noun*
a hotel = un hotel

hour *noun* ▶ p. 319
an hour = una hora
I earn £2 an hour = gano 2 libras por hora

house *noun*
a house = una casa
the bike is at my house = la bicicleta está en mi casa

housewife *noun*
a housewife = un ama de casa (*feminine*)

housework *noun*
housework = tareas domésticas (*feminine plural*)

housing development (*US English*), **housing estate** (*British English*) *noun*
a housing development, a housing estate = un conjunto residencial, una urbanización (*Spa*)

hovercraft *noun*
a hovercraft = un aerodeslizador

how
1 *adverb*
(*in what way*) = cómo
how do you spell your name? = ¿cómo se escribe su nombre?
I know how [to swim | to ride a horse | to skate ...] = yo sé [nadar | cabalgar | patinar ...]
she showed me how to send a fax = me enseño cómo mandar un fax
(*in polite questions*)
how are you? = ¿cómo estás?
how's the job going? = ¿cómo marcha el trabajo?
how was your holiday? = ¿qué tal las vacaciones?
how do you do? = ¡mucho gusto!
(*in questions requiring specific information*)
how tall are you? = ¿cuánto mides?
how old is he? = ¿cuántos años tiene?, ¿qué edad tiene?
(*in exclamations*) = qué
how strange = ¡qué raro!
how about Friday? = ¿qué te parece el viernes?
I'd love to go, how about you? = me encantaría ir ¿y a ti?
2 *conjunction*
I still don't know how she did it = todavía no sé cómo lo hizo

however *adverb*
(*nevertheless*) = sin embargo, no obstante

hug *verb*
= abrazar

huge *adjective*
= enorme

human *adjective*
= humano/humana

human being *noun*
a human being = un ser humano

humid *adjective*
= húmedo

humor (*US English*), **humour** (*British English*) *noun*
humor = humor (*masculine*)
a good sense of humor = un buen sentido del humor

humorous *adjective*
a humorous book = un libro humorístico
a humorous remark = un comentario gracioso

hundred *number* ▶ p. 154
one hundred, a hundred = cien (*masculine*)
(**!** *never changes*)
one hundred people = cien personas
one hundred and ninety-eight = ciento noventa y ocho

The human body

When it is clear who owns the part of the body being mentioned, Spanish tends to use the definite article, where English uses a possessive adjective:

*he closed **his** eyes*	= cerró **los** ojos
*she raised **her** arm*	= levantó **el** brazo

For expressions such as *he hurt his ankle* or *she brushed her teeth*, where the action involves more than the simple movement of a body part, use a reflexive verb in Spanish:

*she **has broken her** leg*	= **se ha roto** la pierna
*he **was washing his** hair*	= **se lavaba** el pelo

Note also the following:

*she touched **my** arm*	= me tocó **el** brazo
	(*literally* she touched to me the arm)

Describing people

When describing people, Spanish mainly uses the verb **tener**:

his hair is long	= tiene el pelo largo
he has long hair	= tiene el pelo largo
the boy with long hair	= el niño de pelo largo
her eyes are green	= tiene (los) ojos verdes
she has green eyes	= tiene (los) ojos verdes
his nose is red	= tiene la nariz roja
he has a red nose	= tiene la nariz roja

Illnesses, aches and pains

where does it hurt?	= ¿dónde te duele?
his leg hurts	= le duele la pierna
I have a bad back	= me duele la espalda
I have a sore throat	= tengo dolor de garganta
he had a heart attack	= le dio un ataque al corazón

! Ciento *is used to translate* one hundred *in numbers between 101 and 199*

two hundred = doscientos/doscientas
two hundred and fifty = doscientos cincuenta (**!** *never changes*)
three hundred = trescientos/trescientas
four hundred = cuatrocientos/cuatrocientas
five hundred = quinientos/quinientas
six hundred = seiscientos/seiscientas
seven hundred = setecientos/setecientas
eight hundred = ochocientos/ochocientas
nine hundred = novecientos/novecientas

Hungary *noun* ▶ **p. 187**
Hungary = Hungría (*feminine*)

hungry *adjective*
to be hungry = tener hambre

hunter *noun*
a hunter = un cazador/una cazadora

hunting *noun*
hunting = caza (*feminine*)
to go hunting = ir de caza

hurrah, hurray *exclamation*
hurrah! = ¡hurra!

hurry
1 *verb*
to hurry = darse prisa, apurarse (*Lat Am*)
to hurry someone = meter prisa a alguien, apurar a alguien (*Lat Am*)
2 *noun*
to be in a hurry = tener prisa, estar apurado/apurada (*Lat Am*)
she was in a hurry to leave = tenía prisa por irse, estaba apurada por irse (*Lat Am*)
I did my homework in a hurry = hice los deberes deprisa, hice las tareas apurado (*Lat Am*)

hurt
1 *verb*
(*to injure*)
to hurt oneself = hacerse daño, lastimarse (*Lat Am*)
to hurt one's leg = hacerse daño en la pierna, lastimarse la pierna (*Lat Am*)
many people were hurt = hubo muchos heridos
(*to be painful*)
my throat hurts = me duele la garganta

- (*to cause emotional pain*)
  to hurt someone's feelings = ofender a
  alguien
2 *adjective*
  she was badly hurt = estaba gravemente
  herida
  to feel hurt = sentirse dolido/dolida

husband *noun*
  a husband = un marido, un esposo

hut *noun*
- (*a shed*)
  a hut = una cabaña
- (*for living in*)
  a hut = una choza

hygienic *adjective*
  = higiénico/higiénica

hypnotize *verb*
  = hipnotizar

hysterical *adjective*
  = histérico/histérica

I

I *pronoun*
  I = yo
  I went to the theater = fui al teatro
  I did it = yo lo hice
  I was singing, he was playing the piano =
  yo cantaba y él tocaba el piano

  ! *Although* **yo** *is given as the translation
  of* **I**, *it is in practice used only for
  emphasis or to avoid ambiguity*

ice
1 *noun* = hielo (*masculine*)
2 *verb*
  to ice a cake = glasear un pastel

ice cream *noun*
- (*the product*)
  ice cream = helado (*masculine*)
- (*on a stick or cone*)
  an ice cream = un helado

ice rink *noun*
  an ice rink = una pista de hielo

ice skating *noun*
  ice skating = patinaje sobre hielo
  (*masculine*)

icing *noun*
  icing = glaseado (*masculine*)

idea *noun*
  an idea = una idea
  I haven't the slightest idea! = ¡no tengo ni
  la menor idea!

identical *adjective*
  = idéntico/idéntica

identity card *noun*
  an identity card = un carné de identidad

idiot *noun*
  an idiot = un idiota/una idiota

if *conjunction*
  = si
  if you like = si quieres
  if you see him don't speak to him = si lo
  ves no le hables
  if I were rich, I would travel = si fuera rica,
  me iría de viaje
  I wonder if they will come = me pregunto si
  vendrán
  if I were you, I wouldn't go = yo que tú, no
  me iría

ignore *verb*
  to ignore a person = ignorar a alguien
  to ignore a problem = no hacer caso de un
  problema
  to ignore the rules = hacer caso omiso de
  las reglas

ill *adjective*
  = enfermo/enferma
  to be ill = estar enfermo/enferma
  to fall ill = caer enfermo/enferma,
  enfermarse (*Lat Am*)

illegal *adjective*
  = ilegal

illness *noun*
  an illness = una enfermedad

illustration *noun*
  an illustration = una ilustración

imagination *noun*
  imagination = imaginación (*feminine*)

imagine *verb*
  = imaginar(se)

imitate *verb*
  = imitar

immediately *adverb*
  = inmediatamente

immigrant
1 *noun*
  an immigrant = un/una inmigrante
2 *adjective*
  an immigrant worker = un obrero
  inmigrante
  an immigrant community = una
  comunidad de inmigrantes

C Am Central America   **Lat Am** Latin America   **Mex** Mexico

impatient *adjective*
= impaciente
to get impatient = impacientarse

import
1 *verb* = importar
2 *noun*
an import = un artículo de importación

important *adjective*
= importante

impossible *adjective*
= imposible

impress *verb*
to impress someone = causarle una buena impresión a alguien
we were impressed by your work = tu trabajo nos causó muy buena impresión

impression *noun*
an impression = una impresión

improve *verb*
• (*to make better*) = mejorar
she wants to improve her Spanish = quiere mejorar su español
• (*to get better*) = mejorar
the situation has improved = la situación ha mejorado

improvement *noun*
an improvement = una mejora

in
1 *preposition*
• (*in a place or position*) = en
in the house = en la casa
he went in the shop = entró en la tienda, entró a la tienda (*Lat Am*)
I read it in the newspaper = lo leí en el periódico
the woman in the photograph = la mujer de la foto
there's a letter in it = tiene una carta adentro
in Ireland = en Irlanda
in Rome = en Roma
• (*dressed in*)
the woman in the red skirt = la mujer de la falda roja
she was dressed in black = estaba vestida de negro
• (*showing the way in which something is done*) = en
written in Spanish = escrito en castellano
in a low voice = en voz baja
• (*during*)
in October = en octubre
in the night = durante la noche
at two o'clock in the morning/afternoon = a las dos de la mañana/de la tarde
• (*within*) = dentro de
I'll be ready in ten minutes = estaré listo dentro de diez minutos

• (*with superlatives*)
the biggest city in the world = la ciudad más grande del mundo
• (*other uses*)
in the rain = bajo la lluvia
one in ten = uno de cada diez
to cut something in two = cortar algo en dos
2 *adverb*
• (*indoors*)
to come in = entrar
• (*at home*)
tell him I'm not in = dile que no estoy

inch *noun*
an inch = una pulgada (*2,54 cm*)

incident *noun*
an incident = un incidente, un episodio

include *verb*
= incluir

including *preposition*
they all liked it, including Paul = a todos les gustó, incluso a Paul

income *noun*
income = ingresos (*masculine plural*)

income tax *noun*
income tax = impuesto sobre la renta (*masculine*)

incompetent *adjective*
= incompetente

inconsiderate *adjective*
= desconsiderado/desconsiderada

inconvenient *adjective*
= inconveniente

incorrect *adjective*
an incorrect answer = una respuesta incorrecta
that is incorrect = eso no es cierto

increase
1 *verb* = aumentar
to increase someone's salary = aumentarle el sueldo a alguien
to increase in value = aumentar de valor
2 *noun*
an increase = un aumento
a price increase = un aumento de precio

incredible *adjective*
= increíble

independent *adjective*
= independiente

India *noun* ▶ p. 187
India = la India

Indian ▶ p. 187
1 *noun*
• (*a person from India*)
an Indian = un indio/una india

• (*a Native American*)
  an Indian = un/una indígena, un indio/una india
2 *adjective*
• (*of India*) = indio/india
• (*of America*) = indígena, indio/india

indicate *verb*
  = indicar

indigestion *noun*
  to have indigestion = tener indigestión

individual
1 *noun*
  an individual = un individuo
2 *adjective* = individual

indoor *adjective*
  (*if it's a pool or court*) = cubierto/cubierta, techado/techada

indoors *adverb*
  = dentro, adentro (*Lat Am*)

industrial *adjective*
  = industrial

industry *noun*
  an industry = una industria

inevitable *adjective*
  = inevitable

infant *noun*
• (*a baby*)
  an infant = un bebé, un niño/una niña
• (*British English—a young child*)
  an infant = un niño/una niña

infection *noun*
  an infection = una infección

influence
1 *noun*
  an influence = una influencia
2 *verb*
  to influence a person = influir a una persona
  to influence someone's decision = influir en la decisión de alguien

inform *verb*
• (*to tell, to give information to*) = informar
• (*to denounce*)
  to inform on someone = delatar a alguien

informal *verb*
• (*if it's a person or a person's manner*) = informal
• (*if it's a discussion or interview*) = informal
• (*if it's language*) = coloquial, familiar

information *noun*
  information = información (*feminine*)
  a piece of information = un dato

information desk *noun*
  the information desk = el mostrador de información

ingredient *noun*
  an ingredient = un ingrediente

inhabitant *noun*
  an inhabitant = un/una habitante

injection *noun*
  an injection = una inyección

injured *adjective*
  = herido/herida

injury *noun*
  an injury = una herida

ink *noun*
  ink = tinta (*feminine*)

inn *noun*
• (*a hotel*)
  an inn = una hostería
• (*a tavern*)
  an inn = una taberna

innocent *adjective*
  = inocente

inquiry *noun*
• (*a question*)
  to make inquiries about prices = pedir información sobre precios
• (*an investigation*)
  an inquiry = una investigación

insect *noun*
  an insect = un insecto

inside
1 *noun*
• **the inside** = el interior
• **to put a shirt on inside out** = ponerse una camisa al revés
2 *preposition* = dentro de
  inside the house = dentro de la casa
3 *adverb* = dentro, adentro (*Lat Am*)
4 *adjective* = interior

inspect *verb*
  to inspect a school/a factory = inspeccionar una escuela/una fábrica
  to inspect the evidence = inspeccionar las pruebas

inspector *noun*
• (*of a school*)
  an inspector = un inspector/una inspectora
• (*in the police*)
  a police inspector = un inspector/una inspectora (de policía)
• (*British English—of passengers' tickets*)
  an inspector = un inspector/una inspectora, un revisor/una revisora (*Spa*)

instead *adverb*
• **we didn't drive there: we walked instead** = en vez de ir allí en coche fuimos a pie
• **instead of** = en vez de, en lugar de

instruction *noun*
  an instruction = una instrucción
  'instructions for use' = 'instrucciones',
  'modo de empleo'

instrument *noun*
  an instrument = un instrumento

insult
1 *noun*
  an insult = un insulto
2 *verb* = insultar

insurance *noun*
  insurance = seguro (*masculine*)

insure *verb*
  = asegurar
  to insure something against theft =
  asegurar algo contra robo

intelligent *adjective*
  = inteligente

intend *verb*
  to intend to do something = pensar hacer
  algo

interest
1 *noun*
• (*felt by a person*)
  interest = interés (*masculine*)
• (*financial*)
  interest = interés (*masculine*)
2 *verb* = interesar

interested *adjective*
  = interesado/interesada
  they are very interested = están muy
  interesados
  I am interested in politics = me interesa la
  política

interesting *adjective*
  = interesante

interfere *verb*
  to interfere in someone's affairs =
  entrometerse en los asuntos de alguien
  he doesn't want these problems to
  interfere with his work = no quiere que
  estos problemas afecten a su trabajo

intermission *noun*
  (*during a performance*)
  the intermission = el intermedio

internal *adjective*
  = interno/interna

international *adjective*
  = internacional

Internet *noun*
  the Internet = el Internet

interpreter *noun*
  an interpreter = un/una intérprete

interrupt *verb*
  = interrumpir

interval *noun*
• (*in time or space*)
  an interval = un intervalo
  at regular intervals = a intervalos regulares
• (*British English—during a performance*)
  the interval = el intermedio
  (*in a play*) = el entreacto

interview
1 *noun*
  an interview = una entrevista
2 *verb*
  to interview someone = entrevistar a
  alguien

into *preposition*
• (*when referring to a place or location*)
  to go into the house = entrar en la casa,
  entrar a la casa (*Lat Am*)
  to get into a car = subir a un coche
  to get into bed = meterse en la cama
• to translate a letter into Spanish = traducir
  una carta al castellano
• five into twenty goes five times = veinte
  dividido por cinco es cinco, veinte
  dividido entre cinco es cinco

introduce *verb*
• (*when people meet*) = presentar
  he introduced me to Peter = me presentó a
  Peter
• (*on radio or television*)
  to introduce a program = presentar un
  programa
• to introduce [a law | change | reform ...] =
  introducir [una ley | un cambio | una
  reforma ...]

introduction *noun*
• (*to a book*)
  an introduction = una introducción
• (*to a speech*)
  an introduction = una presentación
• the introduction of a law = la introducción
  de una ley

invade *verb*
  = invadir

invent *verb*
  = inventar

invention *noun*
  an invention = un invento

investigate *verb*
  = investigar

investigation *noun*
  an investigation = una investigación

invisible *adjective*
  = invisible

invitation *noun*
  an invitation = una invitación

invite *verb*
= invitar

involved *adjective*
  he was involved in an accident = se vio
    envuelto en un accidente
  to be involved in a project = participar en
    un proyecto

Ireland *noun* ▶ p. 187
  Ireland = Irlanda (*feminine*)

Irish ▶ p. 187, p. 245
1 *noun*
• (*the people*)
  the Irish = los irlandeses
• (*the language*)
  Irish = irlandés (*masculine*)
2 *adjective* = irlandés/irlandesa

iron
1 *noun*
• (*the metal*)
  iron = hierro (*masculine*), fierro
    (*masculine*) (*Lat Am*)
• (*for clothes*)
  an iron = una plancha
2 *verb* = planchar

irritating *adjective*
= irritante

island *noun*
  an island = una isla

it *pronoun*
• (*when used as a subject*)
  where is the newspaper?—it's on the table
    = ¿dónde está el periódico?—está en la
    mesa
  where is it? (*of an object*) = ¿dónde está?
  (*of a place*) = ¿dónde queda?
• (*when used as a direct object*) = lo/la
  that's my book/pen and I need it = ése/ésa
    es mi libro/pluma y lo/la necesito

  ! *Note that* lo *and* la *come before the*
  verb in Spanish

• (*when telling someone to do something*)
  that's my book/pen—give it to me = ése/ésa
    es mi libro/pluma—dámelo/la

  ! *Note that* lo *and* la *come after the verb*
  in Spanish

• (*when telling someone not to do*
  something)
  that's my book/pen—don't give it to him! =
    ése/ésa es mi libro/pluma—¡no se lo/la des!

  ! *Note that* lo *and* la *come before the*
  verb in Spanish

• (*in impersonal constructions*)
  who is it? = ¿quién es?
  it's me = soy yo
  it's a nice house = es una casa linda
  it's [difficult | easy | complicated ...] = es [difícil |
    fácil | complicado ...]
  it's cold/warm = hace frío/calor

• (*where it is used after a preposition*)
  I've heard about it = he oído hablar de ello

Italian ▶ p. 187, p. 245
1 *noun*
• (*a person*)
  an Italian = un italiano/una italiana
• (*the language*)
  Italian = italiano (*masculine*)
2 *adjective* = italiano/italiana

Italy *noun* ▶ p. 187
  Italy = Italia (*feminine*)

itchy *adjective*
  my leg is itchy = me pica la pierna

its *adjective*
= su (+ *singular*), sus (+ *plural*)
  its nose = su nariz

itself *pronoun*
• (*translated by a reflexive verb in Spanish*) =
  se
  the cat washed itself = el gato se lavaba
• (*used for emphasis*)
  the house itself is quite large = la casa en sí
    (misma) es bastante grande
  by itself = solo

Jj

jacket *noun*
  a jacket (*formal*) = una chaqueta
  (*casual*) = una americana, un saco (*Lat*
  Am)

jail
1 *noun*
  a jail = una cárcel, una prisión
2 *verb*
  to jail someone = encarcelar a alguien

jam *noun*
  jam = mermelada (*feminine*), dulce
    (*masculine*) (*R Pl*)

January *noun* ▶ p. 192
  January = enero (*masculine*)

Japan *noun* ▶ p. 187
  Japan = (el) Japón

Japanese ▶ p. 187, p. 245
1 *noun*
• (*the people*)
  the Japanese = los japoneses
• (*the language*)
  Japanese = japonés (*masculine*)
2 *adjective* = japonés/japonesa

jar *noun*
  a jar = un tarro, un bote

jaw *noun* ▶ p. 235
  the jaw = la mandíbula

jazz *noun*
  jazz = jazz (*masculine*)

jealous *adjective*
  = celoso/celosa
  he is jealous of her = le tiene celos

jeans *noun*
  (a pair of) jeans = unos vaqueros, unos
    jeans, unos tejanos (*Spa*), unos
    pantalones de mezclilla (*Mex*)

Jesus *noun*
  Jesus = Jesús

jet *noun*
  (*a plane*)
  a jet = un avión

jewelry (*US English*), **jewellery** (*British English*) *noun*
  jewelry = alhajas (*feminine plural*), joyas
    (*feminine plural*)
  a piece of jewelry = una alhaja, una joya

Jewish *adjective*
  = judío/judía

jigsaw *noun*
  a jigsaw = un rompecabezas, un puzzle

job *noun*
• (*a post*)
  a job = un empleo, un trabajo
• (*a task*)
  a job = una tarea

jogging *noun*
  jogging = jogging (*masculine*), footing
    (*masculine*)
  to go jogging = salir a hacer jogging, salir a
    hacer footing

join *verb*
• (*to connect*) = unir
• (*to meet up with*)
  I'll join you in half an hour = los encuentro
    dentro de media hora
  may I join you? = ¿lo puedo acompañar?
• (*become a member of*)
  to join a club/an organization = hacerse
    socio de un club/una organización
  to join the army = alistarse en el ejército
join in
  to join in a game = participar en un juego

joke
1 *noun*
  a joke = (*verbal*) un chiste
    (*practical*) = una broma
2 *verb* = bromear

journalist *noun*
  a journalist = un/una periodista

journey *noun*
  a journey = un viaje

joy *noun*
  joy = alegría (*feminine*)

judge
1 *noun*
• (*in a court*)
  a judge = un juez/una jueza
• (*at a sporting event*)
  a judge = un juez/una jueza
• (*in a competition*)
  the judges = los miembros del jurado
2 *verb* = juzgar

jug *noun*
  a jug = una jarra

juice *noun*
  juice = jugo (*masculine*), zumo (*masculine*)
    (*Spa*)
  fruit juice = jugo de frutas, zumo de frutas
    (*Spa*)

July *noun* ▶ p. 192
  July = julio (*masculine*)

jump
1 *verb* = saltar
  he jumped across the stream = cruzó el
    arroyo de un salto
  to jump rope (*US English*) = saltar a la
    cuerda, saltar a la comba (*Spa*)
2 *noun*
  a jump = un salto
jump out
  he jumped out of the window = saltó por la
    ventana

jumper *noun* (*British English*)
  a jumper = un suéter, un pulóver, un jersey
    (*Spa*)

June *noun* ▶ p. 192
  June = junio (*masculine*)

junior *adjective*
• (*of lower rank*)
  (*if it's a person*) = subalterno/subalterna
  (*if it's a position*) = de subalterno
• (*younger*) = más joven

jury *noun*
  the jury = el jurado

just[1] *adverb*
• (*very recently*)
  I have just arrived = acabo de llegar, recién
    llego (*Lat Am*)
  I saw him just now = lo vi hace un
    momento, recién lo vi (*Lat Am*)
• (*immediately*)
  just before the weekend = justo antes del
    fin de semana
• (*exactly*)
  it's just what I wanted = es justo lo que
    quería

J

R Pl River Plate area SC Southern Cone Spa Spain

- (*barely*) = justo
  I got there just in time = llegué justo a
  tiempo
- (*at this or that very moment*)
  I was just about to phone = estaba a punto
  de llamar
- (*equally*)
  he's just as clever as she is = es tan listo
  como ella

just² *adjective*
= justo/justa

justice *noun*
justice = justicia (*feminine*)

kangaroo *noun*
a kangaroo = un canguro

karate *noun*
karate = kárate (*masculine*), karate
(*masculine*) (*Lat Am*)

keen *adjective*
(*eager, enthusiastic*)
he is a keen footballer = es un futbolista
entusiasta
a keen student = un alumno aplicado/una
alumna aplicada
he is keen on football = le encanta el fútbol

keep *verb*
- (*not to throw away, to reserve for use*) =
  guardar
- (*to cause to remain*)
  to keep the house clean = mantener la
  casa limpia
  to keep someone waiting = hacer esperar a
  alguien
- (*to detain*)
  what kept you? = ¿por qué tardaste?
  they kept him in hospital = lo dejaron
  ingresado, lo dejaron internado (*SC*)
- (*to store*) = guardar
  where do you keep the cups? = ¿dónde
  guardas las tazas?
- (*not break*)
  to keep a promise = cumplir una promesa
  to keep a secret = guardar un secreto
- (*to maintain*)
  to keep the accounts = llevar la
  contabilidad
- (*to continue*)
  to keep walking = seguir caminando
  to keep going = seguir
- (*to remain*)
  to keep calm = mantener la calma

- (*of food: to stay in good condition*) =
  conservarse
keep back = retener
  he kept the children back after school =
  retuvo a los chicos después de las clases
keep down
  to keep down prices = mantener bajos los
  precios
  keep your voice down = no levantes la voz
keep off
  '**keep off the grass**' = 'prohibido pisar el
  césped'
keep on
  to keep on [walking | talking | singing …] =
  seguir [caminando | hablando | cantando …]
keep out
  keep out of the kitchen! = ¡no entres en la
  cocina!
keep up
  **he finds it hard to keep up with the other
  pupils** = le resulta difícil mantenerse al
  nivel de los demás alumnos

kennel, kennels (*British English*) *noun*
(*where dogs are kept while their owners are
away*)
a kennel, kennels = una residencia canina,
un hotel de perros

kerb *noun* (*British English*)
the kerb = el bordillo (de la acera), el borde
de la banqueta (*Mex*), el cordón de la
vereda (*R Pl*)

kettle *noun*
a kettle = una pava, una tetera (para
calentar agua)

key *noun*
- a key = una llave
- (*on a computer or piano*)
  a key = una tecla
key in = teclear

keyhole *noun*
a keyhole = un ojo de la cerradura

kick
1 *verb*
  to kick someone = darle una patada a
  alguien
  he kicked the ball = pateó la pelota
2 *noun*
  a kick = una patada
kick off
  (*in a football match*)
  to kick off = empezar un partido
kick out
  to kick someone out = echar a alguien

kid *noun*
- (*a young goat*)
  a kid = un cabrito/una cabrita, un
  choto/una chota (*Spa*)

- (*a child*)
  a kid = un niño/una niña, un chaval✱/una chavala✱ (*Esp*), un chavalo✱/una chavala✱ (*C Am*), un escuincle✱/una escuincla✱ (*Mex*), un pibe✱/una piba✱ (*R Pl*)

kidnap *verb*
= secuestrar

kill *verb*
= matar
to kill oneself = suicidarse

killer *noun*
a killer = un asesino/una asesina

kilometer *noun* (*US English*),
kilometre (*British English*)
a kilometer = un kilómetro

kind
1 *adjective*
(*if it's a person or gesture*) = amable
to be kind to someone = ser amable con alguien
2 *noun*
a kind [of fish | novel | hotel …] = un tipo [de pescado | de novela | de hotel …]
all kinds of animals = todo tipo de animal

king *noun*
a king = un rey

kingdom *noun*
a kingdom = un reino

kiss
1 *verb* = besar
2 *noun*
a kiss = un beso

kitchen *noun*
a kitchen = una cocina

kite *noun*
a kite = una cometa, un papalote (*Mex*), un barrilete (*R Pl*)

kitten *noun*
a kitten = un gatito/una gatita

knee *noun* ▶ **p. 235**
the knee = la rodilla

kneel *verb*
to kneel (**down**) (*to get down on one's knees*) = arrodillarse
(*to be on one's knees*) = estar arrodillado/arrodillada

knife *noun*
a knife = un cuchillo

knit *verb*
= tejer, hacer punto (*Spa*)
she knitted a scarf = hizo una bufanda, tejió una bufanda (*Lat Am*)

knock
1 *verb*
to knock at the door = llamar a la puerta, golpear a la puerta (*Lat Am*), tocar a la puerta (*Lat Am*)
he knocked his head against the door = se dio un golpe en la cabeza contra la puerta
he knocked the vase off the table = tiró el florero de la mesa
2 *noun*
a knock = un golpe
a knock on the head = un golpe en la cabeza
there was a knock at the door = llamaron a la puerta
knock down
he was knocked down by a car = lo atropelló un coche
to knock down a door = derribar una puerta
knock out
(*to make unconscious*) = dejar sin sentido
knock over = tirar
he knocked over the vase = tiró el florero

knot *noun*
a knot = un nudo

know *verb*
- (*to be acquainted with*) = conocer
  I don't know him = no lo conozco
- (*to understand, to possess knowledge of*) = saber
  how do you know that? = ¿cómo lo sabes?
  I don't know how to drive = no sé manejar
  let me know if you have any more news = avísame si recibes más noticias

knowledge *noun*
- (*learning*)
  knowledge (*in general*) = saber (*masculine*)
  (*facts known by a particular person*) = conocimientos (*masculine plural*)
- (*awareness*)
  knowledge = conocimiento (*masculine*)
  not to my knowledge = no que yo sepa

Ll

laboratory *noun*
a laboratory = un laboratorio

lace *noun*
- (*the material*)
  lace = encaje (*masculine*)
- (*on a shoe*)
  a lace = un cordón, una agujeta (*Mex*)

lack
1 *noun*
  a lack of food = una falta de comida
2 *verb*
  he lacks confidence = le falta confianza en
  sí mismo

ladder *noun*
  a ladder = una escalera de mano

lady *noun*
  a lady = una dama

lake *noun*
  a lake = un lago

lamb *noun*
  a lamb = un cordero

lamp *noun*
  a lamp = una lámpara

lampshade *noun*
  a lampshade = una pantalla (de lámpara)

land
1 *noun*
• (*as opposed to sea*)
  land = tierra (*feminine*)
• (*farmland*)
  land = tierra (*feminine*)
• (*property*)
  a piece of land = un terreno
2 *verb*
• (*of an aircraft*) = aterrizar
• (*from a ship*) = desembarcar
• (*to fall*) = ir a parar
  the ball landed on the roof = la pelota fue a
  parar en el tejado

landlady *noun*
  a landlady = una dueña
  my landlady = la dueña de la casa que
  alquilo

landlord *noun*
  a landlord = un dueño
  my landlord = el dueño de la casa que
  alquilo

landscape *noun*
  a landscape = un paisaje

language *noun*
• (*of a particular nation*)
  a language = un idioma, una lengua
• (*as a general concept or system*)
  language = lenguaje (*masculine*)
• (*way of speaking or expressing oneself*)
  language = lenguaje (*masculine*)
  bad language = malas palabras (*feminine
  plural*) (*Lat Am*), palabrotas (*feminine
  plural*)

lap *noun*
  to sit on someone's lap = sentarse en las
  rodillas de alguien

large *adjective*
  = grande

! *Note that* grande *becomes* gran *when it
is used before a singular noun*
  a large garden = un jardín grande, un gran
  jardín
  a large sum of money = una gran cantidad
  de dinero

last
1 *pronoun*
  the last = el último/la última
  the week before last = la semana
  antepasada
2 *adjective*
• (*final*) = último/última (**!** *before noun*)
  the last episode in the series = el último
  capítulo de la serie
• (*previous*)
  last Tuesday = el martes pasado
  in my last letter = en mi última carta
3 *adverb*
• (*in final position*)
  he came last in the race = quedó en último
  lugar en la carrera, terminó último en la
  carrera (*SC*)
• (*most recently*)
  I was last here in 1978 = la última vez que
  estuve aquí fue en 1978
4 *verb* = durar

late
1 *adjective*
• (*not on time*)
  sorry I'm late = perdón por llegar tarde
  the train was two hours late = el tren llegó
  con dos horas de retraso, el tren llegó dos
  horas atrasado (*Lat Am*)
• (*far into the day or night*)
  to have a late lunch = comer tarde,
  almorzar tarde (*Lat Am*)
• (*toward the end of*)
  in late September = a fines de septiembre
  in the late 1930s = hacia el final de la
  década de los treinta
2 *adverb*
• (*not on time*)
  they arrived late = llegaron tarde
  they arrived half an hour late = llegaron
  con media hora de retraso, llegaron
  media hora atrasados (*Lat Am*)
• (*far into the day or night*)
  it's getting late = se hace tarde

later *adverb*
  = más tarde
  later on = más tarde
  see you later! = ¡hasta luego!

latest *adjective*
  (*most recent*) = último/última
  the latest fashion = la última moda

Latin *noun* ▶ **p. 245**
  Latin = latín (*masculine*)

Latin America *noun* ▶ **p. 187**
  Latin America = América Latina (*feminine*),
  Latinoamérica (*feminine*)

C Am Central America   **Lat Am** Latin America   **Mex** Mexico

Languages

Note that the names of languages in Spanish are always written with a small letter, not a capital as in English; also, Spanish often uses the definite article with languages while English does not.

In the following examples, the name of any language may be substituted for **Spanish** and **español**:

Spanish is a Romance language	= el español es una lengua románica
to translate something into Spanish	= traducir algo al español

There are exceptions:

Spanish is spoken in Chile	= en Chile se habla español
I speak Spanish	= hablo español

The article is never used after **en**:

*he said it **in** Spanish*	= lo dijo **en** español

When **Spanish** means *in Spanish* or *of the Spanish*, it is translated by **español/española**:

a Spanish movie	= una película española
a Spanish word	= una palabra española

If you wish to make it clear that you mean *in Spanish* and not *from Spain,* use **en español**:

a Spanish book	= un libro en español
a Spanish program	= un programa en español

When *Spanish* means *relating to Spanish* or *about Spanish*, it is translated by **de español**:

a Spanish class	= una clase de español
a Spanish dictionary	= un diccionario de español

but

a Spanish-English dictionary	= un diccionario español-inglés

Latin American *adjective* ▶ p. 187
= latinoamericano/latinoamericana

laugh
1 *verb* = reírse
　they laughed at him = se rieron de él
2 *noun*
　a laugh = una risa

laughter *noun*
　laughter = risas *(feminine plural)*

laundry *noun*
• *(a shop or a firm)*
　a laundry = una lavandería, un lavadero *(R Pl)*
• *(washing)*
　the laundry *(clean)* = la ropa limpia
　(dirty) = la ropa sucia
　to do the laundry = lavar la ropa, hacer la colada *(Spa)*

law *noun*
• *(a regulation)*
　a law = una ley
• *(a set of rules in a country)*
　the law = la ley
　it's against the law = está prohibido por la ley
• *(as a university subject)*
　law = derecho *(masculine)*

lawn *noun*
　a lawn = un césped, un pasto *(Lat Am)*, una grama *(C Am)*

lawnmower *noun*
　a lawnmower = una cortadora de céseped, una cortadora de pasto *(Lat Am)*, un cortagrama *(C Am)*

lawyer *noun*
　a lawyer = un abogado/una abogada

lay *verb*
• *(to put)* = poner
　she laid her hand on his shoulder = le puso la mano en el hombro
• *(to set)*
　to lay the table = poner la mesa
• *(of a chicken)*
　to lay an egg = poner un huevo

lazy *adjective*
　= perezoso/perezosa

lead¹
1 *verb*
• *(to guide or escort)* = llevar
　he led me into the garden = me llevó al jardín
• *(to cause)*
　this led him to believe that she was right = esto le hizo llegar a creer que tenía razón

- *(to result in)*
  this led to an accident = esto resultó en un accidente
- *(to have or conduct)* = llevar
  to lead an active life = llevar una vida activa
- *(to be ahead or in front)*
  they were leading by two goals = iban ganando por dos goles

2 *noun*
  (in a match or contest)
  to be in the lead = llevar la delantera
- *(initiative)*
  to take the lead = tomar la iniciativa
- *(British English—for a dog)*
  a lead = una correa
- *(a wire)*
  a lead = un cable

lead² *noun*
- *(the metal)*
  lead = plomo *(masculine)*
- *(in a pencil)*
  the lead = la mina

leader *noun*
- *(of a group or political party)*
  a leader = un/una líder
- *(of a gang)*
  a leader = un/una cabecilla

leaf *noun*
  a leaf = una hoja

leak
1 *verb*
  (if it's a container) = gotear, perder *(R Pl)*
  the roof is leaking = hay una gotera en el techo
2 *noun*
  a leak *(in a roof)* = una gotera
  (in a container) = un agujero

lean
1 *verb*
  to lean against/on something = apoyarse contra/en algo
  she leaned out of the window = se asomó por la ventana
2 *adjective*
  (if it's meat) = magro/magra
lean back = echarse hacia atrás

leap
1 *verb* = saltar, brincar
2 *noun*
  a leap = un salto, un brinco

learn *verb*
  = aprender

leash *noun*
  a leash = una correa

least
1 *adjective*
  they have the least money = son los que tienen menos dinero

2 *pronoun*
- **it was the least I could do** = fue lo menos que pude hacer
- **at least**
  (at the minimum) = por lo menos
  he's at least thirty = tiene por lo menos treinta años
3 *adverb*
  (when used with adjectives or nouns)
  the least expensive shop = la tienda menos cara
  the least difficult question = la pregunta menos difícil
- *(when used with verbs)*
  I like that color the least = ese color es el que menos me gusta

leather
1 *noun*
  leather = cuero *(masculine)*, piel *(feminine)* *(Spa)*
2 *adjective* = de cuero, de piel *(Spa)*

leave
1 *verb*
- *(to depart from)*
  the train left London at 11 o'clock = el tren salió de Londres a las once
  she left the room = se fue del cuarto
  he left home when he was 18 = se fue de la casa a los 18 años
  to leave school = dejar los estudios
  she left her husband = dejó a su marido
- *(to depart)* = irse, marcharse *(Spa)*
  he left the next day = se fue al día siguiente, se marchó al día siguiente *(Spa)*
- *(to put or deposit)* = dejar
  I left my keys on the table = dejé mis llaves sobre la mesa
  he didn't leave a message = no dejó recado
- *(to postpone)* = dejar
  leave it until tomorrow = déjalo para mañana
- *(to allow to remain)* = dejar
  she left the window open = dejó la ventana abierta
- *(to remain)*
  to be left = quedar
  we have ten minutes left = nos quedan diez minutos
2 *noun*
  (authorized absence) = permiso *(masculine)*, licencia *(feminine)* *(Lat Am)*
  to be on leave = estar de permiso, estar de licencia *(Lat Am)*
leave behind
  (not take with one) = dejar
leave out
- *(not to show or mention)* = omitir
- *(to exclude)* = excluir
leave over
  to be left over = quedar

lecture noun
• (British English—in a university)
  a lecture = una clase
• (a public talk)
  a lecture = una conferencia

left
1 noun
  left = izquierda (feminine)
  the first street on your left = la primera
    calle a tu izquierda
2 adjective = izquierdo/izquierda
3 adverb = a la izquierda, hacia la izquierda

left-handed adjective
= zurdo/zurda

leg noun
• (of a person) ▶ p. 235
  a leg = una pierna
• (of an animal, a bird)
  a leg = una pata
• (of a chair or table)
  a leg = una pata
• (of a pair of trousers)
  a leg = una pierna
• (of meat)
  a leg of lamb = una pierna de cordero

legal adjective
= legal

leisure noun
  leisure = ocio (masculine)

lemon noun
  a lemon = un limón

lemonade noun
• (made with fresh lemons)
  lemonade = limonada (feminine)
• (British English—fizzy drink)
  lemonade = gaseosa (feminine)

lend verb
= prestar

length noun
• (in measurement)
  length = largo (masculine), longitud
    (feminine)
  to be 30 cm in length = medir 30
    centímetros de largo, tener 30
    centímetros de largo
• (duration)
  length =duración (feminine)

lens noun
• (for spectacles)
  a lens = una lente
• (on a camera)
  a lens = un objetivo

Leo noun
• (the sign)
  Leo = Leo
  I'm Leo = soy Leo, soy de Leo
• (a person)
  a Leo = un/una leo

leopard noun
  a leopard = un leopardo

less
1 adjective = menos
  less money = menos dinero
  I have less work than he does = tengo
    menos trabajo que él
2 pronoun = menos
  to cost less = costar menos
  they have less than you = tienen menos
    que ustedes
  in less than half an hour = en menos de
    media hora
3 adverb = menos
  we travel less in the winter = viajamos
    menos en el invierno
  less and less = cada vez menos
4 preposition = menos
  less 10% discount = menos 10% de
    descuento

lesson noun
  a lesson = una clase

let¹ verb
• (used in suggestions)
  let's eat = comamos
  let's go home = vamos a casa
  let's go! = ¡vámonos!
• (to allow) = dejar
  to let someone in = dejarle entrar a alguien
  let me help him = deja que yo lo ayude
let down
  (to disappoint) = fallar
let go
  (to stop holding, to release) = soltar
  let go of me! = ¡suéltame!
  he let the prisoners go = soltó a los
    prisioneros
let in
  (to allow to penetrate)
  to let in the rain = dejar entrar la lluvia
let off
  (not to punish) = perdonar
let out
• (to allow to go out)
  let me out! = ¡déjame salir!
  he let the cat out = dejó salir al gato
• (to utter)
  to let out a scream = soltar un grito
• (to release)
  to let a prisoner out = soltar a un
    prisionero

let² verb (British English)
= alquilar
  'to let' = 'se alquila'

letter noun
  a letter = una carta

letter box noun
  a letter box = un buzón

lettuce noun
  a lettuce = una lechuga

L

level

1 *noun*
  a level = un nivel
  at sea level = a nivel del mar
2 *adjective*
- (*flat or even*) = plano/plana, parejo/pareja
  (*Lat Am*)
  a level teaspoonful of sugar = una
    cucharada rasa de azúcar
- (*at same height*)
  level with the ground = al nivel del suelo

liar *noun*
  a liar = un mentiroso/una mentirosa

Libra *noun*
- (*the sign*)
  Libra = Libra
  I'm Libra = soy Libra, soy de Libra
- (*a person*)
  a Libra = un/una libra

library *noun*
  a library = una biblioteca

license (*US*), licence (*GB*) *noun*
  (*for driving or fishing*)
  a license = un permiso, una licencia

license number *noun* (*US English*)
  a license number = un número de
    matrícula, un número de patente (*SC*)

license plate *noun* (*US English*)
  a license plate = una matrícula, una plata
    (*Lat Am*), una patente (*SC*)

lick *verb*
  = lamer

lid *noun*
  a lid = una tapa

lie

1 *verb*
- (*on the ground or on a bed etc*) = tenderse
  he was lying on the sofa = estaba tendido
    en el sofá
- (*to be situated*) = encontrarse
  the village lies in a valley = el pueblo se
    encuentra en un valle
- (*not tell the truth*) = mentir
2 *noun*
  a lie = una mentira
  to tell a lie = mentir
lie down = tenderse, recostarse

life *noun*
  life = vida (*feminine*)

lift

1 *verb* = levantar
  he lifted his arm = levantó el brazo
2 *noun*
- (*British English—an elevator*)
  a lift = un ascensor

- (*in a car*)
  he gave me a lift to the station = me llevó
    hasta la estación en coche, me dio un
    aventón hasta la estación (*Mex*)
lift up = levantar

light

1 *noun*
- (*brightness*)
  light = luz (*feminine*)
- (*in a room , on a machine*)
  a light = una luz
- (*in a street*)
  a light = un farol, una farola (*Spa*)
- (*for traffic*)
  traffic lights = semáforo (*masculine*)
  the lights are green = el semáforo está (en)
    verde
- (*for a cigarette*)
  have you got a light? = ¿tienes fuego?
- (*on a vehicle*)
  the lights = las luces
2 *adjective*
- (*not nighttime*)
  it's already light = ya es de día
- (*if it's a color or piece of clothing*) =
    claro/clara
  light blue = azul claro
- (*not heavy*) = ligero/ligera, liviano/liviana
  (*Lat Am*)
3 *verb*
- (*with a match*) = encender, prender (*Lat
  Am*)
- (*illuminate*) = iluminar

light bulb *noun*
  a light bulb = una bombilla, una bombita
    (*R Pl*), una bujía (*C Am*), un foco (*Mex*)

lighthouse *noun*
  a lighthouse = un faro

lightning *noun*
  a flash of lightning = un relámpago

like[1] *preposition* = como
  people like you and me = la gente como tú
    y yo
  what's it like? = ¿cómo es?

> **!** *Note that* como *becomes* cómo *in
> questions*

like[2] *verb*
- (*to be keen on*)
  I like [swimming | reading | dancing …] = me
    gusta [nadar | leer | bailar …]
  I like Paul but I don't like Peter = me gusta
    Paul pero no Peter
- (*to wish*) = querer
  I would like a coffee please = quiero un
    café por favor
  would you like some cake? = ¿quieres un
    poco de pastel?
  if you like = si quieres

likely *adjective*
= probable
it is likely that he will come = es probable
que venga

> ❗ *Note the use of the subjunctive after* **es**
> **probable que**

limit
1 *noun*
a limit = un límite
2 *verb* = limitar

limited *adjective*
= limitado/limitada

limp *verb*
= cojear, renguear (*Lat Am*)

line
1 *noun*
a line = una línea
a straight line = una línea recta
• (*in poetry*)
a line = un verso
• (*US English—a queue*)
a line = una cola
to stand in line = hacer cola
• (*a row*)
a line = una fila, una hilera
• (*for fishing*)
a line = un sedal
• (*of a telephone*)
a line = una línea
• **a railroad line, a railway line** (*a route*) = una
línea de ferrocarril
(*a track*) = una vía de ferrocarril
2 *verb*
• (*to border*)
an avenue lined with trees = una avenida
bordeada de árboles
• (*with material*) = forrar

linen *noun*
• (*the fabric*)
linen = lino (*masculine*)
• (*for household use*)
linen (*for a bed*) = ropa blanca (*feminine*),
ropa de cama (*feminine*)
(*for a table*) = mantelería (*feminine*)

link
1 *noun*
• (*a connection*)
a link = una conexión
• (*in a chain*)
a link = un eslabón
2 *verb*
• (*to connect physically*) = conectar
to link A to B = conectar A a B
• (*to establish a relation between*) =
relacionar

lion *noun*
a lion = un león

lip *noun*
a lip = un labio

lipstick *noun*
lipstick = lápiz de labios (*masculine*), lápiz
labial (*masculine*) (*Lat Am*)

liquid *noun*
a liquid = un líquido

Lisbon *noun* ▶ **p. 187**
Lisbon = Lisboa (*feminine*)

list *noun*
a list = una lista

listen *verb*
= escuchar

liter *noun* (*US English*)
a liter = un litro

literature *noun*
literature = literatura (*feminine*)

litre *noun* (*British English*) ▶ **liter**

litter *noun*
• (*garbage*)
litter = basura (*feminine*)
• (*of puppies, kittens etc*)
a litter = una camada

little¹
1 *adjective* = poco/poca
little [time | wine | money ...] = poco [tiempo |
vino | dinero ...]
a little [wine | money | Spanish ...] = un poco
de [vino | dinero | español ...]
2 *pronoun*
a little = un poco
I only ate a little = sólo comí un poco
3 *adverb* = poco
a little (*bit*) = un poco
a little (*bit*) **slow** = un poco lento
little by little = poco a poco

little² *adjective*
= pequeño/pequeña
a little house = una casa pequeña
a little dog = un perrito

live¹ *verb*
= vivir
he lives in London = vive en Londres
live on
that's not enough to live on = eso no es
suficiente para vivir

live²
1 *adjective*
• (*alive*) = vivo/viva
• (*of a broadcast or performance*)
this program is live = este programa es en
directo, este programa es en vivo
2 *adverb*
to be transmitted live = transmitirse en
directo, transmitirse en vivo

lively *adjective*
• (*if it's a person, imagination*) = vivo/viva
• (*if it's a party, discussion*) = animado/
animada

living *noun*
to make a living = ganarse la vida
living room *noun*
a living room = una sala (de estar), un living (*Lat Am*), un salón (*Spa*)
load
1 *noun*
• (*on a truck etc*)
a load = una carga
• (*a lot of*)
loads of [food | money | work ...] = cantidad de [comida | dinero | trabajo ...], montones de [comida | dinero | trabajo ...]
2 *verb*
to load a truck = cargar un camión
to load a camera = poner un rollo en una cámara
loaf *noun*
a loaf (of bread) = un pan
loan *noun*
a loan = un préstamo
lobster *noun*
a lobster = una langosta, un bogavante (*Spa*)
local *adjective*
the local newspapers = los periódicos locales
the local shops = las tiendas del barrio
the local people = los lugareños
location *noun*
a location = una situación
lock
1 *verb* = cerrar (con llave)
2 *noun*
a lock = una cerradura, un cerrojo
lock in = encerrar
I got locked in = me quedé encerrado
lock up
to lock up a house = cerrar una casa con llave
locker *noun*
• (*in a locker room*)
a locker = un armario, un locker (*Lat Am*)
• (*at a bus or railroad station*)
a locker = una (casilla de la) consigna automática
locker room *noun* (*American English*)
a locker room = un vestuario, un vestidor (*Mex*)
log *noun*
a log = un tronco
(*as fuel*) = un leño
logical *adjective*
= lógico/lógica
London *noun* ▶ p. 187
London = Londres

lonely *adjective*
a lonely person = una persona sola
a lonely life = una vida solitaria
to feel lonely = sentirse solo/sola
long
1 *adjective* = largo/larga
to have long hair = tener el pelo largo
how long is this room? = ¿cuánto mide de largo este cuarto?
the room is 20 meters long = el cuarto tiene 20 metros de largo
how long is the movie? = ¿cuánto dura la película?
the movie is two hours long = la película dura dos horas
he has been ill for a long time = hace mucho que está enfermo
2 *adverb*
• long ago = hace mucho
I won't be long = no tardo, no demoro (*Lat Am*)
it doesn't take long = no lleva mucho tiempo, no se demora nada (*Lat Am*)
• as long as (*provided that*) = con tal de que
as long as the weather is nice all will be well = con tal de que haga buen tiempo todo estará bien

! Note the use of the subjunctive after con tal de que

look
1 *verb* = mirar
to look at a picture = mirar un cuadro
he looked out of the window = miró por la ventana
• (*to appear*)
he looks tired = parece cansado
he looks well = tiene buena cara
she looks like her mother = se parece a la madre
2 *noun*
• (*appearance*)
the look = el aspecto
I don't like the look of the house = no me gusta el aspecto que tiene la casa
• (*an expression*)
a look = una cara
a look of sadness = una cara triste
look after = cuidar
look around
• he looked around = miró a su alrededor
• (*to inspect*)
they're coming to look around the house = vienen a ver la casa
look back = mirar hacia atrás
look for = buscar
look forward to
I am looking forward to meeting him = tengo muchas ganas de conocerlo
look out
look out! = ¡cuidado!
look out for snakes = cuidado con las serpientes

C Am Central America   Lat Am Latin America   Mex Mexico

look up
 (*to search for*) = buscar

loose *adjective*
• (*if it's a knot or a screw*) = flojo/floja,
  suelto/suelta
• (*if it's a tooth*)
  this tooth is loose = tengo este diente flojo
• (*if it's clothes*) = suelto/suelta,
  holgado/holgada

lorry *noun* (*British English*)
 a lorry = un camión

lose *verb*
 = perder

loss *noun*
 a loss = una pérdida

lost *adjective*
 = perdido/perdida
 to get lost = perderse

lot *pronoun*
 he drinks a lot = bebe mucho
 a lot of money = mucho dinero
 a lot of patience = mucha paciencia
 **I don't need a lot—three or four will be
   enough** = no necesito muchos—con tres o
   cuatro basta
 there's not a lot left = no queda mucho

loud *adjective*
 (*if it's a sound*) = fuerte
 to have a loud voice = tener una voz fuerte
 to say something in a loud voice = decir
   algo en voz alta
 the music was too loud = la música estaba
   demasiado fuerte

loudspeaker *noun*
 a loudspeaker = un altavoz, un
   (alto)parlante (*Lat Am*)

lounge *noun*
• (*in a hotel*)
  a lounge = un salón
• (*in an airport*)
  the departure lounge = la sala de embarque
• (*US English—a bar*)
  a lounge = un bar
• (*British English—in a house*)
  a lounge = una sala (de estar), un living
   (*Lat Am*), un salón (*Spa*)

love
 1 *verb*
• (*if it's a person*) = querer, amar
  they love each other = se quieren, se aman
• (*if it's a thing or activity*)
  I love chocolate = el chocolate me encanta
  I love reading = me encanta leer

2 *noun*
 love = amor (*masculine*)
 to be in love = estar enamorado/enamorada

lovely *adjective*
 (*beautiful*) = precioso/preciosa, lindo/linda
  (*Lat Am*)

low
 1 *adjective* = bajo/baja
 2 *adverb* = bajo

lower
 1 *adjective*
  at a lower price = a un precio más bajo
 2 *verb* = bajar

loyal *adjective*
 (*if it's a friend or customer*) = fiel

luck *noun*
 luck = suerte (*feminine*)
 good luck! = ¡(buena) suerte!

lucky *adjective*
 to be lucky = tener suerte
 a lucky number = un número de la suerte

luggage *noun*
 luggage = equipaje (*masculine*)

lump *noun*
• (*on the body*)
  a lump = un bulto
• (*as the result of a blow to the head*)
  a bump = un chichón
• (*in a sauce or liquid*)
  a lump = un grumo
• (*of coal, cheese etc*)
  a lump = un trozo
• (*of sugar*)
  a lump = un terrón

lunch *noun*
 lunch = almuerzo (*masculine*), comida
  (*feminine*) (*Mex, Spa*)
 to have lunch = almorzar, comer (*Mex,
   Spa*)

lung *noun* ▶ p. 235
 a lung = un pulmón

Luxembourg *noun* ▶ p. 187
 Luxembourg = Luxemburgo (*masculine*)

luxury
 1 *noun*
  luxury = lujo (*masculine*)
 2 *adjective* = de lujo

L

Mm

machine *noun*
a machine = una máquina

machinery *noun*
machinery = maquinaria *(feminine)*

mad *adjective*
* *(crazy)* = loco/loca
* *(very angry)* = furioso/furiosa
* *(enthusiastic, keen)*
to be mad about someone = estar loco/loca por alguien
he's mad about sports = es un fanático de los deportes

magazine *noun*
a magazine = una revista

magic
1 *noun*
magic = magia *(feminine)*
2 *adjective* = mágico/mágica

magnet *noun*
a magnet = un imán

magnificent *adjective* = magnífico/magnífica

magnifying glass *noun*
a magnifying glass = una lupa

maiden name *noun*
a maiden name = un apellido de soltera

mail
1 *noun*
* *(the system)*
the mail = el correo
* *(letters, packages)*
the mail = la correspondencia, el correo
2 *verb (US English)*
to mail a letter to someone = mandarle una carta a alguien

mailbox *noun (US English)*
a mailbox = un buzón

mailman *noun (US English)*
a mailman = un cartero

main *adjective*
= principal

main course *noun*
the main course = el plato principal, el plato fuerte

main road *noun (British English)*
a main road = una carretera principal

maintain *verb*
* *(to preserve)* = mantener
* *(to take care of)*
to maintain a house = ocuparse del mantenimiento de una casa

maize *noun*
maize = maíz *(masculine)*

major
1 *adjective*
a major event = un acontecimiento muy importante
a major crisis = una crisis seria
2 *noun*
a major = un/una mayor *(Lat Am)*, un/una comandante *(Spa)*
3 *verb (US English)*
to major in Spanish = especializarse en español

majority *noun*
a majority = una mayoría

make

> **!** *The word* make *can often be translated by* hacer. *This entry covers the most frequent uses of* make, *but to find translations for other expressions like* to make a fuss, to make a mistake, to make sure *etc, look up the entries at* fuss, mistake, sure *etc*

1 *verb*
to make = hacer
to make [a cake | the bed | noise …] = hacer [un pastel | la cama | ruido …]
to make a phone call = hacer una llamada telefónica
to make friends = hacer amigos
to make oneself understood = hacerse entender
to make breakfast = preparar el desayuno
to be made of [wood | plastic | gold …] = ser de [madera | plástico | oro …]
'made in Argentina' = 'industria argentina'
'made in Mexico/Spain' = 'hecho en México/España'
* *(to cause a particular reaction)*
to make someone happy = hacer feliz a alguien
to make someone [sad | tired | annoyed …] = [entristecer | cansar | enojar …] a alguien
it makes you thirsty = da sed
* *(to have someone do something)*
to make someone wait = obligar a alguien a esperar
* *(to earn)*
to make a lot of money = ganar mucho dinero
to make a living = ganarse la vida
2 *noun*
a make = una marca

make do
to make do with something = arreglárselas con algo

make out
* *(to understand)* = entender
* *(to write out)* = hacer

make up
* *(to be friends again)* = reconciliarse, hacer las paces
* *(to invent)* = inventar

makeup *noun*
makeup = maquillaje (*masculine*)
to put on makeup = maquillarse

male
1 *adjective*
• (*when talking about animals*) =
macho/macha
• (*when talking about humans*) =
masculino/masculina
2 *noun*
• (*a man*)
a male = un hombre
• (*an animal*)
a male = un macho

man *noun*
• a man = un hombre
• (*all human beings*)
man = el hombre

manage *verb*
• (*to run*) = dirigir
to manage a shop = dirigir una tienda
• (*to be able*)
to manage to find work = lograr encontrar
trabajo
• (*to cope*) = arreglárselas

manager *noun*
a manager (*of a company, a department*) =
un director/una directora
(*of a shop*) = un/una gerente
(*of a soccer team*) = un entrenador/una
entrenadora, un director técnico/una
directora técnica (*Lat Am*)

manner *noun*
• (*a way*)
a manner = una manera
• (*an attitude*)
a manner = una actitud

manners *noun*
manners = modales (*masculine plural*)
it's bad manners not to say hello = es de
mala educación no saludar

manual *noun*
a manual = un manual

manufacture *verb*
= fabricar

many
1 *adjective*
• (*a lot of*) = muchos/muchas
• (*when used with* how, too, so, as)
how many plates? = ¿cuántos platos?
how many cups? = ¿cuántas tazas?
there are too many cars = hay demasiados
coches
there are so many things to do here = hay
tantas cosas que hacer aquí
I got as many presents as you did = recibí
tantos regalos como tú

2 *pronoun*
are there many left? = ¿quedan
muchos/muchas?
I've got too many = tengo
demasiados/demasiadas
how many? = ¿cuántos/cuántas?
as many as you like = todo lo que quieras
there were too many of them = había
demasiados/demasiadas

map *noun*
a map (*of a country, or region*) = un mapa
(*of a transport system*) = un plano
a street map of New York = un plano de
Nueva York

marble *noun*
• (*the rock*)
marble = mármol (*masculine*)
• (*used in a game*)
a marble = una canica, una bolita (*S Am*)

march
1 *verb*
• (*in the army*) = marchar
• (*in a demonstration*) = manifestarse
2 *noun*
a march = una marcha

March *noun* ▶ p. 192
March = marzo (*masculine*)

M

margarine *noun*
margarine = margarina (*feminine*)

margin *noun*
a margin = un margen

mark
1 *noun*
• a mark (*on a surface*) = una mancha
(*on a person's body*) = una marca
• (*a grade*)
a mark = una nota
• (*in races*)
on your marks! = ¡a sus marcas!
2 *verb*
• (*to stain*) = manchar
• (*to correct*)
to mark the homework = corregir los
deberes
• (*to indicate*) = señalar, marcar

market
1 *noun*
• (*the place*)
a market = un mercado
• (*the system of trade, the people or things
concerned*)
the market = el mercado
the Spanish market = el mercado español
2 *verb*
(*to sell*) = comercializar

marmalade *noun*
marmalade = mermelada (*feminine*)

marriage noun
• (the institution)
  marriage = matrimonio (masculine)
• (a ceremony)
  a marriage = un casamiento

married adjective
  to be married to someone = estar
  casado/casada con alguien
  to get married = casarse

marry verb
  to marry someone, to get married to
  someone = casarse con alguien

marvelous (US English), **marvellous**
(British English) adjective
= maravilloso/maravillosa

masculine
1 noun (in grammar)
  the masculine = el masculino
2 adjective = masculino/masculina

mash verb
= hacer puré de, moler (Mex), chafar (Spa),
pisar (R Pl)

mashed potatoes noun
  mashed potatoes = puré de papas (Lat
  Am), puré de patatas (Spa)

mask noun
• (in a ceremony, for disguise)
  a mask = una máscara
• (in sports)
  a mask = una careta

mass noun
• (a large number)
  a mass of people = una gran cantidad de
  gente
• (in a church)
  a mass = una misa

massive adjective
= enorme

mast noun
  (on a ship, for flags)
  a mast = un mástil

master
1 noun
• (an owner of a dog)
  a master = un amo
• (British English—a teacher)
  a master (in primary school) = un maestro
  (in secondary school) = un profesor
2 verb
  to master a language = dominar un idioma

masterpiece noun
  a masterpiece = una obra maestra

mat noun
  a mat (at a door) = un felpudo

(in a bathroom) = una alfombrita, una
alfombrilla (Spa), un tapete del baño
(Méx)

match
1 noun
• (a game)
  a match = un partido
• (a matchstick)
  a match = un fósforo, una cerilla (Spa)
2 verb
  the shoes match the skirt = los zapatos
  hacen juego con la falda

matchbox noun
  a matchbox = una caja de fósforos, una
  caja de cerillas (Spa)

mate
1 noun (British English)
  (a friend)
  a mate = un amigo/una amiga
2 verb = aparearse

material noun
• (a substance)
  a material = un material
• (cloth)
  a material = una tela
• (written information)
  material = material (masculine)

math noun (US English)
  math = matemáticas (feminine plural)

mathematics noun
  mathematics = matemáticas (feminine
  plural)

maths noun (British English) ▶ math

matter
1 noun
• (a situation, an event)
  a matter = un asunto
• (a question)
  it's only a matter of time = sólo es cuestión
  de tiempo
• (the problem)
  what's the matter? = ¿qué pasa?
  what's the matter with her? = ¿qué le pasa?
2 verb = importar
  it doesn't matter = no importa

mattress noun
  a mattress = un colchón

mature adjective
= maduro/madura

maximum
1 adjective = máximo/máxima
2 noun
  the maximum = el máximo

may verb
• (when talking about a possibility)
  they may be able to come = es posible que
  vengan
  she may not have seen him = es posible
  que no lo haya visto

C Am Central America   Lat Am Latin America   Mex Mexico

! *Note the use of the subjunctive after* es
posible que
- (*when asking for or giving permission*)
may I come in? = ¿puedo entrar?
you may sit down = pueden sentarse

May *noun* ▶ **p. 192**
May = mayo (*masculine*)

maybe *adverb*
= quizás, tal vez, a lo mejor
maybe he'll arrive later = quizás llegue más
tarde, tal vez llegue más tarde, a lo mejor
llega más tarde

! *Note the use of the subjunctive after*
quizás *and* tal vez

mayor *noun*
a mayor = un alcalde/una alcaldesa

maze *noun*
a maze = un laberinto

me *pronoun*
- (*when used as a direct object*) = me
they know/don't know me = me
conocen/no me conocen

! *Note that* me *comes before the verb in*
Spanish

- (*when used as an indirect object*) = me
he never talks to me = no me habla nunca
he wrote me a letter = me escribió una
carta

! *Note that* me *comes before the verb in*
Spanish

don't send them to me! = ¡no me los
mandes!
- (*when used as an indirect object pronoun
together with a direct object pronoun*) =
me
you have to give them to me = tienes que
dármelos, me los tienes que dar
he said it to me = me lo dijo

! *Note that* me *comes before the direct
object pronoun*

- (*when telling someone to do something*) =
me
help me! = ¡ayúdame!
give the money to me = dame el dinero
give them to me! = ¡dámelos!

! *Note that* me *comes after the verb in*
Spanish

- (*when telling someone not to do
something*) = me
don't leave me! = ¡no me dejes!
don't send them to me! = ¡no me los
mandes!

! *Note that* me *comes before the verb in*
Spanish

- (*when used after prepositions*) = mí
did you buy it for me? = ¿lo compraste
para mí?
come with me = ven conmigo
- (*when used with* to be)
it's me = soy yo

meadow *noun*
a meadow = un prado, una pradera

meal *noun*
a meal = una comida
to go out for a meal = salir a comer (fuera)

mean
1 *verb*
- (*when talking about the sense of
something*) = querer decir
what does that mean? = ¿qué quiere decir
eso?
- (*to have as a result*)
it means giving up my job = significa que
tengo que dejar el trabajo
- (*to intend*)
I meant to tell you the news but I forgot =
tenía la intención de contarte la noticia
pero se me olvidó
she didn't mean to upset you = no quiso
ofenderte
- (*to intend to say*) = querer decir
what do you mean by that? = ¿qué quieres
decir con eso?
I know what you mean = entiendo
- (*to be of importance or value*)
her work means a lot to her = su trabajo es
muy importante para ella
to be meant to
I'm meant to collect the books = se supone
que tengo que recoger los libros
it's meant to be a dictionary for beginners
= se supone que es un diccionario para
principiantes
2 *adjective*
- (*not generous*) = tacaño/tacaña
- (*nasty, unkind*) = malo/mala

meaning *noun*
a meaning = un significado

means *noun*
- (*a way*)
a means = un medio
a means of transport = un medio de
transporte
- (*when talking about money*)
means = medios (económicos) (*masculine
plural*), recursos (*masculine*)
he lives beyond his means = lleva un tren
de vida que no se puede costear

meanwhile *adverb*
(*during this time*) = mientras tanto

measles *noun*
measles = sarampión (*masculine*)

measure
1 *verb* = medir
the window measures 40 cm by 60 cm = la
ventana mide 40 centímetros por 60
centímetros

M

2 *noun*
(*a step*)
a measure = una medida
to take measures to do something = tomar medidas para hacer algo

measurement *noun*
(*of a person*)
measurements = medidas (*feminine plural*)
to take someone's measurements = tomarle las medidas a alguien

meat *noun*
meat = carne (*feminine*)

mechanical *adjective*
= mecánico/mecánica

medal *noun*
a medal = una medalla

media *noun*
the media = los medios de comunicación

medical *adjective*
= médico/médica

medicine *noun*
• (*the subject, the profession*)
medicine = medicina (*feminine*)
• (*a drug*)
a medicine = un medicamento, una medicina

Mediterranean *noun*
the Mediterranean = el Mediterráneo

medium *adjective*
= mediano/mediana

meet *verb*
• (*by accident or appointment*) = encontrar
she met him in the bar = lo encontró en el bar
to meet during the vacation = encontrarse durante las vacaciones
• (*to make the acquaintance of*) = conocer
have you met Liz? = ¿conoces a Liz?
Nicky, meet Carol = Nicky, te presento a Carol
pleased to meet you! = ¡encantado/encantada!
• (*to wait for*) = esperar
is there someone meeting you at the station? = ¿alguien te espera en la estación?
• (*to fetch*)
(*when going to a place*) = ir a buscar,
(*when coming to a place*) = venir a buscar
• (*to have a formal meeting*) = reunirse
meet up
• (*after being apart*) = encontrarse
• (*regularly*) = verse

meeting *noun*
a meeting = una reunión

melon *noun*
a melon = un melón

melt *verb*
• (*to become liquid*)
(*of ice, butter, snow, metal*) = fundirse
(*of wax*) = derretirse
• (*to make liquid*)
(*if it's butter, ice, metal*) = fundir
(*if it's wax*) = derretirse

member *noun*
a member (*of a committee or international organization*) = un/una miembro
(*of a club*) = un socio/una socia
a member of staff (*in a school*) = un/una miembro del personal docente
(*in a bank, firm*) = un empleado/una empleada

memory *noun*
• (*the ability to remember*)
memory = memoria (*feminine*)
to have a good/bad memory = tener buena/mala memoria
• (*of a person, place or time*)
a memory = un recuerdo

mend *verb*
• (*to fix*) = arreglar
to have the roof mended = hacer arreglar el tejado
• (*by sewing*) = coser, arreglar

mental *adjective*
= mental

mention *verb* = mencionar
she mentioned that she is looking for another job = dijo que está buscando otro trabajo
thank you very much—don't mention it! = muchas gracias—¡no hay de qué!

menu *noun*
a menu = un menú

mercy *noun*
mercy = clemencia (*feminine*)

merry-go-round *noun*
a merry-go-round = unos caballitos, un carrusel (*Lat Am*), una calesita (*R Pl*), un tiovivo (*Spa*)

mess *noun*
a mess = un desorden
your room is in a mess = tu cuarto está todo desordenado
to make a mess in the kitchen = dejar la cocina hecha un desastre
mess around, mess about (*British English*) = tontear

message *noun*
a message = un mensaje
(*when phoning*) = un recado

messenger
a messenger = un mensajero/una mensajera

metal
1 *noun*
  a metal = un metal
2 *adjective* = metálico/metálica

meter *noun*
• (*for gas, electricity, water*)
  a meter = un contador, un medidor (*Lat Am*)
• (*US English—a measure*)
  a meter = un metro

method *noun*
  a method = un método
  a method of payment = una forma de pago

metre *noun* (*British English*)
  a metre = un metro

Mexico *noun* ▶ p. 187
  Mexico = México (*masculine*)

microphone *noun*
  a microphone = un micrófono

microscope *noun*
  a microscope = un microscopio

microwave (**oven**) *noun*
  a microwave (**oven**) = un microondas

midday *noun* ▶ p. 319
  midday = mediodía (*masculine*)
  at midday = al mediodía

middle *noun*
  the middle = el medio
  in the middle of the road = en medio de la calle
  in the middle of August = a mediados de agosto
  I'm in the middle of cooking something = estoy preparando algo

middle-aged *adjective*
  = de mediana edad (! *never changes*)

Middle Ages *noun*
  the Middle Ages = la Edad Media

midnight *noun*
  midnight = medianoche (*feminine*)
  at midnight = a medianoche

midwife *noun*
  a midwife = una partera

might *verb*
• (*when talking about a possibility*)
  she might be right = puede que tenga razón
  will you come?—I might = ¿vas a venir?—quizás
  we might miss the plane = a lo mejor perdemos el avión

! *Note the use of the subjunctive after* puede que

• (*when implying that something did not happen*)
  she might have warned us = podría habernos avisado

mild *adjective*
• (*not harsh*)
  a mild winter = un invierno no muy frío
• (*gentle on the hair, skin*) = suave
• (*not strong in taste*)
  a mild cheese = un queso suave
  a mild curry = un curry no muy picante
• (*not serious*)
  a mild infection = una infección leve

mile *noun*
  a mile = una milla

military *adjective*
  = militar

milk
1 *noun*
  milk = leche
2 *verb* = ordeñar

million *number*
  one million, a million = un millón
  a million inhabitants = un millón de habitantes
  three million dollars = tres millones de dólares

millionaire *noun*
  a millionaire = un millonario/una millonaria

mince
1 *noun* (*British English*)
  mince = carne molida, carne picada (*R Pl, Spa*)
2 *verb* = moler, picar (*R Pl, Spa*)

mind
1 *noun*
• (*when talking about a person's thoughts*)
  the mind = la mente
  what's on your mind? = ¿qué es lo que te preocupa?
  I can't get it out of my mind = no puedo quitármelo de la cabeza
• (*when talking about a person's opinions or attitudes*)
  to make up one's mind to live alone = decidirse vivir solo
  to change one's mind = cambiar de opinión
2 *verb*
• (*when expressing an opinion*)
  there's a lot of noise but I don't mind = hay mucho ruido pero no me importa
  she doesn't mind the heat = el calor no le molesta
  I wouldn't mind a drink = no me vendría mal un trago

M

• (*in polite questions or requests*)
  do you mind if I smoke? = ¿te importa si
  fumo?
  would you mind closing the window? = ¿le
  importaría cerrar la ventana?
• (*when telling someone to be careful*)
  mind the steps! = ¡cuidado con las
  escaleras!
• (*to take care of*) = cuidar
  to mind the children = cuidar a los niños
  to mind the shop = atender la tienda
• (*to worry*)
  never mind, I'll get the next train = no te
  preocupes, tomaré el próximo tren

mine¹ *pronoun*
  (*singular*) = mío/mía
  (*plural*) = míos/mías
  mine is here = el mío/la mía está aquí
  a friend of mine = un amigo mío

mine² *noun*
• (*for coal, metals*)
  a mine = una mina
• (*type of bomb*)
  a mine = una mina

miner *noun*
  a miner = un minero/una minera

mineral *noun*
  a mineral = un mineral

mineral water *noun*
  a mineral water = un agua mineral
  (*feminine*)

minimum
  1 *adjective* = mínimo/mínima
  2 *noun*
  the minimum = el mínimo

miniskirt *noun*
  a miniskirt = una minifalda

minister *noun*
• (*in government*)
  a minister = un ministro/una ministra, un
  secretario/una secretaria (*Mex*)
• (*in religion*)
  a minister = un pastor/una pastora

ministry *noun*
  a ministry = un ministerio, una secretaría
  (*Mex*)

minor
  1 *adjective*
  some minor changes = unos pequeños
  cambios
  a minor injury = una herida leve
  2 *noun*
  a minor = un/una menor (de edad)

minority *noun*
  a minority = una minoría

mint *noun*
• (*the herb*)
  mint = menta

• (*a sweet*)
  a mint = una pastilla de menta

minus *preposition*
  = menos
  six minus three is three (6 − 3 = 3) = seis
  menos tres es igual a tres (6 − 3 = 3)

minute *noun* ▶ **p. 319**
  a minute = un minuto

minutes *noun*
  the minutes = el acta
  to take the minutes = levantar el acta

miracle *noun*
  a miracle = un milagro

mirror *noun*
  a mirror (*on a wall*) = un espejo
  (*on a vehicle*) = un (espejo) retrovisor

mischievous *adjective*
  = travieso/traviesa

miserable *adjective*
• (*unhappy*) = triste
• (*depressing*)
  the weather's miserable = el tiempo está
  pésimo

miss *verb*
• (*to fail to hit*)
  to miss the target = no dar en el blanco
  the stone just missed her head = la piedra
  por poco le da en la cabeza
  you missed! = ¡fallaste!
• (*to fail to see*)
  you can't miss it = lo va a ver enseguida
• (*to fail to take*)
  to miss an opportunity = perder una
  oportunidad
  he missed the chance to work abroad =
  perdió la oportunidad de trabajar al
  extranjero
• (*to fail to understand*)
  you've missed the point = no lo has
  entendido
• (*to feel sad not to see*) = echar de menos,
  extrañar (*Lat Am*)
  I miss you = te echo de menos, te extraño
• (*to fail to catch*) = perder
  to miss a train = perder un tren
  to miss a party = perder una fiesta

Miss *noun*
  = señorita

missile *noun*
  a missile = un misil

missing *adjective*
  to be missing = faltar
  the missing jewels = las joyas
  desaparecidas
  to go missing (*British English*) =
  desaparecer

mist *noun*
  mist = neblina (*feminine*)

mistake *noun*
  a mistake = un error
  to make a mistake = cometer un error
  a spelling mistake = una falta de ortografía
  by mistake = por error

misunderstand *verb*
  = entender mal

misunderstanding *noun*
  a misunderstanding = un malentendido

mix *verb*
• (*to put together*) = mezclar
• (*to go together*) = mezclarse
  oil doesn't mix with water = el aceite no se
    mezcla con el agua

mix up
  (*to get confused*)
  to mix up the two languages, to get the
    two languages mixed up = confundir los
    dos idiomas

mixture *noun*
  a mixture = una mezcla

moan *verb*
• (*to groan*) = gemir
• (*to complain*) = quejarse

mobile phone *noun*
  a mobile phone = un celular, un teléfono
    móvil

model *noun*
• (*of a train, a car, a building*)
  a model = un modelo, una maqueta
• (*of fashions*)
  a model = un/una modelo

modern *adjective*
  = moderno/moderna

mole *noun*
• (*the animal*)
  a mole = un topo
• (*a spot on the skin*)
  a mole = un lunar

mom *noun* (*US English*)
  Mom = mamá✱ (*feminine*)

moment *noun*
  a moment = un momento
  it will be ready in a moment = estará listo
    enseguida
  at the moment = en este momento

mommy *noun* (*US English*)
  my mommy = mi mamá✱

Monday *noun* ▶ **p. 192**
  Monday = lunes (*masculine*)

money *noun*
  money = dinero (*masculine*), plata
    (*feminine*) (*S Am*)

monkey *noun*
  a monkey = un mono/una mona

monster *noun*
  a monster = un monstruo

month *noun* ▶ **p. 192**
  a month = un mes

monument *noun*
  a monument = un monumento

mood *noun*
• to be in a good/bad mood = estar de
    buen/mal humor
• (*a bad humor*)
  he's in a mood = está de mal humor

moody *adjective*
  to be moody (*unpredictable*) = ser
    temperamental
  (*in a bad mood*) = estar de mal humor

moon *noun*
  the moon = la luna

moonlight *noun*
  the moonlight = la luz de la luna

moor
1 *noun*
  a moor = un páramo
2 *verb*
  to moor a boat = amarrar un barco

moral *adjective*
  = moral

more
1 *adjective* = más
  more [books | time] = más [libros | tiempo]
  I have more work than him = tengo más
    trabajo que él
  there's no more bread = no hay más pan
  he bought two more tickets = compró dos
    boletos más
2 *pronoun* = más
  to cost more = costar más
  I did more than you = hice más que tú
  more than = más de
  there were more than 20 people = había
    más de 20 personas
  we need more (of them/of it) = necesitamos
    más
3 *adverb*
• (*when comparing*) = más
  it's more complicated than that = es más
    complicado que eso
• (*when talking about time*)
  he doesn't live here any more = ya no vive
    aquí
• more and more = cada vez más
• more or less = más o menos

M

morning *noun* ▶ p. 319
 a morning = una mañana
 Friday morning = el viernes en la mañana,
  el viernes por la mañana (*Spa*)
 in the morning = en la mañana, por la
  mañana (*Spa*)
 tomorrow morning = mañana por la
  mañana
 at six o'clock in the morning = a las seis de
  la mañana
 good morning = buenos días

mosquito *noun*
 a mosquito = un mosquito, un zancudo
  (*Lat Am*)

most
1 *adjective*
 • (*the majority of*) = la mayoría de, la mayor
  parte de
 • (*in superlatives*)
  who has the most money? = ¿quién es el
   que tiene más dinero?
2 *pronoun*
 • = la mayoría, la mayor parte
 • at (**the**) most = como mucho
3 *adverb*
 • (*in superlatives*) = más
  the most expensive shop in London = la
   tienda más cara de Londres
  the most difficult problems = los problemas
   más difíciles
 • most of all
  I like this one most of all = éste es el que
   más me gusta
  most of all I want to visit Buenos Aires = lo
   que más quisiera es visitar Buenos Aires

mostly *adverb*
 (*for the most part*)
 the students are mostly Japanese = la
  mayoría de los estudiantes son japoneses

moth *noun*
 a moth = una mariposa de la luz, una
  palomilla
 (*in clothes*) = una polilla

mother *noun*
 a mother = una madre

mother-in-law *noun*
 a mother-in-law = una suegra

motive *noun*
 a motive = un motivo

motor *noun*
 a motor = un motor

motorbike *noun*
 a motorbike = una motocicleta, una moto

motorist *noun*
 a motorist = un/una automovilista

motor racing *noun*
 motor racing = carreras automovilísticas
  (*feminine plural*)

motorway *noun* (*British English*)
 a motorway = una autopista

mountain *noun*
 a mountain = una montaña

mouse *noun*
 a mouse = un ratón, una laucha (*SC*)

moustache (*British English*)
 a moustache = un bigote

mouth *noun*
 • (*of a person, an animal*) ▶ p. 235
  the mouth = la boca
 • (*of a cave, tunnel*)
  the mouth = la entrada
 • (*of a river*)
  the mouth = la desembocadura

move
1 *verb*
 • (*to make a movement*) = moverse
  I can't move = no puedo moverme
  when the train is moving = cuando el tren
   está en marcha
 • (*to put elsewhere*)
  to move the television = cambiar de lugar
   la televisión
  could you move the chair (**out of the way**)?
   = ¿podrías quitar la silla de en medio?
 • (*to make a movement with*) = mover
  to move one's head = mover la cabeza
  don't move the camera = no muevas la
   cámara
 • (*to act*) = actuar
  to move fast = actuar rápido
 • to move (**house**) (*British English*) =
   mudarse de casa
 • (*to touch, to move emotionally*) = conmover
  to be moved = estar conmovido/conmovida
2 *noun*
 • (*a movement*)
  a move = un movimiento
 • (*a step, a decision*)
  a good move = una buena decisión
  to make the first move = dar el primer paso
 • (*a change of location*)
  a move = una mudanza
 • (*in a game*)
  it's your move = te toca mover
move around
 • (*to travel around*) = moverse
 • (*to put elsewhere*) = cambiar de lugar
  to move the furniture around = cambiar los
   muebles de lugar
move away
 • (*to live elsewhere*) = mudarse
 • (*to make a movement away*) = alejarse
move back = retroceder
move forward = avanzar
move in = mudarse
move out = irse
move over = correrse

movement *noun*
• a movement = un movimiento
• *(a group)*
a movement = un movimiento
the women's movement = el movimiento
feminista

movie *noun (US English)*
a movie = una película

mow *verb*
= cortar

MP *noun (British English)*
an MP = un diputado/una diputada

Mr *noun*
= Señor, Sr.

Mrs *noun*
= Señora, Sra.

Ms *noun*
= Señora, Sra.

much
1 *adverb*
• *(a lot)* = mucho
her house is much smaller than ours = su
casa es mucho más pequeña que la
nuestra
• *(often)* = mucho
they don't go out much = no salen mucho
• *(when used with* very, too *or* so*)*
I don't like driving very much = no me
gusta mucho manejar
you talk too much = hablas demasiado
she loves her so much = la quiere tanto
2 *pronoun* = mucho
how much does it cost? = ¿cuánto cuesta?
3 *adjective* = mucho/mucha
there isn't much water = no hay mucha
agua
• *(when used with* very, too, so *or* how*)*
she doesn't eat very much meat = no come
mucha carne
I spent too much money = gasté demasiado
dinero
don't use so much salt = no pongas tanta
sal
how much coffee? = ¿cuánto café?
how much milk? = ¿cuánta leche?

mud *noun*
mud = barro *(masculine)*, fango
(masculine)

mug
1 *noun*
a mug = una taza (alta y sin platillo), un
tarro *(Mex)*
2 *verb* = atracar

mule *noun*
a mule = una mula

multiply *verb*
(in arithmetic) = multiplicar
to multiply 10 by 10 = multiplicar 10 por 10

mumble *verb*
= farfullar

mum *noun (British English)*
Mum = mamá✱ *(feminine)*

mummy *noun (British English)*
(mother)
my mummy = mi mamá✱

murder
1 *noun*
a murder = un asesinato
2 *verb* = asesinar

murderer *noun*
a murderer = un asesino/una asesina

muscle *noun*
a muscle = un músculo

museum *noun*
a museum = un museo

mushroom *noun*
(edible)
a mushroom = un champiñón

music *noun*
music = música

musical
1 *adjective*
to be musical *(to have talent)* = tener
aptitudes para la música
2 *noun*
a musical = un musical

musician *noun*
a musician = un músico/una música

Muslim
1 *noun*
a Muslim = un musulmán/una musulmana
2 *adjective* = musulmán/musulmana

mussel *noun*
a mussel = una mejillón

must *verb*

> ! The verbs **deber** *and* **tener que** *are
> used to translate* must

• *(when stressing the importance of
something)*
you must go to the doctor = tienes que ir al
médico, debes ir al médico
she must do the exam in June = tiene que
hacer el examen en junio
• *(when assuming that something is true)*
it must be nice to live there = debe (de) ser
lindo vivir allí
• *(when talking about what you intend to do)*
I must phone her this evening = tengo que
llamarla esta tarde

mustache *noun (US English)*
a mustache = un bigote

mutton *noun*
mutton = carne de ovino *(feminine)*

M

my *adjective*
= mi (+ *singular*), mis (+ *plural*)

! *For* my *used with parts of the body,*
▶ **p. 235**

myself *pronoun*
• (*when translated by a reflexive verb in Spanish*)
I didn't hurt myself = no me hice daño, no me lastimé (*Lat Am*)
I bought myself a hat = me compré un sombrero
• (*when used for emphasis*)
I told them myself = se lo dije yo mismo/yo misma
I did it all by myself = lo hice yo solo

mysterious *adjective*
= misterioso/misteriosa

mystery *noun*
• a mystery = un misterio
• (*a story*)
a mystery = una novela de misterio

Nn

nail
1 *noun*
• (*for use in hanging, attaching, repairing*)
a nail = un clavo
• (*on the fingers or toes*)
a nail = una uña
2 *verb* = clavar

nail polish, nail varnish (*British English*) *noun*
nail polish = esmalte de uñas (*masculine*)

naïve *adjective*
= ingenuo/ingenua

naked *adjective*
= desnudo/desnuda

name
1 *noun*
• (*of a person*)
a name = un nombre
what's your name? = ¿cómo te llamas?, ¿cómo se llama?
my name is Joan = me llamo Joan
• (*of a book, play or film*)
a name = un título
2 *verb* = ponerle nombre a
a man named Bob Jones = un hombre llamado Bob Jones

napkin *noun*
a napkin = un servilleta

nappy *noun* (*British English*)
a nappy = un pañal

narrow *adjective*
= estrecho/estrecha, angosto/angosta (*Lat Am*)

nasty *adjective*
• (*unkind*) = malo/mala
to be nasty to someone = ser malo/mala con alguien
• (*unpleasant*) = desagradable

nation *noun*
a nation = una nación

national *adjective*
= nacional

national anthem *noun*
a national anthem = un himno nacional

native
1 *adjective*
his native language = su lengua materna
a native Spanish speaker = un hablante nativo de español
2 *noun*
a native = un nativo/una nativa

natural *adjective*
• (*not artificial*) = natural
• (*normal*) = normal, natural

naturally *adverb*
= naturalmente

nature *noun*
• (*the natural world*)
nature = naturaleza (*feminine*)
• (*part of a person's personality*)
nature = carácter (*masculine*)

naughty *noun*
= travieso/traviesa

navel *noun*
the navel = el ombligo

navy *noun*
the navy = la armada

navy blue *adjective* ▶ **p. 183**
= azul marino (**!** *never changes*)

near
1 *preposition* = cerca de
it's near the station = está cerca de la estación
2 *adverb*
they live quite near = viven muy cerca
to move nearer = acercarse
3 *adjective*
the school is quite near = la escuela está bastante cerca
the nearest shops = las tiendas más cercanas
in the near future = en un futuro próximo

---

nearby *adverb*
= cerca

nearly *adverb*
= casi
I'm nearly ready = estoy casi listo
we're nearly there = ya casi llegamos, ya casi hemos llegado
I nearly forgot = por poco me olvido

nearsighted *adjective*
= miope, corto/corta de vista

neat *adjective*
* (*if it's a person*) = pulcro/pulcra, prolijo/prolija (*R Pl*)
* (*tidy*)
your room is always very neat = tu cuarto siempre está muy ordenado

necessary *adjective*
= necesario/necesaria

neck *noun*
* (*of a person*) ▶ **p. 235**
the neck = el cuello
the back of the neck = la nuca
* (*of a garment*)
the neck = el cuello, el escote

necklace *noun*
a necklace = un collar

need
1 *verb*
* (*to have to*)
you didn't need to ask for permission = no tenías que pedir permiso
you needn't pay now = no hace falta que pagues ahora
they'll need to come early = tendrán que venir temprano
you needn't have come = no hacía falta que vinieras

> **!** Note the use of the subjunctive after no hace falta que

* (*to want*) = necesitar
to need money = necesitar dinero
we need to talk to her = tenemos que hablar con ella
2 *noun*
there's no need (for you) to worry = no tienes por qué preocuparte
I'll do it—there's no need, it's done = yo lo hago—no hace falta, ya está hecho

needle *noun*
a needle = una aguja

negative
1 *adjective* = negativo/negativa
2 *noun*
(*of a photo*)
a negative = una negativa

neglect *verb*
to neglect a child = desatender a un niño
to neglect a house = descuidar

negotiations *noun*
negotiations = negociaciones (*feminine plural*)

neighbor (*US English*), **neighbour** (*British English*) *noun*
a neighbor = un vecino/una vecina

neither
1 *conjunction*
* (*in* neither . . . nor *sentences*)
she speaks neither Spanish nor English = no habla (ni) español ni inglés
they drink neither coffee nor tea = no beben (ni) café ni té
* (*nor*)
I can't sleep—neither can I = no puedo dormir—yo tampoco
2 *adjective*
neither book is useful = ninguno de los libros es útil
neither girl answered = ninguna de las chicas contestó
3 *pronoun* = ninguno/ninguna
neither of them is coming = ninguno (de ellos) viene, no viene ninguno (de ellos)

nephew *noun*
a nephew = un sobrino

nerve *noun*
* **a nerve** = un nervio
* (*courage*)
nerve = valor (*masculine*)
to have the nerve to refuse = tener el valor de rehusar
(*when criticizing*) = tener la frescura de rehusar

nerves *noun*
nerves = nervios (*masculine plural*)
to get on someone's nerves = ponerle los nervios de punta a alguien

nervous *adjective*
= nervioso/nerviosa

nest *noun*
a nest = un nido

net
1 *noun*
a net = una red
2 *adjective* = neto/neta

Netherlands *noun* ▶ **p. 187**
the Netherlands = los Países Bajos

nettle *noun*
a nettle = una ortiga

network *noun*
a network = una red

neutral
1 *adjective*
* (*impartial*) = neutral
* (*not bright*) = neutro/neutra
a neutral color = un color neutro

N

2 *noun*
(*when driving*)
to be in neutral = estar en punto muerto

never *adverb*
• (*not ever*)
they never come to see us = nunca vienen a vernos, no vienen nunca a vernos
never again! = ¡jamás!
I'll never go back there again = no volveré allí nunca, nunca volveré allí
• (*when used for emphasis*)
I never knew that = no lo sabía
she never even apologized = nunca se disculpó siquiera

nevertheless *adverb*
= sin embargo

new *adjective*
= nuevo/nueva

newborn *adjective*
a newborn baby = un bebé recién nacido

news *noun*
• **a piece of news** = una noticia
have you heard the news? = ¿te enteraste de lo que pasó?
have you any news of John? = ¿sabes algo de John?
• (*on radio, TV*)
the news = las noticias

newsagent *noun* (*British English*)
▶ newsdealer

newscaster *noun*
a newscaster = un locutor/una locutora

newsdealer *noun* (*US English*)
a newsdealer = un vendedor/una vendedora de periódicos

newspaper *noun*
a newspaper = un periódico, un diario

newsreader *noun* (*British English*)
a newsreader = un locutor/una locutora

New Year *noun*
the New Year = el Año Nuevo
Happy New Year! = ¡Feliz Año Nuevo!

New Year's (*US English*), **New Year's Day** (*British English*) *noun*
New Year's (Day) = el día de Año Nuevo

New Zealand *noun* ▶ p. 187
New Zealand = Nueva Zelanda (*feminine*), Nueva Zelandia (*feminine*) (*Lat Am*)

next
1 *adjective*
• (*when talking about what is still to come*) = próximo/próxima
the next train = el próximo tren
she's leaving next Friday = se va el viernes que viene

• (*when talking about what followed*) = siguiente
I took the next train = tomé el tren siguiente
the next day = el día siguiente
• (*in a line*)
who's next? = ¿quién sigue?
I'm next = (yo) soy el siguiente
2 *adverb*
• (*in the past*) = luego, después
what happened next? = ¿y luego qué pasó?, ¿y después qué pasó?
• (*now*) = ahora
what'll we do next? = ¿qué vamos a hacer ahora?
• (*in the future*)
when you next go to Leeds, give Gary a call = la próxima vez que vas a Leeds, llama a Gary
• **next to**
we live next to the school = vivimos al lado de la escuela
3 *pronoun*
they're coming the week after next = vienen la semana que viene no, la siguiente

next door *adverb*
= al lado
they live next door = viven al lado

nice *adjective*
• (*enjoyable*) = agradable, lindo/linda (*Lat Am*)
it's nice to be able to relax = es agradable poder descansar
I had a nice time = lo pasé bien
• (*pleasant, kind*) = simpático/simpática
to be nice to someone = ser amable con alguien
• (*attractive*) = bonito/bonita, lindo/linda (*Lat Am*)
you look very nice in that suit = ese traje te queda muy bien
• (*tasty*) = bueno/buena
the meal was nice = la comida estuvo buena

nickname *noun*
a nickname = un apodo

niece *noun*
a niece = una sobrina

night *noun* ▶ p. 319
a night = una noche
to work at night = trabajar de noche
I didn't sleep last night = no dormí anoche

nightclub *noun*
a nightclub = un club (nocturno)

nightdress, nightie *noun*
a nightdress = un camisón

nightmare *noun*
a nightmare = una pesadilla

nil *noun* (*British English*)
(*in sport*)
nil = cero (*masculine*)

nine *number* ▶ **p. 154, p. 319**
nine = nueve (*masculine*) (**!** *never changes*) *see also* five

nineteen *number* ▶ **p. 154, p. 319**
nineteen = diecinueve (*masculine*) (**!** *never changes*) *see also* five

ninety *number* ▶ **p. 154**
ninety = noventa (*masculine*) (**!** *never changes*) *see also* five

ninth
1 *adjective* = noveno/novena
2 *noun* ▶ **p. 192**
(*a part*)
a ninth = una novena parte

no
1 *exclamation*
no = no
no thanks = no gracias
2 *adjective*
• (*not any*)
we have no money = no tenemos dinero
where is he?—I've no idea = ¿dónde está? —no tengo idea
• (*when refusing permission*)
no smoking = prohibido fumar
no talking! = ¡silencio!
• (*when used for emphasis*)
there is no time to argue = no hay tiempo para discutir
it's no problem = no hay problema
3 *adverb*
he no longer works here = ya no trabaja aquí

nobody ▶ no one

nod *verb*
to nod (one's head) (*to say 'yes'*) = asentir con la cabeza
(*to make a sign*) = indicar con la cabeza

noise *noun*
noise = ruido (*masculine*)

noisy *adjective*
= ruidoso/ruidosa
it's too noisy here = hay demasiado ruido aquí

none *pronoun*
= ninguno/ninguna
none of the girls went to the class = ninguna de las chicas fue a la clase
none of what he says is true = nada de lo que dice es cierto
there's none left = no queda ninguno
I have none, I've got none = no tengo

nonsense *noun*
nonsense = tonterías (*feminine plural*)

noodles *noun*
noodles = fideos (*masculine plural*)

noon *noun*
noon = mediodía (*masculine*)
at noon = al mediodía

no one *pronoun* (*also* nobody)
no one = nadie
no one saw him = nadie lo vio
there's no one in the office = no hay nadie en la oficina

nor *conjunction*

> **!** *For translations of* nor *when used in combination with* neither, *look at the entry for* neither *in this dictionary*

I don't like him—nor do I = no me gusta—a mí tampoco
she didn't understand anything and nor did we = ella no entendió nada y nosotros tampoco

normal
1 *adjective* = normal
2 *noun*
to get back to normal = volver a la normalidad

normally *adverb*
= normalmente

north
1 *noun*
the north = el norte
in the north of France = en el norte de Francia
2 *adverb*
we went north = fuimos hacia el norte
it is north of Madrid = está al norte de Madrid
3 *adjective*
= norte (**!** *never changes*)
the north coast = la costa norte
the north wind = el viento norte

N

North America *noun* ▶ **p. 187**
North America = Norteamérica (*feminine*), América del Norte (*feminine*)

northeast *noun*
the northeast = el noreste

Northern Ireland *noun* ▶ **p. 187**
Northern Ireland = Irlanda del Norte (*feminine*)

northwest *noun*
the northwest = el noroeste

Norway *noun* ▶ **p. 187**
Norway = Noruega (*feminine*)

Norwegian ▶ **p. 187, p. 245**
1 *adjective* = noruego/noruega
2 *noun*
• (*a person*)
a Norwegian = un noruego/una noruega

• (*the language*)
Norwegian = noruego (*masculine*)

nose *noun* ▶ p. 235
the nose = la nariz

nostril *noun*
a nostril = una ventana de la nariz

not
1 *adverb* = no
she's not at home = no está en casa
has he not phoned you?, hasn't he
phoned you? = ¿no te ha llamado?
I hope not = espero que no
2 not at all
• (*in no way*)
he's not at all worried = no está nada
preocupado
• (*don't mention it*)
thanks a lot—not at all = muchas
gracias—de nada

note
1 *noun*
• (*to remind oneself*)
a note = una nota
to make a note of an address = anotar una
dirección
to take note of a name = tomar nota de un
nombre
• (*a short letter*)
a note = una nota
• (*British English—paper money*)
a note = un billete
• (*in music*)
a note = una nota
2 *verb*
to note that something has happened =
notar que algo ha pasado
note down = apuntar

notebook *noun*
• (*an exercise book*)
a notebook = un cuaderno
• (*for shorthand*)
a notebook = una libreta

nothing *pronoun*
nothing = nada
nothing has changed = nada ha cambiado
nothing happens in this town = no pasa
nada en esta ciudad
there's nothing else to say = no hay nada
más que decir
they do nothing but complain = no hace
más que quejarse

notice
1 *verb* = notar
2 *noun*
• (*a written sign*)
a notice = un letrero

• (*advance warning*)
notice = aviso (*masculine*)
without any notice = sin previo aviso
to give two month's notice = avisar con dos
meses de antelación
to cancel something at short notice =
cancelar algo con muy poca antelación
to hand in one's notice = presentar su
renuncia
he was given his notice = lo despidieron
• (*attention*)
to take notice of someone = hacerle caso a
alguien

novel *noun*
a novel = una novela

November *noun* ▶ p. 192
November = noviembre (*masculine*)

now *adverb*
= ahora
we have to do it now = tenemos que
hacerlo ahora
do it right now = hazlo ahora
it's three weeks now since she wrote us =
ya hace tres semanas que nos escribió
I should have told you before now =
tendría que habértelo dicho antes
from now on = a partir de ahora
now and again, now and then = de vez en
cuando

nowhere *adverb*
where are you going this summer?
—nowhere = ¿adónde vas este verano?—a
ningún lado
there's nowhere to sit = no hay dónde
sentarse

nuclear *adjective*
= nuclear

nude *adjective*
= desnudo/desnuda
in the nude = desnudo/desnuda

nuisance *noun*
• (*an annoying person*)
a nuisance = un pesado/una pesada
• (*an annoying thing, situation*)
it's a nuisance having to pay in cash = es
una molestia tener que pagar en efectivo,
es un fastidio tener que pagar en efectivo
what a nuisance! = ¡qué molestia!, ¡que
fastidio!

numb *adjective*
(*due to the cold*) =
entumecido/entumecida
to go numb = entumecerse
my hands are numb = tengo las manos
entumecidas

number *noun*
• a number = un número
I gave him my number = le di mi número

(*when talking about quantities*)
a number of people = varias personas
they don't want to leave for a number of reasons = no quieren irse por una serie de razones

numberplate noun (*British English*)
a numberplate = una matrícula, una placa (*Lat Am*), una patente (*SC*)

nun noun
a nun = una monja

nurse noun
a nurse = un enfermero/una enfermera

nursery noun
(*for children*)
a nursery = una guardería
(*for plants*)
a nursery = un vivero

nursery school noun
a nursery school = un parvulario, un kindergarten (*AmL*)

nut noun
a nut = un fruto seco
(*for use with a bolt*)
a nut = una tuerca

nylon noun
nylon = nylon (*masculine*)

oak noun
(*the tree*)
an oak = un roble

oar noun
an oar = un remo

obedient adjective
= obediente

obey verb
= obedecer

object
1 noun
(*a thing*)
an object = un objeto
(*an aim*)
an object = un objetivo
2 verb
to object to something = oponerse a algo

objection noun
an objection = una objeción

oblige verb
(*to require*)
to oblige someone to do something = obligar a alguien a hacer algo
to be obliged to give up work = verse obligado/obligada a dejar el trabajo
(*to be grateful*)
I'd be much obliged if you could help me = le quedaría muy agradecido si pudiera ayudarme

obscene adjective
= obsceno/obscena

obsessed adjective
= obsesionado/obsesionada

obsession noun
an obssession = una obsesión

obstacle noun
an obstacle = un obstáculo

obstinate adjective
= obstinado/obstinada

obstruct verb
(*to slow down*)
to obstruct the traffic = bloquear el tráfico
(*to block*)
to obstruct the road = obstruir la carretera

obtain verb
= obtener, conseguir

obvious adjective
= obvio/obvia

obviously adverb
= obviamente

occasion noun
an occasion = una ocasión

occasionally adverb
= de vez en cuando

occupy verb
(*to live in*) = ocupar
(*to take*) = ocupar
the seats are occupied = los asientos están ocupados
(*to keep busy*)
to keep oneself occupied = entretenerse
it keeps me occupied = me entretiene

occur verb
(*to take place*) = ocurrir
(*to cross someone's mind*)
it never occurred to me = nunca se me ocurrió

ocean noun
the ocean = el océano

o'clock adverb ▶ p. 319
it's 5 o'clock = son las cinco

October noun ▶ p. 192
October = octubre (*masculine*)

O

octopus noun
an octopus = un pulpo

odd adjective
(strange) = raro/rara, extraño/extraña
(not matching) = desparejado/desparejada
odd socks = calcetines desparejados
the odd one out = la excepción
(when talking about numbers) = impar
an odd number = un número impar

odor (US English), **odour** (British English)
noun
an odor = un olor

of preposition
of = de
it's in the center of London = estó en el
centro de Londres
have you heard of her? = ¿has oído hablar
de ella?
of the = del (masculine), de la (feminine),
de los/las (plural)
the names of the pupils = los nombres de
los estudiantes
(when talking about quantities)
a kilo of apples = un kilo de manzanas
a glass of wine = una copa de vino
the flowers were lovely so we bought
some of them = las flores eran bonitas así
que compramos algunas
there are a lot of them = son
muchos/muchas
(US English—when talking about time)
▶ p. 319
it's ten (minutes) of five = son diez para
las cinco (Lat Am), son las cinco menos diez
(R Pl, Spa)

off

! Off is often used in combinations with
verbs, for example, fall off, get off, go off,
take off. To find the correct translations
for this type of verb, look up the separate
dictionary entries at fall, get, go, take etc

1 adverb
(leaving)
I'm off = me voy
(away)
the coast is a long way off = la costa está
muy lejos de aquí
the town is about 30 km off = la ciudad está
a unos 30 kilómetros de aquí
to take a day off = tomar un día libre
(not working, switched off)
the lights are all off = todas las luces están
apagadas
why is the television off? = ¿por qué está
apagada la televisión?
the water's off = el agua está cortada
(canceled)
the match is off because of the bad
weather = el partido está cancelado
debido al mal tiempo

2 adjective
the milk is off = la leche está cortada
I think the meat is off = creo que la carne
está mala
3 preposition
(away from)
just off the coast of Florida = a poca
distancia de la costa de Florida
three feet off the ground = a tres pies del
suelo
(near)
the bathroom's off the bedroom = el baño
da al dormitorio
it's just off Oxford Street = está en una
bocacalle de Oxford Street

offence noun (British English) ▶ offense

offend verb
= ofender

offense (US English) noun
(a crime)
an offense = un delito
to take offense = ofenderse

offer
1 verb = ofrecer
I offered her a sweet = le ofrecí un
caramelo
to offer to water the plants = ofrecerse a
regar las plantas
2 noun
an offer = una oferta

office noun
an office = una oficina
a doctor's office (US English) = un
consultorio, una consulta

office hours noun
office hours = horas de oficina (feminine
plural)

officer noun
an officer (in the army or navy) = un/una
oficial
(in the police force) = un/una policía

official
1 adjective = oficial
2 noun
an official (in the public service) = un
funcionario/una funcionaria
(in a party, a union) = un/una dirigente

often adverb
= a menudo

oil
1 noun
(for fuel)
oil = petróleo (masculine)
(for a vehicle)
oil = aceite (masculine)
(for cooking, in medicine, for the skin)
oil = aceite (masculine)
2 verb = lubricar

ointment *noun*
an ointment = un ungüento

okay, OK
1 *adjective*
(*when asking or giving opinions*)
is it okay if I smoke? = ¿está bien si fumo?
it's okay to invite them = está bien si los
invitas
(*when talking about health*) = bien
are you okay? = ¿estás bien?
2 *exclamation* = ¡bueno!, ¡okey! (*Lat Am*),
¡vale! (*Spa*)

old *adjective*
(*not new, not young*) = viejo/vieja
an old man/woman = un viejo/una vieja
(*when talking about a person's age*)
▶ p. 154
how old are you? = ¿cuántos años tienes?,
¿qué edad tienes?
a three-year old girl = una niña de tres años
her older sister = su hermana mayor
to be the oldest = ser el/la mayor
(*previous*)
that's my old address = esa es mi antigua
dirección
(*long-standing*)
an old friend = un viejo amigo

old-fashioned *adjective*
(*outdated*)
= anticuado/anticuada
(*traditional*)
= tradicional

olive *noun*
(*the fruit*)
an olive = una aceituna
(*the tree*)
an olive (**tree**) = un olivo

olive oil *noun*
olive oil = aceite de oliva (*masculine*)

Olympics *noun*
the Olympics = los juegos Olímpicos

omelet (*US English*), **omelette** (*British
English*) *noun*
an omelet = una omelette, una tortilla
francesa (*Spa*)

on

> **!** On *is often used in combinations with
> verbs, for example,* count on, get on,
> keep on. *To find the correct translations
> for this type of verb, look up the separate
> dictionary entries for* count, get, keep *etc*

1 *preposition*
on = en, sobre
it's on the table = está en la mesa, está
sobre la mesa
there's a spot on the carpet = la alfombra
tiene una mancha
to fall on the floor = caerse al suelo
I like the picture on the wall = me gusta el
cuadro en la pared
to live on Park Avenue = vivir en Park
Avenue

(*when talking about transport*) = en
to travel on the train = viajar en tren
(*about*) = sobre
a book on Africa = un libro sobre (el) África
(*when talking about time*)
she was born on the 6th of December =
nació el 6 de diciembre
I'll be there on Saturday = estaré allí el
sábado
they go to the gym on Mondays = van al
gimnasio los lunes
(*when talking about the media*)
on television = en la televisión
I heard it on the radio = lo oí por la radio
(*using*)
to be on antibiotics = estar tomando
antibióticos
to be on drugs = drogarse
the clock runs on batteries = el reloj
funciona con pilas
2 *adverb*
(*when talking about what one wears*)
to have a hat on = llevar un sombrero
(*working, switched on*) =
encendido/encendida, prendido/prendida
(*Lat Am*)
(*taking place, due to take place*)
there's a lecture on in there = hay una
conferencia allí
I don't have anything on that day = no
tengo ningún compromiso ese día
(*showing*)
what's on at the Renoir? = ¿que dan en el
Renoir?, ¿que ponen en el Renoir? (*Spa*)
(*when talking about time*)
from Tuesday on = a partir del martes

once
1 *adverb*
(*one time*) = una vez
once a day = una vez al día
once in a while = de vez en cuando
(*in the old days*)
once upon a time there was a princess =
érase una vez una princesa
at once
(*immediately*) = inmediatamente
(*at the same time*) = al mismo tiempo, a la
vez
2 *conjunction* = una vez que
I feel better once I'm sitting down = me
siento mejor una vez que estoy sentado

one
1 *number* ▶ p. 154, p. 319
one = uno/una

> **!** Note that uno *becomes* un *before a
> masculine singular noun*

one child = un niño/una niña
one of my colleagues = uno/una de mis
colegas

O

2 *adjective*
(*the only*)
she's the one person who can persuade him = es la única persona que lo puede persuadir
it's the one thing that annoys me = es la única cosa que me fastidia
3 *pronoun*
I need a cigarette—have you got one? = necesito un cigarrillo—¿tienes?
the cakes are delicious—I'll have another one = los pasteles están deliciosos—voy a comer otro
(*when referring to a specific person or thing*)
I've decided to wear the black one = he decidido llevar el negro
he's the one who told me to be quiet = es él quien me dijo que me callara
which one? = ¿cuál?
this one = éste/ésta
(*when used as a personal pronoun*) = uno/una
one never knows = uno nunca sabe
one by one = uno a uno, uno por uno

one another *pronoun*
to love one another = quererse el uno al otro
to help one another = ayudarse el uno al otro

oneself *pronoun*
(*when translated by a reflexive verb in Spanish*) = se
to enjoy oneself = divertirse
to hurt oneself = hacerse daño
(*when used for emphasis*) = uno mismo/una misma

one-way street *noun*
a one-way street = una calle de sentido único, una calle de un solo sentido

one-way ticket *noun* (*US English*)
a one-way ticket (*on a ship or plane*) = un pasaje de ida (*Lat Am*), un billete de ida (*Spa*)
(*on a bus or train*) = un boleto de ida (*Lat Am*), un billete de ida (*Spa*)

onion *noun*
an onion = una cebolla

only
1 *adverb*
only = sólo, solamente
it's only a game = es sólo un juego
he only reads novels = solamente lee novelas
the lift is for staff only = el ascensor es sólo para el personal
only I saw them = soy el único que los vio
I've only just arrived = acabo de llegar, recién acabo de llegar (*Lat Am*)
she had only just bought a car = acababa de comprar un coche, recién acababa de comprar un coche (*Lat Am*)

2 *adjective* = único/única
they are our only neighbors = son nuestros únicos vecinos
she was the only one who didn't speak English = era la única que no hablaba inglés
an only child = un hijo único/una hija única

onto *preposition*
the vase fell onto the sofa = el florero cayó sobre el sofá
my room looks onto the garden = mi cuarto da al jardín

open
1 *verb*
to open = abrir
(*to start*) = **the movie opens next week** = la película se estrena la semana que viene
2 *adjective*
(*not closed*) = abierto/abierta
(*frank*) = abierto/abierta, franco/franca

opener *noun*
an opener (*for bottles*) = un abrebotellas, un destapador (*Lat Am*)
(*for cans*) = un abrelatas

opening hours *noun*
opening hours = horario comercial (*masculine*)

opera *noun*
an opera = una ópera

operate *verb*
(*to make something work*) = manejar, operar
to operate a machine = manejar una máquina, operar una máquina
(*to carry out an operation*) = operar
to operate on someone = operar a alguien

operation *noun*
an operation = una operación
he had an operation = lo operaron

operator *noun*
an operator = un/una telefonista, un operador/una operadora

opinion *noun*
an opinion = una opinión
in my opinion = en mi opinión

opponent *noun*
(*in a contest*)
an opponent = un/una contrincante
(*of a government, a regime*)
an opponent = un opositor/una opositora

opportunity *noun*
an opportunity = una oportunidad, una ocasión
to have an opportunity to go abroad = tener la oportunidad de ir al extranjero
to take the opportunity to go to Boston = aprovechar la ocasión para ir a Boston

oppose *verb*
= oponerse a
to be opposed to something = oponerse a algo

opposite
1 *preposition*
= enfrente de, frente a
it's opposite the park = está enfrente del parque, está frente al parque
2 *adjective*
he was walking in the opposite direction = caminaba en dirección opuesta
I sat on the opposite side of the room = me senté al otro lado de la habitación
3 *adverb* = enfrente
who lives opposite? = ¿quién vive enfrente?
4 *noun*
the opposite = lo contrario

opposition *noun*
opposition = oposición (*feminine*)

optician *noun*
(*selling glasses*)
an optician = un óptico/una óptica
(*British English—an eye specialist*)
an optician = un/una oculista

optimistic *adjective*
= optimista

or *conjunction*
or = o

> **!** *Note that the usual translation* o *becomes* u *when it precedes a word beginning with* o *or* ho-

with or without milk? = ¿con o sin leche?
one or the other = uno u otro
we'll stay here or at Philip's = nos vamos a quedar aquí o en casa de Philip
(*in negative sentences*)
I can't come today or tomorrow = no puedo ir ni hoy ni mañana
he doesn't speak Spanish or English = no habla ni español ni inglés

orange ▶ p. 183
1 *noun*
(*the fruit*)
an orange = una naranja
(*the color*)
orange = naranja (*masculine*)
2 *adjective*
= naranja (**!** *never changes*)

orchard *noun*
an orchard = un huerto

orchestra *noun*
an orchestra = una orquesta

order
1 *verb*
(*to tell*)
to order someone to leave = ordenarle a alguien que se vaya

> **!** *Note the use of the subjunctive after* ordenarle a alguien que

(*to ask for*) = pedir
you have to order the flowers the day before = hay que pedir las flores el día anterior
to order white wine = pedir vino blanco
are you ready to order? = ¿ya han decidido lo que van a pedir?
(*to reserve*)
to order a book = encargar un libro
to order a taxi = llamar un taxi
2 *noun*
(*an instruction*)
an order = una orden
(*a request*)
an order = un pedido
to place an order for something = hacer un pedido de algo, encargar algo
(*the way something is arranged*)
order = orden (*masculine*)
in alphabetical order = en orden alfabético
(*control*)
order = orden (*masculine*)
in order to = para

ordinary *adjective*
(*not unusual*) = normal
an ordinary family = una familia normal
I was wearing my ordinary clothes = llevaba la ropa de todos los días

organ *noun*
(*the musical instrument*)
an organ = un órgano
(*part of the body*)
an organ = un órgano

organization *noun*
an organization = una organización

organize *verb*
(*to arrange*) = organizar
to get organized = organizarse
(*to tidy*) = ordenar

original *adjective*
= original

ornament *noun*
an ornament = un adorno

orphan *noun*
an orphan = un huérfano/una huérfana

other
1 *adjective* = otro/otra (+ *singular*), = otros/otras (+ *plural*)
they sold the other shop = vendieron la otra tienda
she met them the other day = los conoció el otro día
2 *pronoun*
the others = los otros/las otras
3 *adverb*
other than = aparte de
no one other than you knows = nadie sabe aparte de ti

otherwise *conjunction*
= si no
it's not dangerous, otherwise I wouldn't go
= no es peligroso, si no no me iría

ought *verb*
(*when talking about what should be done*)
we ought to fix the radiator = deberíamos
arreglar el radiador
you ought not to say things like that = no
deberías decir semejantes cosas
(*when saying that something is likely to
happen*)
they ought to arrive tomorrow = deberían
llegar mañana
(*when implying that something did not
happen*)
someone ought to have gone with them =
alguien debería haberlos acompañado

our *adjective*   ·
= nuestro/nuestra (+ *singular*),
nuestros/nuestra (+ *plural*)

> **!** For our *used with parts of the body,*
> ▶ **p. 235**

ours *pronoun*
(*singular*) = nuestro/nuestra
(*plural*) = nuestros/nuestras
ours is blue = el nuestro/la nuestra es azul
a friend of ours = un amigo nuestro

ourselves *pronoun*
(*when translated by a reflexive verb in
Spanish*)
we didn't hurt ourselves = no nos hicimos
daño, no nos lastimamos (*Lat Am*)
we bought ourselves a new car = nos
compramos un coche nuevo
(*when used for emphasis*)
we organized everything ourselves = lo
organizamos todo nosotros
mismos/nosotras mismas
we like to be by ourselves = nos gusta
estar solos/solas

out *adverb*

> **!** Out *is often used in combinations with
> verbs, for example,* blow out, come out,
> find out, give out. *To find the correct
> translations for this type of verb, look up
> the separate dictionary entries for* blow,
> come, find, give *etc*

(*outside*) = fuera, afuera (*Lat Am*)

> **!** Note that it is not always necessary to
> translate out in this sense

they're out there = están fuera, están
afuera
she's out in the garden = está en el jardín
to go out = salir
I'm looking for the way out = estoy
buscando la salida

(*absent*)
he's out, so you'll have to come back later
= no está, así que tendrás que volver más
tarde
someone called while you were out =
alguien llamó cuando no estabas
(*available to the public*)
the book will be out in November = el libro
saldrá en noviembre
(*not lighted, not on*) = apagado/apagada

out of
(*from*)
to walk out of the building = salir del
edificio
to take a pencil out of the drawer = sacar
un lápiz del cajón
(*away from*)
it's good to get out of the city = es bueno
salir de la ciudad

outdoor *adjective*
(*if it's a pool*) = descubierto/descubierta, al
aire libre
(*taking place outside*)
outdoor games = juegos al aire libre

outdoors *adverb*
= al aire libre

outfit *noun*
an outfit = un conjunto

outlaw *noun*
an outlaw = un forajido/una forajida

outlook *noun*
(*an attitude*)
an outlook = una actitud
(*for the future*)
the outlook = las perspectivas (*feminine
plural*)
the outlook for the future is excellent = las
perspectivas para el futuro son excelentes

outside
1 *noun*
the outside = el exterior
2 *preposition*
(*in front of*)
I'll see you outside the theater = te veo
fuera del teatro, te veo afuera del teatro
(*Lat Am*)
(*beyond*)
outside the city = fuera de la ciudad
3 *adverb* = fuera, afuera (*Lat Am*)
4 *adjective* = exterior

oval *adjective*
= ovalado/ovalada, oval

oven *noun*
an oven = un horno

over

> **!** Over *is often used in combinations with
> verbs, for example,* get over, hand over,
> move over, roll over. *To find the correct
> translations for this type of verb, look up
> the separate dictionary entries for* get,
> hand, move, roll *etc*

1 *preposition*
  to wear a sweater over a shirt = usar un
    suéter encima de una camisa
  (*across*)
  the bridge over the river = el puente sobre
    el río
  it's over there = está allí
  come over here = ven aquí
  (*above*) = encima de
  the office is over a bookshop = la oficina
    está encima de una librería
  young people over 18 = los jóvenes
    mayores de 18 años
  (*during*)
  we saw them over the weekend = lo vimos
    durante el fin de semana
  we'll be in Italy over the summer =
    pasaremos el verano en Italia
  (*using*)
  over the phone = por teléfono
  (*everywhere*)
  I've looked all over the house for my keys
    = he buscado mis llaves por toda la casa
2 *adverb*
  (*finished*)
  the term is over = el trimestre ha
    terminado
  is the movie over? = ¿terminó la película?
  (*to one's home*)
  to ask someone over = invitar a alguien (a
    casa)
  (*when something is repeated*)
  to start all over again = volver a empezar
  I've told him over and over again = se lo he
    dicho una y otra vez

overcast *adjective*
  an overcast sky = un cielo cubierto

overcoat *noun*
  an overcoat = un abrigo, un sobretodo
    (*R Pl*)

overdose *noun*
  an overdose = una sobredosis

overdraft *noun*
  an overdraft = un sobregiro, un descubierto

overlook *verb*
  my room overlooks the sea = mi cuarto da
    al mar

overtake *verb* (*British English*)
  (*of a car*)
  = adelantar, rebasar (*Mex*)

overthrow *verb*
  = derrocar

overweight *adjective*
  (*if it's a person*) = demasiado gordo/gorda
  (*if it's baggage*)
  your case is overweight = su maleta pesa
    más de la cuenta, su maleta tiene
    sobrepeso (*Lat Am*)

owe *verb*
  = deber
  to owe money to someone = deberle
    dinero a alguien

owl *noun*
  an owl = un búho, un tecolote (*Mex*)

own
1 *adjective* = propio/propia
  she has her own house = tiene su propia
    casa
2 *pronoun*

> **!** Note that, when describing objects,
> people etc, the translations given for the
> pronouns mine, yours, his, hers or theirs
> work for my own, your own, his own etc.
> To work out which translation to use, find
> out whether the object, person etc which
> is being described is masculine,
> feminine or plural

  I didn't use his pencil, I have my own = no
    usé su lápiz, tengo el mío
  **they lent us their chairs because our own
    are broken** = nos prestaron sus sillas
    porque las nuestras están rotas
  they have a house of their own = tienen su
    propia casa
  on one's own = solo/sola
  she lives on her own now = ahora vive sola
3 *verb* = tener
  she owns two houses = tiene dos casa
  he owns a shop = es dueño de una tienda
  who owns that dog? = ¿de quién es ese
    perro?
  own up = confesarse culpable

owner *noun*
  an owner = un dueño/una dueña

oxygen *noun*
  oxygen = oxígeno (*masculine*)

oyster *noun*
  an oyster = una ostra, un ostión (*Mex*)

ozone layer *noun*
  the ozone layer = la capa de ozono

Pp

Pacific *noun*
  the Pacific = el Pacífico

pack
1 *verb* = hacer la(s) maleta(s), empacar (*Lat
    Am*)

2 *noun*
  a pack = un paquete
  a pack of cigarettes = un paquete de cigarrillos, una cajetilla de cigarrillos
  a pack of cards (*British English*) = una baraja, un mazo de cartas (*SC*)
pack up
  to pack up one's belongings = recoger sus bártulos

package *noun*
  a package = un paquete

packed *adjective*
  = lleno/llena

packet *noun*
  a packet = un paquete

page *noun*
  a page = una página

pain *noun*
  pain = dolor (*masculine*)
  I have a pain in my back = me duele la espalda
  to be in pain = tener dolores

painful *adjective*
  = doloroso/dolorosa

paint
1 *noun*
  paint = pintura (*feminine*)
2 *verb* = pintar

paintbrush *noun*
  a paintbrush (*for art*) = un pincel
  (*for decorating*) = una brocha

painter *noun*
  a painter = un pintor/una pintora

painting *noun*
  (*a picture*)
  a painting = un cuadro
  (*the activity*)
  painting = pintura (*feminine*)

pair *noun*
  (*of objects*)
  a pair = un par
  (*of people, animals*)
  a pair = una pareja

pajamas *noun* (*US English*)
  pajamas = un pijama, un/una piyama (*Lat Am*)

Pakistan *noun* ▶ p. 187
  Pakistan = Paquistán (*masculine*)

palace *noun*
  a palace = un palacio

pale *adjective*
  = pálido/pálida
  to go pale, to turn pale = palidecer

pancake *noun*
  a pancake = un crep, un panqueque (*Lat Am*), una crepa (*Mex*)

panic *verb*
  = dejarse llevar por el pánico

panties *noun* (*US English*)
  panties = calzones (*masculine plural*) (*S Am*), pantaletas (*feminine plural*) (*Mex*), bragas (*feminine plural*) (*Spa*)

pantihose *noun* (*US English*)
▶ pantyhose

pants *noun*
  (*US English—trousers*)
  pants = pantalones (*masculine plural*)
  (*British English—underwear*)
  pants (*men's*) = calzoncillos (*masculine plural*)
  (*women's*) ▶ panties

pantyhose *noun*
  pantyhose = panty (*masculine*), medias (*feminine plural*) (*Spa*), pantimedias (*feminine plural*) (*Mex*), medias bombacha (*feminine plural*) (*R Pl*)

paper *noun*
  (*for writing or drawing on*)
  paper = papel (*masculine*)
  a piece of paper = un papel
  (*a newspaper*)
  a paper = un periódico, un diario

parade
1 *noun*
  a parade = un desfile
2 *verb*
  to parade through the streets = desfilar por las calles

parcel *noun* (*British English*)
  a parcel = un paquete

parents *noun*
  parents = padres (*masculine plural*)

park
1 *noun*
  (*in a town*)
  a park = un parque
  (*US English—a stadium*)
  a park = un estadio
2 *verb* = estacionar, aparcar (*Spa*)
  to park a car = estacionar un coche, aparcar un coche (*Spa*)

parking lot *noun* (*US English*)
  a parking lot = un estacionamiento, un aparcamiento (*Spa*)

parking meter *noun*
  a parking meter = un parquímetro

parliament *noun*
  a parliament = un parlamento

parrot *noun*
a parrot = un loro, un papagayo

part *noun*
a part = una parte
a part [of the book | the movie | the time ...] = una parte [del libro | de la película | del tiempo ...]
(*a piece for a machine, a car*)
a part = una pieza
(*a section*)
a part (*in a program*) = una parte
(*in a series*) = un capítulo
(*a role*)
a part = un papel
to play the part of Tommy = hacer el papel de Tommy
to take part in a demonstration = participar en una manifestación

participate *verb*
= participar, tomar parte
to participate in something = participar en algo, tomar parte en algo

particular
1 *adjective*
(*specific*)
we don't sell that particular model = no vendemos ese modelo en particular
in this particular case = en este caso particular
2 *noun*
in particular = en particular

partner *noun*
(*in a relationship*)
a partner = un compañero/una compañera
(*in dancing, sport*)
a partner = una pareja

part-time *adverb*
= a tiempo parcial

party *noun*
(*a social event*)
a party = una fiesta
(*a political organization*)
a party = un partido

pass *verb*
(*to go past*) = pasar
a lot of cars passed = pasaron muchos coches
to pass the school = pasar (por) delante de la escuela
to pass a car = adelantar un coche, rebasar un carro (*Mex*)
to pass someone in the street = cruzarse con alguien en la calle
(*to give*) = pasar
pass me the salt, please = pásame la sal, por favor
(*in football, rugby etc*) = pasar

(*to spend*) = pasar
to pass the time [reading | painting | listening to the radio ...] = pasar el tiempo [leyendo | pintando | escuchando el radio ...]
(*to succeed in an exam*) = aprobar
to pass an exam = aprobar un examen
pass on = pasar
to pass on a message to someone = pasarle un mensaje a alguien

passage *noun*
a passage (*indoors*) = un pasillo
(*outdoors*) = un pasaje

passenger *noun*
a passenger = un pasajero/una pasajera

passport *noun*
a passport = pasaporte

past
1 *noun*
the past = el pasado
2 *adjective*
(*last*) = último/última (**!** *before the noun*)
the past few days have been very difficult = los últimos días han sido muy difíciles
3 *preposition* ▶ **p. 319**
(*British English—when talking about time*)
it's twenty past four = son las cuatro y veinte
it's past eleven = son las once pasadas
(*by*)
I went past your house = pasé por delante de tu casa
she walked straight past me = pasó de largo por mi lado
(*beyond*)
it's just past the traffic lights = queda un poco más allá del semáforo
4 *adverb*
to go past, to walk past = pasar

pastry *noun*
pastry = masa (*feminine*)

patch *noun*
(*on a garment*)
a patch = un parche
(*on a tire*)
a patch = un parche
(*an area*)
a patch of ground = un área (*feminine*) de terreno

path *noun*
a path = un camino, un sendero

patient
1 *noun*
a patient = un/una paciente
2 *adjective* = paciente

pattern *noun*
(*a design*)
a pattern = un diseño
(*when making garments*)
a pattern = un patrón, un molde (*SC*)

P

pavement noun (British English)
a pavement = una acera, una banqueta (Mex), una vereda (SC)

paw noun
a paw = una pata

pay
1 verb
to pay = pagar
to pay for the shopping = pagar las compras
he paid for my meal = me pagó la comida (when talking about wages)
I'm paid $5 an hour = me pagan 5 dólares la hora
(to give)
to pay someone a visit = hacerle una visita a alguien
to pay someone a compliment = hacerle un cumplido a alguien
2 noun
pay = sueldo (masculine)

pay back
to pay someone back = devolverle el dinero a alguien

PE noun
PE = educación física (feminine)

pea noun
a pea = una arveja, un guisante (Spa), un chícharo (Mex)

peace noun
peace = paz (feminine)

peach noun
a peach = un durazno, un melocotón (Spa)

peacock noun
a peacock = un pavo real

peanut noun
a peanut = un maní, un cacahuate (Mex), un cacahuete (Spa)

pear noun
a pear = una pera

pearl noun
a pearl = una perla

pebble noun
a pebble = un guijarro, una piedrecita, una piedrita (Lat Am)

pedestrian noun
a pedestrian = un peatón/una peatona

pedestrian crossing noun
a pedestrian crossing = un paso de peatones

peel verb
= pelar

pen noun
a pen = una pluma

penalty noun
a penalty (in US football) = un castigo
(in soccer) = un penalty, un penal (Lat Am)
(in rugby) = un penalty

pencil noun
a pencil = un lápiz

pencil case noun
a pencil case = un estuche para lápices, una cartuchera (R Pl), un plumier (Spa)

pencil sharpener noun
a pencil sharpener = un sacapuntas

pen pal noun
a pen pal = un amigo/una amiga por correspondencia

penknife noun
a penknife = una navaja, un cortaplumas

pensioner noun
a pensioner = un jubilado/una jubilada

people noun
people (in general) = gente (feminine)
(if counting) = personas (feminine plural)
we met very nice people = conocimos a gente muy simpática
there were three people waiting = había tres personas esperando

pepper noun
(the spice)
pepper = pimienta (feminine)
(the vegetable)
a pepper = un pimiento, un pimentón (S Am), un ají (R Pl)

per preposition
per person = por persona

per cent, percent
1 noun
per cent = porcentaje (masculine)
2 adverb = por ciento

percentage noun
a percentage = un porcentaje

perfect adjective
= perfecto/perfecta
it's the perfect place for a picnic = es el lugar ideal para un picnic

perform verb
(to do)
to perform a task = ejecutar una tarea
(to act) = actuar
(to play) = tocar

perfume noun
perfume = perfume (masculine)

perhaps adverb
= quizás, tal vez, a lo mejor
perhaps he'll arrive later = quizás llegue más tarde, tal vez llegue más tarde, a lo mejor llega más tarde

! *Note the use of the subjunctive after* quizás *and* tal vez

period *noun*
(*in time*)
a period = un período
(*in history*)
a period = una época
(*in a woman's cycle*)
a period = una regla, un período
to have one's period = estar con la regla, estar con el período
(*a school lesson*)
a period = una clase
(*in punctuation—US English*)
a period = un punto

permanent *adjective*
= permanente

permission *noun*
permission = permiso (*masculine*)

person *noun*
a person = una persona

personal *adjective*
= personal

personality *noun*
a personality = una personalidad

persuade *verb*
= persuadir
to persuade someone to give up smoking = persuadir a alguien para que deje de fumar

! *Note the use of the subjunctive after* persuadir a alguien para que

pessimistic *adjective*
= pesimista

pet *noun*
a pet = un animal doméstico

petrol *noun* (*British English*)
petrol = gasolina (*feminine*), nafta (*feminine*) (*R Pl*)

petrol station *noun* (*British English*)
a petrol station = una gasolinera, una estación de nafta (*R Pl*)

pharmacist *noun*
a pharmacist = un farmaceútico/una farmaceútica

pharmacy *noun*
a pharmacy = una farmacia

phone
1 *noun*
a phone = un teléfono
he's on the phone = está hablando por teléfono
2 *verb* = llamar (por teléfono)
to phone for a taxi = llamar para pedir un taxi

phone book *noun*
a phone book = una guía telefónica, un directorio (*Lat Am*)

phone booth, phone box (*British English*) *noun*
a phone booth = una cabina telefónica

phone call *noun*
a phone call = una llamada (telefónica)

phonecard *noun*
a phonecard = una tarjeta telefónica

phone number *noun*
a phone number = un número de teléfono

photo *noun*
a photo = una foto
to take a photo = sacar una foto

photocopier *noun*
a photocopier = una fotocopiadora

photocopy
1 *noun*
a photocopy = una fotocopia
2 *verb* = fotocopiar

photograph *noun*
a photograph = una fotografía

photographer *noun*
a photographer = un fotógrafo/una fotógrafa

physical *adjective*
= físico/física

physics *noun*
physics = física (*feminine*)

piano *noun*
a piano = un piano

pick *verb*
(*to choose*) = elegir, escoger
(*to collect*)
to pick strawberries = recoger fresas
to pick flowers = recoger flores, cortar flores (*SC*)
pick up
(*to lift*)
to pick up the clothes from the floor = recoger la ropa del suelo, alzar la ropa del suelo (*Lat Am*)
to pick up a baby = levantar a un bebé, alzar a un bebé (*Lat Am*)
to pick up the phone = agarrar el teléfono, coger el teléfono (*Spa*)
(*to collect*) = recoger

picnic *noun*
a picnic = un picnic

picture *noun*
a picture (*painted*) = un cuadro
(*drawn*) = un dibujo
(*a photograph*)
a picture = una foto

P

(*a movie*)
a picture = una película

piece *noun*
(*a bit*)
a piece = un pedazo, un trozo
a piece of cheese = un pedazo de queso, un trozo de queso
a piece of string = un cordel
(*a part of a machine*)
a piece = una pieza
to take a machine to pieces = desarmar una máquina
(*a broken part*)
a piece = un pedazo, un trozo
to fall to pieces = hacerse pedazos
(*a coin*)
a 50-pence piece = una moneda de 50 peniques
(*other uses*)
a piece of furniture = un mueble
a piece of advice = un consejo

pierce *verb*
she's had her ears pierced = se ha hecho agujeros en las orejas

pig *noun*
a pig = un cerdo, un chancho (*Lat Am*)

pigeon *noun*
a pigeon = una paloma

pile
a pile = un montón, una pila

pill *noun*
(*a tablet*)
a pill = una pastilla, una píldora
(*a method of contraception*)
the pill = la píldora

pillow *noun*
a pillow = una almohada

pilot *noun*
a pilot = un/una piloto

pimple *noun*
a pimple = un grano, una espinilla (*Lat Am*)

pin *noun*
a pin = un alfiler

pinch *verb*
= pellizcar
he pinched my arm = me pellizcó el brazo
my shoes are pinching = mis zapatos me aprietan

pineapple *noun*
a pineapple = una piña, un ananá (*R Pl*)

pine tree *noun*
a pine tree = un pino

pink *adjective* ▶ **p. 183**
= rosa (**!** *never changes*), rosado/rosada

pint *noun*
(*the quantity*)
a pint = una pinta

> **!** *Note that a* pint *= 0.57 l in Britain and 0.47 l in the US*

a pint of milk = una pinta de leche

pipe *noun*
(*for gas, water*)
a pipe = una cañería, un caño
(*for smoking*)
a pipe = una pipa

pirate *noun*
a pirate = un pirata

Pisces *noun*
(*the sign*)
Pisces = Piscis
I'm Pisces = soy Piscis, soy de Piscis
(*a person*)
a Pisces = un/una piscis

pitch *noun* (*British English*)
a pitch = un campo, una cancha (*Lat Am*)
a football pitch = un campo de fútbol, una cancha de fútbol

pity
1 *noun*
(*when showing regret*)
it's a pity you can't come = es una lástima que no puedas venir

> **!** *Note the use of the subjunctive after* es una lástima que

what a pity! = ¡qué lástima!
2 *verb*
to pity someone = tenerle lástima a alguien

place
1 *noun*
a place = un lugar, un sitio
it's the best place to buy fruit = es el mejor lugar para comprar frutas
they come from all over the place = vienen de todas partes
(*a home*)
at Alison's place = en casa de Alison, donde Alison (*Lat Am*), en lo de Alison (*R Pl*)
I'd like a place of my own = quisiera tener mi propia casa
(*in a line or queue, in a car park*)
a place = un lugar
(*on a team, in a firm*)
a place = un puesto
(*in a contest*)
a place = un puesto, un lugar
to take first place = obtener el primer puesto, obtener el primer lugar
2 *verb*
(*to position carefully*) = colocar

(*in a race*)
this victory places her among the top three
= este triunfo la sitúa entre las tres
primeras

plain *adjective*
(*simple*) = sencillo/sencilla
(*not good-looking*) = feucho/feucha✱

plait *noun*
a plait = una trenza

plan
1 *noun*
(*an arrangement*)
a plan = un plan
(*a map*)
a plan = un plano
2 *verb*
(*to prepare, to organize*)
to plan [a trip | a timetable | a meeting ...] =
planear [un viaje | un horario | una reunión ...]
(*to intend*)
I'm planning to go to Scotland = pienso ir a
Escocia

plane *noun*
a plane = un avión

planet *noun*
a planet = un planeta

plant
1 *noun*
a plant = una planta
2 *verb* = plantar

plaster *noun*
(*a powder, a mixture*)
plaster = yeso (*masculine*)
his leg is in plaster = tiene la pierna
enyesada, tiene la pierna escayolada
(*Spa*)
(*on walls*)
plaster = revoque (*masculine*)
(*British English—for a cut, a wound*)
a plaster = una curita   , una tirita   (*Spa*)

plastic
1 *noun*
plastic = plástico (*masculine*)
2 *adjective* = de plástico

plate *noun*
a plate = un plato

platform *noun*
a platform = un andén

play
1 *verb*
(*to have fun*) = jugar
to play with friends = jugar con amigos
to play cards = jugar a las cartas
(*when talking about sports*) = jugar
to play [football | cricket | tennis ...] = jugar
[fútbol | cricket | tenis ...], jugar [al fútbol | al
cricket | al tenis ...] (*R Pl, Spa*)
France is playing (against) Ireland =
Francia juega contra Irlanda

(*if it's music*) = tocar
to play [the flute | the piano | the drums ...] =
tocar [la flauta | el piano | la batería ...]
(*to put on*) = poner
to play [a video | a CD | a record ...] = poner
[un video | un CD | un disco ...]
(*when talking about theater, cinema*)
to play Hamlet = hacer el papel de Hamlet
2 *noun*
a play = una obra de teatro

player *noun*
a player = un jugador/una jugadora
a tennis player = un jugador/una jugadora
de tenis

playground *noun*
(*British English—of a school*)
a playground = un patio de recreo

please *adverb*
= por favor

pleased *adjective*
(*satisfied*) = satisfecho/satisfecha
I'm very pleased with myself = estoy muy
satisfecha conmigo misma
(*happy*) = contento/contenta
he's very pleased with the results = está
muy contento con los resultados
pleased to meet you = mucho gusto en
conocerlo/conocerla

plenty *pronoun*
to have [plenty of time | plenty of money | plenty
of friends ...] = tener [mucho tiempo | mucho
dinero | muchos amigos ...]

plot *noun*
(*a plan*)
a plot = un complot
(*the story in a movie, novel, play*)
a plot = un argumento

plug *noun*
(*on an appliance*)
a plug = un enchufe
(*in a sink or bath*)
a plug = un tapón
plug in = enchufar
to plug in the radio = enchufar la radio

plum *noun*
a plum = una ciruela

plumber *noun*
a plumber = un plomero/una plomera (*Lat
Am*), un fontanero/una fontanera (*Spa*)

plus *preposition*
= más
three plus three is six (3 + 3 = 6) = tres
más tres son seis (3 + 3 = 6)

pocket *noun*
a pocket = un bolsillo, una bolsa (*Mex*)

pocket money *noun* (*British English*)
pocket money = dinero de bolsillo
(*masculine*), mesada (*feminine*) (*Lat Am*)

poem *noun*
a poem = un poema

poet *noun*
a poet = un/una poeta

point
1 *noun*
(*a statement in a discussion*)
a point = una observación
(*the most important idea*)
to get to the point = ir al grano
the point is that … = la cuestión es que …
that's not the point = no se trata de eso
(*the use*)
there's no point in [arguing | shouting |
  rushing …] = no sirve de nada [discutir |
  gritar | darse prisa …]
(*talking about time*)
to be on the point of [moving | leaving | selling
  the house …] = estar a punto de [mudarse |
  irse | vender la casa …]
(*the sharp end*)
the point = la punta
(*in a contest, a game*)
a point = un punto
2 *verb*
(*to indicate*)
to point one's finger at someone = apuntar
  a alguien con el dedo
to point at [a house | a street | a store …] =
  señalar [una casa | una calle | una tienda …]
point out = señalar

poison
1 *noun*
poison = veneno (*masculine*)
2 *verb* = envenenar

Poland *noun* ▶ p. 187
Poland = Polonia (*feminine*)

pole *noun*
a pole = un poste

police *noun*
the police = la policía

policeman *noun*
a policeman = un policía

police station *noun*
a police station = una comisaría

policewoman *noun*
a policewoman = una policía

polish *verb*
to polish one's shoes = limpiarse los
  zapatos, lustrarse los zapatos (*Lat Am*),
  embolarse los zapatos (*Mex*)
to polish the car = darle brillo al coche,
  sacarle brillo al coche

polite *adjective*
= bien educado/educada, cortés

political *adjective*
= político/política

politician *noun*
a politician = un político/una política

politics *noun*
politics = política (*feminine*)

pollution *noun*
pollution = contaminación (*feminine*)

pond *noun*
a pond (*man-made*) = un estanque
(*natural*) = una laguna

pony *noun*
a pony = un poni

ponytail *noun*
a ponytail = una cola de caballo

pool *noun*
(*a swimming pool*)
a pool = una piscina, una alberca (*Mex*),
  una pileta (*R Pl*)
(*on the ground, the floor*)
a pool of water = un charco de agua
(*the game*)
pool = billar americano (*masculine*), pool
  (*masculine*)

poor *adjective*
(*having little money*) = pobre
(*not satisfactory*)
a poor result = un resultado pobre
(*expressing sympathy*) = pobre (**!** *before
  the noun*)
the poor boy is exhausted = el pobre chico
  está agotado

popular *adjective*
a popular hobby = un pasatiempo popular
she's very popular = tiene muchos amigos

population *noun*
the population = la población

pork *noun*
pork = carne de cerdo (*feminine*), carne de
  puerco (*feminine*) (*Mex*)

port *noun*
a port = un puerto

porter *noun*
a porter (*at a station, airport*) = un
  maletero, un mozo
(*at a hotel, apartment block*) = un portero

Portugal *noun* ▶ p. 187
Portugal = Portugal (*masculine*)

Portuguese ▶ p. 187, p. 245
1 *adjective* = portugués/portuguesa
2 *noun*
(*the people*)
the Portuguese = los portugueses
(*the language*)
Portuguese = portugués (*masculine*)

positive *adjective*
= positivo/positiva

C Am Central America   Lat Am Latin America   Mex Mexico

possibility *noun*
  a possibility = una posibilidad

possible *adjective*
  = posible
  I did as much as possible = hice todo lo
    posible
  they came as quickly as possible =
    vinieron lo más rápido posible

post[1] (*British English*)
1 *noun*
  (*the system*)
  the post = el correo
  (*letters, packages*)
  the post = la correspondencia, el correo
2 *verb* = echar al correo
  I posted the letter yesterday = eché la carta
    al correo ayer

post[2] *noun*
  (*a pole*)
  a post = un poste

postbox *noun* (*British English*)
  a postbox = un buzón

postcard *noun*
  a postcard = una tarjeta postal, una postal

postcode *noun* (*British English*)
  a postcode = un código postal

poster *noun*
  a poster = un cartel, un póster

postman *noun* (*British English*)
  a postman = un cartero

post office *noun*
  a post office = un correo, una oficina de
    correos

postpone *verb*
  = aplazar, posponer, postergar (*Lat Am*)

pot *noun*
  (*for jam, honey*)
  a pot = un tarro
  (*for cooking*)
  a pot = una olla
  (*for a plant*)
  a pot = una maceta, un tiesto

potato *noun*
  a potato = una papa (*Lat Am*), una patata
    (*Spa*)

pottery *noun*
  pottery = cerámica (*feminine*)

pound *noun*
  (*the currency*)
  a pound = una libra
  (*the measurement*)
  a pound = una libra

  ┃ **!** *Note that a* **pound** = 453.6 g

pour *verb*
  (*from a container*) = echar
  (*to serve*) = servir
  she poured me a vodka = me sirvió un
    vodka
  (*to rain*)
  it's pouring (**with rain**) = está lloviendo a
    cántaros

powder *noun*
  powder = polvo (*masculine*)

power *noun*
  (*control, influence*)
  power = poder (*masculine*)
  to be in power = estar en el poder
  (*electricity*)
  power = electricidad (*feminine*)

power cut *noun*
  a power cut = un apagón

practical *adjective*
  = práctico/práctica

practice (*US English*), **practise** (*British
English*) *verb*
  = practicar

practice *noun*
  practice (*training, rehearsal*) = práctica
    (*feminine*)

praise *verb*
  = elogiar

pram *noun* (*British English*)
  a pram = un cochecito

prawn *noun*
  a prawn = un camarón (*Lat Am*), una
    gamba (*Spa*)

prayer *noun*
  a prayer = una oración

precious *adjective*
  = precioso/preciosa

precise *adjective*
  (*accurate*) = exacto/exacta
  (*specific*) = preciso/precisa
  at that precise moment = en ese preciso
    momento

prefer *verb*
  = preferir
  to prefer chocolate to vanilla = preferir el
    chocolate a la vainilla
  I'd prefer to phone = preferiría llamar por
    teléfono

pregnant *adjective*
  = embarazada

prejudice *noun*
  a prejudice = un prejuicio

P

prepare *verb*
  (*to get something or someone ready*) =
    preparar
  (*to get ready*) = prepararse

prepared *adjective*
  (*willing*)
  to be prepared to wait = estar
    dispuesto/dispuesta a esperar
  (*ready*) = listo/lista

prescription *noun*
  a prescription = una receta

present
1 *noun*
  (*a gift*)
  a present = un regalo
  to give someone a present = hacerle un
    regalo a alguien
  (*now*)
  the present = el presente
  at present = en este momento
2 *verb*
  (*to give*)
  to present a prize to someone = entregarle
    un premio a alguien
  (*on radio or TV*)
  to present a program = presentar un
    programa

president *noun*
  a president = un presidente/una presidenta

press
1 *verb* = apretar
2 *noun*
  the press = la prensa

pressure *noun*
  pressure = presión (*feminine*)
  to put pressure on someone = presionar a
    alguien

pretend *verb*
  = fingir

pretty
1 *adjective* = bonito/bonita, lindo/linda (*Lat
    Am*)
2 *adverb* = bastante

prevent *verb*
  to prevent a war = evitar una guerra
  to prevent someone from working =
    impedir que alguien trabaje

  ! Note the use of the subjunctive after
  impedir que

previous *adjective*
  = anterior
  the previous day = el día anterior

price *noun*
  a price = un precio

pride *noun*
  pride = orgullo (*masculine*)

priest *noun*
  a priest = un cura

primary school *noun*
  a primary school = una escuela primaria

prime minister *noun*
  the prime minister = el primer mininstro/la
    primera ministra

prince *noun*
  a prince = un príncipe

princess *noun*
  a princess = una princesa

principal *noun*
  a principal (*in a school*) = un director/una
    directora
  (*at a university*) = un rector/una rectora

print
1 *verb* = imprimir
2 *noun*
  (*of a photo*)
  a print = una copia
  (*in a book*)
  the print = la letra

prison *noun*
  a prison = una cárcel

prisoner *noun*
  (*a captive*)
  a prisoner = un prisionero/una prisionera
  (*in jail*)
  a prisoner = un preso/una presa

private
1 *adjective* = privado/privada
2 *noun*
  in private
  he told me in private = me lo dijo en
    confianza
  the meeting was held in private = la
    reunión se celebró en privado

prize *noun*
  a prize = un premio

probably *adverb*
  = probablemente

problem *noun*
  a problem = un problema

process *noun*
  a process = un proceso
  to be in the process of writing a letter =
    estar escribiendo una carta

produce
1 *verb*
  (*to make*) = producir
  the company produces soft drinks = la
    compañía produce refrescos
  (*to create*)
  to produce a movie = producir una
    película
  to produce a play = poner en escena una
    obra de teatro

2 *noun*
produce = productos (*masculine plural*)

product *noun*
a product = un producto

production *noun*
production = producción (*feminine*)

profession *noun*
a profession = una profesión

professional *adjective*
= profesional

professor *noun*
a professor = un catedrático/una catedrática

profit *noun*
profit = ganancias (*feminine plural*), beneficios (*masculine plural*)
to make a profit = obtener ganancias, obtener beneficios

program[1] *noun*
(*for a computer*)
a program = un programa

program[2] (*US English*), **programme** (*British English*)
1 *noun*
(*on radio, TV*)
a program = un programa
(*for a play, a concert*)
a program = un programa
2 *verb* = programar

progress *noun*
progress = progreso (*masculine*)
to make progress (*of a student*) = hacer progresos
(*of a patient*) = mejorar

project *noun*
a project = un proyecto
(*at school*) = un trabajo

promise
1 *verb* = prometer
to promise to do something = prometer hacer algo
2 *noun*
a promise = una promesa

pronounce *verb*
= pronunciar

proof *noun*
proof = prueba (*feminine*), pruebas (*feminine plural*)
I have proof that they lied = tengo pruebas de que mintieron

properly *adverb*
= bien

property *noun*
property = propiedad (*feminine*)

protect *verb*
= proteger

protest *verb*
= protestar

proud *adjective*
= orgulloso/orgullosa
she's proud of her work = está orgullosa de su trabajo

prove *verb*
= probar

provide *verb*
to provide a meal = proporcionar una comida
to provide work for people = dar trabajo a la gente

provided *conjunction*
I'll lend you my jacket provided you wash the dishes = te presto mi chaqueta con tal de que friegues los platos

> **!** *Note the use of the subjunctive after* con tal de que

psychiatrist *noun*
a psychiatrist = un/una psiquiatra

pub *noun* (*British English*)
a pub = un bar

public
1 *noun*
the public = el público
in public = en público
2 *adjective*
= público/pública

public holiday *noun*
a public holiday = un día festivo, un día feriado (*Lat Am*)

public transportation (*US English*), **public transport** (*British English*) *noun*
public transportation = transporte público (*masculine*)

pudding *noun* (*British English*)
a pudding = un postre

puddle *noun*
a puddle = un charco

pull *verb*
to pull = tirar de, jalar (*Lat Am*)
to pull (on) a rope = tirar de una cuerda, jalar una cuerda
he pulled my hair = me tiró del pelo, me jaló el pelo
(*to take out*)
to pull a handkerchief out of one's pocket = sacar un pañuelo del bolsillo
to pull someone out of the river = sacar a alguien del río
pull down
(*to knock down*) = echar abajo, tumbar (*Mex*)

P

(*to lower*) = bajar
pull out
  to pull a tooth out = sacar una muela
pull up
  (*to stop*) = parar
  (*to remove*)
  to pull up a plant = arrancar una planta

pullover *noun*
  a pullover = un suéter, un pulóver, un
  jersey (*Spa*)

pump *noun*
  a pump = una bomba
  a gasoline pump (*US English*), a petrol
  pump (*British English*) = un surtidor

pumpkin *noun*
  a pumpkin = una calabaza, un zapallo (*SC*)

punch *verb*
  = darle un puñetazo a
  she punched him in the face = le dio un
  puñetazo en la cara

punctual *adjective*
  = puntual

puncture *noun*
  a puncture = un pinchazo, una
  ponchadura (*Mex*)

punish *verb*
  = castigar

pupil *noun*
  a pupil = un alumno/una alumna

puppet *noun*
  a puppet = una marioneta, un títere

puppy *noun*
  a puppy = un cachorro/una cachorra

pure *adjective*
  = puro/pura

purple *adjective* ▶ p. 183
  = morado/morada

purpose *noun*
  a purpose = un propósito
  on purpose = a propósito

purse *noun*
  (*for money*)
  a purse = un monedero
  (*US English—a handbag*)
  a purse = una cartera, un bolso (*Spa*), una
  bolsa (*Mex*)

push *verb*
  = empujar
  to push someone out of the way = apartar
  a alguien de un empujón

pushchair *noun* (*British English*)
  a pushchair = una sillita de paseo, una
  carreola (*Mex*), un changuito   (*R Pl*)

put *verb*
  = poner
  to put the cards on the table = poner las
  cartas sobre la mesa
  don't put sugar in my coffee = no me
  pongas azúcar en el café
  to put someone in prison = meter a alguien
  en la cárcel
put away = guardar
put back
  (*to return to its place*) = volver a poner
  to put a book back on the shelf = volver a
  poner un libro en el estante
  (*to change the time*)
  to put the clocks back = atrasar los relojes
put down
  (*on a surface*) = dejar
  put your cases down here = deja tus
  maletas aquí
  to put the phone down = colgar el teléfono
put forward
  to put forward the clocks = adelantar los
  relojes
put off
  (*to delay*) = aplazar, posponer, postergar
    (*Lat Am*)
  (*British English—to switch off*) = apagar
put on
  (*when dressing*) = ponerse
  (*to switch on*)
  to put the lights on = encender las luces,
  prender las luces (*Lat Am*)
  to put a CD on = poner un CD
put out
  (*to extinguish*) = apagar
put up
  to put one's hand up (*in class*) = levantar
  la mano
  to put a sign up = poner un letrero
  to put up a tent = armar una carpa
  (*to increase*) = aumentar
  to put the rent up = aumentar el alquiler
  (*to give someone a place to stay*) = alojar
put up with = aguantar, soportar

puzzle *noun*
  a puzzle = un rompecabezas (**!** *never
  changes*)

pyjamas *noun* (*British English*)
  pyjamas = un pijama, un/una piyama (*Lat
  Am*)

qualified *adjective*
(*having certificates*) = titulado/titulada

quality *noun*
quality = calidad (*feminine*)

quantity *noun*
a quantity = una cantidad

quarrel
1 *noun*
a quarrel = una pelea
2 *verb* = pelearse

quarter
1 *noun*
a quarter = un cuarto
a quarter of an hour = un cuarto de hora
2 *pronoun*
(*when talking about quantities, numbers*)
a quarter of the population = la cuarta
parte de la población
(*when talking about time*) ▶ **p. 319**
an hour and a quarter = una hora y cuarto
it's a quarter after five, it's (a) quarter past
five (*British English*) = son las cinco y
cuarto

quay *noun*
a quay = un muelle

queen *noun*
a queen = una reina

question
1 *noun*
(*a request for information*)
a question = una pregunta
(*a problem, matter*)
a question = una cuestión, un asunto
2 *verb*
(*to interrogate*) = interrogar
(*to doubt*) = cuestionar

queue (*British English*)
1 *noun*
a queue = una cola
2 *verb* = hacer cola

quick *adjective*
= rápido/rápida

quickly *adverb*
(*speedily*) = rápido, rápidamente
(*promptly*) = pronto

quiet
1 *adjective*
(*silent*)
a quiet street = una calle silenciosa
be quiet! = ¡cállense!
quiet please! = ¡silencio, por favor!

(*not talkative*) = callado/callada
(*calm*) = tranquilo/tranquila
2 *noun*
quiet = silencio (*masculine*)

quietly *adverb*
to speak quietly = hablar en voz baja
to play quietly = jugar sin hacer ruido

quit *verb*
(*to resign*) = dejar el trabajo
(*US English—to give up*)
to quit smoking = dejar de fumar

quite *adverb*
(*fairly*) = bastante
(*completely*)
you're quite right = tienes toda la razón
are you quite sure? = ¿estás
completamente seguro?
(*exactly*)
is it true?—not quite = ¿es cierto?—no
exactamente

quiz *noun*
a quiz = un concurso

rabbit *noun*
a rabbit = un conejo

race
1 *noun*
(*a contest*)
a race = una carrera
(*in horse-racing*)
the races = las carreras de caballos
(*an ethnic group*)
a race = una raza
2 *verb*
to race (**against**) **someone** = echarle una
carrera a alguien, jugarle una carrera a
alguien (*R Pl*)
(*to take part in a contest*) = correr

racecourse *noun*
a racecourse = un hipódromo

racetrack *noun*
a racetrack (*for runners*) = una pista de
atletismo
(*for cars*) = un circuito

racket, **racquet** *noun*
a racket = una raqueta

radiator noun
a radiator = un radiador

radio noun
a radio = un radio (Lat Am), una radio (SC, Spa)
I heard it on the radio = lo oí por el radio, lo oí por la radio

radish noun
a radish = un rábano

rage noun
rage = furia (feminine)

raid
1 verb
to raid a bank = asaltar un banco
the police raided the building = la policía hizo una redada en el edificio
2 noun
a raid (by thieves) = un atraco
(by the police) = una redada

rail noun
(for holding on to)
a rail = un pasamanos
(for trains)
the rails = los rieles, los railes (Spa)

railroad (US English), **railway** (British English) noun
(a track)
a railroad, a railway = una vía férrea
(the rail system)
the railroad, the railway = el ferrocarril

railroad station (US English),
railway station (British English) noun
a railroad station, a railway station = una estación de ferrocarril

rain
1 noun
rain = lluvia (feminine)
2 verb = llover

rainbow noun
a rainbow = un arco íris

raincoat noun
a raincoat = un impermeable

raise verb
(to lift) = levantar
to raise one's hand = levantar la mano
(to increase) = aumentar
to raise prices = aumentar los precios
to raise one's voice = levantar la voz
to raise a subject = sacar un tema
to raise a child = criar a un niño

raisin noun
a raisin = una pasa

range noun
(a selection)
a range (of goods) = una línea
(of prices) = una gama

(of mountains)
a range = una cadena

rare adjective
(not common) = poco común

raspberry noun
a raspberry = una frambuesa

rat noun
a rat = una rata

rather adverb
(when saying what one would prefer)
I'd rather leave = preferiría irme
I'd rather you came with me = preferiría que vinieras conmigo

! Note that the subjunctive is used after preferiría que
(quite) = bastante

raw adjective
= crudo/cruda

razor noun
a razor (cutthroat) = una navaja de afeitar, una navaja de rasurar (Mex)
(with safety blade) = una cuchilla de afeitar, un rastrillo (Mex)
(electric) = una máquina de afeitar, una máquina de rasurar (Mex), una maquinilla de afeitar (Spa)

razor blade noun
a razor blade = una cuchilla

reach verb
(to arrive at) = llegar a
to reach a decision = llegar a una decisión
(to be delivered to)
the letter never reached her = la carta nunca le llegó
(by stretching)
I can't reach the shelf = no alcanzo al estante
(to contact by phone) = contactar
you can reach me at this number = me puedes contactar llamando a este número

react verb
= reaccionar

read verb
= leer
read out = leer en voz alta
read through
(once) = leer
(a second time) = releer

ready adjective
(prepared) = listo/lista
are you ready to leave? = ¿estás listo para irte?
to get ready = prepararse, aprontarse (SC)

real adjective
(not imagined) = real, verdadero/verdadera
in real life = en la vida real

(*actual*) = verdadero/verdadera
is that his real name? = ¿es ése su nombre verdadero?
(*not artificial*) = auténtico/auténtica
are they real diamonds? = ¿son diamantes auténticos?
(*when used for emphasis*) = verdadero/verdadera
it was a real disaster = fue un verdadero desastre

realize *verb*
= darse cuenta
I didn't realize (that) he was your boss = no me di cuenta de que era tu jefe

really *adverb*
it's really easy = es facilísimo
I don't really know them = en realidad no los conozco
realiy? = ¿de verdad?

rear
1 *noun*
the rear (*of a building*) = la parte trasera
(*of a train*) = los últimos vagones
2 *adjective*
the rear door = la puerta trasera
the rear wheel = la rueda de atrás
3 *verb*
(*if it's a child*) = criar

reason *noun*
a reason = una razón
there's no reason to get annoyed = no hay por qué enojarse

reassure *verb*
= tranquilizar

receipt *noun*
a receipt = un recibo

receive *verb*
= recibir

recent *adjective*
= reciente

recently *adverb*
= recientemente

reception *noun*
(*in a hotel, hospital, company*)
a reception = una recepción
(*a formal event*)
a reception = una recepción

receptionist *noun*
a receptionist = un/una recepcionista

recipe *noun*
a recipe = una receta

recognize *verb*
= reconocer

recommend *verb*
= recomendar

record
1 *noun*
(*of events*)
a record = un registro
to keep a record of something = llevar un registro de algo
(*information*)
the records (*historical, public*) = los archivos
(*personal, medical*) = el historial
(*for playing music*)
a record = un disco
(*in sport*)
a record = un récord
2 *verb*
(*on a tape*) grabar

recorder *noun*
a recorder = una flauta dulce

record player *noun*
a record player = un tocadiscos

recover *verb*
(*recuperate*) = recuperarse

rectangle *noun*
a rectangle = un rectángulo

recycle *verb*
= reciclar

red *adjective* ▶ p. 183
= rojo/roja, colorado/colorada (*SC*)
to go red = ponerse rojo/roja, ponerse colorado/colorada
to have red hair = ser pelirrojo/pelirroja
red wine = vino tinto

reduce *verb*
to reduce prices = rebajar los precios
to reduce the number of employees = reducir el número de empleados
to reduce speed = disminuir la velocidad

reduction *noun*
(*in numbers, size, spending*)
a reduction = una reducción
(*in prices*)
a reduction = una rebaja

redundant *adjective* (*British English*)
he was made redundant = lo despidieron por reducción del personal, quedó cesante

refer *verb*
(*to mention*)
to refer to a subject = hacer referencia a un tema
(*to allude*)
to refer to someone = referirse a alguien

referee *noun*
(*in a match, a dispute*)
a referee = un árbitro/una árbitra

R

reflect *verb*
= reflejar
the lights were reflected in the water = las luces se reflejaban en el agua

reflection *noun*
a reflection = un reflejo

refreshing *adjective*
= refrescante

refrigerator *noun*
a refrigerator = un refrigerador (*Lat Am*), un frigorífico (*Spa*), una heladera (*R Pl*)

refugee *noun*
a refugee = un refugiado/una refugiada

refuse¹ *verb*
= rechazar
he refused my offer = rechazó mi oferta
to refuse to listen = negarse a escuchar

refuse² *noun*
refuse = residuos (*masculine plural*), desperdicios (*masculine plural*)

regards *noun*
give her my regards = dale saludos de mi parte, dale recuerdos de mi parte

region *noun*
a region = una región

registration number *noun* (*British English*)
a registration number = un número de matrícula, una matrícula

regret
1 *verb* = arrepentirse de
he regrets that he can't come = lamenta no poder venir
2 *noun*
to have regrets = arrepentirse

regular *adjective*
to take regular exercise = hacer ejercicio con regularidad
a regular customer = un cliente habitual

regularly *adverb*
= con regularidad

rehearsal *noun*
a rehearsal = un ensayo

rehearse *verb*
= ensayar

reject *verb*
= rechazar

relationship *noun*
a relationship = una relación
to have a good relationship with one's parents = llevarse bien con sus padres

relative *noun*
a relative = un/una pariente, un familiar

relax *verb*
= relajarse

relaxed *adjective*
= relajado/relajada

release *verb*
(*to free*) = liberar

reliable *adjective*
a reliable person = una persona de confianza
a reliable car = un coche fiable

relieved *adjective*
= aliviado/aliviada

religion *noun*
religion = religión (*feminine*)

religious *adjective*
= religioso/religiosa

rely *verb*
to rely on
(*to depend on*) = depender de
(*to count on*) = contar con
can we rely on you? = ¿podemos contar contigo?

remain *verb*
(*to continue to be*) = seguir
we have remained friends = seguimos siendo amigos
(*to continue to stay*) = quedarse
they will remain here until December = se quedarán aquí hasta diciembre
(*to be left*) = quedar
is this all that remains? = ¿es esto todo lo que queda?

remark *noun*
a remark = un comentario

remarkable *adjective*
= extraordinario/extrordinaria

remember *verb*
= acordarse de, recordar
I remember writing down the address = recuerdo haber anotado la dirección
to remember to water the plants = acordarse de regar las plantas

remind *verb*
to remind someone to buy milk = recordarle a alguien que compre leche

> **!** *Note the use of the subjunctive after* recordarle a alguien que

she reminds me of my sister = me recuerda a mi hermana

remove *verb*
= quitar

rent
1 *verb* = alquilar, rentar (*Mex*)
2 *noun*
the rent = el alquiler, la renta (*Méx*)

rent out = alquilar, rentar (*Mex*)

rental *noun*
 car rental (*US English*) = alquiler de coches (*masculine*)

repair *verb*
 = arreglar
 to have a bicycle repaired = hacer arreglar una bicicleta

repeat *verb*
 = repetir

replace *verb*
 to replace a teacher = sustituir a un profesor
 they replaced the fence with a wall = cambiaron la cerca por una pared

reply
 1 *verb* = responder, contestar
 2 *noun*
 a reply = una respuesta, una contestación

report
 1 *verb*
 (*to tell about*)
 to report an accident = informar de un accidente
 (*in the news*)
 to report on an event = informar sobre un acontecimiento
 (*to complain about*)
 to report someone (to someone) = denunciar a alguien (a alguien)
 2 *noun*
 (*in the news*)
 a report = una noticia
 (*in a newspaper*)
 a report = un reportaje
 (*an official document*)
 a report = un informe, un reporte (*Mex*)
 (*British English—at school*)
 a (school) report = un boletín de notas, un reporte (*Mex*)

report card *noun* (*US English*)
 a report card = un boletín de notas, un reporte (*Mex*)

reporter *noun*
 a reporter = un/una periodista, un reportero/una reportera

represent *verb*
 = representar

republic *noun*
 a republic = una república

request *noun*
 a request = una petición

rescue *verb*
 (*from danger*) = rescatar, salvar

resemble *verb*
 = parecerse a
 they resemble each other = se parecen

resent *verb*
 to resent someone = guardarle rencor a alguien
 he resented her success = le molestaba que ella tuviera éxito

> **!** *Note that the subjunctive is used after* le molestaba que

reservation *noun*
 a reservation = una reserva, una reservación (*Lat Am*)

reserve *verb*
 = reservar

resign *verb*
 = renunciar, dimitir

resist *verb*
 = resistir

respect
 1 *verb* = respetar
 2 *noun*
 respect = respeto (*masculine*)

responsibility *noun*
 responsibility = responsabilidad (*feminine*)

responsible *adjective*
 = responsable
 to be responsible for the damage = ser responsable del daño
 to be responsible for organizing a trip = ser responsable de organizar un viaje

rest
 1 *noun*
 (*what is left*)
 the rest of them have gone = los demás se han ido
 the rest of the class = el resto de la clase
 we spent the rest of the day in the garden = pasamos el resto del día en el jardín
 (*a break*)
 a rest = un descanso
 to have a rest = descansar
 2 *verb* = descansar

restaurant *noun*
 a restaurant = un restaurante, un restaurant

result *noun*
 a result = un resultado
 as a result of the accident = como consecuencia del accidente

resumé *noun* (*American English*)
 a resumé = un currículum, un historial personal

retire *verb*
 = jubilarse

return *verb*
 (*to go back, to come back*) = volver, regresar
 (*to give back*) = devolver, regresar (*Mex*)

R

return ticket noun (British English)
   a return ticket (on a ship or plane) = un
      pasaje de ida y vuelta (Lat Am), un billete
      de ida y vuelta (Spa), un boleto (de viaje)
      redondo (Mex)
   (on a bus or train) = un boleto de ida y
      vuelta (Lat Am), un billete de ida y vuelta
      (Spa), un boleto (de viaje) redondo (Mex)

reveal verb
   to reveal a secret = revelar un secreto

revenge noun
   revenge = venganza (feminine)

revolution noun
   a revolution = una revolución

reward
1 noun
   a reward = una recompensa
2 verb = recompensar

rhythm noun
   rhythm = ritmo (masculine)

rib noun
   a rib = una costilla

ribbon noun
   a ribbon = una cinta

rice noun
   rice = arroz (masculine)

rich adjective
   = rico/rica

rid: to get rid of verb
   to get rid of something = deshacerse de
      algo
   to get rid of someone = quitarse a alguien
      de encima

ride
1 verb
   to go riding = ir a montar a caballo, ir a
      andar a caballo (Lat Am)
   to ride a horse = montar a un caballo
   to ride a bike = montar en bici, andar en
      bici (Lat Am)
2 noun
   to go for a ride = ir a dar una vuelta, ir a
      dar un paseo

ridiculous adjective
   = ridículo/ridícula

right
1 adjective
   (not left) = derecho/derecha
   (honest, good)
   it's not right to steal = no está bien robar
   (correct) = correcto/correcta
   the right answer = la respuesta correcta
   you're right = tienes razón
   that's right = eso es
2 noun

   (the direction)
   right = derecha (feminine)
   the first street on the right = la primera
      calle a la derecha
   (what one is entitled to do)
   a right = un derecho
   human rights = derechos humanos
      (masculine plural)
3 adverb
   = a la derecha, hacia la derecha

right-handed adjective
   = diestro/diestra

ring
1 verb
   (British English—to phone) = llamar
   to ring for a taxi = llamar un taxi
   (to make a sound) = sonar
   the bell rang = sonó el timbre
   the phone's ringing = está sonando el
      teléfono
   to ring the bell = tocar el timbre
2 noun
   (a piece of jewelry)
   a ring = un anillo
   a wedding ring = una alianza, un anillo de
      boda
   (a circle)
   a ring = un círculo
ring back (British English) = volver a llamar
ring up (British English) = llamar

rinse verb
   = enjuagar

ripe adjective
   = maduro/madura

rise verb
   (of smoke, water, a plane) = subir
   (of prices) = aumentar
   (of the sun or the moon) = salir

risk
1 noun
   a risk = un riesgo
2 verb
   to risk one's life = arriesgar la vida
   to risk losing one's job = correr el riesgo de
      perder el trabajo

rival noun
   a rival = un/una rival

river noun
   a river = un río

road noun
   a road (in town) = una calle
   (out of town) = una carretera
   the road to London = la carretera que va a
      Londres

road sign noun
   a road sign = una señal vial, una señal de
      tránsito (Lat Am)

---

roar *verb*
(*of a lion, an engine*) = rugir
(*of a person*)
to roar with laughter = reírse a carcajadas

roast
1 *verb* = asar
2 *adjective* = asado/asada

roast beef *noun*
roast beef = rosbif (*masculine*)

rob *verb*
to rob someone = robarle a alguien
they robbed her of her savings = le
robaron los ahorros
to rob a bank = asaltar un banco

robbery *noun*
a robbery = un robo

robot *noun*
a robot = un robot

rock *noun*
(*the material*)
rock = roca (*feminine*)
(*a large stone*)
a rock = una roca
(*music*)
rock = rock (*masculine*)

rocket *noun*
a rocket = un cohete

role *noun*
a role = un papel

roll
1 *verb* = rodar
the ball rolled under the car = la pelota
rodó debajo del coche
2 *noun*
(*of paper, cloth, plastic*)
a roll = un rollo
a roll of film = un rollo, un carrete, una
película
(*bread*)
a roll = un pancito, un panecillo (*Spa*), un
bolillo (*Mex*)
roll about, roll around = rodar
roll out = estirar
roll over = darse la vuelta, voltearse
(*Lat Am*), darse vuelta (*SC*)
roll up
to roll up one's sleeves = arremangarse

roller skate *noun*
a roller skate = un patín

roller skating *noun*
roller skating = patinaje (*masculine*)
to go roller skating = ir a patinar

Romania *noun* ▶ p. 187
Romania = Rumania (*feminine*)

romantic *adjective*
= romántico/romántica

roof *noun*
a roof = un tejado, un techo (*Lat Am*)

room *noun*
a room = una habitación, una pieza (*Lat
Am*)
(*for sleeping*) = un dormitorio, un cuarto,
una pieza (*Lat Am*), una recámara (*Lat
Am*)
(*for teaching, holding meetings*) = una sala
(*space*)
room = espacio (*masculine*), lugar
(*masculine*)

root *noun*
a root = una raíz

rope *noun*
a rope = una cuerda

rose *noun*
a rose = una rosa

rot *verb*
= pudrir

rotten *adjective*
= podrido/podrida

rough *adjective*
(*not smooth*) = áspero/áspera
to have rough skin = tener la piel áspera
(*not gentle*) = brusco/brusca
don't be so rough! = ¡no seas tan brusco!
(*not exact, precise*)
a rough figure = una cifra aproximada
a rough sea = un mar agitado

round

! Often **round** *occurs in combinations
with verbs. For more information, see the
note at* **around**

1 *preposition* (*British English*) = alrededor de
to be sitting round a table = estar
sentados/sentadas alrededor de una mesa
2 *adverb* (*British English*)
to go round and round = dar vueltas y
vueltas,
to invite someone round = invitar a
alguien a casa
3 *noun*
a round (*in a quiz*) = una vuelta
(*in boxing*) = un round, un asalto
4 *adjective* = redondo/redonda

roundabout *noun* (*British English*)
(*for traffic*)
a roundabout = una rotonda, una glorieta
(*Mex, Spa*)
(*in an amusement park*)
a roundabout = unos caballitos, un
carrusel (*Lat Am*), una calesita (*R Pl*), un
tiovivo (*Spa*)

round-trip ticket *noun* (*US English*)
a round-trip ticket (*on a ship or plane*) = un
pasaje de ida y vuelta (*Lat Am*), un billete
de ida y vuelta (*Spa*), un boleto (de viaje)
redondo (*Mex*)

(*on a bus or train*) = un boleto de ida y
vuelta (*Lat Am*), un billete de ida y vuelta
(*Spa*), un boleto (de viaje) redondo (*Mex*)

route *noun*
a route = un camino, una ruta
(*of a bus*) = un recorrido

routine *noun*
a routine = una rutina

row¹
1 *noun*
a row (*of trees, houses*) = una hilera
(*of people, seats*) = una fila
to be absent five days in a row = faltar tres
días seguidos
2 *verb* = remar

row² *noun*
(*quarrel*)
a row = una pelea
to have a row with someone = tener una
pelea con alguien

royal *adjective*
= real

rub *verb*
to rub one's eyes = restregarse los ojos
rub out = borrar

rubber *noun*
(*the material*)
rubber = goma (*feminine*), caucho
(*masculine*), hule (*masculine*) (*Mex*)
(*British English—an eraser*)
a rubber = una goma de borrar

rubber band *noun*
a rubber band = una goma (elástica), una
liga (*Mex*), una gomita (*R Pl*)

rubbish *noun* (*British English*)
(*garbage*)
rubbish = basura (*feminine*)
(*poor quality goods*)
rubbish = porquerías (*feminine plural*)
(*nonsense*)
rubbish = tonterías (*feminine plural*)

rubbish bin *noun* (*British English*)
a rubbish bin = un cubo de la basura, un
tacho de la basura (*SC*), un bote de la
basura (*Mex*)

rucksack *noun*
a rucksack = una mochila

rude *adjective*
(*not polite*) = maleducado/maleducada,
grosero/grosera
to be rude to someone = ser
grosero/grosera con alguien
(*vulgar*) = grosero/grosera
a rude word = una grosería, una palabrota

rug *noun*
a rug = una alfombra, un tapete (*Mex*)

rugby *noun* ▶ p. 306
rugby = rugby (*masculine*)

ruin
1 *verb*
(*to destroy*) = destruir
(*to spoil*) = arruinar, estropear
to ruin a meal = arruinar una comida,
estropear una comida
(*to damage*) = estropear
you'll ruin your shoes = vas a estropear tus
zapatos
2 *noun*
a ruin = una ruina

rule
1 *noun*
a rule = una regla, una norma
it's against the rules to smoke in the
building = está prohibido fumar en el
edificio
2 *verb* = gobernar

ruler *noun*
(*for measuring*)
a ruler = una regla
(*a leader*)
a ruler = un/una gobernante

rumor (*US English*), **rumour** (*British
English*) *noun*
a rumor = un rumor

run
1 *verb*
to run = correr
to run after someone = correr tras alguien
to run a race = correr una carrera
(*to manage*) = dirigir
to run a company = dirigir una compañía
(*to work, to operate*)
it runs on batteries = funciona con pilas
the system runs well = el sistema funciona
bien
(*to organize*) = organizar
to run a competition = organizar un
concurso
(*when talking about transport*)
the trains don't run after 12 o'clock = no
hay trenes después de las doce
(*to flow*) = correr
to leave the water running = dejar el agua
corriendo
(*to fill with water*)
to run a bath = preparar un baño
(*of colors*) = desteñirse
(*of makeup*) = correrse
2 *noun*
to go for a run = salir a correr
run around, **run about** (*British English*)
= corretear
run away = huir
run off = salir corriendo

C Am Central America   Lat Am Latin America   Mex Mexico

run out
   we ran out of milk = quedamos sin leche
run over = atropellar

rush
1 *verb*
   (*to hurry*)
   to rush out of the house = salir de la casa
     corriendo
   she was rushed to hospital = fue
     trasladada rápidamente al hospital
2 *noun*
   to be in a rush = tener mucha prisa, estar
     muy apurado/apurada (*Lat Am*)

rush hour *noun*
   the rush hour = la hora pico (*Lat Am*), la
     hora punta (*Spa*)

Russia *noun* ▶ **p. 187**
   Russia = Rusia (*feminine*)

Russian ▶ **p. 187, p. 245**
1 *adjective* = ruso/rusa
2 *noun*
   (*a person*)
   a Russian = un ruso/una rusa
   (*the language*)
   Russian = ruso (*masculine*)

rusty *adjective*
   = oxidado/oxidada

S s

sad *adjective*
   = triste

saddle *noun*
   a saddle (*on a horse*) = una silla de montar,
     una montura
   (*on a bicycle*)= un asiento, un sillín

safe
1 *adjective*
• (*without risk, free from danger*) =
     seguro/segura
   a safe place = un lugar seguro
   it's not safe for children = es peligroso para
     los niños
   to feel safe = sentirse seguro/segura
• (*unharmed*)
   safe and sound = sano y salvo/sana y salva
2 *noun*
   a safe = una caja fuerte

safety *noun*
   safety = seguridad (*feminine*)

Sagittarius *noun*
• (*the sign*)
   Sagittarius = Sagitario
   I'm Sagittarius = soy Sagitario, soy de
     Sagitario
• (*a person*)
   a Sagittarius = un/una sagitario

sail
1 *noun*
   a sail = una vela
   to set sail = zarpar, hacerse a la mar
2 *verb* = ir en barco, navegar
   to go sailing = salir a navegar

sailboat *noun* (*US English*)
   a sailboat = un velero, un barco de vela

sailing boat *noun* (*British English*)
▶ sailboat

sailor *noun*
   a sailor = un marinero

saint *noun*
   a saint = un santo/una santa

salad *noun*
   a salad = una ensalada

salary *noun*
   a salary = un sueldo

sale *noun*
• to put a house up for sale = poner una casa
     en venta, poner una casa a la venta
   to be on sale (*US English*) = estar en
     liquidación
   (*British English*) = estar a la venta
   'for sale' = 'se vende'
• (*with reduced prices*)
   a sale = una liquidación, unas rebajas

salesclerk *noun* (*US English*)
   a salesclerk = un empleado/una empleada
     (*Lat Am*), un dependiente/una
     dependienta (*Spa*), un vendedor/una
     vendedora (*SC*)

salmon *noun*
   salmon = salmón (*masculine*)

salt *noun*
   salt = sal (*feminine*)

same
1 *adjective* = mismo/misma
   she's got the same coat as me = tiene el
     mismo abrigo que yo
   they go to the same school = van a la
     misma escuela
   it's all the same to me = me da igual
   the houses all look the same = las casa son
     todas parecidas
2 *pronoun*
   the same = lo mismo

sand *noun*
   sand = arena (*feminine*)

S

R Pl River Plate area   SC Southern Cone   Spa Spain

sandal *noun*
a sandal = una sandalia

sandwich *noun*
a sandwich = un sándwich

Santa (Claus) *noun*
Santa (Claus) = Papá Noel (*masculine*)

satellite TV *noun*
satellite TV = televisión vía satélite

satisfactory *adjective*
= satisfactorio/satisfactoria

satisfied *adjective*
= satisfecho/satisfecha

Saturday *noun* ▶ p. 192
Saturday = sábado (*masculine*)

sauce *noun*
a sauce = una salsa

saucepan *noun*
a saucepan = una cacerola, un cazo (*Spa*)

saucer *noun*
a saucer = un platillo

sausage *noun*
a sausage = una salchicha

save *verb*
• (*to rescue*) = salvar
  they saved his life = le salvaron la vida
• (*to avoid spending*)
  to save (up) = ahorrar
• (*to avoid wasting*) = ahorrar
  to save [time | money | energy ...] = ahorrar
  [tiempo | dinero | energía ...]
• (*to keep*) = guardar
  he saved me a piece of cake = me guardó
  un pedazo de pastel
• (*to spare*)
  it saved me a lot of work = me ahorró
  mucho trabajo
• (*in computing*) = guardar

savings *noun*
savings = ahorros (*masculine plural*)

saw *noun*
a saw = una sierra

saxophone *noun*
a saxophone = un saxofón, un saxófono

say *verb*
= decir
he said to wait here = dijo que
  esperáramos aquí

> ! *Note the use of the subjunctive after*
> decir que

scandal *noun*
a scandal = un escándalo

scare *verb*
= asustar

scared *adjective*
to be scared = tener miedo
to be scared of someone/something =
  tenerle miedo a alguien/algo

scarf *noun*
a scarf (*long*) = una bufanda
  (*square*) = un pañuelo

scenery *noun*
scenery = paisaje (*masculine*)

school *noun*
• (*in primary, secondary education*)
  a school = una escuela, un colegio
• (*for learning languages, learning to drive*)
  a school = una academia
• (*US English—a university*)
  a school = una universidad

schoolboy *noun*
a schoolboy = un colegial, un escolar

schoolchild *noun*
a schoolchild = un colegial/una colegiala,
  un/una escolar

schoolgirl *noun*
a schoolgirl = una colegiala, una escolar

science *noun*
science = ciencia (*feminine*)
to study science = estudiar ciencias

scientist *noun*
a scientist = un científico/una científica

scissors *noun*
scissors = tijeras (*feminine plural*)
a pair of scissors = unas tijeras

score *verb*
= marcar
to score a goal = marcar un gol

Scorpio *noun*
• (*the sign*)
  Scorpio = Escorpio
  I'm Scorpio = soy Escorpio, soy de Escorpio
• (*a person*)
  a Scorpio = un/una escorpio

Scotch tape *noun* (*US English*)
Scotch tape = cinta Scotch   (*feminine*),
  cinta Durex   (*feminine*) (*Lat Am*), cello
  (*masculine*) (*Spa*)

Scotland *noun* ▶ p. 187
Scotland = Escocia (*feminine*)

Scottish *adjective* ▶ p. 187
= escocés/escocesa

scratch *verb*
• (*when itchy*) = rascarse
  to scratch one's arm = rascarse el brazo
• (*to hurt*) = arañar, rasguñar
• (*to mark, to damage*) = rayar

scream *verb*
= gritar

screen *noun*
  a screen = una pantalla

screw *noun*
  a screw = un tornillo

sea *noun*
  the sea = el mar

seafood *noun*
  seafood = mariscos (*masculine plural*),
  marisco (*masculine*) (*Spa*)

seagull *noun*
  a seagull = una gaviota

seal *noun*
  a seal = una foca

search *verb*
 • to search = buscar
  to search for someone = buscar a alguien
 • (*to examine a place, a person*) = registrar,
  catear (*Mex*)

seasick *adjective*
  to be seasick = estar mareado/mareada

seaside *noun*
  the seaside = la costa, la playa

season *noun*
 • (*autumn, winter, summer or spring*)
  a season = una estación
 • (*for a specific activity*)
  a season = una temporada
  strawberries are in season = es temporada
  de fresas

seat *noun*
 • (*a chair, a bench, on transport*)
  a seat = un asiento
 • (*in a theater, a cinema*)
  a seat = una localidad

seatbelt *noun*
  a seatbelt = un cinturón de seguridad

second
 1 *adjective* = segundo/segunda
 2 *noun* ▶ **p. 192, p. 319**
 • (*in order*)
  the second = el segundo/la segunda
 • (*when talking about time*)
  a second = un segundo
 3 *adverb* = en segundo lugar
  to come second = quedar en segundo
  lugar

secondary school *noun*
  a secondary school = un colegio de
  enseñanza secundaria

second-hand *adjective*
  = de segunda mano (**!** *never changes*)

secret
 1 *adjective* = secreto/secreta
 2 *noun*
 • a secret = un secreto
 • in secret = en secreto

secretary *noun*
  a secretary = un secretario/una secretaria

see *verb*
 • to see = ver
  I can't see them = no los veo
  see you tomorrow! = ¡hasta mañana!
  what time?—let's see = ¿a qué hora?—a ver
 • (*to make sure*)
  to see that the work is finished quickly =
  asegurarse de que el trabajo se termine
  rápido

  | **!** Note the use of the subjunctive after
  | asegurarse de que

 • (*to accompany*)
  I'll see you home = te voy a acompañar a
  casa
see out
  to see someone out = acompañar a
  alguien a la puerta
see to = ocuparse de

seem *verb*
 • (*to appear*)
  she seems happy = parece contenta, se ve
  contenta (*Lat Am*)
  they seem to be looking for someone =
  parece que están buscando a alguien
 • (*when talking about one's impressions*)
  it seems (**that**) there are a lot of problems
  = parece que hay muchos problemas

seldom *adverb*
  = rara vez

self-confident *adjective* = seguro/segura
 de sí mismo/misma

selfish *adjective*
  = egoísta

sell *verb*
  = vender
  stamps sold here = los sellos se venden
  aquí

sellotape *noun* (*British English*)
  Sellotape = cinta Scotch® (*feminine*), cinta
  Durex® (*feminine*) (*Lat Am*), celo
  (*masculine*) (*Spa*)

semidetached *adjective*
  a semidetached house = una casa pareada,
  una casa adosada

send *verb*
  = mandar
  to send a package to someone = mandarle
  un paquete a alguien, enviarle un
  paquete a alguien
  he sent me a letter = me mandó un carta
  to send someone to buy the paper =
  mandar a alguien a comprar el diario
send away
  they sent him away = le dijeron que se
  fuera
send back = devolver

S

send for = mandar a buscar, mandar llamar (*Lat Am*)
they sent for the doctor = mandaron a buscar al médico, mandaron llamar al médico

senior *adjective*
• (*higher in rank*)
those in senior positions = quienes ocupan puestos de responsabilidad
I need to ask advice from a senior colleague = tengo que consultar a un superior
• (*older*)
the senior members of a club = los socios más antiguos de un club

senior high school (*US English*) *noun*
a senior high school = un colegio secundario

sense *noun*
• (**common**) **sense** = sentido común (*masculine*)
• (*allowing one to see, hear, smell etc*)
a sense = un sentido
• (*a meaning*)
a sense = un sentido
it doesn't make sense = no tiene sentido

sensible *adjective*
• (*if it's a person*) = sensato/sensata
• (*if it's a decision*) = prudente
• (*if it's clothes*) = cómodo y práctico/cómoda y práctica

sensitive *adjective*
• (*if it's a person*) = sensible
• (*if it's a situation*) = delicado/delicada

sentence
1 *noun*
• (*in grammar*)
a sentence = una frase
• (*for a crime*)
the maximum sentence = la pena máxima
a life sentence = una condena a cadena perpetua
2 *verb* = sentenciar

separate
1 *adjective* = separado/separada
2 *verb*
• to separate = separar
• (*if it's a couple*) = separarse

separately *adjective*
= por separado

September *noun* ▶ p. 192
September = septiembre (*masculine*), setiembre (*masculine*)

serial *noun*
(*on radio, television*)
a serial = una serie

series *noun*
a series = una serie

serious
• (*causing worry*) = grave
a serious accident = un accidente grave
• (*if it's someone's personality*) = serio/seria

serve *verb*
• (*British English—in a shop*) = atender
are you being served? = ¿lo/la atienden?
• (*at table*) = servir
• (*in sport*) = servir, sacar

service *noun*
• (*which people need or find useful*)
a service = un servicio
• (*in a shop*)
the service = el servicio
• (*a religious ceremony*)
a service = un oficio religioso

service station *noun*
a service station = una estación de servicio

serviette *noun* (*British English*)
a serviette = una servilleta

set
1 *noun*
• (*a collection*)
a set of keys = un juego de llaves
a set of stamps = una serie de sellos
• (*in tennis*)
a set = un set
2 *verb*
• (*to decide on*) = fijar
to set [a date | a time | a price ...] = fijar [una fecha | una hora | un precio ...]
• (*to adjust*) = poner
to set an alarm clock = poner un despertador
to set a video = poner un video
• (*in school*)
to set homework = mandar los deberes, dejar tareas (*Mex*)
to set an exam = poner un examen
• (*to be responsible for*)
to set a record = establecer un récord
to set a good example = dar buen ejemplo
• (*if it's a story, movie*)
the novel is set in Paris = la novela está ambientada en París
• (*of the sun*) = ponerse
set off
• (*to leave*) = salir
• to set off a bomb = hacer explotar una bomba
set up
to set up in business = poner un negocio

settle *verb*
• (*to end*)
to settle an argument = resolver una discusión
• to settle a bill = pagar una cuenta
• (*to make one's home*) = establecerse

seven *number* ▶ **p. 154, p. 319**
  seven = siete (*masculine*) (! *never changes*) *see also* **five**

seventeen *number* ▶ **p. 154, p. 319**
  seventeen = diecisiete (*masculine*) (! *never changes*) *see also* **five**

seventh
1 *adjective* = séptimo/séptima
2 *noun* ▶ **p. 192**
• (*a part*)
  a seventh = una séptima parte

seventy *noun* ▶ **p. 154**
  seventy = setenta (*masculine*) (! *never changes*) *see also* **five**

several *adjective*
  = varios/varias

severe *adjective*
• (*if it's an illness or injury*) = grave
  (*if it's pain*) = fuerte
• (*harsh*) = severo/severa

sew *verb*
  = coser

sewing machine *noun*
  a sewing machine = una máquina de coser

sex *noun*
  sex = sexo (*masculine*)
  to have sex = tener relaciones sexuales

shade *noun*
• (*out of the sun*)
  shade = sombra (*feminine*)
  to sit in the shade = sentarse a la sombra
• (*a color*)
  a shade = un tono
• (*for a lamp*)
  a shade = una pantalla

shadow *noun*
  a shadow = una sombra

shake *verb*
• to shake = sacudir
  to shake a bottle = agitar una botella
  to shake hands with someone = darle la mano a alguien
• to shake one's head = negar con la cabeza
• (*with cold, fear, shock*) = temblar
  he was shaking with fear = temblaba de miedo
• (*during an explosion, earthquake*) = temblar

shall *verb*

> ! *When referring to the future, Spanish uses the future tense of the verb to translate* shall + *verb:* I shall leave = me iré

• (*when talking about the future*)
  I shall see you next Tuesday = te veré el martes que viene

• (*when making suggestions*)
  shall we go to the cinema? = ¿vamos al cine?

shame *noun*
• shame = vergüenza (*feminine*)
• (*when expressing regret*)
  what a shame = ¡qué lástima!

shampoo *noun*
  shampoo = champú (*masculine*)

shape *noun*
• (*a form*)
  a shape = una forma
  in the shape of a cross = en forma de cruz
• (*when talking about health*)
  to be in good shape = estar en forma
  to get into shape = ponerse en forma

share
1 *verb* = compartir
2 *noun*
  a share = una parte
  to pay one's share = pagar su parte
share out = repartir, distribuir

shark *noun*
  a shark = un tiburón

sharp *adjective*
• (*able to cut*) = afilado/afilada, filoso/filosa (*Lat Am*)
• (*sudden*) = cerrado/cerrada
  a sharp bend = una curva cerrada
• (*clever*) = despierto/despierta
• (*harsh, aggressive*)
  a sharp comment = un comentario cáustico
  a sharp reply = una respuesta cortante
• (*violent*)
  a sharp pain = un dolor agudo
• (*in taste*) = ácido/ácida

shave *verb*
  = afeitarse, rasurarse (*Mex*)

she *pronoun*
  she = ella
  she went to the theater = fue al teatro
  she did it = ella lo hizo
  he works in London but she doesn't = él trabaja en Londres pero ella no

> ! *Although* ella *is given as the translation of* she, *it is in practice used only for emphasis, or to avoid ambiguity*

sheep *noun*
  a sheep = una oveja

sheet *noun*
• (*for a bed*)
  a sheet = una sábana
• (*of paper*)
  a sheet = una hoja

shelf *noun*
  a shelf (*for books, ornaments*) = un estante

S

(*in an oven*) = una parrilla
a set of shelves = unos estantes, una
estantería

shell *noun*
a shell (*of an egg, a nut*) = una cáscara
(*of a crab, a snail, a tortoise*) = un/una
caparazón
(*of a sea mollusk*) = una concha

shelter
1 *noun*
• (*from rain, danger*)
to take shelter = refugiarse
• (*for homeless people*)
a shelter = un refugio
2 *verb*
• (*to take shelter*) = refugiarse
• (*to help*) = proteger

shine *verb*
• (*to give out light*) = brillar
• **to shine a light on someone** = alumbrar a
alguien con una luz

ship *noun*
a ship = un barco

shirt *noun*
a shirt = una camisa

shiver *verb*
= temblar, tiritar

shock
1 *noun*
• (*an upsetting experience*)
a shock = un shock
to get a shock = llevarse un shock
• (*a scare*)
what a shock you gave me! = iqué susto
me diste!
• (*the medical state*)
to be in shock = estar en estado de shock
• (*from electricity*)
a shock = una descarga
2 *verb*
• (*to upset*) = conmocionar
• (*to cause a scandal*) = escandalizar

shoe *noun*
a shoe = un zapato

shoelace *noun*
a shoelace = un cordón, una agujeta (*Mex*)

shoot *verb*
• (*using a weapon*)
to shoot someone = pegarle un tiro a
alguien
they shot him in the leg = le pegaron un
tiro en la pierna
• (*to move very fast*)
to shoot past = pasar como un bólido

shop
1 *noun*
a shop = una tienda, un negocio (*SC*)

2 *verb*
to go shopping = ir de compras

shop assistant *noun* (*British English*)
a shop assistant = un empleado/una
empleada (*Lat Am*), un dependiente/una
dependienta (*Spa*), un vendedor/una
vendedora (*SC*)

shopkeeper *noun* (*British English*)
a shopkeeper = un/una comerciante

shopping *noun*
shopping = compras (*feminine plural*)
to do the shopping = hacer la compra,
hacer los mandados (*Mex*), hacer las
compras (*SC*)

shopping cart *noun* (*US English*)
a shopping cart = un carrito

shopping mall (*US English*),
shopping centre (*British English*) *noun*
a shopping mall, a shopping centre = un
centro comercial

shopping trolley *noun* (*British English*)
a shopping trolley = un carrito

shop window *noun*
a shop window = un escaparate, una
vidriera (*Lat Am*), un aparador (*Mex*)

shore *noun*
• (*the coast*)
the shore = la costa, la ribera
• (*the edge of the sea*)
the shore = la orilla
• (*dry land*)
to go on shore = bajar a tierra (firme)

short *adjective*
• (*not lasting long*) = corto/corta
a short visit = una visita corta
a short speech = un breve discurso
• (*not long*) = corto/corta
to have short hair = tener el pelo corto
• (*not tall*) = bajo/baja
• (*lacking*)
to be short of money/time = andar
corto/corta de dinero/tiempo
• **in short** = en resumen

short cut *noun*
a short cut = un atajo

shortly *adverb*
• (*soon*) = dentro de poco
• (*not long*)
shortly before we left = poco antes de que
nos fuéramos

shorts *noun*
• (*short trousers*)
shorts = shorts (*masculine plural*)
a pair of shorts = unos shorts
• (*US English—men's underwear*)
shorts = calzoncillos (*masculine plural*)

shortsighted *adjective* (*British English*)
= miope, corto/corta de vista

shot *noun*
- (*from a gun*)
  a shot = un disparo, un tiro
- (*in sports*)
  a shot (*in football*) = un tiro, un disparo
  (*in tennis, golf, cricket*) = un tiro

should *verb*
- (*when talking about what ought to be done*)
  she should learn to drive = debería
  aprender a manejar
  you shouldn't have said that = no deberías
  haber dicho eso
- (*when saying something is likely to
  happen*)
  it shouldn't be too difficult = no debería ser
  demasiado difícil
- (*when implying that something, though
  likely, didn't happen*)
  the letter should have arrived yesterday =
  la carta debería haber llegado ayer

shoulder *noun* ▶ p. 235
  the shoulder = el hombro

shout
1 *verb* = gritar
2 *noun*
  a shout = un grito

shovel *noun*
  a shovel = una pala

show
1 *verb*
- (*to let someone see*) = mostrar, enseñar
  I'll show you how it works = te muestro
  cómo funciona
- (*to go with*)
  I'll show you to your room = le acompaño a
  su cuarto
- (*to be on TV, at the cinema*)
  the movie is showing at the Phoenix =
  están dando la película en el Phoenix,
  ponen la película en el Phoenix (*Spa*)
2 *noun*
- **a show** (*on a stage*) = un espectáculo
  (*on TV, radio*) = un programa
- (*an exhibition*)
  a show = una exposición
  to be on show = estar expuesto/expuesta
show off = lucirse

shower *noun*
- (*for washing*)
  a shower = una ducha, una regadera (*Mex*)
  to take a shower (*US English*), **to have a
  shower** (*British English*) = ducharse
- (*rain*)
  a shower = un chaparrón, un chubasco

shrimp *noun*
  a shrimp = un camarón

shrink *verb*
= encogerse

shut
1 *adjective* = cerrado/cerrada
2 *verb* = cerrar
shut down = cerrar
shut up
  (*to be quiet*) = callarse
  shut up! = ¡cállate!

shy *adjective*
= tímido/tímida

sick *adjective*
- (*ill*) = enfermo/enferma
  to be sick = estar enfermo/enferma
  (*if one vomits*) = vomitar
  to feel sick = tener ganas de vomitar
  to get sick (*US English*) = caer
  enfermo/enferma, enfermarse (*Lat Am*)
- (*fed up*)
  he's sick of work = está harto del trabajo

sickness *noun*
  a sickness = una enfermedad

side *noun*
- **a side** = un lado
  on my right side = a mi derecha
  by the side of the river = a la orilla del río
- (*of a person's body*)
  the side = el costado, el lado
- (*in a conflict, a contest*)
  to take sides = tomar partido
- (*a team*)
  a side = un equipo

sidewalk *noun* (*US English*)
  a sidewalk = una acera, una banqueta
  (*Mex*), una vereda (*SC*)

sigh *verb*
= suspirar

sight *noun*
- **sight** = vista (*feminine*)
  to lose sight of someone = perder a
  alguien de vista
- **to see the sights** = visitar los lugares de
  interés

sightseeing *noun*
  to go sightseeing = visitar los lugares de
  interés

sign
1 *noun*
- (*a mark*)
  a sign = un signo
- (*for traffic*)
  a sign = una señal
- (*a notice*)
  a sign = un letrero
2 *verb* = firmar

signal
1 *noun*
  a signal = una señal

S

2 *verb*
• (*to make signs*) = hacer señas
• (*when driving*) = poner el intermitente

signature *noun*
   a signature = una firma

signpost *noun*
   a signpost = una señal

silence *noun*
   silence = silencio (*masculine*)

silent *adjective*
   a silent night = una noche silenciosa
   he remained silent = se quedó callado

silk *noun*
   silk = seda (*feminine*)

silly *adjective*
   = tonto/tonta

silver
1 *noun*
   silver = plata (*feminine*)
2 *adjective* = de plata

similar *adjective*
   = parecido/parecida

simple *adjective*
   = sencillo/sencilla

since
1 *preposition* = desde
   I haven't seen him since yesterday = no lo
      he visto desde ayer
   she has been living here since 1988 = vive
      aquí desde 1988
   I haven't been feeling well since Monday =
      desde el lunes que no me siento bien
2 *conjunction*
• (*from the time when*) = desde que
   since she left = desde que se fue
   it's ten years since she died = hace diez
      años que se murió
• (*because*)
   since she was ill, she couldn't go = como
      estaba enferma, no pudo ir
3 *adverb* = desde entonces
   I haven't seen them since = no los he visto
      desde entonces

sincere *adjective*
   = sincero/sincera

sing *verb*
   = cantar

singer *noun*
   a singer = un/una cantante

single
1 *adjective*
• (*one*) = solo/sola (**!** *before noun*)
   we visited three towns in a single day =
      visitamos tres ciudades en un solo día
   not a single word = ni una palabra

• (*when used for emphasis*)
   every single day = todos los días sin
      excepción
   there wasn't a single person = no había ni
      una sola persona
• (*without a partner*) = soltero/soltera
2 *noun*
   (*in tennis*)
   singles = individuales (*masculine plural*),
      singles (*masculine plural*) (*Lat Am*)

single bed *noun*
   a single bed = una cama individual, una
      cama de una plaza (*Lat Am*)

single room *noun*
   a single room = una habitación individual

single ticket *noun* (*British English*)
   a single ticket (*on a ship or plane*) = un
      pasaje de ida (*Lat Am*), un billete de ida
      (*Spa*)
   (*on a bus or train*) = un boleto de ida
      (*Lat Am*), un billete de ida (*Spa*)

sink
1 *noun*
   a sink (*in a kitchen*) = un fregadero, un
      lavaplatos (*Mex*), una pileta (*R Pl*)
   (*in a bathroom*) = un lavabo, un lavamanos,
      un lavatorio (*SC*)
2 *verb* = hundirse

sister *noun*
   a sister = una hermana

sister-in-law *noun*
   a sister-in-law = una cuñada

sit *verb*
• (*to take a seat*) = sentarse
   he sat down on the floor = se sentó en el
      suelo
   to be sitting on the floor = estar
      sentado/sentada en el suelo
   sit down = sentarse
   to be sitting down = estar sentado/sentada
   sit up = ponerse derecho/derecha

situated *adjective*
   = situado/situada
   it is situated near the town center = está
      situado cerca del centro de la ciudad, está
      ubicado cerca del centro de la ciudad
      (*Lat Am*)

situation *noun*
   a situation = una situación

six *number* ▶ **p. 154, p. 319**
   six = seis (*masculine*) (**!** *never changes*)
      see also **five**

sixteen *number* ▶ **p. 154, p. 319**
   sixteen = dieciseis (*masculine*) (**!** *never
      changes*) *see also* **five**

sixth
1 *adjective* = sexto/sexta

C Am Central America   **Lat Am** Latin America   **Mex** Mexico

2 *noun* ▶ **p. 192**
(*a part*)
a sixth = una sexta parte

sixty *noun* ▶ **p. 154**
sixty = sesenta (*masculine*) (**!** *never
changes*) *see also* **five**

size *noun*
• (*when talking about clothes*)
a size (*of garment*) = una talla, un talle
(*R Pl*)
(*of shoe*) = un número
what size do you take? (*in clothes*) = ¿qué
talla tiene?, ¿qué talle tiene?
(*in shoes*) = ¿qué número calza?
• (*when talking about how big something is*)
the size (*of a building, a wardrobe*) = el
tamaño
(*of a problem, an operation*) = la magnitud

skating *noun*
skating = patinaje (*masculine*)

skating rink *noun*
a skating rink = una pista de patinaje

skeleton *noun*
a skeleton = un esqueleto

sketch *noun*
• (*a drawing*)
a sketch = un bosquejo
(*rougher*) = un esbozo
• (*a funny scene*)
a sketch = un sketch

ski
1 *noun*
a ski = un esquí
2 *verb*
to go skiing = ir a esquiar

skiing *noun*
skiing = esquí (*masculine*)

skillful (*US English*), **skilful** (*British
English*) *adjective*
= habilidoso/habilidosa
to be skillful at sewing = ser
habilidoso/habilidosa para la costura

skill *noun*
• (*the quality*)
skill = habilidad (*feminine*)
• (*a particular ability*)
typing is a very useful skill = saber escribir
a máquina es muy útil

skin *noun*
skin = piel (*feminine*)
to have dry skin = tener la piel seca

skip *verb*
• (*to give little jumps*) = brincar
• (*with a rope*)
to skip rope (*US English*), **to skip** (*British
English*) = saltar a la cuerda, saltar a la
comba (*Spa*)

• (*to miss*) = saltarse
to skip a page = saltarse una página

skirt *noun*
a skirt = una falda, una pollera (*SC*)

sky *noun*
the sky = el cielo

skyscraper *noun*
a skyscraper = un rascacielos

slap *verb*
to slap someone (*on the arm, the leg*) =
darle una palmada a alguien
(*in the face*) = darle una bofetada a alguien,
darle una cachetada a alguien (*Lat Am*)

sled (*US English*), **sledge** (*British
English*)
a sled = un trineo

sleep
1 *noun*
sleep = sueño
to go to sleep = dormirse
2 *verb*
• (*to be asleep*) = dormir
• (*to have sex*)
to sleep with someone = acostarse con
alguien

sleeping bag *noun*
a sleeping bag = un saco de dormir, una
bolsa de dormir (*R Pl*)

sleepy *adjective*
to be sleepy, to feel sleepy = tener sueño

sleet *noun*
sleet = aguanieve (*feminine*)

sleeve *noun*
a sleeve = una manga

slice
1 *noun*
a slice (*of bread*) = una rebanada
(*of meat*) = una tajada
(*of cheese*) = un trozo, un pedazo
(*of lemon, cucumber*) = una rodaja
2 *verb*
to slice bread = cortar pan en rebanadas

slide
1 *verb*
• (*intentionally*) = deslizarse
• (*accidentally*) = resbalarse
the plates slid off the table = los platos se
resbalaron y cayeron al suelo
2 *noun*
• (*an image*)
a slide = una diapositiva
• (*in a playground*)
a slide = un tobogán, una resbaladilla
(*Mex*)

slightly *adverb*
= ligeramente

S

slim *adjective*
= delgado/delgada

slip *verb*
• (*to slide, to fall*) = resbalarse
  it just slipped out of my hands = se me resbaló de las manos
• (*to go quietly*)
  he slipped out of the room = salió de la habitación sin que lo vieran

slipper *noun*
  a slipper = una zapatilla, una pantufla (*Lat Am*)

slippery *adjective*
= resbaladizo/resbaladiza

slow *adjective*
• (*not fast*) = lento/lenta
• (*if it's a clock or watch*) = atrasado/atrasada
  the clock is 20 minutes slow = el reloj está 20 minutos atrasado

slowly *adverb*
= lentamente, despacio

sly *adjective*
= astuto/astuta

small *adjective*
= pequeño/pequeña, chico/chica (*Lat Am*)

smart *adjective*
• (*clever*) = listo/lista
• (*British English—elegant*) = elegante

smash *verb*
  (*to break*) = romper
smash up = destrozar

smell
1 *noun*
• (*an odor*)
  a smell = un olor
• **the sense of smell** = el olfato
2 *verb* = oler
  to smell of soap = oler a jabón

smelly *adjective*
  to be smelly = oler mal

smile
1 *verb* = sonreír
  to smile at someone = sonreírle a alguien
2 *noun*
  a smile = una sonrisa

smoke
1 *noun*
  smoke = humo (*masculine*)
2 *verb* = fumar

smooth *adjective*
  (*if it's cloth, stone*) = liso/lisa
  (*if it's skin*) = suave

snack *noun*
  a snack = un tentempié

snail *noun*
  a snail = un caracol

snake *noun*
  a snake = una serpiente

sneaker *noun* (*US English*)
  a sneaker = una zapatilla de deporte, un tenis

sneeze *verb*
= estornudar

snore *verb*
= roncar

snow
1 *noun*
  snow = nieve (*feminine*)
2 *verb* = nevar

snowball *noun*
  a snowball = una bola de nieve

snowflake *noun*
  a snowflake = un copo de nieve

snowman *noun*
  a snowman = un muñeco de nieve

so
1 *adverb*
  he's so happy = está tan contento
  they speak so fast = hablan tan rápido
  he worries so much = se preocupa tanto
  she has so many clothes = tiene tanta ropa
  I've so much work to do = tengo tanto trabajo que hacer
• (*also*)
  I'm fifteen and so is he = tengo quince años y él también
  if you go, so will I = si vas tú, voy yo también
• (*other uses*)
  I think so = creo que sí
  I'm afraid so = me temo que sí
  I told you so = te lo dije
  so what? = ¿y qué?
  and so on = etcétera
2 *conjunction*
• **so that** = para que
  be quiet so that I can work = cállate para que yo pueda trabajar

  ! Note the use of the subjunctive after para que

• **so as** = para
  we left early so as not to miss the train = salimos temprano para no perder el tren
• (*therefore*) = así que, de manera que
  he wasn't at home so I called again = no estaba en casa, así que volví a llamar más tarde, no estaba en casa, de manera que volví a llamar más tarde

soap *noun*
  soap = jabón (*masculine*)

soccer noun ▶ **p. 306**
   soccer = fútbol (*masculine*), futbol
   (*masculine*) (*Mex*)

social adjective
   = social

sock noun
   a sock = un calcetín

sofa noun
   a sofa = un sofá

soft adjective
• (*not hard or tough*) = blando/blanda
• (*not harsh or severe*) = suave
   a soft light = una luz suave
• (*not strict*) = blando/blanda, indulgente

soft drink noun
   a soft drink = un refresco

software noun
   software = software (*masculine*)

soil noun
   soil = tierra (*feminine*)

soldier noun
   a soldier = un/una soldado

sole noun
• (*of the foot*)
   the sole = la planta
• (*of a shoe*)
   a sole = una suela

solicitor noun (*British English*)
   a solicitor = un abogado/una abogada

solution noun
   a solution = una solución

solve verb
   to solve a problem = solucionar un
      problema
   to solve a mystery = resolver un misterio

some
1 adjective
• (*an amount or a number of*)
   I have to buy some bread = tengo que
      comprar pan
   have some water = toma un poco de agua
   we bought some beer = compramos
      cerveza
   she ate some strawberries = comió unas
      fresas
• (*certain*) = algunos/algunas
   some people don't like traveling by plane
      = a algunas personas no les gusta viajar
      en avión
2 pronoun
• (*an amount or number*)
   **I need some nails—I know where you can
      find some** = necesito unos clavos—yo sé
      dónde puedes encontrar algunos
   have some more = toma más

• (*certain people or things*) =
      algunos/algunas
   some are very expensive = algunos son
      muy caros
   some (of them) are Italian = algunos son
      italianos

somebody, **someone** pronoun
   = alguien

something pronoun
   = algo

sometimes adverb
   = a veces

somewhere adverb
   to go somewhere else = ir a otro lado
   I saw your pen somewhere = vi tu pluma
      en algún lado

son noun
   a son = un hijo

song noun
   a song = una canción

son-in-law noun
   a son-in-law = un yerno

soon adverb
   = pronto
   see you soon! = ¡hasta pronto!
   the sooner the better = cuanto antes mejor
   as soon as possible = lo más pronto
      posible, lo antes posible

sore adjective
   = dolorido/dolorida
   my legs are sore = tengo las piernas
      doloridas
   she has a sore throat = le duele la garganta

sorry
1 exclamation
• (*when apologizing*)
   sorry! = ¡lo siento!, ¡perdón!
• (*when asking someone to repeat*)
   sorry? = ¿cómo?
2 adjective
• (*when apologizing*)
   I'm sorry I'm late = siento llegar tarde
   to say sorry = pedir perdón
• (*when expressing regret*)
   I'm sorry you can't come = siento que no
      puedas venir

   ! Note the use of the subjunctive after
   sentir que

• (*to feel pity for*)
   I feel sorry for them = los compadezco

sort
1 noun
   a sort = un tipo
   it's a sort of bird = es un tipo de pájaro

S

2 *verb*
to sort the papers = ordenar los documentos
to sort the books into piles = separar los libros en montones
sort out
* *(to solve)* = solucionar
* *(to organize)* = ordenar
* *(to pick out)*
to sort out the old clothes from the new = separar la ropa vieja de la nueva

sound
1 *noun*
* *(a noise)*
a sound = un ruido
* *(of an instrument, a bell)*
a sound = un sonido
I heard the sound of voices = oí unas voces
* *(of a radio, a television)*
the sound = el sonido
2 *verb*
it sounds interesting = suena interesante
it sounds like a piano = suena como un piano

soup *noun*
a soup = una sopa

sour *adjective*
= agrio/agria

south
1 *noun*
the south = el sur
in the south of France = en el sur de Francia
2 *adverb*
we went south = fuimos hacia el sur
it is south of Newark = está al sur de Newark
3 *adjective*
= sur (**!** *never changes*)
the south coast = la costa sur
the south wind = el viento del sur

South Africa *noun* ▶ **p. 187**
South Africa = Sudáfrica *(feminine)*

southeast *noun*
the southeast = el sureste

southwest *noun*
the southwest = el suroeste

souvenir *noun*
a souvenir = un recuerdo

space *noun*
* *(room)*
space = espacio *(masculine)*, lugar *(masculine)*, sitio *(masculine)*
* *(outer space)*
space = espacio *(masculine)*
* *(a gap)*
a space = un espacio

spade *noun*
a spade = una pala

Spain *noun* ▶ **p. 187**
Spain = España *(feminine)*

Spaniard *noun* ▶ **p. 187**
a Spaniard = un español/una española

Spanish ▶ **p. 187, p. 245**
1 *adjective* = español/española
2 *noun*
* *(the language)*
Spanish = español *(masculine)*, castellano *(masculine)*
* *(the people)*
the Spanish = los españoles

spare
1 *adjective*
* *(extra)* = de más
to have a spare key = tener una llave de más
I've got a spare ticket = tengo un boleto de más
spare time = tiempo libre
2 *verb*
* **to have money to spare** = tener dinero de sobra
* *(from a bad experience)*
you can spare me the details = te puedes ahorrar los detalles

spare room *noun*
a spare room = un cuarto de huéspedes

speak *verb*
= hablar
who's speaking, please? *(on the phone)* = ¿quién habla?
speak up = hablar más fuerte

special *adjective*
= especial

specialty *(US English)*, **speciality** *(British English)* noun
a specialty = una especialidad

spectator *noun*
a spectator = un espectador/una espectadora

speech *noun*
a speech = un discurso

speed
1 *noun*
speed = velocidad *(feminine)*
2 *verb*
* *(to travel fast)*
to speed away = alejarse a toda velocidad
* *(to drive too fast)* = ir a exceso de velocidad
speed up = acelerar

speed limit *noun*
a speed limit = una velocidad máxima, un límite de velocidad

spell *verb*
- (*when speaking*) = deletrear
- (*when writing*) = escribir
  how do you spell it? = ¿cómo se escribe?

spelling *noun*
  spelling = ortografía (*feminine*)

spend *verb*
- (*to pay money*) = gastar
- (*to pass*)
  to spend time reading = pasar el tiempo
  leyendo

spider *noun*
  a spider = una araña

spill *verb*
  = derramar
  the milk spilled everywhere = la leche se
    derramó por todas partes

spinach *noun*
  spinach = espinacas (*feminine plural*)

spine *noun* ▶ p. 235
  the spine = la columna vertebral

spit *verb*
  = escupir

spite: in spite of *preposition*
  = a pesar de
  we went out in spite of the weather =
    salimos a pesar del tiempo

spiteful *adjective*
- (*mean*)
  a spiteful person = una persona mala
  a spiteful comment = un comentario
  malicioso
- (*resentful*) = rencoroso/rencorosa

spoil *verb*
- (*to ruin*) = arruinar, estropear
- (*as a parent*) = mimar, malcriar

sponge *noun*
  a sponge = una esponja

sponge cake *noun*
  a sponge cake = un bizcocho, un
  bizcochuelo (*SC*)

spoon *noun*
  a spoon = una cuchara

sport *noun* ▶ p. 306
  a sport = un deporte

sports center (*US English*), **sports
centre** (*British English*) *noun*
  a sports center = un centro deportivo

spot
1 *noun*
- (*on an animal*)
  a spot = una mancha
- (*British English—pimple*)
  a spot = un grano, una espinilla (*Lat Am*)

- (*a place*)
  a spot = un lugar, un sitio
  I had to decide on the spot = tuve que
    decidir en ese mismo momento
2 *verb* = ver, divisar
  he spotted her in the crowd = la vio entre
    el gentío, la divisó entre el gentío
  to spot a mistake = descubrir un error

sprain *verb*
  to sprain one's ankle = hacerse un
  esguince en el tobillo

spring *noun*
  spring = primavera (*feminine*)
  in spring = en primavera

spy
1 *noun*
  a spy = un/una espía
2 *verb*
  to spy on someone = espiar a alguien

square
1 *noun*
- (*the shape*)
  a square = un cuadrado
- (*in a town*)
  a square = una plaza
2 *adjective* = cuadrado/cuadrada

squash
1 *noun*
- (*the sport*) ▶ p. 306
  squash = squash (*masculine*)
- (*British English—a drink*)
  orange squash = naranjada (*feminine*)
2 *verb* = aplastar

squeak *verb*
  (*of an animal*) = chillar
  (*of a door*) = chirriar
  (*of a shoe*) = crujir

squeeze *verb*
  to squeeze a lemon = exprimir un limón
  he squeezed her hand = le apretó la mano

squirrel *noun*
  a squirrel = una ardilla

stable *noun*
  a stable = una caballeriza

stadium *noun*
  a stadium = un estadio

staff *noun*
  the staff (*of a company*) = el personal
  (*of a school, college*) = el personal docente

stage *noun*
- (*a phase*)
  a stage = una etapa
- (*in a theater*)
  a stage = un escenario

S

Sports and games

Spanish normally uses the definite article with names of sports and games:

football	= **el** fútbol
bridge	= **el** bridge
chess	= **el** ajedrez

Names of games and sports follow the same pattern as **chess** in the following phrases:

to play chess	= jugar ajedrez, jugar al ajedrez (*RPl, Spa*)
he beat me at chess	= me ganó al ajedrez
to win at chess	= ganar al ajedrez
she's good at chess	= juega bien ajedrez, juega bien al ajedrez (*RPl, Spa*)

Players and events

a chess player	= un jugador de ajedrez .
but
I'm not a chess player	= no juego ajedrez, no juego al ajedrez (*RPl, Spa*)
a chess champion	= un campeón de ajedrez
a chess championship	= un campeonato de ajedrez
a game of chess	= una partida de ajedrez, un partido de ajedrez (*Lat Am*)
but
| a game of football | = un partido de fútbol |

---

stain
1 *noun*
  a stain = una mancha
2 *verb* = manchar

stairs *noun*
  the stairs = la escalera

stamp *noun*
• (*for an envelope*)
  a stamp = un sello, una estampilla (*Lat Am*), un timbre (*Mex*)
• (*on a document, a passport*)
  a stamp = un sello

stand *verb*
• **to be standing** = estar de pie, estar parado/parada (*Lat Am*)
• (*to step*)
  to stand on a nail = pisar un clavo
• (*to bear*)
  I can't stand German = no soporto el alemán
  I can't stand him = no lo aguanto, no lo soporto
stand back = apartarse
stand for = significar
  what does SA stand for? = ¿qué significa SA?
stand out = destacarse
stand up
  to stand up = ponerse de pie, levantarse, pararse (*Lat Am*)
stand up for = defender
  to stand up for oneself = defenderse

star *noun*
• (*in space*)
  a star = una estrella

• (*a famous person*)
  a star = una estrella

stare *verb*
  to stare at someone = mirar fijamente a alguien

start
1 *verb*
• (*to begin*) = empezar, comenzar
  to start work, to start working = empezar a trabajar, comenzar a trabajar
• (*to set up*)
  to start a business = abrir un negocio
• (*to begin working*)
  the car won't start = el coche no arranca
• (*to put into action*)
  to start a car = arrancar un coche
  to start a machine = hacer funcionar una máquina
2 *noun*
  a start = un comienzo
  at the start of the week = al principio de la semana
start off = empezar
  to start off by painting the walls = empezar por pintar las paredes
start over (*US English*) = volver a empezar

state *noun*
• (*a territory*)
  a state = un estado
• (*a government*)
  the State = el Estado
• (*the condition something or someone is in*)
  a state = un estado
  to be in a bad state (**of repair**) = estar en mal estado

C Am Central America **Lat Am** Latin America **Mex** Mexico

statement noun
a statement = una declaración

station noun
• (for trains)
a station = una estación
• (a channel)
a station (on radio) = una emisora, una estación (Lat Am)
(on TV) = un canal

stationery noun
stationery = artículos de papelería (masculine plural)

statue noun
a statue = una estatua

stay
1 verb = quedarse
we stayed there for a week = nos quedamos allí una semana
to stay with friends = quedarse con amigos
2 noun
a stay = una estadía (Lat Am), una estancia (Mex, Spa)
stay in = quedarse en casa
stay out
to stay out late = volver tarde
stay up = quedarse levantado/levantada

steady adjective
• (continuous) = constante
• (not likely to move) = firme

steak noun
a steak = un bistec, un filete, un churrasco (S Am), un bife (R Pl)

steal verb
= robar
to steal money from someone = robarle dinero a alguien

steam noun
steam = vapor (masculine)
steam up = empañarse

steel noun
steel = acero (masculine)

steep adjective
= empinado/empinada

steering wheel noun
a steering wheel = un volante

step
1 noun
• (when walking)
a step = un paso
to take a step = dar un paso
• (in stairs, at a door)
a step = un escalón
• (in a series of actions)
to take steps = tomar medidas
2 verb
to step in a puddle = pisar un charco
step aside = hacerse a un lado

stepbrother noun
a stepbrother = un hermanastro

stepfather noun
a stepfather = un padrastro

stepmother noun
a stepmother = una madrastra

stepsister noun
a stepsister = una hermanastra

stereo noun
a stereo = un estéreo

stewardess noun
a stewardess = una azafata, una aeromoza (Lat Am)

stick
1 verb
• (using glue or tape) = pegar
• (to become attached) = pegar
• (to get blocked)
the door is stuck = la puerta está atascada
2 noun
• (a piece of wood)
a stick = un palo
• (for walking)
a stick = un bastón
stick out = sobresalir
his ears stick out = tiene las orejas salidas

stiff adjective
• (not soft, not supple)
a stiff material = una tela tiesa
to have stiff legs (after sport, walking) = tener las piernas entumecidas
• (not easy to use)
to be stiff (if it's a door, a drawer) = ser difícil de abrir

still[1] adverb
= todavía, aún

still[2]
1 adverb
to sit/stand still = quedarse tranquilo/tranquila
2 adjective
the lake was still = el lago estaba en calma

sting verb
= picar

stir verb
= revolver, remover (Spa)

stomach noun ▶ p. 235
the stomach = el estómago

stomachache noun
stomachache = dolor de estómago (masculine)

stone noun
a stone = una piedra

stop
1 verb

S

- (*to put an end to*)
  to stop smoking = dejar de fumar
  stop it! = ¡basta ya!
- (*to prevent*)
  to stop someone from leaving = impedir
  que alguien se vaya

  > **!** Note the use of the subjunctive after
  > impedir que

- (*to cease moving*) = parar
  the bus didn't stop = el autobús no paró
- (*to cease, to stop operating*)
  it's stopped raining = ha dejado de llover
  the clock stopped = el reloj se paró
  2 *noun*
  a (bus) stop = una parada, un paradero
  (*Lat Am*)

store *noun*
  a store = una tienda

storekeeper *noun* (*US English*)
  a storekeeper = un/una comerciante

storey *noun* (*British English*)
  a storey = un piso, una planta

storm *noun*
  a storm = una tormenta

story[1] *noun*
- **a story** = una historia
- (*in a newspaper*)
  a story = un artículo
- (*a rumor*)
  a story = un rumor

story[2] *noun* (*US English*)
  a story = un piso, una planta

straight
  1 *adjective*
- (*not curved*) = recto/recta
  a straight line = una línea recta
- (*not curly*) = liso/lisa
- (*in the right position*)
  the picture isn't straight = el cuadro está
  torcido, el cuadro está chueco (*Lat Am*)
- (*honest*)
  a straight question = una pregunta directa
  2 *adverb*
- (*erect*) = derecho
  sit up straight = ponte derecho
- (*without delay*) = directamente

strange *adjective*
- (*odd*) = raro/rara, extraño/extraña
  **it's strange that she doesn't come here
  any more** = es raro que no venga más por
  aquí

  > **!** Note the use of the subjunctive after es
  > raro que

- (*which or whom one doesn't know*) =
  desconocido/desconocida

stranger *noun*
  a stranger (*a person one hasn't met before*)
  = un desconocido/una desconocida

(*from another place*) = un forastero/una
  forastera

straw *noun*
- (*for feeding animals*)
  straw = paja (*feminine*)
- (*for drinking through*)
  a straw = una pajita, una paja, un popote
  (*Mex*), una caña (*Spa*)

strawberry *noun*
  a strawberry = una fresa, una frutilla (*SC*)

stream *noun*
  a stream = un riachuelo, un arroyo

street *noun*
  a street = una calle

streetlamp *noun*
  a streetlamp = un farol, una farola (*Spa*)

strength *noun*
  strength = fuerza (*feminine*)

stress *noun*
  stress = estrés (*masculine*), tensión
  (*feminine*)

stretch *verb*
  = estirar
  to stretch one's legs (*by walking*) = estirar
  las piernas

strict *adjective*
  = estricto/estricta

strike *noun*
  a strike = una huelga, un paro (*Lat Am*)
  to go on strike = ir a la huelga, ir al paro
  (*Lat Am*)

string *noun*
  string = cordel (*masculine*), bramante
  (*masculine*) (*Spa*), mecate (*masculine*)
  (*Mex*), piolín (*masculine*) (*R Pl*)

striped *adjective*
  = rayado/rayada

stroke *verb*
  = acariciar

stroller *noun* (*US English*)
  a stroller = una sillita de paseo, una
  carreola (*Mex*), un changuito® (*R Pl*)

strong *adjective*
- (*having physical, mental strength*) = fuerte
- (*not easily damaged*) = fuerte, resistente
- (*having force, power*) = fuerte
  a strong wind = un viento fuerte
  strong coffee = café fuerte, café cargado
- (*obvious, noticeable*)
  a strong Spanish accent = un acento
  español muy marcado
  a strong smell of garlic = un fuerte olor a
  ajo

stubborn *adjective*
  = terco/terca

student *noun*
　a student (*at university*) = un/una
　　estudiante
　(*at school*) = un alumno/una alumna

study
1 *verb* = estudiar
　to study to be a teacher = estudiar
　　docencia
2 *noun*
　a study = un estudio

stuff
1 *noun*
• stuff (*things, belongings*) = cosas (*feminine
　plural*)
2 *verb*
　(*to put*) = poner
　she stuffed her clothes in the drawer =
　　puso la ropa en el cajón

stuffing *noun*
　stuffing = relleno (*masculine*)

stupid *adjective*
　= tonto/tonta

style *noun*
• (*a way of dressing, behaving*)
　a style = un estilo
　to have style = tener estilo
• (*a design, a type*)
　a style = un diseño
• (*a fashion*)
　a style = una moda

stylish *adjective*
　= elegante

subject *noun*
• (*of a conversation*)
　a subject = un tema
　to change the subject = cambiar de tema
• (*being studied*)
　a subject (*at school, college*) = una
　　asignatura, una materia (*Lat Am*)
　(*for an essay, a report*) = un tema

suburb *noun*
　a suburb = un barrio residencial de las
　　afueras, una colonia (*Mex*)

subway *noun*
• (*US English—the rail system*)
　the subway = el metro, el subterráneo
　　(*R Pl*)
• (*British English—an underground passage*)
　a subway = un paso subterráneo

succeed *verb*
　to succed in doing something = lograr
　　hacer algo

success *noun*
　success = éxito (*masculine*)

successful *adjective*
　to be successful = tener éxito

such
1 *adjective*
　there's no such thing as ghosts = no
　　existen los fantasmas
　I said no such thing! = ¡yo no dije tal cosa!
2 *adverb*
　they have such a lot of money = tienen
　　tanto dinero
　I've never seen such a mess = nunca vi
　　semejante desorden

suddenly *adverb*
　= de repente, de pronto

suffer *verb*
　= sufrir
　to suffer from headaches = sufrir de
　　dolores de cabeza

sugar *noun*
　sugar = azúcar (*masculine or feminine*)

suggest *verb*
　= sugerir

suggestion *noun*
　a suggestion = una sugerencia

suit
1 *noun*
　a suit = un traje
2 *verb*
• (*to be convenient*) = convenirle a
　does Friday suit you? = ¿le conviene el
　　viernes?
• (*to look well on*)
　the hat suits you = el sombrero te queda
　　bien

suitable *adjective*
　= apropiado/apropiada

suitcase *noun*
　a suitcase = una maleta, una petaca (*Mex*),
　　una valija (*R Pl*)

sum *noun*
• (*an amount*)
　a sum of money = una cantidad de dinero
• (*in arithmetic*)
　a sum = una suma
　sum up = resumir

summer *noun*
　summer = verano (*masculine*)
　in summer = en (el) verano

sun *noun*
　the sun = el sol

sunbathe *verb*
　= tomar el sol, asolearse (*Lat Am*)

sunburned, sunburnt *adjective*
　to get sunburned = quemarse

Sunday *noun* ▶ p. 192
　Sunday = domingo (*masculine*)

S

sunglasses *noun*
sunglasses = gafas de sol (*feminine plural*), lentes de sol (*masculine plural*) (*Lat Am*), anteojos de sol (*masculine plural*) (*Lat Am*)

sunny *adjective*
a sunny day = un día de sol
it's going to be sunny = va a hacer sol

sunrise *noun*
sunrise = salida del sol (*feminine*)

sunset *noun*
sunset = puesta de(l) sol (*feminine*)

sunshine *noun*
sunshine = sol (*masculine*)

suntan *noun*
a suntan = un bronceado
to get a suntan = broncearse

supermarket *noun*
a supermarket = un supermercado

superstitious *adjective*
= supersticioso/supersticiosa

supper *noun*
a supper = una cena, una comida (*Lat Am*)

support *verb*
• (*to back*) = apoyar
• (*to hold, to help physically*)
the roof is supported by these columns = el tejado se apoya en estas columnas

supporter *noun*
a supporter (*of a team*) = un/una hincha
(*of a party*) = un partidario/una partidaria

suppose *verb*
• (*to imagine*) = suponer, imaginarse
I suppose so = supongo que sí, me imagino que sí
• (*to be meant to*)
we're supposed to start at 8 o'clock = se supone que tenemos que empezar a las ocho

sure *adjective*
• (*certain*) = seguro/segura
I'm sure he said 9 o'clock = estoy segura de que dijo las nueve
are you sure? = ¿estás seguro?
to make sure that the door is closed = asegurarse de que la puerta esté cerrada
• (*bound*)
he's sure to win = seguro que va a ganar
• to be sure of oneself = estar seguro/ segura de sí mismo/misma

surf *verb*
= hacer surf

surface *noun*
a surface = una superficie

surgeon *noun*
a surgeon = un cirujano/una cirujana

surgery *noun*
• (*an operation*)
to have surgery = operarse, someterse a una intervención quirúrgica
• (*British English—the place*)
a surgery = un consultorio, una consulta

surname *noun*
a surname = un apellido

surprise
1 *noun*
surprise = sorpresa (*feminine*)
to take someone by surprise = sorprender a alguien
2 *verb* = sorprender

surprised *adjective*
= sorprendido/sorprendida
I'm not surprised = no me sorprende

surround *verb*
= rodear

survey *noun*
a survey = una encuesta, un sondeo

survive *verb*
= sobrevivir
to survive an accident = salir con vida de un accidente

suspect *verb*
= sospechar
they suspect him of lying = sospechan que miente

suspicious *adjective*
• (*mistrustful*) = desconfiado/desconfiada
to be suspicious of someone = desconfiar de alguien
• (*arousing suspicion*) = sospechoso/sospechosa

swan *noun*
a swan = un cisne

swap *verb*
to swap something for something = cambiar algo por algo

sweat
1 *noun*
sweat = transpiracion (*feminine*), sudor (*masculine*)
2 *verb* = transpirar, sudar

sweater *noun*
a sweater = un suéter, un pulóver, un jersey (*Spa*)

Swede *noun* ▶ p. 187
a Swede = un sueco/una sueca

Sweden *noun* ▶ p. 187
Sweden = Suecia (*feminine*)

Swedish ▶ p. 187, p. 245
1 *adjective*
= sueco/sueca

2 *noun*
  Swedish = sueco (*masculine*)

sweep *verb*
  = barrer

sweet
1 *adjective*
• (*tasting of sugar*) = dulce,
  azucarado/azucarada
  (*not bitter or dry*) = dulce
  to have a sweet tooth = ser goloso/golosa
• (*if it's a smell*) = agradable
• (*kind, gentle*) = dulce
• (*cute*) = rico/rica
2 *noun* (*British English*)
• (*confectionery*)
  a sweet = un caramelo, un dulce (*Mex*)
• (*a dessert*)
  a sweet = un postre

swim
1 *verb* = nadar
2 *noun*
  to go for a swim = ir a nadar

swimming *noun*
  swimming = natación (*feminine*)

swimming pool *noun*
  a swimming pool = una piscina, una
  alberca (*Mex*), una pileta (*R Pl*)

swimsuit *noun*
  a swimsuit = un traje de baño, un bañador
  (*Spa*), una malla (*R Pl*)

swimming trunks *noun*
  swimming trunks = traje de baño
  (*masculine*), bañador (*masculine*) (*Spa*)

swing
1 *verb*
• (*to move back and forth*) = balancearse
  to swing by one's hands from a tree =
  balancearse colgando de un árbol
• (*to move something back and forth*) =
  balancear
  to swing one's legs = balancear las piernas
2 *noun*
  a swing = un columpio, una hamaca (*R Pl*)

Swiss ▶ **p. 187**
1 *adjective*
  = suizo/suiza
2 *noun*
  the Swiss = los suizos

switch
1 *noun*
  a switch = un interruptor
2 *verb* = cambiar
  to switch seats = cambiar de asiento
  to switch from English to Spanish = pasar
  del inglés al español
switch off = apagar
switch on = encender, prender (*Lat Am*)

Switzerland *noun* ▶ **p. 187**
  Switzerland = Suiza (*feminine*)

sympathetic *adjective*
  = comprensivo/comprensiva

symptom *noun*
  a symptom = un síntoma

syringe *noun*
  a syringe = una jeringa, una jeringuilla

system *noun*
  a system = un sistema

Tt

table *noun*
  a table = una mesa

tablet *noun*
  a tablet = una pastilla, un comprimido

table tennis *noun* ▶ **p. 306**
  table tennis = ping-pong (*masculine*), tenis
  de mesa (*masculine*)

tackle *verb*
• (*in soccer*) = entrarle a
• (*in American football, rugby*) = placar

tactful *adjective*
  = diplomático/diplomática

tail *noun*
  a tail (*of a horse, a fish, a bird*) = una cola
  (*of a dog, a pig*) = un rabo

take *verb*
• (*to take hold of*) = tomar, agarrar (*Lat Am*)
  to take someone by the hand = tomar a
  alguien de la mano, agarrar a alguien de
  la mano
• (*to carry with one*) = llevar
  I'll take the letters to Jack = yo le llevo las
  cartas a Jack
• (*to accompany, to bring*) = llevar
  to take someone home = llevar a alguien a
  casa
• (*to remove*)
  to take a book off the shelf = tomar un
  libro del estante
• (*to cope with, to bear*) = aguantar
  I can't take any more = no aguanto más
• (*when talking about what is necessary*)
  it takes [time | courage | patience …] = hace
  falta [tiempo | valentía | paciencia …]
  it takes two hours to get to London = se
  tarda dos horas en llegar a Londres
• (*to accept*) = aceptar
  we don't take checks = no aceptamos
  cheques

T

R Pl River Plate area   **SC** Southern Cone   **Spa** Spain

- (to react to)
  she took it the wrong way = se lo tomó a mal
- **take the first turn on the right** = tome la primera a la derecha
- **to take an exam** = hacer un examen, examinarse (Spa), dar un examen (SC)
- (to wear)
  to take a size 10 (in clothes) = usar la talla 14, usar el talle 14 (R Pl)
  to take a size 5 (in shoes) = calzar un número 5
- (if it's a medicine or drugs) = tomar
  I don't take sugar in my coffee = no le pongo azúcar al café

take apart = desmontar, desarmar

take away
  (to carry or lead away) = llevarse

take back = devolver, regresar (Mex)

take down
  (to remove)
  to take down a poster = quitar un cartel

take off
- (from an airport) = despegar
- (to remove)
  to take off one's clothes = quitarse la ropa
  I took off my shoes = me quité los zapatos

take out
- (from a box, a pocket, a bag) = sacar
- (from a bank account) = sacar, retirar

take part = participar
  to take part in something = participar en algo, tomar parte en algo

take place = tener lugar

take up
  to take up time = llevar tiempo
  to take up space = ocupar espacio

talented adjective
  = talentoso/talentosa

talk
1 verb
- (to speak) = hablar
  to talk to someone = hablar con alguien
  they were talking about you = estaban hablando de ti
  to talk to oneself = hablar solo/sola
- (to chat) = hablar, platicar (Mex)
2 noun
- (a conversation)
  a talk = una conversación, una plática (Mex)
- (about a special subject)
  a talk = una charla, una plática

talkative adjective
  = hablador/habladora

tall adjective
  = alto/alta
  how tall is he? = ¿cuánto mide?
  he's 2 meters tall = mide dos metros

tame adjective
- (by nature) = manso/mansa
- (domesticated) = domado/domada

tan noun
  a tan = un bronceado
  to get a tan = broncearse

tank noun
- (in a car, for water)
  a tank = un tanque
- (vehicle)
  a tank = un tanque

tanned adjective
  = bronceado/bronceada

tap
1 noun (British English)
  a tap = una llave, una canilla (R Pl), un grifo (Spa)
2 verb
  to tap on the door = dar un golpecito en la puerta

tape
1 noun
- (for a tape recorder, a video)
  a tape = una cinta
- (for repairs, sticking)
  tape = cinta adhesiva (feminine)
2 verb = grabar

tape measure noun
  a tape measure = una cinta métrica

tape recorder noun
  a tape recorder = un grabador, una grabadora

target noun
  a target = un blanco, un objetivo

task noun
  a task = una tarea

taste
1 noun
- (when eating, drinking)
  a taste = un sabor, un gusto
- (when talking about preferences)
  taste = gusto (masculine)
2 verb
- (when describing a flavor)
  it tastes bitter = tiene un sabor amargo
  it tastes like cabbage = sabe a repollo
- (to try) = probar

Taurus noun
- (the sign)
  Taurus = Tauro
  I'm Taurus = soy Tauro, soy de Tauro
- (a person)
  a Taurus = un/una tauro

tax noun
  a tax = un impuesto

taxi noun
  a taxi = un taxi

---

tea *noun*
• (*the product*)
  tea = té
• (*a cup of tea*)
  a tea = un té
• (*British English—a meal*)
  tea (*in the afternoon*) = té (*masculine*)
  (*in the evening*) = cena (*feminine*), comida
  (*feminine*) (*Lat Am*)

teach *verb*
• (*to help someone to learn skills*)
  to teach someone (how) to read =
  enseñarle a leer a alguien
• (*to work as a teacher*) = enseñar

teacher *noun*
  a teacher (*in a primary school*) = un
  maestro/una maestra
  (*in a secondary school*) = un profesor/una
  profesora

team *noun*
  a team = un equipo

teapot *noun*
  a teapot = una tetera

tear[1] *verb*
• (*to cause damage to*)
  to tear a piece of paper = romper un papel
  to tear a page out of a book = arrancar una
  página de un libro
• (*to become damaged*) = romperse
  tear off = arrancar
  tear up = romper

tear[2] *noun*
  (*when crying*)
  a tear = una lágrima

tease *verb*
  to tease someone = tomarle el pelo a
  alguien

teaspoon *noun*
  a teaspoon = una cucharita

technical *adjective*
  = técnico/técnica

teenager *noun*
  a teenager = un/una adolescente

telegram *noun*
  a telegram = un telegrama

telephone *noun*
  a telephone = un teléfono

telephone call *noun*
  a telephone call = una llamada (telefónica)

telephone directory *noun*
  a telephone directory = una guía
  telefónica, un directorio (*Lat Am*)

telescope *noun*
  a telescope = un telescopio

television *noun*
  a television = un televisor
  I saw it on television = lo vi en la televisión

tell *verb*
• (*to say to*) = decir
  tell me the truth = dime la verdad
• (*to recount, to relate*) = contar
  to tell a joke = contar un chiste
• (*when giving instructions*)
  to tell someone to do something = decirle
  a alguien que haga algo

  | **!** Note the use of the subjunctive after
  | decirle a alguien que

• (*to work out, to know*)
  I can tell (that) she's annoyed = sé que está
  enojada
• (*when making distinctions*)
  to tell the difference = notar la diferencia
  to tell which is which = distinguir cuál es
  cuál
• (*to reveal*)
  don't tell anyone = no le cuentes a nadie
  tell off = regañar, reñir (*Spa*), retar (*SC*)

temper *noun*
  to be in a temper = estar furioso/furiosa
  to lose one's temper = perder los estribos

temperature *noun*
  a temperature = una temperatura
  to have a temperature = tener fiebre, tener
  calentura, tener temperatura (*SC*)
  to take someone's temperature = tomarle
  la temperatura a alguien

temporary *adjective*
• (*if it's a job*) = eventual, temporal
• (*if it's accommodation*) = temporal,
  temporario/temporaria (*Lat Am*)

ten *number* ▶ **p. 154, p. 319**
  ten = diez (*masculine*) (**!** *never changes*)
  see also **five**

tennis *noun* ▶ **p. 306**
  tennis = tenis

tense *adjective*
  = tenso/tensa

tent *noun*
  a tent = una tienda, una carpa (*Lat Am*)

tenth
  1 *adjective*
  = décimo/décima
  2 *noun* ▶ **p. 192**
  (*a part*)
  a tenth = una décima parte

term *noun*
  (*at school, university*)
  a term = un trimestre

T

terrible *adjective*
(*very bad*)
  the film is terrible = la película es espantosa
  I've got a terrible headache = tengo un
    terrible dolor de cabeza

terrified *adjective*
= aterrorizado/aterrorizada

terror *noun*
  terror = terror (*masculine*)

test
1 *verb*
• (*to try out*) = probar
• (*in school, college*)
  to test the students = hacerles una prueba
    a los estudiantes
2 *noun*
• (*of a person or a person's ability*)
  a test = un test
  (*in school, college*) = una prueba
  a driving test = un examen de conducir, un
    examen de manejar (*Lat Am*)
  a blood test = un análisis de sangre
  an eye test = un examen de la vista

textbook *noun*
  a textbook = un libro de texto

text message *noun*
  a text message = un texto

than
1 *preposition*
• (*in comparisons*) = que
  he is stronger than me = es más fuerte que
    yo
  I've got more money than you = tengo más
    dinero que tú
• (*when talking about quantities*) = de
  more than half the pupils = más de la
    mitad de los alumnos
  less than $100 = menos de cien dólares
2 *conjunction* = que
  he's older than I am = es mayor que yo

thank *verb*
  to thank someone = darle las gracias a
    alguien
  thank you = gracias

thanks
1 *exclamation*
  thanks! = ¡gracias!
2 *noun*
  thanks to = gracias a

that

> **!** *See the usage note on* that *for more
> detailed information*

1 *pronoun*
  what's that? = ¿qué es eso?
  who's that? = ¿quién es él/ella?
  is that Joe? = ¿ése es Joe?
  that's how they make butter = así es como
    se hace la mantequilla
  that's not true = eso no es cierto
  that's the kitchen = allí está la cocina

2 *adjective*
= ese/esa
• (*if it's more distant or in the remote past*) =
  aquél/aquella
  I know that girl = conozco a esa chica
  he didn't go to work that day = no fue a
    trabajar aquél día

the *definite article*

> **!** *See the usage note on* the *for
> translations*

theater (*US English*), **theatre** (*British
English*) *noun*
  a theater = un teatro

their *adjective*
= su (+ *singular*), sus (+ *plural*)

> **!** *For* their *used with parts of the body,*
> ▶ **p. 235**

theirs *pronoun*
  (*singular*) = suyo/suya
  (*plural*) = suyos/suyas
  theirs is blue = el suyo/la suya es azul, el/la
    de ellos es azul
  a friend of theirs = un amigo suyo, un
    amigo de ellos

them *pronoun*
• (*when used as a direct object*) = los/las
  I know them = los/las conozco
  I don't know them = no los/las conozco

> **!** *Note that* los *and* las *come before the
> verb in Spanish; when talking about
> mixed groups, the masculine form* los *is
> used*

• (*when used as an indirect object*) = les
  I never talk to them = nunca les hablo
  I wrote them a letter = les escribí una carta

> **!** *Note that* les *comes before the verb in
> Spanish*

• (*when used as an indirect object pronoun
  together with a direct object pronoun*) =
  se
  I gave it to them = se lo di
  I'm not going to say it to them = no se lo
    voy a decir

> **!** *Note that* se *comes before the direct
> object pronoun*

• (*when telling someone to do something*)
  catch them! = ¡atrápenlos!/¡atrápenlas!
  give them the money = dales el dinero
  give it to them = dáselo

> **!** *Note that* los, las, les, *and* se *come after
> the verb in Spanish*

• (*when telling someone not to do
  something*)
  don't look at them! = ¡no los/las mires!
  don't show it to them! = ¡no se lo muestres!

C Am Central America   Lat Am Latin America   Mex Mexico

That

As an adjective **that** is translated by:

ese + masculine singular noun	**ese** libro
esa + feminine singular noun	**esa** mesa

Note that the gender and number agree with the noun that follows.

To refer to something more distant or something that occurred in the remote past, the following forms are used:

aquel + masculine singular noun	**aquel** libro
aquella + feminine singular noun	**aquella** época

As a pronoun

In Spanish, pronouns reflect the gender and number of the noun that they represent. So **that** meaning *that one* is translated by **ése** or **aquél** for a masculine singular noun, **ésa** or **aquélla** for a feminine singular noun, and **those** is translated by **ésos** or **aquéllos** for a masculine plural noun and by **ésas** or **aquéllas** for a feminine plural noun:

that is my favorite **aquélla** es la que más me gusta

When used to mean **who** or **which**, **that** is translated by **que** when it is the subject or direct object:

*the woman **that** bought them* la mujer **que** los compró
*the books **that** I bought* los libros **que** compré

When followed by a preposition, **that** is translated by **el que** when representing a masculine singular noun, by **la que** when representing a feminine singular noun, by **los que** when representing a masculine plural noun, and by **las que** when representing a feminine plural noun:

*the chair **that** he was sitting on* la silla en **la que** estaba sentado
*the children **that** I bought the books for* los niños para **los que** compré los libros

Where **that** as a pronoun is used to refer to something which is not specified for gender, it is translated by the neuter **eso** or **aquello**, according to context:

*what's **that**?* = ¿qué es **eso**?
*what's **that** over there?* = ¿qué es **aquello** que se ve allá?

As a conjunction

When used as a conjunction, **that** can always be translated by **que**:

*he said **that** he would go* dijo **que** iría

! *Note that* los, las, les, *and* se *come after the verb in Spanish*

- *(when used after prepositions and with* to be) = ellos/ellas
  we bought it for them = lo compramos para ellos/ellas
  I have nothing against them = no tengo nada en contra de ellos/ellas, no tengo nada en contra suya
  they had their dog with them = tenían el perro consigo
  it's them = son ellos

themselves *pronoun*
- *(when translated by a reflexive verb in Spanish)*
  they didn't hurt themselves = no se hicieron daño, no se lastimaron (*Lat Am*)
  they bought themselves a new car = se compraron un coche nuevo

- *(when used for emphasis)*
  they said it themselves = ellos mismos/ellas mismas lo dijeron
  they did it all by themselves = lo hicieron ellos solos/ellas solas

then *adverb*
- *(at that point in time)*= entonces
  I was living in Germany then = entonces yo vivía en Alemania
- *(after, next)* = después, luego

there
1 *pronoun*
  there is = hay
  there are = hay
  there is a problem = hay un problema
  there are no shops = no hay tiendas
  there was no room = no había lugar
  there will be a lot of people = habrá mucha gente

The

In Spanish the definite article agrees in gender and number with the noun that follows, so **the** is translated as follows:

el + masculine singular noun	**el** perro
la + feminine singular noun	**la** silla
los + masculine plural noun	**los** papeles
las + feminine plural noun	**las** mujeres

When **el** follows the preposition **de** the two words combine to form one word **del**:

los hijos **del** profesor (**not** los hijos **de el** profesor)

Similarly, when **el** follows the preposition **a** the two words combine to form **al**:

fuimos **al** colegio (**not** fuimos **a el** colegio)

In general, when the definite article is used in English, it is also used in Spanish. There are however important exceptions:

Before the ordinal number in titles of kings, popes, etc

Elizabeth **the** Second	= Isabel Segunda
Henry **the** Eighth	= Enrique Octavo

There are some occasions where there is no definite article in English but it is needed in Spanish.

There are two main cases of this:

a) with generic and abstract nouns when they are the subject of a sentence:

modesty is a good virtue	= **la** modestia es una buena virtud
silk is very delicate	= **la** seda es muy delicada
international Communism	= **el** comunismo internacional
blue is my favourite color	= **el** azul es mi color favorito

b) with nouns that refer to the members of a group:

children are often very selfish	= **los** niños son a menudo muy egoístas
Brazilians speak Portuguese	= **los** brasileños hablan portugués

---

2 *adverb*
- *(when talking about location) (close by)* = ahí
  (further away) = allí, ahí (*Lat Am*)
  (less precise, further) = allá
  put the books there = pon los libros ahí
  go over there = vete allí
  when do we get there? = ¿cuándo llegamos allá?
- *(when drawing attention)*
  there they are = allí están
  there you are, there you go = toma

therefore *adverb*
= por lo tanto

thermometer *noun*
a thermometer = un termómetro

these
1 *adjective*
= estos/estas
these books aren't mine = estos libros no son míos
2 *pronoun*
= éstos/éstas
what are these? = ¿qué son éstos/éstas?
these are your things = éstas son tus cosas

they *pronoun*
- **they** = ellos/ellas

  ! *When talking about mixed groups the masculine form* **ellos** *is used*
  they went to the theater = fueron al teatro
  they did it = ellos/ellas lo hicieron

  ! *Although* **ellos** *and* **ellas** *are given as translations of* **they**, *they are in practice used for emphasis, or to avoid ambiguity*
- *(when talking in an impersonal or vague way about people)*
  that's how they make butter = así es como se hace la mantequilla
  they've dug up the road = han levantado la calle

thick *adjective* .
- *(if it's a fabric, a book)* = grueso/gruesa
  (if it's a soup, a sauce) = espeso/espesa
- *(stupid)* = burro✱/burra✱

thief *noun*
a thief = un ladrón/una ladrona

thigh *noun* ▶ p. 235
the thigh = el muslo

✱ in informal situations   **C Am** Central America   **Lat Am** Latin America   **Mex** Mexico

thin *adjective*
• *(not thick)*
a thin slice of ham = una tajada fina de jamón
a thin sauce = una salsa clara
• *(not fat)* = delgado/delgada
to get thin = adelgazar

thing *noun*
• **a thing** = un cosa
I've got things to do = tengo cosas que hacer
the best thing would be to call = lo mejor sería llamarlo
I can't hear a thing = no oigo nada
• *(belongings)*
things = cosas *(feminine plural)*
• *(when talking about a situation)*
how are things? = ¿qué tal?

think *verb*
• *(when talking about opinions)* = pensar, creer
what do you think? = ¿tú qué piensas?
I think it's unfair = pienso que es injusto
will they come?—I don't think so = ¿van a venir?—pienso que no
• *(to concentrate on an idea)* = pensar
think hard before answering = piénsalo bien antes de contestar
• *(to remember)*
I can't think of his name = no recuerdo su nombre
• *(to take into account, to have in mind)*
to think of someone = pensar en alguien
I hadn't thought of that = eso no se me había ocurrido
• *(to have vague plans to)*
I'm thinking of leaving school = estoy pensando dejar los estudios
• *(to have an idea about)*
to think of a solution = encontrar una solución

third
1 *adjective* = tercero/tercera

> **!** *Note that* **tercero** *becomes* **tercer** *when it appears before a masculine singular noun*

2 *noun* ▶ **p. 192**
• *(in a series)*
the third = el tercero/la tercera
• *(a part)*
a third = una tercera parte, un tercio
3 *adverb* = en tercer lugar
to come third = terminar en tercer lugar

thirsty *adjective*
to be thirsty = tener sed

thirteen *number* ▶ **p. 154, p. 319**
thirteen = trece *(masculine)* (**!** *never changes) see also* **five**

thirty *noun* ▶ **p. 154, p. 319**
thirty = treinta *(masculine)* (**!** *never changes) see also* **five**

this
1 *adjective* = este/esta
I like this garden = me gusta este jardín
who is this woman? = ¿quién es esta mujer?
2 *pronoun* = éste/ésta *(masculine/feminine)*, esto *(neuter)*
this (one) is mine = éste es el mío/ésta es la mía
what's this? = ¿qué es esto?

thorn *noun*
a thorn = una espina

those
1 *adjective* = esos/esas
(if it's more distant or in the remote past) = aquellos/aquellas
those keys are Pete's = esas llaves son de Pete
in those times = en aquellos tiempos
2 *pronoun* = ésos/ésas
(if it's more distant or in the remote past) = aquéllos/aquéllas
those (ones) cost five dollars and those (ones) over there ten dollars = ésos cuestan cinco dólares y aquéllos (de allá) diez dólares
those who have been less fortunate = los que no han tenido tanta suerte

though *conjunction*
= aunque

thought *noun*
a thought = un pensamiento

thousand *number*
one thousand, a thousand = mil
four thousand pounds = cuatro mil libras

thread *noun*
thread = hilo *(masculine)*

threat *noun*
a threat = una amenaza

threaten *verb*
= amenazar

three *number* ▶ **p. 154, p. 319**
three = tres *(masculine)* (**!** *never changes) see also* **five**

throat *noun* ▶ **p. 235**
the throat = la garganta

through *preposition*

> **!** *Through is often used in combinations with verbs, for example,* **get through**, **go through**. *To find the correct translations for this type of verb, look up the separate dictionary entries at* **get**, **go** *etc*

• *(from one side to the other)*
to drive through the desert = cruzar el desierto en coche

T

- (*via, by way of*) = por
  to go through the town center = pasar por el centro de la ciudad
  to look through a window = mirar por una ventana
- (*past*)
  to go through customs = pasar por la aduana
- (*when talking about time*)
  right through the day = todo el día
  from Friday through to Sunday = de viernes a domingo
  open April through September (*US English*) = abierto/abierta desde abril hasta septiembre

throw *verb*
- (*to hurl*)
  to throw a ball = tirar una pelota, aventar una pelota (*Mex*)
  she threw stones at him = le tiró piedras, le aventó piedras (*Mex*)
  she threw the book on the floor = tiró el libro al suelo
- **to throw a party** = dar una fiesta
  throw away, throw out = tirar

thumb *noun* ▶ p. 235
  the thumb = el pulgar

thunder *noun*
  thunder = truenos (*masculine plural*)

thunderstorm *noun*
  a thunderstorm = una tormenta eléctrica

Thursday *noun* ▶ p. 192
  Thursday = jueves (*masculine*)

ticket *noun*
  a ticket (*for a bus, a train*) = un boleto (*Lat Am*), un billete (*Spa*)
  (*for a plane*) = un pasaje
  (*for a theater, a museum*) = una entrada

tickle *verb*
  to tickle someone = hacerle cosquillas a alguien

tide *noun*
  the tide = la marea
  the tide is in/out = la marea está alta/baja
  a high/low tide = una marea alta/baja

tidy *adjective*
  = ordenado/ordenada, prolijo/prolija (*R Pl*)
  tidy up = ordenar

tie
  1 *verb* = atar, amarrar (*Lat Am*)
  he tied the dog to a tree = ató el perro a un árbol, amarró el perro a un árbol (*Lat Am*)
  to tie a package (up) with string = atar un paquete con cuerda, amarrar un paquete con cuerda (*Lat Am*)
  2 *noun*
- (*worn with a shirt*)
  a tie = una corbata

- (*in sport*)
  a tie = un empate
  tie up = atar, amarrar (*Lat Am*)

tiger *noun*
  a tiger = un tigre

tight *adjective*
  a tight dress (*fitting closely*) = un vestido ajustado
  (*uncomfortable*) = un vestido apretado
  these shoes are too tight = estos zapatos me aprietan

tights *noun* (*British English*)
  tights = panty (*masculine*), medias (*feminine plural*) (*Spa*), pantimedias (*feminine plural*) (*Mex*), medias bombacha (*feminine plural*) (*R Pl*)

tile *noun*
  a tile (*on a wall*) = un azulejo
  (*on a floor*) = una baldosa

till¹ ▶ until

till² *noun*
  a till = una caja

timber *noun*
  timber = madera (*feminine*)

time *noun* ▶ p. 319
- **time** = tiempo (*masculine*)
  we haven't seen them for a long time = hace mucho tiempo que no los vemos
- (*when talking about a specific hour or period of time*)
  the time = la hora
  to arrive on time = llegar a tiempo
  it's time we left = es hora de irnos
- (*a moment*)
  at times = a veces
  we arrived at the right time = llegamos en un buen momento
  for the time being = por el momento, de momento
- (*a period in the past*)
  a time = una época
- (*an experience*)
  we had a good time = lo pasamos bien
- (*an occasion*)
  a time = una vez
  several times a day = varias veces al día
  the first time we met = la primera vez que nos encontramos
  from time to time = de vez en cuando
- (*when comparing*)
  three times more expensive = tres veces más caro

times *preposition*
  three times four is twelve (3 × 4 = 12) = tres (multiplicado) por cuatro (son) doce (3 × 4 = 12)

timetable *noun*
  a timetable = un horario

Time of day

What time is it?

what time is it?	= ¿qué hora es?
can you tell me the time?	= ¿me dice(s) la hora?, ¿me da(s) la hora?
do you have the time?	= ¿tiene(s) hora?

It is ...

it is one o'clock	= es la una
it is three o'clock	= son las tres
it is exactly one o'clock	= es la una en punto
it is exactly three o'clock	= son las tres en punto

Note that **y** is used for times **after** the hour

it is 1:15	= es la una **y** cuarto
it is 6:20	= son las seis **y** veinte
it is 2:30	= son las dos **y** media

For times **before** the hour **para** is used in Latin America (with the exception of the River Plate area) and **menos** is used in Spain and the River Plate. Note the different constructions:

it's 7:45	= son un cuarto **para** las ocho (*Lat Am excluding R Pl*)
	= son las ocho **menos** cuarto (*Spa, R Pl*)
it's 4:50	= son diez **para** las cinco (*Lat Am excluding R Pl*)
	= son las cinco **menos** diez (*Spa, R Pl*)

a.m./p.m.

To specify a.m. or p.m. Spanish adds one of the following:

in the morning	= de la mañana
in the afternoon/evening	= de la tarde
in the evening/at night	= de la noche
in the morning (early hours)	= de la madrugada

De la tarde is used from midday until about 8 p.m. and **de la madrugada** is used for the early hours of the morning, between 2 a.m. and 5 a.m.

Midday

twelve o'clock midday	= las doce del mediodía

Note that **el mediodía** refers in Spanish to the hours between 12 and 3 o'clock in the afternoon:

It's one o'clock (p.m.)	= es la una del mediodía

When?

Spanish always uses the word **a**, whether or not English includes the word **at**. The only exception is when there is another preposition present, as in **alrededor de las tres** (about three o'clock), **antes de las tres** (before three o'clock):

what *time did you arrive?*	= ¿**a qué** hora llegaste?	
at *two o'clock*	= **a** las dos	
at about *one o'clock*	= **alrededor de** la una	= **sobre** la una (*Spa*)
Just after *three*	= **a** las tres **y pico**	
it must be ready **by** *five*	= tiene que estar listo **para** las cinco	
it is open **from** *nine* **to** *five*	= está abierto **de** nueve **a** cinco	

The 24-hour clock

This is used a lot more in Spanish than it is in English (in timetables etc):

21:30 (9:30 p.m.)	= las veintiuna treinta
13:15 (1:15 p.m.)	= las trece quince

When the time is on the hour, you add the word **horas**:

17:00 (5 p.m.)	= las diecisiete horas

T

tin *noun*
• (*the metal*)
  tin = estaño (*masculine*)
• (*British English—a can*)
  a tin = una lata, un bote (*Spa*)

tin opener *noun* (*British English*)
  a tin opener = un abrelatas

tiny *adjective*
  = minúsculo/minúscula

tip *noun*
• (*the point, the end*)
  the tip = la punta
• (*given in a hotel, restaurant*)
  a tip = una propina
• (*a piece of advice*)
  a tip = un consejo

tire *noun* (*US English*)
  a tire = un neumático, una llanta (*Lat Am*),
  una goma (*R Pl*)

tired *adjective*
• (*needing rest*) = cansado/cansada
  to get tired = cansarse
• (*needing a change*) = harto/harta
  I'm tired of being a waitress = estoy harta
  de ser camarera

tissue *noun*
  a tissue = un pañuelo de papel

to
1 *preposition*
• (*talking about destination*) = a
  we went to London = fuimos a Londres
  they went to the airport = fueron al
  aeropuerto
  move a little to the right = córrete un poco
  hacia la derecha
• (*talking about position*)
  to the left/right of something = a la
  izquierda/derecha de algo
  to the north of Madrid = al norte de Madrid
• (*as far as, until*) = hasta
  she can count to ten = sabe contar hasta
  diez
  I can't stay to the end = no puedo
  quedarme hasta el final ▶ **from**
• (*when used with the indirect object*)
  give the book to me = dame el libro
  I gave it to Rachel = se lo di a Rachel
  what did you say to him/them? = ¿qué
  le/les dijiste?
• (*talking about proportion, relation*)
  Barcelona won by two goals to one =
  Barcelona ganó por dos (goles) a uno
  there's a ten to one chance of . . . = hay
  una probabilidad de uno en diez de . . .
• (*indicating a reaction, showing an attitude*)
  to my horror . . . = para mi horror . . .
  to the best of my knowledge = que yo sepa
• (*indicating belonging to*) = de
  the key to the front door = la llave de la
  puerta de la calle

• (*British English—when talking about time*)
    ▶ **p. 319**
  it's ten (**minutes**) to five = son diez para las
  cinco (*Lat Am*), son las cinco menos diez
  (*R Pl, Spa*)
2 *used in infinitives*
• to sing/sew/go = cantar/coser/ir
  it's easy to do = es fácil de hacer
  she had to do it = tuvo que hacerlo
  I tried to phone you = traté de llamarte
  she was the first to arrive = fue la primera
  en llegar
  he has a lot to do = tiene mucho que hacer
• (*in order to*) = para
  I do it to save money = lo hago para
  ahorrar dinero

toast *noun*
  toast = tostadas (*feminine plural*), pan
  tostado (*masculine*)

toaster *noun*
  a toaster = una tostadora

today *adverb*
  = hoy

toe *noun* ▶ **p. 235**
  a toe = un dedo (del pie)

together *adverb*
  = juntos/juntas

toilet *noun*
  a toilet = un baño (*Lat Am*), un servicio
  (*Spa*)

toilet paper *noun*
  toilet paper = papel higiénico

tomato *noun*
  a tomato = un tomate, un jitomate (*Mex*)

tomorrow *noun*
  tomorrow = mañana

tongue *noun* ▶ **p. 235**
  the tongue = la lengua

tonight *adverb*
  = esta noche

too *adverb*
• (*also*) = también
  I'm going too = yo voy también
• (*more than is necessary or desirable*)
  it's too big = es demasiado grande
  there were too many people = había
  demasiada gente
  I ate too much = comí demasiado
• (*very*) = muy
  I'm not too sure = no estoy muy segura

tool *noun*
  a tool = una herramienta

tooth *noun* ▶ **p. 235**
  a tooth = un diente

toothache *noun*
  to have toothache = tener dolor de muela

toothbrush *noun*
  a toothbrush = un cepillo de dientes

toothpaste *noun*
  toothpaste = pasta de dientes (*feminine*)

top
1 *noun*
• (*the highest part*)
  the top of the hill = la cumbre de la colina
  at the top of the stairs = en lo alto de la
  escalera
  at the top of the page = en la parte superior
  de la página
  the socks are on top of the radiator = los
  calcetines están encima del radiador, los
  calcetines están sobre el radiador
• (*a cover, a lid*)
  a top (*on a bottle, a pan*) = una tapa
  (*on a pen*) = el capuchón
• (*the highest level*)
  to be at the top of the class = ser el
  primero/la primera de la clase
2 *adjective* = superior, de arriba
  the top shelf = el estante superior, el
  estante de arriba

torch *noun* (*British English*)
  a torch = una linterna

tortoise *noun*
  a tortoise = una tortuga

total
1 *noun*
  a total = un total
2 *adjective* = total

touch
1 *verb* = tocar
2 *noun*
  [to be | get | stay …] **in touch with someone** =
  [estar | ponerse | mantenerse …] en contacto
  con alguien

tough *adjective*
• (*not soft, not sensitive*) = duro/dura
  to be tough with someone = ser duro/dura
  con alguien
• (*difficult*) = difícil
• (*severe*) = severo/severa
  a tough law = una ley severa

tour *noun*
• (*by a team, band, theater group*)
  a tour = una gira
  to be on tour = estar de gira
• (*by tourists, pupils, visitors*)
  a tour = una visita

tourism *noun*
  tourism = turismo (*masculine*)

tourist *noun*
  a tourist = un/una turista

toward(s) *preposition*
• (*when talking about place, time*) = hacia

• (*when talking about attitudes*)
  his attitude toward her = su actitud para
  con ella

towel *noun*
  a towel = una toalla

tower *noun*
  a tower = una torre

town *noun*
  a town = una ciudad
  to go into town = ir a la ciudad

town hall *noun*
  the town hall = el ayuntamiento, la
  intendencia (*Mex*)

toy *noun*
  a toy = un juguete

track *noun*
• (*a path*)
  a track = un sendero
• (*for sports*)
  a track = una pista
• (*the rails*)
  the track(**s**) = la vía férrea
• (*left by a person, animal, vehicle*)
  a track = una pista, unas huellas

tracksuit *noun*
  a tracksuit = un equipo de deportes, unos
  pants (*Mex*), un chándal (*Spa*), un
  jogging (*R Pl*)

trade *noun*
• (*business*)
  trade = comercio (*masculine*)
• (*a profession*)
  a trade = un oficio

traffic *noun*
  traffic = tráfico (*masculine*), tránsito
  (*masculine*) (*Lat Am*)

traffic circle *noun* (*US English*)
  a traffic circle = una rotonda, una glorieta
  (*Mex, Spa*)

traffic jam *noun*
  a traffic jam = un embotellamiento, un
  atasco

traffic lights *noun*
  the traffic lights = el semáforo

trailer *noun* (*US English*)
  a trailer = una caravana, un rulot (*Esp*),
  una casa rodante (*SC*)

train
1 *noun*
  a train = un tren
2 *verb*
• (*to teach, to prepare*)
  to train an employee = capacitar a un
  empleado/una empleada

T

- (*to learn a job*)
  to train as a doctor/teacher = estudiar medicina/docencia
- (*for a sporting event*) = entrenarse

trainer *noun*
- (*sports coach*)
  a trainer = un entrenador/una entrenadora
- (*British English—sports shoe*)
  a trainer = una zapatilla de deporte, un tenis

tramp *noun*
  a tramp = un vagabundo/una vagabunda

translate *verb*
  = traducir

translator *noun*
  a translator = un traductor/una traductora

transport, transportation (*US English*) *noun*
  transport = transporte (*masculine*)
  a means of transport = un medio de transporte

trap *noun*
  a trap = una trampa

trash *noun* (*US English*)
  trash = basura (*feminine*)

trash can *noun* (*US English*)
  a trash can = un cubo de la basura, un tacho de la basura (*SC*), un bote de la basura (*Mex*)

travel *verb*
  = viajar

travel agency *noun*
  a travel agency = una agencia de viajes

traveler (*US English*), **traveller** (*British English*)
  a traveler = un viajero/una viajera

traveler's check (*US English*), **traveller's cheque** (*British English*) *noun*
  a traveler's check = un cheque de viaje

tray *noun*
  a tray = una bandeja

treat *verb*
- (*to deal with, to behave with*) = tratar
  he treated me badly = me trató mal
- (*to provide medical care for*) = tratar
- (*to pay for*)
  he treated me to lunch = me invitó a almorzar

treatment *noun*
  treatment = tratamiento (*masculine*)

tree *noun*
  a tree = un árbol

tremble *verb*
  = temblar

trial *noun*
  a trial = un proceso

triangle *noun*
  a triangle = un triángulo

trick
1 *noun*
- (*a joke*)
  a trick = una broma
  to play a trick on someone = hacerle una broma a alguien
- (*a means of deceiving*)
  a trick = una trampa
- (*to entertain*)
  a trick = un truco
2 *verb* = engañar

trip
1 *noun*
  a trip (*abroad*) = un viaje
  (*a day out*) = una excursión
2 *verb*
  to trip (**up**) = tropezar
  to trip someone (**up**) = hacerle una zancadilla a alguien

trouble *noun*
- (*difficulties*)
  trouble = problemas (*masculine plural*)
  to be in trouble = estar en apuros
  to get someone into trouble = meter a alguien en problemas
- (*an effort*)
  to take the trouble to do something = molestarse en hacer algo

trousers *noun*
  trousers = pantalones (*masculine plural*)

trout *noun*
  a trout = una trucha

truck *noun* (*US English*)
  a truck = un camión

true *adjective*
  is it true that he's leaving? = ¿es cierto que se va?
  it's a true story = es una historia verídica
  to come true = hacerse realidad

trumpet *noun*
  a trumpet = una trompeta

trunk *noun*
- (*of a tree*)
  a trunk = un tronco
- (*a large case*)
  a trunk = un baúl
- (*of an elephant*)
  a trunk = una trompa
- (*US English—of a car*)
  the trunk = el maletero, la cajuela (*Mex*), el baúl (*R Pl*)

trust *verb*
= confiar en
to trust a friend = confiar en un amigo
I don't trust them = no me fío de ellos

truth *noun*
the truth = la verdad

try *verb*
• (*to attempt*) = intentar
to try to understand = intentar entender
• (*to test*) = probar
to try (out) a recipe = probar una receta
to try (on) a pair of trousers = probarse
unos pantalones
• (*to taste*) = probar
• (*in court*) = juzgar

T-shirt *noun*
a T-shirt = una camiseta

tube *noun*
a tube = un tubo

Tuesday *noun* ▶ **p. 192**
Tuesday = martes (*masculine*)

tuna *noun*
tuna = atún (*masculine*)

tunnel *noun*
a tunnel = un túnel

turkey *noun*
a turkey = un pavo, un guajolote (*Mex*)

Turkey *noun* ▶ **p. 187**
Turkey = Turquía (*feminine*)

turn
1 *verb*
• (*to move one's body*) = volverse, voltearse
(*Lat Am*), darse vuelta (*SC*)
• (*to change direction*) = doblar
to turn right = doblar a la derecha
to turn the corner = doblar la esquina
• (*to twist*) = girar
to turn the handle = girar la manilla
• (*to become*)
to turn into a butterfly = transformarse en
una mariposa
to turn red = ponerse rojo/roja
2 *noun*
• (*a bend*)
a turn = una curva
• (*a change of direction*)
a turn = una vuelta, un giro
• (*in games*)
whose turn is it? = ¿a quién le toca?
it's my turn = me toca a mí
turn around, turn round (*British English*)
• (*to face the other way*) = darse la vuelta,
volverse, voltearse (*Lat Am*), darse vuelta
(*SC*)
• (*to change the position of*)
to turn the table around = dar la vuelta a la
mesa, voltear la mesa (*Lat Am*), dar
vuelta la mesa (*SC*)

turn back = volver, regresar
turn down
• (*to lower*) = bajar
to turn down the volume = bajar el
volumen
• (*to reject*) = rechazar
turn off = apagar
to turn [the light | the oven | the radio …] off =
apagar [la luz | el horno | la radio …]
to turn the faucet/tap off = cerrar la llave
turn on = encender, prender (*Lat Am*)
to turn on the TV = encender el televisor,
prender el televisor
to turn the faucet/tap on = abrir la llave
turn over
• (*to roll over*) = darse la vuelta, voltearse
(*Lat Am*), darse vuelta (*SC*)
• **to turn over the page** = dar la vuelta a la
página, dar vuelta la página
(*SC*)
turn up
• (*shorten*)
(*if it's trousers*) = acortar
(*if it's a hem*) = subir
• (*to increase*) = subir
to turn up the heating = subir la calefacción
• (*British English—arrive*) = aparecer

turtle *noun*
• **a (sea) turtle** = una tortuga marina
• (*US English—a tortoise*)
a turtle = una tortuga

TV *noun*
a TV = un televisor
I saw it on TV = lo vi en la televisión

twelve *number* ▶ **p. 154, p. 319**
twelve = doce (*masculine*) (**!** *never
changes*) see also **five**

twenty *number* ▶ **p. 154, p. 319**
twenty = veinte (*masculine*) (**!** *never
changes*) see also **five**

twice *adverb*
= dos veces
twice a week = dos veces por semana
twice as many people = el doble de
gente

twin
1 *noun*
a twin = un mellizo/una melliza, un
gemelo/una gemela (*Spa*)
2 *adjective*
my twin brother = mi hermano mellizo, mi
hermano gemelo (*Spa*)

twist *verb*
• (*to bend out of shape*) = retorcer
• (*to injure*)
to twist one's ankle = torcerse el tobillo
• (*of a road, a river*)
to twist and turn = serpentear

T

two *number* ▶ **p. 154, p. 319**
two = dos (*masculine*) (**!** *never changes*)
see also **five**

type
1 *noun*
a type = un tipo
he's not my type = no es mi tipo
2 *verb* = escribir a máquina

typewriter *noun*
a typewriter = una máquina de escribir

typical *adjective*
= típico/típica

typist *noun*
a typist = un mecanógrafo/una
mecanógrafa

tyre *noun* (*British English*)
a tyre = un neumático, una llanta (*Lat Am*),
una goma (*R Pl*)

Uu

ugly *adjective*
= feo/fea

umbrella *noun*
an umbrella = un paraguas

unbearable *adjective*
= insoportable

unbelievable *adjective*
= increíble

uncle *noun*
an uncle = un tío

uncomfortable *adjective*
= incómodo/incómoda

unconscious *adjective*
= inconsciente

under *preposition*
under = debajo de, abajo de (*Lat Am*)
to hide under the bed = eesconderse debajo
de la cama, esconderse abajo de la cama
(*below*)
to go under the bridge = pasar por debajo
del puente, pasar por abajo del puente
(*less than*)
to earn under $3 an hour = ganar menos de
3 dólares la hora
children under 5 = los niños menores de
cinco años

underground
1 *adjective* = suterráneo/suterránea

2 *noun* (*British English*)
the underground = el metro, el subterráneo
(*R Pl*)

underline *verb*
= subrayar

underneath
1 *adverb* = debajo, abajo
2 *preposition* = debajo de, abajo de (*Lat Am*)

underpass *noun*
an underpass (*for traffic*) = un paso
inferior
(*for pedestrians*) = un paso subterráneo

undershirt *noun* (*US English*)
an undershirt = una camiseta

understand *verb*
= entender
to make oneself understood = hacerse
entender

understanding *adjective*
= comprensivo/comprensiva

underwater *adjective*
= submarino/submarina

underwear *noun*
underwear = ropa interior (*feminine*)

undo *verb*
(*if it's a button*) = desabrochar
(*if it's a zipper*) = abrir
(*if it's a knot or shoelace*) = desatar,
desamarrar (*R Pl*)

undress *verb*
= desvestirse

unemployed *adjective*
= desempleado/desempleada,
desocupado/desocupada, parado/parada
(*Spa*)

unemployment *noun*
unemployment = desempleo (*masculine*),
desocupación (*feminine*), paro
(*masculine*) (*Spa*)

unfair *adjective*
= injusto/injusta

unfortunate *adjective*
= desafortunado/desafortunada

unfortunately *adverb*
= desafortunadamente

unfriendly *adjective*
(*if it's a person*) = antipático/antipática
(*if it's a place*) = hostil

ungrateful *adjective*
= desagradecido/desagradecida

unhappy *adjective*
(*sad*) = triste
(*not satisfied*) = descontento/descontenta

C Am Central America   Lat Am Latin America   Mex Mexico

unhealthy *adjective*
(*if it's food*) = malo/mala para la salud
(*if it's a person*) = de mala salud
(*if it's conditions*) = poco saludable

uniform *noun*
a uniform = un uniforme

union *noun*
a union = un sindicato

unique *adjective*
= único/única

United Kingdom *noun* ▶ p. 187
the United Kingdom = el Reino Unido

United States (**of America**) *noun*
▶ p. 187
the United States (of America) = los
Estados Unidos

universe *noun*
the universe = el universo

university *noun*
a university = una universidad

unkind *adjective*
(*if it's a person, an action*)
to be unkind = ser cruel
an unkind remark = un comentario
hiriente

unknown *adjective*
= desconocido/desconocida

unless *conjunction*
= a no ser que
he won't come unless you're there = no
vendrá a no ser que estés tú

! *Note that the subjunctive is used after* a
no ser que

unlock *verb*
= abrir

unlucky *adjective*
(*having bad luck*) =
desafortunado/desafortunada
you were unlucky = tuviste mala suerte
(*bringing bad luck*)
it's unlucky to walk under a ladder = pasar
debajo de una escalera trae mala suerte

unpack *verb*
= deshacer las maletas, desempacar (*Lat
Am*)

unsuccessful *adjective*
to be unsuccessful in doing something =
no lograr hacer algo
the movie was unsuccessful = la película
fracasó

unsuitable *adjective*
unsuitable clothing = ropa inapropiada
he is unsuitable for the job = no es la
persona indicada para el trabajo

untidy *adjective*
(*in habits*) = desordenado/desordenada,
desprolijo/desprolija (*R Pl*)
(*in appearance*) = descuidado/descuidada,
desprolijo/desprolija (*R Pl*)
your room is untidy = tu cuarto está
desordenado

until
1 *preposition* = hasta
2 *conjunction* = hasta que
we'll stay until they come = nos
quedaremos hasta que vengan

! *Note the use of the subjunctive after*
hasta que

unusual *adjective*
(*rare*) = poco común, fuera de lo corriente
it's unusual to see so few people = es raro
ver a tan poca gente
(*different, out of the ordinary*) =
distintivo/distintiva

up

! Up *is often used in combinations with
verbs, for example,* blow up, give up, sit
up. *To find the correct translations for this
type of verb, look up the separate
dictionary entries at* blow, give, sit *etc*

1 *preposition*
to go up the street = subir por la calle
she ran up the stairs = subió las escaleras
corriendo
2 *adverb*
up in the sky = en el cielo
to go up = subir
to go up to Scotland = ir a Escocia
up there = allí arriba
put the picture a bit further up = pon el
cuadro un poco más arriba
3 *adjective*
(*out of bed*)
he's not up yet = no se ha levantado
todavía
to be up all night = pasar la noche en vela
(*wrong*)
what's up? = ¿qué pasa?
up to
(*well enough*)
to be up to going out = sentirse con fuerzas
para salir
(*when talking about who is responsible*)
it's up to me to decide = me corresponde a
mí decidir
(*until*) = hasta

upset
1 *adjective*
to be upset (*annoyed*) = estar
disgustado/disgustada, estar
molesto/molesta
(*distressed*) = estar alterado/alterada
to get upset (*annoyed*) = disgustarse
(*distressed*) = alterarse

U

2 *verb*
  (*to make someone unhappy*) = molestar
  (*to annoy*) = disgustar

upside down *adverb*
  = al revés

upstairs *adverb*
  = arriba
  he's upstairs = está arriba
  to go upstairs = subir

urgent *adjective*
  = urgente

us *pronoun*
  (*when used as a direct object*) = nos
  they know/don't know us = nos conocen/no
    nos conocen

  > **!** *Note that* nos *comes before the verb in*
  > *Spanish*

  (*when used as an indirect object*) = nos
  he never talks to us = no nos habla nunca
  they wrote us a letter = nos escribió una
    carta

  > **!** *Note that* nos *comes before the verb in*
  > *Spanish*

  (*when used as an indirect object pronoun*
    together with a direct object pronoun) =
    nos
  you have to give them to us = nos los
    tienes que dar, tienes que dárnoslos
  he said it to us = nos lo dijo

  > **!** *Note that* nos *comes before the direct*
  > *object pronoun*

  (*when telling someone to do something*)
  help us! = ¡ayúdanos!
  give the money to us = danos el dinero
  give them to us! = ¡dánoslos!

  > **!** *Note that* nos *comes after the verb in*
  > *Spanish*

  (*when telling someone not to do*
    something)
  don't leave us! = ¡no nos dejes!
  don't send them to us! = ¡no nos los
    mandes!

  > **!** *Note that* nos *comes after the verb in*
  > *Spanish*

  (*when used after prepositions and with* **to**
    be) = nosotros/nosotras
  did you buy it for us? = ¿lo compraste para
    nosotros?
  come with us = ven con nosotros
  it's us = somos nosotros

  > **!** *Note that, when talking about mixed*
  > *groups, the masculine form* nosotros *is*
  > *used*

USA *noun* ▶ p. 187
  the USA = los EEUU, los EE UU
  (*in spoken language*) = los Estados Unidos,
    USA✱ (*masculine*)

use
1 *verb*
  (*to make use of*) = usar
  he uses this room as an office = usa este
    cuarto como oficina
  (*to use up*)
  to use gas = consumir gasolina
2 *noun*
  to make use of a room = hacer uso de un
    cuarto
  to have the use of the car = poder usar el
    coche
  (*when talking about what is useful*)
  to be of use to someone = serle útil a
    alguien
  to be of no use = no servir
  what's the use of complaining? = ¿de qué
    sirve quejarse?

use up
  to use up all the money = gastar todo el
    dinero
  to use up the milk = acabar la leche

used
1 *verb*

  > **!** *Note that the imperfect tense in*
  > *Spanish is generally used to translate*
  > used to + *verb:* **she used to live in**
  > **London** = vivía en Londres

  I used to read a lot = leía mucho
  there used to be a castle here = antes
    había un castillo aquí
2 *adjective*
  to be used to animals = estar
    acostumbrado/acostumbrada a los
    animales
  to get used to a new job = acostumbrarse a
    un trabajo nuevo

useful *adjective*
  = útil

useless *adjective*
  = inútil

usual *adjective*
  (*if it's a method*) =
    acostumbrado/acostumbrada
  (*if it's a place, route*) = de siempre
  (*if it's clothes*) = de costumbre

usually *adverb*
  = normalmente

Vv

vacant *adjective*
a vacant room = un cuarto libre
the post is vacant = el puesto está vacante

vacation *noun (US English)*
a vacation = unas vacaciones
to go on vacation = ir de vacaciones

vacuum *verb* = pasar la aspiradora,
aspirar *(Lat Am)*
to vacuum a room = pasar la aspiradora
por un cuarto, aspirar un cuarto

vacuum cleaner *noun*
a vacuum cleaner = una aspiradora, un
aspirador

vain *adjective*
= vanidoso/vanidosa

valley *noun*
a valley = un valle

valuable *adjective*
= valioso/valiosa

van *noun*
a van = una furgoneta, una camioneta, una
vagoneta *(Mex)*

variety *noun*
variety = variedad *(feminine)*
there are a variety of flavors = hay varios
sabores

various *adjective*
= varios/varias

vary *verb*
= variar

vase *noun*
a vase *(for flowers)* = un florero
(ornamental) = un jarrón

veal *noun*
veal = ternera *(feminine)*

vegetable *noun*
a vegetable = una verdura

vegetarian *noun*
a vegetarian = un vegetariano/una
vegetariana

vein *noun*
a vein = una vena

velvet *noun*
velvet = terciopelo *(masculine)*

very
1 *adverb* = muy
to eat very little = comer muy poco
we like them very much = nos gustan
mucho
for the very first time = por primera vez

2 *adjective*
to stay to the very end = quedarse hasta el
fin
you are the very person I wanted to see =
eres justo la persona que quería ver

vest *noun*
(US English—a waistcoat)
a vest = un chaleco
(British English—a piece of underwear)
a vest = una camiseta

vet *noun*
a vet = un veterinario/una veterinaria

vicious *adjective*
(if it's an attack) = feroz, salvaje
(if it's a dog) = fiero/fiera

victory *noun*
a victory = una victoria

video
1 *noun*
(a recorded film, program, event)
a video = un video, un vídeo *(Spa)*
▶ video cassette, video recorder
2 *verb* = grabar

video camera *noun*
a video camera = una videocámara

videocassette *noun*
a videocassette = un videocasete

video recorder *noun*
a video recorder = un aparato de video, un
aparato de vídeo *(Spa)*

view *noun*
a view = una vista
you're blocking my view = me estás
tapando
(an opinion, an attitude)
a view = una opinión
a point of view = un punto de vista

village *noun*
a village = un pueblo

vinegar *noun*
vinegar = vinagre *(masculine)*

vineyard *noun*
a vineyard = una viña

violent *adjective*
= violento/violenta

violin *noun*
a violin = un violín

Virgo *noun*
(the sign)
Virgo = virgo
I'm Virgo = soy Virgo, soy de Virgo
(a person)
a Virgo = un/una virgo

V

visit
1 *verb* = visitar
  to visit Bilbao = visitar Bilbao
  we visited Helen yesterday = fuimos a ver
    a Helen ayer
  to visit with someone (*US English*) = ir a
    ver a alguien
2 *noun*
  a visit = una visita
  to pay someone a visit = hacerle una visita
    a alguien

visitor *noun*
  (*a guest*)
  a visitor = una visita
  to have visitors = tener visitas
  (*a tourist*)
  a visitor = un/una visitante

vocabulary *noun*
  vocabulary = vocabulario (*masculine*)

voice *noun*
  a voice = una voz
  to speak in a low voice = hablar en voz
    baja

volleyball *noun* ▶ p. 306
  volleyball = vóleibol (*masculine*)

vomit *verb*
  = vomitar

vote
1 *noun*
  (*a ballot*)
  a vote = un voto
2 *verb* = votar
  I did not vote for her = no voté por ella

wage *noun*
  a wage = un sueldo

waist *noun*
  the waist = la cintura

waistcoat *noun* (*British English*)
  a waistcoat = un chaleco

wait *verb*
• **to wait** = esperar
  to wait for something/someone = esperar
    algo/a alguien
  to wait for someone to leave = esperar a
    que alguien se vaya

  ! *Note the use of the subjunctive after*
  esperar a que

  I can't wait to see them = me muero de
    ganas de verlos
• (*in a restaurant*)
  to wait on table (*US English*), **to wait at**
    table (*British English*) = atender una mesa

wait up
  to wait up for someone = esperar a alguien
    levantado/levantada

waiter *noun*
  a waiter = un camarero, un mesero (*Lat*
    Am), un mozo (*SC*)

waiting room *noun*
  a waiting room = una sala de espera

waitress *noun*
  a waitress = una camarera, una mesera
    (*Lat Am*)

wake *verb*
  = despertar
wake up = despertarse
  he woke me up = me despertó

Wales *noun* ▶ p. 187
  Wales = (el País de) Gales

walk
1 *verb*
• (*rather than run*) = caminar, andar
• (*rather than drive or ride*) = ir a pie
• (*for pleasure*) = pasear
  to walk the dog = sacar al perro a pasear
2 *noun*
  a walk = un paseo
  to go for a walk = ir a pasear
  it's five minutes walk from here = está a
    cinco minutos de aquí a pie
walk around = pasear
  to walk around the town = pasear por la
    ciudad
walk back = volver a pie, regresar a pie

wall *noun*
  a wall (*freestanding*) = un muro
  (*of a city*) = una muralla
  (*of a room, a building*) = una pared, una
    muralla (*Chi*)

wallet *noun*
  a wallet = una billetera, un billetero

wallpaper *noun*
  wallpaper = papel de empapelar
    (*masculine*)

wander *verb*
  to wander around town = pasear por la
    ciudad
wander away, wander off = alejarse

want *verb*
• **to want** = querer
  he wants to go out = quiere salir
  I want you to come with me = quiero que
    me acompañes

  ! *Note the use of the subjunctive after*
  querer que
• (*to need*) = necesitar

war *noun*
a war = una guerra

wardrobe *noun*
a wardrobe = un armario, un ropero

warm *adjective*
• (*not cold*)
the water is warm = el agua está tibia
the climate is warm = el clima está cálido
to feel warm, to be warm = tener calor
it's warm in here = hace calor aquí dentro
to get warm = calentarse
• (*enthusiastic*)
a warm reception = una acogida cálida
warm up
• (*to get warm*) = calentarse
• (*for a sporting event*) = hacer ejercicios de calentamiento
• (*to make warm*) = calentar

warn
= advertir
I warned him not to take the car = le advertí que no llevara el coche

> ! Note the use of the subjunctive after advertir que

warning *noun*
• (*a piece of advice*)
a warning = una advertencia
• (*prior notice*)
they arrived without warning = llegaron sin avisar

wash *verb*
• (*to clean*) = lavar
to wash one's clothes = lavar la ropa
to wash one's face = lavarse la cara
to wash the dishes = fregar los platos, lavar los trastes (*C Am, Mex*)
• (*to clean oneself*) = lavarse
wash up
• (*US English—to clean oneself*) = lavarse
• (*British English—to do the dishes*) = fregar los platos, lavar los trastes (*C Am, Mex*)

washbowl (*US English*), **washbasin** (*British English*) *noun*
a washbowl = un lavamanos, un lavabo, un lavatorio (*SC*)

washing *noun*
the washing (*dirty*) = la ropa para lavar
(*clean*) = la ropa lavada
to do the washing = lavar la ropa, hacer la colada (*Spa*)

washing machine *noun*
a washing machine = una máquina de lavar, una lavadora, un lavarropas (*R Pl*)

washing-up *noun* (*British English*)
to do the washing-up = fregar los platos, lavar los trastes (*C Am, Mex*)

wasp *noun*
a wasp = una avispa

waste
1 *verb*
to waste electricity = despilfarrar la electricidad
we're wasting time = estamos perdiendo el tiempo
2 *noun*
it's a waste of money = es tirar el dinero
a waste of time = una pérdida de tiempo

watch
1 *verb*
• (*to look at*) = mirar
to watch television = ver la televisión, mirar televisión
• (*to keep under observation*) = vigilar
• (*to pay attention to*)
watch what you're doing = mira lo que haces
2 *noun*
a watch = un reloj
watch out = tener cuidado
watch out! = ¡cuidado!

water
1 *noun*
water = agua (*feminine*)
the water's cold = el agua está fría
2 *verb* = regar

waterfall *noun*
a waterfall (*small*) = una cascada
(*large*) = una catarata

wave
1 *verb*
• (*to signal with one's hand*)
to wave to someone = saludar a alguien con la mano
to wave goodbye = hacer adiós con la mano
• (*to direct*)
the policeman waved them on = el policía les hizo señas de que siguieran
2 *noun*
(*on the sea*)
a wave = una ola

way *noun*
• (*a manner, a method*)
a way = una forma, una manera, un modo
he does it the wrong way = no lo hace bien
that's not the way to do it = no se hace así
I like the way she dresses = me gusta como se viste
I prefer to do it my way = prefiero hacerlo a mi manera
• (*a route, a road*)
a way = un camino
on the way to Leeds = de camino a Leeds
where's the way out? = ¿dónde está la salida?
to lose one's way = perderse
• (*a direction*)
they went that way = fueron por ahí
this way! = ¡por aquí!

to be in the way = estorbar
to get out of the way = apartarse
it's a long way from here = está muy lejos
de aquí
she likes to get her own way = le gusta
salirse con la suya
• **by the way** = a propósito

we *pronoun*
we = nosotros/nosotras

> ❗ *When talking about mixed groups the*
> *masculine form* **nosotros** *is used*

we went to the theater = fuimos al teatro
we **did it** = nosotros/nosotras lo hicimos

> ❗ *Although* **nosotros** *and* **nosotras** *are*
> *given as translations of* **we**, *they are in*
> *practice used only for emphasis*

weak *adjective*
• (*not healthy*) = débil
• (*not good or able*) = flojo/floja
• (*having very little power*) = débil
weak coffee = café poco cargado

wealthy *adjective*
= rico/rica

wear *verb*
• (*to be dressed in*)
to be wearing trousers = llevar pantalones
to wear black = vestirse de negro
• (*to put on*) = ponerse
wear out
to wear one's shoes out = gastar los
zapatos
to wear someone out = agotar a alguien

weather *noun*
the weather = el tiempo
what's the weather like? = ¿qué tiempo
hace?, ¿cómo está el tiempo?
the weather is [**bad** | **nice** | **hot** …] = hace [mal
tiempo | buen tiempo | calor …]

weather forecast *noun*
the weather forecast = el pronóstico del
tiempo

Web *noun*
the Web = el Web, la Red
a website = un sitio web

wedding *noun*
a wedding = una boda

Wednesday *noun* ▶ p. 192
Wednesday = miércoles (*masculine*)

week *noun*
a week = una semana

weekend *noun*
a weekend = un fin de semana

weigh *verb*
= pesar
what do you weigh? = ¿cuánto pesas?

weight *noun*
weight = peso
to put on weight = engordar
to lose weight = adelgazar

weird *adjective*
= raro/rara, extraño/extraña

welcome
1 *verb*
to welcome someone = darle la bienvenida
a alguien
2 *adjective*
• (*when receiving people*)
to be welcome = ser bienvenido/bienvenida
welcome to the United States =
bienvenidos a los Estados Unidos
• (*when acknowledging thanks*)
thanks—you're welcome = gracias—de
nada

well
1 *adverb*
• **well** = bien
he is well paid = le pagan bien
• **as well** = también
as well as = además de
we may as well go home = más vale que
vayamos a casa

> ❗ *Note the use of the subjunctive after*
> más vale que

2 *adjective*
to feel well = sentirse bien
I'm very well = estoy muy bien

well-known *adjective*
= conocido/conocida

Welsh ▶ p. 187, p. 245
1 *adjective* = galés/galesa
2 *noun*
• (*the people*)
the Welsh = los galeses
• (*the language*)
Welsh = galés (*masculine*)

west
1 *noun*
the west = el oeste
in the west of England = en el oeste de
Inglaterra
2 *adverb*
we went west = fuimos hacia el oeste
it is west of London = está al oeste de
Londres
3 *adjective*
= oeste (❗ *never changes*)
the west coast = la costa oeste
a west wind = un viento del oeste

West Indies *noun* ▶ p. 187
the West Indies = las Antillas

wet *adjective*
• (*moist*) = mojado/mojada
to get wet = mojarse
she got her feet wet = se mojó los pies
• (*if it's the weather*) = lluvioso/lluviosa

what
1 *pronoun*
• **do what you want** = haz lo que quieras
what we need is a timetable = lo que
necesitamos es un horario
• (*used in questions*)
what do you want? = ¿qué quieres?
what's her phone number? = ¿cuál es su
número de teléfono?
what's this button for? = ¿para qué sirve
este botón?
what's the Spanish for 'boring'? = ¿cómo
se dice 'boring' en español?
what's she like? = ¿cómo es?
what if I don't get there on time? = ¿y si no
llego a tiempo?
2 *adjective*
do you know what train to take? = ¿sabes
qué tren hay que tomar?
what a great idea! = ¡qué buena idea!

whatever *pronoun*
• (*when anything is possible*)
take whatever you want = toma lo que
quieras
• (*when it doesn't matter*)
**whatever they do, it won't change
anything** = hagan lo que hagan, no va a
cambiar nada

wheat *noun*
wheat = trigo (*masculine*)

wheel *noun*
a wheel = una rueda

wheelchair *noun*
a wheelchair = una silla de ruedas

when
1 *adverb* = cuándo
when did she leave? = ¿cuándo se fue?
I don't know when the film starts = no sé
cuándo empieza la película
2 *conjunction* = cuando
I was asleep when the phone rang = estaba
dormida cuando sonó el teléfono
3 *pronoun*
(*used in questions*) = cuándo
until when? = ¿hasta cuándo?

where
1 *adverb* = dónde
where are you going? = ¿dónde vas?
do you know where he is? = ¿sabes dónde
está?
2 *conjunction* = donde
that's where she fell = allí es donde se cayó
I'll leave the key where you can see it =
voy a dejar la llave donde la puedes ver

whether *conjunction*
= si

which
1 *pronoun*
• **the house which I told you about** = la casa
de la que te hablé
• (*used in questions*)
which of the girls is his sister? = ¿cuál de
las chicas es su hermana?
do you know which she chose? = ¿sabes
cuál eligió?
2 *adjective*
in which European city is it? = ¿en qué
ciudad europea está?, ¿en cuál ciudad
europea está?
ask her which chapters we have to read =
pregúntale qué capítulos hay que leer,
pregúntale cuáles capítulos hay que leer

while
1 *conjunction* = mientras
2 *noun*
a while ago = hace un rato
after a while = después de un rato

whisper *verb*
= susurrar

whistle
1 *verb* = silbar
2 *noun*
• (*an instrument*)
a whistle = un silbato
• (*a sound*)
a whistle = un silbido

white *adjective* ▶ p. 183
= blanco/blanca

who *pronoun*
• **my friend who lives in Miami** = mi amigo
que vive en Miami
those who can't come by car = los que no
pueden venir en coche
• (*used in questions*) = quién
who did he buy the book for? = ¿para
quién compró el libro?

whole
1 *noun*
the whole of the country = todo el país
we're staying the whole of August = nos
quedamos todo agosto
2 *adjective* = entero/entera
three whole weeks = tres semanas enteras

whom *pronoun*
• **the person to whom I spoke on the phone**
= la persona con la que hablé por
teléfono
• (*used in questions*)
whom did you meet? = ¿a quién conociste?

whose
1 *pronoun*

W

- **the boy whose bike was stolen** = el chico al que le robaron la bicicleta
  the woman whose house I'm buying = la mujer cuya casa voy a comprar
- (*used in questions*)
  whose is the dog? = ¿de quién es el perro?
2 *adjective*
  whose car is that? = ¿de quién es ese coche?
  do you know whose jacket this is? = ¿sabes de quién es esta chaqueta?

why
1 *adverb*
- (*used in questions*) = por qué
  why did you do that? = ¿por qué hiciste eso?
  why not? = ¿por qué no?
- (*when making suggestions*)
  why don't we go away this weekend? = ¿por qué no vamos a algún lado este fin de semana?
2 *conjunction*
  that's why I can't stand him = por eso es que no lo aguanto

wide
1 *adjective*
- (*in size*) = ancho/ancha
  how wide is it? = ¿cuánto tiene de ancho?, ¿cuánto mide de ancho?
  the room is 10 meters wide = el cuarto tiene 10 metros de ancho
- (*in range*) = amplio/amplia (**!** *before the noun*)
  a wide range of games = una amplia gama de juegos
2 *adverb*
  to open the window wide = abrir la ventana de par en par

wife *noun*
  a wife = una esposa, una mujer

wild *adjective*
- (*if it's an animal*) = salvaje
- (*if it's a plant*) = silvestre
- (*noisy, out of control*)
  to go wild = volverse loco/loca

will *verb*
- (*when talking about the future*)

  > **!** When referring to the future, the future tense is not always the first option for translating **will** + verb into Spanish. The present tense of **ir** + **a** + verb is common in Latin American countries

  she won't agree = no aceptará, no va a aceptar
  it will be sunny tomorrow = mañana hará sol, mañana va a hacer sol
  what will we do? = ¿qué vamos a hacer?
- (*in invitations and requests*)
  will you have some coffee? = ¿quiere un café?
  won't you stay for dinner? = ¿se queda a cenar?

- (*when making assumptions*)
  they won't know what's happened = no sabrán lo que ha pasado
- (*in short questions and answers*)
  that will be cheaper, won't it? = ¿eso será más barato, no?
  will it be ready?—yes it will = ¿estará listo? —sí

win *verb*
  = ganar

wind *noun*
  the wind = el viento

window *noun*
  a window (*in a house*) = una ventana
  (*in a shop*) = un escaparate, una vidriera (*Lat Am*), un aparador (*Mex*)
  (*in a vehicle*) = una ventanilla

windy *adjective*
  a windy day = un día de viento
  it's windy = hace viento

wine *noun*
  wine = vino (*masculine*)

wing *noun*
  a wing = un ala (*feminine*)

winter *noun*
  winter = invierno (*masculine*)
  in winter = en invierno

wipe *verb*
  = limpiar
  to wipe one's nose = limpiarse la nariz
wipe up = limpiar

wise *adjective*
- (*if it's a person*) = sabio/sabia
- (*if it's a decision, a choice*) = acertado/acertada

wish
1 *noun*
- **a wish** = un deseo
  to make a wish = pedir un deseo
- (*in greetings*)
  best wishes, Helen = saludos de Helen, un abrazo de Helen
2 *verb*
- (*expressing what one would like*)
  I wish they would come = ojalá (que) vinieran

  > **!** Note the use of the subjunctive after ojalá (que)

  she wished she hadn't told him = lamentó habérselo dicho
- (*in greetings*) = desear

with *preposition*

  > **!** Note that **with** is used after many adjectives, eg **to be angry with** someone, **to be pleased with** something. To find the translation, look up the separate dictionary entries at **angry**, **pleased** etc

- **with** = con
  to go out with friends = salir con amigos
  I'm living with my parents = vivo con mis
    padres
- (*when describing*)
  a girl with black hair = una chica de pelo
    negro
  his clothes were covered with mud = su
    ropa estaba cubierta de barro
- (*as a result of*)
  trembling with fear = temblando de miedo

without *preposition*
  = sin
  we got in without paying = entramos sin
    pagar

wolf *noun*
  a wolf = un lobo

woman *noun*
  a woman = una mujer

wonder
1 *verb*
- (*to ask oneself*) = preguntarse
  I wonder why? = ¿me pregunto por qué?
- (*in polite requests*)
  I wonder if you could help me? = ¿me
    podría ayudar?
2 *noun*
  it's a wonder that no one was injured = es
    asombroso que nadie resultara herido
  it's no wonder he's always late = no es de
    extrañar que siempre llegue tarde

> **!** *Note the use of the subjunctive after* es
> asombroso que *and* no es de extrañar
> que

wonderful *adjective*
  = maravilloso/maravillosa

wood *noun*
- (*timber*)
  wood = madera (*feminine*)
- (*a small forest*)
  a wood = un bosque

wool *noun*
  wool = lana (*feminine*)

word *noun*
  a word = una palabra
  I didn't say a word = yo no dije nada
  in other words you don't want to go = es
    decir que no quieres ir

word processor *noun*
  a word processor = un procesador de
    textos

work
1 *verb*
- (*to have or do a job*) = trabajar
- (*to operate properly*) = funcionar
  the TV isn't working = la televisión no
    funciona

- (*to be successful*) (*of an idea, a trick*) =
    resultar
  (*of a medicine, a treatment, a plan*) = surtir
    efecto
- (*to use, to operate*)
  do you know how to work the computer? =
    ¿sabes manejar la computadora?
2 *noun*
- **work** = trabajo (*masculine*)
  to be out of work = estar sin trabajo
  it's hard work learning German = es difícil
    aprender alemán
- (*by an artist, a musician*)
  a work = una obra

work out
- (*to solve*)
  to work out a problem = resolver un
    problema
- (*to understand*) = entender
- (*to calculate*) = calcular
- (*to go well*) = salir bien

work up
  to get worked up = exaltarse

worker *noun*
  a worker (*in a factory*) = un obrero/una
    obrera
  (*in an office, a bank*) = un empleado/una
    empleada

world *noun*
  the world = el mundo

World Cup *noun*
  the World Cup = la Copa Mundial

worm *noun*
  a worm = un gusano

worried *adjective*
  = preocupado/preocupada
  to be worried about someone =
    preocuparse por alguien

worry *verb*
- (*to be worried*) = preocuparse
- (*to make someone worried*) = preocupar
  it's worrying me = me preocupa

worse *adjective*
  = peor
  this book is worse than the others = este
    libro es peor que los demás
  to get worse = empeorar

worst
1 *noun*
  the worst = el/la peor
2 *adjective* = peor
  the worst hotel in town = el peor hotel de la
    ciudad

worth *adjective*
  to be worth $100 = valer 100 dólares
  how much is it worth? = ¿cuánto vale?
  it's not worth the trouble = no vale la pena

would *verb*

> ! *Spanish usually uses verbs in the conditional to translate* **would** *or* **'d** + *verb:* I would buy, I'd buy = compraría

- (*when talking about hypothetical rather than real situations*)
  If I had more money, I would buy a car = si tuviera más dinero, me compraría un coche
- (*in reported speech*)
  I thought you'd forget to come = pensé que te olvidarías de venir
- (*to be prepared to*)
  he wouldn't listen to me = no me quería escuchar
- (*when talking about wishes*)
  I'd like a beer = me gustaría una cerveza, quisiera una cerveza
- (*when asking, offering, or advising*)
  would you switch the television off? = ¿podrías apagar la televisión?
  would you like something to eat? = ¿quieres comer algo?

wrap *verb*
= envolver

wreck *verb*
= destrozar

wrestling *noun*
wrestling = lucha (*feminine*)

wrist *noun* ▶ p. 235
the wrist = la muñeca

write *verb*
= escribir
to write a letter = escribir una carta
to write someone a check = hacerle un cheque a alguien
write back = contestar
write down = apuntar
write out = escribir

writing *noun*
(*written material*)
to put something in writing = poner algo por escrito

writing pad *noun*
a writing pad = un bloc

wrong
1 *adjective*
- (*not as it should be*)
  there's something wrong = pasa algo
  what's wrong? = ¿qué pasa?
  what's wrong with you? = ¿qué te pasa?, ¿qué tienes?
- (*not proper or suitable*)
  I took the wrong key = llevé la llave equivocada
  to go the wrong way = equivocarse de camino
- (*not correct*)
  a wrong answer = una respuesta equivocada
  you're wrong = estás equivocado/equivocada
- (*not good, not honest*)
  it's wrong to steal = robar está mal
  she hasn't done anything wrong = no ha hecho nada malo
2 *adverb*
  to get the time wrong = equivocarse de hora
  everything went wrong = todo salió mal

Xx

X-ray
1 *noun*
  an X-ray = una radiografía
  I had an X-ray = me hicieron una radiografía
2 *verb* = hacer una radiografía de

Yy

yacht *noun*
  a yacht = un yate

yard *noun*
- (*when measuring*)
  a yard = una yarda

  > ! *Note that a yard = 0.9144 m*

- (*US English—a garden*)
  a yard = un jardín
- (*of a school*)
  a yard = un patio
- (*British English—of a house*)
  a yard = un patio

yawn *verb*
= bostezar

year *noun* ▶ p. 154, p. 192
- **a year** = un año
  he's lived there for years = hace años que vive allí
- (*when talking about age*)
  to be 15 years old, to be 15 years of age = tener 15 años
  a four-year old = un niño/una niña de cuatro años

You

In English **you** is used to address everybody, whereas Spanish has four forms: **tú**, **vosotros** (feminine form **vosotras**), **usted**, and **ustedes**.

Generally speaking, the pronoun **tú** and the **tú** form of the verb are used between friends and family, between people on first-name terms, among young people even if they do not know each other, and when addressing children and animals.

The pronouns **usted** and the **usted** form of the verb are used when addressing an older person, someone in authority, or, in general, as a show of respect.

Ustedes and vosotros

In Latin America, the Canary Islands and parts of Andalusia, **ustedes** is the plural of both **usted** and **tú**. In the rest of Spain, the informal plural, that is, the plural form of **tú**, is **vosotros**, which takes the second person plural form of the verb.

Vos

In some Latin American countries, the form **vos** is used instead of **tú**. This usage is known as **voseo** and is common in the River Plate and parts of Central America.

- *(in a school system)*
  the first year, year 1 = el primer curso, el primer año

yell
1 *verb* = gritar
2 *noun*
  a yell = un grito

yellow *adjective* ▶ **p. 183**
  = amarillo/amarilla

yes *adverb*
  yes = sí
  are you coming with us?—yes I am = ¿vienes con nosotros?—sí

yesterday *adverb*
  = ayer

yet
1 *adverb* = todavía
  not yet = todavía no
  have they arrived yet? = ¿han llegado ya?
2 *conjunction* = pero

yield *verb*
  to yield one's right of way (*US English—when driving*) = ceder el paso

yoghurt *noun*
  yoghurt = yogur (*masculine*)

you *pronoun*
- *(when used as the subject)*
  (*informal—singular*) = tú, vos (*R Pl*)
  (*informal—plural*) = ustedes, vosotros/vosotras (*Spa*)

  ! *When talking about mixed groups the masculine form* **vosotros** *is used*

  (*formal—singular*) = usted

  (*formal—plural*) = ustedes
  you are my best friends = ustedes son mis mejores amigos, (vosotros) sois mis mejores amigos (*Spa*)
  you **did it** = tú lo hiciste
  I was singing and you were playing the piano = yo cantaba y usted tocaba el piano
  be quiet, you two = ustedes dos: ¡cállense!, vosotros dos: ¡callaos! (*Spa*)
  poor you! = ¡pobrecito!/¡pobrecita!

  ! *Note that the main translations given above are in practice used only for emphasis, or to avoid ambiguity*

- *(when used as a direct object)*
  (*informal—singular*) = te
  (*informal—plural*) = los/las, os (*Spa*)
  (*formal—singular*) = lo/la, le/la (*Spa*)
  (*formal—plural*) = los/las, les/las (*Spa*)
  I know/don't know you = te conozco/no te conozco
  did he see you? = ¿los/las vio?, ¿les/las vio? (*Spa*)

  ! *Note that the direct object pronoun comes before the verb in Spanish*

- *(when used as an indirect object)*
  (*informal—singular*) = te
  (*informal—plural*) = les, os (*Spa*)
  (*formal—singular*) = le
  (*formal—plural*) = les
  he gave you the book = les dio el libro, os dio el libro (*Spa*)
  I wrote you a letter = le escribí una carta

  ! *Note that the indirect object pronoun comes before the verb in Spanish*

- *(when used as an indirect object pronoun together with a direct object pronoun)*
  (*informal—singular*) = te

R Pl River Plate area   **SC** Southern Cone   **Spa** Spain

(*informal—plural*) = se, os (*Spa*)
(*formal—singular*) = se
(*formal—plural*) = se
I gave it to you = se lo di
I'm not going to say it to you = no te lo voy
a decir

! Note that the indirect object pronoun
comes before the direct object pronoun
in Spanish

---

* (*when used after prepositions*)
(*informal—singular*) = ti, vos (*R Pl*)
(*informal—plural*) = ustedes,
vosotros/vosotras (*Spa*)
(*formal—singular*) = usted
(*formal—plural*) = ustedes
we bought it for you = lo compramos para
ustedes
a letter for you = una carta para usted
he arrived after you = llegó después de ti
I'll go with you = iré contigo
* (*when talking in an impersonal or vague
way about people*)
(*when used as the subject*)
you can't do that here = no se puede hacer
eso aquí, uno no puede hacer eso aquí, no
puedes hacer eso aquí (*Spa*)
(*when used as a direct object*)
**people stop you in the street and ask for
money** = la gente lo para a uno en la calle
y le pide dinero, la gente te para en la
calle y te pide dinero (*Spa*)
(*when used as an indirect object*)
they can cause you a lot of trouble = le
pueden a uno crear muchos problemas,
te pueden crear muchos problemas (*Spa*)

young *adjective*
= joven
a young lady = una joven
young people = los jóvenes
she is a year younger than me = tiene un
año menos que yo, es un año menor que
yo
a younger brother/sister = un
hermano/una hermana menor

your *adjective*
* (*belonging to one person*)
(*informal*) = tu (+ *singular*), tus (+ *plural*)
(*formal*) = su (+ *singular*), sus (+ *plural*)
* (*belonging to more than one person*)
(*informal*) = su (+ *singular*), sus (+ *plural*),
vuestro/vuestra (+ *singular*) (*Spa*),
vuestros/vuestras (+ *plural*) (*Spa*)
(*formal*) = su (+ *singular*), sus (+ *plural*)
* (*one's*)
if your name begins with A ... = si el
nombre de uno empieza con A ..., si tu
nombre empieza con A ... (*Spa*)
**you have to take your shoes off in a
mosque** = hay que quitarse los zapatos
en una mezquita

! For your *used with parts of the body,*
▶ **p. 235**

---

yours *pronoun*
* (*belonging to one person*)
(*informal—singular*) = tuyo/tuya
(*informal—plural*) = tuyos/tuyas
(*formal—singular*) = suyo/suya
(*formal—plural*) = suyos/suyas
yours is blue = el tuyo/la tuya es azul
a friend of yours = un amigo suyo
* (*belonging to more than one person*)
(*informal—singular*) = suyo/suya,
vuestro/vuestra (*Spa*)
(*informal—plural*) = suyos/suyas,
vuestros/vuestras (*Spa*)
(*formal—singular*) = suyo/suya
(*formal—plural*) = suyos/suyas
yours are blue = los suyos/las suyas son
azules
a friend of yours = un amigo suyo, un
amigo vuestro (*Spa*)

yourself *pronoun*
* (*when translated by a reflexive verb in
Spanish*)
(*informal*)
did you hurt yourself? = ¿te hiciste daño?,
¿te lastimaste? (*Lat Am*)
describe yourself = descríbete
(*formal*)
did you hurt yourself? = ¿se hizo daño?,
¿se lastimó? (*Lat Am*)
describe yourself = descríbase
* (*when used for emphasis*)
(*informal*) = tú mismo/tú misma
(*formal*) = usted mismo/usted misma
by yourself = solo/sola
* (*oneself*) = uno mismo/una misma

yourselves *pronoun*
* (*when translated by a reflexive verb in
Spanish*)
(*informal*)
did you hurt yourselves? = ¿se hicieron
daño *or* se lastimaron? (*Lat Am*), ¿os
hicisteis daño? (*Spa*)
(*formal*)
did you hurt yourselves? = ¿se hicieron
daño?, ¿se lastimaron? (*Lat Am*)
* (*when used for emphasis*)
(*informal*) = ustedes mismos/mismas,
vosotros mismos/vosotras mismas (*Spa*)
(*formal*) = ustedes mismos/mismas
by yourselves = solos/solas

youth *noun*
(*a young man*)
a youth = un joven

youth club *noun*
a youth club = un club de jóvenes

youth hostel *noun*
a youth hostel = un albergue juvenil

C Am Central America   **Lat Am** Latin America   **Mex** Mexico

Zz

zebra *noun*
  a zebra = una cebra

zebra crossing *noun* (*British English*)
  a zebra crossing = un paso de cebra

zero *noun*
  a zero = un cero

zip (*British English*) *noun* ▶ zipper

zip code *noun* (*US English*)
  a zip code = un código postal

zipper *noun* (*US English*)
  a zipper = una cremallera, un cierre (*Lat Am*), un zíper (*Mex*)

zodiac *noun*
  the zodiac = el zodíaco, el zodiaco

zone *noun*
  a zone = una zona

zoo *noun*
  a zoo = un zoológico, un zoo (*Spa*)

Verb tables

Spanish verb tables

Present indicative
   canto = *I sing, I'm singing*

Imperfect indicative
   cantaba = *I was singing, I used to sing*

Past simple indicative
   canté = *I sang*

Future indicative
   cantaré = *I will sing*

Conditional (present)
   si hubiera un coro, cantaría =
   if there was a choir, I would sing

Present subjunctive
   es posible que cante = *he might sing*

Imperfect subjunctive
   aunque yo cantara = *even if I sang*

Imperative
   canta/cantad = *sing!*

Verbs ending in -ar

1 hablar

Present indicative	Conditional (present)
hablo	hablaría
hablas	hablarías
habla	hablaría
hablamos	hablaríamos
habláis	hablaríais
hablan	hablarían

Imperfect indicative	Present subjunctive
hablaba	hable
hablabas	hables
hablaba	hable
hablábamos	hablemos
hablabais	habléis
hablaban	hablen

Past simple indicative	Imperfect subjunctive*
hablé	hablara
hablaste	hablaras
habló	hablara
hablamos	habláramos
hablasteis	hablarais
hablaron	hablaran

Future indicative	Imperative
hablaré	habla (tú)
hablarás	hable (usted)
hablará	hablemos (nosotros)
hablaremos	hablad (vosotros)
hablaréis	hablen (ustedes)
hablarán	

Gerund
hablando

Past participle
hablado

* all **-ar** verbs have an alternative form of the Imperfect
subjunctive in which the **-ara** ending is replaced by
-ase, eg: hablase, hablases, hablase, hablásemos,
hablaseis, hablasen

2 sacar   formed as **1 hablar** except:

Past simple indicative	Present subjunctive
saqué	saque
sacaste	saques
sacó	saque
sacamos	saquemos
sacasteis	saquéis
sacaron	saquen

	Imperative
	saca (tú)
	saque (usted)
	saquemos (nosotros)
	sacad (vosotros)
	saquen (ustedes)

3 pagar   formed as **1 hablar** except:

Past simple indicative	Present subjunctive
pagué	pague
pagaste	pagues
pagó	pague
pagamos	paguemos
pagasteis	paguéis
pagaron	paguen

	Imperative
	paga (tú)
	pague (usted)
	paguemos (nosotros)
	pagad (vosotros)
	paguen (ustedes)

4 cazar formed as 1 hablar except:

Past simple indicative	Present subjunctive
cacé	cace
cazaste	caces
cazó	cace
cazamos	cacemos
cazasteis	cacéis
cazaron	cacen

Imperative
caza (tú)
cace (usted)
cacemos (nosotros)
cazad (vosotros)
cacen (ustedes)

8 regar formed as 1 hablar except:

Present indicative	Present subjunctive
riego	riegue
riegas	riegues
riega	riegue
regamos	reguemos
regáis	reguéis
riegan	rieguen

Past simple indicative	Imperative
regué	riega (tú)
regaste	riegue (usted)
regó	reguemos (nosotros)
regamos	regad (vosotros)
regasteis	rieguen (ustedes)
regaron	

5 empezar formed as 1 hablar except:

Present indicative	Present subjunctive
empiezo	empiece
empiezas	empieces
empieza	empiece
empezamos	empecemos
empezáis	empecéis
empiezan	empiecen

Past simple indicative	Imperative
empecé	empieza (tú)
empezaste	empiece (usted)
empezó	empecemos (nosotros)
empezamos	empezad (vosotros)
empezasteis	empiecen (ustedes)
empezaron	

9 colgar formed as 1 hablar except:

Present indicative	Present subjunctive
cuelgo	cuelgue
cuelgas	cuelgues
cuelga	cuelgue
colgamos	colguemos
colgáis	colguéis
cuelgan	cuelguen

Past simple indicative	Imperative
colgué	cuelga (tú)
colgaste	cuelgue (usted)
colgó	colguemos (nosotros)
colgamos	colgad (vosotros)
colgasteis	cuelguen (ustedes)
colgaron	

6 contar formed as 1 hablar except:

Present indicative	Present subjunctive
cuento	cuente
cuentas	cuentes
cuenta	cuente
contamos	contemos
contáis	contéis
cuentan	cuenten

Imperative
cuenta (tú)
cuente (usted)
contemos (nosotros)
contad (vosotros)
cuenten (ustedes)

10 forzar formed as 1 hablar except:

Present indicative	Present subjunctive
fuerzo	fuerce
fuerzas	fuerces
fuerza	fuerce
forzamos	forcemos
forzáis	forcéis
fuerzan	fuercen

Past simple indicative	Imperative
forcé	fuerza (tú)
forzaste	fuerce (usted)
forzó	forcemos (nosotros)
forzamos	forzad (vosotros)
forzasteis	fuercen (ustedes)
forzaron	

7 pensar formed as 1 hablar except:

Present indicative	Present subjunctive
pienso	piense
piensas	pienses
piensa	piense
pensamos	pensemos
pensáis	penséis
piensan	piensen

Imperative
piensa (tú)
piense (usted)
pensemos (nosotros)
pensad (vosotros)
piensen (ustedes)

11 actuar formed as 1 hablar except:

Present indicative	Present subjunctive
actúo	actúe
actúas	actúes
actúa	actúe
actuamos	actuemos
actuáis	actuéis
actúan	actúen

Imperative
actúa (tú)
actúe (usted)
actuemos (nosotros)
actuad (vosotros)
actúen (ustedes)

12 jugar   formed as **1 hablar** except:

Present indicative	Present subjunctive
juego	juegue
juegas	juegues
juega	juegue
jugamos	juguemos
jugáis	juguéis
juegan	jueguen

Past simple indicative	Imperative
jugué	juega (tú)
jugaste	juegue (usted)
jugó	juguemos (nosotros)
jugamos	jugad (vosotros)
jugasteis	jueguen (ustedes)
jugaron	

13 vaciar   formed as **1 hablar** except:

Present indicative	Present subjunctive
vacío	vacíe
vacías	vacíes
vacía	vacíe
vaciamos	vaciemos
vaciáis	vaciéis
vacían	vacíen

Imperative
vacía (tú)
vacíe (usted)
vaciemos (nosotros)
vaciad (vosotros)
vacíen (ustedes)

14 andar   formed as **1 hablar** except:

Past simple indicative	Imperfect subjunctive
anduve	anduviera
anduviste	anduvieras
anduvo	anduviera
anduvimos	anduviéramos
anduvisteis	anduvierais
anduvieron	anduvieran

15 dar   formed as **1 hablar** except:

Present indicative	Present subjunctive
doy	dé
das	des
da	dé
damos	demos
dais	deis
dan	den

Past simple indicative	Imperfect subjunctive
di	diera
diste	dieras
dio	diera
dimos	diéramos
disteis	dierais
dieron	dieran

16 estar   formed as **1 hablar** except:

Present indicative	Present subjunctive
estoy	esté
estás	estés
está	esté
estamos	estemos
estáis	estéis
están	estén

Past simple indicative	Imperfect subjunctive
estuve	estuviera
estuviste	estuvieras
estuvo	estuviera
estuvimos	estuviéramos
estuvisteis	estuvierais
estuvieron	estuvieran

Imperative
está (tú)
esté (usted)
estemos (nosotros)
estad (vosotros)
estén (ustedes)

Verbs ending in -er

17 meter

Present indicative	Conditional (present)
meto	metería
metes	meterías
mete	metería
metemos	meteríamos
metéis	meteríais
meten	meterían

Imperfect indicative	Present subjunctive
metía	meta
metías	metas
metía	meta
metíamos	metamos
metíais	metáis
metían	metan

Past simple indicative	Imperfect subjunctive*
metí	metiera
metiste	metieras
metió	metiera
metimos	metiéramos
metisteis	metierais
metieron	metieran

Future indicative	Imperative
meteré	mete (tú)
meterás	meta (usted)
meterá	metamos (nosotros)
meteremos	meted (vosotros)
meteréis	metan (ustedes)
meterán	

Gerund
metiendo

Past Participle
metido

* all **-er** verbs have an alternative form of the Imperfect subjunctive in which the **-era** ending is replaced by **-ese**, eg: meti**ese**, meti**eses**, meti**ese**, meti**ésemos**, meti**eseis**, meti**esen**

18 vencer formed as 17 meter except:

Present indicative	Present subjunctive
venzo	venza
vences	venzas
vence	venza
vencemos	venzamos
vencéis	venzáis
vencen	venzan

Imperative
vence (tú)
venza (usted)
venzamos (nosotros)
venced (vosotros)
venzan (ustedes)

19 conocer formed as 17 meter except:

present indicative	Present subjunctive
conozco	conozca
conoces	conozcas
conoce	conozca
conocemos	conozcamos
conocéis	conozcáis
conocen	conozcan

Imperative
conoce (tú)
conozca (usted)
conozcamos (nosotros)
conoced (vosotros)
conozcan (ustedes)

20 coger formed as 17 meter except:

Present indicative	Present subjunctive
cojo	coja
coges	cojas
coge	coja
cogemos	cojamos
cogéis	cojáis
cogen	cojan

Imperative
coge (tú)
coja (usted)
cojamos (nosotros)
coged (vosotros)
cojan (ustedes)

21 entender formed as 17 meter except:

Present indicative	Present subjunctive
entiendo	entienda
entiendes	entiendas
entiende	entienda
entendemos	entendamos
entendéis	entendáis
entienden	entiendan

Imperative
entiende (tú)
entienda (usted)
entendamos (nosotros)
entended (vosotros)
entiendan (ustedes)

22 **mover** formed as **17 meter** except:

Present indicative
muevo
mueves
mueve
movemos
movéis
mueven

Present subjunctive
mueva
muevas
mueva
movamos
mováis
muevan

Imperative
mueve (tú)
mueva (usted)
movamos (nosotros)
moved (vosotros)
muevan (ustedes)

25 **oler** formed as **17 meter** except:

Present indicative
huelo
hueles
huele
olemos
oléis
huelen

Present subjunctive
huela
huelas
huela
olamos
oláis
huelan

Imperative
huele (tú)
huela (usted)
olamos (nosotros)
oled (vosotros)
huelan (ustedes)

23 **torcer** formed as **17 meter** except:

Present indicative
tuerzo
tuerces
tuerce
torcemos
torcéis
tuercen

Present subjunctive
tuerza
tuerzas
tuerza
torzamos
torzáis
tuerzan

Imperative
tuerce (tú)
tuerza (usted)
torzamos (nosotros)
torced (vosotros)
tuerzan (ustedes)

26 **leer** formed as **17 meter** except:

Gerund
leyendo

Past participle
leído

Past simple indicative
leí
leíste
leyó
leímos
leísteis
leyeron

Imperfect subjunctive
leyera
leyeras
leyera
leyéramos
leyerais
leyeran

24 **volver** formed as **17 meter** except:

Past participle
vuelto

Present indicative
vuelvo
vuelves
vuelve
volvemos
volvéis
vuelven

Present subjunctive
vuelva
vuelvas
vuelva
volvamos
volváis
vuelvan

Imperative
vuelve (tú)
vuelva (usted)
volvamos (nosotros)
volved (vosotros)
vuelvan (ustedes)

27 **caber** formed as **17 meter** except:

Present indicative
quepo
cabes
cabe
cabemos
cabéis
caben

Past simple indicative
cupe
cupiste
cupo
cupimos
cupisteis
cupieron

Future indicative
cabré
cabrás
cabrá
cabremos
cabréis
cabrán

Conditional (present)
cabría
cabrías
cabría
cabríamos
cabríais
cabrían

Present subjunctive
quepa
quepas
quepa
quepamos
quepáis
quepan

Imperfect subjunctive
cupiera
cupieras
cupiera
cupiéramos
cupierais
cupieran

28 caer formed as 17 meter except:

Gerund
cayendo

Past participle
caído

Present indicative
caigo
caes
cae
caemos
caéis
caen

Past simple indicative
caí
caíste
cayó
caímos
caísteis
cayeron

Present subjunctive
caiga
caigas
caiga
caigamos
caigáis
caigan

Imperfect subjunctive
cayera
cayeras
cayera
cayéramos
cayerais
cayeran

Imperative
cae (tú)
caiga (usted)
caigamos (nosotros)
caed (vosotros)
caigan (ustedes)

29 haber formed as 17 meter except:

Present indicative
he
has
ha
habemos
habéis
han

Past simple indicative
hube
hubiste
hubo
hubimos
hubisteis
hubieron

Future indicative
habré
habrás
habrá
habremos
habréis
habrán

Conditional (present)
habría
habrías
habría
habríamos
habríais
habrían

Present subjunctive
haya
hayas
haya
hayamos
hayáis
hayan

Imperfect subjunctive
hubiera
hubieras
hubiera
hubiéramos
hubierais
hubieran

30 hacer formed as 17 meter except:

Past participle
hecho

Present indicative
hago
haces
hace
hacemos
hacéis
hacen

Past simple indicative
hice
hiciste
hizo
hicimos
hicisteis
hicieron

Future indicative
haré
harás
hará
haremos
haréis
harán

Conditional (present)
haría
harías
haría
haríamos
haríais
harían

Present subjunctive
haga
hagas
haga
hagamos
hagáis
hagan

Imperfect subjunctive
hiciera
hicieras
hiciera
hiciéramos
hicierais
hicieran

Imperative
haz (tú)
haga (usted)
hagamos (nosotros)
haced (vosotros)
hagan (ustedes)

31 poder formed as 17 meter except:

Present indicative
puedo
puedes
puede
podemos
podéis
pueden

Past simple indicative
pude
pudiste
pudo
pudimos
pudisteis
pudieron

Future indicative
podré
podrás
podrá
podremos
podréis
podrán

Conditional (present)
podría
podrías
podría
podríamos
podríais
podrían

Present subjunctive
pueda
puedas
pueda
podamos
podáis
puedan

Imperfect subjunctive
pudiera
pudieras
pudiera
pudiéramos
pudierais
pudieran

Imperative
puede (tú)
pueda (usted)
podamos (nosotros)
poded (vosotros)
puedan (ustedes)

32 poner formed as **17 meter** except:

Past participle
puesto

Present indicative
pongo
pones
pone
ponemos
ponéis
ponen

Past simple indicative
puse
pusiste
puso
pusimos
pusisteis
pusieron

Future indicative
pondré
pondrás
pondrá
pondremos
pondréis
pondrán

Conditional (present)
pondría
pondrías
pondría
pondríamos
pondríais
pondrían

Present subjunctive
ponga
pongas
ponga
pongamos
pongáis
pongan

Imperfect subjunctive
pusiera
pusieras
pusiera
pusiéramos
pusierais
pusieran

Imperative
pon (tú)
ponga (usted)
pongamos (nosotros)
poned (vosotros)
pongan (ustedes)

34 querer formed as **17 meter** except:

Present indicative
quiero
quieres
quiere
queremos
queréis
quieren

Past simple indicative
quise
quisiste
quiso
quisimos
quisisteis
quisieron

Future indicative
querré
querrás
querrá
querremos
querréis
querrán

Conditional (present)
querría
querrías
querría
querríamos
querríais
querrían

Present subjunctive
quiera
quieras
quiera
queramos
queráis
quieran

Imperfect subjunctive
quisiera
quisieras
quisiera
quisiéramos
quisierais
quisieran

Imperative
quiere (tú)
quiera (usted)
queramos (nosotros)
quered (vosotros)
quieran (ustedes)

33 traer formed as **17 meter** except:

Gerund
trayendo

Past participle
traído

Present indicative
traigo
traes
trae
traemos
traéis
traen

Past simple indicative
traje
trajiste
trajo
trajimos
trajisteis
trajeron

Present subjunctive
traiga
traigas
traiga
traigamos
traigáis
traigan

Imperfect subjunctive
trajera
trajeras
trajera
trajéramos
trajerais
trajeran

Imperative
trae (tú)
traiga (usted)
traigamos (nosotros)
traed (vosotros)
traigan (ustedes)

35 saber formed as **17 meter** except:

Present indicative
sé
sabes
sabe
sabemos
sabéis
saben

Past simple indicative
supe
supiste
supo
supimos
supisteis
supieron

Future indicative
sabré
sabrás
sabrá
sabremos
sabréis
sabrán

Conditional (present)
sabría
sabrías
sabría
sabríamos
sabríais
sabrían

Present subjunctive
sepa
sepas
sepa
sepamos
sepáis
sepan

Imperfect subjunctive
supiera
supieras
supiera
supiéramos
supierais
supieran

Imperative
sabe (tú)
sepa (usted)
sepamos (nosotros)
sabed (vosotros)
sepan (ustedes)

36 ser formed as 17 meter except:

Gerund	Present subjunctive
siendo	sea
	seas
Past participle	sea
sido	seamos
	seáis
	sean

Present indicative

	Imperfect subjunctive
soy	fuera
eres	fueras
es	fuera
somos	fuéramos
sois	fuerais
son	fueran

Imperfect indicative

	Imperative
era	sé (tú)
eras	sea (usted)
era	seamos (nosotros)
éramos	sed (vosotros)
erais	sean (ustedes)
eran	

Past simple indicative
fui
fuiste
fue
fuimos
fuisteis
fueron

37 tener formed as 17 meter except:

Present indicative	Present subjunctive
tengo	tenga
tienes	tengas
tiene	tenga
tenemos	tengamos
tenéis	tengáis
tienen	tengan

Past simple indicative	Imperfect subjunctive
tuve	tuviera
tuviste	tuvieras
tuvo	tuviera
tuvimos	tuviéramos
tuvisteis	tuvierais
tuvieron	tuvieran

Future indicative	Imperative
tendré	ten (tú)
tendrás	tenga (usted)
tendrá	tengamos (nosotros)
tendremos	tened (vosotros)
tendréis	tengan (ustedes)
tendrán	

Conditional (present)
tendría
tendrías
tendría
tendríamos
tendríais
tendrían

38 valer formed as 17 meter except:

Present indicative	Present subjunctive
valgo	valga
vales	valgas
vale	valga
valemos	valgamos
valéis	valgáis
valen	valgan

Future indicative	Imperfect subjunctive
valdré	valiera
valdrás	valieras
valdrá	valiera
valdremos	valiéramos
valdréis	valierais
valdrán	valieran

Conditional (present)	Imperative
valdría	vale (tú)
valdrías	valga (usted)
valdría	valgamos (nosotros)
valdríamos	valed (vosotros)
valdríais	valgan (ustedes)
valdrían	

39 ver formed as 17 meter except:

Gerund	Present subjunctive
viendo	vea
	veas
Past participle	vea
visto	veamos
	veáis
	vean

Present indicative	Imperative
veo	ve (tú)
ves	vea (usted)
ve	veamos (nosotros)
vemos	ved (vosotros)
veis	vean (ustedes)
ven	

Imperfect indicative
veía
veías
veía
veíamos
veíais
veían

Past simple indicative
vi
viste
vio
vimos
visteis
vieron

40 romper formed as 17 meter except:

Past participle
roto

Verbs ending in -ir

41 partir

Gerund
partiendo

Past participle
partido

Present indicative
parto
partes
parte
partimos
partís
parten

Imperfect indicative
partía
partías
partía
partíamos
partíais
partían

Past simple indicative
partí
partiste
partió
partimos
partisteis
partieron

Future indicative
partiré
partirás
partirá
partiremos
partiréis
partirán

Conditional (present)
partiría
partirías
partiría
partiríamos
partiríais
partirían

Present subjunctive
parta
partas
parta
partamos
partáis
partan

Imperfect subjunctive*
partiera
partieras
partiera
partiéramos
partierais
partieran

Imperative
parte (tú)
parta (usted)
partamos (nosotros)
partid (vosotros)
partan (ustedes)

* all **-ir** verbs have an alternative form of the Imperfect subjunctive in which the **-era** ending is replaced by **-ese**, eg: partiese, partieses, partiese, partiésemos, partieseis, partiesen

42 distinguir formed as **41 partir** except:

Present indicative
distingo
distingues
distingue
distinguimos
distinguís
distinguen

Present subjunctive
distinga
distingas
distinga
distingamos
distingáis
distingan

Imperative
distingue (tú)
distinga (usted)
distingamos (nosotros)
distinguid (vosotros)
distingan (ustedes)

43 reducir formed as **41 partir** except:

Present indicative
reduzco
reduces
reduce
reducimos
reducís
reducen

Present subjunctive
reduzca
reduzcas
reduzca
reduzcamos
reduzcáis
reduzcan

Past simple indicative
reduje
redujiste
redujo
redujimos
redujisteis
redujeron

Imperfect subjunctive
redujera
redujeras
redujera
redujéramos
redujerais
redujeran

Imperative
reduce (tú)
reduzca (usted)
reduzcamos (nosotros)
reducid (vosotros)
reduzcan (ustedes)

44 dirigir formed as **41 partir** except:

Present indicative
dirijo
diriges
dirige
dirigimos
dirigís
dirigen

Present subjunctive
dirija
dirijas
dirija
dirijamos
dirijáis
dirijan

Imperative
dirige (tú)
dirija (usted)
dirijamos (nosotros)
dirigid (vosotros)
dirijan (ustedes)

45 corregir formed as **41 partir** except:

Present indicative
corrijo
corriges
corrige
corregimos
corregís
corrigen

Present subjunctive
corrija
corrijas
corrija
corrijamos
corrijáis
corrijan

Past simple indicative
corregí
corregiste
corrigió
corrigieron
corregisteis
corrigieron

Imperative
corrige (tú)
corrija (usted)
corrijamos (nosotros)
corregid (vosotros)
corrijan (ustedes)

46 sentir formed as 41 partir except:

Gerund
sintiendo

Present indicative
siento
sientes
siente
sentimos
sentís
sienten

Past simple indicative
sentí
sentiste
sintió
sentimos
sentisteis
sintieron

Present subjunctive
sienta
sientas
sienta
sintamos
sintáis
sientan

Imperfect subjunctive
sintiera
sintieras
sintiera
sintiéramos
sintierais
sintieran

Imperative
siente (tú)
sienta (usted)
sintamos (nosotros)
sentid (vosotros)
sientan (ustedes)

47 adquirir formed as 41 partir except:

Present indicative
adquiero
adquieres
adquiere
adquirimos
adquirís
adquieren

Present subjunctive
adquiera
adquieras
adquiera
adquiramos
adquiráis
adquieran

Imperative
adquiere (tú)
adquiera (usted)
adquiramos (nosotros)
adquirid (vosotros)
adquieran (ustedes)

48 pedir formed as 41 partir except:

Gerund
pidiendo

Present indicative
pido
pides
pide
pedimos
pedís
piden

Past simple indicative
pedí
pediste
pidió
pedimos
pedisteis
pidieron

Present subjunctive
pida
pidas
pida
pidamos
pidáis
pidan

Imperfect subjunctive
pidiera
pidieras
pidiera
pidiéramos
pidierais
pidieran

Imperative
pide (tú)
pida (usted)
pidamos (nosotros)
pedid (vosotros)
pidan (ustedes)

49 dormir formed as 41 partir except:

Gerund
durmiendo

Past participle
dormido

Present indicative
duermo
duermes
duerme
dormimos
dormís
duermen

Past simple indicative
dormí
dormiste
durmió
dormimos
dormisteis
durmieron

Present subjunctive
duerma
duermas
duerma
durmamos
durmáis
duerman

Imperfect subjunctive
durmiera
durmieras
durmiera
durmiéramos
durmierais
durmieran

Imperative
duerme (tú)
duerma (usted)
durmamos (nosotros)
dormid (vosotros)
duerman (ustedes)

50 reír formed as 41 partir except:

Gerund
riendo

Past participle
reído

Present indicative
río
ríes
ríe
reímos
reís
ríen

Imperfect indicative
reía
reías
reía
reíamos
reíais
reían

Past simple indicative
reí
reíste
rió
reímos
reísteis
rieron

Future indicative
reiré
reirás
reirá
reiremos
reiréis
reirán

Conditional (present)
reiría
reirías
reiría
reiríamos
reiríais
reirían

Present subjunctive
ría
rías
ría
riamos
riáis
rían

Imperfect subjunctive
riera
rieras
riera
riéramos
rierais
rieran

Imperative
ríe (tú)
ría (usted)
riamos (nosotros)
reíd (vosotros)
rían (ustedes)

51 **huir** formed as **41 partir** except:

Gerund
huyendo

Past participle
huido

Present indicative
huyo
huyes
huye
huimos
huís
huyen

Past simple indicative
huí
huiste
huyó
huimos
huisteis
huyeron

Present subjunctive
huya
huyas
huya
huyamos
huyáis
huyan

Imperfect subjunctive
huyera
huyeras
huyera
huyéramos
huyerais
huyeran

Imperative
huye (tú)
huya (usted)
huyamos (nosotros)
huid (vosotros)
huyan (ustedes)

52 **prohibir** formed as **41 partir** except:

Present indicative
prohíbo
prohíbes
prohíbe
prohibimos
prohibís
prohíben

Present subjunctive
prohíba
prohíbas
prohíba
prohibamos
prohibáis
prohíban

Imperative
prohíbe (tú)
prohíba (usted)
prohibamos (nosotros)
prohibid (vosotros)
prohíban (ustedes)

53 **decir** formed as **41 partir** except:

Gerund
diciendo

Past participle
dicho

Present indicative
digo
dices
dice
decimos
decís
dicen

Past simple indicative
dije
dijiste
dijo
dijimos
dijisteis
dijeron

Future indicative
diré
dirás
dirá
diremos
diréis
dirán

Conditional (present)
diría
dirías
diría
diríamos
diríais
dirían

Present subjunctive
diga
digas
diga
digamos
digáis
digan

Imperfect subjunctive
dijera
dijeras
dijera
dijéramos
dijerais
dijeran

Imperative
di (tú)
diga (usted)
digamos (nosotros)
decid (vosotros)
digan (ustedes)

54 **ir** formed as **41 partir** except:

Gerund
yendo

Past participle
ido

Present indicative
voy
vas
va
vamos
vais
van

Imperfect indicative
iba
ibas
iba
íbamos
ibais
iban

Past simple indicative
fui
fuiste
fue
fuimos
fuisteis
fueron

Present subjunctive
vaya
vayas
vaya
vayamos
vayáis
vayan

Imperfect subjunctive
fuera
fueras
fuera
fuéramos
fuerais
fueran

Imperative
ve (tú)
vaya (usted)
vayamos (nosotros)
id (vosotros)
vayan (ustedes)

55 **oír** formed as **41 partir** except:

Gerund
oyendo

Past participle
oído

Present indicative
oigo
oyes
oye
oímos
oís
oyen

Imperfect indicative
oía
oías
oía
oíamos
oíais
oían

Past simple indicative
oí
oíste
oyó
oímos
oísteis
oyeron

Future indicative
oiré
oirás
oirá
oiremos
oiréis
oirán

Conditional (present)
oiría
oirías
oiría
oiríamos
oiríais
oirían

Present subjunctive
oiga
oigas
oiga
oigamos
oigáis
oigan

Imperfect subjunctive
oyera
oyeras
oyera
oyéramos
oyerais
oyeran

Imperative
oye (tú)
oiga (usted)
oigamos (nosotros)
oíd (vosotros)
oigan (ustedes)

56 **salir** formed as **41 partir** except:

Present indicative
salgo
sales
sale
salimos
salís
salen

Past simple indicative
salí
saliste
salió
salimos
salisteis
salieron

Future indicative
saldré
saldrás
saldrá
saldremos
saldréis
saldrán

Conditional (present)
saldría
saldrías
saldría
saldríamos
saldríais
saldrían

Present subjunctive
salga
salgas
salga
salgamos
salgáis
salgan

Imperfect subjunctive
saliera
salieras
saliera
saliéramos
salierais
salieran

Imperative
sal (tú)
salga (usted)
salgamos (nosotros)
salid (vosotros)
salgan (ustedes)

57 seguir formed as **41 partir** except:

Gerund
siguiendo

Present indicative
sigo
sigues
sigue
seguimos
seguís
siguen

Past simple indicative
seguí
seguiste
siguió
seguimos
seguisteis
siguieron

Present subjunctive
siga
sigas
siga
sigamos
sigáis
sigan

Imperfect subjunctive
siguiera
siguieras
siguiera
siguiéramos
siguierais
siguieran

Imperative
sigue (tú)
siga (usted)
sigamos (nosotros)
seguid (vosotros)
sigan (ustedes

58 venir formed as **41 partir** except:

Gerund
viniendo

Present indicative
vengo
vienes
viene
venimos
venís
vienen

Past simple indicative
vine
viniste
vino
vinimos
vinisteis
vinieron

Future indicative
vendré
vendrás
vendrá
vendremos
vendréis
vendrán

Conditional (present)
vendría
vendrías
vendría
vendríamos
vendríais
vendrían

Present subjunctive
venga
vengas
venga
vengamos
vengáis
vengan

Imperfect subjunctive
viniera
vinieras
viniera
viniéramos
vinierais
vinieran

Imperative
ven (tú)
venga (usted)
vengamos (nosotros)
venid (vosotros)
vengan (ustedes)

59 abrir formed as **41 partir** except:

Past participle
abierto

60 escribir formed as **41 partir** except:

Past participle
escrito

61 freír formed as **41 partir** except:

Gerund
friendo

Past participle
frito

Present indicative
frío
fríes
fríe
freímos
freís
fríen

Imperfect indicative
freía
freías
freía
freíamos
freíais
freían

Past simple indicative
freí
freíste
frió
freímos
freísteis
frieron

Future indicative
freiré
freirás
freirá
freiremos
freiréis
freirán

Conditional (present)
freiría
freirías
freiría
freiríamos
freiríais
freirían

Present subjunctive
fría
frías
fría
friamos
friáis
frían

Imperfect subjunctive
friera
frieras
friera
friéramos
frierais
frieran

Imperative
fríe (tú)
fría (usted)
friamos (nosotros)
freíd (vosotros)
frían (ustedes)

62 morir formed as **41 partir** except:

Gerund
muriendo

Past participle
muerto

Present indicative
muero
mueres
muere
morimos
morís
mueren

Past simple indicative
morí
moriste
murió
morimos
moristeis
murieron

Present subjunctive
muera
mueras
muera
muramos
muráis
mueran

Imperfect subjunctive
muriera
murieras
muriera
muriéramos
murierais
murieran

63 **pudrir** formed as **41 partir** except:

past participle
podrido

64 **reunir** formed as **41 partir** except:

Present indicative
reúno
reúnes
reúne
reunimos
reunís
reúnen

Present subjunctive
reúna
reúnas
reúna
reunamos
reunáis
reúnan

Imperative
reúne (tú)
reúna (usted)
reunamos (nosotros)
reunid (vosotros)
reúnan (ustedes)

65 **ceñir** formed as **41 partir** except:

Gerund
ciñendo

Present indicative
ciño
ciñes
ciñe
ceñimos
ceñís
ciñen

Past simple indicative
ceñí
ceñiste
ciñó
ceñimos
ceñisteis
ciñeron

Present subjunctive
ciña
ciñas
ciña
ciñamos
ciñáis
ciñan

Imperfect subjunctive
ciñera
ciñeras
ciñera
ciñéramos
ciñerais
ciñeran

Imperative
ciñe (tú)
ciña (usted)
ciñamos (nosotros)
ceñid (vosotros)
ciñan (ustedes)